The Movie Companion

The Movie Companion

MARIO READING

Published by SILVERDALE BOOKS
An imprint of Bookmart Ltd
Registered number 2372865
Trading as Bookmart Ltd
Blaby Road
Wigston
Leicester LE18 4SE

Previously published as *Dictionary of Cinema* by House of Stratus, 2001

This revised, paperback edition published by Magpie Books,
an imprint of Constable & Robinson Ltd, for Silverdale Books, 2006

Designed by
Katherine Winterson, Spokes Design

ISBN-10: 1-84509-463-8
ISBN-13: 9-781-84509-463-8

Printed and bound in China

1 3 5 7 9 10 8 6 4 2

Introduction

My first visceral memory of film, and one that I have never quite succeeded in shaking off, is of fear. Fear of the unseen. The image came in David Lean's *Oliver Twist* (1948), and I'm still not one hundred percent certain that I remember it correctly, for I've never, for obvious reasons, chosen to watch the film again. As I recall it now (and I last saw the film around 1958, when I was five years old), Robert Newton's Bill Sykes, in an ungovernable fit of temper, kills the innocent Nancy, played by Kay Walsh, but Lean, being the consummate and inventive filmmaker that he is (and possibly swayed by censorship considerations), chooses to show the murder only in shadow – the shadow of the rise and fall of Sykes's club, accompanied by Nancy's terrified and increasingly feeble screams and the demented scrabbling of Sykes's dog at the door. The recollection of this appalling scene has haunted me for years (and continues to do so), and provides an awesome example of the simple power of the moving image to imbrue reality.

Later images from my childhood viewing are less unsettling but equally forceful, and comprise the shooting of the dog in Robert Stevenson's *Old Yeller* (1957), a memory which has forever barred me from discovering the ending to Lewis Milestone's *Of Mice And Men* (1939), (for even to this day I can never get past the scene where the old man's dog is taken out of the bunkhouse to be shot, without bursting into tears and asking someone to switch off the television set), and curious flashbacks to a film in which a murderer finds himself sealed up in an entirely electrified room – heaven alone knows what the film was called, but I, for sure, never wish to find out.

No happy memories, you ask? Hundreds, but they are usually non-specific, as though one tends to remember simply the feeling of happiness rather than any particular scene to that effect. No, the visceral memories are reserved for psychological horror (analysts, please don't call me – I'll call you), and are unnervingly specific. Oh dear. Another one has just sprung to mind concerning a torture sequence (probably very mild) in a Second World War-based spy movie. It was the screams of course, and my imagining of what was happening, that were so very much more telling than the brutal, and probably not very descriptive reality.

These films certainly distressed me, but they probably also prepared me, much as Grimm's *Fairy Tales*, Heinrich Hoffmann's *Der Struwelpeter* (*Shock-headed Peter*), and Wilhelm Busch's *Max and Moritz* had done before, for the understanding that life was not necessarily always going to be sweetness and light. To that extent it was right of my parents to let me watch the films, and I don't at all regret the uneasiness some of the scenes may have engendered. Later, movies became a source of comfort rather than unease, and to this day I get an excited and fluttery feeling in my stomach when I am finding my seat in a cinema before the showing of a film I particularly want to see, and which I suspect will have 'heart'.

Now to *The Movie Companion*. I wrote it because I love film. It is also a sly effort to justify a misspent youth, teenager-hood, young adulthood, early middle age and middle age spent watching extraordinary numbers of the things, often when I should have been otherwise occupied. This way I can console myself that all those tens of thousands of hours glued to the screen or to the television set were simply research for the *magnum opus* I always knew I would perpetrate on an unsuspecting world. During all those solitary (but never lonely) hours, I developed opinions which inevitably find themselves reflected here – opinions which I hope you will find stimulating, occasionally enervating, but always, I trust, honest. If I tell you that I have had to leave out over eighty single-spaced pages chock-full with potential entrants, you will realise that space, and a desire to give full value to the people who do appear, has inevitably engendered casualties – I also admit that there are a number of individuals whom one might expect to see but who I have refused to include because, in my opinion, they simply don't merit the space.

The layout, I trust, is self-evident. Everything is in pure alphabetical order, with cross-references to guide you to related snippets throughout the book. Under each entry there is a list entitled Other Key Films – this is my entirely subjective choice, from the often extensive filmographies available to me, of movies that I think best reflect that individual's skills. In the case of still-living, still-working personalities, I have added as many of their most recent films as space allows simply to reflect the state of that particular person's career as it is, rather than as they would have it be. Also, on occasion, I have added, under the title Key Line (s), a *bon mot*, quip or quote that I trust may add a little extra enjoyment to my summation. As far as foreign titles go, I have tended to leave them in the original, except where they are better known to English-speaking audiences in their English versions – in that case I give both (unless they are exceedingly well-known) with the original title first, followed by the English title. Film release dates present further difficulties, because they vary, according to the mores of the country, depending on whether the film is an American, a British, a Continental, or an International film, so that what may initially appear as an anomaly is simply the release date in a different country.

Now to birth dates and death dates. I don't give them. In my opinion they get in the way. A quick glance at the dates in the filmographies together with an even cursory reading of the text will give a passable idea of what age a person was when they did what film. Neither do I show courtesy titles – as far as I am concerned 'Lord This', 'Dame That', or 'Sir Somebody Other', usually didn't start out that way, and it's their *career* I'm writing about, not the end result of it – it wasn't Lord Olivier, for example, who starred as Heathcliff in William Wyler's *Wuthering Heights* (1939); it was plain, simple, common-or-garden Laurence Olivier.

Within the main body of the text, I invariably attach the director's name to films they are known to have directed; however I don't carry this over to the Key Films section for reasons of space, except when the Key Films refer to the career of a non-actor or a non-director (cinematographers, screenwriters, composers, etc.) in which case I do include them for ease of reference. In addition to the main body of the text, I have included a few highlighted sections that I hope will amuse, entertain and engender discussion. These include my personal choice of films in the following classes: Adventure Films, All-time Best Films, Animated Films, Big-budget Action Films, Children's Films, Comedy Films, Crime Films, Cult Films, Detective Films, Documentary Films, Dramas, Epics, *Film Noirs*, Gangster Films, Ghost Films, Horror Films, Love Films, Monster Films, Musical Films, Political/Satirical Films, Psychological Dramas, Science Fiction Films, Sentimental Films, Silent Films, Spy Films, Swashbucklers, Thrillers, War Films, Weepies, and Western Films. These lists, culled from more than 25,000 movies, are not intended to be definitive (such an ambition would be palpably absurd), but are simply designed as a quick guide to readers who may be setting out on – rather than on their way back from – a lifetime's voyage of cinematic discovery. Finally, I've added a small section of Worst Films (limiting myself to the last fifteen years or so), Erotic Moments, and a separate section entitled Heartstopping Moments, which consists of a small series of subjective, but, one hopes, perspicaciously chosen peak moments in cinema.

Books with such an extensive reach as *The Movie Companion* are usually written by committees, with all the disadvantages in terms of consistency and wit, and the advantages in terms of shared responsibility and multi-tasking. The shared responsibility for this book is entirely mine. The opinions are also mine, for better or worse, as is the choice of entries. I admit that the book is idiosyncratic. So am I. But it was a labour of love, for film has been both my comfort and my educator – a prop in times of sickness, a joy in times of health, and a boon at moments (rare, these) of intellectual growth.

Well, there you have it. I've made my excuses, explained what I'm doing here, and now all that's left is to wish you the same enjoyment reading *The Movie Companion*, that I've had writing and researching it. 'Salud, y forza al canuto.'

Mario Reading 2006

Aardman Animations

Home to Plasticine superheroes Wallace and Gromit, Aardman is one of the most successful of all the independent animation studios. Founded by Peter Lord and David Sproxton in 1972, Aardman now has the blessing – and the mountains of cash that go with it – of **Steven Spielberg's** DreamWorks SKG. Based in Bristol, Aardman was originally responsible for Morph, of BBC TV's *Take Hart* fame, after which it branched out into music videos and advertising. Nick Park joined as co-director in 1985, bringing Wallace and Gromit with him, and the rest is history. Park now has three Oscars under his belt, and is still as committed to Plasticine, rather than to computer animation, as ever. A warehouse fire on 20th October 2005 destroyed thirty years' worth of Aardman memorabilia, but stiff-upper-lipped Park brushed off the disaster with, 'in the light of other tragedies, today isn't a big deal.'
Other Key Films: *A Grand Day Out* (1989); *Creature Comforts* (1991); *The Wrong Trousers* (1993); *A Close Shave* (1995); *Chicken Run* (2000); *The Curse Of The Were-Rabbit* (2005)
Key Line: 'Maybe I love Gromit because he's the dog I never had.' [Nick Park]

Abbott and Costello

A hit-and-miss comedy duo that never really matched the heights achieved by their famous antecedents, **Laurel and Hardy**. Arthur Lubin's *Buck Privates* (1941) began their rise, Charles Riesner's *Lost in a Harem* (1944) consolidated it, Charles Barton's *Abbott and Costello Meet Frankenstein* (1948) steadied them on their way down, while the same director's *Dance With Me Henry* (1956) saw them finally hit rock bottom.
Other Key Films: *Hold That Ghost* (1941); *The Naughty Nineties* (1945)

Abril, Victoria

Best known for being one of director **Pedro Almodóvar's** favourite stars, Abril is considerably more famous in her native Spain than internationally, despite twin art-house successes in Almodóvar's sexually explicit *Tie Me Up! Tie Me Down!* [*Átame!*] (1989) and Josiane Balasko's sexually and emotionally convoluted *French Twist* [*Gazon Maudit*] (1995). In *French Twist*, Abril, fed up to the back teeth with her macho and serially unfaithful husband, takes up with a lesbian drifter who is then impregnated by the despondent husband (in a particularly weird *ménage à trois*) after which the two women bring up the child as their own while the husband is outed for the closet gay he has always been by a rich bisexual playboy whose drinking toast of choice is '*Salud, y forza al canuto.*' [Cheers, and more power to the p★★★★] Wow!
Other Key Films: *Robin And Marian* (1976); *Law Of Desire* [uncredited] (1987); *High Heels* (1991); *Kika* (1993); *Libertarias* (1996); *Entre Las Piernas* (1999); *Mari Del Sud* (2001); *Incautos* (2004); *El Camino De Los Ingleses* (2006)
Key Line: 'She moves like a panther prowling to a flamenco beat...' [Robert J Pardi on Abril's feline appeal]

Best Big-budget Action Films

Luc Besson's *Léon* (1994); **John Boorman's** *Excalibur* (1981); **James Cameron's** *The Terminator* (1984) and *Terminator 2 – Judgement Day* (1991); Richard Fleischer's *The Vikings* (1957); Brian G Hutton's *Where Eagles Dare* (1969); Ted Kotcheff's *First Blood* (1982); George Lucas's *Star Wars*

Adam, Ken

Influential and multi-talented production designer responsible for the overall look of some of the most successful of the **James Bond** films, including Guy Hamilton's

Goldfinger (1964), Terence Young's *Dr No* (1963) and *Thunderball* (1965), and Lewis Gilbert's *The Spy Who Loved Me* (1977). Other highlights of this extraordinary man's career include the multitude of inventive set pieces on Michael Anderson's *Around the World in 80 Days* (1956), the brilliantly conceived war room in **Stanley Kubrick's** *Dr Strangelove* (1963), and the gorgeous look of the whole of Kubrick's *Barry Lyndon* (1975). In recent years he's even designed a video game.

Other Key Films: **Thorold Dickinson's** *The Queen of Spades* (1949); **Robert Siodmak's** *The Crimson Pirate* (1952); **Sydney J Furie's** *The Ipcress File* (1965); **Herbert Ross's** *Pennies From Heaven* (1981); **Barry Sonnenfeld's** *Addams Family Values* (1991); **Nicholas Hytner's** *The Madness Of King George* (1994); **Frank Oz's** *In & Out* (1997); **István Szabó's** *Taking Sides* (2001)

Addinsell, Richard

English romantic composer whose many screen credits include the wildly popular Warsaw Concerto for piano and orchestra, heard for the first time in Brian Hurst's *Dangerous Moonlight* (1941), and which featured a Paderewski-like and elegantly dashing **Anton Walbrook** playing the piece in a bombed-out house.

Other Key Films: **Sam Wood's** *Goodbye Mr Chips* (1939); **Thorold Dickinson's** *Gaslight* (1940); **David Lean's** *Blithe Spirit* (1945); **Alfred Hitchcock's** *Under Capricorn* (1949); **Laurence Olivier's** *The Prince And The Showgirl* (1958); **Ted Kotcheff's** *Life At The Top* (1965)

Addison, John

Successful composer of an impressive number of the key British films of the 1960s (many of which just happen to have been directed by **Tony Richardson**) and which include *The Entertainer* (1960), and *Tom Jones* (1963), Addison is best seen in the context of his predecessor and compatriot, **Richard Addinsell**, with both men proving to be so totally professional and self-effacing that no one, apart from the occasional keen-eyed film buff, has ever heard of them.

Other Key Films: **Tony Richardson's** *Look Back In Anger* (1959), *A Taste Of Honey* (1961), *The Loneliness Of The Long Distance Runner* (1962), *The Loved One* (1965) and *The Charge Of The Light Brigade* (1968); **Guy Green's** *Luther* (1973); **Herbert Ross's** *The Seven Per Cent Solution* (1976)

Adjani, Isabelle

Glacially beautiful and politically uncompromising star of **François Truffaut's** *The Story of Adèle H* (1975), Adjani also shone in **Werner Herzog's** *Nosferatu the Vampyre* (1979), **Luc Besson's** *Subway* (1985) and Bruno Nuytten's *Camille Claudel* (1989). She made something of a comeback in Patrice Chereau's *La Reine Margot* (1994), but, despite her cult status, she still remains (voluntarily, one suspects) on the periphery of her profession. Adjani, who has an Algerian/Turkish father and a German mother, is the only person in French cinema history to have received four César awards.

Other Key Films: *Possession* (1980); *Quartet* (1981); *One Deadly Summer* (1983); *Diabolique* (1996); *Paparazzi* (1998); *Bon Voyage* (2003)

Best Adventure Films

Henri-Georges Clouzot's *Le Salaire De La Peur* [*The Wages Of Fear*] (1953); Jacques Feyder's *Knight Without Armour* (1937); **John Ford's** *The Hurricane* (1937); **Henry Hathaway's** *The Lives Of A Bengal Lancer* (1935); **Howard Hawks's** *To Have And Have Not* (1945); **Werner Herzog's** *Aguirre, Wrath Of God* (1972) and *Fitzcarraldo*

(1982); **Alfred Hitchcock's** *The 39 Steps* (1935); **John Huston's** *The African Queen* (1951) and *The Man Who Would Be King* (1975); **Zoltan Korda's** *The Four Feathers* (1939); **Akira Kurosawa's** *Throne Of Blood* (1961); Ernest B Schoedsack and Ernest Pichel's *The Most Dangerous Game* (1932); **Ridley Scott's** *The Duellists* (1977); **Steven Spielberg's** *Jaws* (1975) and *Raiders Of The Lost Ark* (1981); **John Sturges's** *The Great Escape* (1963); J Lee Thompson's *North West Frontier* (1959)

Agee, James

Influential and often acerbic film critic for *Time* and *The Nation* magazines, Agee scripted **John Huston's** *The African Queen* (1951) and **Charles Laughton's** *Night of the Hunter* (1955), proving that, unlike most film critics, he was also able to produce the creative goods when called upon. His film reviews have recently been republished, and go a long way towards confirming his critical prescience in a world fogged by the effects of the Second World War and its aftermath – one can, in the circumstances, just about forgive him for his curious blindness to the merits of *film noir*. He received a posthumous Pulitzer Prize for his novel, *A Death in the Family*, crowning his all too brief forty-five-year life span of achievement.

Albers, Hans

One of Germany's greatest screen actors, Albers had an unusually wide range, acting in comedy, in tragedy, and as a romantic lead. Towards the end of his life, age and decrepitude consigned him to character roles, but he remained much loved, and his wartime incarnation as Baron Münchhausen proved immensely popular on both sides of the conflict.
Other Key Films: *Zigeunerblut* (1911); *Lola Montez* (1919); *Grand Hotel Babylon* (1919); *Der Prinz Und Die Tänzerin* (1926); *The Blue Angel* (1930); *Münchhausen* (1943); *Blue-Beard* (1951); *Der Letzte Mann* (1955)

Alda, Alan

Popular character actor (born Alphonso D'Abruzzo) who made his mark in the smash hit TV series *M*A*S*H*, Alda has successfully run parallel careers on stage, screen, and as a writer and director with *The Four Seasons* (1981), *Sweet Liberty* (1986) and *A New Life* (1988). He was outstanding as a self-obsessed film director in **Woody Allen's** *Crimes And Misdemeanours* (1989), but many consider his best screen performance to have been in Jerry Schatzberg's *The Seduction Of Joe Tynan* (1979), which he also scripted. In recent years he has made a triumphant return to the small screen as Senator Arnold Vinick in TV's *The West Wing*.
Other Key Films: *The Extraordinary Seaman* (1969); *To Kill A Clown* (1972); *California Suite* (1978); *Betsy's Wedding* (1990); *Manhattan Murder Mystery* (1993); *Everyone Says I Love You* (1996); *Mad City* (1997); *The Object Of My Affection* (1998); *What Women Want* (2000); *The Aviator* (2004)

Aldrich, Robert

Cult filmmaker who alternately hit and missed the spot with a succession of fascinating and often shocking films. Pick of the bunch must be *Kiss Me Deadly* (1955), in which Aldrich came closer than anyone has ever done to transferring no-holds-barred hardboiled **pulp fiction** onto the screen. He resuscitated the careers of **Bette Davis, Joan Crawford** and **Olivia de Havilland** with the melodramatic *Whatever Happened to Baby Jane?* (1962) and its follow-up, *Hush...Hush Sweet Charlotte* (1964), and set the seal on his own success as a commercial director with the

evergreen *The Dirty Dozen* (1967).
Other Key Films: *Vera Cruz* (1954); *Apache* (1954); *The Big Knife* (1956); *The Killing of Sister George* (1968); *Too Late The Hero* (1970); *Ulzana's Raid* (1972); *The Choirboys* (1977); *The Angry Hills* (1981)

Allégret, Marc
A nephew of André Gide, Allégret made his reputation with *Fanny* (1932), which, with the two other films in the trilogy, **Alexander Korda's** *Marius* (1931) and author Marcel Pagnol's own *César* (1936), represented, perhaps, the first tentative emergence onto the screen of the since rather dumbed-down 'soap opera' genre. Allégret went on to specialise in romantic melodrama, a style typified by the fervid *Blanche Fury* (1948), in which the illegitimate but passionately cold **Stewart Granger** tries to claim his dubious inheritance by murdering his legitimate brother and uncle in a gothic atmosphere that sometimes borders on the fay.
Other Key Films: *Heart of Paris* (1935); *Les Amants Terribles* (1936); *L'Arlésienne* (1942); *Lunegarde* (1946); *Blackmailed* (1951); *Les Démons De Minuit* (1961); *Les Parisiennes* (1962)

Allen, Woody
Critically acclaimed director whose turbulent private life has occasionally tended to overshadow his undoubted talents as a film-maker, Allen began his career as a stand-up comedian, before progressing to screenwriting with Clive Donner's *What's New Pussycat?* (1965) and Herbert Ross's film version of Allen's Broadway hit *Play It Again, Sam* (1972). More popular in France than in his native New York, Allen is renowned for using the women in his life as the main female protagonists in his films – **Diane Keaton** graced both *Annie Hall* (1977) and *Manhattan* (1979), while Mia Farrow (with whom he later had an injurious bust-up) appeared in, amongst other films, *Hannah and her Sisters* (1986) and *Husbands and Wives* (1992). A rarity among American filmmakers, Allen always retains full creative control over his own material, and he has recently undergone a welcome return to form with the UK based *Match Point* (2005).
Other Key Films: *Zelig* (1982); *The Purple Rose of Cairo* (1985); *Radio Days* (1988); *Crimes and Misdemeanors* (1989); *Manhattan Murder Mystery* (1993); *Bullets Over Broadway* (1994); *Mighty Aphrodite* (1995); *Deconstructing Harry* (1997); *Celebrity* (1998); *Sweet And Lowdown* (2000); *Small Time Crooks* (2000); *The Curse Of The Jade Scorpion* (2001); *Scoop* (2006)
Key Lines:
1. 'When I die I want to come back as **Warren Beatty's** little finger.' [Allen on sex]
2. 'Los Angeles is not good for me – it's carcinogenic.' [Allen on the Big Orange]
3. 'Hey, don't knock masturbation. It's sex with someone I love.' [Allen on onanism]

Best All-time Films
Ingmar Bergman's *The Seventh Seal* (1957) and *Wild Strawberries* (1957); **Robert Bresson** *Le Journal D'Un Curé De Campagne* (1951); **Marcel Carné's** *Les Enfants Du Paradis* (1943-1944); **Jean Cocteau's** *La Belle Et La Bête* (1945); **Michael Curtiz's** *Casablanca* (1942); **Jean Eustache's** *La Maman Et La Putain* (1973); **Federico Fellini's** *8_* (1963); **Victor Fleming's** *Gone With The Wind* (1939); **John Ford's**

The Searchers (1956); **Akira Kurosawa's** *The Seven Samurai* (1954); **Yasujiro Ozu's** *Tokyo Story* (1953); **Roman Polanski's** *Chinatown* (1974); **Satyajit Ray's** *The Music Room* (1963); **Carol Reed's** *The Third Man* (1949); **Jean Renoir's** *La Règle Du Jeu* (1939) and *Une Partie De Campagne* (1936); **Vittorio de Sica's** *Bicycle Thieves* (1948); **Andrei Tarkovsky's** *Andreï Rublev* (1966-1967); **Jean Vigo's** *L'Atalante* (33-34); **Orson Welles's** *Citizen Kane* (1941); **Billy Wilder's** *Some Like It Hot* (1959)

Allyson, June

With her torch singer's voice and impishly sweet smile, Allyson was a dead cert to play girl-next-door roles and good, unthreatening female chums, and wholesome old MGM made certain that those were the parts that she got. Following nearly a decade in musicals, Allyson moved into drama, probably at the instigation of her husband, **Dick Powell**, but the studio only once let her stretch her wings and play completely against type, as the shrewish wife in José Ferrer's *The Shrike* (1955). They then proceeded to scupper the whole shebang by tacking on a ridiculously upbeat ending.
Other Key Films: *Thousands Cheer* (1943); *The Sailor Takes A Wife* (1946); *Secret Heart* (1946); *Words And Music* (1948); *Little Women* (1949); *The Glenn Miller Story* (1954); *Executive Suite* (1954); *Woman's World* (1954); *Stranger In My Arms* (1959)

Almendros, Néstor

Influential cinematographer who first made his mark in **Barbet Schroeder's** sun-drenched drug-culture curiosity *More* (1969), which he soon followed with **Eric Rohmer's** exquisitely carnal *My Night at Maud's* (1969) and *Claire's Knee* (1971). Almendros worked frequently with **François Truffaut**, most notably on *The Story of Adèle H* (1975) and *The Last Metro* (1980), but his global reputation rests strongly on his miraculous camerawork for **Terrence Malick's** *Days of Heaven* (1978), and on the superlative job he did for **Alan J Pakula** on *Sophie's Choice* (1982).
Other Key Films: Eric Rohmer's *La Collectioneuse* (1971) and *Pauline at the Beach* (1983); Barbet Schroeder's *Maîtresse* (1976); Robert Benton's *Kramer vs. Kramer* (1979), *Places In The Heart* (1984) and *Billy Bathgate* (1991)

Almodóvar, Pedro

Scabrous and anarchic, Almodóvar has been obsessed, ever since his earliest underground films, with the delirious convolutions of gay and female sexual desire. A stylist of the first order (and the coincidental discoverer of **Antonio Banderas**), Almodóvar found a large international audience with *Women on the Verge of a Nervous Breakdown* (1988), closely followed by *Tie Me Up! Tie Me Down!* (1989), *High Heels* (1991), and *Kika* (1994), which the United States misguidedly banned as a result of feminist pressure. His latest films, including *The Flower Of My Secret* (1995), *Live Flesh*

Claude Laydu and Nicole Ladmiral in Journal d'Un Curé de Campagne (Diary of a Country Priest), directed by Robert Bresson (1951).

UGC/The Kobal Collection/Roger Corbeau

(1997), *All About My Mother* [*Todo Sobre Mi Madre*] (1999), and *Talk To Her* [*Habla Con Ella*] (2002), have proved immensely popular with European oriented and iconoclastically inclined audiences.

Other Key Films: *Pepi, Luci, Bom* (1980); *Matador* (1986); *Law of Desire* (1987); *La Mala Educación* (2004); *Volver* (2006)

Altman, Robert

After his extraordinary breakthrough with *M*A*S*H* in 1970, Altman took his improvisatory techniques to new heights in *Nashville* (1975), which cemented his reputation as an actor's director. Over the ensuing twenty-five years he has followed his own star on the outer edge of the Hollywood system, alternating flops and triumphs with a commendably independent nonchalance. Highlights of his career include *The Long Goodbye* (1973), a radical reworking of **Raymond Chandler** that somehow contrives to remain true to the original, and *The Player* (1992), which boasts the longest and most successful first travelling shot since **Orson Welles's** scintillating *Touch Of Evil* (1958) set the standard in these matters. Altman also had a tremendous late-career hit (he was seventy-six at the time), with *Gosford Park* (2001).

Other Key Films: *McCabe And Mrs Miller* (1971); *California Split* (1974); *Thieves Like Us* (1974); *A Wedding* (1978); *Come Back To The Five And Dime Jimmy Dean Jimmy Dean* (1982); *Streamers* (1983); *Short Cuts* (1993); *Prêt-A-Porter* [*Ready To Wear*] (1994); *Kansas City* (1996); *Wild Card* (1997); *The Gingerbread Man* (1998); *Cookie's Fortune* (1999); *Dr T And The Women* (2000); *The Company* (2003); *A Prairie Home Companion* (2006)

Alwyn, William

A fine screen composer as well as a prolific and successful mainstream conductor and musician, Alwyn's name appears on the score of a remarkable number of prestigious 1940s and 1950s British films, including Sidney Gilliat's *The Rake's Progress* [a.k.a. *Notorious Gentleman*] (1945), **Carol Reed's** *Odd Man Out* (1947) and Anthony Pelissier's *The Rocking Horse Winner* (1949). His most popular and affecting score was for Reed's brilliant psychological study of childhood, *The Fallen Idol* (1948).

Other Key Films: Anthony Asquith's *The Winslow Boy* (1948); **Jean Negulesco's** *The Mudlark* (1950); **David Lean's** *Madeleine* (1950); **Robert Siodmak's** *The Crimson Pirate* (1952); Ken Annakin's *Swiss Family Robinson* (1960)

Anderson, Lindsay

Politically committed and awesomely well-informed about cinema (he wrote the best-ever book about **John Ford**) this ex-theatre director and occasional documentarist shattered British middle and lower middle class illusions about the working classes in *This Sporting Life* (1963), and went on to attack the middle classes themselves in *If...* (1968), a masterpiece of poeto-anarchic fabulism in which the inmates of an English public school turn the tables on their masters and massacre them with machine guns, rifles, and hand grenades from the very edifices they are being trained to protect. The film went on, quite rightly, to win the Palme D'Or at the Cannes Film Festival.

Other Key Films: *Every Day Except Christmas* (1958); *O Lucky Man* (1973); *Britannia Hospital* (1982); *The Whales Of August* (1987); *Glory! Glory!* (1989); *Is That All There Is?* (1992)

Andersson, Bibi

Along with **Liv Ullmann**, Andersson is the best-known actress to emerge from director **Ingmar Bergman's** extraordinary body of work. Catching sight of her on stage at Malmö during a theatrical production, Bergman immediately cast her in his gentle comedy of manners, *Smiles Of A Summer Night* (1955) – just three years later she followed up her success with a significant triumph at the Cannes Film Festival with Bergman's *Brink Of Life* (1958). Although she later moved into the commercial mainstream, it is as the complex heroine of such powerful and uncompromising emotional dramas as Bergman's *Persona* (1966) and *The Touch* (1971) that she will always be remembered.

Other Key Films: *The Seventh Seal* (1956); *Wild Strawberries* (1958); *The Magician* (1958); *The Devil's Eye* (1960); *The Pleasure Garden* (1961); *All These Women* (1964); *The Rape* (1967); *The Passion Of Anna* (1969); *Scenes From A Marriage* (1973); *Babette's Feast* (1987); *Dreamplay* (1994); *Shit Happens* (2000); *Elina* (2002)

Andress, Ursula

No great shakes as an actress, Andress was, nevertheless, something of an event in cinematic history, bursting onto the screen in what, in retrospect no doubt, seemed a rather sturdy white bikini, in Terence Young's *Dr No* (1962) – for the next few years her poster image, complete with Freudian knife at belt, graced the walls and the minds of an untold number of spotty teenagers. Trading on her newfound fame she went on to appear in a succession of blatantly commercial British films which culminated in her public cuckolding of her husband John Derek (of *Tarzan The Ape Man* (1981) and Bo Derek fame), with actor **Jean-Paul Belmondo**, in a primitive version of what has now become the much-loved modern paparazzi-fest tradition. And that's about it.

Other Key Films: *She* (1965); *What's New Pussycat?* (1965); *The Blue Max* (1966); *Clash Of The Titans* (1981); *Liberté, Égalité, Choucroute* (1985); *Cremaster 5* (1997); *Die Vogelpredigt* (2005)

Andrews, Dana

Curiously unquantifiable (he wasn't *really* handsome) but invariably interesting lead actor who shone as the obsessed detective (a perennial Hollywood genre favourite, this) in **Otto Preminger's** fascinating whodunit *Laura* (1944), and much later as the unbelieving psychic investigator in **Jacques Tourneur's** cult horror masterpiece *Curse Of The Demon* (1958). *Film noir* aficionados will cherish the often-underrated Andrews's performance in Preminger's little-known (and **Ben Hecht** scripted) *Where The Sidewalk Ends* (1950), in which he plays a cop gone seriously to the bad, with the gorgeous **Gene Tierney**, who also played the elusive *Laura*, featuring once again as his love interest.

Other Key Films: *Ball Of Fire* (1941); *Swamp Water* (1941); *Boomerang!* (1947); *Beyond A Reasonable Doubt* (1956); *While The City Sleeps* (1956); *Battle Of The Bulge* (1965)

Andrews, Harry

A fine and in many ways scurrilously underrated actor (one presumes on account of his typecast, square-jawed, military look) Andrews always appeared comfortable in front of the cameras, and exuded that rare thing – spontaneous integrity. He moved from the stage to a thirty-year career in films, and finally to television, where he also excelled, producing some of his best work in that medium, most notably in Michael

Wilcox's 1985 BBC TV drama, *Lent*. On film he was particularly good as the gruff but tender sergeant Tom Pugh in J Lee Thompson's *Ice Cold In Alex* (1958), and also as **Trevor Howard's** obstreperous elder brother, Lord Raglan, in **Tony Richardson's** *The Charge Of The Light Brigade* (1968).

Other Key Films: *The Red Beret* (1952); *The Black Knight* (1954); *Saint Joan* (1958); *Barabbas* (1962); *55 Days At Peking* (1964); *The Hill* (1965); *The Sea Gull* (1968); *Entertaining Mr Sloane* (1970); *The Ruling Class* (1972); *The Mackintosh Man* (1973)

Andrews, Julie

Always eager to belie the squeaky-clean, perpetual virgin image which the studios foisted upon her in such perennial family fare as Robert Stevenson's *Mary Poppins* (1964) and **Robert Wise's** *The Sound Of Music* (1965), Andrews has also chosen to act in more 'adult' material, such as husband Blake Edwards's *S.O.B.* (1981), in which she famously bared her breasts at the not-so-advanced age of forty-six. Many of her die-hard fans felt that by doing so she had rather missed the point.

Other Key Films: *Torn Curtain* (1966); *Star!* (1968); *Victor/Victoria* (1981); *Duet For One* (1986); *Relative Values* (2000); *Shrek 2 & 3* (2004/2007)

Key Line: 'Working with her is like being hit over the head with a Valentine's card.' [Attributed to Christopher Plummer, her co-star in The Sound Of Music]

Anger, Kenneth

Famous in film buff circles for his schlock exposé of Hollywood's most grotesque secret lives in his books *Hollywood Babylon* (1958) and *Hollywood Babylon 2* (1984) (must reading for all aficionados of camp), Anger is also a very talented avant-garde filmmaker (and occasional actor), obsessed with mysticism and the occult, whose work includes the notorious and orgiastic *Inauguration Of The Pleasure Dome* (54-66).

Other Key Films: *Fireworks* (1947); *The Story Of O* (1959-1961); *Scorpio Rising* (1964); *Lucifer Rising* (1973); *Jonas In The Desert* (1993); *Anger Sees Red* (2004)

Best Animated Films

Tex Avery's *The Cat That Hated People* (1948) and *Little Rural Ridinghood* (1949); Frédéric Back's *L'Homme Qui Plantait Des Arbres* (1987); Brad Bird's *The Incredibles* (2004); **Tim Burton's** *The Nightmare Before Christmas* (1994); **Walt Disney's** *Snow White And The Seven Dwarfs* (1937), *Pinocchio* (1940), *Fantasia* (1940) and *The Jungle Book* (1967); Paul Grimault's *Le Roi Et L'Oiseau* (1979); Hanna/Barbera's *The Cat's Concerto* (Tom & Jerry) (1947); John Lasseter's *Toy Story* (1995); Nick Park's *Wallace & Gromit Tetralogy* (1989-2005); Robert Zemeckis's *Who Framed Roger Rabbit* (1988)

Annaud, Jean-Jacques

Annaud's career runs parallel, in many ways, to his near contemporary **Ridley Scott**. Both started out in advertising, moved smoothly through their own domestic markets, and have since ended up making large, internationally promoted middlebrow films. *Quest For Fire* (1981) was Annaud's first big success in this sphere, notable for the fact that its dialogue consisted of an entirely made-up language (by novelist Anthony Burgess) with subtitles, ensuring the film the widest possible commercial airing. Annaud pulled off a similar trick with *The Bear* (1988) [the dialogue this time consisting of grunts and screams], which followed his very successful foray into Umberto Eco territory with *The Name Of The Rose* (1986). Very popular in France, where he is seen as living proof that French sensibility can indeed attract a mass international following, Annaud is also notable for the very few projects he takes up.

See **Worst Films**

Other Key Films: *Black And White In Colour* (1976); *Hothead* (1979); *The Lover* (1992); *Wings Of Courage* (1995); *Seven Years In Tibet* (1997); *Enemy At The Gates* (2001); *Two Brothers* (2004)

Antonioni, Michelangelo

One of the undoubted masters of the Italian cinema, Antonioni's uncanny visual sense was evident from his very first directing job, the black-and-white documentary *The People Of The Po Valley* (1947). Everything counts in an Antonioni film, from the colour of a fur coat to the positioning of two alienated people on a bridge. In his famous trilogy comprising *L'Avventura* (1959), *La Notte* (1960) and *L'Eclisse* (1962), Antonioni uses the marvellous faces of Monica Vitti and **Jeanne Moreau** to mirror the breakdown of a series of intense interrelationships. With *Blow-Up* (1966), Antonioni turned his attention to swinging London, and in *Zabriskie Point* (1970) to irony-free California, which he proceeded (paradoxically really, given the title of his previous film) to blow up, in one of the longest and most graphic explosion shots in film history. **Jack Nicholson** gave one of his best-ever screen performances in Antonioni's *The Passenger* (1975), which explored, at times painfully, the sometimes tenuous fragmentation of personal identity, a subject of which this director has proved himself a master.

Other Key Films: *Story Of A Love Affair* (1950); *Red Desert* (1964); *The Three Faces Of A Woman* (1965); *Identification Of A Woman* (1982); *Beyond The Clouds* (1995); *Eros* [Segment] (2004)

Apted, Michael

Director Michael Apted's debut feature, *Triple Echo* (1972), was a curious, rather underrated piece of work, in which a Second World War deserter disguises himself as the sister of his mistress (by cross-dressing) in order to avoid capture and a certain firing squad, only to find himself the object of a Military Police sergeant's lewd advances (in the form of a gloriously gloating **Oliver Reed**) – a hell of a plot, when you come to think of it, and considerably in advance of its time in its investigation of sexual identity. Apted went on to international success with *Coal Miner's Daughter* (1980), *Gorky Park* (1983), *Gorillas In The Mist* (1988) and *Nell* (1994), as well as trying his hand, very effectively, at a **James Bond** movie, in *The World Is Not Enough* (1999) – but none have had quite the same mystery or sense of place as *Triple Echo*. *Extreme Measures* (1996), with **Gene Hackman** and **Hugh Grant**, was an outstanding thriller, however, and Apted remains a director to watch.

Other Key Films: *Stardust* (1974); *Critical Condition* (1987); *The Long Way Home* (1989); *Class Action* (1990); *Thunderheart* (1992); *Moving The Mountain* (1995); *Inspiration* (1997); *Always Outnumbered* (1998); *Enigma* (2001)

Arau, Alfonso

Mexican director of *Like Water For Chocolate* (1992), which was written by his ex-wife Laura Esquivel, and the even more 'chocolaty' *A Walk In The Clouds* (1995), Arau began life as an actor on such movies as **Sam Peckinpah's** *The Wild Bunch* (1969) and Robert Zemeckis's *Romancing The Stone* (1984). His own films vary from out-and-out thrillers to social commentaries, and he now runs his own LA production company, specialising in films for a predominantly Latin American audience.

Other Key Films: *The Barefoot Eagle* (1967); *Calzonzin Inspector* (1974); *Wetback Power* (1980); *Chido Guan* (1984); *Picking Up The Pieces* (2000); *Zapata* (2004)

Arbuckle, Fatty

'Poor' Fatty tasted both the fruits of heady success and the bitter aloes of public contumely. The former 'king of comedy' (who was earning $5,000 a week in 1917) saw his career plummet when he was accused of rape and murder after inadvertently causing the death of gaiety girl Virginia Rappe by rupturing her bladder *in flagrante delicto* at an orgy. Though finally acquitted on all charges (for lack of evidence – most of the other revellers were drunk at the time and the chief witness was dead) Fatty was banned from acting and his $3,000,000 contract with Paramount torn up. The disgraced former plumber eventually ended up drunk and dead himself, aged only forty-six, in a New York apartment. **James Ivory** later made a film inspired by the Arbuckle affair, starring James Coco, called *The Wild Party* (1975).

Other Key Films: *The Rounders* (1914); *A Cream Puff Romance* (1916); *Rough House* (1917); *The Cook* (1918); *The Garage* (1919); *The Dollar-A-Year Man* (1921)

Ardant, Fanny

A favourite actress of avant-garde director **Alain Resnais** (and the widow of film director **François Truffaut**) the Monte-Carlo born Ardant has been notably successful on both stage and screen, as much on account of her offbeat, bluestocking looks, as for her undoubted talent. Her filmography is astonishing, the more so as she is virtually unknown outside France except in enlightened film buff circles. Her recent performance in **Patrice Leconte's** majestically comic *Ridicule* (1996) has, of course, done absolutely nothing to change this unreasonable state of affairs.

Other Key Films: *Les Chiens* (1979); *The Woman Next Door* (1981); *Vivement Dimanche!* (1983); *Un Amour De Swann* (1984); *Next Summer* (1985); *Mélo* (1986); *Afraid Of The Dark* (1992); *The Deserter's Wife* (1992); *Colonel Chabert* (1994); *Beyond The Clouds* (1996); *Pédale Douce* (1997); *Elizabeth* (1998); *La Cena* (1998); *La Débandade* (1999); *Le Fils Du Français* (1999); *Le Libertin* (2000); *Callas Forever* (2002)

Arkin, Alan

A much-garlanded character actor, Arkin is best known for his portrayal of the deaf-mute in Robert Ellis Miller's *The Heart Is A Lonely Hunter* (1968) and for his bravura performance as Yossarian in **Mike Nichols's** otherwise disappointing *Catch 22* (1970). He was absolutely outstanding in James Foley's film version of David Mamet's stage play, *Glengarry Glen Ross* (1992), and more recent turns in **Tim Burton's** *Edward Scissorhands* (1990), Joe Johnston's *The Rocketeer* (1991) and Andrew Niccol's *Gattaca* (1997) prove that his career is still in gear.

Other Key Films: *The Russians Are Coming! The Russians Are Coming!* (1966); *Wait Until Dark* (1967); *Inspector Clouseau* (1968); *Freebie And The Bean* (1974); *Hearts Of The West* (1975); *Simon* (1980); *Big Trouble* (1985); *Grosse Pointe Blank* (1997); *Jakob The Liar* (1999); *Arigo* (2000) [also dir.]; *Firewall* (2006)

Arlen, Harold

Son of a New York cantor, the multi-talented Arlen composed the music for **Victor Fleming's** *The Wizard Of Oz* (1939) and **Vincente Minnelli's** all-black *Cabin In The Sky* (1943), which united such Jazz luminaries as Lena Horne, **Louis Armstrong**, Duke Ellington and Ethel Waters. The best song in the movie, and one of the best ever written, is Arlen's 'Happiness Is Just A Thing Called Joe.'

Other Key Films: Anatole Litvak's *Blues In The Night* (1941); George Seaton's *The Country Girl* (1954); **George Cukor's** *A Star Is Born* (1954)

Arletty

Quintessential French actress who steadfastly refused all offers to go to Hollywood, Arletty later found herself accused of collaboration with the Germans after her war-time affair with a high-ranking Nazi officer came to light. Her name is now inextricably linked with that of director **Marcel Carné**, for whom she acted in four absolutely outstanding films – *Hôtel Du Nord* (1938), *Le Jour Se Lève* (1939), *Les Visiteurs Du Soir* (1943), and *Les Enfants Du Paradis* (1944), the last of which, thanks in part to her outstanding performance as Garance, is generally recognised as one of the greatest films of all time.

Other Key Films: *Un Chien Qui Rapporte* (1930); *Pension Mimosas* (1935); *Faisons Un Rêve* (1936); *Les Perles De La Couronne* (1937); *Désiré* (1938); *Fric-Frac* (1939); *Madame Sans-Gêne* (1941)

Armendariz, Pedro

He was Mexico's very own version of **Rudolf Valentino**, and his following remains strong to this day in a country still emotionally wedded to its past and to the cult of poetic and sentimental machismo which he personified. Armendariz killed himself at the age of fifty-one on learning that he had cancer, after starring in a succession of great films from the golden age of Mexican cinema, including **Emilio Fernandez's** *Maria Candelaria* (1943) and *The Pearl* (1945). He had a flourishing career, too, across the border with the US, with notable parts in **John Ford's** *Three Godfathers* (1949) and a wonderful last fling as *James Bond's* lasciviously daredevil Turkish friend, Kerim Bey, in *From Russia With Love* (1963).

Other Key Films: *Maria Elena* (1935); *La Reina Del Rio* (1939); *Simon Bolivar* (1941); *Flor Sylvestre* (1944); *Enamorada* (1946); *The Fugitive* (1947); *Fort Apache* (1948); *We Were Strangers* (1949); *La Malquerida* (1949); *The Big Boodle* (1958); *La Cucaracha* (1958)

Armstrong, Gillian

Armstrong's career began strongly with *My Brilliant Career* (1979), to the extent that she seemed on the verge of a heady international breakthrough, but her subsequent choice of resolutely low-profile material seems to have worked against her (while saying much for her integrity). *Mrs Soffel* (1984) may have been a touch worthy, but *High Tide* (1987), with the excellent **Judy Davis**, was a magnificent return to form, and Armstrong's version of *Little Women* (1994) is the best since the 1933 **George Cukor/Katherine Hepburn** movie.

Other Key Films: *The Singer And The Dancer* (1976); *Starstruck* (1982); *Fires Within* (1991); *The Last Days Of Chez Nous* (1992); *Oscar And Lucinda* (1997); *Charlotte Gray* (2001)

Armstrong, Louis

Hardly a film actor (not a lot of people know that...) so much as a walking, singing, trumpet-playing legend, who starred in a number of films simply to please his fans and to boost box office takings – mind you, he had a neat line in repartee and he lit up the screen whenever he appeared, which must put him somewhere near the top rank of the acting profession. He partnered **Bing Crosby** in Norman McLeod's *Pennies From Heaven* (1936), and then again, twenty-one years later, in Charles Walters's *High Society* (1956), but if you *really* want to see Satchmo swing, check out Bert Stern's *Jazz On A Summer's Day* (1959), and in particular his duet with trombonist Jack Teagarden on the evergreen 'Lazy River'. Sublime!

Other Key Films: *Artists And Models* (1937); *Cabin In The Sky* (1943); *Hollywood Canteen* (1944); *A Song Is Born* (1948); *The Glenn Miller Story* (1954); *The Five Pennies* (1959); *Paris Blues* (1961); *Hello Dolly!* (1969)

Arnold, Malcolm

Distinguished composer and coincidental scorer of film soundtracks, Arnold is best known in cinema circles for his work on **David Lean's** *The Sound Barrier* (1952), *Hobson's Choice* (1954), and *The Bridge On The River Kwai* (1958), but he also scored Ronald Neame's *Tunes Of Glory* (1960) and Delbert Mann's rather disappointing – at least when compared with the 1935 **George Cukor** version – *David Copperfield* (1970).

Other Key Films: Anthony Kimmins's *The Captain's Paradise* (1953); Henry Cornelius's *I Am A Camera* (1955); **Carol Reed's** *Trapeze* (1956); Stuart Heisler's *Island In The Sun* (1958); Ronald Neame's *The Chalk Garden* (1964); **Anthony Mann's** *The Heroes Of Telemark* (1966)

Arthur, Jean

Arthur only really shone when **Frank Capra** directed her, but then this husky voiced tomboy of an actress – who always gave the impression that she was game for anything – made movie magic, as in *Mr Deeds Goes To Town* (1936), *You Can't Take It With You* (1938) and *Mr Smith Goes To Washington* (1939). Her career ended on a sour note thanks to a contractual dispute with Columbia Studios, but she lit the screen up one last time as embattled homesteader **Van Heflin's** wife, quietly and decorously in love with gunfighter **Alan Ladd** in **George Stevens's** magnificent **Western** *Shane* (1953).

Other Key Films: *The Whole Town's Talking* (1935); *The Plainsman* (1937); *Arizona* (1940); *The Devil And Miss Jones* (1941); *The Talk Of The Town* (1942)

Key Line: 'I'm hard to get, Geoff. All you have to do is ask me.' [Arthur to Cary Grant in Howard Hawks's *Only Angels Have Wings* (1939)]

Arzner, Dorothy

Along with **Ida Lupino**, who was infinitely her superior in instinct, if not in technique, Arzner was one of the few female film directors to work commercially in the era of the great studios. A superb editor, and a more than competent scriptwriter, Arzner's first directing job was Paramount's *Fashions For Women* (1927). Among her later films, both *Nana* (1934) and *Dance Girl Dance* (1940), with its slight feminist twist, are particularly worthy of mention.

Other Key Films: *Manhattan Cocktail* (1928); *The Wild Party* (1929); *Merrily We Go To Hell* (1932); *Christopher Strong* (1933); *First Comes Courage* (1943)

Ashcroft, Peggy

A great stage actress who gave only a few screen performances, Ashcroft had the rare ability to subsume herself totally inside any part that she was playing. As the downtrodden crofter's wife in **Alfred Hitchcock's** *The Thirty-Nine Steps* (1935), her intense five minutes on film unaccountably linger in the mind long afterwards, and it was only just that she received a belated best-supporting actress Oscar for her role of Mrs Moore, in **David Lean's** *A Passage To India*.

Other Key Films: *The Wandering Jew* (1933); *Rhodes* (1936); *The Nun's Story* (1959); *Secret Ceremony* (1968); *Sunday Bloody Sunday* (1971); *She's Been Away* (1989)

Asquith, Anthony

Known as 'Puffin' to chums such as **John Mills**, Asquith was actually the son of a British Prime Minister, and, coincidentally, the director of several of the most prestigious films in the history of British Cinema. His longest-lasting collaboration was with playwright Terence Rattigan, from whose scripts he directed the haunting *The Way To The Stars* (1945) [a.k.a. *Johnny In The Clouds*], *The Winslow Boy* (1950) and *The Browning Version* (1951). Asquith was a real master at portraying the stultifying inhibitions of the upper and middle classes, and his films were often subtly anarchic, reflecting his deeply held and egalitarian political views.

Other Key Films: *Pygmalion* (1938); *French Without Tears* (1939); *Fanny By Gaslight* (1944); *The Importance Of Being Earnest* (1952); *Carrington VC* (1954); *The Yellow Rolls-Royce* (1964)

Astaire, Fred

The most elegant of all screen dancers, Astaire encapsulated the magic and glamour of Hollywood better than anyone else, whether dancing alone – one has only to think of his 'put her to sleep, sandman' tap-dance in front of Edward Everett Horton in Mark Sandrich's *Top Hat* (1935) – or in partnership with **Ginger Rogers** [check out their magical pairing in **George Stevens's** *Swing Time* (1936)], **Rita Hayworth**, or **Cyd Charisse**, who all did their best work with him. Like every great dancer, he made his partners look beautiful, and his light, apparently untrained tenor voice was perfect for those subtle Cole Porter numbers which prove so very much harder to master than they first appear when one foolishly attempts to sing along to them in the shower. Later, when his dancing days were over, Astaire proved himself a sensitive and modest actor, most notably as Julian Osborn in Stanley Kramer's *On The Beach* (1959). A true master.

Other Key Films: *Flying Down To Rio* (1933); *The Gay Divorcee* (1934); *Follow The Fleet* (1936); *Shall We Dance* (1937); *Carefree* (1938); *Holiday Inn* (1942); *The Sky's The Limit* (1943); *Blue Skies* (1946); *Easter Parade* (1948); *Let's Dance* (1950); *The Band Wagon* (1953); *Silk Stockings* (1958); *Funny Face* (1958); *The Towering Inferno* (1974); *That's Entertainment* [compilation] (1974)

Key Line: 'Can't act. Can't sing. Slightly bald. Can dance a little.' [Verdict on Astaire's first screen test in 1932]

Asther, Nils

If Asther were only ever remembered for one part, that part would be the eponymous effete Chinese warlord in **Frank Capra's** *The Bitter Tea Of General Yen* (1933). Using all the well-honed techniques he learnt during his salad days as a star of silent cinema, Asther somehow transcended the absurdity inherent in a tall, finely chiselled Swede playing a Chinaman, to produce an odd and heady effect that is infinitely seductive, and, by the end of the film, almost unbearably poignant – we are certainly not in the least surprised when gorgeous **Barbara Stanwyck**, as Megan Davis, throws caution (and her boring missionary husband) to the winds on his account. The final scene on board the boat, with Stanwyck and Walter Connolly reminiscing about Yen, never fails to bring a tear (at least to this writer's) eye.

Other Key Films: *The Cossacks* (1928); *Adrian Lecouvreur* (1928); *Wild Orchids* (1929); *The Sea Bat* (1930); *Letty Lynton* (1932); *Madame Spy* (1934); *The Crime Doctor* (1934); *Night Monster* (1942); *That Man From Tangier* (1953); *When Darkness Falls* (1960)

Astor, Mary

Astor is most fondly remembered for her unwanted part in the 'Mary Astor sex diaries scandal', in which she detailed her exotic shenanigans with four-times-a-night curtain-raiser, playwright George S Kaufman. The diaries unaccountably fell into the hands of Astor's then husband, who blatantly used them against her in the ensuing child custody proceedings. Astor's movies could hardly fail after that, and eager fans breathlessly scrutinized (with entirely new eyes, one supposes) her ice cool performance as Brigid O'Shaughnessy opposite **Humphrey Bogart's** Sam Spade in **John Huston's** *The Maltese Falcon* (1941), and her glittering comic turn as sexy serial divorcée Princess Centimillia in **Preston Sturges's** *The Palm Beach Story* (1942) [French title, *Madame Et Ses Flirts!*], which also happens to be one of the funniest films ever made.

Other Key Films: *Beau Brummell* (1924); *Red Dust* (1932); *Dodsworth* (1936); *The Hurricane* (1937); *The Prisoner Of Zenda* (1937); *The Great Lie* (1941); *Across The Pacific* (1942); *Meet Me In St Louis* (1944)

Key Line: 'Ah, desert night – with George's body plunging into mine, naked under the stars…' (A brief excerpt from Astor's diary, unfortunately subsequently burnt by order of the judge.)

Attenborough, Richard

Attenborough made his first real mark as the tormented, razor-toting Pinkie in **John Boulting's** *Brighton Rock* (1947), and followed this up with a seemingly countless number of stiff upper lip and 'cor blimey!' jobs in worthy Second World War films. Talent will always out, however, and he soon matured into more nuanced performances, culminating in his chilling portrayal of serial killer John Reginald Christie in Richard Fleischer's *10 Rillington Place* (1971). By this time Attenborough had transmogrified into a gifted director, most notably with his screen version of Joan Littlewood's stage production of Charles Chilton's play *Oh! What A Lovely War* (1969), which he followed up with the equally successful *Young Winston* (1972), the first of a number of sometimes rather worthy biopics that took him through the 1980s and 1990s. Now a Lord, and something of a power behind the scenes in British Cinema, he delighted his loyal audience by a tremendous return to form as a director with the touching and still underrated *Shadowlands* (1993).

Other Key Films: *In Which We Serve* (1942); *The Gift Horse* (1952); *The Angry Silence* (1960); *The Great Escape* (1963); *Gandhi* (1982); *Cry Freedom* (1987); *Chaplin* (1992); *In Love And War* (1996); *Grey Owl* (1999)

Atwill, Lionel

A fine character actor (and renowned lecher and orgiast) who, like his successor **Vincent Price**, developed a lucrative secondary career in **horror** movies, Atwill's booming English stage voice and lean, tormented features enlivened many a dreary murder scene. The performance for which he is best remembered came as the doomed protagonist in Sidney Lanfield's classic *The Hound Of The Baskervilles* (1939), but he also did sterling supporting work as diplomats, aristocrats, colonial governors and stern fathers in some of the greatest films of Hollywood's golden age.

Other Key Films: *Indiscretion* (1921); *The Mystery Of The Wax Museum* (1933); *Stamboul Quest* (1934); *The Devil Is A Woman* (1935); *Captain Blood* (1935); *The Lives Of A Bengal Lancer* (1935); *The Last Train From Madrid* (1937); *The Great Waltz* (1938); *The Three Musketeers* (1939); *Johnny Apollo* (1940); *Boom Town* (1940); *To Be Or Not To Be* (1942)

Key Line: 'All women love the men they fear. Their preference is… for a Master!' [Atwill on himself]

Audran, Stéphane

A former wife of director **Claude Chabrol** and the star of many of his films, Audran perfectly encapsulated the brittle, sophisticated and sensual French ideal of beauty that **Luis Buñuel** so perfectly satirised in *The Discreet Charm Of The Bourgeoisie* (1972). A highly intelligent actress and markedly careful with her choice of roles, Audran showed a vast and still-expanding international audience just how good she was with the performance of a lifetime in Gabriel Axel's now perennial *Babette's Feast* (1987), although her most famous role is still that of Hélène, **Jean Yanne's** potential victim in Chabrol's *Le Boucher* (1970) [*The Butcher*]. If an American actress had produced the same body and quality of work in the US that Audran has done in France, she would be considered a national treasure.

Other Key Films: *Les Cousins* (1959); *Le Tigre Aime La Chair Fraîche* (1964); *Les Biches* (1968); *Just Before Nightfall* (1971); *Violette Nozière* (1978); *Eagle's Wing* (1979); *Coup De Torchon* [*Clean Slate*] (1981); *Le Choc* (1982); *Quiet Days In Clichy* (1990); *Betty* (1992); *Maximum Risk* (1996); *Arlette* (1997); *Belle Maman* (1999); *Le Pique-Nique De Lulu Kreutz* (2000)

August, Bille

Denmark's most prestigious filmmaker, August soon made his national mark with *Twist And Shout* (1986), and his international one with *Pelle The Conqueror* (1987), with which he won a Palme D'Or at the Cannes Film Festival. His more recent films, such as *The House Of The Spirits* (1993) and *Smilla's Sense Of Snow* (1997) have disappointed some of his fans, and, despite his undoubted talent, he has yet to establish himself firmly as a major international player.

Other Key Films: *Zappa* (1983); *The Best Intentions* (1992); *Jerusalem* (1996); *Les Misérables* (1998); *A Song For Martin* (2000); *Return To Sender* (2004)

August, Joseph H

One of the great unsung cinematographers of the American cinema, August was a master of light and shade, which he used to fine effect in **John Ford's** *The Informer* (1935) and *They Were Expendable* (1945), and particularly in his final film, **William Dieterle's** haunting *Portrait Of Jennie* (1948). The highlight of August's career (for aficionados only, of course) was the scene in Henry Otto's *Dante's Inferno* (1924) where August photographed the interior of Hell in a now notorious ten-minute sequence in which greased up musclemen (complete with helmets and togas) thoroughly enjoy themselves thrashing (for the victim's own good, no doubt) an eclectic assortment of naked and chained starlets.

Other Key Films: Lambert Hillyer's *The Narrow Trail* (1917); **John Ford's** *Up The River* (1930); **Howard Hawks's** *Twentieth Century* (1934); **George Cukor's** *Sylvia Scarlett* (1935); **George Stevens's** *A Damsel In Distress* (1937)

Aurenche, Jean

One of the greatest and most consistent of all French screenwriters, Aurenche is responsible for such brilliantly disparate films as **Marcel Carné's** *Hôtel Du Nord* (1938) and, together with his collaborator, Pierre Bost, **Claude Autant-Lara's** *Le Diable Au Corps* [*Devil In The Flesh*] (1947), and **René Clément's** *Jeux Interdits* [*Forbidden Games*] (1952). Criticised by some **New Wavers** for his adherence to the 'tradition de qualité' which they felt had cramped French films for a generation, with Aurenche finally won through, despite nearly a decade in the doldrums, with **Bertrand Tavernier's** *Coup De Torchon* (1981) and Pierre Granier-Deferre's *L'Étoile Du Nord* (1982), which perfectly illustrate the need for both cinematic traditions.

Other Key Films: Jean Delannoy's La Symphonie Pastorale (1946); Claude Autant-Lara's L'Auberge Rouge [The Red Inn] (1951), Le Rouge Et Le Noir [The Red And The Black] (1954) and En Cas De Malheur [Love Is My Profession] (1958)

Autant-Lara, Claude

That paradoxical figure, an anti-establishment right-winger, Autant-Lara made the notorious *Le Diable au Corps* [*Devil in the Flesh*] (1946) in which a schoolboy conducts a passionate affair with an absent soldier's wife. A stylish, commercially successful filmmaker, Autant-Lara found himself increasingly marginalised during the late 1950s and early 1960s by the arrival of the French **New Wave**, which criticized him for his slick virtuosity and concentration on technique. He made something of a belated riposte, however, with *En Cas De Malheur* [*Love Is My Profession*] (1958), which starred a conspicuously rosy-cheeked Brigitte Bardot [see picture section for an explanation].

Other Key Films: Ciboulette (1933); Le Rouge Et Le Noir (1954); A Pig Across Paris (1956); Le Journal D'Une Femme En Blanc (1965); Gloria (1977)

Auteuil, Daniel

Now internationally known thanks to his performances in **Claude Berri's** *Jean De Florette* (1986) and *Manon Des Sources* (1986), Auteuil descends from a family of itinerant opera singers, and the comic brio he brings to some of his roles, together with a wry, occasionally awkward self-deprecation, reflects this fact, and marks him out as a natural screen presence. Superb as the tormented protestant king, Henri de Navarre, in Patrice Chereau's *Reine Margot* [*Queen Margot*] (1994), he is equally at home in such contemporary dramas as **André Techiné's** *Ma Saison Préférée* [*My Favourite Season*] (1993) and Claude Sautet's *Un Coeur En Hiver* [*A Heart In Winter*] (1993). One can always infer more from Auteuil's sensitive, perpetually tormented face than his skilful use of screen dialogue would suggest, putting him in friendly contention with such great French cinema actors of the past as **Louis Jouvet** and **Jean Gabin**.

Other Key Films: L'Amour En Douce (1985); Romuald Et Juliette (1989); Lacenaire (1990); The Separation (1994); Les Voleurs (1996); Lucie Aubrac (1997); Le Bossu (1997); La Fille Sure Le Pont (1999); Mauvais Passe (1999); La Veuve De Saint-Pierre (2000); Sade (2000); L'Adversaire (2001); Caché [Hidden] (2005); Mon Meilleur Ami (2006)

Auteur Theory

A concept, first put forward in 1954 by **François Truffaut** in Cahiers du Cinéma magazine, equating film with high art, insofar as each film might be considered as the exclusive and identifiable work of the director, rather than as a more conventional collaboration between many.

Autry, Gene

Singing cowboy star who, with his horse, Champion, almost single-handedly kept Republic Studios from going under during the late 1930s and early 1940s, and who became massively wealthy as a result. Writer of more than 200 songs, Autry's films were long on action and short on romance, something that obviously appealed to the youthful pre-war audiences that were his staple.

Key Films: *Tumblin' Tumbleweeds* (1935); *Melody Ranch* (1940); *Heart Of The Rio Grande* (1942); *Rim Of The Canyon* (1949)

Avery, Tex

A far greater cult figure in France than he is in the USA, Avery was the supreme fantasist of cartoon animation, with many of his 1930s and 1940s shorts reaching almost surreal levels of macabre and ironical humour. A classic example is his placard-carrying '*Eat At Joe's*' bear – it is only belatedly that we realise that the bear *is* Joe, and that he lures hungry victims into a fake diner to provide for his own meals. Falsely described as a screwball stylist, Avery actually understood the attraction and cathartic effect of horror just as well as Bruno Bettelheim or the brothers Grimm, and his vital, sexy cartoons, stand up, to this day, as well as ever.

Other Key Films: *Uncle Tom's Bungalow* (1937); *The Blitz Wolf* (1942); *Red Hot Riding Hood* (1943); *The Shooting Of Dan Magoo* (1945); *Uncle Tom's Cabana* (1947); *Señor Droopy* (1949) ...let's face it, watch anything by Avery you can.

Ayres, Lew

Ayres's finest moment came as young German army recruit Paul Baumer, killed by a sniper while reaching out to touch a butterfly, in Lewis Milestone's great anti-war film *All Quiet On The Western Front* (1930), following which he spent long, and no doubt profitable years, dangling his stethoscope as Dr Kildare. A gentle, kindly man, he took both of those parts with him to the Second World War, in which, as a conscientious objector, he agreed only to serve as a medical orderly (albeit under fire). When he was eventually allowed back into the Hollywood fold, he made one or two effective *film noirs*, with **John Sturges's** downbeat *The Capture* (1950) a real standout.

Other Key Films: *Night World* (1932); *The Last Train From Madrid* (1937); *The Unfaithful* (1947); *Johnny Belinda* (1948); *Donovan's Brain* (1953); *Advise And Consent* (1962)

Azéma, Sabine

Along with **Fanny Ardant**, Azéma is a favourite actress of director **Alain Resnais** – he used her in his Alan Ayckbourn inspired curiosity *Smoking/No Smoking* (1993) – and a fine stage performer as well. She invariably gives committed performances, and the highlights of her screen career include **Bertrand Tavernier's** *Un Dimanche À La Campagne* [*A Sunday In The Country*] (1984), Resnais's *Mélo* (1986), and the provision of consummate and touching support for **Philippe Noiret** in Tavernier's majestic *À La Vie Et Rien D'Autre* (1989).

Other Key Films: *La Dentellière* [*The Lacemaker*] (1977); *Cinq Jours En Juin* (1989); *Trois Années* (1990); *On Connaît La Chanson* (1997); *Le Schpountz* (1999); *La Bûche* (1999); *Tanguy, 28 Ans, Habite Encore Chez Ses Parents* (2001); *La Chambre Des Officiers* (2001); *Olé* (2005)

Aznavour, Charles

One of the great French torch singers of the 1950s and 1960s (although he was, in fact, of Armenian extraction), Aznavour was also a surprisingly good actor, a fact first recognized by **François Truffaut** in *Tirez Sur Le Pianiste* [*Shoot The Piano Player*] (1960), in which Aznavour plays Charlie Kohler/Edouard Saroyan, the unwitting and elusive piano-playing brother of a minor crook who subsequently re-enters his life and inveigles him into mayhem. He carried Claude Bernard-Aubert's very funny *Le*

Facteur S'En Va-T-En Guerre [*The Postman Goes To War*] (1966) on his own, and he was about the best thing in **Claude Lelouch's** otherwise rather turgid *Edith Et Marcel* (1983), which told of the brief love affair between *chanteuse* Edith Piaf and boxer Marcel Cerdan. His most celebrated international hit, which he sang in magnificently broken English, was 'She', an American cover version of which appeared on the soundtrack of Garry Marshall's *Pretty Woman* (1990), sung by another artist (how dumb can you get?). Try to catch Aznavour's original French version if you can.

Other Key Films: *Le Testament D'Orphée* (1960); *Taxi For Tobruk* (1961); *The Adventurers* (1973); *The Blockhouse* (1973); *The Tin Drum* (1979); *Viva La Vie* (1984); *Les Années Campagne* (1991); *Le Comédien* (1997)

Babenco, Hector

Argentinian-born Babenco is the prime example of a film director lauded in his own country for the controversial yet committed nature of his early work, who then tries, and fails, to achieve the same trick in the United States under the triple burden of stars, money and his own political expectations. *Pixote* (1981), with its uncomfortable use of real street children whom the audience voyeuristically know stand little chance of eventual survival after the filmmakers no longer need them, finds itself in marked counterpoint to the smooth, equally committed, yet undeniably theatrical *Kiss Of The Spider Woman* (1985) and *Ironweed* (1987), in both of which the audience can be perfectly sure that the stars will return to their lives of luxury and plenty as soon as their low-life makeup is taken off. A paradox? Of course. That is the nature of cinema.

Other Key Films: *King Of The Night* (1975); *At Play In The Fields Of The Lord* (1991); *Foolish Heart* (1998); *Carandiru* (2003)

Bacall, Lauren

Her first film was **Howard Hawks's** *To Have And Have Not* (1944), she was nineteen, and the wiggle she gave future real life husband **Humphrey Bogart** in the last scene of the film is one of the sexiest moments in all cinema – full of invitation and promise and devil-may-care youth. She followed this up with a sizzling performance as Vivien Sternwood in Hawks's *The Big Sleep* (1947) and then, apart from a fine, more mature appearance in **John Huston's** *Key Largo* (1948), she virtually disappeared from the scene as a major Hollywood player, although she was to appear successfully on the stage and in a further mixed bag of twenty-five movies – some reasonably memorable, as in **Jean Negulesco's** *How To Marry A Millionaire* (1953), and others decidedly less so. She did, on the other hand, become something of an icon as the former Mrs Bogart, and this part (despite many protestations) she has always played very well indeed.

Other Key Films: *Dark Passage* (1947); *Young Man With A Horn* (1950); *Blood Alley* (1955); *Written On The Wind* (1958); *North West Frontier* (1959); *Harper* (1966); *Murder On The Orient Express* (1974); *The Shootist* (1976); *Mr North* (1988); *Misery* (1990); *The Mirror Has Two Faces* (1996); *Day And Night* (1997); *The Venice Project* (1999); *Presence Of Mind* (1999); *Dogville* (2003); *These Foolish Things* (2006)

Key Lines:

1. 'Maybe just whistle. You know how to whistle, don't you, Steve? You just put your lips together and blow.' [*To Have And Have Not*]

2. 'I know. I know. You don't give a hoot what I do. But when I do it you get sore.' [To Have And Have Not]

Lauren Bacall and
Humphrey Bogart
in The Big Sleep,
directed by Howard
Hawks (1946).

*Warner Bros/The
Kobal Collection*

Bacharach, Burt

One of the greatest of the 1960s generation of composer/songwriters, Bacharach's
name is on literally dozens of film scores, sometimes for a single song, as in **John
Ford's** *The Man Who Shot Liberty Valance* (1962), and sometimes for the whole score,
as in his Oscar-winning efforts for George Roy Hill's *Butch Cassidy And The Sundance
Kid* (1969), in which he won an additional Oscar for the title song alone, 'Raindrops
Keep Falling On My Head'. Scorning simple melodies, Bacharach's hallmark has
always been the complexity of his rhythms, which, while making his songs seem
eminently hummable when sung by professionals, nevertheless presents significant
difficulties to your average shower singer.

Other Key Films: Clive Donner's *What's New Pussycat?* (1965); Lewis Gilbert's *Alfie*
(1966); Charles Jarrott's *Lost Horizon* (1973); Steve Gordon's *Arthur* (1981); Bud
Yorkin's *Love Hurts* (1991); The Coen Brothers' *Fargo* (1996); P J Hogan's *My Best
Friend's Wedding* (1997); Andrew Bergman's *Isn't She Great* (2000); *Bridget Jones: The
Edge Of Reason* (2004)

Bacon, Kevin

A talented character actor who at first seemed more at ease as part of a group rather
than carrying a film on his own, Bacon had a big hit with Herbert Ross's dance
drama *Footloose* (1984), but has since tended to play the role of a friend, or subsidiary
to the hero, in such movies as John Hughes's *Planes, Trains & Automobiles* (1987) and

Rob Reiner's *A Few Good Men* (1992). Bacon made an excellent directing debut with *Losing Chase* (1996), which starred Helen Mirren and Bacon's wife, Kyra Sedgwick, and this intelligent and increasingly eclectic actor was also on scintillating form as Nicole Kassell's *The Woodsman* (2004).

Other Key Films: *Starting Over* (1979); *Diner* (1982); *Flatliners* (1990); *JFK* (1991); *The River Wild* (1994); *Apollo 13* (1995); *Sleepers* (1996); *Wild Things* (1998); *The Hollow Man* (2000); *Novocaine* (2001); *Where The Truth Lies* (2005)

Bacon, Lloyd

Bacon was a typical Hollywood studio director who turned out dozens of mostly nondescript feature films, with, however, one or two real gems hidden away amongst them. He cut his teeth directing **Mack Sennett** shorts, and later worked extensively for Warners, where he appeared to shine most directing musicals, of which the brilliant 42nd *Street* (1933), great-uncle of all backstage musicals, has best stood the test of time.

Other Key Films: *The Singing Fool* (1928); *Footlight Parade* (1933); *Wonder Bar* (1934); *Gold Diggers Of 1937* (1936); *Marked Woman* (1937); *The Oklahoma Kid* (1939); *Brother Orchid* (1940); *Action In The North Atlantic* (1943)

Baker, Rick

One of the great special effects make-up men, Baker is particularly good at recreating apes, which he has done for John Guillermin in **King Kong** (1976) (acting as the great Kong himself), for Hugh Hudson in *Greystoke* (1984) and for **Michael Apted** in *Gorillas In The Mist* (1988), amongst others. His miraculous transformation of **Eddie Murphy** into a grossly overweight, lovelorn professor in Tom Shadyack's *The Nutty Professor* (1996) and Peter Segal's *Nutty Professor II: The Klumps* (2000) is particularly inspired.

Other Key Films: **William Friedkin's** *The Exorcist* (1973); **George Lucas's** *Star Wars* (1977); **Brian De Palma's** *The Fury* (1978); John Landis's *An American Werewolf In London* (1981); **David Cronenberg's** *Videodrome* (1983); Joel Schumacher's *Batman Forever* (1995); Barry Sonnenfeld's *Men In Black* (1997); **Ron Howard's** *How the Grinch Stole Christmas* (2000); **Tim Burton's** *Planet Of The Apes* (2001); **Wes Craven's** *Cursed* (2005); Frank Coraci's *Click* (2006)

Baker, Stanley

Tough-guy actor who cut his teeth on the new breed of 'realist' British crime films of the 1950s, Baker's brooding, apparently innate talent was quickly recognized by **Joseph Losey**, who used him to good effect in *The Concrete Jungle* (1960), the frustratingly perverse *Eva* (1961), and later in the far more successful (though still perverse) *Accident* (1967). He could play an embittered, angry man better than anyone else in cinema, but he also shone in more complex roles, such as that of Lt. Chard in Cy Endfield's *Zulu* (1963). He later branched out into film production, and latterly, before his early death at the age of forty-nine, in 1976, he seemed to be losing just a little of his earlier edge.

Other Key Films: *Eye Witness* (1950); *The Cruel Sea* (1953); *Hell Drivers* (1958); *Campbell's Kingdom* (1958); *Violent Playground* (1958); *Hard Drivers* (1960); *Hell Is A City* (1960); *Robbery* (1967); *The Games* (1970); *The Last Grenade* (1970)

Balcon, Michael

Founder of Gainsborough Films, and later chief of production at Ealing Studios,

Balcon was one of the mainstays of pre- and post-war British cinema, responsible for successes such as **Alfred Hitchcock's** *The Thirty-Nine Steps* (1935), **Sam Wood's** *Goodbye Mr Chips* (1939), and the multi-directed *Dead Of Night* (1945), possibly the single best ghost film of all time. After the war he produced many of the Ealing comedies, including **Robert Hamer's** *Kind Hearts And Coronets* (1949) and **Alexander Mackendrick's** *Whisky Galore* (1949) and *The Man In The White Suit* (1951).

Other Key Films: **Robert Flaherty's** *Man Of Aran* (1934); Alfred Hitchcock's *The Man Who Knew Too Much* (1934), *Sabotage* (1936) and *The Secret Agent* (1936); Alberto Cavalcanti's *Nicholas Nickleby* (1947); Henry Cornelius's *Passport To Pimlico* (1949); **Basil Dearden's** *The Blue Lamp* (1950); Charles Crichton's *The Lavender Hill Mob* (1951); Charles Frend's *The Cruel Sea* (1953); Alexander Mackendrick's *The Ladykillers* (1955)

Baldwin, Alec

Elegant leading man and gifted screen actor who considers his stage work to be every bit as important as his film parts, Baldwin appeared to hit the big time as Jack Ryan in John McTiernan's *The Hunt For Red October* (1990), but blew his chance for a follow up in Phillip Noyce's *Clear And Present Danger* (1994) after a contract dispute, and has since seemed satisfied to aim at critical rather than commercial success. He was outstanding in James Foley's *Glengarry Glen Ross* (1992), adequate in Roger Donaldson's *The Getaway* (1994), and realistically edgy in Lee Tamahori's aptly named *The Edge* (1997).

Other Key Films: *Beetlejuice* (1988); *Working Girl* (1988); *Malice* (1993); *The Juror* (1996); *Mercury Rising* (1998); *The Confession* (1999); *Thomas And The Magic Railroad* (2000); *Pearl Harbor* (2001); *The Aviator* (2004); *Fun With Dick And Jane* (2005); *Brooklyn Rules* (2006)

Ball, Lucille

You either loved her or you hated her (and America loved her) in the 'I Love Lucy' TV series, but no one can deny that Ball had supreme comic timing, a talent to which her TV filmography amply testifies. One of the most successful producers in Hollywood history with her Desilu production company, Ball started off on the screen as a **Ginger Rogers** clone but soon graduated to her very own brand of slapstick humour in **Lloyd Bacon's** *The Fuller Brush Girl* (1950), followed by a series of **Bob Hope** vehicles, of which the best was undoubtedly George Marshall's *Fancy Pants* (1950). Jamestown, in New York State, where she was born, has become something of a shrine to her memory, and Lucy-Desi Days are held there every year to celebrate her life and achievements.

Other Key Films: *Roman Scandals* (1933); *Top Hat* (1935); *The Big Street* (1942); *Du Barry Was A Lady* (1943); *Ziegfeld Follies* (1946); *Forever Darling* (1956)

Ballard, Lucien

Ballard was one of the greatest of the black-and-white cinematographers, something recognised by that doyen of the monochrome, **Josef von Sternberg**, who used him on *Morocco* (1930), *The Devil Is A Woman* (1935) and *Crime And Punishment* (1935). Ballard's greatest achievement came with **Stanley Kubrick's** *The Killing* (1956), in which he managed to suggest a seemingly washed-out but actually deeply contrasted suburban and rural America, an effect that was later imitated but never bettered by such leading directorial lights as **Martin Ritt**, **Peter Bogdanovich**, and **Terrence Malick**. Ballard's final films were mostly **Westerns**, and include **Sam Peckinpah's**

elegiac *Ride The High Country* (1962), the same director's seminal *The Wild Bunch* (1969) and nostalgic *Junior Bonner* (1972), not to mention **Henry Hathaway's** sensationally good (and sensationally well-shot) **John Wayne** oater, *True Grit* (1969).
Other Key Films: John Brahm's *The Lodger* (1944); **Jacques Tourneur's** *Berlin Express* (1948); **Henry Hathaway's** *Nevada Smith* (1966); **John Sturges's** *Hour Of The Gun* (1967); Tom Gries's *Will Penny* (1968); Sam Peckinpah's *The Ballad Of Cable Hogue* (1970)

Ballhaus, Michael
One of the most innovative of recent cinematographers, Ballhaus made his reputation working for **Rainer Werner Fassbinder** on films as disparate as *Chinese Roulette* (1976) and *The Marriage Of Maria Braun* (1978). In recent years his edgy, constantly moving style has won over the likes of **Martin Scorsese** with *GoodFellas* (1990), *The Age Of Innocence* (1993) and *Gangs Of New York* (2002), and **Robert Redford**, with *Quiz Show* (1994), to his Hollywood camp.
Other Key Films: Rainer Werner Fassbinder's *The Bitter Tears Of Petra Von Kant* (1972) and *The Stationmaster's Wife* (1977); Martin Scorsese's *The Color Of Money* (1986) and *The Last Temptation Of Christ* (1988); Steve Kloves's *The Fabulous Baker Boys* (1989); **Wolfgang Petersen's** *Outbreak* (1995); Barry Levinson's *Sleepers* (1996); **Mike Nichols's** *Primary Colors* (1998); Barry Sonnenfeld's *Wild Wild West* (1999); Robert Redford's *The Legend Of Bagger Vance* (2000)

Balsam, Martin
Fine character actor best known for his heady descent down the stairs at the point of **Anthony Perkins's** knife (sorry, I've given the secret away) in **Alfred Hitchcock's** *Psycho* (1960), Balsam's laconic face and his ability to look hunted, marginally devious and yet still somehow decent stood him in good stead in more than sixty very often distinguished films – he was one of Hollywood's greatest second rankers.
Other Key Films: *On The Waterfront* (1964); *12 Angry Men* (1958); *Breakfast At Tiffany's* (1961); *Seven Days In May* (1964); *Hombre* (1967); *Little Big Man* (1970); *The Stone Killer* (1973); *Cape Fear* (1991); *Soldato Ignoto* (1995); *Legend Of The Spirit Dog* (1997)

Bancroft, Anne
Bancroft was the one and only Mrs Robinson (despite **Kathleen Turner** and Jerry Hall's performances a few years ago on stage in London's West End) and she carried the same acute intelligence and commitment to all her parts. Before her iconic status as Mrs R in **Mike Nichols's** *The Graduate* (1967), Bancroft triumphed in **Arthur Penn's** *The Miracle Worker* (1962) and in Jack Clayton's *The Pumpkin Eater* (1964), and looked set for a major movie career, but her inclinations were obviously otherwise, for she contented herself with the occasional juicy role in such quality vehicles as David Jones's *84 Charing Cross Road* (1987). For forty years, until her death in 2005, she was married to comedian and film director **Mel Brooks**.
Other Key Films: *The Raid* (1954); *Seven Women* (1966); *Young Winston* (1972); *The Elephant Man* (1980); *To Be Or Not To Be* (1983); *Mr Jones* (1993); *How To Make An American Quilt* (1995); *G. I. Jane* (1997); *Great Expectations* (1998); *Up At The Villa* (2000); *Keeping The Faith* (2000); *Heartbreakers* (2001)

Banderas, Antonio
Following his initial success in a number of **Pedro Almodóvar's** films, most notably

Law Of Desire [La Ley Del Deseo] (1987) and *Women On The Verge Of A Nervous Breakdown* (1988), Hollywood picked up this good-looking and athletic Spaniard and imaginatively cast him as a Cuban in Arne Glimcher's *The Mambo Kings* (1992). **Alan Parker's** *Evita* (1996) followed (this time Banderas was Argentinian), and Martin Campbell's rather good *The Mask Of Zorro* (1998), but it is unlikely, on present showing, that Banderas will ever have the range of his illustrious predecessor in the Zorro part, **Tyrone Power**. He has,

Director Pedro Almodóvar working with Antonio Banderas on the set of Mujeres al Borde de un Ataque de Nervios (Women on the Verge of a Nervous Breakdown) in 1988.

El Deseo-Lauren/The Kobal Collection

however, carved out a rather lucrative secondary career in feline voiceovers, *pace* the multi-directed *Shrek 2* (2004), *Shrek 3* (2007), *Shrek 4*, etc. etc... There's even a *Puss In Boots* in the offing, or so the tom-toms tell me. Note For Film Buffs: It was Banderas who introduced Catherine Zeta-Jones to **Michael Douglas**. Isn't that interesting?

Other Key Films: *Labyrinth Of Passion* (1982); *Matador* (1986); *The Law Of Desire* (1987); *Tie Me Up! Tie Me Down!* (1990); *Philadelphia* (1993); *Interview With A Vampire* (1994); *Assassins* (1995); *The 13th Warrior* (1999); *Play It To The Bone* (1999); *The Body* (2001); *Spy Kids* (2001); *Original Sin* (2001); *The Legend Of Zorro* (2005); *Take The Lead* (2006)

Bankhead, Tallulah

A renowned high liver, gaiety girl and wit (and the not entirely coincidental seductress of numerous young Etonians) Bankhead was always a stage actress at heart and rarely turned her hand, or anything else for that matter, to film. However when she did she was great fun (if rather creakingly theatrical), and her best-known role was as millionairess Connie Porter cast adrift in **Alfred Hitchcock's** *Lifeboat* (1944) with Walter Slezak, **William Bendix** and her mink coat for company. She'd have made a great dinner companion, though.

Other Key Films: *The Trap* (1919); *Tarnished Lady* (1931); *Devil And The Deep* (1932); *Main Street To Broadway* (1953)

Key Lines:

1. 'Cocaine habit-forming? Of course not. I should know. I've been using it for years.' [Bankhead on substance abuse]

2. 'I'm as pure as the driven slush.' [Bankhead on virtue]

Banky, Vilma: Banky deserves a place in this book if only for her name, which many people instantly recognize without ever having seen any of her films. She was actually one of the top three or four stars of her day, acting silently alongside the young **Ronald Colman** and the even younger **Gary Cooper**, and simply giving up her career when sound came along. Her most famous part was in George Fitzmaurice's *The Son Of The Sheik* (1926), in which she partnered **Rudolf Valentino** in what was arguably his best film.

Other Key Films: *The Lady From Paris* (1924); *The Dark Angel* (1926); *The Winning*

Of Barbara Worth (1926); *The Night Of Love* (1927); *Two Lovers* (1928); *This Is Heaven* (1929)

Bannen, Ian

An intense character actor who specialised in men under pressure, Bannen acted in dozens of high quality British films and one or two US ones, although he never really looked comfortable on the far side of the Atlantic. He came close to winning an Oscar for his supporting role of Crow, in **Robert Aldrich's** *The Flight Of The Phoenix* (1965), but his best performance was as the putative child molester, Kenneth Baxter, tormented by **Sean Connery's** Detective Sergeant Johnson, in **Sidney Lumet's** *The Offence* (1973). He died tragically, in a car accident near Loch Ness in Scotland, in November 1999.

Other Key Films: *A Tale Of Two Cities* (1958); *The Hill* (1965); *Jane Eyre* (1971); *The Mackintosh Man* (1973); *Eye Of The Needle* (1981); *Ghandi* (1982); *Gorky Park* (1983); *Defence Of The Realm* (1986); *Hope And Glory* (1987); *The Cherry Orchard* (1991); *Damage* (1992); *Braveheart* (1995); *Waking Ned* (1998); *To Walk With Lions* (1998); *Best* (2000)

Bara, Theda

Her name was an anagram of 'Arab Death', and she was Fox's answer to the anodyne **Mary Pickford**. Famous overnight as the 'vamp' following her appearance in *A Fool There Was* (1915) (which was based on Rudyard Kipling's poem 'The Vampire'), Bara made a film a month for Fox in the following three years, incarnating such vampish heroines as Cleopatra, Camille, Du Barry and Cigarette – but the public slowly tired of her, and she ended up parodying her own image during the 1920s in a vain attempt to keep their interest in her alive.

Other Key Films: *Carmen* (1916); *Serpent Of The Nile* (1916); *The She-Devil* (1918)
Key Line: 'Kiss me, my fool.' [A Fool There Was]

Bardem, Juan Antonio

One of Spain's most prestigious filmmakers, Bardem became the visual historian and invisible conscience of all those persecuted during the Franco era through the medium of such films as *Muerte De Un Ciclista* (1955) and *Calle Mayor* (1956). Following the success of his early films with international critics, Bardem became the focus of sustained governmental interference, and it was only after the death of Franco, and until his own death in 2002 at the age of eighty, that Bardem was able to continue systematically mapping the tormented post-war history of the Spanish people.

Other Key Films: *Welcome Mr Marshall* (1952); *Felices Pascuas* (1954); *La Venganza* (1958); *El Ultimo Dia De La Guerra* (1969); *Behind The Shutters* (1973); *El Poder Del Deseo* (1976); *Lorca, La Muerte De Un Poeta* (1987); *Resultado Final* (1998)

Bardot, Brigitte

Known as 'the sex kitten' and also as the 'girl with the best bottom in the business' – which she unabashedly showed in numerous steamy films, most notably in front of her defence lawyer, **Jean Gabin**, in **Claude Autant-Lara's** *Love Is My Profession* [*En Cas De Malheur*] (1959) [**see picture**] – Bardot encapsulated the modern, sexually uninhibited woman well before such a state actually existed. Married, amongst others, to film director Roger Vadim and to multi-millionaire playboy Gunther Sachs, Bardot retired from the screen (with no apparent regrets) at the early age of forty, to devote the remainder of her life to animal welfare.

Brigitte Bardot in 1955, surrounded by a crowd of admirers.

The Kobal Collection

Other Key Films: *Doctor At Sea* (1955); *And Woman Was Created* [*Et Dieu Créa La Femme*] (1956); *Une Parisienne* (1958); *Babette S'En Va-T-En Guerre* (1959); *The Truth* [*La Vérité*] (1960); *Contempt* [*Le Mépris*] (1963); *Viva Maria* (1965); *Masculin-Féminin* (1966); *Les Femmes* (1969); *Don Juan 1973* (1973)

Key Line: 'Garbo's visage had a kind of emptiness into which anything could be projected – nothing can be read into Bardot's face.' [Simone de Beauvoir on Bardot]

Barker, Lex

He was a good ***Tarzan*** in some very bad films, and later the unforgettable Old Shatterhand (to Pierre Brice's Winnetou) in a series of German **Westerns** based on the best-selling books of Karl May – films that were hardly ever seen outside Europe. Barker's most competent straight performance came in **Federico Fellini's** *La Dolce Vita* (1960), but he was perhaps best known for his five (mostly rather brief) marriages to a variety of actresses, including **Lana Turner**, of whom another famous husband, bandleader Artie Shaw, once said, 'Lana was an airhead – she was a beautiful ornament.' [I don't know what this has to do with anything, but there it is]

Other Key Films: *Crossfire* (1947); *Mr Blandings Builds His Dream House* (1948); *Tarzan's Peril* (1951); *The Deerslayer* (1958); *Winnetou* (63 & 64); *Old Shatterhand* (1964)

Barkin, Ellen

An excellent actress with an offbeat, sexy face (her beauty somewhat along the lines of a **Frances McDormand**), Barkin had a real hit with Jim McBride's excellent *The Big Easy* (1986), followed by Harold Becker's equally excellent *Sea Of Love* (1989). Then what? A good but small part in Mike Newell's *Into The West* (1993) and some fun with Walter Hill's *Wild Bill* (1995), but nothing in there to match her obvious talent and screen presence. See **Erotic Moments**

Other Key Films: *Diner* (1982); *Tender Mercies* (1982); *Down By Law* (1986); *Siesta* (1987); *This Boy's Life* (1993); *The Fan* (1996); *Fear And Loathing In Las Vegas* (1998); *Drop Dead Gorgeous* (1999); *Money* (2000); *Crime And Punishment In Suburbia* (2000); *Someone Like You* (2001); *She Hate Me* (2004)

Barnes, George

Barnes plied his camera for virtually all the great names of the Hollywood golden age, and was perhaps the most consummately professional and consistent cinematographer of his day. He worked on George Fitzmaurice's *The Son Of The Sheik* (1926) and *Raffles* (1930), and he was co-photographer on **Henry King's** gorgeously Technicolor-ed *Jesse James* (1939); but his best work came later, for **Alfred Hitchcock** on *Rebecca* (1940) and *Spellbound* (1945), and for Robert Stevenson on *Jane Eyre* (1943), which was chiefly notable for its wildly atmospheric lighting and for a booming and gleefully sado-masochistic **Orson Welles**, as Mr Rochester.

Other Key Films: Ray Enright's *Dames* (1934); **Lloyd Bacon's** *Marked Woman* (1937); Mitchell Leisen's *Frenchman's Creek* (1944); Richard Wallace's *Sinbad The Sailor* (1947); Abraham Polonsky's *Force Of Evil* (1948)

Barrault, Jean-Louis

Politically committed theatrical impresario inevitably paired in the French public's eye with his wife, Madeleine Renaud, Barrault will be remembered by devoted filmgoers for his majestic performance as the mime, Baptiste Deburau, in **Marcel Carné's** masterpiece *Les Enfants Du Paradis* (1945). He made a belated appearance in Ettore Scola's *La Nuit De Varennes* (1982), but Barrault's heart was always in the theatre, and particularly with the Comédie Française and the Théâtre de France, from whose ranks he was unceremoniously jettisoned after supporting the students during the May 1968 riots.

Other Key Films: *Les Beaux Jours* (1935); *Bizarre Bizarre* (1937); *Orage* (1938); *D'Homme À Hommes* (1948); *La Ronde* (1950); *Le Dialogue Des Carmélites* (1960)

Barry, John

Near-ubiquitous during the 1960s, Barry scored just about every big British movie of the decade, and a quick glance at his extended filmography suggests that he must have had precious little time left over from work to taste the swinging side of 1960s London. His first major commission came with Bryan Forbes's *The L-Shaped Room* (1962), but Barry really began to be noticed with his catchy theme and variations for Terence Young's *From Russia With Love* (1963), which one has only to think of momentarily to instantly start humming the tune. The James Hill-directed *Born Free* (1966) theme was his too, together with the beautifully scored Anthony Harvey film, *The Lion In Winter* (1968). His most memorable scoring, however, involves a toss-up between **John Schlesinger's** *Midnight Cowboy* (1969) and **Sydney Pollack's** *Out Of Africa* (1985), with *Out of Africa* winning by a short head. Mind you, his score for **Lawrence Kasdan's** *Body Heat* (1981) was also outstanding.

Other Key Films: Guy Hamilton's *Goldfinger* (1964); James Clavell's *The Last Valley* (1970); **Nicholas Roeg's** *Walkabout* (1971); Graeme Clifford's *Frances* (1982); **Francis Ford Coppola's** *The Cotton Club* (1984); Richard Marquand's *Jagged Edge* (1985); **Kevin Costner's** *Dances With Wolves* (1990); Adrian Lyne's *Indecent Proposal* (1993); Roland Joffé's *The Scarlet Letter* (1995); Beeban Kidron's *Swept From The Sea* (1997); Harold Becker's *Mercury Rising* (1998); **Michael Apted's** *Enigma* (2001); Eric Darnell & Tom McGrath's *Madagascar* (2005)

Barrymores, The

Scions of a famous theatrical family, Ethel, John and Lionel Barrymore succeeded in films almost despite their nineteenth-century selves. Ethel never took films seriously, even when she received a best-supporting Oscar for Clifford Odets's *None But The Lonely Heart* (1944), but her brother John, on the other hand, was a natural show-off to whom films offered a gammon-scented opportunity, and whose career would have been even more astonishing but for his heavy drinking and womanising, which he parodied so beautifully in Edmund Goulding's *Grand Hotel* (1932). Lionel out-hammed even his brother, particularly in **King Vidor's** *Duel In The Sun* (1946), but he somehow contrived to restrain himself during the filming of **John Huston's** *Key Largo* (1948) to turn in a dignified and powerful performance as the paraplegic James Temple. Together, all three notched up a mind-boggling number of film performances, somehow contriving to stifle virtually all critical faculties on the part of their ever-faithful public.

Other Key Films: Ethel: *Rasputin And The Empress* (1933); *The Spiral Staircase* (1946); *The Paradine Case* (1948); *Portrait Of Jenny* (1949); *Deadline USA* (1952); John: *Dr Jekyll And Mr Hyde* (1920); *Moby Dick* (1930); *Dinner At Eight* (1933); *The Great Profile* (1940); Lionel: *The Temptress* (1927); *David Copperfield* (1935); *Camille* (1937); *Captains Courageous* (1937); *It's A Wonderful Life* (1946)

Key Line: 'For an actress to be a success, she must have the face of a Venus, the brains of a Minerva, the grace of a Terpsichore, the memory of a Macaulay, the figure of Juno, and the hide of a rhinoceros.' [Ethel on acting]

Basinger, Kim

A curiously on/off actress who has made more than one comeback and more than one mistake, not least by refusing to appear in Jennifer Chambers Lynch's *Boxing Helena* (1993), for which she was sued by the makers and forced to pay multimillion dollar damages. If looks alone could make a star, Basinger would be it, but her acting ability has always been just a little doubtful, despite good critical reception for her role as a **Veronica Lake** look-alike in Curtis Hanson's excellent *L.A. Confidential* (1997).

Other Key Films: *Never Say Never Again* (1983); *The Natural* (1984); *Fool For Love* (1985); *Blind Date* (1987); *Batman* (1989); *The Getaway* (1994); *I Dreamed Of Africa* (2000); *Bless The Child* (2000); *Cellular* (2004); *The Sentinel* (2006)

Bass, Saul

Bass changed the way movie titles and credit sequences are designed, turning them from the often turgid succession of filmed names an audience is eager to get through, to something which reflects the movie they are about to watch, and acts as a sort of foreword, or amuse-gueule, preparing punters for whatever treat is in store. Notable examples of his work occur in **Billy Wilder's** *The Seven Year Itch* (1955), **Alfred Hitchcock's** *Vertigo* (1958), **Otto Preminger's** *Anatomy Of A Murder* (1959) and **Martin Scorsese's** *GoodFellas* (1990).

Other Key Films: Otto Preminger's *The Man With The Golden Arm* (1956); **Stanley Kubrick's** *Spartacus* (1960); **John Frankenheimer's** *Grand Prix* (1966)

Bates, Alan

Important British stage actor who appeared in a number of seminal films, including **John Schlesinger's** *A Kind Of Loving* (1962) and **Ken Russell's** *Women In Love* (1970), in which he indulged in the infamous naked wrestling scene with **Oliver Reed** – illiterate critics of Russell have often missed the point of this scene, however, for it is completely Lawrentian and totally in keeping with the tone of the book. Bates, for his part, always chose his roles with extreme care, and his filmography is an impressive one, with remarkable few clinkers. His best performances came in Clive Donner's *Nothing But The Best* (1964) and in Schlesinger's *Far From The Madding Crowd* (1967), as the faithful but somewhat ill-starred Gabriel Oak.

Other Key Films: *The Entertainer* (1960); *Whistle Down The Wind* (1961); *Zorba The Greek* (1965); *Georgy Girl* (1966); *King Of Hearts* (1966); *The Fixer* (1968); *The Go-Between* (1971); *A Day In The Death Of Joe Egg* (1972); *The Shout* (1978); *Quartet* (1981); *Return Of The Soldier* (1982); *Britannia Hospital* (1982); *Secret Friends* (1991); *Silent Tongue* (1993); *The Grotesque* (1995); *Varya* (1999); *Gosford Park* (2001); *The Mothman Prophecies* (2002); *The Statement* (2003)

Bates, Kathy

A fine, understated actress, who finally found the international recognition she deserved in Rob Reiner's *Misery* (1990), in which she famously smashed **James Caan's** ankles with a sledgehammer. Jon Avnet's *Fried Green Tomatoes* (1991) followed, but her best role to date has undoubtedly been as the eponymous title character in Taylor Hackford's *Dolores Claiborne* (1995), in which Bates showed just what subtlety and stillness she can bring to difficult and at times unsympathetic parts.

Other Key Films: *Taking Off* (1971); *Come Back To The 5 And Dime, Jimmy Dean Jimmy Dean* (1982); *Dick Tracy* (1990); *Shadows And Fog* (1992); *Used People* (1992); *North* (1994); *Angus* (1995); *Diabolique* (1996); *Titanic* (1997); *Primary Colors* (1998); *Bruno* (2000); *Unconditional Love* (2002); *Relative Strangers* (2006)

Béart, Emmanuelle

The gorgeous, St Tropez-born daughter of French pop star Guy Béart, Emmanuelle first came to general notice playing the part of the vengeful Manon in **Claude Berri's** *Manon Des Sources* (1986), and then proved that she could act as well as look beautiful in Claude Sautet's *Un Coeur En Hiver* (1993), in which she co-starred with her real-life lover (and soon-to-be husband) **Daniel Auteuil**, who had the Herculean task of convincing the audience that his screen persona was frigidly capable of rejecting her – the couple divorced, however, in 1995, after two years of marriage and a daughter.

Other Key Films: *L'Amour En Douce* (1985); *Ruptures* (1993); *Belle Epoque* (1994); *L'Enfer* (1994); *Mission: Impossible* (1996); *Don Juan* (1998); *Voleur Du Vie* (1998); *Le Temps Retrouvé* (1999); *Elephant Juice* (1999); *La Bûche* (1999); *Les Destinées Sentimentales* (2000); *Voyance Et Manigance* (2001); *8 Femmes* (2002); *Natalie* (2003); *L'Enfer* (2005)

Beatles, The

Hardly renowned for their film careers when considered in relation to their musical achievements, their performance as a group in Richard Lester's *A Hard Day's Night* (1964) is nevertheless worthy of mention, if only on account of the film's energy and their iconic presence in it when seen against the miracle of the 1960s and the effect they had on popular culture during that decade. Of the quartet, drummer Ringo Starr has paradoxically enjoyed the most 'successful' acting career, but his performances are, for the most part, simply adequate, and have never indicated either the need or even the possibility of a radical mid-term vocational change on his part. George Harrison, on the other hand, through his production company Handmade Films, acted as either the co- or the executive producer on a number of fine British films, including **Terry Gilliam's** *Time Bandits* (1981), **Neil Jordan's** *Mona Lisa*

(1986) and **Bruce Robinson's** *Withnail & I* (1987).
Other Key Films: *Help!* (1965); *Yellow Submarine* (1968) [in animated form]; *Let It Be* (1970)

Beatty, Warren

Beatty is good-looking, charismatic and politically impeccable (in recent Hollywood terms), but the jury must surely still be out on his acting ability. He has the typical mannerisms of a major star, and these get in the way of any real performance, although, no doubt, they please his many fans. He hasn't acted in that many films compared to, say, his exact contemporary **Jack Nicholson**, but of the films in which he has appeared, particular plaudits must go to **Elia Kazan's** *Splendor In The Grass* (1961), **Alan J Pakula's** *The Parallax View* (1974), and also to *Reds* (1981), which Beatty himself directed.
Other Key Films: *The Roman Spring Of Mrs Stone* (1961); *Lilith* (1964); *Bonnie And Clyde* (1967); *McCabe And Mrs Miller* (1971); *Shampoo* (1975); *Heaven Can Wait* (1978); *Dick Tracy* (1990); *Bugsy* (1991); *Bulworth* (1998); *Town & Country* (2001)

Beineix, Jean-Jacques

Beineix had a well-justified international smash hit with *Diva* (1981), which he followed up with the turgid and mannered *La Lune Dans Le Caniveau* [*The Moon In The Gutter*] (1983). *Betty Blue* (1986) reset the score in his favour (for a while) but Beineix has never really followed up on all the hype that was associated with his name in the early 1980s, and his recent films have been radically disappointing, if the quality of his initial promise is taken into account.
Other Key Films: *Roselyne Et Les Lions* (1989); *IP 5: The Island Of Pachyderms* (1992); *Otaku* (1994); *Mortel Transfert* (2001)

Belafonte, Harry

Belafonte came back into his own again thanks to the role of hoodlum Seldom Seen, in **Robert Altman's** *Kansas City* (1996), after many years spent concentrating on his concert career to the exclusion of films. Despite the fact that he will always be best known for his gorgeous singing of hits like 'Jamaica Farewell', he has turned in some outstanding screen performances, most notably in **Robert Wise's** *Odds Against Tomorrow* (1959), as Johnny Ingram, the butt of fellow crook **Robert Ryan's** inveterate racism.
Other Key Films: *Carmen Jones* (1955); *Island In The Sun* (1958); *The World The Flesh And The Devil* (1959); *Buck And The Preacher* (1972); *Ready To Wear* (1994); *White Man's Burden* (1995); *Bobby* (2006)

Belmondo, Jean-Paul

Quintessential French actor (and son of the sculptor, Paul Belmondo), Belmondo has never managed to secure a true international audience, but came closest with his Bogart influenced young man on the run, Michel Poiccard, in **Jean-Luc Godard's** *À Bout De Souffle* [*Breathless*] (1960). With his wide-boy, ex-boxer's face, and his eyes perpetually screwed up against a cloud of Gitanes smoke, Belmondo personified the free-spirited soul of the 1960s, moving successfully into action roles in the 1970s and 1980s, and then into straight drama in the 1990s, a move which culminated, unfortunately, in Claude Lelouch's disastrously pretentious *Les Misérables* (1995). His best films came early, and include Philippe de Broca's *That Man From Rio* (1964), Godard's excellent *Pierrot Le Fou* (1965), and Jacques Deray's near-ubiquitous

Borsalino (1970). Of Belmondo's extremely successful action-man period, Henri Verneuil's *Night Caller* (1975) stands out as almost perfect of its type.

Other Key Films: *Les Tricheurs* (1958); *Web Of Passion* (1959); *Moderato Cantabile* (1960); *Cartouche* (1962); *Le Doulos* (1963); *Le Voleur* (1967); *Stavisky* (1974); *L'Alpageur* (1976); *L'As Des As* (1982); *Le Marginal* (1983); *Itinéraire D'Un Enfant Gâté* (1988); *Désiré* (1996); *Une Chance Sur Deux* (1998); *Peut-Être* (1999); *Les Acteurs* (2000); *Amazone* (2000)

Benchley, Robert

A successful and sophisticated American humorist with a dry, acerbic, New-Yorker style wit, Benchley was an extremely popular character actor during the 1930s and 1940s, appearing in numerous shorts and feature films, often in the guise of an irascible, fast talking fly-in-the-ointment of the US bourgeois lifestyle.

Key Films: *How To Sleep* [short] (1935); *China Seas* (1935); *A Night At The Movies* [short] (1937); *The Trouble With Husbands* [short] (1940); *Bedtime Story* (1941); *I Married A Witch* (1942); *Practically Yours* (1944); *The Bride Wore Boots* (1946)

Key Line: 'Let's get out of these wet clothes and into a dry Martini.' [Benchley on sex, booze and the 1930s Manhattan lifestyle]

Bendix, William

Bendix was instantly recognisable, with his sloppy, crumpled face and his renowned capacity for playing mentally challenged losers, but his acting was a good deal more intelligent than the good buddy/bad buddy parts he was normally given, and he was particularly memorable as the injured and bewildered ex-GI murderer in George Marshall's **Raymond Chandler**-scripted *The Blue Dahlia* (1946), and, again with **Alan Ladd**, as the ex-flyer's possibly slightly more than platonic crony, in **John Farrow's** *Calcutta* (1947).

Other Key Films: *China* (1943); *Lifeboat* (1944); *The Dark Corner* (1946); *Two Years Before The Mast* (1946); *Streets Of Laredo* (1949); *The Big Steal* (1949); *Macao* (1952)

Bening, Annette

Now married to the much-used **Warren Beatty** (with whom she has four children), Bening is a far better actress than her more famous husband, as she has recently shown in her Oscar-winning turn in Sam Mendes's *American Beauty* (1999). This followed a number of other outstanding performances, notably in **Milos Forman's** disastrously underrated *Valmont* (1989), and in **Stephen Frears's** superb *film noir, The Grifters* (1990). An actress to watch, and almost certainly a stayer. Note For Film Buffs: A false rumour has it that it is Bening's face and figure that we see on Michael Deas's 1992 revamped Columbia film logo – it is in fact model Jenny Joseph's.

Other Key Films: *Postcards From The Edge* (1990); *Bugsy* (1991); *Guilty By Suspicion* (1991); *Regarding Henry* (1991); *Love Affair* (1994); *The American President* (1995); *Richard III* (1995); *Mars Attacks!* (1996); *The Siege* (1998); *In Dreams* (1998); *What Planet Are You From?* (2000); *Open Range* (2003); *Being Julia* (2004); *Mrs Harris* (2005)

Bennett, Charles

Screenwriter of seven early **Alfred Hitchcock** films, including *The Thirty-Nine Steps* (1935) and the much-underrated *Young And Innocent* (1937), the exuberant, polo-playing Bennett eventually moved to Hollywood to script or co-script such wonderfully quirky oddities as **John Farrow's** *Where Danger Lives* (1950), and **Jacques Tourneur's** *Curse Of The Demon* (1958). His later scripts, under the Irwin

Allen aegis, were a little pedestrian, and Bennett was known to opine, in later years, with the ghost of a twinkle in his eye, that he bitterly regretted ever having gone to Hollywood.

Other Key Films: Maurice Elvey's *The Clairvoyant* (1934); Herbert Smith's *Night Mail* (1935); Robert Stevenson's *King Solomon's Mines* (1937)

Benny, Jack

Achingly funny American comedian with an impeccable sense of timing, Benny could make even his silences hilarious, as in his famous 'your money or your life' sketch, in which the miserly Benny, threatened by a highwayman, cannot make up his mind which course he ought to take. He was sublime in **Ernst Lubitsch's** *To Be Or Not To Be* (1942), and widely reckoned to be one of the nicest men in Hollywood. What more can anyone want?

Other Key Films: *The Medicine Man* (1930); *It's In The Air* (1935); *Artists And Models* (1937); *Man About Town* (1939); *Charley's Aunt* (1941); *George Washington Slept Here* (1942); *A Guide for The Married Man* (1967)

Key Line: 'I don't deserve this, but I have arthritis, and I don't deserve that either.' [Benny, on receiving an award]

Berenger, Tom

Berenger has often flirted with the big-time, but he never quite seems to have made it. He suggested what he was capable of in **Richard Brooks's** *Looking For Mr Goodbar* (1977), impressed again in **Lawrence Kasdan's** *The Big Chill* (1983), and finally appeared to have hit his box office stride with **Oliver Stone's** *Platoon* (1986), in which he played the devil-driven and booze-addicted bad angel, Sgt. Barnes, to **Willem Dafoe's** hash-powered quasi-saint, Sgt. Elias. **Ridley Scott**, too, used him to good effect as the smitten cop letting down his blue-collar wife in *Someone To Watch Over Me* (1987), but since then he seems to have had an on/off love affair with the public (and, quite possibly, himself). He was excellent in **Wolfgang Petersen's** *Shattered* (1991), and one cannot help wishing for yet another belated career resurrection for this exceptional screen actor, beyond the straight-to-video and the TV pilots he has been doing of late.

Other Key Films: *Beyond Obsession* (1985); *Love At Large* (1990); *The Field* (1990); *At Play In The Fields Of The Lord* (1991); *Sniper* (1993); *Last Of The Dogmen* (1995); *The Substitute* (1996); *The Gingerbread Man* (1998); *Shadow Of Doubt* (1998); *Takedown* (1999); *Fear Of Flying* (2000); *Eye See You* (2001); *Training Day* (2001)

Beresford, Bruce

Don's Party (1976), *The Getting Of Wisdom* (1977) and *Breaker Morant* (1979) signalled the arrival of a major directing talent, but Hollywood has never quite known how to use this idiosyncratic Australian. His *Tender Mercies* (1983) with the excellent, always understated **Robert Duvall**, was superb, and with an Oscar under his belt for *Driving Miss Daisy* (1989), Beresford's star seemed to have risen for good – but his recent eclectic choice of material (good for him!) and his staunch refusal to be typed, has tended to dilute his box office appeal.

Other Key Films: *King David* (1985); *Crimes Of The Heart* (1985); *Mr Johnson* (1991); *A Good Man In Africa* (1994); *Silent Fall* (1994); *Last Dance* (1996); *Paradise Road* (1997); *Double Jeopardy* (1999); *Ataturk* (2000); *Bride Of The Wind* (2001); *Evelyn* (2002); *The Contract* (2006)

Berger, Helmut

Odd, off-beat star of continental films, the good-looking Berger first made an impression in **Luchino Visconti's** *The Damned* (1969), and his best later parts almost always echoed that same theme of decadence. He was excellent, again, as Alberto, in **Vittorio De Sica's** gorgeous *The Garden Of The Finzi-Continis* (1971), believably wayward as Visconti's *Ludwig* (1973), and seriously disturbing as a bisexual cross-dresser in Tinto Brass's weird and perverse *Salon Kitty* (1976).

Other Key Films: *Dorian Gray* (1970); *Ash Wednesday* (1973); *The Romantic Englishwoman* (1975); *The Godfather Part III* (1990); *Stille Wasser* (1996); *Die 120 Tage Von Bottrop* (1997); *Unter Den Palmen* (1999); *Honey Baby* (2003)

Bergman, Ingmar

Indisputably one of the greatest film directors of all time, Bergman managed to correlate his personal development as a human being with his artistic development as a filmmaker to produce one of the most astonishingly consistent bodies of work on record. It is impossible to over-emphasise the excitement with which his new films were received in intellectual and artistic circles during the 1950s, 1960s and 1970s, and his success must be seen as an object lesson to young filmmaking aspirants that integrity and excellence must always count for more than merely commercial success in the sum total of human endeavour. *Smiles Of A Summer Night* (1955), *The Seventh Seal* (1958), *Wild Strawberries* (1958), *The Virgin Spring* (1960), and *Through A Glass Darkly* (1962) are all masterpieces of the highest order, and even in his lesser films (of which there are few), his commitment to a personal vision is so intense that most forms of criticism seem, in many respects, redundant.

Other Key Films: *Summer Interlude* (1951); *Summer With Monika* (1953); *The Magician* (1958); *The Devil's Eye* (1960); *Winter Light* (1963); *The Silence* (1963); *Persona* (1966); *Hour Of The Wolf* (1968); *The Shame* (1968); *The Touch* (1971); *Cries And Whispers* (1972); *Scenes From A Marriage* (1973); *The Magic Flute* (1974); *The Serpent's Egg* (1977); *Autumn Sonata* (1978); *Fanny And Alexander* (1983); **Liv Ullmann's** *Faithless* [Bergman wrote the script] (2000)

Key Line: 'After years of playing with images of life and death, life has made me shy.' [Bergman on filmmaking]

Bergman, Ingrid

Like the fiery arc of a short-lived meteor, this serenely beautiful but fatally masochistic actress fell foul of a Hollywood system that reckoned it owned her and which knew how to thrust home its dagger, Cassius-like, when she eventually turned her back on its blandishments. After Gregory Ratoff's 1939 remake of her Swedish success *Intermezzo*, it seemed that Bergman could do no wrong; first with **Michael Curtiz's** *Casablanca* (1942), then with **Sam Wood's** *For Whom The Bell Tolls* (1943), followed by **George Cukor's** *Gaslight* (1944) and **Alfred Hitchcock's** *Spellbound* (1945) and *Notorious* (1946) – successes every one, although with a possessive producer (**David O Selznick**) waiting in the wings, and only too ready to start calling all the shots. Crisis-stricken, and feeling that her career was largely out of her own hands, Bergman ran away to Italy at the age of thirty-five, leaving her husband and daughter behind her. She conceived a son with director **Roberto Rossellini** during the filming of *Stromboli* (1950), followed by twin girls, and it took Hollywood all of six long years to forgive her, her punishment being the very mediocrity of nearly all of her future parts within the studio system.

Other Key Films: *Dr Jekyll And Mr Hyde* (1941); *The Bells Of St Mary's* (1945); *Arch*

Of Triumph (1948); *Under Capricorn* (1949); *Voyage To Italy* (1953); *Elena Et Les Hommes* (1956); *Indiscreet* (1958); *Aimez-Vous Brahms?* [*Goodbye Again*] (1961); *Autumn Sonata* (1978)

Berkeley, Busby

Sex was Berkeley's stock-in-trade, and no individual in the history of film purveyed it better. Turning gorgeous chorus girls into gigantic sexual kaleidoscopes through the use of stratospheric fixed lenses, Berkeley revelled in the camera's voyeuristic ability, until all of us, the audience, the filmmaker, the technicians and the actors become voyeurs with him in a giant, musically accompanied orgy of lubricity. Even **Eddie Cantor** became infected by this merry bacchanal, and the scene in Leo McCarey's *The Kid From Spain* (1932) where Cantor emerges from under the bedclothes in a Vassar-style girl's dormitory, which then magically transforms itself into a gigantic swimming pool, seems somehow to sum up all the glories of devil-may-care Hollywood's depression era chutzpah.

Other Key Films *Whoopee!* (1930); *42nd Street* (1933); *Footlight Parade* (1933); *Gold Diggers Of 1933* (1933); *Roman Scandals* (1933); *Dames* (1934); *Fashions Of 1934* (1934); *Twenty Million Sweethearts* (1934); *Stars Over Broadway* (1935); *Babes In Arms* (1939)

Berlin, Irving

A sublimely talented song writer who could hardly play a note on the piano unless it was tuned to the correct key, Berlin was responsible for such perennial hits as 'Alexander's Ragtime Band', 'Cheek To Cheek' and 'White Christmas', which was so memorably and lucratively (it went on to become the bestselling song of all time) sung by **Bing Crosby** in Mark Sandrich's *Holiday Inn* (1942). Recipient of a Medal of Merit, a Congressional Gold Medal, a French Légion D'Honneur and the Medal of Liberty, Berlin survived to the ripe old age of 101, and may, with some justification, be considered the most successful songwriter who has ever lived.

Other Key Films: Alan Crosland's *The Jazz Singer* (1927); Roy Del Ruth's *Kid Millions* (1934); Mark Sandrich's *Top Hat* (1935); Charles Walters's *Easter Parade* (1948); George Sidney's *Annie Get Your Gun* (1950); **Michael Curtiz's** *White Christmas* (1954)

Berri, Claude

High-profile French producer/director whose career has seen him through more ups and downs than most filmmakers – he began his career with an Oscar for his film short, *The Chicken* (1963), then proceeded to blow his chances of an international career with a string of only occasionally successful comedies. Berri is now best known for his **Marcel Pagnol** duet, *Jean De Florette* (1986) and *Manon Des Sources* (1986), and for his more recent true-life resistance thriller, *Lucie Aubrac* (1997) [featuring a luminous performance by Carole Bouquet], which followed a long period in which he concentrated on production rather than direction.

Other Key Films: *Marry Me! Marry Me!* (1969); *Le Cinéma De Papa* (1970); *Le Sex Shop* (1972); *Le Male Du Siècle* (1975); *Le Maître D'Ecole* (1982); *Tchao Pantin* (1983); *Uranus* (1991); *Germinal* (1993); *La Débondade* (1999); *Une Femme De Ménage* (2003); *Ensemble C'Est Tout* (2006)

Berry, Jules

One of the *monstres sacrés* of the 1930s golden era of French cinema, the sinister-voiced Berry worked for just about every director of note at the time, and had screenwriters of the quality of **Jacques Prévert** clamouring to write for him on account of his extraordinary mastery of the spoken French language. His most characteristic performances occur in **Jean Renoir's** early masterpiece *Le Crime De Monsieur Lange* (1936), as the abominable, but nonetheless sympathetic Paul Batala, and in **Marcel Carné's** *Le Jour Se Lève* (1939) and *Les Visiteurs Du Soir* (1942).

Other Key Films:
Rigolboche (1936); *Arsène Lupin Détective* (1937); *Carrefour* (1937); *La Symphonie Fantastique* (1942); *Le Voyageur De La Toussaint* (1943); *Portrait D'Un Assassin* (1949); *Les Maîtres Nageurs* (1950)

Bertolucci, Bernardo

A co-writer on **Sergio Leone's** *Once Upon A Time In The West* (1968), Bertolucci announced

Director Bernardo Bertolucci on the set of The Sheltering Sky with Debra Winger and John Malkovich (1990).

Recorded Picture Co/Sahara Co/The Kobal Collection

himself to the world with *The Spider's Stratagem* (1970), closely followed by his first masterpiece, *The Conformist* (1970), in which he established the complex visual patterns (with the help of his magnificent cinematographer **Vittorio Storaro**) which were to mark the films of his later maturity. *Last Tango In Paris* (1972), for instance, deserved every accolade it was given, if only for daring to challenge the mainstream cinematic parameters of human sexuality, and although Bertolucci may have disappointed his admirers in recent years with his emphasis on surface textures to the detriment of his former emotional honesty, even his relative failures, like *The Sheltering Sky* (1990), retain their ability to seduce both the eye and the mind.

Other Key Films: *1900* (1977); *La Luna* (1979); *The Last Emperor* (1987); *Stealing Beauty* (1996); *Besieged* (1998); *Paradiso E Inferno* (1999); *The Dreamers* (2003)

Besson, Luc

French cult filmmaker who has successfully negotiated the crossover to commercial cinema without the total loss of integrity normally associated with such a move, Besson seduced the film buffs with *Le Dernier Combat* (1984), the quasi-philosophers with *Subway* (1985), and the sea-and-nihilism freaks with *The Big Blue* (1988). He then went on to seduce the feminists with *La Femme Nikita* (1991), the cultists with *Léon* (1994), and the sci-fi action loons with *The Fifth Element* (1997) – not a bad run for this still relatively young (he was born in 1959) Parisian.

Other Key Films: *Atlantis* (1991); *The Messenger: The Story Of Joan Of Arc* (1999); *Angel-A* (2005)

Binoche Juliette

French actress who has the ability to transcend the normal parameters of her all-too-obvious surface sex appeal to produce beautiful, touching performances that leave the spectator with an insight into femininity that few modern actresses ever have the capacity, far less the instinct, to attempt. She was the best thing in Philip Kaufman's otherwise unsatisfactory *The Unbearable Lightness Of Being* (1988), as well as in **Louis**

Malle's sadly underrated *Damage* (1992), but her true possibilities were only belatedly and triumphantly captured by the great **Krzysztof Kieslowski** in the *Blue* (1994) part of his colours trilogy. Her performance as Hana in **Anthony Minghella's** *The English Patient* (1996) simply reinforced the fact that she is one of the best film actresses working anywhere today. Since then, she has produced marvellously nuanced performances in virtually all her films, most notably as the emotionally damaged Alice, in **André Téchiné's** *Alice Et Martin* (1998), finding renewed strength through coping with her younger lovers' breakdown, and as Vianne Rocher in Lasse Hallström's delightful fairy-tale, *Chocolat* (2000). Other Key Films: *Les Nanas* (1984); *La Vie De Famille* (1984); *Mauvais Sang* (1986); *Les Amants Du Pont Neuf* (1991); *Wuthering Heights* (1992); *The Horseman On The Roof* (1996); *Les Enfants Du Siècle* (1999); *La Veuve De Saint-Pierre* (2000); *Code Inconnu* (2000); *Caché [Hidden]* (2005); *Breaking And Entering* (2006)

Juliette Binoche in *The English Patient*, directed by Anthony Minghella (1996).

TigerMoth/Miramax/ The Kobal Collection

Birkin, Jane

Willowy, absurdly English, yet somehow quintessentially European scion of the 1960s, Birkin seemed famous for only two things during much of her career – for being Serge Gainsbourg's mistress, and for her breathy orgasm on the soundtrack of Gainsbourg's song – which was initially due to have been sung by **Brigitte Bardot** – '*Je t'aime...et moi non plus*'. Birkin is better than that of course, as the French have always known, and as the rest of us only belatedly discovered in her exquisite performance opposite **Dirk Bogarde** in **Bertrand Tavernier's** *Daddy Nostalgie* [a.k.a. *These Foolish Things*] (1990).

Other Key Films: *Blow-Up* (1966); *La Piscine* (1969); *Don Juan* (1973); *Dark Places* (1973); *Le Diable Au Coeur* (1976); *Death On The Nile* (1978); *Evil Under The Sun* (1982); *La Belle Noiseuse* (1991); *Noir Comme Le Souvenir* (1995); *On Connaît La Chanson* (1997); *A Soldier's Daughter Never Cries* (1998); *The Last September* (1999); *Reines D'Un Jour* (2001); *Mariées Mais Pas Trop* (2003)

Bitzer, Billy

Bitzer was the man who put director **D W Griffith's** vision up onto the screen in a series of the most famous films ever made. A former silversmith, Bitzer graduated towards the camera only slowly, finally beginning his most famous collaboration at the relatively advanced age of thirty-six. It was Bitzer's genius that captured the very spirit of silent film in Griffith's *The Birth Of A Nation* (1915), *Intolerance* (1916) and *Broken Blossoms* (1919), and it was Bitzer, too, who developed and perfected the numerous technical innovations that Griffith has largely, and no doubt rightly, taken much of the credit for, and which include back lighting and the iris.

Other Key Films: *In Old Kentucky* (1909); *The Fugitive* (1910); *The Lonedale Operator* (1911); *Madame Rex* (1911); *A Tale Of The Wilderness* (1912); *The New York Hat* (1912); *Hearts Of The World* (1918); *Way Down East* [co/camera] (1920); *Orphans Of The Storm* [co/camera] (1922)

Black, Karen

A superb character actress who lit up the screen in **Bob Rafelson's** *Five Easy Pieces* (1970) as good-time-girl Rayette Dipesto, **Jack Nicholson's** dumb yet sensitive blue-collar girlfriend, Black also made her mark in John Flynn's *The Outfit* (1973), **John Schlesinger's** *The Day Of The Locust* (1975) and **Robert Altman's** *Nashville* (1975). For some incomprehensible reason her star began to wane during the 1980s and 1990s, leaving us to chew over the indelible images of her 1970s heyday and ponder what might have been – the scene in *Five Easy Pieces* where Black (with her scrupulously painted toenails perched coquettishly on the car dashboard) sings a country-and-western ballad to the over-educated but under-motivated Nicholson, is one of the most heartrending reflections of almost-love in the history of cinema. Didn't they *know* what she had?

Other Key Films: *Easy Rider* (1969); *Drive He Said* (1971); *Portnoy's Complaint* (1972); *The Great Gatsby* (1975); *Family Plot* (1976); *Come Back To The Five And Dime, Jimmy Dean, Jimmy Dean* (1982); *Children Of The Night* (1992); *The Player* (1992); *Cries Of Silence* (1993); *New York Crossing* (1996); *The Donor* (2000); *House Of 1000 Corpses* (2001); *America Brown* (2004); *Whitepaddy* (2006)

Key Line: 'I'll go out with you, or I'll stay in with you, or I'll do anything that you like for me to do, if you tell me that you love me.' [Black to Nicholson's Robert Eroica Dupea, in *Five Easy Pieces*]

Blanc, Mel

The greatest of all voice-over artists, Blanc provided the voices for the characters in the Looney Tunes and Merrie Melodies series of animated cartoons.

Key Line: 'What's up Doc?' [Bugs Bunny Cartoons]

Blaxploitation Movies

A series of 1970s films which glorified the black experience while at the same time endeavouring to gather in the largest possible paying audience to view the results. First and best of the genre was Gordon Parks's *Shaft* (1971) [remade in 2000 by John Singleton with **Samuel L Jackson** in the title role of John Shaft], closely followed by the even more influential *Superfly* (1972), which was directed by Parks's son, Gordon Parks Jr, who was killed in a plane crash seven years later. **Quentin Tarantino** paid homage to the genre by using a famous blaxploitation actress, Pam Grier, in his excellent *Pulp Fiction* (1994) follow-up, *Jackie Brown* (1997).

Blier, Bernard

Always the most unlikely looking of screen stars, with his chamber-pot belly and his bald head, Blier confounded the Gods of Appearance by constructing a distinguished and lengthy career in French cinema. He appeared in well over 100 films during his more than fifty-year film career, including **Marcel Carné's** *Hôtel Du Nord* (1938) and *Le Jour Se Lève* (1939), and **Henri-Georges Clouzot's** *Quai Des Orfèvres* (1947). Made a Chevalier De La Légion D'Honneur by the French Government for his contribution to cinema history, Blier, who died in 1989, is the father of film director Bertrand Blier, of *Les Valseuses* (1974) and *Trop Belle Pour Toi* (1989) fame.

Other Key Films

L'Enfer Des Anges (1939); *La Symphonie Fantastique* (1942); *Seul Dans La Nuit* (1945); *Monseigneur* (1949); *La Souricière* (1950); *Avant Le Deluge* (1954); *Le Dossier Noir* (1955); *Crime Et Châtiment* (1956); *L'Homme À L'Imperméable* (1958); *Retour De Manivelle* (1958); *Les Misérables* (1958); *La Chatte* (1958); *Germinal* (1962); *Casanova* (1970); *Le Corps De Mon Ennemi* (1976); *Buffet Froid* (1980); *I Picari* (1987)

Boetticher, Budd

One of the best-kept secrets of visually and emotionally literate American cinema, Boetticher was never allowed outside the B-Movie format, but that suited both him and his style just fine. He made a series of **Westerns** with **Randolph Scott** in the final years of the 1950s, the best of which, *The Tall T* (1958), *Buchanan Rides Alone* (1958) and *Ride Lonesome* (1959), must rank among the finest in a genre already over-brimming with talent in the likes of **John Ford**, **Howard Hawks**, **Sam Peckinpah** and **Anthony Mann**. Boetticher understood men and what motivates them, and as if in subconscious echo, he threw up his own burgeoning career to pursue a story in Mexico about an ill-fated matador, Carlos Arruza, that wrecked his health, destroyed his marriage and bankrupted both his future and his bank balance. One likes to imagine him, like Randolph Scott's Buchanan, shrugging off such absurd vicissitudes with a cracked smile and an airy laugh, geeing up his horse, and quietly continuing on his way. But that only happens in the movies…

Other Key Films: *The Bullfighter And The Lady* (1951); *The Magnificent Matador* (1956); *Seven Men From Now* (1956); *Decision At Sundown* (1958); *Westbound* (1959); *Comanche Station* (1960); *The Rise And Fall Of Legs Diamond* (1960); *Arruza* (1971)

Bogarde, Dirk

For fifteen years, between 1948 and 1963, Bogarde winced his way through more than thirty mostly forgettable films [with the possible exception of **Basil Dearden's** *The Blue Lamp* (1950) and *Victim* (1961), and **Michael Powell** and **Emeric Pressburger's** *Ill Met By Moonlight* (1958)] as a matinee idol who was forced to sew the flies of his trousers together to defend himself from overeager female fans. Then **Joseph Losey** cast him as manservant Hugo Barrett in *The Servant* (1963), and the second part of Bogarde's career began, ushering in a golden period in which he took on a series of increasingly challenging roles in a succession of English and European art-house films, which included Losey's *Accident* (1968), **Luchino Visconti's** *The Damned* (1969) and *Death In Venice* (1971), and Liliana Cavani's controversial exercise in sadomasochism, *The Night Porter* (1973). The third part of Bogarde's professional life was taken up with writing, but he gave a final, touching performance opposite **Jane Birkin** in **Bertrand Tavernier's** *Daddy Nostalgie* (1990) [a.k.a. *These Foolish Things*], which neatly and elegantly brought this now eminent actor's filmic career to an end.

Other Key Films: *Doctor In The House* (1954); *The Sleeping Tiger* (1954); *The Spanish Gardener* (1956); *Campbell's Kingdom* (1958); *A Tale Of Two Cities* (1958); *King And Country* (1964); *Darling* (1966); *Le Serpent* (1973); *Permission To Kill* (1975); *Providence* (1977); *A Bridge Too Far* (1977); *Despair* (1979); *The Vision* (1987)

Bogart, Humphrey

Rediscovered and taken to its collective heart by the French **New Wave** of the 1950s and 1960s, Bogart, while remaining quintessentially a man of his own time, also managed, in terms of his image, to transcend it. Born a New York WASP, Bogart shone when playing cynical and worldly men, brought, often despite their own better instincts, to heroism. In this way he differed from **Jean Gabin**, to whom, in many ways, he can be compared. Gabin, though often beaten down, was never cynical – it needed Bogart's genius, particularly as Rick Blaine in **Michael Curtiz's** *Casablanca* (1942), to exemplify the world-weary spleen of a knight in only-so-very-slightly-tarnished armour. In Bogie's final film, Mark Robson's *The Harder They Fall* (1956), **Philip Yordan** (possibly with the help of a friend or two) wrote a cracking script about the boxing industry, and Bogart, as always, played it straight down the line, from heel to hero. A few weeks after the film came out he was diagnosed with the cancer that was eventually to kill him, a little under a year later, just nine days before his fifty-eighth birthday. <u>Note For Film Buffs</u>: Bogie's favourite movie was **William Wellman's** *A Star Is Born* (1937). He used to run a 16-mm print of it every Christmas Eve and cry all the way through it. When asked why, he answered, 'I don't know. It just makes me cry.'

Other Key Films: *The Petrified Forest* (1936); *They Drive By Night* (1940); *High Sierra* (1941); *The Maltese Falcon* (1941); *To Have And Have Not* (1944); *The Big Sleep* (1946); *Key Largo* (1948); *The Treasure Of The Sierra Madre* (1948); *In A Lonely Place* (1950); *The African Queen* (1951); *The Barefoot Contessa* (1954); *The Caine Mutiny* (1954); *The Harder They Fall* (1956)

Key Line: 'Life, every now and then, behaves as though it had seen too many bad movies...' [Joseph L Mankiewicz's The Barefoot Contessa (1954)]

Bogdanovich, Peter

Almost more important in film criticism and conservation than he is in creative cinema (which is a backhanded compliment to just that creativity) Bogdanovich has savoured the highs and lows more than most directors of his generation, and probably acknowledges his own shortcomings and failures as well as anybody. His successes are impressive, and include *Targets* (1968), *The Last Picture Show* (1971), *Saint Jack* (1979) and *Mask* (1985) – his failures can usually be set down to either misplaced ambitions or lubricity – and who would dare to cast the first stone in that direction?

Other Key Films: *What's Up Doc?* (1972); *Paper Moon* (1973); *Daisy Miller* (1974); *Nickelodeon* (1976); *Texasville* (1990); *The Thing Called Love* (1993); *The Cat's Meow* (2001)

Bohringer, Richard

Perennially Gitanes-smoking, hoarse-voiced French character actor, Bohringer made his mark with international audiences in **Jean-Jacques Beineix's** *Diva* (1981), in which he played the quirky Gorodish – he's the one who explains the way to butter the perfect baguette, and who peels onions wearing a snorkel. Bohringer remains very much a local French actor, however, and beloved of Gallic cultural talk shows, despite his second successful foray into international waters with **Peter Greenaway's** *The Cook, The Thief, His Wife And Her Lover* (1989). Film fans who want to sample Bohringer's peculiarly eccentric style of acting should seek out a copy of Michel Deville's *Death In A French Garden* [*Péril En La Demeure*] (1985), or **Patrice Leconte's** ironically misogynistic *Tango* (1993), secure in the knowledge that they won't be let down.

Other Key Films: *Le Dernier Métro* [*The Last Metro*] (1980); *L'Addition* (1984);

Subway (1985); *Le Paltoquet* (1986); *Kamikaze* (1986); *Après La Guerre* (1989); *Dames Galantes* (1990); *Le Parfum D'Yvonne* (1994); *Les Caprices D'Un Fleuve* (1996); *Tykho Moon* (1996); *La Vérité Si Je Mens* (1997); *Comme Une Bête* (1998); *Cinq Minutes De Détente* (1999); *La Soutane Écarlate* (2000); *Ma Folle De Soeur* (2001); *Mauvais Genres* (2001); *Cavalcade* (2005); *Le Poulain* (2006)

Bolt, Robert

An eminent playwright and the screenwriter on such films as **David Lean's** *Lawrence Of Arabia* (1962), *Dr Zhivago* (1965) and *Ryan's Daughter* (1970), Bolt's finest hour came with the filming of his stage play about the tormented and finally doomed relationship between Henry VIII and Sir Thomas More in **Fred Zinnemann's** *A Man For All Seasons* (1966). Bolt, who had been married to actress Sarah Miles, died in 1995, after a long and exhausting battle with illness.

Other Key Films: Roger Donaldson's *The Bounty* (1984); Roland Joffé's *The Mission* (1986)

Bond, James

The brainchild of Ian Lancaster Fleming (and originally blond – of hair colour, not of name) Bond made his literary debut in *Casino Royale* in 1953, and his film debut in Terence Young's *Dr No* (1962). Discounting the turgid, multi-directed and ostensibly comic 1967 version of *Casino Royale* (in which there were any number of Bonds, some even female) the nominally English super-spy has since been played by six different actors on the big screen, in the following, occasionally leap-frogging order: Scots-born **Sean Connery**, English-born **Roger Moore**, Australian-born George Lazenby, Welsh-born Timothy Dalton, Irish-born **Pierce Brosnan** and, most recently, English-born (and the first blond Bond) Daniel Craig. (The Americans did, however, get a look in, way back in 1954, when Bond was played in a one-hour TV special by Barry Nelson.) The best Bond, by popular acclaim, appears to be Connery, but Dalton, Brosnan and Craig are all excellent, and Moore brought a cheerful wryness to the part that was as entertaining, in its way, as Connery's laconic intelligence was menacing. In recent years the Bond brand name has moved from marketing tool to marketing miracle, swept along by the remarkable success of the *Goldeneye* video game, which set a new standard in computer-game graphics. The Bond trademark has proved the most resilient and long lasting of all the great movie brands, a fact testified to by the hundreds of Bond sites listed on the Internet.

Other Key Films: Terence Young's *From Russia With Love* (1963); Guy Hamilton's *Goldfinger* (1964); Lewis Gilbert's *You Only Live Twice* (1967); Guy Hamilton's *Live And Let Die* (1973); John Glen's *The Living Daylights* (1987); Martin Campbell's *Goldeneye* (1995); Roger Spottiswoode's *Tomorrow Never Dies* (1997); **Michael Apted's** *The World Is Not Enough* (1999); Martin Campbell's *Casino Royale* (2006)

Key Line: Bond: 'Do you expect me to talk?' Goldfinger: 'No, Mr Bond, I expect you to die.' [Goldfinger]

Bond, Ward

One of **John Wayne's** greatest chums, and a fine, though limited character actor in his own right, Bond specialised in playing hardened men who won't take any nonsense, despite, or perhaps even because of, their own semi-comical natures. His best part came as Captain The Reverend Samuel Clayton in **John Ford's** *The Searchers* (1956) where he showed a level of incipient humanity that was lacking in many of his other characterizations.

Other Key Films: *Dodge City* (1939); *Young Mr Lincoln* (1939); *Drums Along The*

Mohawk (1939); *The Long Voyage Home* (1940); *They Were Expendable* (1945); *My Darling Clementine* (1946); *The Fugitive* (1947); *Fort Apache* (1948); *Three Godfathers* (1948); *Wagonmaster* (1950); *The Quiet Man* (1952); *Johnny Guitar* (1954); *Rio Bravo* (1959)

Bonham Carter, Helena

Fearful of being forever typecast as the upper-class English Rose she actually is by birth (the film director Anthony Asquith was her great-grand-uncle, and UK Prime Minister Herbert Henry Asquith, first Earl of Oxford, her great-great-grandfather), Bonham Carter has striven, sometimes unsuccessfully, to portray herself as a foul-mouthed, working-class American instead. The logic of this may seem inescapable to some, but the simple fact remains that what she does best is British costume drama, where inhibitions, cruel and corsets reign supreme. She was excellent in **James Ivory's** *Howards End* (1992), and also in Mort Ransen's marginally more contemporary *Margaret's Museum* (1995), and she will almost certainly go on trying to extend her range, which is a great deal more than can be said of most of the actors and actresses who have acquired for themselves such a cosy and potentially lucrative niche.

Other Key Films: *A Room with A View* (1986); *Maurice* (1987); *Getting It Right* (1989); *Hamlet* (1990); *Where Angels Fear To Tread* (1991); *Mary Shelley's* **Frankenstein** (1994); *Mighty Aphrodite* (1995); *Twelfth Night* (1996); *Keep The Aspidistra Flying* (1997); *Fight Club* (1999); *Carnivale* (1999); *Novocaine* (2001); *Planet Of The Apes* (2001); *Big Fish* (2003); *Charlie And The Chocolate Factory* (2005); *Sixty Six* (2006)

Boop, Betty

Max Fleischer's sexy cartoon heroine of the late 1920s and 1930s, Betty was based on the flapper concept behind Helen Kane's famous song rendition (later parodied by **Marilyn Monroe**) of 'I Want To Be Loved By You'. Come to think of it, Monroe's screen persona, particularly in **Billy Wilder's** *Some Like It Hot* (1959), and in her windblown upskirt scene in the same director's *The Seven Year Itch* (1955), seems to owe a lot more than has ever been previously acknowledged to gorgeous Betty's antics – and Marilyn would have been between the ages of five and thirteen at the height of Betty's fame, and no doubt highly impressionable. Hmm. How about a PhD thesis on this, until now it seems, largely unexplored possibility? <u>Note For Film Buffs:</u> A most amusing case of furtive flash framing occurred in the late 1920s, during one of Max Fleischer's risqué Betty Boop cartoons. The quite naturally non-prescient cartoonist, thinking that no one would ever discover his little joke, drew Betty's vagina onto a single frame during a wind-driven upskirt sequence, leaving audiences to speculate on whether they had fantasized Betty's nudity, or really seen it – the invention of video, however, rapidly uncovered Fleischer's delightful and witty erotic conceit.

Boorman, John

A well-informed and fanatical propagandist for film, Boorman is one of Britain's finest directors, and his career is something of a miracle given the shabby way film-makers of talent are often treated by the London-based institutions and governing bodies that should be helping and encouraging them. Many of Boorman's best films have consequently been shot with US and other foreign funding, producing such gems as *Point Blank* (1967), *Hell In The Pacific* (1968) and *Deliverance* (1972) – *Excalibur* (1981), a visually and aurally stunning evocation of the Arthurian legends, and the retrospectively ruminative *Hope And Glory* (1987), showed just what British filmmaking had been missing over the years of its director's enforced creative exile. Boorman's recent John Le Carré outing, *The Tailor Of Panama* (2001), miraculously transformed **Pierce Brosnan** from hunk to successful light comedian, by virtue of a literate script (by Andrew Davies), stunning photography (by Philippe Rousselot), and Boorman's steady and emotionally literate hand on the tiller.

Other Key Films: *Leo The Last* (1970); *Zardoz* (1974); *The Emerald Forest* (1985); *Beyond Rangoon* (1995); *The General* (1998); *Country Of My Skull* (2004)

Borgnine, Ernest

A natural 'heavy' as personified by his sadistic military policeman, Sgt. 'Fatso' Judson, in **Fred Zinnemann's** *From Here To Eternity* (1953), and as **Robert Ryan's** evil henchman, Coley Trimble, in **John Sturges's** *Bad Day At Black Rock* (1954), Borgnine surprised everyone when he received an Oscar for his portrayal of the amorously ill-favoured Bronx butcher in Delbert Mann's *Marty* (1955) [which constituted the first of a new breed of filmed teleplays that revolutionized Hollywood's approach to screen dialogue in the mid 1950s]. His career has varied wildly since then, leaving the impression that, apart from the one blip, Borgnine has never been more than a talented, single-tracked team player.

Other Key Films: *Johnny Guitar* (1954); *Run For Cover* (1955); *Violent Saturday* (1955); *Jubal* (1956); *The Vikings* (1958); *Barabbas* (1962); *The Flight Of The Phoenix* (1965); *The Wild Bunch* (1969); *Hustle* (1975); *Escape From New York* (1981); *Cane Arrabiatto* (1985); *Skeleton Coast* (1987); *Tides Of War* (1990); *Gattaca* (1997); *Abilene* (1999); *Castlerock* (2000); *Hoover* (2000); *The Long Ride Home* (2003); *Oliviero Rising* (2006)

Borzage, Frank

A scurrilously under-appreciated filmmaker whose particular brand of heady romanticism was eaten up and then spat out by the cheerful, rackety, patriotic hoo-hah that followed the United States' belated entry into the Second World War, Borzage could show the poetical side of a love story almost as well as the French, and he had a particular insight into the vulnerabilities and weaknesses of judgement such a love engenders. His best films, which include *Seventh Heaven* (1927), *Bad Girl* (1931), *History Is Made At Night* (1937), *Three Comrades* (1938), *The Mortal Storm* (1940), and the magnificent **Crawford/Gable** turn in *Strange Cargo* (1940), have heart, (a rare thing in Hollywood), and as such deserve to be remembered and shown far more than they are. Borzage cared about love and friendship and the painful losses the one can cause to the other, and with films such as *A Farewell to Arms* (1932), he paved the way for such later poets of the human condition as **Nicholas Ray** and **Charles Laughton**.

Other Key Films: *Lazybones* (1925); *Street Angel* (1928); *The River* (1929); *Man's Castle* (1933); *No Greater Glory* (1934); *Desire* (1936); *Moonrise* (1948)

Boulting, John & Roy

A set of twins who either shared or alternated the producing, writing and directing work on a high-quality sequence of British films and documentaries of the 1940s and 1950s including *Thunder Rock* (1943), a seriously weird paean to proactive wartime commitment, and *The Guinea Pig* [a.k.a. *The Outsider*] (1949), in which the working class recipient of a scholarship, **Richard Attenborough**, struggles to make his way in an upmarket and initially unwelcoming private school. (In our newly enlightened and radically chic age, of course, the private schoolboys would now be struggling against each other, and not Attenborough, in order to take his discarded place at the sub-standard state school his academic brilliance so unwisely caused him to leave!) The Boultings's best joint projects were the **Graham Greene** and Terence Rattigan-scripted *Brighton Rock* (1950), and a little-seen thriller, *Seven Days To Noon* (1950), in which an atomic scientist threatens London in a rather misguided protest in favour of nuclear disarmament. When the brothers belatedly turned to comedy in the 1960s, something of their magic unfortunately gave way in the process.

Other Key Films: *Desert Victory* (1944) [doc.]; *Tunisian Victory* (1945) [doc.]; *Burma Victory* (1947) [doc.]; *Singlehanded* (1954); *The Magic Box* (1956); *Private's Progress* (1956); *Run For The Sun* (1958); *Brothers In Law* (1958); *I'm All Right Jack* (1959); *Lucky Jim* (1963); *Twisted Nerve* (1968); *There's A Girl In My Soup* (1973)

Bourvil

A much-loved comedian who changed his name from André Raimbourg to that of the town, Bourville, in which he had been brought up (in a delightful and typically French tribute to his rural roots), Bourvil had become something of a national treasure by the time of his death at the age of fifty-three in 1970. He was that rare thing, a comedian who could handle both the tragic and the slapstick elements inherent in all great comedy. His greatest success came in Gérard Oury's *La Grande Vadrouille* (1966), in which he, Terry-Thomas and the great **Louis de Funès** play British pilots (!) escaping from the predictably demented Boches. Bourvil's best performance, however, came in another Gérard Oury story, this time directed by André Cayette, the considerably more downbeat *Le Miroir A Deux Faces* (1958), which was later lamentably remade by a narcissistic **Barbra Streisand**, who had most emphatically not learned the lessons of the original.

Other Key Films: *La Ferme Du Pendu* (1945); *Les Trois Mousquetaires* (1953); *Les Misérables* (1958); *Un Drôle De Dimanche* (1958); *Le Bossu* (1959); *Le Corniaud* (1965); *Les Grandes Gueules* (1965); *L'Étalon* (1970)

Bow, Clara

In retrospect a rather tragic figure, Bow, at the height of her brief fame, was known as Elinor Glyn's 'It' girl, and seemed, for a time, to have the world at her feet. But fame and it's gradual loss after the advent of sound had cramped her style and highlighted her brassy accent, served only to undermine her already fragile (and possibly inherited) mental state, and she spent a large part of her later life confined to various institutions. A direct precursor of such tragic goddesses of the screen as **Jean Harlow** and **Marilyn Monroe**, the best of Bow's films span the period 1927-1929 (the run-up to the Great Depression, in other words) and parallel, by an awful sort of spontaneous morphology, Bow's later descent into her own depressive cycle.

Key Films: *It* (1927); *Children Of Divorce* (1927); *Wings* (1927); *Red Hair* (1928); *The Wild Party* (1929); *The Saturday Night Kid* (1929)

Boyer, Charles

Smoothly romantic star and heartthrob for nearly three separate generations of women, Boyer's magnetic powers of attraction may seem a little hard to understand now – but given a small amount of insight and an even smaller capacity for retrospective empathy, it becomes clear that Boyer represented the apparently opposing paradoxes of passion and security for his female audience, and that this otherwise quite unrealistic (and therefore quintessentially filmic) equation, was something that the philosophically-inclined Boyer instinctively understood and chose to make his own. Following a career permeated with lightness, professionalism and charm, Boyer died tragically, by his own hand, just two days after the death of his beloved wife, Pat, and thirteen years following the death, by suicide, of their only son, Michael.

Key Films: *Le Capitaine Fracassé* (1927); *L'Epervier* (1933); *Liliom* (1933); *Shanghai* (1935); *Mayerling* (1936); *The Garden Of Allah* (1936); *Conquest* (1937); *Orage* (1937); *Algiers* (1938); *All This And Heaven Too* (1940); *Back Street* (1941); *The Constant Nymph* (1943); *Gaslight* (1944); *Madame De…* (1953); *Nana* (1955); *La Parisienne* (1958); *Stavisky* (1974)

Brackett, Charles

Renowned for his inspired collaboration with **Billy Wilder** on *The Major And The Minor* (1942), *Five Graves To Cairo* (1943), *The Lost Weekend* (1945), *The Emperor Waltz* (1948) and *Sunset Boulevard* (1950), the near-miraculous Brackett also collaborated on the scripts, or provided the storylines for, **Ernst Lubitsch's** *Ninotchka* (1939), **Howard Hawks's** *Ball Of Fire* (1942) and **Henry Hathaway's** *Niagara* (1953). Hot diggety-dog! How many of the more-lauded, super-cosseted and better-paid directors who traditionally steal a screenwriter's thunder can match that sort of a career tally? And look at the following – not a clinker amongst them.

Other Key Films: Robert Z. Leonard's *Piccadilly Jim* (1937); Ernst Lubitsch's *Bluebeard's Eighth Wife* (1938); Theodore Reed's *What A Life* (1939); Mitchell Leisen's *To Each His Own* (1946); **Jean Negulesco's** *Titanic* (1953)

Branagh, Kenneth

Something of a multi-talented wunderkind who was raised so high after his initial successes on the stage, on the road, on television, and with his first motion picture, *Henry V* (1989), that it was almost inevitable that a *Frankenstein* (1994), or something very much like it, would come along to melt or pare his wings. The fact remains that Branagh is a cultured bringer-together – a leader and galvaniser of men and women – and that this particular talent is in such short supply at the moment that to carp at his occasional excesses is tantamount to wishing that the literate part of the British film industry commit Seppuku with a rusty dagger. Long may he continue striving on his, and our, behalf.

Other Key Films: *Dead Again* (1991); *Peter's Friends* (1992); *Much Ado About Nothing* (1993); *A Midwinter's Tale* (1995); *Hamlet* (1996); *Love's Labour's Lost* (2000); *As You Like It* (2006)

Brandauer, Klaus Maria

A consummate actor and manipulator of the screen, Brandauer is capable of the tricky feat of making us disapprove of the character he is playing while still liking the man who is playing him, thus providing the audience with a pretty moral conundrum indeed. Most notable along these lines was Brandauer's Baron Blor Blixen-Finecke in **Sidney Pollack's** *Out Of Africa* (1985), who, despite giving **Meryl Streep** syphilis, ruining her and then running out on her – not necessarily in that order – remained so much more sympathetic and believable than the two main protagonists in the film that one found oneself cheering him on during each separate perfidy. Brandauer had previously managed a similar trick, as the baddie, Largo, in Irvin Kershner's **James Bond** outing *Never Say Never Again* (1983), and one is left with the feeling that were Brandauer ever to put himself forward as a benevolent dictator, in, say, his native Austria, he might have a darned good chance of snatching the job from under the noses of any notionally democratic opposition.

Other Key Films: *Mephisto* (1981); *Colonel Redl* (1986); *Streets Of Gold* (1986); *Hanussen* (1988); *The French Revolution* (1989); *The Russia House* (1990); *White Fang* (1991); *Mario And The Magician* (1994); *Rembrandt* (1999); *Dykaren* (2000); *Vercingétorix* (2001); *Jedermanns Fest* (2002); *The Fourth Generation* (2006)

Brando, Marlon

A master of Method Acting, Brando cemented his screen career with three films in three years directed by **Elia Kazan** – *A Streetcar Named Desire* (1951), *Viva Zapata* (1952) and *On The Waterfront* (1954). In 1953 he took a brief break from Kazan and starred as Mark Antony in **Joseph L Mankiewicz's** critically acclaimed *Julius Caesar*. Brando directed his own extraordinary first feature, *One-Eyed Jacks*, in 1961, but from then onwards his career has varied enormously. Later highlights include **Gillo Pontecorvo's** *Burn!* (1970), **Francis Ford Coppola's** *The Godfather* (1972) and *Apocalypse Now* (1979), and a phenomenal performance as Paul, in **Bernardo Bertolucci's** *Last Tango in Paris* (1972), in which he single-handedly extended the possibilities of screen acting.

Marlon Brando in The Appaloosa, directed by Sydney J. Furie (1966).

Universal/The Kobal Collection

Other Key Films: *The Men* (1950); *The Wild One* (1954); *Guys And Dolls* (1955); *Teahouse Of The August Moon* (1956); *The Young Lions* (1958); *The Fugitive Kind* (1960); *Mutiny On The Bounty* (1962); *The Chase* (1966); *Reflections In A Golden Eye* (1967); *The Missouri Breaks* (1973); *A Dry White Season* (1989); *Don Juan DeMarco* (1995); *The Island Of Dr Moreau* (1996); *The Brave* (1997); *Free Money* (1998); *The Score* (2001)

Key Lines:

1. 'You don't understand. I could've had class. I could've been a contender. I could've been somebody… instead of a bum, which is what I am.' [*On The Waterfront*]

2. 'An actor's a guy who, if you ain't talking about him, ain't listening.' [Brando on actors]

Brasseur, Pierre

Brasseur was a vastly impressive all-rounder, combining a forty-five-year film career with some exalted stage performances, the writing of numerous plays and the reputation of being a more than passable poet – the sort of civilized Renaissance man, in other words, the cinema so rarely throws up nowadays, except, perhaps, in the person of a **John Sayles** or a **Peter Bogdanovich**. Brasseur made his mark playing the vicious and cowardly little hood in **Marcel Carné's** quasi-nihilistic *Quai Des Brumes* (1938) who ends the film by gunning down hero/anti-hero **Jean Gabin** from a passing car. The quality of many of the films Brasseur appeared in was astonishing, and he never let down either his directors or the screenwriters (particularly **Jacques**

Prévert) who so adored writing for his elusive, ironical voice. His greatest screen performance came, not surprisingly, as Frederick Lemâitre in Carné's miraculous *Les Enfants Du Paradis* (1945).

Other Key Films: *Les Deux Timides* (1925); *La Fille De L'Eau* (1925); *Quick* (1932); *Pattes De Mouche* (1936); *Les Portes De La Nuit* (1946); *Les Amants De Verone* (1948); *Les Mains Sales* (1951); *Barbe-Bleue* (1951); *La Tour De Nèsle* (1954); *Oasis* (1954); *La Tête Contre Les Murs* (1958); *La Loi* (1958); *Vive L'Amour* (1961); *King Of Hearts* (1966)

Brennan, Walter

Winner of no less than three supporting actor Oscars, for **William Wyler's** *Come And Get It!* (1936), David Butler's *Kentucky* (1938), and Wyler's *The Westerner* (1940), Brennan is the most famous character actor of them all, and his magnificent string of performances in **Howard Hawks's** *To Have And Have Not* (1945), where he played **Humphrey Bogart's** gimpy drunk companion Eddie, in **John Ford's** *My Darling Clementine* (1946), as the evil Clanton paterfamilias, and in his supreme comic turn as **John Wayne's** crusty sidekick, Stumpy, in Hawks's sublime and still stubbornly underrated *Rio Bravo* (1959), are surely more than enough to ensure Brennan's eternal seat in the great movie house in the sky.

Other Key Films: *Bride Of Frankenstein* (1935); *Barbary Coast* (1935); *The Three Godfathers* (1936); *Fury* (1936); *The Adventures Of Tom Sawyer* (1938); *Sergeant York* (1941); *Swamp Water* (1941); *Hangmen Also Die* (1943); *Driftwood* (1947); *Best Of The Badmen* (1951); *Bad Day At Black Rock* (1955); *The Proud Ones* (1956)

Key Lines:
1. 'Say? Was you ever bit by a dead bee?' [Brennan to **Lauren Bacall** in *To Have And Have Not*]
2. 'Drinking don't bother my memory. If it did, I wouldn't drink. I couldn't. I'd forget how good it was. Then where'd I be? Start drinking water again.' [*To Have And Have Not*]

Bresson, Robert

Watching any film by Robert Bresson is an experience so distinct from watching a film by any other director that one is forced to review one's expectations of the cinema accordingly. Bresson is a filmmaker of such awesome seriousness and integrity that one sometimes feels as if invited into the garden of a monastery, there to contemplate the human soul in an environment devoted to the noumenal and scrupulously detached from material things. Disdaining 'acting' per se, he uses faces, sounds, images and music, to highlight his search for some elusive truth to which he alone appears to hold the key – there are moments in his films that are so sublimely honest that one stands aghast at the triviality of much of one's normal filmic diet of pap, expediency, and *folie de grandeur*. Yes, there is a place for entertainment and joy and silliness, but there must also be one for art, and Bresson, **Jean Renoir**, **Ingmar Bergman**, and a bare few others remind us of our responsibilities and our humanity, and warn us that we trivialize the transformative power of faith and of exalted emotions at our peril. See **Heartstopping Moments**

Key Films: *Les Anges Du Péché* (1943); *Les Dames Du Bois De Boulogne* (1945); *Le Journal D'Un Curé De Campagne* (1950); *Un Condamné À Mort S'Est Échappé* (1956); *Pickpocket* (1959); *Le Procès De Jeanne D'Arc* (1962); *Au Hasard, Balthazar* (1966); *Mouchette* (1967); *Une Femme Douce* (1969); *Quatre Nuits D'Un Rêveur* (1971); *Lancelot Du Lac* (1974); *Le Diable Probablement* (1977); *L'Argent* (1983)

Bridges, Jeff

Bridges was one of the best young actors of the 1970s and 1980s, appearing in one great movie after another, and then, for some reason, he went mainstream on us and the power of his performances tailed off, along with his youth, until he became merely a good working actor, and not the edgy and slightly dangerous presence he had been in his early prime. Still, his prime was enough (and more than many lesser talents ever had), and his outstanding performances as the lost young Texan, Duane Jackson, in **Peter Bogdanovich's** *The Last Picture Show* (1971); as the young but fatally untalented boxing hopeful, Ernie Munger, in **John Huston's** magnificent film about losers, *Fat City* (1972); as Lightfoot, the crazy boy **Clint Eastwood** takes under his wing only to see him die like a moth in a candle flame, in **Michael Cimino's** superb comedy thriller *Thunderbolt And Lightfoot* (1974); and as Richard Bone in **Ivan Passer's** *Cutter's Way* (1981), a man with no ambitions and no convictions who nonetheless ends up by rising to the quality of his friendships – these are great films and great performances by any standards, and there are more. Bridges remains the unsung hero of post-1960s melancholia, and his place in any discriminating viewer's movie pantheon is assured.

Other Key Films: *Bad Company* (1972); *The Last American Hero* (1973); *Hearts Of The West* (1975); *Stay Hungry* (1976); *Winter Kills* (1979); *Against All Odds* (1984); *Starman* (1984); *Jagged Edge* (1985); *Tucker: The Man And His Dream* (1988); *The Fabulous Baker Boys* (1989); *The Vanishing* (1993); *Wild Bill* (1995); *White Squall* (1996); *The Mirror Has Two Faces* (1996); *The Big Lebowski* (1998); *Arlington Road* (1999); *The Muse* (1999); *Simpatico* (1999); *The Contender* (2000); *Seabiscuit* (2003); *The Door In The Floor* (2004); *The Moguls* (2005); *Tideland* (2005); *Stick It* (2006)

Bronson, Charles

Bronson had one of the finest natural physiques ever seen on an actor, a gift (if that is the right word) from his years working down the Lithuanian coalmines. How such a man, from such a place, should ever have managed to reach the heady heights of Hollywood stardom is a story that almost makes one believe that the streets of the United States are indeed paved with gold. Bronson's greatest success, however, has always been in Europe, with European audiences, and his late flowering (he was almost fifty when he really hit the big-time) is a tribute to his guts and staying power. His epiphany – when, briefly, he attained a quasi-mythological status in Italy and France – came with **Sergio Leone's** *Once Upon A Time In The West* (1968), where his craggy, lived-in features seemed to suggest, in purely visual terms, of course, (something which Leone, of all people, understood), the neutral, desiccated, almost sterile air of the great deserts of the American West.

Other Key Films: *The Magnificent Seven* (1960); *The Great Escape* (1963); *The Dirty Dozen* (1967); *Soleil Rouge* (1971); *The Valachi Papers* (1972); *Chato's Land* (1972); *The Stone Killer* (1973); *Death Wish* (1974); *The White Buffalo* (1977); *The Indian Runner* (1991); *Death Wish V: The Face Of Death* (1994)

Brooks, Louise

Brooks's star shone briefly in **G W Pabst's** *Pandora's Box* (1929) and *Diary Of A Lost Girl* (1929), and then again in the late 1950s and early 1960s when she was 'rediscovered' by film curator James Card, her pageboy bob and kohl-encircled eyes looming from a multitude of fresh posters and stills. But her star faded just as abruptly second time around, leaving the remainder of her life to be spent chasing the furtive image of that rekindled moment, or trying, in vain, to recreate a magic that was as elusive as she, in the end, turned out to be. In the final analysis it was what Pabst made of her that counted, as if she were a canvas hewn from human skin for him to paint on, and it was this sad and bitter and ultimately empty paradox that so

swiftly, and so completely, brought her down.

Other Key Films: *A Girl In Every Port* (1928); *Beggars Of Life* (1928); *Prix De Beauté* (1930)

Brooks, Mel

Brooks made one of the funniest films in cinema history with *The Producers* (1968) – inventive, acute, flamboyant and anarchic, his seemed a genuinely original voice at a time when cinema comedy had hit the post-TV doldrums. *Blazing Saddles* (1974) was brasher and more obvious but still more or less on target (his fans said charitably) and the splendid *Young Frankenstein* (1974) amused by virtue of its skilful rehashing of music-hall and silent film conventions (but the

fans were still having to stretch to keep their boy in contention). But that first brief spurt of originality seemed to have hamstrung its director, and with each post-1974 film he sank lower and lower down the scale, until his most recent films resemble a series of strung-together gags distilled from a how-to book for TV, rather than motion picture entities with some residual purpose beyond the simple fact that they might make money. It's a tragedy, really, and one returns to Brooks's original version of *The Producers* time and again as if to the work of some long-lost comic genius too modest and self-effacing to have ever thought of travestying himself.

Other Key Films: *Silent Movie* (1976); *High Anxiety* (1977); *History Of The World Part One* (1981); *To Be Or Not To Be* (1983); *Spaceballs* (1987); *Life Stinks* (1991); *Robin Hood: Men In Tights* (1993); **Dracula**: *Dead And Loving It* (1995)

Brooks, Richard

A screenwriter turned director (akin, one supposes, to a poacher turned gamekeeper), Brooks made an impressive sequence of literate, high-quality films during the late 1950s and 1960s, including *Cat on A Hot Tin Roof* (1958), *Elmer Gantry* (1960), *Lord Jim* (1965) and *In Cold Blood* (1967). Each one was an adaptation of an existing work, and each one retained just the faintest trace of a *Classics Illustrated* approach, as if Brooks never expected the readers of the original works to bother turning up at the cinema and call his bluff. This is not to say that he wasn't a good director – for he was far more skilful, and brought far better material to the screen than most of his contemporaries – but merely that his work seemed to lack the spark of greatness which great adaptations need. His treatment of Truman Capote's best-selling novel *In Cold Blood* came closest, but one wonders how much of its effect relied on Conrad Hall's exquisite photography, which included the famous shot of droplets of rain streaming down a cell window and reflecting off killer Perry Smith's gut-stricken face as if they were tears.

Other Key Films: *Deadline USA* (1952); *The Blackboard Jungle* (1955); *The Last Hunt* (1956); *The Brothers Karamazov* (1958); *Sweet Bird Of Youth* (1962); *The Professionals* (1966); *Looking For Mr Goodbar* (1977); *Wrong Is Right* (1982); *Fever Pitch* (1985)

Key Lines:
1. 'The images come first, and with images, like music, the primary reaction is emotional...the effect has to be orchestral.' [Brooks on film]
2. 'As long as it has that element in it that you can recognize in yourself, as long as it has a pinch of the truth in it – terrific!' [Brooks, on watching **Gary Cooper** movies in the Cambodian jungle, during the filming of *Lord Jim*]

Brosnan, Pierce

Better-looking and better-preserved than any man his age (he was born in 1953) has any right to be, Brosnan made a suave and believable ***James Bond*** in Martin Campbell's *Goldeneye* (1995), Roger Spottiswoode's *Tomorrow Never Dies* (1997), **Michael Apted's** *The World Is Not Enough* (1999), and Lee Tamahori's *Die Another Day* (2002), and a convincingly heroic figure in Roger Donaldson's *Dante's Peak* (1996) and John McTiernan's *The Thomas Crown Affair* (1999). His career has had a gentle lift-off, and his best part, before Bond rocketed him (briefly?) into the stratosphere, was as the cold-blooded Russian operative in John Mackenzie's *The Fourth Protocol* (1987), an impressively tight, old-fashioned little thriller, and none the worse for that. Come to think of it, Brosnan is a rather old-fashioned sort of a star, and it's a fair bet that he will show considerably more staying power, in consequence, than many of the brasher, rasher, younger generation of rivals snapping at his heels, as his recent 'outing' as a closet light comedian, in **John Boorman's** *The Tailor Of Panama* (2001), so persuasively suggests.

Other Key Films: *The Long Good Friday* (1980); *Mister Johnson* (1990); *The Lawnmower Man* (1992); *Mrs Doubtfire* (1993); *Love Affair* (1994); *The Mirror Has Two Faces* (1996); *Grey Owl* (1999); *Blood And Champagne* (2001); *After The Sunset* (2004); *The Matador* (2005); *Seraphim Falls* (2006)

Brown, Joe E

Brown doesn't really merit a place here, but he's getting one because he was utterly brilliant in **Billy Wilder's** *Some Like It Hot* (1959), where he played spoiled but soft-hearted multi-millionaire Osgood E. Fielding III, to **Jack Lemmon's** Jerry/Josephine. Osgood is the sort of man that everyone would like to have as a favourite uncle, and it takes genius, of a certain sort, to create such an enduring and much-beloved archetype.

Other Key Films: *Song Of The West* (1930); *The Tenderfoot* (1932); *A Midsummer Night's Dream* (1935); *Chatterbox* (1943); *The Tender Years* (1947); *Show Boat* (1951); *Around The World In Eighty Days* (1956); *It's A Mad Mad Mad Mad World* (1963)

Key Line: Jerry: 'We can't get married at all. I'm a man.' Osgood: 'Well. Nobody's perfect.' [*Some Like It Hot*]

Browning, Tod

The one work for which Browning is really known outside the quasi-Masonic and

rarefied world of the film critic and theorist, is his 1932 production *Freaks*. The principal reason for its fame may well lie in the fact that it was banned, and banning inevitably creates interest – but the true reason for its success is far subtler than that, and relies as much on Browning's early experiences as a circus entertainer as it does on the instinctive insights the film contains on the consequences of judging a thing or a person simply by their appearance. No film has ever brought this subject home with greater force, and *Freaks*, which would be virtually unfilmable today because of its non-politically correct subject matter, remains, to all intents and purposes unique.
Other Key Films: *The Unholy Three* (1925); *The Unknown* (1927); *The Thirteenth Chair* (1929); **Dracula** (1931); *The Iron Man* (1932); *Mark Of The Vampire* (1935); *The Devil Doll* (1936)

Brynner, Yul

It's a little hard to fathom the extent of Brynner's screen success, inasmuch as the polished old chestnut (whoops) of women finding bald men irresistible because of their enhanced testosterone count could not possibly have applied to him, as Brynner shaved, rather than lost, his hair. Something of a one-track actor, Brynner could glower with the best of them, and his rugged and deeply masculine Siberian/Russian voice (at least one presumes it was Siberian/Russian, for Brynner was extremely vague about his antecedents) had a certain rough charm. But the real rub comes when one compares roles and actors. Take Brynner's Chris, the boss in **John Sturges's** *The Magnificent Seven* (1960), then match it against Takashi Shimura's Kambei (exactly the same role) in **Akira Kurosawa's** *The Seven Samurai* (1954). Well? Shimura suggested the veteran soldier's tiredness, his feeling for duty, his sense of fun and his noble soul – Brynner simply suggested Chris's eagerness to be at the enemy, and a certain simpering complicity in the various neuroses of his companions.
Other Key Films: *The King And I* (1956); *The Buccaneer* (1958); *The Sound And The Fury* (1959); *Le Testament D'Orphée* (1960); *Taras Bulba* (1962); *Villa Rides* (1968); *The Madwoman Of Chaillot* (1969); *Westworld* (1973)

Buñuel, Luis

It would be naïve to call Buñuel predominantly a surrealist, just as it would be false to call his early collaborator, Salvador Dali, principally a painter – both were concerned with appearances, how little they matter, and how much fun they are to suborn. A comedian of anarchy, Buñuel turned any project he was given (or chose to take) into yet another facet of an all-consuming vision in which the Church, the middle classes, the worthy and the dull became fodder for his explosive visions. He despised the cinema of 'effect', and chose to tell his stories and illustrate his themes in as uncomplicated a way as possible – but the depth of thought behind each image always comes through, and at his best, in *Los Olvidados* (1950), *The Adventures Of Robinson Crusoe* (1952), *Viridiana* (1961), *The Exterminating Angel* (1962), *Tristana* (1970) and *The Discreet Charm Of The Bourgeoisie* (1972), Buñuel reached a sort of paradoxical, because atheistic, sanctity.
Other Key Films: *Un Chien Andalou* (1928); *L'Age D'Or* (1930); *Mexican Bus Ride* (1951); *Wuthering Heights* (1953); *The River And Death* (1954); *The Criminal Life Of Archibaldo De La Cruz* (1955); *Nazarin* (1959); *Le Journal D'Une Femme De Chambre* (1964); *Simon Of The Desert* (1965); *Belle De Jour* (1967); *That Obscure Object Of Desire* (1977)
Key Line: 'Thanks to God, I am still an atheist.' [Buñuel on faith]

Burnett, W R

Either co-screenwriter, original novelist or story consultant on **Mervyn LeRoy's** *Little Caesar* (1930), **Raoul Walsh's** *High Sierra* (1941) and **John Huston's** *The Asphalt Jungle* (1950), Burnett, though a gentle, non-violent man himself, understood the gangster mind wonderfully well, and has heavily influenced just about everybody (including **Quentin Tarantino** and **Martin Scorsese**) who has attempted the genre since. An inveterate gambler who succeeded in virtually bankrupting himself on more than one occasion, Burnett was effectively forgotten by the time of his death in 1982, having, himself, become the 'outsider' character he always depicted so well.

Other Key Films: Howard Hawk's *Scarface: Shame Of A Nation* (1932); Stuart Heisler's *I Died A Thousand Times* (1956); **John Sturges's** *The Great Escape* (1963)

Sue Lyon and Richard Burton in The Night of the Iguana, directed by John Huston (1964).

MGM/The Kobal Collection

Key Line: 'You're born, you're gonna have trouble, and you're gonna die. That you know. There's not much else you know.' [Burnett on life, living, and the pursuit of sapience]

Burton, Richard

Together with **Robert Donat**, Burton was the screen actor with the finest speaking voice in the business, as is amply demonstrated in his definitive recordings of the poetry of Dylan Thomas. At his best (and when he wasn't coasting along in blandly commercial film vehicles) Burton could electrify the screen more effectively even than **Marlon Brando**. He gave a magisterially self-referential performance as the drunken, railing, despairing unfrocked priest, the Reverend T Lawrence Shannon, in **John Huston's** *The Night Of The Iguana* (1964), for unfortunately alcohol, and a fine, but ultimately underused intellect, were Burton's twin crosses in life. His readings in Donald Brittain and John Kramer's magnificent *Volcano: An Inquiry Into The Life And Death Of Malcolm Lowry* (1976) showed what was potentially lost when he didn't get to play the once-in-a-lifetime role of Lowry's alter ego, Geoffrey Firmin, in Huston's *Under The Volcano* (1984).

Other Key Films: *My Cousin Rachel* (1952); *Bitter Victory* (1958); *Look Back In Anger* (1958); *Becket* (1964); *The Spy Who Came In From The Cold* (1965); *Who's Afraid Of Virginia Woolf* (1966); *Where Eagles Dare* (1969); *Villain* (1971); *Under Milk Wood* (1973); *1984* (1984)

Burton, Tim

Burton has becoming something of a one-man cult, and deservedly so, for he brought a new, albeit Gothically inclined look to a 1980s commercial cinema in need of something (anything!) to redeem it from creeping mediocrity. *Batman* (1989) was as good as it should have been thanks to Burton's genuine comic-book vision of a subject that lingers in the souls of most grown-up male children – call it the

subliminal wish to be a hero if you like – and it is Burton's particular strength that he understands the child inherent in the man and caters to it, while bringing a demonstrably adult understanding and skill to the construction of his creations. *Edward Scissorhands* (1990) was enormous fun, and *The Nightmare Before Christmas* (1993) was a genuinely original slant on an overused, and for the most part under-imaginative genre.
Other Key Films: *Pee-Wee's Big Adventure* (1985); *Beetlejuice* (1988); *Batman Returns* (1992); *Ed Wood* (1994); *Mars Attacks!* (1996); *Sleepy Hollow* (1999); *Planet Of The Apes* (2001); *Big Fish* (2003); *Charlie And The Chocolate Factory* (2005); *Corpse Bride* (2005)

Buscemi, Steve

Marvellously offbeat character actor whose scene-stealing turns in **Quentin Tarantino's** *Reservoir Dogs* (1991) and **Joel & Ethan Coen's** *Fargo* (1996) were enough to guarantee him cult status with those viewers who weren't aware of the cult status he already enjoyed thanks to his theatrical forays and appearances in independent, non-mainstream films. Buscemi benefits from a curiously memorable face which he uses as if it were a glove puppet, galvanising its features and eyes until the viewer either laughs, gives in, or in the case of his inept crook, Carl Showalter, in *Fargo*, runs.
Other Key Films: *Parting Glances* (1986); *Coffee And Cigarettes Part Two* (1988); *Mystery Train* (1989); *New York Stories* (1989); *Miller's Crossing* (1990); *Zandalee* (1991); *The Hudsucker Proxy* (1994); *Things To Do In Denver When You're Dead* (1995); *Kansas City* (1996); *Trees Lounge* (1996) [also dir.]; *Con Air* (1997); *The Big Lebowski* (1998); *28 Days* (2000); *The Animal Factory* [also dir.] (2000); *Double Whammy* (2001); *Coffee And Cigarettes* (2003); *Big Fish* (2003); *Romance & Cigarettes* (2005); *Monsterhouse* (2006)

Busch, Niven

Busch either co-scripted, wrote the original novel or provided the story for **Henry King's** *In Old Chicago* (1938), **William Wyler's** *The Westerner* (1940), Tay Garnett's *The Postman Always Rings Twice* (1946), **King Vidor's** *Duel In The Sun* (1947) and **Raoul Walsh's** *Pursued* (1947), which adds up to a pretty good career, even if, unlike that of most directors and actors, a screenwriter's career is far more difficult to pin down. An inveterate field sportsman and rancher, Busch really understood his subject, and this knowledge comes through in both his novels and the screenplays he was so often called upon to make of them.
Other Key Films: Anthony Mann's *The Furies* (1950); John Sturges's *The Capture* (1950); Raoul Walsh's *Distant Drums* (1951)

Byrne, Gabriel

A dark, cerebral actor, whose features often suggest more than one might infer simply from his capacities as an actor, Byrne's career got off to a relatively late start (he was thirty-one) in **John Boorman's** *Excalibur* (1981), in which he played a quick-tempered and utterly self-destructive Uther Pendragon. The image he often portrays on screen is a curious one, as full of apparent lethargy as a lion before the sudden, flashing movement that means death – in other words he hasn't ever been used as effectively as he might have been in **Joel & Ethan Coen's** *Miller's Crossing* (1990), Mike Newell's *Into The West* (1993) and Bryan Singer's *The Usual Suspects* (1995), to suggest a new and possibly more fruitful direction for this rather oddball actor to take.
Other Key Films: *Defence Of The Realm* (1986); *Gothic* (1986); *A Soldier's Tale* (1988);

The End Of Violence (1997); *Smilla's Sense Of Snow* (1997); *This Is The Sea* (1998); *The Man In The Iron Mask* (1998); *Enemy Of The State* (1998); *Stigmata* (1999); *End Of Days* (1999); *Canone Inverso – Making Love* (2000); *Spider* (2002); *Vanity Fair* (2004); *Assault On Precinct 13* (2005); *Played* (2006)

Caan, James

Caan is a throwback to the great character actors of the 1930s and 1940s, and his screen career has been marked more by opportunities missed than by openings taken. He has never really been able to carry a movie on his own, being by nature more of a team player, although, paradoxically, many of his best performances have been of loners. He was the youth in the funny hat in **Howard Hawks's** *El Dorado* (1967) [an excellent remake of Hawks's own *Rio Bravo* (1959)], and then the vivacious, extreme-living Sonny in **Francis Ford Coppola's** *The Godfather* (1972). Weightier parts came and went, most notably with **Michael Mann's** *Thief* (1981), but it seemed that Caan had been sidelined forever. He spent five years away from the screen between 1982 and 1987, but returned, impressively, in Coppola's *Gardens Of Stone* (1987), triumphantly, in Rob Reiner's *Misery* (1990), and sinisterly, in Steve Kloves's excellent but ultimately flawed *Flesh And Bone* (1993). Now Caan hovers (contentedly, one supposes) just outside the normal lanes of the Hollywood mainstream, like an injured rogue shark waiting for the occasional pickings from rich passing ships.

Other Key Films: *The Rain People* (1969); *Rabbit, Run* (1970); *Freebie And The Bean* (1974); *The Gambler* (1974); *The Killer Elite* (1975); *Rollerball* (1975); *Comes A Horseman* (1978); *Alien Nation* (1988); *Dick Tracy* (1990); *Things To Do In Denver When You're Dead* (1995); *Mickey Blue Eyes* (1999); *The Way Of The Gun* (2000); *Viva Las Nowhere* (2000); *Jericho Mansions* (2003); *Dogville* (2003)

Cage, Nicolas

Cage is one of the most interesting of the current crop of Hollywood leading men, largely because he cut his teeth on independent and off-beat movies before graduating to the blockbusters he now appears in with such deadening regularity. A nephew of **Francis Ford Coppola** (a status which doubtless helped him in the early stages of his career but which has since been transcended by his talent) Cage's best roles came before his multi-million dollar leap to superstardom, and include **Alan Parker's** *Birdy* (1984) as bewildered Vietnam vet Al Columbato, **Joel** and **Ethan Coen's** *Raising Arizona* (1987) in which he played soft-hearted ex-hoodlum H I McDonough, **David Lynch's** *Wild At Heart* (1990) in which his Sailor Ripley ran the gamut of emotions from dementia back to dementia again, and, best of all, **Mike Figgis's** *Leaving Las Vegas* (1995), in which Cage was miraculously good as the demon-possessed Ben Sanderson who drinks himself to death, eyes open, in one final, nihilistic binge.

Other Key Films: *Rumble Fish* (1983); *Peggy Sue Got Married* (1986); *Moonstruck* (1987); *Honeymoon In Vegas* (1992); *Red Rock West* (1993); *The Rock* (1996); *Con Air* (1997); *Face/Off* (1997); *Snake Eyes* (1998); *Gone In Sixty Seconds* (2000); *Family Man* (2000); *Captain Corelli's Mandolin* (2001); *Adaptation* (2002); *Matchstick Men* (2003); *Lord Of War* (2005); *The Wicker Man* (2006)

Cagney, James

Cagney was the best at what he did, and what he did was unique and virtually unintelligible to those who had never seen him on screen. He was mannered, small, ugly and obstreperous, and he was also elegant, witty, quick-witted and often

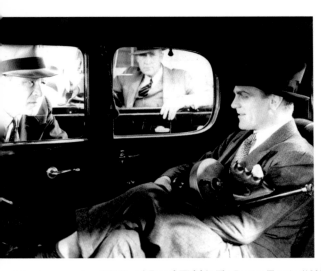

beautiful in movement and design. How to explain him? Only through his films, which failed, thank God, to harness the energy of this half-Norwegian half-Irish walking, darting – even singing and dancing, in **Michael Curtiz's** *Yankee Doodle Dandy* (1942) – idiosyncrasy. Only Hollywood could have produced him, and only Warners really knew how to use him, in such timeless movies as **William Wellman's** *The Public Enemy* (1931), Curtiz's *Angels With Dirty Faces* (1938), William Keighley's *Each Dawn I Die*

Robert Armstrong and James Cagney in G-Men, directed by William Keighley (1935).

Warner Bros/The Kobal Collection

(1939) and **Raoul Walsh's** *The Roaring Twenties* (1939). Perhaps his greatest mature role came in Walsh's *White Heat* (1949), but he was as brilliant in comedy as he was in drama, and **Billy Wilder's** *One Two Three* (1961) provided a suitable valedictory to his magnificent career. <u>Note For Film Buffs</u>: Catch Cagney, if you can, in his later and scurrilously underrated **Westerns**, such as **Nicholas Ray's** *Run For Cover* (1955) and **Robert Wise's** *Tribute To A Bad Man* (1956) and see for yourselves how Cagney brought humanity to a since often dehumanised genre.

Other Key Films: *Blonde Crazy* (1931); *Winner Take All* (1932); *Hard To Handle* (1933); *Footlight Parade* (1933); *Jimmy The Gent* (1934); *A Midsummer Night's Dream* (1935); *Ceiling Zero* (1936); *Blood In The Sun* (1946); *Love Me Or Leave Me* (1955); *Mister Roberts* (1955); *Man Of A Thousand Faces* (1958); *Shake Hands With The Devil* (1959); *Ragtime* (1981)

Cain, James M

Pulp fiction writer and guru of *film noir*, Cain was also an amateur of music, and music and musical forms abound in his crime novels, his screenplays, and in the myriad authorized and unauthorized adaptations made from his stories. The best of the unauthorized borrowings was **Luchino Visconti's** *Ossessione* (1942), which was based, more than merely closely, on Cain's novel *The Postman Always Rings Twice*, but which brought with it a particularly Italianate sense of doomed and earthy passion. Cain also co-scripted John Cromwell's headily romantic *Algiers* (1938), and the sum of his novels that have been made into first-rate feature films is quite simply awe-inspiring – and this despite Cain's oft-repeated reservations about cinema's artistic potential.

Other Key Films: John M Stahl's *When Tomorrow Comes* (1939); **Billy Wilder's** *Double Indemnity* (1944); **Michael Curtiz's** *Mildred Pierce* (1945); Tay Garnett's *The Postman Always Rings Twice* (1946); **Anthony Mann's** *Serenade* (1956)

Key Line: 'Most pictures aren't worth seeing. Let's face it, the moving picture never did lick reality. Pictures don't go deep. If a girl has a pretty face, that's as far as the camera can look.' [Cain on the movies]

Caine, Michael

The recently knighted Caine is a cosy establishment figure now, which is hardly surprising since he started out as a conservatively inclined (though vaguely anarchic) working-class boy made good. He always seemed to know he would make it, and that serene confidence has been his best friend during his successful mainstream career. He was utterly convincing both as Lewis Gilbert's *Alfie* (1966) and as Harry Palmer in Sidney J Furie's *The Ipcress File* (1965), and despite Oscar-winning performances in **Woody Allen's** *Hannah And Her Sisters* (1986) and Lasse Hallström's *The Cider House Rules* (1999), some of Caine's best performances have come in lesser films, such as James Clavell's *The Last Valley* (1971), or films where he has played second lead, as in **Bob Rafelson's** under-appreciated *Blood And Wine* (1996). Caine was always good at comedy but better at coldness, and his most memorable roles have reflected this aspect of his persona, as in the eponymous Jack Carter in Mike Hodges's *Get Carter* (1971), or as Kurt Steiner, the disillusioned German Wehrmacht war hero in **John Sturges's** *The Eagle Has Landed* (1977).

Other Key Films: *Zulu* (1964); *The Italian Job* (1969); *Too Late The Hero* (1970); *Sleuth* (1972); *The Man Who Would Be King* (1975); *California Suite* (1978); *Dressed To Kill* (1980); *Educating Rita* (1983); *The Holcroft Covenant* (1985); *Mona Lisa* (1986); *The Fourth Protocol* (1987); *Noises Off* (1992); *Little Voice* (1998); *Quills* (2000); *Miss Congeniality* (2000); *Last Orders* (2000); *The Quiet American* (2002); *The Statement* (2003); *The Weather Man* (2005); *Children Of Men* (2006)

Key Line: 'Not a lot of people know that.' [Catchphrase attributed to Caine, but vehemently denied by the man himself]

Cameron, James

One of Tinseltown's most successful commercial directors following a lucrative string of hits which include *The Terminator* (1984), *Aliens* (1986), *The Abyss* (1989), *Terminator 2: Judgement Day* (1991) and *Titanic* (1997), Cameron is a fastidious filmmaker who prepares his movies with an intricacy that may go a long way towards explaining their remarkable box office record. His blockbusters often contain something more than mere surface characterization, and this comes as a most welcome innovation in that most inhuman of vehicles, the mega-budgeted, studio-dominated Hollywood hit. A little creative imagination might not go amiss on his film titles, though.

Other Key Films: *Piranha II: The Spawning* (1981); *Rambo: First Blood Part II* [co-script] (1985); *True Lies* (1994)

Campion, Jane

New Zealander Campion began her career making shorts, and her success at Cannes with the ultra-short *Peel* (1982) edged her steadily towards her debut feature, *Sweetie* (1989), which first brought her predilection for plots involving awkward or marginal young women who have been badly let down by their families to the public's notice. She continued this theme with *An Angel At My Table* (1990), the story of author Janet Frame's struggle for acceptance, and she finally found mainstream acceptance with *The Piano* (1993), an intensely irritating and mannered film that some people, it is only fair to say, loved. Her *Portrait Of A Lady* (1996) was little better, and Campion seems to have fallen uncomfortably between two stools in recent years, not being able to decide whether she should concentrate on art-house cinema or on the commercial.

Other Key Films: *Holy Smoke* (1998); *In The Cut* (2001)

Cantinflas

Mexico's most famous comedian and something of a household name in the US after his appearance as Passepartout in Michael Anderson's *Around The World In Eighty Days* (1956). Cantinflas never managed to parlay his brief international success into the longer term, but that can hardly have bothered him since his reputation throughout the Spanish-speaking world began high, with Alejandro Galindo's *Ni Sangre Ni Arena* (1941), and was sustained throughout the rest of his life, ensuring that he remained in demand even after his premature retirement.

Other Key Films: *El Gandarme Desconcido* (1941); *El Circo* (1942); *Los Tres Mosqueteros* (1943); *El Mago* (1949); *Pepe* (1960); *El Extra* (1962); *El Padrecito* (1964); *El Patrullero 777* (1978)

Cantor, Eddie

Cantor was a genuinely funny man, and his demented brand of humour relied on the premise of a cowardly man levering himself out of sticky places through his gift of the gab – Cantor's patter certainly succeeded in levering him back into the fortune he had made on Broadway and lost to the Wall Street Crash of 1929. His films are sometimes hard to watch nowadays, with the gradual changes that have occurred in our perception of humour and its timing, but Leo McCarey's *The Kid From Spain* (1932) remains tremendous and sexy fun (with its bevy of **Busby Berkeley** college girls) and Frank Tuttle's *Roman Scandals* (1933) has a lot to recommend it too – Cantor had a surprisingly mellifluous singing voice which he could use to great effect, and his plots have a marked penchant for involving scantily-clad dancing girls in their various shenanigans (which can't be a bad thing!)

Other Key Films: *Kid Boots* (1926); *Whoopee!* (1930); *Palmy Days* (1931); *Kid Millions* (1934); *Strike Me Pink* (1936); *Ali Baba Goes To Town* (1937); *Thank Your Lucky Stars* (1943); *If You Knew Susie* (1948)

Canutt, Yakima

Most renowned of all Hollywood stuntmen, Canutt doubled for, amongst others, **John Wayne**, **Clark Gable** and **Roy Rodgers**, and was largely responsible for the sensational chariot race in **William Wyler's** *Ben-Hur* (1959), in which **Charlton Heston** gave Stephen Boyd his grisly comeuppance. When Heston queried some new trick Canutt was hatching, Canutt responded with 'Chuck, just make sure you stay in the chariot. I guarantee you're going to win the goddamned race.' Canutt also designed and executed the famous 'man under the galloping horses' stunt in **John Ford's** *Stagecoach* (1939), in which, doubling as an ignoble savage, Canutt jumps from his pinto onto the back of a team of four recklessly galloping horses, clambers to the cross bar, is shot by Big John Wayne (a.k.a. The Ringo Kid), falls between the galloping horses, hangs on to the cross bar for a moment while the stage drags him along the ground, then lets go, disappearing beneath the hooves of the horses and the wheels of the stage, eventually emerging, more or less intact, on the desert floor, where he proceeds, against all the odds, to play dead.

Capra, Frank

Capra certainly started his career from the bottom, as a film splicer and general handyman around various minor studios, ending up as a gagman for **Hal Roach**. This meant that when **Harry Cohn** offered him the hitherto unheard-of opportunity to direct a series of films to counter the prevailing miseries of the depression, Capra was the man for the job. Ever ambitious, Capra rode the depression-era camera tracks to awesome effect, and his masterpiece of the period must be *It Happened One Night* (1934), although *Platinum Blonde* (1931) and *The Bitter Tea Of General Yen* (1932), his magnificent story of a doomed cross-cultural passion in war-torn China between **Barbara Stanwyck's** soon-to-be missionary's wife and **Nils Asther's** blissfully decadent warlord, have considerably more heart to them, and strike one as less cold-bloodedly commercial than Columbia Studio's usual output. A number of Capra's later films, including *Mr Deeds Goes To Town* (1936) and *It's A Wonderful Life* (1946), have entered American folklore, and it would be invidious to criticize them with the public's response to their message verging on the irrational, but his earlier *Lost Horizon* (1937) is a genuinely uplifting film, benefiting from a script by Capra's long-term collaborator **Robert Riskin**, brilliantly gleaned from James Hilton's worldwide bestseller about the utopian never-never-land of Shangri-La. Once cinema's greatest master of populism, Capra was shamefully neglected by the Hollywood hierarchy after 1950. See **Erotic Moments**

Other Key Films: *The Strong Man* (1926); *American Madness* (1932); *Mr Smith Goes To Washington* (1939); *Meet John Doe* (1941); *Arsenic And Old Lace* (1944); *Pocketful Of Miracles* (1961)

Cardiff, Jack

Cardiff (a lifetime achievement award winner at the 2001 Oscar ceremony, and the first ever technician to receive such an honour) understood the camera as few men before or since have understood it, and his black-and-white films, such as **René Clair's** *The Ghost Goes West* (1935) and Jacques Feyder's wondrously romantic *Knight Without Armour* (1937), together with his later rich Technicolor work on **Michael Powell's** *A Matter Of Life And Death* (1946) and *Black Narcissus* (1947), and on **Albert Lewin's** magical *Pandora And The Flying Dutchman* (1951), attest to something more consistent than a mere cameraman's (his own definition of himself) input – call it a cinematographer's eye, if you will. His later films, including those he directed himself [excepting *Sons And Lovers* (1960) and *Young Cassidy* (1965), which he co-directed with **John Ford**] were pedestrian in the extreme, and one remains astonished at how Cardiff could show so much critical acuity for so long behind the camera, only to blow it so consummately at the end of his career when he found himself in front of the lens.

Other Key Films: **Zoltan Korda's** *The Four Feathers* (1939); Gabriel Pascal's *Caesar And Cleopatra* (1945); Michael Powell's *The Red Shoes* (1948); **Alfred Hitchcock's** *Under Capricorn* (1949); **John Huston's** *The African Queen* (1951); **Joseph L Mankiewicz's** *The Barefoot Contessa* (1954); **King Vidor's** *War And Peace* (1956); Lewis Teague's *Cat's Eye* (1985); Jamie Payne's *The Dance Of Shiva* (1998) [short]
Key Line: 'Watch me very carefully when I have my periods.' [**Ava Gardner** to Jack Cardiff, while filming *The Barefoot Contessa*]

Cardinale, Claudia

She wasn't really an actress but more of an image, which is why **Sergio Leone** used her alongside **Charles Bronson** in *Once Upon A Time In The West* (1968), and why **Federico Fellini** used her alongside **Marcello Mastroianni** in *8 1/2* (1963), and why **Luchino Visconti** used her opposite **Alain Delon** in *The Leopard* (1963) – think of the actors, and the parts she played, and the reasons for her choice become clear. Her very voluptuousness was almost deadening, and one sometimes came away from her films feeling strangely tarnished, as if one's voyeurism were being cast back at one for being too obvious and for making the nominal object of it too acute and empty an end. When she spoke, Cardinale sounded like a Neapolitan whore, and it was this paradox which saved her from the mediocrity that so much beauty would normally confer – one didn't watch a Cardinale performance so much as marvel at the vessel containing it, and Leone's undermining of her carefully nurtured image in *Once Upon A Time In The West* can now be seen, in retrospect, as a masterstroke of Italian fabulism.

Other Key Films: *La Prima Notte* (1959); *Rocco And His Brothers* (1960); *Cartouche* (1961); *La Viaccia* (1961); *The Pink Panther* (1963); *Gli Indifferenti* (1964); *The Adventures Of Gerard* (1970); *The Red Tent* (1971); *La Pelle* (1981); *Fitzcarraldo* (1982); *La Storia* (1985); *Briganti* (1999); *Estrenando* **Sueños** (2005); *Tous Frais Payés* (2006)

Carné, Marcel

Carné's later career doesn't matter – all that matters is that in an astonishingly rich period of eight years he distilled the dreams, the ironical spirit of resignation, and the doomed romanticism of France, an ancient nation sold on the existential virtues of living and loving for the moment, rather than of storing up goods for a notional and anti-instinctual future. Carné presented the French to themselves as they wanted to be seen, and the French to us as we wanted to see them, and this was his true gift. With *Quai Des Brumes* (1938), *Hotel Du Nord* (1938), *Le Jour Se Lève* (1939), *Les Visiteurs Du Soir* (1942) and *Les Enfants Du Paradis* (1945), he guaranteed a sort of immortality to a state of mind the direct opposite of the commercial Armageddon we live in today. Carné's characters live briefly, love wildly, and die with their disillusions intact.

Other Key Films: *Jenny* (1937); *Les Portes De La Nuit* (1946); *Juliette Ou La Clé Des Songes* (1951); *Thérèse Raquin* (1953); *L'Air De Paris* (1954); *Terrain Vague* (1960)

Carpenter, John

Carpenter has always drawn much of the inspiration for his films from the B-Movies

of the 1950s, beginning with *Dark Star* (1974), his cult sci-fi classic, continuing with the edgy *Assault On Precinct 13* (1976) – a backhanded tribute to **Howard Hawks's** *Rio Bravo* (1959) – and culminating in *Halloween* (1978), which catapulted him into big-time horror and **slasher movie** territory. His *Escape From New York* (1981) was a male adolescent's dream movie (hero Kurt Russell, as Snake Plissken, even sported an eye-patch, as I recall) and Carpenter has continued referentially entertaining us ever since, with such films as *The Thing* (1982), *Christine* (1983) and *Starman* (1984). His tongue may have, on occasion, been fixed firmly in his cheek, but his films have always been honestly imbued with a real love of cinema, and of the thrills and spills and Jills associated with the best of it.
Other Key Films: *The Fog* (1980); *Big Trouble In Little China* (1986); *Memoirs Of An Invisible Man* (1992); *Village Of The Damned* (1995); *Escape From LA*(1996); *Vampires* (1998); *Ghosts Of Mars* (2001)

A poster for Marcel Carne's 1938 film Le Quai de Brumes (Port of Shadows) in which Jean Gabin, Michel Simon and Michele Morgan acted.

Cinè-Alliance/Pathè/The Kobal Collection

Carrey, Jim

One of the most bankable of all recent box office stars, Canadian born Carrey can be genuinely funny, a talent which is rarer than gold dust in Hollywoodland. Tom Shadyac's *Ace Ventura: Pet Detective* (1994) began Carrey's rise to superstardom, followed by Charles Russell's *The Mask* (1994) and the sensationally sick Farrelly Brothers slapstick masterpiece, *Dumb & Dumber* (1994), which took bad taste to a magnificently sustained new low. After a scene-stealing performance as the Riddler in Joel Schumacher's *Batman Forever* (1995) Carrey briefly suffered from a hefty dose of the worthies, but he has now re-emerged, humour triumphantly intact, in challenging films such as **Peter Weir's** *The Truman Show* (1998) and Michel Gondry's *Eternal Sunshine Of The Spotless Mind* (2004).
Other Key Films: *Ace Ventura:When Nature Calls* (1995); *The Cable Guy* (1996); *Liar Liar* (1997); *Man On The Moon* (1999); *How The Grinch Stole Christmas* (2000); *Me, Myself And Irene* (2000); *Fun With Dick And Jane* (2005)

Irony Warning!! Irony Warning!! Tests have proved that without the aforementioned irony warning, even highly literate readers will take the following tongue-in-cheek and affectionate paean to the *Carry On* version of essential English humour literally. So please read on, bearing in mind that I don't mean what I seem to be saying. Capisco?

Carry On Films

Appalling series of unfunny, would-be comic British films (1958-1992) that even otherwise sane people pretend to like. Gathering together a precociously awful armada of British comic has-beens, audiences have cheered such profoundly unedifying spectacles as Kenneth Williams's travestying of Julius Caesar at the point of his death, crying, 'Infamy! Infamy! They've all got it in for me!' Now is that funny, I ask you? Seriously, though…
Key Films: Gerald Thomas's *Carry On Teacher* (1959), *Carry On Nurse* (1959), *Carry On Constable* (1960), *Carry On Cleo* (1964), *Carry On Cowboy* (1965), *Carry On Up The Khyber* (1968), *Carry On Camping* (1969), *Carry On Henry* (1971), *Carry On Matron*

(1972), *Carry On Behind* (1975); *Carry On Emmanuelle* (1978); *Carry On Columbus* (1992)

Casablanca

Considered by some to be the single most romantic film of all time, **Michael Curtiz's** *Casablanca* (1942) brought together the talents of **Humphrey Bogart, Ingrid Bergman,** Paul Henreid, **Sidney Greenstreet, Claude Rains, Peter Lorre** and **Conrad Veidt,** not to mention a veritable menagerie of screenwriters, three of whom (**Julius J Epstein,** Philip G. Epstein, and Howard Koch) eventually got their name on the credits (and an Oscar apiece). Dooley Wilson sang 'As Time Goes By', but didn't, incidentally, play the piano. Curtiz and his screenwriters stole from just about every genre there was to steal from, creating a heady concoction that had little, if nothing, to do with the Second World War, and a very great deal to do with an inspired escapism from it. Bogart based his character, Richard 'Rick' Blaine, on a mixture of **Jean Gabin,** in **Marcel Carné's** *Quai Des Brumes* (1938), and **Gary Cooper,** in **Josef von Sternberg's** *Morocco* (1930), with the ineffable homespun

Claude Rains, Paul Henreid and Ingrid Bergman in Casablanca, directed by Michael Curtiz (1942).

Warner Bros/The Kobal Collection

Bogart cynicism to leaven the dose. Bergman took the idea for her famous mackintosh from Michèle Morgan in *Quai Des Brumes* too, but the look and the sound of Ilsa Lund were triumphantly her own. The film, unlike many of the other commercial vehicles of the time, improves with every viewing.

Key Lines:

1. 'Play it, Sam, play 'As Time Goes By'.' [Bergman to Wilson]
2. 'Major Strasser has been shot. Round up the usual suspects.' [Rains]
3. 'Of all the gin joints in all the towns in all the world, she walks into mine.' [Bogart]
4. 'Here's looking at you, kid.' [Bogart to Bergman]
5. 'If she can stand it, I can. Play it!' [Bogart to Wilson]
6. 'How extravagant you are, throwing away women like that. Someday they

may be scarce.' [Rains to Bogart]

7. 'I remember every detail. The Germans wore grey. You wore blue.' [Bogart to Bergman]

Cassavetes, John

A notably independent filmmaker and a sometime nervy and not very talented mainstream actor, Cassavetes seduced the liberal intelligentsia in the late 1960s and early 1970s with a sequence of films that seem almost aggressively anti-cinematic, as if their director did not actually like the job he was in. Best of the lot was *Husbands* (1970) which suggested (but only suggested, mind) what Cassavetes could have achieved if he had even a little tightened up his act. Instead, his films too often resembled the vapid meanderings of the town drunk on yet another of his endless sprees.

Other Key Films: *Shadows* (1961); *Faces* (1968); *Minnie And Moskowitz* (1971); *Woman Under The Influence* (1974); *The Killing Of A Chinese Bookie* (1976); *Gloria* (1980); *Love Streams* (1984)

Chabrol, Claude

A sensationally variable director who, at his best, as in *Que La Bête Meure* (*This Man Must Die*) (1969) and *Le Boucher* (1970), could turn out some of the finest and most perspicacious (in terms of human motivation) thrillers ever, and at his worst, as in *Madame Bovary* (1991), could astonish even die-hard fans with the sterility and matter-of-factness of his direction. From his very first film, *Le Beau Serge* (1958), it was obvious that in Chabrol French cinema had something special – a director who could both fascinate and entertain – and in his second film, *Les Cousins* (1959), he extended this range, suggesting rather than explaining, much as a good novelist might do in similar circumstances. Eschewing tricks, Chabrol filmed straight down the line, something which failed to endear him to the **New Wave**, and his mid-period *Les Biches* (1968), which concerns the uneasy affair between two lesbians and the architect who loves them both, is his finest film in this mode; for Chabrol, when he cares to be, is both the reluctant champion and the ultimate castigator of the French petit bourgeoisie, while **Eric Rohmer**, his elder in years, but near-contemporary in terms of film, remains his fondest observer.

Other Key Films: *A Double Tour* (1959); *The Tiger Likes Fresh Blood* (1964); *Le Scandale* (1967); *La Femme Infidèle* (1969); *La Rupture* (1970); *Juste Avant La Nuit* (1971); *Les Innocents Aux Mains Sales* (1976); *Les Magiciens* (1975); *Violette Nozière* (1978); *L'Enfer* (1994); *The Ceremony* (1996); *Au Coeur Du Mensonge* (1999); *Merci Pour Le Chocolat* (2000); *La Fleur Du Mal* (2003); *La Demoiselle D'Honneur* (2004); *L'Ivresse Du Pouvoir* (2006)

Chandler, Raymond

A magnificent though frustrated screenwriter (and a real lover of the film medium) as well as being the novelist/creator of the much-filmed private eye **Philip Marlowe**, Chandler scripted, amongst others, **Billy Wilder's** *Double Indemnity* (1942), George Marshall's *The Blue Dahlia* (1946) and **Alfred Hitchcock's** *Strangers on a Train* (1951). A master of simile and metaphor, and a literate, erudite man, Chandler later succumbed to drink and melancholia following the death of his beloved wife, Cissy.

Other Key Films: Irving Pichel's *And Now Tomorrow* (1944); Lewis Allen's *The Unseen* (1945)

Key Lines:

1. 'Everything written with vitality expresses that vitality; there are no dull

subjects, only dull minds.' [Chandler on the art of writing]

2. 'America seemed to call me in some mysterious way.' [Chandler on his passion for the 'mean streets' of California]

Chaney, Lon

The son of deaf-mute parents, Chaney became, of necessity, a consummate mime. The original 'Man Of A Thousand Faces', he died just as the advent of sound was about to change forever the way people viewed the silent cinematic image. In approaching 150 films Chaney nearly always portrayed the tormented, the deformed and the marginal, giving his characters a nobility that speech would almost certainly have diluted. His was the greatest-ever Quasimodo in Wallace Worsley's *The Hunchback Of Notre Dame* (1923), and no actor has ever understood the Phantom's reluctant donning of the cloak as well as Chaney did in Rupert Julian's *Phantom Of The Opera* (1925). Great actors such as **Charles Laughton** learned much of their craft from watching him, particularly in his capacity for stillness, and his ability to express both extreme languor and sudden, violent resolution.

Charlie Chaplin in The Circus, directed by himself (1928).

Chaplin/United Artists/ The Kobal Collection

Other Key Films: *Hell Morgan's Girl* (1917); *The Miracle Man* (1919); *Oliver Twist* (1922); *The Unholy Three* (1925); *The Blackbird* (1926); *The Unknown* (1927); *London After Midnight* (1927); *Where East Is East* (1929)

Chaplin, Charlie

Sit any child in front of a Chaplin film and a strange change will occur – where before it had sought speed and constant stimulation, the child is now seen to relax, and its expectations simplify. The child will at first chortle, perhaps self-consciously, and then, slowly, it will give itself up to the magic that Chaplin so uniquely possessed. For Chaplin was the great communicator, and he communicates now beyond the grave to all those with the inclination, and the capacity, to see and hear him. When Chaplin touches us we remain touched, and images from his films remain with us as the stuff and dressing of our unconscious. It's easy to pull him down as a man, for he had more than his fair share of faults, but there must surely be a place for genius beyond stricture, for illumination beyond the conjecture of fools, and Chaplin holds firm, despite, or perhaps because of, these very shortcomings.

Other Key Films: *The Tramp* (1915); *Shanghaied* (1915); *The Vagabond* (1916); *The Rink* (1916); *The Immigrant* (1917); *A Dog's Life* (1918); *Shoulder Arms* (1918); *The Kid* (1921); *A Woman Of Paris* (1923); *The Gold Rush* (1925); *The Circus* (1928); *City Lights* (1931); *Modern Times* (1936); *The Great Dictator* (1940); *Monsieur Verdoux* (1947); *Limelight* (1952)

Key Line: 'All I need to make a comedy is a park, a policeman and a pretty girl.' [Chaplin on comedy]

Chase Film

The most comprehensive of all genres, comprising **Westerns**, thrillers, **science-fiction** movies and demented love stories, the chase film involves both itself and the audience in an extended, often over-the-top chase, hopefully leaving everyone happy and exhausted by the final credits. Top of the bunch must be **Alfred Hitchcock's** *The Thirty-Nine Steps* (1935) in which **Robert Donat** finds himself chased, not only by the baddies, but also by the police and an irate, gorgeously be-stockinged Madeleine Carroll in handcuffs.

Chen Kaige

Forced to give up school to work on the land during Mao Tse-Tung's Cultural Revolution, Chen Kaige used this hard-won knowledge in his first film, *Yellow Earth* (1984), which was about the misunderstandings inherent between town and country, worker and peasant. With **Zhang Yimou** as his cinematographer, he went on to make *The Big Parade* (1985) which showed how individuals must learn to relate to the institutions they are forced to join in a communal society, and which fell just as inevitably foul of the communist authorities. *Farewell My Concubine* (1993) was Kaige's first major international success, sharing the Palme D'Or at Cannes, and in 1999 he completed the most expensive Asian film ever made, *The Emperor And The Assassin*, which is safely set in 221 BC, and deals with the reunification of the seven kingdoms by Emperor Ying Zheng, and the love and skulduggery that went hand in hand with it – in the film, Zheng's concubine, the exquisite **Gong Li**, falls in love with the assassin who is meant to fake an attempt on Zheng's life, which just goes to prove that the basic *film noir* plot was comfortably in existence over two thousand years ago.

Other Key Films: *King Of Children* (1987); *Life On A String* (1991); *Temptress Moon* (1997); *Killing Me Softly* (2002); *The Promise* (2005)

Chevalier, Maurice

In his French films Chevalier was tough, caustic, sexy and streetwise, and in his American films he was winsome, charming, coy and rather camp. Could it be the language? Perhaps French encourages candour and English encourages euphemism? Who knows. But the French films (apart from the US ones made by the European oriented **Ernst Lubitsch**) are generally better, and the French Chevalier, with his brilliant vocal skills – he could scat, sing songs and wordplay ballads just as well as **Jean Gabin** and Berthe Sylva, which is really saying something – more accurately reflected Chevalier's music-hall background. He ended his long career (despite a blip after the war when he was accused, then cleared, of collaboration) as the avuncular roué every woman would like to pretend she'd had a love affair with in her prime, shrugging and winking and charming his way through such delightful candyfloss as **Vincente Minnelli's** *Gigi* (1958) and Walter Lang's *Can-Can* (1960).

Other Key Films: *The Love Parade* (1929); *Playboy Of Paris* (1930); *The Merry Widow* (1934); *Folies Bergère* (1935); *Avec Le Sourire* (1937); *Le Silence Est D'Or* (1947); *A Royal Affair* (1950); *My Seven Little Sins* (1954); *Love In The Afternoon* (1958); *Can-Can* (1960)

Best **Children's Films**

Ludwig Berger, Tim Whelan and **Michael Powell's** *The Thief Of Bagdad* (1940); Josef von Baky's *Münchhausen* (1943); Desmond Davis's *Clash Of The Titans* (1980); **Walt Disney's** *Song Of The South* (1946) and *One Hundred And One Dalmatians* (1961); Richard Fleischer's *Twenty Thousand Leagues Under The Sea* (1954); **Victor Fleming's** *The Wizard Of Oz* (1939); **Terry Gilliam's** *Time Bandits* (1981); David Hand and **Walt Disney's** *Bambi* (1942); Nathan Juran's *The Seventh Voyage Of Sinbad* (1958);

Albert Lamorisse's *The White Stallion* [a.k.a. *White Mane*] (1953); **Fritz Lang's** *Moonfleet* (1955); Mike Newell's *Into The West* (1991); **Satyajit Ray's** *The Golden Fortress* (1974); Henry Safran's *Storm Boy* (1976); **John Sayles's** *The Secret Of Roan Inish* (1996); **Steven Spielberg's** *E. T. The Extra-Terrestrial* (1982)

Christie, Julie

Christie seemed unbelievably natural and carefree at a time when her contemporaries were busy tending their beehive hairdos and sanding their five lacquered layers of nail varnish. To see her strolling along a dull northern street, swinging her handbag and looking happy to be alive and young and with the future still ahead of her in **John Schlesinger's** *Billy Liar* (1963), was to suddenly understand, through one moving image, what the 1960s should have been about. She gradually lost that unselfconsciousness (which is hardly surprising given the attention, the pressure, and the quantity of adulation she subsequently received) but in her best films, which include Schlesinger's *Far From The Madding Crowd* (1967), **Nicholas Roeg's** *Don't Look Now* (1973) and **James Ivory's** *Heat And Dust* (1983), she reclaims it, delighting us with her spontaneity, and reminding us of who we might have been had not work, ambition, genes and mediocrity got in the way.

Other Key Films: *Darling* (1965); *Doctor Zhivago* (1965); *Fahrenheit 451* (1966); *The Go-Between* (1971); *McCabe And Mrs Miller* (1971); *Shampoo* (1975); *Demon Seed* (1977); *Memoirs Of A Survivor* (1981); *The Return Of The Soldier* (1983); *Dragonheart* (1996); *Hamlet* (1996); *Afterglow* (1997); *Belphégor* (2000); *Troy* (2004); *Finding Neverland* (2004); *La Vida Secreta De Las Palabras* (2005)

Cimino, Michael

Cimino was a potentially good director who blew it, thanks, no doubt, to the usual character defaults, but also to a far greater than normal vainglory. *Thunderbolt And Lightfoot* (1974) was a first-rate little thriller, which combined comedy, action and pathos to excellent effect, and *The Deer Hunter* (1978) was a flawed but fascinating example of high movie hokum. *Heaven's Gate* (1980), with its disastrously unrealistic production costs, became the symbol for all that was wrong with post-*Easy Rider* Hollywood, until it seemed that Cimino had hoist himself with his own petard. He has only really ever partially redeemed himself with the not bad (but not really very good either) *Year Of The Dragon* (1985).

Other Key Films: *The Sicilian* (1987); *Desperate Hours* (1990); *The Sunchaser* (1996)

Citizen Kane

It is hard to say anything about **Orson Welles's** *Citizen Kane* (1941) that hasn't been said and resaid many times already. Suffice it to say that Welles was given carte blanche, under a virtually unprecedented contract from RKO, to make whatever film he wanted to. Following on from an idea he had sketched out with his co-writer, Herman J Mankiewicz, Welles began filming the story of William Randolph Hearst, newspaper tycoon and media monster, complete with insalubrious details of Hearst's private life with his mistress, Marion Davies (the name Rosebud, which figures so prominently in the film, was rumoured to be Hearst's nickname for Miss Davies's clitoris). Understandably incensed, Hearst did everything he could to get the film banned, and his vituperation continued long after his death, and possibly had something to do with Welles's later cold-shouldering by key elements of the Hollywood hierarchy. What really mattered though, was the film, and it is for its extraordinary originality that Kane is justly renowned, and for which it regularly gets voted the best film of all time. Using virtually every technique the cinema had hitherto thrown up, Welles (already wise enough, aged twenty-five, to employ only the best of collaborators) also added some of his own, gleaned from his experiences in the theatre and in radio – **Gregg Toland's** deep focus photography, Mankiewicz's literate writing skills, **Bernard Hermann's** music and Van Nest Polglase's and Perry Ferguson's art direction all contributed to this masterpiece, but it is indisputable that Welles was the captain of his ship, and as such, while being the first to take credit, he should also be allowed the dubious, but only just privilege, of being last man off.

Key Line: 'As it must to all men, death came to Charles Foster Kane.' [Newsreel announcement of Kane's death]

Clair, René

Clair was a consummate filmmaker who started out by undermining, moved on to delighting, and ended up by challenging his audiences. Some of his silent films showed marked avant-garde tendencies, but Clair fortunately overcame this handicap to produce some of the most innocently happy films of the 1930s, including *Sous Les Toits De Paris* (1930), *Le Million* (1931) and *The Ghost Goes West* (1935), with **Robert Donat** as both the ill-starred scion of a beleaguered Scottish dynasty, and his ghost, who find themselves vicariously removed to Florida by a rich American. *I Married A Witch* (1942) is another gem, and contains **Veronica Lake's** best comedic work (and she *was* a good comedienne) and concerns a notorious family of New England witches who are burnt at the stake but return to haunt (in a delightfully irritating way) the unwitting ancestor of their nemesis, **Frederic March**. *It Happened Tomorrow* (1944) was another US winner, and Clair returned to France after the war, his reputation enhanced, to direct a number of challenging and emotionally mature dramas, including *Les Belles De Nuit* (1952) and *Les Grandes Manoeuvres* (1955), films which harked back to that earlier period in France, before the war, in which he had made his reputation.

Other Key Films: *Paris Qui Dort* (1923); *The Italian Straw Hat* (1927); *Le Dernier Milliardaire* (1934); *The Flame Of New Orleans* (1941); *And Then There Were None* (1945); *La Beauté Du Diable* (1950); *Porte Des Lilas* (1958); *Les Fêtes Galantes* (1965)

Key Line: 'René Clair was amazing. He had the only black pinstripe suit that I had ever seen that had crimson stripes. He was elegant, elegant. He looked like a ballroom dancer, like a Valentino. Very petite, intense, wonderful.' [Screenwriter Stewart Stern on being directed in a play, *The French Touch*, by Clair]

Clément, René

Clément cemented his early reputation with *La Bataille Du Rail* (1946), a heart-rending reconstruction of the often-fatal Resistance activities of French Railway workers during the Second World War; but his greatest war film came later, with *Jeux Interdits* (1952), in which Clément and his scriptwriters, **Jean Aurenche** and **Pierre Bost**, discovered that by filming the war from the point of view of two natural and instinctive children who have no alternative but to create their own realities in the face of its absurdity, he could bring home its message and effect to a wider, still war-weary audience. Clément never quite matched that stroke of genius again, but his antiheroic *Knave Of Hearts* (1954) became something of a cult on both sides of the channel, and *Plein Soleil* (1959), with **Alain Delon** at his coldest and most manipulative, provided **Anthony Minghella** with at least some of the cinematic wherewithal to attempt his *Talented Mr Ripley* (1999), based on the same Patricia Highsmith story.

Other Key Films: *Les Maudits* (1947); *The Walls Of Malapaga* (1949); *Gervaise*

(1956); *Le Jour Et L'Heure* (1963); *Les Félins* (1964); *Is Paris Burning?* (1966); *The Deadly Trap* (1971)

Clift, Montgomery

Elizabeth Taylor noticed Clift's extraordinary intensity during the shooting of **George Stevens's** *A Place In The Sun* (1951), where she was disturbed to find that this method actor would often come off the set literally shaking with unresolved emotion. The highpoint of Clift's career came two years later, however, with his Robert E Lee Prewitt in **Fred Zinnemann's** *From Here To Eternity* (1953), although he had previously given another convincing performance as Matthew Garth, in **Howard Hawks's** *Red River* (1948). Appallingly disfigured in a car accident during the making of **Edward Dmytryk's** *Raintree County* (1958), Clift's face was surgically reconstructed to afford at least a semblance of his former beauty, and he used this new (and real) vulnerability to good effect in **John Huston's** *The Misfits* (1961) and *Freud* (1962). Hounded throughout his career because of his homosexuality, and tragically prone to remorse and self-loathing on the same account, Clift died, four years later, aged just forty-five, of a heart attack.

Other Key Films: *The Search* (1948); *The Heiress* (1949); *The Big Lift* (1950); *I Confess* (1953); *The Young Lions* (1958); *Suddenly Last Summer* (1959); *Wild River* (1960); *Judgement At Nuremberg* (1961); *The Defector* (1966)

Clooney, George

Clooney made his name as Dr Doug Ross in the television series *ER*, and that might have been the end of it, had not this nephew of singer Rosemary Clooney – together with one or two Hollywood studios desperate for a new romantic male action star to replace their ageing crop – decided it was time for him to take his chance on the big screen. The strange thing is that Clooney apparently blew it, with Joel Schumacher's *Batman And Robin* (1997) and Mimi Leder's *The Peacemaker* (1997), but it was so obvious to everyone that he had what it takes, that the studios persisted, the star barely resisted (*pace* Tom Lehrer), and the rest will probably be history. His recent standout performances in the **Coen Brothers'** *O Brother, Where Art Thou?* (2000), in Stephen Gaghan's *Syriana* (2005), and in his own excellent *Good Night, And Good Luck* (2005), proves that he is the nearest thing to a reincarnated **Clark Gable** that Hollywood possesses.

Other Key Films: *Return Of The Killer Tomatoes!* (1988); *Unbecoming Age* (1992); *From Dusk Till Dawn* (1996); *One Fine Day* (1996); *Out Of Sight* (1998); *The Thin Red Line* (1998); *Three Kings* (1999); *The Perfect Storm* (2000); *O Brother, Where Art Thou?* (2000); *Ocean's Eleven* (2001); *Spy Kids* (2001); *Solaris* (2002); *Confessions Of A Dangerous Mind* (2002); *Intolerable Cruelty* (2003); *Ocean's Twelve* (2004); *The Good German* (2006)

Key Line: 'I don't believe in happy endings… it's a mean thing, life.' [Clooney on life]

Close, Glenn

Close is not predominantly a movie actress but a theatrical one, and it is conceivable that when the sum of her career is finally taken, film will only have a walk-on part. She was excellent, however, in a thankless role, that of Alex Forrest in Adrian Lyne's *Fatal Attraction* (1987), but her Marquise De Merteuil in **Stephen Frears's** *Dangerous Liaisons* (1988), despite all the hype, was markedly inferior to **Annette Bening's** Marquise in **Milos Forman's** *Valmont* (1989). Her best screen role came as the ill-fated Sunny von Bulow in **Barbet Schroeder's** *Reversal Of Fortune* (1990).

Clouzot, Henri-Georges

Clouzot was France's master of suspense and sadism, seeking his subjects behind twitching curtains or in crowded rooms. His second film was *Le Corbeau* (1943), a magnificently dark thriller about a poison-pen letterist who turns an otherwise happy town against itself. Seen by many as a brave criticism of French collaboration with the Nazis, it paradoxically got Clouzot into trouble after the war for showing the French as too black and for laying itself open to use in German propaganda! The very sexy *Quai Des Orfèvres* (1947) reinstated him [see **Erotic Moments**], and was followed, six years later, by the finest of all nail-biters, *The Wages Of Fear [Le Salaire De La Peur]* (1953). Clouzot then went on to match *Le Corbeau* with its bourgeois counterpart, *Les Diaboliques* (1955), a truly devious whodunit that leaves one guessing until the very last moment. His *Le Mystère Picasso* (1956) was a brilliant and innovative documentary which had the happy idea of asking Picasso to paint on glass panels through which Clouzot's camera could film him – the feature-length result came perilously close to revealing the very magic that Picasso himself believed in so intensely.

Other Key Films: *L'Assassin Habite Au 21* (1942); *Manon* (1949); *Les Espions* (1958); *La Vérité* (1960); *L'Enfer* (1964); *La Prisonnière* (1968)

Coburn, James

Thin, rangy, laconic – a man of odd movements and languid mien – Coburn was a loner hero in all his best films, and although he was surprisingly good at comedy, one remembers him most fondly for his knife-throwing Britt in **John Sturges's** *The Magnificent Seven* (1960), for his bomb-loving ex-IRA gunslinger, Sean Mallory, in **Sergio Leone's** underrated *A Fistful Of Dynamite* [a.k.a. *Duck, you Sucker/ Once Upon A Time There Was A Revolution*] (1971), and for his disillusioned Sergeant Steiner in **Sam Peckinpah's** sensational *Cross Of Iron* (1977).

Other Key Films: *Ride Lonesome* (1959); *Hell Is For Heroes* (1962); *The Great Escape* (1963); *Major Dundee* (1965); *A High Wind In Jamaica* (1965); *Our Man Flint* (1966); *Pat Garrett And Billy The Kid* (1973); *Death Of A Soldier* (1986); *Maverick* (1994); *Eraser* (1996); *Keys To Tulsa* (1997); *Intrepid* (2000); *Proximity* (2001); *Snow Dogs* (2002); *American Gun* (2002)

Cocteau, Jean

Cocteau was a phenomenon more than a man, and his talents read like the sort of list Narcissus would have drawn up for himself had he ever bothered to put stylus to wax tablet. Cocteau thought of himself predominantly as a poet, however, and this view permeated his films and allowed him the freedom to invent. *La Belle Et La Bête* (1946) is the most successful of these dream fantasies, closely followed by *Orphée* (1950), a film which cannot fail to move viewers when seen for the first time and at a young enough age, and provide them with some understanding of the imaginative possibilities of the cinema. Many further films were made from Cocteau's scripts and stories, and possibly the most successful of these is **Jean-Pierre Melville's** *Les Enfants Terribles* (1950), in which we are drawn in, almost against our will, to the claustrophobic yet strangely liberating world of the semi-insane.

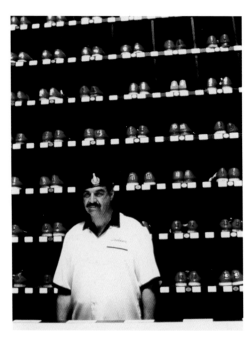

Jerry Haleva in The Big Lebowski, directed by Joel Coen (1998).

Polygram/Working Title/The Kobal Collection

Other Key Films: *Le Sang D'Un Poète* (1930); *L'Aigle À Deux Têtes* (1948); *Les Parents Terribles* (1948); *Le Testament D'Orphée* (1960)

Coen Brothers, The

Love them or hate them (and they are desperately popular with the more pretentious critics) Joel and Ethan Coen very definitely have talent, and for every turkey like *Barton Fink* (1991) [and what a hell of a turkey that was: see **Worst Films**] they come up with three or four successes, including their debut *Blood Simple* (1984), the hilarious *Raising Arizona* (1987), the gloriously pulpy *Miller's Crossing* (1990), and their near-masterpiece *Fargo* (1996), a movie which improves with every viewing. Quirky, individualistic, and just a touch self-conscious, the Coens epitomise the brasher form of artist, not content to step back and let things be, but always aiming for effects that may not come off but certainly seem worth striving for at the time. Their recent *The Big Lebowski* (1998) featured an on-form **Jeff Bridges** playing the sort of man he might have become had he not taken up acting, aged eight, in his father's 'Sea Hunt' TV series, and *O Brother, Where Art Thou?* (2000) is a paean to blues, road movies, jail films, and the magnetic talent of **George Clooney**.

Other Key Films: *The Hudsucker Proxy* (1994); *The Man Who Wasn't There* (2001); *Intolerable Cruelty* (2003); *The Ladykillers* (2004)

Coffee, Lenore

Yet another unsung screenwriter (except to the cognoscenti), Coffee's forty-year career, from silent to sound, included innumerable adaptations, scenarios, and script and dialogue credits, the best of which include Clarence Brown's *Possessed* (1931), **Cecil B De Mille's** *The Squaw Man* (1931) and David Miller's *Sudden Fear* (1952). Like so many of her profession, Coffee ended up penniless and forgotten in a film industry funded rest-home, while television audiences were still thrilling on TV to **Bette Davis's** performance in **Edmund Goulding's** Coffee-scripted *The Great Lie* (1941).

Other Key Films: William Nigh's *Desert Nights* (1929); **Michael Curtiz's** *Four Daughters* (1938); Irving Pichel's *Tomorrow Is Forever* (1946); **Edward Dmytryk's** *The End Of The Affair* (1955)

Key Line: 'I like Graham Greene very much. He's a convert to Catholicism, too. He said something once that I will always remember, "I wouldn't want a God I could understand." ' [Coffee on her collaboration with Greene on *The End Of The Affair* (1955)]

Cohn, Harry

Cohn was the man Hollywood loved to hate, and over the years he came to epitomize everything that was bad and grasping about the studio system. Founder of Columbia Pictures with his later-to-be-ousted brother Jack, Cohn used his new-found power to tyrannise his writers, directors and stars into performing his will, earning himself the nickname 'White Fang' from **Ben Hecht** in the process.

Key Line: 'On your first day there you were invited to lunch with Harry Cohn in the executive dining room. You sat down. At which point he pressed a button, and the chair under you collapsed. And everybody laughed, laughed, laughed.' [**Charles Bennett** on his rite-of-passage at Columbia Pictures]

Colbert, Claudette

Colbert wouldn't even have found a job on TV these days thanks to her currently unfashionable form of beauty, but that would have been televisions', and our, loss. She was a witty, sparkling little thing, unquestionably strong (before feminine strength became an unpleasant buzzword with supremacist connotations). She had a light, pleasantly ironical touch in comedy, which was best brought out by a man's man, like **Clark Gable**, in *It Happened One Night* (1934). She was brilliant at deflation, too, and one remembers her breezy magnificence in **Preston Sturges's** *The Palm Beach Story* (1942), where she dealt, in turn, with the Weenie King, a heroically ineffectual **Joel McCrea**, the entire Ale & Quail club, **Mary Astor's** sexually voracious Princess Centimillia, and, best of all, Rudy Vallee's sublime J D Hackensacker III. All of which goes to prove, in the proverbial nutshell, that she was a consummate screen actress.

Other Key Films: *The Sign Of The Cross* (1932); *Imitation Of Life* (1934); *Under Two Flags* (1936); *Tovarich* (1937); *Bluebeard's Eighth Wife* (1938); *Zaza* (1939); *Drums Along The Mohawk* (1939); *It's A Wonderful World* (1940); *Boom Town* (1940); *Since You Went Away* (1944); *Guest Wife* (1945); *The Egg And I* (1947); *Sleep, My Love* (1948)

Key Lines:
1. 'I proved, once and for all, that the limb is mightier than the thumb.' [*It Happened One Night*]
2. 'I just had the unpleasant sensation of hearing you referred to as my husband.' [*It Happened One Night*]

Colman, Ronald

One of the few actors to retain, and indeed increase, his audience appeal after the move from silent to sound film, Colman was still capable of fluttering female hearts at the relatively advanced age of fifty-seven, when he won an Oscar for his portrayal of a schizophrenic actor in **George Cukor's** *A Double Life* (1947). His best parts came earlier, however, in **John Ford's** *Arrowsmith* (1931), **Jack Conway's** *A Tale Of Two Cities* (1935) and *The Prisoner Of Zenda* (1937), and **Frank Capra's** recently restored *Lost Horizon* (1937), where Colman's supremely elegant and comforting voice perfectly matched the other-worldly atmosphere of Shangri-La.

Other Key Films: *The White Sister* (1923); *Beau Geste* (1926); *Bulldog Drummond* (1929); *Raffles* (1930); *The Unholy Garden* (1931); *Under Two Flags* (1936); *Random Harvest* (1942)

Key Line: 'I may not believe in myself, but I expect others to believe in me.' [*A Double Life*]

Best Comedy Films

Woody Allen's *Radio Days* (1987); **Robert Altman's** *M*A*S*H* (1970); Richard

Benjamin's *My Favourite Year* (1982); John G Blystone's *Blockheads* (1938); **Mel Brooks's** *The Producers* (1968); **Frank Capra's** *Arsenic And Old Lace* (1944); **René Clair's** *I Married A Witch* (1942); **George Cukor's** *The Philadelphia Story* (1940); Bill Forsyth's *Local Hero* (1983); **Terry Gilliam** and Terry Jones's *Monty Python And The Holy Grail* (1974); **Robert Hamer's** *Kind Hearts And Coronets* (1949); **Howard Hawks's** *Bringing Up Baby* (1938), *Ball Of Fire* (1941) and *I Was A Male War Bride* (1949); James W Horne's *Way Out West* (1937); **Buster Keaton's** *The Navigator* (1924); **Stanley Kubrick's** *Dr Strangelove Or: How I Learned To Stop Worrying And Love the Bomb* (1964); **Emir Kusturica's** *Black Cat, White Cat* (1998); **Patrice Leconte's** *Tango* (1992); **Ernst Lubitsch's** *Ninotchka* (1939) and *To Be Or Not To Be* (1942); Leo McCarey's *Duck Soup* (1933) and *The Awful Truth* (1937); **Alexander Mackendrick's** *The Ladykillers* (1955) and *Whisky Galore* (1948); Norman Z McLeod's *It's A Gift* (1934); **Preston Sturges's** *Sullivan Travels* (1941) and *The Palm Beach Story* (1942)

Connery, Sean

Recently voted the sexiest male of the century (and the man who improves most as he gets older) by a significant cross-section of American womanhood, ex-bodybuilder Connery started his international career by pipping the likes of **Trevor Howard**, **Peter Finch**, **James Mason** and **Richard Burton** to the role of Ian Fleming's ***James Bond*** (probably because he came cheap). His increasing box-office success in the Bond part allowed Connery to branch out into more 'worthy' fare, and he made the curiously underrated *Marnie* (1964) for **Alfred Hitchcock**, followed by **Sidney Lumet's** unremittingly brutal *The Hill* (1965). In recent years virtually everything the newly knighted Connery has done has turned to box-office gold, but despite this he remains, when he cares to be – as Daniel Dravot, for instance in **John Huston's** magnificent *The Man Who Would Be King* (1975) and as Barley Blair, in **Fred Schepisi's** *The Russia House* (1991) – an excellent actor and a consummate screen professional.

Other Key Films: *Hell Drivers* (1958); *Dr No* (1962); *From Russia With Love* (1963); *Woman Of Straw* (1964); *The Molly Maguires* (1970); *The Anderson Tapes* (1972); *The Offence* (1973); *The Wind And The Lion* (1975); *Outland* (1981); *Five Days One Summer* (1983); *The Untouchables* (1987); *The Rock* (1996); *Entrapment* (1999); *Finding Forrester* (2000); *The League Of Extraordinary Gentlemen* (2003)

Conway, Jack

Conway learned the directing art under **D W Griffith**, and went on to make some of the best films of Hollywood's golden age, including the definitive *A Tale Of Two Cities* (1935) with **Ronald Colman**. He also directed the one and only **Jean Harlow** in *Red-Headed Woman* (1932), and in her final film, *Saratoga* (1937) [the final scenes of which had to be filmed back on, by a stand-in, due to Harlow's death], and was responsible for the sexiest Tarzan movie ever, *Tarzan And His Mate* (1934), in which the smooth-buttocked **Maureen O'Sullivan** wore the famous cut-away loin cloth that has delighted and titillated discerning moviegoers for nigh on seventy years.

Other Key Films: *Arsène Lupin* (1932); *Libeled Lady* (1936); *Too Hot To Handle* (1938)

Cooper, Chris

One of the finest screen actors currently at work in Hollywood, Cooper is also one of the most self-effacing, and one cries out for him to be used more often while suspecting that he is very cannily managing his own career, thank you very much, and doesn't need any advice from outside parties. His best performance among many has come in **John Sayles's** cross-cultural American masterpiece *Lone Star* (1997), in which Cooper plays Sheriff Sam Deeds, struggling to emerge from beneath the shadow of his hero-worshipped (except by his son) dead father. This is indisputably one of the great films of the last thirty years, and deserves to be paired with the best of **John Ford**, but Cooper's performance is as utterly unlike **John Wayne's**, in, say, Ford's *The Searchers* (1956), as it is possible to be. Deeds is an ordinary man in extraordinary circumstances, and he triumphs (if that is the word) specifically on account of that very, dogged, ordinariness. It takes a master to achieve such a trick.

Other Key Films: *Bad Timing* (1980); *Matewan* (1987); *City Of Hope* (1991); *Guilty By Suspicion* (1991); *This Boy's Life* (1993); *Money Train* (1995); *A Time To Kill* (1996); *Great Expectations* (1998); *The Horse Whisperer* (1998); *American Beauty* (1999); *Me, Myself And Irene* (2000); *The Patriot* (2000); *The Bourne Identity* (2002); *Capote* (2005); *Syriana* (2005)

Cooper, Gary

Awesomely good-looking even in later life and an inveterate womaniser (his mistresses included **Clara Bow**, **Marlene Dietrich**, **Carole Lombard**, **Ingrid Bergman**, Patricia Neal, **Grace Kelly**, Anita Ekberg and Lupe Velez), Cooper epitomised the laconic, slow-speaking (but hardly slow-witted) **Western** heroes the movie public have always yearned for. The son of British immigrants to the US, Cooper was pretty much top of the Hollywood heap for twenty of the thirty-five years of his acting career. Rated by contemporaries as the greatest film star of them all, he was both a fine comedian in films such as **Frank Capra's** *Mr Deeds Goes To Town* (1936) and **Howard Hawks's** *Ball Of Fire* (1941), a sublime romantic hero in **Frank Borzage's** *Farewell To Arms* (1932) and **Henry Hathaway's** *Peter Ibbetson* (1935), and a superb dramatic lead in **Fred Zinnemann's** *High Noon* (1952) and **Anthony Mann's** underrated *Man Of The West* (1958), where he combined all these talents to almost mythic effect.

Gary Cooper in 1929.
Paramount/The Kobal Collection/Richee, E. R.

Other Key Films: *Shopworn Angel* (1928); *Morocco* (1930); *The Lives Of A Bengal Lancer* (1935); *Desire* (1936); *The Plainsman* (1936); *The Westerner* (1940); *Sergeant York* (1941); *For Whom The Bell Tolls* (1943); *The Fountainhead* (1949); *Vera Cruz* (1954); *Love In The Afternoon* (1958)

Key Lines:

1. 'For me it's the first chapter. For what has my life been up to now? A preface? An empty foreword.' [Cooper's over-erudite linguistic expert, Bertram Potts, to **Barbara Stanwyck's** over-sexed gangster's moll, Sugarpuss O'Shea, in *Ball Of Fire*]

2. 'He's hung like a horse and he can go all night.' [Clara Bow, musing on Cooper's jewellery collection]

Cooper, Merian C

Always an adventurer (he joined an expedition against Pancho Villa and was shot down a couple of times during the First World War) Cooper only really made movies as a means of raising money to fund his real love, flying. With his partner, Ernest B Schoedsack, he filmed a number of highly regarded documentaries, including the fictionalised *Chang* (1927) about an embattled Siamese hill-tribe family, and the public's response to these eventually led him to try his hand at feature films. With the success of his first effort, *The Four Feathers* (1929), he, Schoedsack and RKO decided to take a punt on a wild idea involving giant apes and New York skyscrapers, and the result was **King Kong** (1933), the greatest and most original adventure story of all time. The film was so successful that Cooper was shunted upstairs to the executive lounge, and he continued on in film only as a producer – but it is to him, coincidentally, that we owe many of director **John Ford's** greatest early movies.

Coppola, Francis Ford

Coppola is an enigma – a man of extraordinary energy and varied passions whose generous encouragement of others, twinned with his magnificent work on the *Godfather* trilogy (1972-90) and *Apocalypse Now* (1979), should be enough to put him on a par with a **John Ford**, a **Nicholas Ray**, or a **Frank Capra**. The fact that he doesn't quite match his progenitors is not so much a criticism as a warning – recent American film lacks the soul and the poetry of its greatest antecedents, and Coppola, too, falls into this trap – it's as if by being given an enormous, magical box of tricks, directors like Coppola have forgotten that it is people, and not effects that count. Effects however, can best be left to nature – what a movie audience wants to see is how people respond to extremes, and how these extremes bring out a communal and incipient humanity. John Ford understood this in *The Hurricane* (1937) which was never intended to be simply about the storm, but rather about the people whose lives it changed; Nicholas Ray understood it in *They Live By Night* (1949), which was not about crime but about youth; and Frank Capra understood it in *The Bitter Tea Of General Yen* (1932), which wasn't so much about revolution, as about the lives and loves of the people caught up in it. *Apocalypse Now* is magnificent, and bears repeated viewings, but one finally comes to the conclusion, after being bowled over, yet again, by its brilliance – so what? It is impossible to imagine Martin Sheen's Capt. Willard as changed by the end of it. Or even wiser. He and the viewer have simply undergone an extraordinary experience together, and are content to part on those terms. But one never forgets Terangi and Marama, Bowie and Keechie, Megan Davis and General Yen.
Other Key Films: *The Rain People* (1969); *The Conversation* (1974); *One From The Heart* (1982); *The Outsiders* (1983); *Rumble Fish* (1983); *The Cotton Club* (1984); *Peggy Sue Got Married* (1986); *Gardens Of Stone* (1987); *Tucker: The Man And His Dream* (1988); *Bram Stoker's **Dracula*** (1992); *Jack* (1996); *The Rainmaker* (1997); *Youth Without Youth* (2006)

Corman, Roger

Corman may be most renowned for his colourful horror films, but he was always more than simply a master of the macabre, and his innate sense of design and continual encouragement of other directors make him an important player in 1950s and 1960s cinema (he is the producer of 376 films at the last count). As a director his best films were undoubtedly those starring **Vincent Price**, and in particular the **Nicholas Roeg-**photographed *The Masque Of The Red Death* (1964) and the **Robert Towne-**scripted *The Tomb Of Ligeia* (1964), in both of which Price thankfully plays it straight. Both films had a heady visual style to them, and were essentially accurate portrayals of Edgar Allan Poe's interior world. Corman's championing of such 'difficult' European directors as **Ingmar Bergman** and **Federico Fellini** also redounds to his credit, and it is interesting to note that in recent years Corman has moved beyond his cult status to the status of grand old man of low budget cinema.

Other Key Films: *Machine Gun Kelly* (1958); *The House Of Usher* (1960); *The Pit And The Pendulum* (1961); *X – The Man With X-Ray Eyes* (1963); *The St Valentine's Day Massacre* (1967); *Bloody Mama* (1970); *Frankenstein Unbound* (1990)

Key Line: 'He was only interested in saving money, so his intellect ground down to almost nothing...Roger's stuff was 99 percent garbage and 1 percent is of interest.' [Screenwriter Charles B Griffith on his many collaborations with Corman]

Costa-Gavras, Constantin

Costa-Gavras is a political director, and his films invariably reflect his background as the son of a Greek communist and former Second World War resistance fighter. *Z* (1969), with **Yves Montand**, was the first film to signal his particular talents as a truth-seeker and propagandist against tyranny, and he followed this up with *The Confession* (1970), *State Of Siege* (1972) and *Special Section* (1972), which concentrated on Czechoslovakia, Uruguay, and Vichy war-time France respectively. He succeeded in making even the CIA uncomfortable with *Missing* (1973), but his most successful film, in both human and political terms, is the little seen *Betrayed* (1988), which works surprisingly well with its portrayal of an FBI agent, **Debra Winger**, torn apart by her love for a man, **Tom Berenger**, whom at the same time she must inevitably betray for the rabid, though paradoxically attractive Ku Klux Klan activist that he is. Costa-Gavras deals brilliantly with such paradoxes throughout the body of his work, and his strength lies in never forgetting the human in favour of the epic.

Other Key Films: *The Sleeping-Car Murders* (1965); *Shock Troops* (1967); *Clair De Femme* (1979); *Hanna K.* (1983); *Family Business* (1986); *Music Box* (1990); *La Petite Apocalypse* (1993); *The Dreyfuss Affair* (1994); *Rasputin* (1995); *Mad City* (1997); *Amen* (2002); *Le Couperet* (2005)

Costner, Kevin

Now struggling for his commercial life after a sequence of own-goal turkeys, Costner is a genuine talent with an uncanny capacity to miss his own market. After a run of well-chosen hits with **Brian de Palma's** *The Untouchables* (1987), Roger Donaldson's *No Way Out* (1987) and his own well-directed *Dances With Wolves* (1990), not to mention a first-rate performance in **Oliver Stone's** *JFK* (1991), his star position seemed more or less unassailable. Kevin Reynolds's *Robin Hood: Prince Of Thieves* (1991) followed, together with an excellent turn as a convict with a heart of gold in **Clint Eastwood's** *A Perfect World* (1993), and then...yes, Reynolds's *Waterworld* (1995) and Costner's own *The Postman* (1997), both disasters on an epic scale. Why? **Sam Raimi's** *For Love Of The Game* (2000) has done nothing to stop the slide, and despite good reviews in Roger Donaldson's *Thirteen Days* (2000) and his own *Open Range* (2003), Costner remains a man who is struggling. Is a **John Travolta**-like comeback on the cards? Only time, and the next edition of this book, will tell.

Other Key Films: *Silverado* (1985); *Bull Durham* (1988); *Field Of Dreams* (1989); *The Bodyguard* (1992); *Wyatt Earp* (1994); *Tin Cup* (1996); *3000 Miles To Graceland* (2001); *The Upside Of Anger* (2005); *Rumor Has it...* (2005)

Key Line: 'It's a great cultural achievement, now, fame, and it doesn't stand for anything.' [Costner on himself]

Cotten, Joseph

Now seen as something of an **Orson Welles** protégé, Cotten never appeared to take his acting very seriously, and it seems almost by default that he turned in good performances. Apart from the ubiquitous *Citizen Kane* (1941), Cotten's best roles were in Welles's sadly truncated *The Magnificent Ambersons* (1942) and *Journey Into Fear* (1942), and, most notably, **Alfred Hitchcock's** *Shadow Of A Doubt* (1943), in which he played Uncle Charlie, a charmingly ingratiating killer. Once again, in **Carol Reed's** *The Third Man* (1949), he pulled out all the stops alongside his friend Welles, in his incarnation of Holly Martins to Welles's Harry Lime, but, woefully, Cotten's later work was pedestrian in the extreme.

Other Key Films: *Gaslight* (1944); *Duel In The Sun* (1946); *Portrait Of Jenny* (1948); *Under Capricorn* (1949); *Niagara* (1953); *Touch Of Evil* (1958)

Coward, Noel

Coward constructed his own image of himself and resolutely lived by it throughout his extraordinarily successful life. When his plays began losing popularity he moved to films, and when the film work began to dry up he began a new career as an entertainer, chanteur and occasional actor, and when he tired of this he took to writing, yet again about himself, or rather about who he wanted to be. All this is perfectly normal in an actor, and Coward made a virtue of it. The plays serve as his memorial, for it was generally others who made the best films of his stories, most notably director **David Lean** with *Blithe Spirit* (1945) and *Brief Encounter* (1945).

Other Key Films: *In Which We Serve* [co-dir.] (1942); David Lean's *This Happy Breed* (1944)

Cox, Paul

Cox's *Man Of Flowers* (1983) was one of the most curious, but at the same time most exalted films of the 1980s, particularly in its preoccupation with questions of acceptance and redemption. All Cox's films seem to touch on such metaphysical aspects, even when they are at their very bleakest, as in *My First Wife* (1984), in which Cox explores, in excoriating detail, the breakdown of a marriage and of family relationships. Cox is an oasis of emotional daylight in a pretty bleak world, and one can forgive him his tics and his tendency to encourage his actors to underplay their roles, for simply having the courage to try, as in *Cactus* (1986), to reflect on the real and the imagined, and to at least attempt to shuffle them into some sort of acceptable symmetry.

Other Key Films: *Illuminations* (1976); *Inside Looking Out* (1977); *Kostas* (1979); *Lonely Hearts* (1982); *Vincent: The Life And Death Of Vincent Van Gogh* (1987); *Island* (1989); *The Golden Braid* (1990); *A Woman's Tale* (1991); *Lust And Revenge* (1996); *Innocence* (2000); *Human Touch* (2004)

Craven, Wes

A master of schlock horror and shock tactics (try saying that fast!), Craven has moved from the periphery to the commercial mainstream in tandem with society's changing tastes and widening standards of acceptance. The *Hills Have Eyes* (1977) [remade by Alexandre Aja in 2006], while not being his first success, was at least characteristic, in its concentration on the gruesome and the grotesque, of what was to come. Commercial heaven (in the guise of the Hollywood money-men) came to Craven in recognition of the infinitely repeatable thrills of *Nightmare In Elm Street* (1984), and Craven has doggedly followed (ghosted?) the same scenario and the same ghoul-strewn path ever since, most recently with the *Scream* series.

Other Key Films: *Last House On The Left* (1972); *Deadly Blessing* (1981); *Swamp Thing* (1982); *Deadly Friend* (1986); *Shocker* (1990); *The People Under The Stairs* (1991); *Scream* (1996); *Scream 2* (1997); *Music Of The Heart* (1999); *Scream 3* (2000); *Cursed* (2005); *Red Eye* (2005)

Crawford, Joan

Crawford spent her life being dragged through the mud – posthumously by her adopted daughter and the gossips, and during her lifetime through her predilection for such gorgeously pulpy, soap-dish material as **Michael Curtiz's** *Mildred Pierce* (1945) and the later, wilder, *Flamingo Road* (1949), parts that appeared to reflect her non-acting life. This could be construed as a curiously backhanded compliment to her star power, for her audience believed so strongly in the roles that she played that they found it hard to accept that they weren't seeing the real Joan Crawford on the screen. And perhaps they were right. Crawford was a 'wannabe', the redneck daughter of poor Texans, and the sum total of her life consisted in the relegation and eventual extinguishing of that reality. And she achieved this, up to a point. But her later choice of films show her despair all too clearly, together with the sad carapace of the self-sufficient woman that she forcibly constructed around herself to disguise it. If you have trouble connecting to Crawford, try watching her in **Frank Borzage's** curious and heady *Strange Cargo* (1940), and daylight may dawn.

Other Key Films: *This Modern Age* (1931); *Grand Hotel* (1932); *Sadie McKee* (1934); *Mannequin* (1938); *The Women* (1939); *Above Suspicion* (1943); *Humoresque* (1946); *Possessed* (1947); *Daisy Kenyon* (1947); *Harriet Craig* (1950); *Johnny Guitar* (1954); *What Ever Happened To Baby Jane?* (1962)

Key Line: 'A woman can do anything, get anywhere, as long as she doesn't fall in love.' [Curtis Bernhardt's *Possessed*]

Best Crime Films

Robert Altman's *The Long Goodbye* (1973); **Claude Chabrol's** *Le Boucher* (1969) and *Que La Bête Meure* [*This Man Must Die*] (1969); **Joel and Ethan Coen's** *Fargo* (1996); **Jules Dassin's** *Du Rififi Chez Les Hommes* (1954); Michel Deville's *Eaux Profondes* (1981); **William Friedkin's** *French Connection* (1971); Curtis Hanson's *L.A. Confidential* (1997); **Alfred Hitchcock's** *Rear Window* (1954); **John Huston's** *The Asphalt Jungle* (1950); **Fritz Lang's** *Beyond A Reasonable Doubt* (1956); **Jean-Pierre Melville's** *Bob Le Flambeur* (1955); **Otto Preminger's** *Anatomy Of A Murder* (1959); **Raoul Walsh's** *High Sierra* (1941); **Orson Welles's** *The Lady From Shanghai* (1946)

Cronenberg, David

Cronenberg tried to make the horror film an art form, and failed, although **James Whale** had achieved just that, without being particularly aware of it, many years before him. *The Fly* (1986), a remake of Kurt Neumann's 1958 movie, was wildly over-praised, but with *Dead Ringers* (1988) Cronenberg came closest to his aim, inso-far as he moved beyond horror into the territory of the fetishist – of man as the slave of his machines – and the film works wonderfully on that level. *Crash* (1997) was another good try, but there was no humanity at all at its centre, and one felt almost grateful, by the end, for the gradual disintegration of its demented protagonists. Cronenberg is the intellect made metal, and until he realises that metal cuts when sharpened, and that those cuts bleed and cause pain, he will remain the half-successful director that he is.

Other Key Films: *Shivers* (1975); *The Brood* (1979); *Scanners* (1981); *Videodrome* (1982); *The Dead Zone* (1983); *Naked Lunch* (1991); *eXistenZ* (1999) *Camera* [short] (2000); *Spider* (2002); *A History Of Violence* (2005)

Crosby, Bing

Crosby was perhaps the best and most versatile popular singer of all time – he could do jazz and ballads, comic and sentimental, swing and sweetheart. His film career certainly didn't reflect this versatility, but an easy-going and likeable charm came through on the screen that was enough to comfort his audience, and to suggest to them that if a simple everyday sort of a guy like Crosby could make it, then so, perhaps, might they. Crosby made the old-fashioned seem modern, and his best part, unsurprisingly, came in a **Billy Wilder** film, *The Emperor Waltz* (1948), in which modesty and simplicity (surprise, surprise) win out over royalty. But Crosby *was* royalty, of course, and he was successful also when he acknowledged this fact, as in Charles Walters's *High Society* (1956). His screen persona was the most likeable thing about him, and his matching of it so beautifully and so seamlessly to his singing personality showed a kind of genius.

Other Key Films: *The Big Broadcast* (1932); *Mississippi* (1936); *Pennies From Heaven* (1936); *Road To Singapore* (1940); *Holiday Inn* (1942); *Going My Way* (1944); *Road To Rio* (1947); *A Connecticut Yankee In King Arthur's Court* (1949); *White Christmas* (1954); *The Country Girl* (1954); *Stagecoach* (1966)

Key Line: 'You know, if the world was run right, only women would get married.' [Victor Schertzinger's *Road To Singapore*]

Crowe, Russell

New Zealander Russell Crowe began his film career aged 8, in the Australian *Spyforce* TV Series, but it was his Hando in Geoffrey Wright's *Romper Stomper* (1992) that alerted the movie world to his talent. Curtis Hanson's *L.A. Confidential* (1997) reinforced the message, and the brawling, macho Rusty Crowe we all know and love was on his way. He's since turned into one of the most dependable (if accident prone) of Hollywood's leading men, with bravura performances in Michael Mann's *The Insider* (1999), **Ridley Scott's** *Gladiator* (2000), and **Peter Weir's** *Master And Commander: The Far Side Of The World* (2003).

Other Key Films: *The Quick And The Dead* (1995); *Heaven's Burning* (1997); *Proof Of Life* (2000); *A Beautiful Mind* (2001); *Cinderella Man* (2005); *A Good Year* (2006)

Key Line: 'I'd like to play passionate women, but no one will let me.' [Crowe on the limitations of achievable ambition]

Cruise, Tom

Possibly the most successful big box office attraction of the past fifteen years, Thomas Cruise Mapother IV first made his mark in Harold Becker's *Taps* (1981) at the tender age of nineteen. His big break came with Tony Scott's *Top Gun* (1986), closely followed by critical success in **Martin Scorsese's** *The Color Of Money* (1986) and Barry Levinson's *Rain Man* (1988). That rare being, a major league star who can act, Cruise's best work came in Rob Reiner's *A Few Good Men* (1992) and **Sydney Pollack's** *The Firm* (1993), but Hollywood loves him more for the *Mission: Impossible* series (1995-2006), an apparently blue chip guarantee to print money, following the knock-on success of *Mission: Impossible II* (2000) and *Mission: Impossible III* (2006) – all this despite the series' palpable absurdities. In one scene, for instance, we have Cruise worthily and responsibly struggling to put on a seat belt during a hot-dogging race despite, minutes before, voluntarily dangling by his fingers from a piece of naked rock one thousand feet above the earth without a safety harness. Cruise and his ex-wife **Nicole Kidman** took time out from money-making to act in **Stanley Kubrick's** last film, *Eyes Wide Shut* (1999), and the result, while critically hammered at the time, may still prove to be a sleeper in disguise – as if to drive his point home, Cruise reiterated his acting credentials with his recent stand-out performances as Frank 'T J' Mackey in Paul Thomas Anderson's *Magnolia* (1999), and as Vincent in **Michael Mann's** excellent *Collateral* (2004).

Other Key Films: *The Outsiders* (1983); *Risky Business* (1983); *Legend* (1985); *Cocktail* (1988); *Born On The Fourth Of July* (1989); *Days Of Thunder* (1990); *Far And Away* (1992); *Interview With The Vampire* (1994); *Jerry Maguire* (1996); *Vanilla Sky* (2001); *Minority Report* (2002); *The Last Samurai* (2003); *War Of The Worlds* (2005)

Cukor, George

Cukor is now celebrated as much for his homosexuality (he was one among many) as for his perceived sensitivity in directing women, although both facets have been exaggerated and made the expedient realities of otherwise unenlightened self-interest groups. He was quite simply a first-rate director, honed in the theatre, who had the nous and commercial intelligence to play to his strengths, and to those of his actors and actresses. He had a magical six years with *Dinner At Eight* (1933), *Little Women* (1933), *David Copperfield* (1935), *Sylvia Scarlett* (1936), *Camille* (1937) and *Holiday* (1938), although the run was somewhat curtailed when **David Selznick** eased him off *Gone With The Wind*. But he soon made a skilful return with *The Women* (1939) and *The Philadelphia Story* (1940), and later consolidated his brilliant career even more (as if that were possible) with *Adam's Rib* (1949), *Pat And Mike* (1952) and *A Star Is Born* (1954). Always the perfect entertainer, Cukor's films had heart, and a curious, almost spontaneous integrity, and his existence is something of a miracle in the environment in which he chose to function.

Other Key Films: *Tarnished Lady* (1931); *A Bill Of Divorcement* (1932); *Romeo And Juliet* (1936); *Keeper Of The Flame* (1943); *Gaslight* (1944); *Winged Victory* (1944); *A Double Life* (1947); *Born Yesterday* (1950); *Bhowani Junction* (1956); *Let's Make Love* (1960); *My Fair Lady* (1964); *Travels With My Aunt* (1973); *Rich And Famous* (1981)

Cult Film

Any film that has a cult, rather than a mainstream following. Such films frequently outlast their theatrical releases, finding themselves repeated, often at Art-House cinemas, ad infinitum. Jim Sharman's *The Rocky Horror Picture Show* (1975) is a case in point, as is **Robert Wise's** *The Sound Of Music* (1965), both of which see cult followers dressing up as characters out of the movie and re-enacting certain scenes inside the cinema in exact parallel to what is happening on the screen.

Key Line: 'What's a cult? It just means not enough people to make a minority.' [**Robert Altman** on cult status]

Best Cult Films

Robert Aldrich's *Kiss Me Deadly* (1955); **Robert Altman's** *Nashville* (1975); **Jean-Jacques Beineix's** *Diva* (1980); Walerian Borowczyk's *Blanche* (1971); Philippe de Broca's *Le Roi De Coeur [King Of Hearts]* (1966); **Tod Browning's** *Freaks* (1932); **Luis Buñuel** and Salvador Dali's *L'Age D'Or* (1930); Luis Buñuel's *Belle De Jour* (1966); **Frank Capra's** *The Bitter Tea Of General Yen* (1932); **Jean Cocteau's** *Orphée* (1949); **Paul Cox's** *Man Of Flowers* (1983); **Jonathan Demme's** *Caged Heat* (1974);

Georges Franju's *Les Yeux Sans Visages* [a.k.a. *Eyes Without A Face*, or *Horror Chamber Of Dr Faustus*] (1960); **Jean-Luc Godard's** *A Bout De Souffle* (1959) and *Vivre Sa Vie* (1962); **Edmund Goulding's** *Nightmare Alley* (1947); Robin Hardy's *The Wicker Man* (1973); **Hal Hartley's** *Simple Men* (1992); **Howard Hughes's The Outlaw** (1941); Alejandro Jodorowsky's *Santa Sangre* (1989); Edward Ludwig's *Wake Of The Red Witch* (1948); **David Lynch's** *Blue Velvet* (1986); **Michael Powell** and Emeric Pressburger's *I Know Where I'm Going* (1945), *Black Narcissus* (1947) and *Gone To Earth* (1950); **Alain Resnais's** *Hiroshima Mon Amour* (1958) and *Last Year At Marienbad* (1961); **Bruce Robinson's** *Withnail & I* (1986); **Josef von Sternberg's** *The Shanghai Gesture* (1941); **Quentin Tarantino's** *Pulp Fiction* (1994); **Edgar G Ulmer's** *Detour* (1945); **King Vidor's** *Duel In The Sun* (1947); **John Waters's** *Cry-Baby* (1990)

Curtis, Jamie Lee

A fine comedienne and an outstanding screamer (although not quite in the same league as Fay Wray, of **King Kong** fame), particularly in **John Carpenter's** *Halloween* (1978), Curtis has worked consistently since her corpse-strewn beginnings, but it is only belatedly that directors have begun to recognise her inherited talent (she is the daughter of **Tony Curtis** and **Janet Leigh**). Amy Jones's *Love Letters* (1983) first revealed her potential for drama, and Charles Crichton's *A Fish Called Wanda* (1988) proved how adept she was at feather-light comedy. Her career has already been a long one by current Hollywood standards (she was born in 1958), and seems set fair, given her versatility, to continue indefinitely, as has recently been manifested by her excellent turn in **John Boorman's** *The Tailor Of Panama* (2001).

Other Key Films: *The Fog* (1980); *Trading Places* (1983); *Blue Steel* (1990) *Forever Young* (1992); *True Lies* (1994); *Fierce Creatures* (1997); *Homegrown* (1998); *Virus* (1999); *Daddy And Them* (2000); *Halloween 8* (2001); *Freaky Friday* (2003)

Curtis, Tony

Curtis has had two high points in his career, and they came within two years of each other – his reptilian Sidney Falco in **Alexander Mackendrick's** magnificent *Sweet Smell Of Success* (1958), and his sublimely harassed Joe/Josephine in **Billy Wilder's** *Some Like It Hot* (1959). His other successes have always seemed variations on those themes, but the two movies revealed a genuine and surprising talent, given his inauspicious beginnings as part of Universal's soul-destroying star production line.

Other Key Films: *Houdini* (1953); *The Black Shield Of Falworth* (1954); *Trapeze* (1956); *The Vikings* (1958); *Spartacus* (1960); *Great Imposter* (1960); *Taras Bulba* (1962); *The Boston Strangler* (1968); *The Last Tycoon* (1976); *Insignificance* (1985); *Stargames* (1998); *Reflections Of Evil* (2002)

Curtiz, Michael

As well as directing that perennial favourite, **Casablanca** (1942), Curtiz made an astonishing average of four films a year for Warner Brothers during his quarter of a century tenure as one of their in-house directors, no less than twelve of which starred **Errol Flynn**. Renowned for his temperamental exigencies on set, Curtiz stories abound, many relating to his often-idiosyncratic use of the English language (he was Hungarian by birth). **David Niven** named the second volume of his autobiography *Bring On The Empty Horses* after one of Curtiz's shouted commands on the set of *The Charge Of The Light Brigade* (1936). Even a brief look at Curtiz's key films will show what an astonishing capacity the man had to reinvent himself – his directing credits include thrillers, *film noirs*, musicals, horror movies, gangster pictures and even a jazz film. To cap an extraordinary career, nearly forty-six years after directing his first silent feature he took on the **Elvis Presley** star vehicle *King Creole* (1958), and made a success of it.

Other Key Films: *20,000 Years In Sing Sing* (1933); *Mystery Of The Wax Museum* (1933); *Captain Blood* (1935); *The Adventures Of Robin Hood* (1938); *Angels With Dirty Faces* (1938); *The Private Lives Of Elizabeth and Essex* (1939); *The Sea Wolf* (1941); *Yankee Doodle Dandy* (1942); *Mildred Pierce* (1945); *Young Man With A Horn* (1950); *White Christmas* (1954)

Cusack, John

An interesting and careful actor who has husbanded his talent well and chosen his parts with great care and attention, Cusack's star is definitely rising, and he has enough versatility to make the most of the opportunities that will no doubt keep flooding in after his recent success in Spike Jonze's *Being John Malkovich* (1999) and James Mangold's *Identity* (2003). He was excellent, too, in **Stephen Frears's** *The Grifters* (1990), and wonderfully edgy in **Woody Allen's** *Shadows And Fog* (1991) and *Bullets Over Broadway* (1994), and if he can only manage to keep the lid on his self-destructive urges (in 1990 he was put on probation for three years for drunk driving) he should have a great career ahead of him.

Other Key Films: *Class* (1983); *Stand By Me* (1986); *Broadcast News* (1987); *True Colors* (1991); *Bob Roberts* (1992); *The Road To Wellville* (1994); *City Hall* (1996); *Grosse Point Blank* (1997); *High Fidelity* (2000); *Serendipity* (2001); *Runaway Jury* (2003); *The Ice Harvest* (2005)

Cushing, Peter

The Hammer actor par excellence, Cushing usually played the straight man to **Christopher Lee's** warped monster, and this suited his inhibited, old-fashioned style of acting (Cushing would have been entirely at home in Victorian stage melodrama). He was the ultimate Baron Frankenstein in Terence Fisher's *The Curse Of Frankenstein* (1958), if only because his fall was so long, and from so erudite and informed a height. Professing himself a little fed up with the unwanted form of celebrity his horror roles brought him, Cushing nevertheless always gave of his best, and his Van Helsing, in Fisher's *Dracula* (1958), was equally grave and informed by the seriousness that had become his trademark.

Other Key Films: *The Revenge Of Frankenstein* (1958); *The Hound Of The Baskervilles* (1959); *The Mummy* (1959); *The Brides Of Dracula* (1960); *Dr Terror's House Of Horrors* (1964); *The Gorgon* (1964); *Torture Garden* (1967); *Asylum* (1972); *The Beast Must Die* (1974); *Star Wars* (1977)

Dafoe, Willem

A fine character actor with an indie movie face, Dafoe is yet another of the elite 1980s school of Hollywood actors (see **Tom Berenger**, **Christopher Walken** and **Kevin Bacon**) who have flirted with stardom but never quite attained it. His breakthrough came when he was allowed to play a hero (virtually for the first time) in **Oliver Stone's** *Platoon* (1986), which gave him the opportunity to move on to the greatest of all heroes, Jesus Christ, in **Martin Scorsese's** *The Last Temptation Of Christ* (1988). Now somewhat inured to heroic roles, Dafoe stayed on track as an investigator into the Ku Klux Klan in **Alan Parker's** *Mississippi Burning* (1988), but then delighted all the fans of his darker side with an evil gem of a performance in

David Lynch's *Wild At Heart* (1990), in which he played the blinding car headlights to Laura Dern's fascinated rabbit. Rarely out of work, Dafoe has become the steady candle that burns behind many a brighter, briefer flame.

Other Key Films: *The Loveless* (1983); *Streets Of Fire* (1984); *To Live And Die In L.A.* (1985); *Off Limits* (1988); *Triumph Of The Spirit* (1989); *Body Of Evidence* (1993); *Tom & Viv* (1994); *Clear And Present Danger* (1994); *The English Patient* (1996); *Lulu On The Bridge* (1998); *American Psycho* (2000); *Edges Of The Lord* (2001); *Bullfighter* (2001); *The Life Aquatic With Steve Zissou* (2005); *The Aviator* (2004); *Ripley Under Ground* (2005); *Inside Man* (2006)

Damon, Matt

Often paired in the public's imagination with his boyhood buddy Ben Affleck – two years his junior and also born in Cambridge MA – Damon proved in **Gus Van Sant's** *Good Will Hunting* (1997) that not only could he act, but also that he could co-write a mean screenplay. His recent outing in **Anthony Minghella's** *The Talented Mr Ripley* (2000) was most emphatically not a copy of **Alain Delon's** brilliant portrayal of Ripley in **René Clément's** *Plein Soleil* (1960), and none the worse for that. Damon is obviously talented, and, more importantly, not too showy, which bodes well for the length of any future Hollywood career he may have. Plus he already has his very own *James Bond* franchise, in ex-agent Jason Bourne. Definitely one to watch.

Other Key Films: *Mystic Pizza* (1988); *School Ties* (1992); *Geronimo: An American Legend* (1994); *Courage Under Fire* (1996); *John Grisham's The Rainmaker* (1997); *Saving Private Ryan* (1998); *The Legend Of Bagger Vance* (2000); *All The Pretty Horses* (2000); *Ocean's Eleven* (2001); *The Bourne Identity* (2002); *Ocean's Twelve* (2004); *The Bourne Supremacy* (2004); *Syriana* (2005)

Dassin, Jules

Dassin was always a political director, even when he swam with the sharks in the Hollywood mainstream of the 1940s, and those politics eventually got him into trouble with the 1947-1957 House Committee On Un-American Activities (HUAC), leading to his subsequent exile in Europe. His early films showed great promise, and include the superb prison drama *Brute Force* (1947), the cop rite-of-passage movie *The Naked City* (1948), and two of the very best *film noir* thrillers ever produced, *Thieves' Highway* (1949), in which Dassin conjures up something resembling a French film in an American setting, and *Night And The City* (1950), which has a doomed **Richard Widmark** running for his life through the dark streets of London and becoming progressively more demented the closer he comes to death. Dassin's hokum period only began when he arrived in Europe and met Melina Mercouri, and its apogee came with the cheery, teary, weary, *Never On Sunday* (1960).

Other Key Films: *The Canterville Ghost* (1944); *Rififi* (1955); *He Who Must Die* (1958); *Phaedra* (1962); *Topkapi!* (1964) *10:30 PM Summer* (1966); *Circle Of Two* (1980)

Davis, Bette

Star of more than ninety films, chain-smoking Ruth Davis took her new screen name from the title of Balzac's lowlife novel *Cousin Bette*. After posing nude, aged sixteen, to model for the making of a statue of the young goddess Diana, Davis disastrously failed her first screen test, and eventually made her debut at the age of twenty-five in Hobart Henley's *Bad Sister* (1931). Davis was renowned for her roles in a series of 'women's movies' during the 1930s and 1940s, in which she incarnated the tough but tender heroine who, despite girl-next-door looks, still manages to steal her man from under the noses of her more glamorous rivals. A steadfast foe of studio boss Jack Warner, with whom she conducted an extended court battle, Davis had the ability, above all the other actresses of her time, to make her audience want to believe in melodrama, and in the heightened words and exalted passions that are its foundation. A victim, like her near contemporary **Joan Crawford**, of the vicious daughter syndrome, Davis died as she had lived – unapologetically, and on her way back from somewhere.

Other Key Films: *The Cabin In The Cotton* (1932); *The Petrified Forest* (1936); *Jezebel* (1938); *Dark Victory* (1939); *Juarez* (1939); *The Private Lives Of Elizabeth And Essex* (1939); *The Letter* (1940); *The Great Lie* (1941); *The Little Foxes* (1941); *Now, Voyager* (1942); *All About Eve* (1950); *Whatever Happened To Baby Jane?* (1962); *Hush…Hush Sweet Charlotte* (1965); *The Whales Of August* (1987)

Key Lines:
1. 'Fasten your seat belts, it's going to be a bumpy night.' [*All About Eve*].
2. 'Oh, Jerry, don't let's ask for the moon. We have the stars!' [*Now, Voyager*]
3. 'If she hadn't been a film star, Davis would probably have made it as the first female US president.' [BBC *Mastermind* contestant, on Davis's force of character]

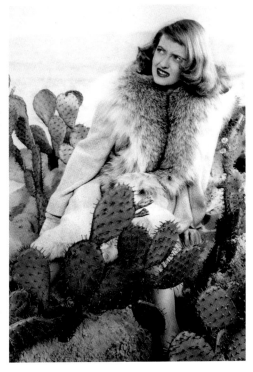

Bette Davis in The Bride Came C. O. D., directed by William Keighley (1941).

Warner Bros/First National/The Kobal Collection

Davis, Judy

One of the most interesting and talented of all present day screen performers, Davis has flirted with the limelight but the limelight has never quite reciprocated. She should be one of the most celebrated actresses of her generation, but in fact she is known only to dedicated movie buffs, **Woody Allen** freaks, Australians, and as an occasional character player in other people's blockbusters. She seemed set to hit the Hollywood heights following her role in **David Lean's** *A Passage To India* (1984), but she contented herself with the more challenging parts offered by non-mainstream films such as Tim Burstall's excellent *Kangaroo* (1986), **Gillian Armstrong's** *High Tide* (1987), James Lupine's *Impromptu* (1991) and Woody Allen's *Husbands And Wives* (1992). Her splendidly eccentric performance in **Bob Rafelson's** seriously underrated *Blood And Wine* (1997) simply adds more fuel to the Davis mystique – she's a stayer, and her reputation should definitely outlast those of her glitzier, more celebrated rivals.

Other Key Films: *My Brilliant Career* (1979); *The Winter Of Our Dreams* (1981); *Heatwave* (1983); *Barton Fink* (1991); *Naked Lunch* (1991); *Where Angels Fear To Tread* (1991); *Absolute Power* (1997); *Deconstructing Harry* (1997); *Celebrity* (1998); *A Colder Climate* (1999); *Gaudi Afternoon* (2000); *Marie Antoinette* (2006)

Day, Doris

Part of the triumvirate of apparently perpetual virgins that includes **Debbie Reynolds** and **Julie Andrews**, Doris Day was actually the best actress of the bunch and a very fine singer, but she still found it impossible to shed her squeaky-clean image in any tangible (or non-tangible) way. She came closest in **Alfred Hitchcock's** *The Man Who Knew Too Much* (1956) – just as Andrews did later in Hitchcock's *Torn Curtain* (1966) – but her mumsie appeal was too much even for **Rock Hudson's** passion in Michael Gordon's *Pillow Talk* (1959), and one is inevitably forced to assume that the 'talk' in question took place on separate pillows, in resolutely separate beds, and concerned the office picnic. Despite all this, she contrived to remain the Number 1 female star in the US and the UK pretty much continuously between 1959 and 1965.

Other Key Films: *Romance On The High Seas* (1948); *Young Man With A Horn* (1950); *Tea For Two* (1950); *Calamity Jane* (1953); *Love Me Or Leave Me* (1958); *The Pajama Game* (1958); *That Touch Of Mink* (1962); *Move Over, Darling* (1963); *The Ballad Of Josie* (1967); *Caprice* (1967)

Day-Lewis, Daniel

One of the best screen actors of recent years, Day-Lewis is yet another stage goodie turned movie bandit, and is renowned for his meticulous preparation for each screen role that he accepts (and they are few). He had a striking success as Johnny, the gay punk, in **Stephen Frears's** *My Beautiful Laundrette* (1985), and further plaudits followed for his insufferable prig, Cecil Vyse, in **James Ivory's** *A Room With A View* (1985). Hollywood suddenly took notice of him, and he appeared as a magnificently athletic Hawkeye in **Michael Mann's** *The Last Of The Mohicans* (1992). His best roles to date have been as Christy Brown in Jim Sheridan's *My Left Foot* (1989), and as Gerry Conlon in the same director's *In The Name Of The Father* (1993). A brief glance at Day-Lewis's filmography leads one to conclude that he seems perfectly happy turning out one quality film every two years or so, with a sensible gap for hols in between.

Other Key Films: *Sunday Blood Sunday* (1971); *Gandhi* (1982); *The Bounty* (1984); *The Unbearable Lightness Of Being* (1988); *The Age Of Innocence* (1993); *The Crucible* (1995); *The Boxer* (1997); *Gangs Of New York* (2002); *The Ballad Of Jack And Rose* (2005)

Dean, James

With his strangely tormented features and fervid method style acting, Dean seemed to embody all the alienation and anger felt by teenagers brought up in the restrictive atmosphere of the Eisenhower Cold War years. The James Dean cult, however, only really began after the twenty-four-year-old manic-depressive killed himself in his Porsche on his way to a sports-car rally on 30th September 1955. It has been alleged that Dean's mangled body was covered in partially healed cigarette burns (testimony to a more than passing interest in sadomasochistic practices) and these and other posthumous acknowledgments of Dean's bisexuality mean that he has become something of a gay icon in recent years, ensuring that the titles of his earlier films now take on the appearance of a belatedly camp, Joe Orton-esque style in-joke. The star of **Nicholas Ray's** *Rebel Without A Cause* (1955), **Elia Kazan's** *East of Eden* (1955) and **George Stevens's** *Giant* (1956), Dean's cult status is now equalled only by that of **Rudolf Valentino** and **Marilyn Monroe**.

Other Key Films: *Fixed Bayonets* (1951); *Sailor Beware* (1951); *Has Anybody Seen My Gal?* (1952); *Trouble Along The Way* (1953)

Key Lines:

1. 'Why did you run out on me? Why did you leave me alone?' [*Rebel Without A Cause*]
2. 'It was like a strange wind that came right through the streets of Hollywood. People's rhythm changed. They began to pool into little groups like mercury rolling across a tabletop, collecting other little pieces of itself.' [Stewart Stern, who scripted Nicholas Ray's *Rebel Without A Cause* (1955) and **Robert Altman** and George W Georges's *The James Dean Story* (1958), on Hollywood, the day of Dean's death]

Dearden, Basil

A professional, socially conscious director who began his work at a time when British Cinema was happiest forgetting its wartime traumas in a sudsy bathful of melodramatic tosh, Dearden's subtlest film is *Frieda* (1947), in which he tried to confront Britain's inevitable post-World-War-Two anti-German prejudice – *Sapphire* (1959), too, was a valiant pitch (in the light of its times) for racial tolerance, and *Victim* (1961) made a brave stab at reversing middle England's phobic prejudices against homosexuality. Dearden is best known among film buffs, however, for directing *The Smallest Show On Earth* (1958), a gentle paean to cinema and to English eccentricity, which he followed with the amusing heist caper *The League Of Gentlemen* (1960) and the less amusing *Khartoum* (1966), in which **Laurence Olivier** did his notorious turn as the Mahdi, masquerading as Othello, masquerading as Richard III.

Other Key Films: *The Captive Heart* (1946); *Saraband For Dead Lovers* (1948); *The Blue Lamp* (1949); *The Ship That Died Of Shame* (1955); *The Secret Partner* (1961); *Woman Of Straw* (1963); *The Man Who Haunted Himself* (1970)

Decaë, Henri

Brilliant French cinematographer renowned for his naturalistic photography on such key French **New Wave** films as **Louis Malle's** *Ascenseur Pour L'Echafaud* (1958) and *Les Amants* (1958), **Claude Chabrol's** *Le Beau Serge* (1958) and *Les Cousins* (1958) (one hell of a run for a single year!) and **François Truffaut's** *Les Quatre Cents Coups* (1959). Decaë's later films were more commercial, less exploratory, and include Anatole Litvak's pleasantly quirky *The Night Of The Generals* (1967) and Franklin Schaffner's really rather turgid *The Boys From Brazil* (1978).

Other Key Films: **René Clément's** *Plein Soleil* (1960); Serge Bourguignon's *Sundays And Cybele* (1962); Gérard Oury's *Le Corniaud* (1965); Louis Malle's *Viva Maria* (1965); Sydney Pollack's *Bobby Deerfield* (1977); Georges Lautner's *Le Professionel* (1981); Georges Lautner's *Attention! Une Femme Peut En Cacher Une Autre* (1983); Gérard Oury's *La Vengeance Du Serpent À Plumes* (1984)

De Funès, Louis

Outstanding French comedian who specialized in demented, short-tempered, and accident-prone little men, De Funès worked particularly well with **Bourvil** as his calmer, more bovine partner, most notably in Gérard Oury's *Le Corniaud* (1964) and *La Grande Vadrouille* (1966), two films which enjoyed a spectacular success throughout the Francophone nations in the late 1960s.

Other Key Films: *La Tentation De Barbizon* (1946); *Capitaine Pantoufle* (1953); *La Belle Américaine* (1961); *Le Gendarme De St Tropez* (1964); *Oscar* (1967); *Les Aventures De Rabbi Jacob* (1973); *La Zizanie* (1978)

De Havilland, Olivia

Now best known for her longstanding feud with sister **Joan Fontaine** and for being the real-life object of **Errol Flynn's** attentions (she was the only one that got away), De Havilland was one of the few stars who ever bested the Hollywood studio system, winning a ground-breaking court case against Warner's. Squeaky-clean and saintly as Melanie in **Victor Fleming's** *Gone with The Wind* (1939), she proved that she could really act in Anatole Litvak's *The Snake Pit* (1948), and in **William Wyler's** *The Heiress* (1949), for both of which she won well-deserved Oscars.

Other Key Films: *Anthony Adverse* (1936); *The Charge of the Light Brigade* (1936); *The Adventures Of Robin Hood* (1939); *The Private Lives Of Elizabeth And Essex* (1938); *Hold Back The Dawn* (1941); *The Dark Mirror* (1946); *My Cousin Rachel* (1952); *Hush…Hush Sweet Charlotte* (1965)

Delerue, Georges

An extraordinarily successful film composer, and one whom a remarkable array of top directors trusted to fulfil even their most outrageous wishes, Delerue's haunting scores have graced such seminal films as **Alain Resnais's** *Hiroshima Mon Amour* (1959), **François Truffaut's** *Shoot The Piano Player* [*Tirez Sur Le Pianiste*] (1960) and *Jules Et Jim* (1962), **Jean-Luc Godard's** *Le Mépris* (1963), **Ken Russell's** *Women In Love* (1969), **Bernardo Bertolucci's** *The Conformist* (1970) and **Oliver Stone's** *Platoon* (1986). Very few other film composers can remotely challenge his record.

Other Key Films: François Truffaut's *La Peau Douce* (1964); Philippe De Broca's *King Of Hearts* (1966); **Fred Zinnemann's** *A Man For All Seasons* (1966) and *The Day Of The Jackal* (1974); Herbert Ross's *Steel Magnolias* (1989); **Bruce Beresford's** *Mister Johnson* (1990); Pierre Schoendorffer's *Diên Biên Phu* (1992); Jean-Claude Brisseau's *Céline* (1992)

Delli Colli, Tonino

Master cinematographer and photographer of choice for **Sergio Leone** in both *The Good, The Bad, And The Ugly* (1966) and his masterpiece, *Once Upon A Time In The West* (1968), Delli Colli also shot *Pigsty* (1969), *The Decameron* (1971) and *The Canterbury Tales* (1972) for **Pier Paolo Pasolini**, as well as **Louis Malle's** magnificent and still underrated *Lacombe Lucien* (1973), the single best feature film ever made about French collaboration during the Second World War.

Other Key Films: Pier Paolo Pasolini's *The Gospel According To St Matthew* (1964) and *Salo 120 Days Of Sodom* (1975); Marco Ferreri's *Tales Of Ordinary Madness* (1981); Sergio Leone's *Once Upon A Time In America* (1984); **Federico Fellini's** *Ginger And Fred* (1985); **Jean-Jacques Annaud's** *The Name Of The Rose* (1986); **Roman Polanski's** *Bitter Moon* (1992) & *Death And The Maiden* (1994); Roberto Benigni's *Life Is Beautiful* (1997)

Delon, Alain

Although sometimes known to curse his good looks ('I am an actor!' he has been heard to say, in weaker moments) Delon owes his career to them, and it is a somewhat surprising fact that he has never managed to seduce audiences across the

Atlantic in the same way that he has seduced those of his native France. He was a very good screen Ripley in **René Clément's** superb thriller *Plein Soleil* (1960) [though it is only fair to mention that **Matt Damon** was equally good, forty years later, in **Anthony Minghella's** *The Talented Mr Ripley* (1999)], but Delon really comes into his own playing cold, marginalised characters, such as the hit-man in **Jean-Pierre Melville's** *Le Samouraï* (1967), and the corrupt art-dealer in **Joseph Losey's** *Monsieur Klein* (1975).

Other Key Films: *Rocco And His Brothers* (1960); *L'Eclisse* (1962); *The Leopard* (1963); *Borsalino* (1970); *Un Flic* (1972); *Red Sun* (1971); *Le Choc* (1982); *Swann In Love* (1984); *Le Jour Et La Nuit* (1997); *Les Acteurs* (2000)

Del Rio, Dolores

A gorgeous and extremely talented Mexican actress who got fed up with being typecast as exotic plunder in films such as Thornton Freeland's *Flying Down To Rio* (1933) and **Lloyd Bacon's** *Wonder Bar* (1934), Del Rio threw up Hollywood in 1943 and returned to her native land where she constructed a second, and critically far more successful career, in such masterpieces as **Emilio Fernández's** *Flor Silvestre* (1943) and *Maria Candelaria* (1943) [see **Gabriel Figueroa**], only occasionally returning across the border to work for more enlightened gringo directors such as **John Ford**, in *The Fugitive* (1947).

Other Key Films: *Bird Of Paradise* (1932); *In Caliente* (1935); *Journey Into Fear* (1942); *Bugambilia* (1944); *La Otra* (1946); *Historia De Una Mala Mujer* (1948); *Cheyenne Autumn* (1964); *The Children Of Sanchez* (1978)

De Mille, Cecil B.

Somewhat underrated now thanks to the false perception that all he ever did was to marshal gigantic numbers of men and women and even more gigantic sets to fulfil his megalomaniacal aims, De Mille tapped into a puritanical (call it Christian nonconformist if you like) vein in the US which likes to see and taste what it will, in private, condemn. His films mirrored, in consequence, those twin daemons of popular American culture, money and sex – money, in the enormous sets, the multifarious casts and the top-name actors he brought to the screen, and sex in his commercially astute choice of tableau style biblical and **Western** epics and in such voluptuous and shimmering leading ladies as **Gloria Swanson**, surreally reprised in **Billy Wilder's** *Sunset Boulevard* (1950); **Claudette Colbert**, in her famous naked bath in ass's milk in *The Sign Of The Cross* (1932) and the carpet-rolling episode in *Cleopatra* (1934); and last but not least **Hedy Lamarr**, the memory of whose naked swim in Gustav Machaty's *Ecstasy* (1933) imbued each and every lubricious frame of *Samson And Delilah* (1949).

Other Key Films: *The Squaw Man* (1913); *The Girl Of The Golden West* (1915); *The Woman God Forgot* (1917); *The Squaw Man* [remake] (1918); *The Ten Commandments* (1923); *The King Of Kings* (1927); *Madame Satan* (1930); *The Plainsman* (1937); *Union Pacific* (1939); *Reap The Wild Wind* (1942); *The Greatest Show On Earth* (1952); *The Ten Commandments* [remake] (1956)

Demme, Jonathan

A former exploitation director who seemed only to benefit from his experiences directing such cult classics as *Caged Heat* (1974) [a more intelligent film than the name, or the women's prison subject matter would at first glance suggest] Demme has also made *Cousin Bobby* (1991) a brilliant portrait of his fundamentalist cousin, the Rev. Robert Castle, and the riveting *Silence Of The Lambs* (1991), in which he both revealed and transcended his exploitation movie background. That rare thing, a mainstream director who can still stimulate and surprise his audience, Demme was also responsible for *Swimming To Cambodia* (1987), a semi-documentary in which oddball commentator Spalding Gray sounds off, in his enlightened, reactionary way, about life, films, and the absurdities inherent in being an American journalist on the razz in a country which literally massacred itself.

Other Key Films: *Crazy Mama* (1975); *Melvin And Howard* (1980); *Something Wild* (1986); *Married To The Mob* (1988); *Philadelphia* (1993); *Beloved* (1998); *The Manchurian Candidate* (2004)

Catherine Deneuve in
Le Vice et la Vertu (Vice
and Virtue), directed by
Roger Vadim (1962).

*Gaumont/Trianon/Ultra/
The Kobal Collection*

Deneuve, Catherine

Glacially beautiful star of **Roman Polanski's** *Repulsion* (1965) and **Luis Buñuel's** *Tristana* (1970), and never afraid of a challenge, Deneuve has become something of a French icon in recent years, retaining her elegant and sexually enticing good looks well into middle age. Erstwhile wife of photographer David Bailey, and mistress of **Roger Vadim** and **Marcello Mastroianni**, Deneuve's most famous role was that of the bored but loving housewife who took to dabbling at prostitution during the long afternoons, in Buñuel's recently reissued *Belle De Jour* (1967). After a quiet period in the early 1980s, Deneuve's career took a sudden turn for the better – if one ignores Manoel de Oliviera's appalling clinker *The Convent* (1995) – with well-received performances in **André Techiné's** *Ma Saison Preferée* (1992) and its follow-up, *Les Voleurs* (1996).

Other Key Films: *Les Parapluies De Cherbourg* (1964); *Les Demoiselles De Rochefort*

(1967); *Tristana* (1970); *The Last Métro* (1980); *The Hunger* (1983); *Indochine* (1992) *L'Inconnu* (1996); *Belle Maman* (1999); *Le Temps Retrouvé* (1999); *The Last Napoleon* (1999); *Dancer In The Dark* (2000); 8 *Femmes* (2002); *Um Filme Falado* (2003); *Rois Et Reines* (2004); *The Stone Council* (2006)

Key Line: 'Sexuality is such a part of life, but sexuality in the movies – I have a hard time finding it.' [Deneuve on sex]

De Niro, Robert

After a stint emoting at the Actor's Studio, De Niro got good notices for his part in the otherwise awful **Roger Corman** flick, *Bloody Mama* (1970), and this indirectly led to him being cast in John Hancock's magnificent *Bang The Drum Slowly* (1973), in which his real potential showed through for the first time. **Martin Scorsese's** *Mean Streets* (1973) cemented his reputation, and De Niro's filmography now reads like a guided tour through the late twentieth century Cinematic Hall of Fame. To be fair, De Niro has made his share of turkeys, but he has also saved such otherwise shaky vehicles as **Elia Kazan's** *The Last Tycoon* (1977) and Scorsese's *New York, New York* (1977). His least mannered performances, and the ones in which he showed a real potential for humour, came in Martin Brest's *Midnight Run* (1988) and John McNaughton's *Mad Dog And Glory* (1992), but he is destined to be remembered, above all, for the roles of Vito Corleone in **Francis Ford Coppola's** *The Godfather Part II* (1974), and of the grotesquely alienated Travis Bickle, in Scorsese's *Taxi Driver* (1976).

Other Key Films: *1900* (1977); *The Deer Hunter* (1978); *Raging Bull* (1980); *Once Upon A Time In America* (1984); *The Mission* (1986); *Jacknife* (1989); *Awakenings* (1990); *GoodFellas* (1990); *Cape Fear* (1991); *Heat* (1995); *Ronin* (1998); *Analyze This* (1999); *Flawless* (1999); *Meet The Parents* (2000); *15 Minutes* (2001); *The Score* (2001); *Meet The Fockers* (2004); *Hide And Seek* (2005); *The Good Shepherd* (2006)

De Palma, Brian

De Palma is a pretty shrewd operator – one has only to look at the steady progress of his career to realise that he's forced Hollywood to take him on his own merits rather than having Hollywood's foisted upon him. A Hitchcock devotee, De Palma's first real success came with *Sisters* (1973), but this effective little movie was totally eclipsed by *Carrie* (1976) three years later, which was also notable for an early appearance by **John Travolta** receiving what proved to be a particularly costly blow-job from gorgeous Nancy Allen, while attempting to drive her home in his car (no mobile phones in those days). De Palma's first dedicated blockbuster was *The Untouchables* (1987), a first-class action movie, intelligently directed, and this was followed, in quality if not in chronological order, by the underrated *Carlito's Way* (1993). De Palma then touched stratospheric heights with the absurd but enjoyable *Mission: Impossible* (1995), which grossed a stupendous $475 million at the box office coincidentally netting its producer and star, **Tom Cruise**, a cool $100 million in the process. In the final analysis, De Palma is an interesting and skilful director, well versed in film lore and movie history, and something of a welcome throwback to an earlier age of eclectic studio directors.

Other Key Films: *Greetings* (1968); *The Wedding Party* (1969); *Hi Mom!* (1970); *Phantom Of The Paradise* (1974); *The Fury* (1978); *Dressed To Kill* (1980); *Blow Out* (1981); *Scarface* (1983); *Body Double* (1984); *Wise Guys* (1986); *Casualties Of War* (1989); *Raising Cain* (1992); *Snakes Eyes* (1998); *Mission To Mars* (2000); *Femme Fatale* (2002); *The Black Dahlia* (2006)

Depardieu, Gérard

Depardieu is a true force of nature (something reflected in his wildly fluctuating weight and girth) and for twenty years, between 1974 and 1994, he was France's most successful and hard-working screen actor. He has something of **Jean Gabin's** skill in depicting simple yet sensitive men who can rise to every occasion, but he has far more of an acting span than Gabin – which is not to say that his is a greater or more effective screen presence – for Depardieu falls more readily into the *Acteur De Composition* range rather than that of the glitzier *Monstre Sacré* which Gabin inhabited so triumphantly. Depardieu's greatest role came late, with **Jean-Paul Rappeneau's** *Cyrano De Bergerac* (1990), a part that lay in waiting for him and which only someone with his acquired capacity for spouting Alexandrines could even have attempted. An international star despite (or perhaps because of?) his endearing incapacity to learn an acceptable standard of English, Depardieu regularly throws caution to the winds both in his everyday life and in his acting, and as such should be cherished over the safer, more boring stars that are spewed up so regularly and so unimaginatively from *outre-mer*.

Other Key Films: *Les Valseuses* (1974); *Maîtresse* (1975); *Baxter – Vera Baxter* (1977); *Le Camion* (1977); *Les Chiens* (1979); *Le Dernier Métro* (1980); *Mon Oncle D'Amérique* (1980); *Loulou* (1980); *The Return Of Martin Guerre* (1982); *Danton* (1983); *Jean De Florette* (1986); *Sous Le Soleil De Satan* (1987); *Camille Claudel* (1988); *Trop Belle Pour Toi* (1989); *Tous Les Matins Du Monde* (1992); *Le Colonel Chabert* (1994); *The Man In The Iron Mask* (1998); *The Bridge* (1999); *Vatel* (2000); *102 Dalmatians* (2000); *Le Placard* (2000); *Concorrenza Sleale* (2001); *Vidocq* (2001); *36 Quai Des Orfèvres* (2004); *Olé* (2005); *Quand J'Étais Chanteur* (2006)

Depp, Johnny

Something of an iconoclast, Depp has always tried to go his own way in movies while still retaining a wary speculator's eye on the main chance. Following TV success with *21 Jump Street* and a minor part in **Oliver Stone's** *Platoon* (1986), Depp hit the big-time with the title role in **Tim Burton's** *Edward Scissorhands* (1990), which unfortunately eclipsed a far better film he made in the same year, **John Waters's** *Cry-Baby* (1990), whose heady and imaginative mix of music and the grotesque has ensured it long-lasting cult success in such enlightened movie-going countries as France. Depp showed us he could act both in Lasse Hallström's quirky and enjoyable *What's Eating Gilbert Grape* (1993) and in Burton's *Ed Wood* (1994), and he seems to be that rare thing, an actor who is equally as popular with European art-house audiences as he is with American mainstreamers. <u>Note For Film Buffs</u>: 'Depp' means idiot in colloquial German.

Other Key Films: *American Dreamers* (1992); *Don Juan DeMarco* (1995); *Dead Man* (1996); *Donnie Brasco* (1997); *Sleepy Hollow* (1999); *The Ninth Gate* (2000); *Chocolat* (2000); *Blow* (2001); *Pirates Of The Caribbean* (2003); *Finding Neverland* (2004); *The Libertine* (2004); *Charlie And The Chocolate Factory* (2005); *Pirates Of The Caribbean: Dead Man's Chest* (2006)

Key Line: 'I don't want to be stared at while I'm mowing my lawn. I want to wake up and wander in my yard nude, or dressed as Abe Lincoln if I feel like it.' [Depp on the price of fame]

Deren, Maya

A genuinely innovative avant-garde filmmaker, Deren collaborated, with her Czech cinematographer husband Alexander Hammid, on the dense, surrealistic eighteen-minute short, *Meshes In The Afternoon* (1943), which still retains its power to surprise and seduce to this day. Obsessed with magic, myth and symbolic movement, Deren was moving towards a sequence of increasingly abstract structures when she fell prey to a brain haemorrhage at the tragically early age of forty-four.

Other Key Films: *Ritual In Transfigured Time* (1949); *Meditation In Violence* (1953)

De Sica, Vittorio

A former romantic actor turned director (although he still acted on occasion to fund his other ventures), De Sica was that most Italian of creatures, a man who saw nothing strange in spanning three or even four different genres throughout his career, varying from the avant-garde to the blatantly commercial. A founder member of the neo-realist school with his extraordinary *Bicycle Thieves* (1948), De Sica gradually returned to the sort of mainstream films in which he had begun his career, with *Stazione Termini* [*Indiscretion Of An American Wife*] (1954) and *Two Women* (1960). He reverted briefly and belatedly to the art cinema form with the lush and haunting *The Garden Of The Finzi-Continis* (1971), which he completed just three years before his death, proving, in the process, that he had lost nothing of his consummate and golden touch behind the camera.

Other Key Films: *Shoeshine* (1946); *Miracle In Milan* (1951); *Umberto D* (1952); *L'Oro Di Napoli* (1954); *Marriage, Italian Style* (1964); *After The Fox* (1966); *Una Breva Vacanza* (1973); *The Journey* (1974)

Best Detective Films

Harold Becker's *Sea Of Love* (1988); **Henri-Georges Clouzot's** *L'Assassin Habite Au 21* (1942) and *Quai Des Orfèvres* (1947); **Howard Hawks's** *The Big Sleep* (1946); Bruce Humberstone's *I Wake Up Screaming* (1942); **John Huston's** *The Maltese Falcon* (1941); **Fritz Lang's** *The Big Heat* (1953); **Joseph H Lewis's** *So Dark The Night* (1946); Claude Miller's *Mortelle Randonnée* (1982); **Alan Pakula's** *Klute* (1971); **Alan Parker's** *Angel Heart* (1987); **Otto Preminger's** *Laura* (1944); Richard Quine's *Pushover* (1954); **Carol Reed's** *The Fallen Idol* (1947); Dick Richards's *Farewell, My Lovely* (1975); Franco Rosi's *Cadavres Exquis* (1975); **Ridley Scott's** *Blade Runner* (1982); Bryan Singer's *The Usual Suspects* (1995); W S Van Dyke's *The Thin Man* (1934); **Orson Welles's** *Touch Of Evil* (1958); **Billy Wilder's** *The Private Life Of Sherlock Holmes* (1970); **William Wyler's** *Detective Story* (1951)

DeVito, Danny

A diminutive but important player in the Hollywood ball game, DeVito first came to the viewing public's attention playing one of **Jack Nicholson's** bewildered fellow asylum inmates in **Milos Forman's** *One Flew Over The Cuckoo's Nest* (1975). He went on to star in TV's successful *Taxi* series (1978-1983), and from there to directing, with *Throw Momma From The Train* (1987), *The War Of The Roses* (1989), *Hoffa* (1992) and *Matilda* (1996). Interspersed with these only occasionally successful films, DeVito has had key parts in Barry Levinson's *Tin Men* (1987), Ivan Reitman's *Twins* (1988), Barry Sonnenfeld's *Get Shorty* (1995) and Curtis Hanson's *L.A. Confidential* (1997), proving both his versatility and his astuteness at manipulating the Hollywood game to his own advantage.

Other Key Films: *Car Wash* (1976); *Terms Of Endearment* (1983); *Romancing The Stone* (1984); *Wise Guys* (1986); *Ruthless People* (1986); *Batman Returns* (1992); *Junior* (1994); *Mars Attacks* (1996); *The Rainmaker* (1997); *Man On The Moon* (1999); *Drowning Mona* (2000); *Heist* (2001); *Big Fish* (2003); *Even Money* (2006)

Diaz, Cameron

A gorgeous and exotic-looking actress (the happy product, one supposes, of her Cuban, American Indian and Anglo-German ancestry) Diaz first made her mark opposite **Jim Carrey** in Charles Russell's *The Mask* (1994), and consolidated her position as sex symbol of the 1990s and teenage heart-throb, with Jim Wilson's *Head Above Water* (1997) and P J Hogan's *My Best Friend's Wedding* (1997). Her recent success in Spike Jonze's *Being John Malkovich* (1999) will have done nothing whatsoever to stunt her lucrative career growth.

Other Key Films: *Feeling Minnesota* (1996); *She's The One* (1996); *A Life Less Ordinary* (1997); *There's Something About Mary* (1998), *Charlie's Angels* (2000); *The Invisible Circus* (2001); *Vanilla Sky* (2001); *Gangs Of New York* (2001); *In Her Shoes* (2005); *The Holiday* (2006)

DiCaprio, Leonardo

Still remarkably young (he was born in 1974) for the position he has won for himself, DiCaprio is a canny operator who has made the most of his carefully chosen roles and looks set to continue the miraculous run he started with Baz Luhrmann's *Romeo And Juliet* (1996), **James Cameron's** *Titanic* (1997) and Randall Wallace's *The Man In The Iron Mask* (1998), despite the blip in his rise through the stratosphere created by Danny Boyle's clinker *The Beach* (2000). DiCaprio is so newsworthy, however, that even a relative failure like that is barely perceived as such by the popular press, and his largely female fans are likely to continue their worship until a similar, younger version of their hero comes mincing along. Rather surprisingly, DiCaprio *can* act, as he once showed to good advantage in his excellent turn as the brain-damaged Arnie Grape in Lasse Hallström's *What's Eating Gilbert Grape?* (1993), and as he more recently showed in **Martin Scorsese's** *The Aviator* (2004), in which he played an elegantly paranoiac Howard Hughes.

Other Key Films: *Critters 3* (1991); *Poison Ivy* (1992); *This Boy's Life* (1993); *The Basketball Diaries* (1995); *A Hundred And One Nights* (1995); *The Quick And The Dead* (1995); *Total Eclipse* (1995); *Marvin's Room* (1996); *Gangs Of New York* (2002); *Catch Me If You Can* (2002); *The Departed* (2006)

Dickinson, Angie

There was something unbelievably sexy about Angie Dickinson, and her sex appeal proved enough to secure her numerous parts in films of which better actresses could only dream. But overt sex appeal is no small thing in the movies – in fact it's an art in itself – and Dickinson deserves considerable credit for refining it in such a luridly enticing way. Her best film was **Howard Hawks's** *Rio Bravo* (1959) in which, while seeming to subsume herself within the star egos that surrounded her, she cannily contrived to remain in the memory even when the film was over and the gunplay complete. More good roles came with **Don Siegel's** *The Killers* (1964) and **John Boorman's** *Point Blank* (1967), in both of which she played, very effectively, women on the edge of their tether and not a little out of their depth. Finally, in **Brian De Palma's** *Dressed To Kill* (1980) (made when she was perilously close to 50), Angie knocked her younger rivals into a cocked hat in terms of her almost palpable lubricity.

Other Key Films: *China Gate* (1958); *The Bramble Bush* (1960); *Ocean's 11* (1960); *The Sins Of Rachel Cade* (1961); *The Chase* (1966); *Cast A Giant Shadow* (1966); *Big Bad Mama* (1974); *Even Cowgirls Get The Blues* (1994); *Sabrina* (1995); *Pay It Forward* (2000); *Big Bad Love* (2001); *Ocean's Eleven* (2001)

Dickinson, Thorold

A much-respected director and cinema theoretician who sadly gave up making films in mid-career, Dickinson directed both the atmospheric *Gaslight* (1940), and the beautifully designed but uncomfortable to watch *Queen Of Spades* (1948). Football fans (*cinéphiles*, no doubt, to a man) still cherish his now cult-status *The Arsenal Stadium Mystery* (1940). Dickinson's true importance to cinema, however, lies in his chairmanship of the British Film Academy (1952-1953), and his presidency of the International Federation of Film Societies, in both of which roles he excelled.

Other Key Films: *Next Of Kin* (1942); *Secret People* (1952); *Hill 24 Doesn't Answer* (1955)

Dieterle, William

A former silent era actor who, astonishingly, played a bit role in **F W Murnau's** *Faust* (1926), Dieterle made a niche for himself directing such luxury biopics as *Juarez* (1939) and the excellent *Dr Ehrlich's Magic Bullet* (1940), before he discovered where his real talent lay and branched out into romantic melodramas with *Love Letters* (1945) and the haunting *Portrait Of Jennie* (1948). His best films came earlier,

Marlene Dietrich.
The Kobal Collection

however, with *The Last Flight* (1931), *The Hunchback Of Notre Dame* (1939), and *The Devil And Daniel Webster* (1941) [a.k.a. *All That Money Can Buy*]. A committed anti-fascist, Dieterle was yet another director who fell foul of Senator Joe McCarthy's 1947-1957 House Committee On Un-American Activities (HUAC), and he never really recovered from the deeply unfair blow to his reputation that McCarthy's witch-hunters fomented on him.

Other Key Films: *A Midsummer Night's Dream* (1935); *Another Dawn* (1937); *Blockade* (1938); *Tennessee Johnson* (1941); *Dark City* (1950)

Dietrich, Marlene

Fêted in Hollywood after the release of **Josef von Sternberg's** *The Blue Angel* (1930), the bisexual Dietrich went on to enjoy a near fifty-year career on stage and screen. Held in high esteem for her bravely declared anti-Nazi sympathies during the second World War (she was affectionately nicknamed 'The Kraut' by her friend Ernest Hemingway), she starred in more than thirty films, of which seven were directed by von Sternberg, her most obsessive fan, whose wife eventually divorced him after citing the cross-dressing Dietrich for having 'alienated her husband's affections'. The high-point of her career came in von Sternberg's *Shanghai Express* (1932) in which the director perfectly encapsulated Dietrich's beauty and the mystery of her allure – for she seemed at one and the same time visually available, yet materially unattainable – whilst making a virtue of her voice and her highly-accented English through the heightened use of slowed down, abbreviated, and brilliantly mannered dialogue. When her film roles eventually began to dry up, Dietrich skilfully recreated herself [remember the lesbian kiss in von Sternberg's *Blonde Venus* (1932)?] as a *chanteuse* throughout Europe and the Americas. Note for Film Buffs: watch out for a sensational Dietrich performance opposite a top-form **Robert Donat** in Jacques Feyder's rarely-screened *Knight Without Armour* (1937).

Other Key Films: *Morocco* (1930); *Dishonored* (1931); *The Scarlet Empress* (1934); *The Devil Is A Woman* (1935); *Desire* (1936); *Angel* (1937); *Destry Rides Again* (1939); *Stage Fright* (1950); *No Highway* (1951); *A Touch Of Evil* (1958); *Judgement At Nuremberg* (1961)

Key Line: 'It took more than one man to change my name to Shanghai Lily.' [*Shanghai Express*]

Di Palma, Carlo

A first-rate director of photography who added his own distinctive visual voice to **Michelangelo Antonioni's** films, most notably in *Red Desert* (1964) and *Blow-Up* (1966), Di Palma later went on to become one of **Woody Allen's** preferred cinematographers in *Hannah And Her Sisters* (1986), the sublime *Radio Days* (1987), *Husbands And Wives* (1992) and *Mighty Aphrodite* (1995), amongst others. Somewhat surprisingly, given his artistic track record, Di Palma also shot **Brian De Palma's** [no relation] *Mission: Impossible* (1996).

Other Key Films: *Omicron* (1963); *I Tre Volti* (1965); *The Appointment* (1969); *Tragedy Of A Ridiculous Man* (1981); *Identification Of A Woman* (1982); *The Secret Of My Success* (1987); *Manhattan Murder Mystery* (1993); *Everyone Says I Love You* (1996); *Deconstructing Harry* (1997)

Disney, Walt

Creator of Mickey Mouse, Donald Duck, Goofy and Pluto, the mercurial Disney was also responsible for such ground-breaking animated cartoons as *Snow White And The*

Seven Dwarfs (1937) and *Fantasia* (1940). His jealously guarded trade name has since become synonymous with squeaky-clean family entertainment and a multi-billion dollar entertainment industry legacy that includes numerous theme parks and film production companies; but what Disney really achieved, and what the company that bears his name has so singularly failed to do in the decades since his death in 1966, was to tap into popular culture while still retaining the archetypal power of the original, often literary, idea. Whereas the loss of Bambi's mother, in *Bambi* (1942), would now be portrayed as a maudlin, mock-sentimental farce, in the original *Bambi* Disney refused to sentimentalise the lot of animals and showed the loss as merely part of the natural order of things, thus infinitely magnifying its power – more, as Hollywood still resolutely refuses to acknowledge, is not necessarily better. Disney was a true master who correctly identified the need both for enlightened sentiment in popular culture and for something to bridge the gap between the adult and the child's world, and who then went on to triumphantly fill that gap with his animated films. Note For Film Buffs: A delightful urban myth [à la **Orson Welles's** *The Immortal Story* (1968)] has been making the rounds for many years that the notionally American-as-apple-pie Disney was in fact born in Mojacar, Spain, and dubbed 'Waldo' by his doctor father and village washerwoman mother – nothing can be proved, however, as all records were lost during the Spanish Civil War. It might be apposite to mention here that apple pie is actually an English invention, dating back to the time of William Chaucer, and has no relation whatsoever to its cheeky American attribution.

Other Key Films: *Pinocchio* (1940); *Dumbo* (1940); *Cinderella* (1950); *Alice In Wonderland* (1951); *Peter Pan* (1953); *The Living Desert* (1953); *Old Yeller* (1958); *Sleeping Beauty* (1959); *The Swiss Family Robinson* (1960); *101 Dalmatians* (1961); *The Incredible Journey* (1963); *Mary Poppins* (1964); *The Jungle Book* (1967)

Key Line: 'Fancy being remembered around the world for the invention of a mouse!' [Disney on his deathbed]

Di Venanzo, Gianni

Before **Carlo Di Palma** (in director **Michelangelo Antonioni's** life) came Di Venanzo, a master cinematographer who contributed greatly to the almost hypnotic visual effect exerted by the last two parts of Antonioni's brilliant trilogy, *La Notte* (1961) and *L'Eclisse* (1962). Di Venanzo also lit and photographed **Joseph Losey's** otherwise vicariously disappointing and wantonly perverse *Eva* (1962), **Federico Fellini's** masterpiece *8 1/2* (1963), and the same director's underrated *Juliet Of The Spirits* (1965). A brilliant and instinctive photographer, Di Venanzo looked set fair, before his untimely death in 1966 at the age of forty-five, to become a key player in the Italian Renaissance of the 1960 and early 1970s.

Other Key Films: *Il Grido* (1958); *Salvatore Giuliano* (1962); *Le Mani Sulla Città* (1963); *Gli Indifferenti* (1964); *Il Momento Della Verità* (1965); *La Decima Victima* (1965)

Dmytryk, Edward

Dmytryk, one of the original Hollywood Ten, fell foul of the House Un-American Activities Committee (what outrageous nomenclature – a worthy precursor to the modern-day scourge of political correctness in its grotesque ersatz logic) in 1947, and ended up, before he recanted, with a brief blacklisting. His career followed a similar pattern. He directed a trilogy of tight little thrillers in the 1940s, notable for their tough dialogue, enlightened use of location filming, and expressionistic camerawork, – *Murder My Sweet* [*Farewell My Lovely*] (1945), *Cornered* (1945) and *Crossfire* (1947). He then recanted, just as he had done before the HUAC. His remaining work varied wildly, with belated highpoints occurring in *The Caine Mutiny* (1954), *The Young Lions* (1958) and *Warlock* (1959), although all these later films manifested a rather sorry looseness when compared to the tight, lowly budgeted gems that preceded them. **Other Key Films**: *Hitler's Children* (1943); *Tender Comrade* (1944); *Till The End Of Time* (1946); *The Sniper* (1952); *Broken Lance* (1954); *The End Of The Affair* (1954); *Soldier Of Fortune* (1955); *The Left Hand Of God* (1955); *Mirage* (1965); *Shalako* (1968)

Best Documentary Films

Donald Brittain and John Kramer's *Volcano: An Inquiry Into The Life And Death Of Malcolm Lowry* (1976); **Henri-Georges Clouzot's** *Le Mystère Picasso* (1955); **Robert Flaherty's** *Nanook Of The North* (1923) and *Man Of Aran* (1934); **Georges Franju's** *Le Sang Des Bêtes* (1948); Kon Ichikawa's *Tokyo Olympiad* (1966); **F W Murnau** and Robert Flaherty's *Tabu* (1931); Marcel Ophüls's *Le Chagrin Et La Pitié* [*The Sorrow And The Pity*] (1969) and *Hotel Terminus* (1988); **Alain Resnais** and Robert Hessens's *Guernica* (1950) & Resnais's *Nuit Et Brouillard* (1955); **Leni Riefenstahl's** *Olympia Parts 1 & 2* (1938); Georges Rouquier's *Farrebique* (1945); **Jean Vigo's** *A Propos De Nice* (1930)

Donat, Robert

This quintessential and beautifully spoken Englishman was in fact half-Polish, and overcame a stammer and a lifetime of chronic asthma to become one of the most popular and best-loved stars of his generation. A consummate screen actor, Donat imbued every role (and there were, sadly, few) with his own particular brand of playful integrity. Catch him in **Alfred Hitchcock's** *The Thirty-Nine Steps* (1935) or in the wonderful and little seen Jacques Feyder movie, *Knight Without Armour* (1937). Donat died, aged only fifty-three, after having recorded some achingly beautiful readings from his favourite English poets for Argo records.

Other Key Films: *The Private Life of Henry VIII* (1933); *The Count Of Monte Cristo* (1934); *The Ghost Goes West* (1935); *The Citadel* (1938); *Goodbye Mr Chips* (1939); *The Young Mr Pitt* (1942); *The Adventures Of Tartu* (1943); *Perfect Strangers* (1945); *The Winslow Boy* (1948); *The Cure For Love* (1949); *The Magic Box* (1951); *Lease Of Life* (1954); *The Inn Of The Sixth Happiness* (1958)

Donen, Stanley

One of the greats of the Hollywood musical (whatever one may think of the genre in terms of its extrinsic relevance), **Gene Kelly** and Donen's *Singin' In The Rain* (1952) became one of the most successful of all crossovers, and proved that entertainment need not presuppose stupidity on the part of an audience. *Seven Brides For Seven Brothers* (1954) and *Funny Face* (1958), while not threatening the status quo in any profound way, entertained pleasantly and without depth, as did his two comedy thrillers *Charade* (1963) and *Arabesque* (1966) – in fact Donen could be said to encapsulate virtually everything the Soviet Union thought was decadent about the West at the height of the Cold War (something which should endear him to his bewildered crossover audience far more than many of his post-*Singin'* movies). *Two For The Road* (1967) was a delightful late career surprise, and showed the same sharpness of vision which characterized Donen's brilliant early work, *On The Town* (1949), which he co-directed with Gene Kelly.

Other Key Films: *Deep In My Heart* (1954); *It's Always Fair Weather* (1955); *The Pajama Game* (1958); *Indiscreet* (1958); *Staircase* (1969); *Movie Movie* (1978); *Blame It On Rio* (1984)

Dors, Diana

She was intended to be the British National Serviceman's sex symbol during the early part of the 1950s, rather as Betty Grable had been to US draftees during the Second World War, but, apart from a few small successes, Dors's career did not turn out as planned. Surprisingly, twenty-five years before her early death, aged fifty-two, from cancer, Dors (originally Diana Fluck, from Swindon) took off the make-up and the glitz and played against type as Ruth Ellis, the last British woman to be hanged for murder, in J Lee Thompson's *Yield To The Night* (1956). Given the absurd hype surrounding her at the time, the very existence of such an unlikely piece of work in her filmography is something of a miracle – in fact it signalled her increasing desire, especially towards the end of her career, to be regarded as a serious actress.

Other Key Films: *Holiday Camp* (1947); *Oliver Twist* (1948); *Value For Money* (1955); *I Married A Woman* (1958); *On The Double* (1961); *The Sandwich Man* (1966); *Berserk* (1967); *There's A Girl In My Soup* (1970); *Deep End* (1970); *Steaming* (1984)

Douglas, Kirk

Douglas played tough men from the very beginning – he was born Issur Danielovitch of poor Russian immigrant parents, so he knew what it was like to struggle – although through some curious trick of the camera he always appeared considerably taller and broader on screen than he was in real life. Wisely, though, he leavened this toughness with a physical vulnerability and a most up-to-date capacity for angst (whether existential or otherwise is a moot point) and the films in which he succeeds best are those which reflect both sides of his Janus-like nature – the capacity not only to call down the punches on himself, but also to recover from them. Whit Sterling, in **Jacques Tourneur's** *Out Of The Past* [a.k.a. *Build My Gallows High*] (1947), was Douglas's first really juicy role, and he already looked the complete pro he was to remain throughout his astonishing career. It was Douglas, for instance, who gave **Stanley Kubrick** the directing job on *Spartacus* (1960), while cannily retaining the copyright of the film for himself (making it the only film of Kubrick's that was effectively outside the director's control). Douglas was superb at playing loners, and of all the glitzy roles he eventually filled, one remembers best his ageing, iconoclastic modern cowboy, Jack Burns, in David Miller's *Lonely Are The Brave* (1962), doggedly getting into a fight in order to spring his best friend from jail and ending up bowled over by a water-closet-carrying pantechnicon on the concrete highway, his eyes cold as a bird of prey's, and with his dying horse beside him.

Other Key Films: *I Walk Alone* (1948); *A Letter To Three Wives* (1949); *Young Man With A Horn* (1950); *Ace In The Hole* (1951); *Detective Story* (1951); *The Bad And The Beautiful* (1953); *Man Without A Star* (1955); *Lust For Life* (1956); *Gunfight At The O. K. Corral* (1958); *Last Train From Gun Hill* (1959); *Spartacus* (1960); *Seven Days In May* (1964); *The War Wagon* (1967); *The Arrangement* (1969); *Tough Guys* (1986); *Diamonds* (1999); *Illusion* (2004)

Douglas, Michael

Being **Kirk Douglas's** son was always going to be a hard act to follow, and to give him credit, Michael Douglas has made a pretty good stab at it. Power was the stock-in-trade in this family, and Douglas showed early on that he was, in symbolically Freudian terms at least, perfectly prepared to kill his own dad by persuading him (quite rightly as it turned out – for **Jack Nicholson** was born for the part) that he was too old to play the Randle Patrick McMurphy role in **Milos Forman's** *One Flew Over The Cuckoo's Nest* (1975), which the thirty-three-year-old

Michael just happened to be co-producing with **Saul Zaentz**. Never the actor his father was, Douglas has made up for this shortcoming by highlighting his charm, his butt, and his sardonic sense of humour, and his best parts, as Jack Colton, in Robert Zemeckis's *Romancing The Stone* (1984), and as Gordon Gekko, in **Oliver Stone's** *Wall Street* (1987), have used these assets to the full.

Other Key Films: *Coma* (1978); *The China Syndrome* (1979); *Jewel Of The Nile* (1985); *Fatal Attraction* (1987); *Black Rain* (1989); *The War Of The Roses* (1989); *Basic Instinct* (1992); *Falling Down* (1993); *Disclosure* (1994); *The Game* (1997); *A Perfect Murder* (1998); *Wonder Boys* (2000); *Traffic* (2000); *One Night At McCool's* (2001); *Don't Say A Word* (2001); *The Sentinel* (2006)

Key Line: 'Greed – for lack of a better word – is good. Greed is right. Greed works.' [*Wall Street*]

Downey, Robert, Jr.

A perennial bad boy, Downey seems like a flashback to the **Errol Flynn** years of Hollywood, where acting was simply a means to a self-indulgent end, but hardly the end in itself. Downey flits from part to part, sometimes well, sometimes indifferently, with newspaper headlines and probationary terms as half-humorous, half-tragic interstices. He was surprisingly good in Michael Hoffman's *Restoration* (1995), leading one to suppose that perhaps rip-roaring Stuart England, rather than liberal bleeding-heart Hollywood, should have been his natural stamping ground.

Other Key Films: *To Live And Die In L.A.*(1985); *Less Than Zero* (1987); *Chaplin* (1992); *Natural Born Killers* (1994); *Only You* (1994); *Richard III* (1995); *One Night Stand* (1997); *Black And White* (1999); *Wonder Boys* (2000); *The Singing Detective* (2003); *Good Night, And Good Luck* (2005); *A Guide To Recognizing Your Saints* (2006)

Dracula

Filmed more than 150 times to date, Bram Stoker's 1897 novel has tapped into the subconscious of more than five separate generations of filmgoers. Bela Lugosi played him most famously in 1931, but Max Schreck's incarnation of him as *Nosferatu* in the 1922 **F W Murnau** silent film version was far more frightening. Recent Draculas have included **Christopher Lee**, Frank Langella, and **Gary Oldman,** but most impressive of all was the demented **Klaus Kinski** in **Werner Herzog's** *Nosferatu The Vampyre* (1979).

Key Lines:
1. 'There are far worse things facing man than death.' [Lugosi in **Tod Browning's** *Dracula* (1931)]
2. 'For one who has not lived even a single lifetime, you are a wise man, Van Helsing.' [Lugosi (you'll have to imagine the Transylvanian accent) to Edward Van Sloan]

Best Dramas

Marcel Carné's *Hotel Du Nord* (1938); **Carl Dreyer's** *Dies Irae* [*Day Of Wrath*] (1943); Julien Duvivier's *La Fin Du Jour* (1938); **Federico Fellini's** *La Strada* (1954); Jacques Feyder's *La Kermesse Héroïque* (1935); Mike Figgis's *Leaving Las Vegas* (1995); **Georges Franju's** *Thérèse Desqueyroux* (1962); **Howard Hawks's** *Only Angels Have Wings* (1939); **John Huston's** *The Night Of The Iguana* (1964); **Krzysztof Kieslowski's** *The Decalogue* (1989); **Fritz Lang's** *M* (1931); **Charles Laughton's** *The Night Of The Hunter* (1955); **David Lean's** *Great Expectations* (1946); **Joseph L**

Mankiewicz's *All About Eve* (1950); **Kenji Mizoguchi's** *Ugetsu Monogatari* (1953); **Jean Renoir's** *Les Bas-Fonds* (1936); **John Sayles's** *Lone Star* (1995); **John Schlesinger's** *Sunday, Bloody Sunday* (1971); **Josef von Sternberg's** *The Scarlet Empress* (1934); **George Stevens's** *Giant* (1956); Albert Valentin's *Marie-Martine* (1942); **Luchino Visconti's** *Senso* (1954); **Orson Welles's** *Chimes At Midnight* (1966); **William Wellman's** *A Star Is Born* (1937); **Fred Zinnemann's** *From Here To Eternity* (1953)

Dreyer, Carl Theodor

Dreyer is one of that small band of undisputedly great directors (**Abel Gance** is another example) whose films, by some extraordinary oversight, are rarely, if ever, shown outside art theatres and university film clubs. A Dane of Swedish extraction, born illegitimately, and the product of a strictly Lutheran adoptive household following the death of his mother when he was two years old, Dreyer's art reflects the tensions inherent in such an emotionally deprived upbringing, tensions which imbue the sometimes over-fastidious visual and affective quality of his films. It seems extraordinary to us now, but most of Dreyer's films, including the magnificent *The Passion Of Joan Of Arc* (1928), were commercial disasters, and he was viewed with a mixture of distaste and condescension by the mainstream Nordic film community. *Day Of Wrath* (1943), *Ordet* [a.k.a. *The Word*] (1955) and *Gertrud* (1964) are now acknowledged as masterpieces, and it is to be hoped that enlightened Festival Directors and television programmers will one day give both these, and his lesser-known shorts, the belated status they deserve.

Other Key Films: *Leaves From Satan's Book* (1920); *Vampyr* (1932); *Two People* (1945)

Dreyfuss, Richard

He has hit the heights and plumbed the depths, and still Dreyfuss remains a difficult actor to categorize. He brings an intelligence to parts that could easily have been played unintelligently, such as that of oceanographer Matt Hooper in **Steven Spielberg's** *Jaws* (1975), and he shines in light comedies, such as Herbert Ross's *The Goodbye Girl* (1977), without really being a comedian. He was as excellent in Paul Mazursky's *Down And Out In Beverley Hills* (1985), as he was maudlin in Stephen Herek's *Mr Holland's Opus* (1995) – the jury, in the final analysis, must still be considered out.

Other Key Films: *The Apprenticeship Of Duddy Kravitz* (1974); *Close Encounters Of The Third Kind* (1977); *The Big Fix* (1978); *Whose Life Is It Anyway?* (1981); *Stakeout* (1987); *Always* (1989); *Lost In Yonkers* (1993); *Night Falls On Manhattan* (1997); *A Fine And Private Place* (1998); *The Crew* (2000); *Who Is Cletis Tout?* (2001); *Silver City* (2004); *Poseidon* (2006)

Dunaway, Faye

Dunaway's is a fragile talent, best used, paradoxically, by a director – **Roman Polanski**, for instance, in *Chinatown* (1974) – with whom she is temperamentally unsuited. Her face has always been her fortune, and her cold features, which bear an almost Asiatic cast despite her blonde hair and green eyes, have been well utilized by directors as disparate as **Arthur Penn**, in *Bonnie And Clyde* (1967), **Sidney Lumet**, in *Network* (1976), and **Sydney Pollack**, in *Three Days Of The Condor* (1975). Dunaway's best acting role came in **Barbet Schroeder's** underrated *Barfly* (1987), in which she bravely scraped off the paint and the glamour to reveal the soft emotional underside she normally does so much to conceal.

Other Key Films: *The Thomas Crown Affair* (1968); *The Arrangement* (1969); *Little Big Man* (1970); *The Towering Inferno* (1974); *Eyes Of Laura Mars* (1978); *Mommie Dearest* (1981); *The Wicked Lady* (1983); *The Handmaid's Tale* (1990); *Don Juan DeMarco* (1995); *In Praise Of Older Women* (1997); *The Thomas Crown Affair* [remake] (1999); *Messenger: The Story Of Joan Of Arc* (1999); *The Yards* (2000); *Stanley's Gig* (2000); *Last Goodbye* (2004); *Ghosts Never Sleep* (2005); *Cut Off* (2006)

Dunne, Philip

Dunne's extraordinary screenwriting career was defined by quality, wit and a literate sophistication, and his scripts for **John Ford's** *How Green Was My Valley* (1941), **Joseph L Mankiewicz's** *The Ghost And Mrs Muir* (1947) and **Carol Reed's** *The Agony And The Ecstasy* (1965) do a great deal more than merely illustrate that fact. A committed liberal, Dunne was one of the main organizers of the anti-blacklist committee, and his career provides proof, if proof were needed, that the writers of popular movies can and do influence public perceptions and opinions.
Other Key Films: George B Seitz's *The Last Of The Mohicans* (1936); **Henry King's** *Stanley And Livingstone* (1939); **Henry Hathaway's** *Johnny Apollo* (1940); **Elia Kazan's** *Pinky* (1949); Henry Koster's *The Robe* (1953)

Duras, Marguerite

Duras was a literary novelist and doyenne of the *nouveau roman* who contributed, either as a director or screenwriter, to some of the most challenging avant-garde art house films of the past fifty years. Her first cinematic masterpiece was her elusive but ultimately overwhelming script for **Alain Resnais's** brilliant *Hiroshima Mon Amour* (1959). She followed this up with the screenplay (from her own book) for Peter Brooks's highly-charged *Moderato Cantabile* (1964), in which **Jeanne Moreau** suggests the obsessive quality of a Duras heroine better than any other actress either before or since. Preoccupied throughout her life with memories of her childhood in French Indochina, Duras's own directorial efforts were not always as satisfying as her collaborations, and it occasionally seemed as though the very collaborative nature of filmmaking was in some way alien to the essentially solitary state of an artist of her calibre.
Other Key Films: René Clément's *Barrage Contre Le Pacifique* (1958); **Tony Richardson's** *The Sailor From Gibraltar* (1967); *India Song* [dir.] (1975); *Le Camion* [dir.] (1977); *Baxter – Vera Baxter* [dir.] (1977); **Jean-Jacques Annaud's** *The Lover* (1992); Michelle Porte's *L'Après-Midi De Monsieur Andesmas* (2004)

Duvall, Robert

Duvall is a perfectionist and one of the finest of all recent screen actors. From his very first appearance as the retarded 'Boo' Radley in Robert Mulligan's *To Kill A Mockingbird* (1962), it was obvious that Duvall possessed the rare quality of being able to communicate emotion through facial and bodily expression, as well as by more conventional, verbal means. His finest parts have come with Joseph Anthony's unjustly neglected *Tomorrow* (1972) (based on a William Faulkner story) in which Duvall showed his extraordinary capacity for subsuming himself inside a seemingly thankless part and making it sing, and in Randa Haines's *Wrestling Ernest Hemingway* (1993), in which Duvall miraculously transforms himself into the very image of an expatriate Cuban, complete with Guayabera and slicked back hair. His most memorable part came in **Francis Ford Coppola's** *Apocalypse Now* (1979), in which his monstrous but all-too-credible Lt. Col. Kilgore utters his famous napalm line [see

Key Line], a phrase which has now taken on almost mythic proportions to become one of the most memorable lines in the history of movies. Let's be brutally frank – Duvall could play just about any part, however inauspicious it might at first appear, and make it interesting.

Other Key Films: *The Chase* (1966); *True Grit* (1969); *M*A*S*H* (1970); *The Godfather* (1972); *The Outfit* (1973); *The Conversation* (1974); *The Great Santini* (1979); *Tender Mercies* (1983); *The Natural* (1984); *Belizaire The Cajun* (1986); *The Lightship* (1986); *Colors* (1988); *Rambling Rose* (1991); *The Stars Fell On Henrietta* (1995); *Sling Blade* (1996); *The Apostle* (1997); *Deep Impact* (1998); *A Civil Action* (1998); *Gone In 60 Seconds* (2000); *The 6th Day* (2000); *Open Range* (2003); *Kicking & Screaming* (2005); *Lucky You* (2006)

Key Line: 'I love the smell of napalm in the morning. It smells like…victory!' [*Apocalypse Now*]

Dwan, Allan

Dwan was an innovator, devising one of the earliest dolly devices for **D W Griffith**, and he was undoubtedly one of the first pioneers to film from the back of a moving motor vehicle. He directed more than 400 films during his fifty-year career (1911-1961), a career in which he started at the bottom, at Essanay Studios, as a scenario editor, rose to the top, at Paramount and Fox, making such **Gloria Swanson** and **Douglas Fairbanks** vehicles as *The Iron Mask* (1929) and *What A Widow!* (1930), then sank to the bottom again after the coming of sound, with the occasional belated surge back to the surface, with *Frontier Marshal* (1937), *Suez* (1938), *Brewster's Millions* (1945) and *The Sands Of Iwo Jima* (1949). Like many of his contemporaries, he turned to **Westerns** during the 1950s, with considerable success, and the career of this remarkable man finally shuddered to a halt with an excellent *film noir*, *The River's Edge* (1958) (featuring an unmitigatingly evil **Ray Milland**), and an underrated little sci-fi potboiler, *Most Dangerous Man Alive* (1961).

Other Key Films: *The Gold Lust* (1911); *The County Chairman* (1914); *The Dark Star* (1919); *Robin Hood* (1922); *Big Brother* (1923); *Manhandled* (1924); *East Side West Side* (1927); *While Paris Sleeps* (1932); *Heidi* (1937); *Rebecca Of Sunnybrook Farm* (1938); *Rise And Shine* (1941); *Driftwood* (1947); *I Dream Of Jeanie* (1952); *The Queen Of Montana* (1954); *Slightly Scarlet* (1956); *Hold Back The Night* (1956)

Eastwood, Clint

While Eastwood first made his name in **Sergio Leone's** low-budget and ground-breaking trilogy of spaghetti **Westerns**, *A Fistful Of Dollars* (1964), *For A Few Dollars More* (1965) and *The Good, The Bad And The Ugly* (1966), his career since then has proved that it is perfectly possible to be both commercially successful and critically discriminating at one and the same time. Using big-budget movie projects such as mentor **Don Siegel's** *Dirty Harry* (1971) and James Fargo's *Every Which Way But Loose* (1978) to fund his own, rather more esoteric directing projects, Eastwood has played his full part in bringing the American myth, in all its elusive subtlety, to the big screen. With films like Siegel's *The Beguiled* (1971), **Michael Cimino's** *Thunderbolt and Lightfoot* (1974), and his own *The Outlaw Josie Wales* (1976), *Honkytonk Man* (1982), *Unforgiven* (1992), *Mystic River* (2003) and *Million Dollar Baby* (2004), Eastwood has charted the psychological course of the American male (and, in the case of *Million Dollar Baby*, female) better than any other actor/director of his time. During his most commercially lucrative decade, 1974-1984, Eastwood's films grossed a total of $1,400 million.

Other Key Films: *Where Eagles Dare* (1969); *Play Misty For Me* [also dir.] (1971); *High Plains Drifter* [also dir.] (1973); *Escape From Alcatraz* (1979); *Tightrope* (1984); *Pale Rider* [also dir.] (1985); *Bird* [dir.] (1988); *A Perfect World* [also dir.] (1993); *The Bridges Of Madison County* [also dir.] (1995); *Absolute Power* [also dir.] (1997); *True Crime* [also dir.] (1999); *Space Cowboys* [also dir.] (2000); *Blood Work* [also dir.] (2002); *Flags Of Our Fathers* [dir.] (2006)

Key Line: 'Go ahead, make my day.' [Clint Eastwood's *Sudden Impact*]

Easy Rider

Costing a mere $375,000 to make, and raking in a thousand times that over the years, this influential **Road Movie**, directed by **Dennis Hopper** and starring himself, **Peter Fonda** and **Jack Nicholson**, garnered Harvard Lampoon's worst movie award for 1970. Despite its many shortcomings, *Easy Rider* (1969) did a great deal to free up the tide-bound Hollywood system in the 1970s, leading to a brief Second Golden Age of mainstream cinema.

Edison, Thomas Alva

Edison is the man generally credited with being the inventor of motion pictures, but his assistant, W K L Dickson, was the man who actually perfected the machines that were to become Edison's Kinetograph and Kinetoscope. Edison himself considered that the moving picture was simply a novelty, which would soon pall on the paying public, but he had the foresight to take out patents on his two machines in 1892, and to buy the rights to Thomas Armat's projector in 1896, something which proved to be a wise investment when rivals began to use the same technology to make money. In 1908 Edison joined with a number of other film producers to set up The Motion Picture Patents Company, which claimed royalties to the tune of $25,000 a week on any film made using Dickson's technology, only to see the Company's monopoly formally broken, in 1917, following an Antitrust action.

Eisenstein, Sergei

Massively influential in technical terms, and a social propagandist of heroic proportions, Eisenstein made a total of fourteen films in his brief fifty-year lifespan, most of which were either never completed or were hardly ever seen. Obsessed by design to the occasional detriment of humanity, Eisenstein struggled under the tyranny of Soviet bureaucracy as well as from the physical depredations caused by his own fervid lifestyle. His silent masterpiece *Battleship Potemkin* (1925) (and in particular the scene on the Odessa steps) has achieved a strange sort of anthropomorphic immortality, and his finest film, *Alexander Nevsky* (1938), paradoxically (and perversely, given Hitler's abrupt about-turn on the so-called Germano/Soviet alliance) got the filmmaker into serious trouble with Stalin for criticizing the Germans.

Other Key Films: *Strike* (1924); *October* (1928); *Que Viva Mexico* (1932); *Ivan The Terrible Trilogy* (1943-1946)

Epic

The most recent in the sun, sand, sex and sandals field are **Ridley Scott's** *Gladiator* (2000), **Peter Jackson's** *Lord Of The Rings* Trilogy (2001-2003) and **Wolfgang Petersen's** *Troy* (2004), whose lavish spectacle and exotic locations perfectly encapsulate a genre that boasts such distinguished precursors as **Cecil B De Mille's** *The Ten Commandments* (1956) and **Stanley Kubrick's** *Spartacus* (1960). Prerequisites for any epic worth the name is the inclusion of enormous armies of either computerised or run-of-the-mill live extras, a historical setting that allows for numerous pitched battles to take place, and heroic stars with exaggerated muscular or glandular cleavages (depending on sex) – the term 'wide sweep' occurring somewhere in the publicist's blurb also helps.

Best Epics
Bernardo Bertolucci's *1900* (1976) and *The Last Emperor* (1987); Sergei Bondarchuk's *War And Peace* (1967); Mario Camerini's *Ulysses* (1955); **Basil Dearden's** *Khartoum* (1966); **Cecil B DeMille's** *King Of Kings* (1927), *The Sign Of The Cross* (1932), *Samson And Delilah* (1949) and *The Ten Commandments* (1956); **D W Griffith's** *Birth Of A Nation* (1915) and *Intolerance* (1916); **Henry Hathaway**, **John Ford** and George Marshall's *How The West Was Won* (1962); **Howard Hawks's** *Land Of The Pharaohs* (1955); **Peter Jackson's** *Lord Of The Rings* Trilogy (2001-2003); **Chen Kaige's** *The Emperor And The Assassin* (1999); **Akira Kurosawa's** *Kagemusha* (1980); **Stanley Kubrick's** *Spartacus* (1960); **David Lean's** *Lawrence Of Arabia* (1962) and *Doctor Zhivago* (1965); **Anthony Mann's** *El Cid* (1961) and *The Fall Of The Roman Empire* (1964); Fred Niblo's *Ben-Hur* (1925); **Laurence Olivier's** *Henry V* (1944); **Wolfgang Petersen's** *Troy* (2004); **Ridley Scott's** *Gladiator* (2000); **William Wyler's** *Ben-Hur* (1959)

Episodic Film
Particularly popular in 1940s British cinema, episodic films contain two or more separate episodes, often linked by a narrator or contiguous storyline, and requiring one or more directors. The most successful of all is *Dead Of Night* (1945), a truly eerie mandala-like series of ghost stories which boasts **Alberto Cavalcanti**, **Basil Dearden**, **Robert Hamer** and Charles Crichton among its plethora of directing talent.
Other Key Films: D W Griffith's *Intolerance* (1916); Julien Duvivier's *Tales Of Manhattan* (1942); W Somerset Maugham's *Quartet* (1948) and *Trio* (1950); Sidney Cole's *Train Of Events* (1949); **Max Ophüls's** *La Ronde* (1950); **Pier Paolo Pasolini's** *The Canterbury Tales* (1971); Neil Simon's *California Suite* (1978); **Jim Jarmusch's** *Mystery Train* (1989); **Woody Allen**, **Francis Ford Coppola** and **Martin Scorsese's** *New York Stories* (1989)

Epstein, Julius J
Influential co-screenwriter of **Michael Curtiz's** *Casablanca* (1942) and **Frank Capra's** *Arsenic and Old Lace* (1944), Epstein professed himself mystified by *Casablanca*'s success, calling it 'slick shit!'. Always the consummate professional, he had, without knowing it, answered his own question. His screenwriting career spanned fifty years, and men such as he are the unsung heroes of Hollywood.
Other Key Films: Vincent Sherman's *Mr Skeffington* (1944); Charles Walters's *The Tender Trap* (1955); **Sam Peckinpah's** *Cross of Iron* (1977); Robert Ellis Miller's *Reuben, Reuben* (1983)

Erice, Victor
Downbeat and emotionally subtle Spanish director of such luminous masterpieces as *The Spirit Of The Beehive* (1973), *El Sur* (1983) and that punctilious and absorbing paean to artistic creation, *The Quince Tree Sun* (1992), Erice has stayed resolutely clear of Hollywood and all its manifold temptations, and seems content to turn out roughly one exquisite and well-thought out film each decade. His philosophically

inclined filmic meditations move slowly, but reward those with patience enough to follow them through to completion.

Other Key Films: *Los Desafíos* [part only] (1968); *Ten Minutes Older: The Trumpet* [part only] (2002)

Erotic Moments

A random, subjective, but, one hopes, enlightened selection of a few choice erotic moments from the annals of film;

1.   **Samuel Fuller's** *Underworld USA* (1961), when Dolores Dorn sucks on a phallic piece of ice as she is waiting in the park to meet Cliff Robertson. When slowed down on video (as if anyone would do such a thing) Sam Fuller's intention becomes very clear indeed.

2.   **Henri–Georges Clouzot's** *Quai des Orfèvres* (1947), when Suzy Delair, having returned home from a glamour photo session wearing only a fur coat and a basque, reveals herself for her husband, Bertrand Blier, by opening her mouth and her coat to him in unmistakeable invitation (and in swooping close-up). See ***The Outlaw***

3.   **Frank Capra's** *Platinum Blonde* (1931), when the much-lamented Robert Williams asks **Jean Harlow** to close her eyes, and she does so, turning her face up to be kissed in what has to be one of the most astonishingly erotic moments in any film, ever.

4.   **Jean Renoir's** La *Bête Humaine* (1938), in which **Jean Gabin** gives Simone Simon a kiss '*à la cannibale*' – meaning they virtually eat each other. This kiss stands as a perfect symbol for the effect they have on one another during the subsequent course of the film.

5.   The **Ellen Barkin**/**Dennis Quaid** masturbation scene in Jim McBride's *The Big Easy* (1986). What to say? Just watch the movie for a lesson in onscreen erotic chemistry – and Barkin's nose has to be the sexiest in the business.

See also **Best Films**, **Best Titles**, **Heartstopping Moments** and **Worst Films**

Eustache, Jean

There are few men or women who deserve their place in cinema history on the strength of only one film, but Eustache (who died at the age of 43 in 1981) is one of them. His *La Maman Et La Putain* [*The Mother And The Whore*] (1973) is so extraordinary and unique an achievement that it almost beggars belief. On seeing it on its re-release in London in 1998, this author came out of the cinema after 219 of the shortest minutes of his life, convinced, afresh, (as if he ever needed convincing), that cinema, in the right hands, can be one of the greatest, noblest, and most subversively illuminating of all art forms.

Other Key Films: Les *Mauvaises Fréquentations* (1967); *Mes Petites Amoureuses* (1975)

Expressionism

Inflamed by the ideas of Freud and exacerbated by the horrors of the First World War, Expressionism took early root in German filmmaking, culminating in a remarkable series of films made during the 1920s in which exterior architecture was seen as a mirror to the interior world – twisted staircases, wildly disproportionate buildings and streets, dark shadows, and a gruesome concentration on the freakish and the macabre became, for a brief while, German cinema's stock-in-trade. Directors such as **Fritz Lang**, **F W Murnau** and **G W Pabst** are Expressionism's best-known adherents, but less well-known directors such as Paul Leni and Robert Wiene, who made the extraordinary *The Cabinet Of Dr Caligari* (1919), were also devotees of expressionism's curious, and massively influential, morphology.

Other Key Films: Carl Boese & Paul Wegener's *The Golem* (1920); Fritz Lang's *Der Müde Tot* (1921) and *Dr Mabuse The Gambler* (1922); F W Murnau's *Nosferatu* (1922); Leo Birinsky & Paul Leni's *Waxworks* (1924)

Fairbanks Jr., Douglas

Son of **Douglas Fairbanks Sr.** and his first wife, Anna Sully, 'Junior', as he was known by his father, made his first real mark in Paul Czinner's *Catherine The Great* (1934), but only came close to matching his father's charisma when he played the swashbuckling Rupert von Hentzau in **John Cromwell's** *The Prisoner Of Zenda* (1937). Highly decorated during the Second World War, Fairbanks was the recipient of an honorary British knighthood for his work in cementing Anglo-US relations, and died at the advanced age of 91 in 2000.

Other Key Films: *The Dawn Patrol* (1930); *The Narrow Corner* (1933); *Gunga Din* (1939); *The Corsican Brothers* (1941); *Sinbad the Sailor* (1947)

Fairbanks Sr., Douglas

Famous silent swashbuckling star who never really made the transition to sound, Fairbanks was known as the King of Hollywood in his time, reigning jointly alongside his wife, **Mary Pickford's**, Queen. A founder of United Artists with Pickford, **D. W. Griffith** and **Charlie Chaplin**, the magically athletic Fairbanks was a charismatic master of evocative action in a long series of screen successes which included Fred Niblo's *The Mark Of Zorro* (1920), **Allan Dwan's** *Robin Hood* (1922) and **Raoul Walsh's** *The Thief Of Bagdad* (1924).

Other Key Films: *The Three Musketeers* (1921); *Don Q Son Of Zorro* (1925); *The Black Pirate* (1926); *The Iron Mask* (1929); *The Taming Of The Shrew* (1929)

Farrar, David: There was something devil-may-care about David Farrar, epitomised by him throwing in his career in 1962 'when things got boring' and moving to Africa. This quality was best revealed in two **Michael Powell**/Emeric Pressburger films, *Black Narcissus* (1947), in which he played the decadent and virile Mr Dean, who flutters the sentimental heart of **Deborah Kerr's** Sister Clodagh (particularly when singing sentimental hymns in his velvety drunken baritone) and in *Gone To Earth* (1950), as Squire Reddin, where he fluttered the elemental heart of **Jennifer Jones**, particularly when she's laid over the pommel of his hunter or trying on the Stuart finery of his ancestors that he just happens to keep in an old trunk. There's a peculiar quality about *Gone To Earth*, some 'rightness', as though Powell and Farrar, Hugh Griffith and Cyril Cusack had managed to put their finger on a piece of Old England and encapsulate it – for it is rare for any film to give such an overwhelming, unprejudiced and honest impression of the past. Farrar was a throwback, an eighteenth-century man in a twentieth-century world, and it is for this that some of his films, particularly *The Small Back Room* (1948) and *Cage Of Gold* (1950), deserve reassessment.

Other Key Films: *Went The Day Well* (1942); *The Lisbon Story* (1946); *Frieda* (1947); *Mr. Perrin And Mr. Traill* (1948); *Night Without Stars* (1951); *Duel In The Jungle* (1954); *The Black Shield Of Falworth* (1954); *Tears For Simon* (1956); *I Accuse!* (1958); *Solomon And Sheba* (1959)

Farrow, John

Farrow was a weird sort of mainstream director, in that he disdained nothing in the way of work while remaining curiously literate and slightly out of place in the brash surroundings in which he found himself. His films have very little in common with each other beyond a marked emphasis on character, though never, happily, to the exclusion of action. He made one of the greatest of all **Westerns**, *Hondo* (1953), and a few first-rate *film noirs*, which include *The Big Clock* (1948), *The Night Has A Thousand Eyes* (1948), *Where Danger Lives* (1950) and *His Kind Of A Woman* (1951). He was particularly good with actors, and one is left with the impression, viewing the sum total of Farrow's work, that maybe he knew something we didn't, for his films are oddly enjoyable. All in all, an extremely underrated director.

Other Key Films: *Reno* (1939); *A Bill Of Divorcement* (1940); *Wake Island* (1942); *Two Years Before The Mast* (1946); *California* (1947); *Calcutta* (1947); *Alias Nick Beal* (1949); *Ride Vaquero* (1953); *A Bullet Is Waiting* (1954)

Fassbinder, Rainer Werner

Very few directors have ever worked at the breakneck speed Fassbinder did during the 1970s, and one can only conjecture whether he instinctively sensed that he would die early, or whether his death at the age of thirty-six from a drug overdose was simply the result (and not the intuitive upshot) of his unbearably manic creative urges. Whatever the case, it remains indisputable that Fassbinder melded his political convictions to his cinematic artistry in a way that few directors since **Sergei Eisenstein** have achieved, and it is enlightening to note that Eisenstein, too, burnt himself out at the early age of fifty. Fassbinder's is the cinema of demoralization, and his *Der Händler Der Vier Jahreszeiten* [*The Merchant Of The Four Seasons*] (1972), *The Bitter Tears Of Petra Von Kant* (1972), *Chinese Roulette* (1976), *The Marriage Of Maria Braun* (1979) and *Veronika Voss* (1982) are masterpieces of alienated urban angst. Fassbinder hated the world in which he lived but loved its people, and it is in his humanity in the face of an unwanted but very real existential torment that his genius lies.

Other Key Films: *Katzelmacher* (1969); *Warum Läuft Herr R Amok?* (1970); *Beware The Holy Whore* (1971); *Wildwechsel* (1973); *Fontane's Effi Briest* (1974); *Fox And His Friends* (1975); *Fear Of Fear* (1976); *Satan's Brew* (1976); *Despair* (1978); *Berlin Alexanderplatz* (1980); *Lili Marlene* (1981); *Lola* (1982); *Querelle* (1982)

Fellini, Federico

Fellini is the great showman, a man at ease with himself and with the direction he has taken while remaining mildly amused that so many people have chosen to take it with him. He is the Pied Piper to our enchanted child, and his strengths lie, not in the viewer's inevitable disenchantment and just as inevitable enforced maturity, but in the hope he holds out that we could all remain as children if only we would listen, and watch, and accept. Fellini springs his voluptuous vision upon us, confident that we will follow him, but he relies as much upon his reputation as our judgement. When watching how he uses his wife, Giulietta Masina, as the bewildered Gelsomima to **Anthony Quinn's** brutish Zampano in *La Strada* (1954), it is us who become Gelsomima, with Fellini himself as the Quinn figure, forcing us onto his stage and making us twirl and caper for his amusement. In retrospect *I Vitelloni*, (1953) now seems to be his masterpiece, simply because it managed to encapsulate the boredom and the random but natural desire for existential recognition that underlie all his later, more self-consciously contrived films. Fellini remains a master, but a flawed one, capable of raising us briefly on his waxen wings, and making us forget that what we are seeing below us is only make believe and papier-mâché. See **Heartstopping Moments**

Other Key Films: *The White Sheik* (1952); *The Swindle* (1955); *The Nights Of Cabiria* (1958); *La Dolce Vita* (it was Fellini's film that gave rise to this now-common phrase) (1960); *8_* (1963); *Juliet Of The Spirits* (1965); *Satyricon* (1969); *The Clowns* (1970); *Roma* (1972); *Amarcord* [Fellini's filmic autobiography] (1973); *Casanova* (1976); *Orchestra Rehearsal* (1979); *And The Ship Sails On* (1983); *Ginger And Fred* (1985)

Fernandel

Fernandel is the man most French people think about when they think of comedy – not **Jacques Tati**, not **Charlie Chaplin**, but Fernandel. With his elongated face, mischievous grin and strangely disingenuous eyes, Fernandel encapsulated an image of France that offered the small man a chance in the larger scheme of things if he was either cunning enough, lucky enough or stupid enough to take it. Fernandel embodied all these qualities in one man, and his humour was consequently a great deal more subtle (verging, dare one say it, on the archetypal) than at first meets the eye. His first great success came as Marcel Pagnol's *Angèle* (1934), and his subsequent successes were legion, stretching across the Atlantic and even, God forbid, across the English Channel. His most consistently-played character was the Catholic Priest, opposite Gino Cervi's intransigent communist mayor, in the Don Camillo series (once again, a reinforcement rather than an undermining of the status quo), and his most satisfying film was Henri Verneuil's *The Cow And I* (1959), in which he came perilously and effectively close to playing straight.

Other Key Films: *Le Rosier De Madame Husson* (1932); *Josette* (1936); *Ignace* (1937); *Le Schpountz* (1939); *The Italian Straw Hat* [remake] (1940); *Emile L'Africain* (1949); *The Red Inn* (1951); *Le Petit Monde De Don Camillo* (1952); *The Sheep Has Five Legs* (1954); *Ali Baba* (1954); *Dynamite Jack* (1961); *Heureux Qui Comme Ulysse* (1970)

Fernández, Emilio

Fernández was Mexico's greatest film director (and in international terms, one of the greatest directors that ever lived) and his art was to take the innate sentimentality of the Mexican character and turn it into tragic and beautiful poetry. He was a man who lived life to full, even overpowering, effect, as on the occasion when he once shot a critic during a heated altercation, and later killed a farm labourer in a similar dispute, for which, in traditional Mexican fashion, he served only six months in jail. A veteran of the revolution, Fernández was a true Mestizo (of mixed Indian and Spanish/American blood) and his best films, *Flor Silvestre* (1943), *María Candelaria* (1943), *La Perla* (1945) and *Río Escondido* (1947) put Mexico and its people back onto the map at a time when President Lázaro Cárdenas was alienating much of the rest of the industrial word by nationalising his country's oil industry. With the great cinematographer **Gabriel Figueroa** at his side, and the sublime **Pedro Armendariz** and **Dolores Del Rio** to act for him, Fernández, at his best, showed that an ancient and ill-understood country, unfairly swamped by its more recent, rather brasher neighbour, may have its **John Fords** too.

Other Key Films: *Los Abandonadas* (1944); *Bugambilla* (1944); *Pepita Jimenez* (1945); *Enamorada* (1946); *Salón México* (1948); *La Malquerida* (1949); *Victimas Del Pecado* (1950); *El Rapto* (1953); *Una Cita De Amor* (1956); *Pueblito* (1962); *Un Dorado De Pancho Villa* (1968); *La Choca* (1973); *Zona Roja* (1976)

Ferrara, Abel

A violent, visceral filmmaker who began his directing career with the serially banned *Driller Killer* (1979), which he then followed with *Ms. 45* (1981), a blood-curdling wish-fulfilment tale of a raped woman's revenge on her rapists. Ferrara's quest into the instinctive depths of his own Catholicism reached its fervidly (a)stigmatic height in *Bad Lieutenant* (1992), which began with the sickeningly violent gang rape of a nun using a Church crucifix, and continued with **Harvey Keitel's** misguided though ultimately redemption-seeking policeman, at first reluctantly, then righteously, and finally fetishistically, investigating her case. Ferrara is a brilliant though equally misguided filmmaker, and one suspects that Keitel's compulsively exploitative cop bears a not inconsiderable spiritual resemblance to its progenitor.

Other Key Films: *Fear City* (1984); *China Girl* (1987); *King Of New York* (1989); *Dangerous Game* (1993); *Snake Eyes* (1994); *The Blackout* (1997); *New Rose Hotel* (1998); *'R Xmas* (2001); *Mary* (2005)

Fields, W C

Fields was a second-generation American with an English cockney father from whom he ran away, and he began his stage career as a juggler – God knows why this should be important, but it is. Suffice it to say that Fields was one of the world's greatest comic geniuses and that whatever he did, however awful and cowardly he seemed, his creations were always imbued with an overwhelming humanity. One recalls with joy his Mr Micawber, in **George Cukor's** magnificent *David Copperfield* (1935), in which his playing of the role, so far from Dickens on the surface, was yet indisputably and utterly true to the Dickensian spirit – he purportedly questioned producer **David O Selznick** closely as to why there should be no juggling allowed in the part. Cuthbert J Twillie, Egbert Souse, Ambrose Wolfinger, Charles Bogle, Karl La Fong, Larson E Whipsnade, Eustace McGargle, Mahatma Kane Jeeves, Augustus Q Winterbottom, T Frothingwell Bellows, and Otis J Criblecoblis were only some of his expedient alter egos (still running away), and it was with a sort of sublime joy that one finally saw him settled, at the end of Norman Z McLeod's *It's A Gift* (1934), on his well-earned Californian orange groves. Fields was the inheritor of a typically English sense of humour, transcendently and serendipitously transplanted to a puritan, prohibition-minded United States, offering, God Bless it, untold fresh opportunities for its exalted furtherance.

Other Key Films: *Pool Sharks* [short] (1915); *That Royle Girl* (1926); *Fools For Luck* (1928); *The Dentist* [short] (1932); *The Barber Shop* [short] (1933); *Mrs. Wiggs Of The Cabbage Patch* (1934); *The Man On The Flying Trapeze* (1935); *You Can't Cheat An Honest Man* (1939); *My Little Chickadee* (1940); *The Bank Dick* (1940); *Never Give A Sucker An Even Break* (1941)

Key Lines:

1. 'It's a funny old world – a man's lucky if he gets out of it alive.' [Charles Lamont's *You're Telling Me* (1934)]
2. 'Some weasel took the cork out of my lunch.' [George Marshall's *You Can't Cheat An Honest Man* (1939)]
3. 'Any man who hates dogs and small children can't be all bad.' [Fields on sentimentality]
4. 'I'd rather be in Pennsylvania.' [Fields on his death-bed]
5. 'Women are like elephants to me. I like to look at them, but I wouldn't want to own one.' [Edward Sutherland's *Mississippi* (1935)]
6. 'Don't wait up for me, my dear. I may play a little Parcheesi before

coming to bed.' [William Beaudine's *The Old-Fashioned Way* (1934)]

7. 'I was in love with a beautiful blonde once. She drove me to drink. It's the one thing I'm indebted to her for.' [Edward F Cline's *Never Give A Sucker An Even Break*]

Fiennes, Ralph

Fiennes's finest moment to date has come in **Steven Spielberg's** *Schindler's List* (1993) in which he played concentration-camp commandant Amon Goeth with such astonishing veracity that one actually found oneself beginning to understand how the barbarities of the Nazi era could have occurred as much by moral default as by scrupulous intention. His Charles Van Doren, in **Robert Redford's** *Quiz Show* (1994), was another tour de force, and even when he is in a film that fails, as with Jeremiah Chechik's *The Avengers* (1998), Fiennes impresses with the seriousness with which he approaches even such a ludicrously underwritten role. His Almasy, in **Anthony Minghella's** *The English Patient* (1996), is a prime example of Fiennes's greatest quality, his capacity for enlightened and constructive empathy even when the character he is playing is morally compromised.

Other Key Films: *The Baby Of Macon* (1993); *Strange Days* (1995); *Oscar And Lucinda* (1997); *Onegin* (1999); *The End Of The Affair* (1999); *Spider* (2002); *Red Dragon* (2002); *Maid In Manhattan* (2002); *Chromophobia* (2005); *The Constant Gardener* (2005); *The White Countess* (2005); *Land Of The Blind* (2006); *Bernard And Doris* (2006)

Key Line: 'I veer away from trying to understand why I act. I just know I need to do it.' [Fiennes on acting]

Figueroa, Manuel

The favoured partner of director **Emilio Fernández**, (with whom he made the celebrated *María Candelaria* (1943) and *La Perla* (1945)) and one of the ten greatest cinematographers of all time, Figueroa was the supreme master of dramatic light, preferring the deeper contrasts and heightened dramatic force of black & white to the softer, more dispersed tones of colour. An orphan, Figueroa was largely self-taught, only going to Hollywood when he was nearly thirty years of age to study with the great **Gregg Toland**, **Orson Welles's** mentor and the progenitor of deep focus photography. Although he was constantly wooed by Hollywood throughout his career, Figueroa resolutely nailed his colours to the nascent Mexican Film Industry (to whose renaissance he contributed not a little), only occasionally sallying across the frontier to film **John Ford's** *The Fugitive* (1947) and later **Don Siegel's** *Two Mules For Sister Sara* (1969). On Figueroa's own side of the legally dubious Mexican/US border, that wise old bird and old Mexico hand **John Huston** wooed Figueroa to shoot his sublime *Night Of The Iguana* (1964), as well as the immaculately coloured *Under The Volcano* (1984), which may rightly be seen to stand as Figueroa's epitaph.

Other Key Films: Fernando De Fuente's *Allá En El Ranch Grande* (1936); Emilio Fernández's *Flor Silvestre* (1943), *Enamorada* (1946), *Río Escondido* (1947), *Maclovia* (1948), *Pueblerina* (1949) and *Salón México* (1949); **Luis Buñuel's** *Los Olvidados* (1950), *Él* (1952), *Nazarín* (1958), *The Exterminating Angel* (1962) and *Simon Of The Desert* (1965); Brian G. Hutton's *Kelly's Heroes* (1970)

Key Line: 'Lighting is the privilege of the cinematographer. He owns the light.' [Figueroa on the cinematographer's art]

Film Noir

Generic term applied by French critics to a series of 1940s and 1950s Hollywood movies, mostly directed by European émigrés, which highlighted the dark and fatalistic side of the human condition. Using a style that incorporated elements of German **expressionism**, **pulp fiction** and the French poetic melodrama of the 1930s [see **Poetic Realism**], the disparate pantheon of noir directors includes **Billy Wilder, Fritz Lang, Nicholas Ray, Edgar G. Ulmer**, and **Edward Dmytryk**. Some of the greatest noir *auteurs* were in fact B-Movie directors who contrived to slip their strange films triumphantly through the Hollywood net – most notable among these was **Joseph H. Lewis** whose *Gun Crazy* (1949) has become massively influential in recent years, spawning an entire series of imitative, but on the whole, lesser, movies. Some contemporary directors such as **Lawrence Kasdan** with *Body Heat* (1981) and **Joel** and **Ethan Coen's** debut movie *Blood Simple* (1985), have made superb stabs at continuing the genre, and every few years or so there is a sudden resurgence of interest in the genre when a new film appears, such as **Dennis Hopper's** *The Hot Spot* (1990), **Stephen Frears's** *The Grifters* (1990), John Dahl's *The Last Seduction* (1994), the Coen Brothers' *Fargo* (1996), or **Oliver Stone's** *U-Turn* (1997), that sees fit to acknowledge its debt to its exalted precursors.

Key Lines:

1. 'What do you want, Joe, my life history? Here it is in four words. Big ideas, small results.' [**Barbara Stanwyck** to Keith Andes in Fritz Lang's *Clash By Night* (1952)]

2. 'You never can depend on girls named Dolores.' [**George Raft** in Edwin L Marin's *Nocturne* (1946)]

3. 'It was the bottom of the barrel and I scraped it. But I didn't care. I had her.' [**Robert Mitchum**, about **Jane Greer**, in *Out Of The Past* [a.k.a. *Build My Gallows High*] (1947)]

Best Film Noir:

Jacques Becker's *Le Trou* (1959); John Dahl's *Red Rock West* (1992); **Jules Dassin's** *Night And The City* (1950); **Edward Dmytryk's** *Murder My Sweet* [a.k.a. *Farewell My Lovely*] (1944) and *Crossfire* (1947); **Stephen Frears's** *The Grifters* (1989); Tay Garnett's *The Postman Always Rings Twice* (1946); **Henry Hathaway's** *Kiss Of Death* (1947); **Lawrence Kasdan's** *Body Heat* (1981); **Stanley Kubrick's** *The Killing* (1956); **Fritz Lang's** *The Big Heat* (1953) and *Human Desire* (1954); **Joseph H Lewis's** *Gun Crazy* (1949); Robert Montgomery's *Ride The Pink Horse* (1947); **Otto Preminger's** *Where The Sidewalk Ends* (1949); **Nicholas Ray's** *They Live By Night* (1949) and *In A Lonely Place* (1950); **Don Siegel's** *The Big Steal* (1949); **Robert Siodmak's** *The Killers* (1946) and *Criss Cross* (1948); **Jacques Tourneur's** *Out of The Past* [a.k.a. *Build My Gallows High*] (1947); Frank Tuttle's *This Gun For Hire* (1942); **Edgar G. Ulmer's** *Detour* (1945); **Charles Vidor's** *Gilda* (1946); **Luchino Visconti's** *Ossessione* (1942); **Billy Wilder's** *Double Indemnity* (1944); **Robert Wise's** *The Set-Up* (1949)

Finch, Peter

Finch was a subtle actor with a gentle manner and a handsome and particularly well-ageing face, and his most complex performance came in **John Schlesinger's** brilliantly sustained *Sunday Bloody Sunday* (1971), as the vulnerable and civilized Dr Daniel Hirsh, who is forced, much against his will, to share his male lover with **Glenda Jackson's** equally vulnerable Alex Greville. Finch never gave a poor or ill-considered performance, and his premature death of a heart-attack, aged only sixty-three, just after he had completed **Sidney Lumet's** *Network* (1976), was greeted with particular sadness by all advocates of the enlightened, sensitive school of screen acting, a talent ideally characterized by Finch's portrayal of the bewildered Squire Boldwood in Schlesinger's *Far From The Madding Crowd* (1967).

Other Key Films: *The Heart Of The Matter* (1953); *Father Brown* (1954); *A Town Like Alice* (1956); *The Battle Of The River Plate* (1956); *The Nun's Story* (1959); *The Trials Of Oscar Wilde* (1960); *The Pumpkin Eater* (1964); *Judith* (1966); *England Made Me* (1973); *A Bequest To The Nation* (1973); *Raid On Entebbe* (1977)

Key Line: 'I'm mad as hell and I'm not going to take it anymore.' [*Network*]

Finney, Albert

Finney was just the sort of talented working-class boy that post post-war Britain felt it needed during the 1960s to blow away the inhibited mists of an antediluvian class consciousness, and Finney dutifully joined the ranks of **Terence Stamp** and **Michael Caine** in an attempt to do just this. The result was a series of only vaguely subversive films and the creation, needless to say, an entirely new and equally exclusive caste to replace the one whose apparent downfall he had so recently celebrated. If Finney were French he would be a *monstre sacré*, for his talent lies in his innumerable variations on himself – his consul, Geoffrey Firmin, in **John Huston's** *Under The Volcano* (1984), was genuinely affecting, however, but still suffered from inevitable speculation about what a railing, drink-sodden **Richard Burton** might have made of the same role.

Other Key Films: *Saturday Night And Sunday Morning* (1960); *Tom Jones* (1963); *Two For The Road* (1967); *Charlie Bubbles* (1967); *Gumshoe* (1971); *Wolfen* (1981); *Shoot The Moon* (1982); *The Dresser* (1983); *Miller's Crossing* (1990); *The Browning Version* (1994); *Washington Square* (1997); *Breakfast Of Champions* (1999); *Simpatico* (1999); *Erin Brockovich* (2000); *Traffic* (2000); *Delivering Milo* (2000); *Hemingway* (2001); *The Hunter of Death* (2001); *Big Fish* (2003); *A Good Year* (2006)

Fitzgerald, Barry: He was the stock Irishman in any number of forgettable, and some not-so-forgettable, Hollywood films, and even fellow Irishman **John Ford** did not disdain to use him as such – in fact it might be said that Fitzgerald *encapsulated* the sentimental view of Irishness that American audiences so greedily lapped up during the three decades of his screen career, and still lap up, green plastic bowler hats and all, to this day. Fitzgerald's hokum was at its most memorable in Ford's *The Long Voyage Home* (1940) in which it was at least leavened by a modicum of seriousness, and again in Ford's *The Quiet Man* (1952), which was so chock-full of hokum (and jolly nice hokum it was too) that Fitzgerald's performance did not, for once, stand out.

Other Key Films: *Juno And The Paycock* (1930); *Ebb Tide* (1937); *Bringing Up Baby* (1938); *The Dawn Patrol* (1938); *The Sea Wolf* (1941); *How Green Was My Valley* (1941); *Going My Way* (1944); *The Naked City* (1948); *Union Station* (1950)

Flaherty, Robert

Known by some as 'the father of the documentary', a title which he viewed with bemused tolerance, Flaherty was the son of a gold-miner, and from an early age he began to build up an interest in the natural world of day-to-day survival as opposed to the ever more artificial world of his native United States. His first completed film, *Nanook Of The North* (1922) was made almost by chance as the result of previous expeditions he had made among the Eskimo, around Hudson's Bay in Canada, and it remains one of the best films ever about survival in the face of intense natural odds – Nanook himself died of starvation just after the film was completed. It was followed by the softer, similarly heartfelt, but more self-consciously beautiful *Moana* (1926), which detailed the diurnal life of a band of fishermen in the Polynesian archipelago. Flaherty's greatest achievement, however, came with *Man Of Aran* (1934), which he filmed over a period of three years off the Irish coast. His final, lyrical, *Louisiana Story* (1948) also deserves mention, as does Flaherty's wife, Frances, who was his companion, muse, helpmeet and collaborator on many of his extraordinary and ground-breaking ventures.

Other Key Films: *The Pottery-Maker* (1925); *The Twenty-Four Dollar Island* (1927); *White Shadows Of The South Seas* (1928); *Tabu* (1933); *Industrial Britain* (1933); *Elephant Boy* (1937); *The Land* (1942)

Fleming, Victor

Fleming's posthumous fame lies mainly in two films, **Gone With The Wind** (1939) which he directed almost by default after **George Cukor** had been sacked, and *The Wizard Of Oz* (1939). These came almost at the end of his career, however, and this macho man's man (he used to brothel crawl with **Clark Gable**), had already made his mark during the 1920s and 1930s with such classics as *The Virginian* (1929), *Red Dust* (1932), and *Captains Courageous* (1937), a grossly sentimental film which is nevertheless still able to raise the odd furtive tear in this particular correspondent (hem, hem).

Other Key Films: *Lord Jim* (1925); *The Way Of All Flesh* (1927); *Bombshell* (1933); *Treasure Island* (1934); *Test Pilot* (1938); *Dr Jekyll And Mr Hyde* (1941); *Tortilla Flat* (1942)

Flynn, Errol

More renowned for his off-screen antics than for his on-screen acting, Flynn was actually a consummate professional. Astonishingly handsome, and with an athlete's physique to boot, Flynn's breakthrough came with **Michael Curtiz's** *Captain Blood* (1935), which set the pattern for a succession

Errol Flynn photographed in 1936 at the wheel of a Rolls-Royce.

Kenner Parker/Nelvana/ The Kobal Collection/ Fryer, Elmer

of swashbuckling roles that ensured him his place in Hollywood legend. Hopelessly (and one-sidedly) infatuated with eight time co-star **Olivia de Havilland**, Flynn took solace from drink, drugs, brawling and an increasingly crazed round of sexual shenanigans, all of which contributed to his early death at the age of fifty. He last successfully buckled-his-swash in William Keighley's *The Master Of Ballantrae* (1953), which is far better than it has any right to be given Flynn's deplorable condition at the time. One prefers to remember him as Robert Devereux, Earl of Essex, ardently proclaiming his love for both **Bette Davis** and her throne, yet still scorning the chance to use that love, at the expense of truth, to save his skin.

Other Key Films: *The Charge Of The Light Brigade* (1936); *The Adventures Of Robin Hood* (1938); *The Private Lives Of Elizabeth and Essex* (1938); *The Sea Hawk* (1939); *Objective Burma!* (1945); *The Sun Also Rises* (1958)

Key Line: 'My dear friend, there's a little bit of Don Juan in every man. But since I *am* Don Juan, there must be more of it in me.' [Vincent Sherman's *Adventures Of Don Juan* (1949)]

Fonda, Henry

Fonda personified integrity on the screen, and became **John Ford's** actor of choice in such American classics as *Young Mr Lincoln* (1939), *The Grapes Of Wrath* (1940) and the sublime *My Darling Clementine* (1946). A surprisingly good straight man, Fonda also shone in **Preston Sturges's** comedy masterpiece *The Lady Eve* (1941), opposite a scintillating **Barbara Stanwyck**. After exemplary wartime service in the US Navy, Fonda played a variety of tormented heroes in such movies as **Alfred Hitchcock's** *The Wrong Man* (1956) and **Sidney Lumet's** electrifying courtroom drama *Twelve Angry Men* (1958). In a rare outing as a bad guy, Fonda elegantly out-acted and (mostly) out-shot the opposition in **Sergio Leone's** majestic *Once Upon A Time In The West* (1968).

Other Key Films: *The Farmer Takes A Wife* (1935); *Jezebel* (1938); *Drums Along The Mohawk* (1939); *Jesse James* (1939); *The Fugitive* (1947); *Fort Apache* (1948); *Mister Roberts* (1955); *Warlock* (1959); *Fail-Safe* (1964) *On Golden Pond* (1981)

Fonda, Jane

Excoriated by the political right for her extreme opposition to the Vietnam War, Fonda soon succeeded in living down the sex-doll image which **Roger Vadim** had foisted on her in *Barbarella* (1968). An intense, occasionally unsympathetic actress, she finally found her feet in **Alan J Pakula's** *Klute* (1971) playing hard-bitten prostitute Bree Daniels to **Donald Sutherland's** bewildered investigator, John Klute. Some politically exemplary movies followed, including **Fred Zinnemann's** *Julia* (1977), Hal Ashby's *Coming Home* (1978), and James Bridges's *The China Syndrome* (1980). Her career has tailed off somewhat in recent years, and she has become more renowned for her choice of husbands (Roger Vadim, Tom Hayden and Ted Turner), her autobiography and her fitness videos, than for her screen work.

Other Key Films: *Cat Ballou* (1965); *Barefoot In The Park* (1967); *They Shoot Horses, Don't They?* (1969); *California Suite* (1978); *The Electric Horseman* (1979); *On Golden Pond* (1981); *Stanley & Iris* (1990); *Monster-In-Law* (2005)

Fonda, Peter

Renowned for his part in **Dennis Hopper's** *Easy Rider* (1969), and for being the son of Henry, the brother of Jane, and the father of Bridget, Peter Fonda has been making something of a comeback in recent years with movies such as Michael Almereyda's *Nadja* (1994), and Victor Nuñez's *Ulee's Gold* (1997). His directorial debut, *The Hired Hand* (1971), boded rather well for this Hollywood scion, but, son of a famous father that he is, Fonda has never quite seemed able to get a full grip on his undoubted talent.

Other Key Films: *The Last Movie* (1971); *Dirty Mary Crazy Larry* (1974); *Race With The Devil* (1975); *Wanda Nevada* [also directed] (1979); *The Cannonball Run* (1981); *The Limey* (1999); *South Of Heaven, West Of Hell* (2000); *Wooly Boys* (2001); *Japan* (2006)

Fontaine, Joan

Sister and occasional public enemy of **Olivia de Havilland**, Fontaine tended towards the demure in such roles as the second Mrs de Winter, in **Alfred Hitchcock's** *Rebecca* (1940) and poor Jane, in Robert Stephenson's *Jane Eyre* (1944) [surely the cinema's most relentless passive/aggressive ever], but in real life Fontaine was something of a derring-do, mixing pilotage, fishing and ballooning with the more decorous de Winter-like pursuits of cooking and interior design. What she had on screen, especially in her younger years, was an innocent vulnerability perfect for virile bounders such as **Cary Grant**, **Laurence Olivier** and **Orson Welles** to threaten, thus guaranteeing the audience its fair share of thrills. Her later career marked something of a turning point, and she was allowed to stretch herself a little in more taxing, and occasionally more unsympathetic roles, such as the scheming wife in **Nicholas Ray's** *Born To Be Bad* (1950).

Other Key Films: *Gunga Din* (1939); *Suspicion* (1941); *The Constant Nymph* (1943); *Frenchman's Creek* (1944); *Ivy* (1947); *The Emperor Waltz* (1948); *Kiss The Blood Off My Hands* (1948); *Letter From An Unknown Woman* (1948); *The Bigamist* (1953); *Serenade* (1956); *Island In The Sun* (1958); *A Certain Smile* (1958); *The Witches* (1966)

Ford, Glenn
Ford could turn his hand to just about anything, as befitted the son of a rough, tough, railroad man, and he forged a successful career through being relaxed and at his ease in more or less any situation. His first big break came with **Charles Vidor's** *Gilda* (1946), in which he played a down-at-heel chiseller who is taken up by a bisexual casino owner, in whose wife, **Rita Hayworth**, they both have a shared interest (kinky, or what?). His best performance came in **Fritz Lang's** terrific *film noir The Big Heat* (1953), and in later years Ford profitably mined the **Western** trail (where a few wrinkles more or less don't count) along with so many of his ageing male contemporaries. Out of favour now in an age that wrongly fancies it understands the subtleties better than its ancestors, Ford was always a sensitive actor in a pretty much un-sensitive business.

Other Key Films: *A Stolen Life* (1946); *The Undercover Man* (1949); *The Secret Of Convict Lake* (1951); *Affair In Trinidad* (1952); *The Violent Men* (1955); *The Blackboard Jungle* (1955); *3:10 To Yuma* (1958); *Cowboy* (1958); *Santee* (1973)

Ford, Harrison
A far better actor than he has any right to be given the wonderfully obscene amount of money his most successful movies have made, Ford is equally at home as a laconic light comedian in Ivan Reitman's *Six Days And Seven Nights* (1998), and as the tormented, almost *noir* protagonist of **Peter Weir's** *Witness* (1985) and **Ridley Scott's** *Blade Runner* (1982). It would be churlish not to give him credit for his professionalism in roles such as Han Solo in **George Lucas's** *Star Wars* series, and as Indiana Jones in **Steven Spielberg's** tetralogy of the same name, but Ford really showed what he could do with an adventurous role in Andrew Davis's superb *The Fugitive* (1993) in which he played the falsely accused Dr Richard Kimble, and which, almost alone in recent years, restored one's faith in the capacity of the Hollywood mainstream to entertain, without at the same time despising, its audience.

Other Key Films: *American Graffiti* (1973); *The Conversation* (1974); *Apocalypse Now* (1979); *The Mosquito Coast* (1986); *Frantic* (1988); *Presumed Innocent* (1990); *Regarding Henry* (1991); *Random Hearts* (1999); *What Lies Beneath* (2000); *K-19: The Widowmaker* (2002); *Firewall* (2006)

Key Line: 'It's not the age. It's the mileage.' [Steven Spielberg's, *Raiders Of The Lost Ark*]

Ford, John
The former Sean Aloysius O'Feeney won six Oscars during his career, and deserved

a number more. A true poet of the screen, he incorporated song, sound and image in a series of masterpieces that, even today, have no serious parallel in American cinema – in films like *Young Mr Lincoln* (1939), *The Grapes of Wrath* (1940), *My Darling Clementine* (1946) and *The Searchers* (1956), he became, quite literally, the emotional historian of the American soul. All his films had heart – a rare thing in the commercial world in which he operated – and a strong belief in community. Ford's people were courteous to each other (even to their enemies, when this was possible) and it was no coincidence that he chose either **John Wayne** or **Henry Fonda** to incarnate the finest of his realistically flawed heroes. Ford's conservative view of the family as the essential prop of any civilized and civilizing society has received its fair share of brickbats from the self-appointed liberal and intellectual elite of his own and more recent times, but his films obstinately retain their magic and their power to move the instincts, while the words and works of his assailants have, more often than not, simply crumbled into dust and been forgotten. See **Heartstopping Moments**

Other Key Films: *The Informer* (1935); *The Hurricane* (1937); *Stagecoach* (1939); *Drums Along the Mohawk* (1939); *They Were Expendable* (1945); *Fort Apache* (1948); *She Wore A Yellow Ribbon* (1949); *Rio Grande* (1950); *Wagon Master* (1950); *The Quiet Man* (1952); *Mogambo* (1953); *Mister Roberts* (1955); *The Man Who Shot Liberty Valance* (1962)

Key Line: 'It is easier to get an actor to be a cowboy than to get a cowboy to be an actor.' [Ford on acting and cowboys]

The illustration used in posters for Milos Forman's 1984 film Amadeus.

Saul Zaentz Company/ The Kobal Collection

Forman, Milos

A native Czechoslovakian who lost both his parents to a Nazi concentration camp, the critically-acclaimed director of *A Fireman's Ball* (1968) was stranded in Paris in 1968 after the Russian takeover of his country, and eventually forsook Europe altogether and moved to Hollywood. His first big US success was *One Flew Over The Cuckoo's Nest* (1975), proving, yet again, that it often takes a foreigner to best interpret a country for its own citizens. The hybrid *Amadeus* (1984) followed the disappointing *Ragtime* (1981) as Forman's next international success, but his excellent *Valmont* (1989) was unjustly overlooked in favour of **Stephen Frears's** *Dangerous Liaisons* (1988), both of which were based on the same Choderlos de Laclos epistolary novel. Forman is a fastidious director with a marked flair for atmosphere, character, and eccentricity, and his distinctly personal slant on American subjects is particularly welcome given the turgid repetitions and rank sentimentality inherent in so many home-baked productions.

Other Key Films: *Loves Of A Blonde* [*A Blonde In Love*] (1965); *Taking Off* (1971); *Hair* (1979); *The People Vs. Larry Flint* (1996); *Man On The Moon* (1999); *Goya's Ghosts* (2006)

Foster, Jodie

Foster was a movie brat even before the term was invented, acting in TV commercials from age three, and feature films from age ten, with Jerrold Freedman's inappropriately named *Kansas City Bomber* (1972). 1976 was her *annus mirabilis*, in which she made her mark in two very different films, as Tallulah, in **Alan Parker's** *Bugsy Malone*, and as Iris Steensman, in **Martin Scorsese's** *Taxi Driver*. In her adult career (post 1983) she has sometimes verged on the worthy, almost as if she wants to be both a critical success and a mainstream darling at one and the same time, without having tumbled to the fact that the two aspirations are not necessarily compatible. But when directors have succeeded in channelling her away from her Joan-of-Arc syndrome, she has been extremely effective, most notably in **Jonathan Demme's** *The Silence Of The Lambs* (1991) as the hawk-like Clarice Starling, and in Richard Donner's *Maverick* (1994).

Other Key Films: *Candleshoe* (1978); *Foxes* (1980); *Carny* (1980); *The Hotel New Hampshire* (1984); *The Accused* (1988); *Little Man Tate* [also dir.] (1991); *Shadows And Fog* (1992); *Sommersby* (1993); *Nell* (1994); *Contact* (1997); *Anna And The King* (1999); *The Dangerous Lives Of Altar Boys* (2001); *Panic Room* (2002); *Flightplan* (2005); *Inside Man* (2006)

Francis, Freddie

Francis is something of a paradox – his films as a director consist almost entirely of such thoughtfully-made and entertaining little thrillers as *Paranoiac* (1963), *Dr Terror's House Of Horrors* (1965), *Torture Garden* (1968) and *The Ghoul* (1975), whereas the films he has collaborated on as a cinematographer are of another ilk entirely, and include Jack Clayton's *Room At The Top* (1959) and *The Innocents* (1961), **Jack Cardiff's** *Sons And Lovers* (1960) [Cardiff was yet another gamekeeper-cinematographer turned poacher-director], **Karel Reisz's** *Saturday Night And Sunday Morning* (1960) and *The French Lieutenant's Woman* (1981), **David Lynch's** *The Elephant Man* (1980), and **Martin Scorsese's** *Cape Fear* (1991). How to equate the two? It is almost as if it were belatedly to be discovered that Salvador Dali had stooped to painting set designs for some rogue filmmaker's dream sequence. But then he did, didn't he? For **Alfred Hitchcock's** *Spellbound* (1945).

Other Key Films: Karel Reisz's *Night Must Fall* (1964); Edward Zwick's *Glory* (1989); Michael Austin's *Princess Caraboo* (1994); **Bob Hoskins's** *Rainbow* (1995); David Lynch's *Dune* (1984) and *The Straight Story* (1999)

Franju, Georges

Some reckon him one of the greatest of all French film directors; others don't reckon him at all. Franju is **cult** material par excellence, and from his first bravura documentary release, *Le Sang Des Bêtes* (1949), in which he casts an unswerving eye on the brutal business of meat slaughtering, it was obvious that Franju was not to be conveniently filed and docketed. A co-founder of the French national film archive, *La Cinémathèque Française*, he alternately stimulates and shocks, as for example, with his sensationally surreal horror classic *Les Yeux Sans Visages* [a.k.a. *Eyes Without A Face*, or *Horror Chamber Of Dr Faustus*] (1960), which has been a staple of University film clubs for decades. Franju's feature film masterpiece is probably *Judex* (1964), in which he successfully recreates the adventurous and dreamlike silent world of Louis Feuillade, the original creator of the Judex and Fantomas characters.

Other Key Films: *Hôtel Des Invalides* [doc.] (1951); *Le Grand Méliès* [doc.] (1952); *La Tête Contre Les Murs* [a.k.a. *The Keepers*] (1959); *Thomas L'Imposteur* [a.k.a. *Thomas*

The Imposter] (1965); *L'Homme Sans Visage* [a.k.a. *Shadowman*] (1974)
Key Line: Franju: 'Movies should have a beginning, a middle and an end. **Jean-Luc Godard**: 'Certainly, but not necessarily in that order.' [Franju and Godard on film]

Frankenheimer, John

A variable director, Frankenheimer has a rigorous technique which he sometimes uses to mask a lack of emotional depth in his characters. His *The Manchurian Candidate* (1962), however, still stands up very well, and the recent (and finally litigation-free) re-release of *Seven Days In May* (1964) confirms his reputation as a fine weaver of suspense. *French Connection II* (1975) and *Black Sunday* (1979) were both excellent thrillers, and one is irresistibly drawn to the conclusion, particularly in the light of his recent **Robert de Niro** vehicle *Ronin* (1998), that Frankenheimer is actually a first-class *Boy's Own* director reluctantly masquerading as a grown up.
Other Key Films: *The Young Stranger* (1958); *Birdman Of Alcatraz* (1962); *The Train* (1965); *The Horsemen* (1971); *The Challenge* (1982); *The Holcroft Covenant* (1985); *Reindeer Games* (2000); *Ambush* (2001)

Frankenstein

Something of a genre in itself, nearly every budding director has taken a shot at Mary Shelley's *Frankenstein* (either literally or figuratively) since the birth of the cinema circa 1895. **James Whale's** 1931 *Frankenstein* is the movie most people remember, with a sad-eyed **Boris Karloff** playing the nameless monster, but Whale's follow-up, *The Bride Of Frankenstein* (1935) is equally good, and benefits from an electrifying performance (forgive the pun) from the one and only Elsa Lanchester. Later movie versions have varied from the comic, with Charles Barton's *Abbott And Costello Meet Frankenstein* (1948) and **Mel Brooks's** *Young Frankenstein* (1974) to the worthy with David Wickes's *Frankenstein* (1993), to the dotty with Frank Henenlotter's *Frankenhooker* (1990), to the misguided with William Beaudine's *Jesse James Meets Frankenstein's Daughter* (1965) and **Kenneth Branagh's** *Mary Shelley's Frankenstein* (1993), to the genuinely frightening with Jack Smight's *Frankenstein: The True Story* (1973).
Other Key Films: Erle C Kenton's *The Ghost Of Frankenstein* (1942); Roy William Neill's *Frankenstein Meets The Wolf Man* (1943); Terence Fisher's *Frankenstein Must Be Destroyed!* (1970); Stuart Gordon's *Re-Animator* (1985)
Key Line: 'It's alive! It's alive!' [Colin Clive's Henry Frankenstein, on first seeing Boris Karloff twitch in James Whale's *Frankenstein*]

Frears, Stephen

Something of a star on his home-grown British cinema circuit (and latterly in the US) Frears is a director of integrity who has the rare capacity to tease out an actor's performance beyond its normal range. From his debut feature *Gumshoe* (1972), in which **Albert Finney's** obsession with **Raymond Chandler** and **Humphrey Bogart** leads him into more trouble than he is capable of handling let alone explaining, through *The Hit* (1984), a somewhat nihilistic and beautifully-scored Costa del Sol gangster movie, to the films that have really made his name, *My Beautiful Laundrette* (1985), *Prick Up Your Ears* (1987) and *Dangerous Liaisons* (1988), Frears has produced thoughtful and well-founded work. His best film is *The Grifters* (1990), in which he effectively inhabits novelist Jim Thompson's head by unsentimentally portraying a world of small-town, penny ante American con artists who are enmeshed in moral, amoral, and proto-Oedipal relations, far beyond their understanding.

Other Key Films: *Bloody Kids* (1980); *Sammy And Rosie Get Laid* (1987); *Hero* (1992); *The Snapper* (1993); *Mary Reilly* (1996); *The Van* (1997); *The Hi-Lo Country* (1998); *High Fidelity* (2000); *Liam* (2000); *Dirty Pretty Things* (2002); *Mrs Henderson Presents* (2005); *The Queen* (2006)

Friedkin, William

A brilliant technician, Friedkin struck pay-dirt with two blockbusters in three years, *The French Connection* (1971), with its famous (and illegal – Friedkin had not asked permission to film where and what he did) car chase, and *The Exorcist* (1973), a green-vomit-stained masterpiece of inspired exploitation which spawned a host of inferior copies, and which totally changed the way Hollywood viewed word-of-mouth advertising. Friedkin seemed to lose his touch following *The Exorcist* (perhaps bemused by the film's extraordinary success), and his work since then has varied from the outrageously exploitative to the marginally pretentious.

Other Key Films: *The Birthday Party* (1968); *The Night They Raided Minsky's* (1970); *The Boys In The Band* (1970); *Sorcerer* (1977); *To Live And Die In L.A.* (1985); *Rampage* (1992); *Jade* (1995); *Rules of Engagement* (2000); *The Hunted* (2003); *Bug* (2006)

Fröbe, Gert

Rotund German character actor even more famous in his homeland than abroad, Fröbe was renowned for his comic prowess and ability to send himself – and the German bourgeoisie – hilariously up. International audiences remember him most fondly for his Colonel Manfred von Holstein 'running on the water scene' in Ken Annakin's *Those Magnificent Men In Their Flying Machines* (1965) [in which he also demonstrated his unique ability to imitate an entire brass band through his nose] and for his sinister Mr Auric Goldfinger, in Guy Hamilton's *Goldfinger* (1964).

Other Key Films: *Berliner Ballade* (1948); *Heroes And Sinners* (1955); *The 1000 Eyes Of Dr Mabuse* (1960); *The Longest Day* (1962); *Die Dreigroschenoper* (1963); *Tonio Kröger* (1964); *A High Wind In Jamaica* (1965); *Chitty Chitty Bang Bang* (1968)

Key Line: 'This is gold, Mr Bond. All my life I've been in love with its colour, its brilliance, it's divine heaviness.' [*Goldfinger*]

Fuller, Samuel

Fuller used the B-Movie format to its full extent, writing, producing and directing his own work and retaining control over it at a time, during the 1950s and 1960s, when such a thing was virtually impossible in a mainstream context. A master of the camera and its movement, Fuller was a conservative/anarchist obsessed with criminality who refused to be bound by the conventional subject matter of Cold War America. Like **pulp fiction** writer Jim Thompson (whom in some ways he resembles) Fuller's view of morality and its voluble adherents is an arch one, and his characters often function more through expediency and unenlightened self-interest than through any established code. An instinctive Darwinist who believed in the rough process of natural selection, Fuller's *House Of Bamboo* (1955) and *Underworld USA* (1961) were devastating attacks on cupidity, human frailty and the emptiness of the revenge motive, whilst *Shock Corridor* (1963) was a heady paean to the incipient insanity of those who think themselves sane, a view Fuller brought to final fruition in his magnificent but ultimately pessimistic war film, *The Big Red One* (1980). Fuller is that uncomfortable thing, a man who falls between the two stools of high art and schlock commerciality, and his films are disturbing, disquieting, occasionally comically bad, and very often misunderstood. See **Erotic Moments**

Other Key Films: *I Shot Jesse James* (1949); *Fixed Bayonets* (1951); *Pickup On South Street* (1953); *Hell And High Water* (1954); *Run Of The Arrow* (1958); *Verboten!* (1959); *Merrill's Marauders* (1962); *The Naked Kiss* (1965); *White Dog* (1982); *Thieves After Dark* (1984); *Street Of No Return* (1989)

Key Line: 'When you're in the battlefield, survival is all there is. Death is the only great emotion.' [Fuller's dearth]

Gabin, Jean

Born Jean-Alexis Moncorgé to a family of itinerant entertainers on the Café circuit, Gabin, at his consummate best, outclassed even **Humphrey Bogart** as a tough guy with a tender heart. In films like **Marcel Carné's** poetic *Quai Des Brumes* (1938) and

Jean Gabin (left) and Brigitte Bardot (centre) in En Cas de Malheur (In Case of Adversity/ Love Is My Profession), directed by Claude Autant-Lara (1957).

UCIL/IENA/INCOM/ The Kobal Collection/Limot

Jean Renoir's masterpiece *La Grande Illusion* (1937), Gabin played working-class men with the capacity to transcend, even if only very fleetingly, the brutalization of their lot. Although he continued acting for more than thirty years after serving with the Free French during the Second World War, Gabin's greatest moments undoubtedly came in the 1930s, during the magnificent golden era of French cinema, which, to all intents and purposes, he encapsulated. Gabin could transmit passion, pain or disillusionment with a single glance, and his rough way with women, leavened with an innate romanticism that came as something of a pleasurable shock from a broken-nosed man who could have doubled as a middleweight boxer, endeared him to both sexes. By the time of his death, in 1974, he had become one of France's national treasures.

Other Key Films: *Méphisto* (1931); *Zouzou* (1934); *La Belle Équipe* (1936); *Les Bas-Fonds* (1936); *Pépé Le Moko* (1936); *Gueule D'Amour* (1937); *La Bête Humaine* (1938); *Le Jour se Lève* (1939); *The Walls Of Malapaga* (1949); *La Nuit Est Mon Royaume* (1951); *Le Plaisir* (1952); *La Minute De Vérité* (1952); *Touchez Pas Au Grisbi* (1954);

Archimède Le Clochard (1958); *Les Misérables* (1958); *En Cas De Malheur* (1958); *Le Soleil Des Voyous* (1967); *Le Clan Des Siciliens* (1969); *Le Testament* (1975); *L'Année Sainte* (1976)

Key Line: 'He had the most beautiful loins I've ever seen in a man.' [**Marlene Dietrich** to a journalist, *à propos* of her one-time lover, Gabin]

Gable, Clark

Despite the big ears and the alleged bad breath and all the other myriad faults that also-rans persist in seeing in him, Gable was the undisputed King of Hollywood during the 1930s, 1940s and a hefty part of the 1950s too – King not in box office necessarily, but in stature and star ranking. When people thought of Hollywood, they thought of Gable, just as when they thought of literature, they thought of Hemingway. It was something beyond the rational. And Gable played up to it wonderfully, wooing both men and women with his on-screen virility – men wanted to emulate him, women to be approved by him. He was fortunate to have begun acting at a time when licence, innuendo and sheer sex weren't frowned upon and euphemised. With films such as Robert Z Leonard's *Susan Lenox: Her Fall And Rise* (1931), **Victor Fleming's** *Red Dust* (1931) and Tay Garnett's *China Seas* (1935), Gable forged an image of the male that has lasted, more or less untainted, to the present day. He conducted passionate affairs with **Joan Crawford** and **Jean Harlow**, contracted a tender and loving marriage with the ill-fated **Carole Lombard** (whose death in a freak air accident broke his heart), and never lived to see the birth of his only son, John Clark Gable. **Frank Capra's** *It Happened One Night* (1934) was Gable creating Gable, Victor Fleming's *Gone With The Wind* (1939) was Gable out-Gabling himself, **John Ford's** *Mogambo* (1953) was Gable proving that he still was Gable and that he didn't give a two-penny half-penny damn if people knew it, and **John Huston's** *The Misfits* (1960) was Gable's wise, virile and utterly en-Gabled swansong, the swansong also to an era of men who chose not to subjugate their lives to the tyranny and the oppressiveness of a neurotic and sometimes debilitating over-analysis.

Other Key Films: *Possessed* (1931); *Hell Divers* (1932); *Strange Interlude* (1932); *No Man Of Her Own* (1933); *Manhattan Melodrama* (1934); *Call Of The Wild* (1935); *Mutiny On The Bounty* (1935); *Wife vs. Secretary* (1936); *Test Pilot* (1938); *Strange Cargo* (1940); *Comrade X* (1940); *Somewhere I'll Find You* (1942); *Lone Star* (1952); *The Tall Men* (1955)

Key Lines:

1. 'Frankly, my dear, I don't give a damn!' [*Gone With The Wind*]
2. 'Being near him gave me twinges of a sexual urge beyond belief.' [**Joan Crawford** on the King]
3. 'Quiet, determined – no, not determined, just quiet. I said to Hunt [Stromberg] once, "This guy's got eyes like a child and a build like a bull."' [**John Lee Mahin**, who scripted **Victor Fleming's** *Red Dust* (1932) and co-scripted Clarence Brown's *Wife Versus Secretary* (1936), on Gable]

Gance, Abel

Gance had been virtually ignored for thirty years before Kevin Brownlow's detailed reconstruction of his final masterpiece, *Napoléon* (1927), triumphantly reappeared before an unprepared public in 1980. *Napoléon* seemed to sum up the three brief but unbelievably rich decades of the silent era, reuniting for the first and last time all the ground-breaking cinematic techniques that had been thrown up in their passing. A pioneer of the split-screen technique, in which he used three separate cameras and screens to achieve a triptych-like effect, Gance achieved early and lasting critical success with *Mater Dolorosa* (1917), *La Dixième Symphonie* (1918), *J'Accuse* (1919) and *La Roue* (1923), films in which he honed the rapid-fire editing skills he was later to use in *Napoléon*, and which were to become his trademark. The latter part of his career was distinguished by a series of superb screen biographies, *Lucrezia Borgia* (1935), *The Queen And The Cardinal* (1935), *The Life And Loves Of Beethoven* (1936) and *La Reine Margot* (1953), but it is for the wonders of *Napoléon* that he is now rightly, if somewhat belatedly, acclaimed.

Other Key Films: *Le Nègre Blanc* (1912); *La Fleur Des Ruines* (1915); *Barberousse* (1917); *La Fin Du Monde* (1931); *Le Voleur De Femmes* (1936); *Louise* (1939); *Le Capitaine Fracasse* (1943); *La Tour De Nesles* (1955); *Cyrano Et D'Artagnan* (1963)

Best Gangster Films

Jacques Becker's *Casque D'Or* (1952); **Francis Ford Coppola's** *The Godfather Parts I, II, & III* (1972-1990); **Marcel Carné's** *Le Jour Se Lève* (1939); **Michael Curtiz's** *Angels With Dirty Faces* (1938); **Brian De Palma's** *Scarface* (1983) and *The Untouchables* (1987); Julien Duvivier's *Pépé Le Moko* (1936); **Howard Hawks's** *Scarface* (1932); Mike Hodges's *Get Carter* (1971); **John Huston's** *Key Largo* (1948) and *Prizzi's Honor* (1985); **Mervyn LeRoy's** *Little Caesar* (1930); **Louis Malle's** *Atlantic City* (1981); John Mackenzie's *The Long Good Friday* (1981); Michael Mann's *Heat* (1995); Mike Newell's *Donnie Brasco* (1997); **Martin Scorsese's** *Goodfellas* (1989) and *Casino* (1995); **Quentin Tarantino's** *Reservoir Dogs* (1992); **Raoul Walsh's** *White Heat* (1949)

Garbo, Greta

She was the most famous screen actress of them all, although, ironically, many of the people who know her name have probably never seen a single one of her films. She was a woman whose beauty emerged from the screen as if by magic, and it is arguable that the sadness we see reflected in her face stemmed from the profoundest parts of a psyche bruised, almost beyond endurance, by a deprived and poverty-stricken childhood. When, as **George Cukor's** *Camille* (1937), Garbo takes a curiously childlike pleasure in baubles and bangles and the beautiful fripperies only rich men can provide, we are not repelled by her shallowness, but are instead forced to understand the very deprivations that can cause such a compensatory passion. In **Rouben Mamoulian's** *Queen Christina* (1933), Garbo throws away a kingdom for an already-lost love, and in **Ernst Lubitsch's** *Ninotchka* (1939) she gives up her country and her identity for the capacity to laugh. In real life she quit the screen, dramatically, at the height of her fame, arguing for the right to be herself and to live her life in all its unadorned banality, but she left behind enough of herself in the fleeting images of her brief and glittering star to remind her audience, in the decades and centuries to come, that magic contains its very own capacity for liberation.

Other Key Films: *The Temptress* (1926); *Flesh And The Devil* (1927); *The Divine Woman* (1928); *The Kiss* (1929); *Anna Christie* (1930); *Susan Lenox: Her Rise And Fall* (1931); *Mata Hari* (1931); *Grand Hotel* (1932); *As You Desire Me* (1932); *The Painted Veil* (1934); *Anna Karenina* (1935); *Conquest* (1937); *Two-Faced Woman* (1941)

Key Lines:

1. 'I want to be alone.' [*Grand Hotel*]
2. 'What, when drunk, one sees in other women, one sees in Garbo sober.' [Kenneth Tynan on Garbo]

3.　'I have been memorizing this room. In future, in my mind, I shall live a great deal in this room.' [To her lover, **John Gilbert**, in *Queen Christina*]

Gardner, Ava

A stunningly beautiful share-cropper's daughter from North Carolina, Gardner flummoxed her critics by proving that she could act as well as look scenic in movies such as **Robert Siodmak's** *The Killers* (1946), **Alfred Lewin's** headily romantic

Frank Sinatra and Ava Gardner in 1951.

Universal/The Kobal Collection

Pandora and the Flying Dutchman (1951), and **John Ford's** *Mogambo* (1953), in which she more than matched the formidable **Grace Kelly**. The swansong of her beauty (and incidentally one of her finest performances) came in **John Huston's** sublime *Night of the Iguana* (1964), as transplanted hotelier and devil-may-care existentialist Maxine Faulk [see **Heartstopping Moments**]. Famously married (at different times, needless to say) to **Mickey Rooney**, Artie Shaw and **Frank Sinatra**, Gardner lived her life in the fast lane and resolutely refused to complain when the time finally came to pay the piper.

Other Key Films: *Lost Angel* (1943); *The Hucksters* (1947); *The Bribe* (1949); *My Forbidden Past* (1951); *Show Boat* (1951); *The Snows Of Kilimanjaro* (1952); *The Barefoot Contessa* (1954); *Bhowani Junction* (1956); *The Sun Also Rises* (1958); *On The Beach* (1959); *Seven Days In May* (1964); *Mayerling* (1968)

Key Line: 'Do you really think I could be a star?' [**Joseph L Mankiewicz's** *The Barefoot Contessa*]

Garfield, John

A hard-bitten, left-leaning precursor to **Marlon Brando** and **Steve McQueen**, Garfield died at the early age of forty-one, of a heart attack following his blacklisting by the House Committee On Un-American Activities (HUAC) for refusing to name names. Garfield personified the loner – the man who came through the Great Depression and had been changed by it. His boxer's face fitted him perfectly for hard-boiled roles, often as working men with the courage of their convictions, but also for tragic, fatalistic roles, such as that of drifter Frank Chambers in Tay Garnett's *The Postman Always Rings Twice* (1946). Capable of appearing in oddities like **Michael Curtiz's** *The Sea Wolf* (1941) and **John Huston's** *We Were Strangers* (1949), and also of improving potboilers such as Delmer Daves's *Pride Of The Marines* (1945), Garfield's finest moments came in mainstream movies that still somehow managed to hit home, most notably as tormented boxer Charlie Davis in Robert Rossen's *Body and Soul* (1947), and as a self-confident lawyer, Joe Morse, who gradually allows himself to be corrupted by the underworld milieu he frequents, in Abraham Polonsky's *Force of Evil* (1948).

John Garfield and Lana Turner in The Postman Always Rings Twice, directed by Tay Garnett (1946).

MGM/The Kobal Collection

Other Key Films: *Juarez* (1939); *East Of The River* (1940); *Tortilla Flat* (1942); *Fallen Sparrow* (1943); Nobody *Lives Forever* (1946); *Humoresque* (1946); *The Breaking Point* (1950); *He Ran All The Way* (1951)

Key Line: 'Stealing a man's wife, that's nothing. But stealing a man's car, that's larceny.' [*The Postman Always Rings Twice*]

Garland, Judy

Erstwhile wife of **Vincente Minnelli** and mother of Liza, Garland received more hype, for a more variable talent, than did even Lassie, and her messy, self-obsessed life has become so bound up with her screen career that it is almost impossible to watch **George Cukor's** melodramatic *A Star Is Born* (1954) without assuming the film is about her. (It wasn't, of course. Cukor had originally shot the story as *What Price Hollywood?* in 1932, when Garland was only ten, and **William Wellman** made the original, and better, *A Star Is Born*, based loosely on the lives of **John Gilbert** and **Greta Garbo**, in 1937.) Even Garland's singing voice was overrated, although she could certainly belt out a tune loudly enough when she chose to, while utterly ignoring any particular need for characterization beyond the strictly vocal. (Try listening first to Billie Holiday or Connie Boswell, and then go back to Garland – impossible). Garland always seemed to be acting, and her main appeal seems to lie in this very staginess, rather as **Barbra Streisand's** (a rather similar schmaltz-merchant come to think of it) does now. All right, she *was* genuinely winsome as Dorothy, in **Victor Fleming's** *The Wizard Of Oz* (1939), but then again, can winsomeness ever *be* genuine?

Other Key Films: *Love Finds Andy Hardy* (1938); *Babes In Arms* (1939); *Strike Up The Band* (1940); *Girl Crazy* (1943); *Meet Me In St. Louis* (1944); *The Clock* (1945); *The Pirate* (1948); *Easter Parade* (1948); *Words And Music* (1948)

Key Line: 'I was born at the age of twelve on a Metro-Goldwyn-Mayer lot.' [Garland on stardom]

Garmes, Lee

Garmes was one of the greatest of all the black-and-white cinematographers, pioneering the centrally concentrated use of light, while leaving the periphery of a scene in low-key. He was an expert on the dolly as well as the static set-up, and the picture of Garmes one always remembers is of him soaring and swooping into the air, with his camera, implausibly, under total control, on such films as **Josef von Sternberg's** *Shanghai Express* (1932) and **King Vidor's** blissfully absurd *Duel In The Sun* (1946).

Other Key Films: Josef Von Sternberg's *Morocco* (1930) and *Dishonored* (1931); **Howard Hawks's** *Scarface* (1932); Julien Duvivier's *Lydia* (1941); **Edmund Goulding's** *Nightmare Alley* (1947); **William Wyler's** *Detective Story* (1951)

Garson, Greer

A popular actress who specialized in five-hanky films, Garson first shone playing **Robert Donat's** wife, Katherine Ellis, in **Sam Wood's** *Goodbye Mr Chips* (1939), a success which led to her role as the eponymous heroine in **William Wyler's** *Mrs Miniver* (1942), alongside the man with whom she was to co-star on eight different occasions, Walter Pidgeon. Her finest moment, however, came as the self-willed Elizabeth Bennett in Robert Z Leonard's well-nigh perfect *Pride and Prejudice* (1940), which boasted, among its many other felicities, a brilliant script co-written by novelist Aldous Huxley.

Other Key Films: *Blossoms In The Dust* (1941); *Random Harvest* (1942); *The Youngest Profession* (1943); *Madame Curie* (1943); *Adventure* (1946); *Desire Me* (1947); *Julius Caesar* (1953)

Gere, Richard

With his mincing, city boy's walk, and his all too self-conscious tics (the flicking of the hair, the cannibal kissing) Gere is an odd candidate for enduring stardom, but he has lasted longer, and at a higher level, than many of his more talented contemporaries. Does he pick his roles better, or is it that he simply reinvents himself every five or six years, chooses an on-the-make actress to reinforce his continuing sex appeal, and takes it from there? His best role came as Jesse, the perky, existential hero of Jim McBride's *Breathless* (1983), in which Gere took the Julian Kay character from **Paul Schrader's** *American Gigolo* (1980) and extended him with a touch more style and a lot more energy. He was fine, too, in **Taylor Hackford's** brilliantly populist *An Officer And A Gentleman* (1982), particularly in the early scenes with his father, played by the excellent Robert Loggia, in which Gere suggested the sort of edgy, working-class boys he might have played if fame, and the Hollywood shredding machine, hadn't so consummately eaten him up.

Other Key Films: *Looking For Mr. Goodbar* (1977); *Days Of Heaven* (1978); *No Mercy* (1986); *Internal Affairs* (1990); *Pretty Woman* (1990); *Sommersby* (1992); *Mr. Jones* (1993); *Primal Fear* (1996); *The Jackal* (1997); *Runaway Bride* (1999); *Autumn In New York* (2000); *Dr. T And The Women* (2000); *The Mothman Prophecies* (2002); *Chicago* (2002); *Shall We Dance* (2004); *Bee Season* (2005); *The Flock* (2006)

Gershwin, George

The extraordinarily precocious but short-lived Gershwin (1898-1937) provided the music (his brother Ira supplied the lyrics) for well over fifty films, most, unfortunately, posthumously. The best of these, namely John Murray Anderson's *The King Of Jazz* (1930), **Vincente Minnelli's** *An American In Paris* (1951) and **Otto**

Preminger's *Porgy And Bess* (1959), conspired to push the musical off the stage and into what passes, in Hollywood Musical terms at least, for real life. Gershwin's song-writing capacity was sublime, and his rigorous technique and respect for the concert hall and for the classical repertoire allowed jazz, for almost the first time, to become something of a mainstream interest – no matter what its adherents felt about it.

Other Key Films: Norman McLeod's *Lady Be Good* (1941); Norman Taurog's *Girl Crazy* (1943); Irving Rapper's *Rhapsody In Blue* (1945); Charles Walters's *The Barkleys Of Broadway* (1949); **Stanley Donen's** *Funny Face* (1958); **Robert Wise's** *Star!* (1968)

Best **Ghost Films**

Lewis Allen's *The Uninvited* (1944); **Claude Autant-Lara's** *Sylvie Et Le Fantôme* (1945); Alberto Cavalcanti, **Basil Dearden**, **Robert Hamer** and Charles Crichton's *Dead of Night* (1945); **René Clair's** *The Ghost Goes West* (1935); Jack Clayton's *The Innocents* (1961); **Basil Dearden's** *The Halfway House* (1943); **William Dieterle's** *Portrait Of Jenny* (1949); **David Lean's** *Blithe Spirit* (1945); **Anthony Minghella's** *Truly, Madly, Deeply* (1991); **Peter Weir's** *Picnic At Hanging Rock* (1975)

Gibson, Mel

Mel Columcille Gerard Gibson only moved from his native New York to Australia when he was twelve (not a lot of people know that), and so it's hardly surprising that he feels so at home in both cultures. **George Miller's** cult favourite *Mad Max* (1979) started him on the long return path to America, **Peter Weir's** *Gallipoli* (1981) saw him briefly hesitate, but his success in Miller's *Mad Max 2: The Road Warrior* (1981) made lucrative repatriation a foregone conclusion. A more than competent stage actor, Gibson was wonderful as journalist Guy Hamilton in Weir's *The Year Of Living Dangerously* (1983), and one can forgive him the block-busting *Lethal Weapon* series (1987-1998) because he used his ensuing box-office clout to turn out a more than respectable *Hamlet* (1990) for **Franco Zeffirelli**, followed by his own, Oscar-winning *Braveheart* (1995) and *The Passion Of Christ* (2004). Obviously that rare thing, a film star with integrity, Gibson still lives in rural Australia with his wife and their seven children.

Other Key Films: *Tim* (1979); *The Bounty* (1984); *Mrs Soffel* (1984); *The River* (1984); *Tequila Sunrise* (1988); *Bird On A Wire* (1990); *Forever Young* (1992); *The Man Without A Face* (1993); *Maverick* (1994); *Ransom* (1998); *Conspiracy Theory* (1997); *Payback* (1999); *The Patriot* (2000); *The Million Dollar Hotel* (2000); *What Women Want* (2000); *We Were Soldiers* (2002); *Signs* (2002); *Under And Alone* (2006); *Apocalypto* [dir.] (2006)

Gielgud, John

Gielgud's ninety-six-year life almost spanned the entire century, from 1904 to 2000, and he died with his mellifluous voice and unparalleled verse-speaking talents intact. Predominantly a stage actor, and a Shakespearian at that, Gielgud rarely chose to make films, but when he did he brought the same elegantly puckish grace and polish to what were often scandalously underwritten parts. Given a token Oscar for his beautifully modulated performance as Dudley Moore's manservant in Steve Gordon's *Arthur* (1981), Gielgud really deserves his place in cinema history for having discovered and generously supported the careers of a quite extraordinary number of outstanding English actors and actresses. His own career briefly hung in the balance, in 1953, when he was fined for 'cottaging' and his misdemeanour was maliciously broadcast by the press – at his first appearance on stage after the event, his

Liverpool audience gave him a standing ovation, ensuring that justice was both done, and seen to be done.

Other Key Films: *The Secret Agent* (1936); *The Prime Minister* (1941); *Julius Caesar* (1953); *The Barretts Of Wimpole Street* (1958); *Becket* (1964); *Chimes At Midnight* (1966); *The Charge Of The Light Brigade* (1968); *Providence* (1976); *The Shooting Party* (1984); *Prospero's Books* (1991); *Shine* (1996); *Elizabeth* (1998); *The Tichborne Claimant* (1998)

Gilbert, John

Renowned as Garbo's great love (although she vehemently denied the rumour) and the only real rival to **Rudolf Valentino**, Gilbert knew how to manipulate the Hollywood system to his ends, and his brief and memorable career was as lucrative and as meteoric as it was, eventually, tragic. Dead of a heart attack at forty-one, after sound, and the audience's decreasing greed for the passion he so convincingly provided had let him down, Gilbert, at his best, encapsulated the romance and sensuality a woman might want to give herself utterly to, rather than the more cerebral, witty type of lover which came into fashion during the 1930s. Unable or unwilling to make the change, Gilbert's only real success during the sound era was as Don Antonio de la Prada, in **Rouben Mamoulian's** *Queen Christina* (1933), but the reversal of roles with Garbo, after the heady days of Clarence Brown's *Flesh And The Devil* (1926), when he was her mentor, protector and passionate friend, must have cut this proto-alcoholic to the quick. With his fortune already lost in the 1929 stock market crash, Gilbert lasted a further three years, and ended up as the model for **Frederic March's** bittersweet performance as Norman Maine in **William Wellman's** *A Star Is Born* (1937).

Other Key Films: *Heart O' The Hills* (1919); *Arabian Love* (1922); *Monte Cristo* (1922); *He Who Gets Slapped* (1924); *The Merry Widow* (1925); *The Big Parade* (1925); *Bardelys The Magnificent* (1926); *Man Woman And Sin* (1927); *Desert Nights* (1929); *Downstairs* (1932)

Gilliam, Terry

The most precociously talented of all the Monty Python team in that he not only has a sense of humour but also the nous to use it creatively, Gilliam was behind the titles and animated interstices that did so much to raise the surreal Python humour to something approaching an art form. *Time Bandits* (1981) was his first extra-Pythonian venture, and it worked surprisingly well as historical fantasy, becoming something of a favourite with the adults for whose children it was apparently intended. *Brazil* (1985), too, was a critical success, but *The Adventures Of Baron Munchausen* (1988), while being genuinely engaging, unaccountably fell foul of the paying public, and it was only with the over-praised *The Fisher King* (1990) and the assertively curious *Twelve Monkeys* (1995) that Gilliam finally succeeded in levering himself back from the corner of the classroom.

Other Key Films: *Jabberwocky* (1977); *Fear And Loathing In Las Vegas* (1998); *The Brothers Grimm* (2005); *Tideland* (2005)

Gish Sisters, The

Dorothy and Lillian appeared together most famously in **D W Griffith's** *The Birth Of A Nation* (1915), but it was Lillian who had the more natural screen presence, and it was not long before she had become a major star, while Dorothy's career, though a worthwhile, and in any other context, a distinguished one, was forced to take second place. The sisters never fell out, however, and Lilian (ever the lady) went on to what was, at seventy-five years, one of the longest screen careers in Hollywood history. But it was Griffith who brought out the best in the demure but determined Lillian, and who understood and used her capacity for moving the audience, and it is for his *Intolerance* (1916), *Hearts Of The World* (1918), *Broken Blossoms* (1919), and *Orphans Of The Storm* (1922) that she is best known. She matured slowly, however, and in retrospect it is also for her work in Victor Sjöström's *The Scarlet Letter* (1926), and especially *The Wind* (1928), that she deserves to be remembered, roles which foretold the most notable of her numerous majestic but all-too-brief comebacks, as Rachel, in **Charles Laughton's** magnificent adult fairy-tale *The Night Of The Hunter* (1955).

Other Key Films: *The Madonna Of The Storm* (1913); *Way Down East* (1920); *Romola* (1924); *Annie Laurie* (1927); *His Double Life* (1933); *Duel In The Sun* (1947); *Portrait Of Jennie* (1949); *The Unforgiven* (1960); *The Comedians* (1967); *A Wedding* (1978); *Sweet Liberty* (1986); *The Whales Of August* (1987)

Key Line: 'Lillian had certain qualities that *seemed* ethereal, and at moments, she had great spirituality, but she was as tough as a pine knot.' [Screenwriter Horton Foote on Gish, who starred in the original stage version of his *The Trip To Bountiful* (1953)]

Godard, Jean-Luc

Godard was a post-structuralist before the term was even invented, glorying in cinema for cinema's sake, and refusing to kow-tow (ever) to his audience's expectations. A superb critic as well as a ground-breaking director, Godard's films irritate, entertain, enlighten and obfuscate in about equal measure. *Breathless* [*À Bout De Souffle*] (1960) still has the power to engender a heady sense of excitement about the very medium of cinema, and *Pierrot Le Fou* (1965) takes slapstick and returns it to something resembling the innocent and anarchic art form it originally stemmed from. *Alphaville* (1965) was way ahead of its time in melding *film noir* with **science fiction**, and *Weekend* (1967) can now be seen as an almost unbearably prescient commentary on the roots of our own society's technologically advanced but morally tormented condition. In recent years Godard has busied himself with a series of documentaries about the cinema, the eight-part *Histoire(s) Du Cinéma* (89-98), and these follow a similarly instinctual and awesomely well-informed path.

Other Key Films: *Une Femme Est Une Femme* (1960); *Le Mépris* (1963); *Vivre Sa Vie* (1963); *Made In USA* (1966); *Masculine Feminine* (1966); *La Chinoise* (1967); *Tout Va Bien* (1972); *Passion* (1982); *First Name: Carmen* (1983); *Detective* (1985); *Forever Mozart* (1996); *Éloge De L'Amour* (2001); *Notre Musique* (2004)

Key Lines:

1. 'Photography is truth. The cinema is truth twenty-four times per second.' [*Le Petit Soldat*]
2. 'Ce n'est pas une image juste, c'est juste une image.' (This isn't a just image, it's just an image) [Godard on truth and paradox: see the quote above!]

Goldman, William

Goldman is the best-known screenwriter in the world thanks to his brilliant 'how to get on in the Hollywood jungle' book, *Adventures In The Screen Trade* (1983), and its follow-up about the Cannes Film Festival, *Hype And Glory* (1990). It was *Adventures* that made him, though, for every would-be screenwriter the world over bought it in the fond hope that some of its caustic and down-to-earth magic would rub off onto them. Goldman is also famous for writing the original script for George Roy Hill's *Butch Cassidy And The Sundance Kid* (1969), and for being the writing brains behind **Alan Pakula's** *All The President's Men* (1976). His real genius lies in his talent for script-doctoring (the highly-paid prinking of other people's dud scripts), and for his sanity in continuing to write novels, like *Marathon Man* and *Magic*, which are then picked up by desperate directors who ensure that he is paid far more than the novel alone would ever have brought him for subsequently scripting them onto the screen: that said, Goldman's is a welcome voice of sanity in a rather insane trade.

Other Key Films: Jack Smight's *Harper* (1966); George Roy Hill's *The Great Waldo Pepper* (1975); Rob Reiner's *The Princess Bride* (1987) and *Misery* (1990); Richard Donner's *Maverick* (1994); **Clint Eastwood's** *Absolute Power* (1997); Simon West's *The General's Daughter* (1999); Scott Hicks's *Hearts In Atlantis* (2001); **Lawrence Kasdan's** *Dreamcatcher* (2003)

Goldwyn, Sam: The most famous independent producer of them all (and probably the most pretentious) Goldwyn came up the hard way and never allowed anyone to forget it. He liked to spend money on high-profile books and properties, stuff the set with talent, and then choose the wrong star to front the piece. On the other hand he was a great philanthropist and something of a saint when compared to, say, a **Harry Cohn**. Now renowned more for his malapropisms than for his movies, he was nevertheless responsible for a pretty extraordinary list of movies by anyone's standards, which included Leo McCarey's *The Kid From Spain* (1932) (watch it – it will grow on you), **William Wyler's** *Dodsworth* (1936), **John Ford's** *The Hurricane* (1937), and **Howard Hawks's** *Ball Of Fire* (1942).

Other Key Films: William Wyler's *Wuthering Heights* (1939), *The Westerner* (1940), *The Little Foxes* (1941) and *The Best Years Of Our Lives* (1946); **Joseph L Mankiewicz's** *Guys And Dolls* (1955)

Key Lines:

1. 'Goldwyn filled the room with wonderful panic and beat at your mind like a man in front of a slot machine, shaking it for the jackpot.' [**Ben Hecht** on Goldwyn]
2. 'Pictures are for entertainment. Messages should be delivered by Western Union.' [Goldwyn on high-minded worthiness]
3. 'Let me tell you, he wasn't the clown or ignoramus that the Goldwyn stories would indicate… He talked as any other sharp, intelligent man would talk and with only a slight trace of an accent.' [*Noir* writer **James M Cain** on Goldwyn]

Goldwynisms:

1. 'That's the way with these directors, they're always biting the hand that lays the golden egg.'
2. 'A verbal contract isn't worth the paper it's written on.'
3. 'Any man who goes to a psychiatrist should have his head examined.'
4. 'We're overpaying him but he's worth it.'
5. 'We have all passed a lot of water since then.'

Gong Li

One of China's finest screen actresses, and the star of choice for director **Zhang Yimou**, who has used her in *Red Sorghum* (1987), *Ju-Dou* (1989) and *To Live* (1994), amongst other films, and also for **Chen Kaige**, for whom she played Pang Ruyi in *Temptress Moon* (1997) and the Emperor Ying Zheng's concubine in *The Empress And The Assassin* (1999). Li differs from her trans-Pacific counterparts in that her emotional core moves from inside out, rather than in the opposite direction, as defined by the tenets of the Western acting tradition, where the idea always comes first.

Other Key Films: *Raise The Red Lantern* (1991); *The Stories of Qiu Ju* (1992); *Farewell, My Concubine* (1993); *Shanghai Triad* (1995); *Breaking The Silence* (1999); *2046* (2004); *Memoirs Of A Geisha* (2005); *Miami Vice* (2006)

Gone With The Wind

The most famous movie of them all, and rightly so, director **Victor Fleming** and producer **David O Selznick's** *Gone With The Wind* (1939) was the greatest crossover film ever made, for it contained something for just about everyone. If you wanted battles, it had battles, if you wanted romance, well then, **Clarke Gable's** passion for **Vivien Leigh**, and Vivien Leigh's passion for **Leslie Howard**, and Leslie Howard's passion for **Olivia de Havilland**, and Olivia de Havilland's passion for Leslie Howard, and everyone's passion for Tara, and the Southland, and money, were enough to send the punters away happy. And Selznick, of all men, understood the fact that films are there to make people happy – they are comfort food, placebos that people turn to in times of trouble, and a vicarious way to tell oneself that all is not bad in a world in which such elegant fripperies can still be made.

Key Lines:

1. 'As God is my witness, they're not going to lick me. I'm going to live through this. And when it's all over, I'll never be hungry again – no, nor any of my folk. If I have to lie, steal, cheat or kill, as God is my witness, I'll never be hungry again!' [Vivien Leigh as Scarlett O'Hara]

2. 'You come out of *Gone With The Wind* feeling that history isn't so disturbing after all. One can always make a dress out of a curtain.' [Film critic, Dilys Powell]

Goodrich, Frances

With her husband, Albert Hackett, Goodrich co-scripted some of the very best and most witty Hollywood mainstream films of the 1930s and 1940s, including W S Van Dyke's *The Thin Man* (1934) and *After The Thin Man* (1936), **Frank Capra's** *It's A Wonderful Life* (1946) (together with Capra and Jo Swerling), **Michael Curtiz's** *Father Of The Bride* (1950) and **George Stevens's** *The Diary Of Anne Frank* (1959). Irremediably modest, Goodrich and Hackett both steadfastly refused to play on their extraordinary, though largely unsung success.

Other Key Films: **Clarence Brown's** *Ah, Wilderness!* (1935); **Robert Z Leonard's** *The Firefly* (1937); Stuart Gilmore's *The Virginian* (1946); Charles Walters's *Easter Parade* (1948); **Jean Negulesco's** *A Certain Smile* (1958)

Gould, Elliott

Gould's acting (if not his commercial) star has rather set of recent years, but there was a time when he was considered cool by young America (which should be enough to coax anyone from following fashion) and his crumpled self-awareness enticing. Let's forget the dross, then, and look at the gems – Gould's quirky, contemporised Philip Marlowe in **Robert Altman's** *The Long Goodbye* (1973); his rather predictable but still effective casting as Jewish/American archaeologist David Kovac in **Ingmar Bergman's** *The Touch* (1970); and his bewildered but ultimately triumphant bank teller, Miles Cullen, in Daryl Duke's excellent and underrated little thriller, *The Silent Partner* (1978).

Other Key Films: *The Night They Raided Minsky's* (1968); *M*A*S*H* (1970); *California Split* (1974); *A Bridge Too Far* (1977); *The Lady Vanishes* (1979); *The Big Hit* (1998); *Picking Up The Pieces* (2000); *Puckoon* (2001); *Ocean's Eleven* (2001); *Ocean's Twelve* (2002); *Open Window* (2006)

Goulding, Edmund

Goulding was a quirky director, and it is almost impossible to apply the **auteur theory** to him (not that one would necessarily wish to do so anyway), as his films are so wildly disparate. *Grand Hotel* (1932) would top anyone's list of Goulding favourites, but *Dawn Patrol* (1938) was a great little war movie, and *Dark Victory* (1939), *The Old Maid* (1939) and *The Great Lie* (1941) were magnificent **Bette Davis** melodramas by anyone's standards. Like the somewhat younger **George Cukor**, Goulding was particularly good at coaxing outstanding performances from actresses with ego problems, but it is for his weird *Nightmare Alley* (1947), in which **Tyrone Power** subverts his pretty boy image to such an extent that he ends up as a live chicken munching fairground geek, that Goulding will be most fondly remembered by aficionados. **Other Key Films**: Henry King's *Tol'able David* [script] (1921); Henry Otto's *Dante's Inferno* [script] (1924); *Sally, Irene And Mary* (1925); *That Certain Woman* (1937); *The Constant Nymph* (1943); *Claudia* (1943); *Of Human Bondage* (1946); *The Razor's Edge* (1946); *Mister 880* (1950)

Grahame, Gloria

There are some people who are so right for just one or two roles that the remainder of their careers don't really matter. Grahame was one of those. Married first to director **Nicholas Ray**, and then to one of Ray's sons from a previous marriage, Grahame's screen career was as variable as her love-life. Possibly the ultimate half-tough, half-vulnerable *film noir* heroine, she starred in a quintet of films that are the stuff of **cult** legends – **Edward Dmytryk's** *Crossfire* (1947), **Fritz Lang's** *The Big Heat* (1953) and *Human Desire* (1954), David Miller's *Sudden Fear* (1952) and Nicholas Ray's sensational *In A Lonely Place* (1953), where she brought out the dark and sadistic side of **Humphrey Bogart** as no other woman before or since. Her Laurel Gray was so good in that film, which glimmered with substrata from her troubled marriage with director Ray, that everything she did afterwards was inevitably somewhat anti-climactic. A tragic figure, Grahame had the rare talent of being able to suggest far more than her lines dictated on the screen, and one found oneself speculating not so much about the present, but about her character's past, of where she came from, and of what she would do next. It was a spontaneous gift, of which she was probably unaware, but which Ray, above all men, had the genius to spot. Watch any of the films below, and it's unlikely that you'll be disappointed.

Other Key Films: *It's A Wonderful Life* (1946); *A Woman's Secret* (1949); *Roughshod* (1949); *Macao* (1952); *The Bad And The Beautiful* (1952); *The Glass Wall* (1953); *Man On A Tightrope* (1953); *Naked Alibi* (1954); *The Man Who Never Was* (1956); *Odds Against Tomorrow* (1959)

Key Lines:

1. Bogart: 'You said you liked my face.' Grahame: 'I said I liked it, I didn't say I wanted to kiss it.' [*In A Lonely Place*]

2. 'I was born when you kissed me. I died when you left me. I lived a few weeks while you loved me.' [Grahame quoting Bogart's script back to him for real, in *In A Lonely Place*]

Granger, Stewart

Granger was the perfect example of a straight-down-the-line commercial actor who invariably gave excellent value and who occasionally surpassed himself (when he wasn't watching) by suggesting a deeper resonance in his roles. Second only to **Errol**

Flynn in the swashbuckling stakes, Granger's beautiful diction, splendid physique, and long-nosed, virile profile, set female hearts a-flutter for more than twenty years, and Granger was sufficiently sure of himself to even get away with playing bounders and murderers, as in **Marc Allégret's** impassioned *Blanche Fury* (1948), without queering his box-office pitch. He was a believable big-game hunter in Andrew Marton and Compton Bennett's *King Solomon's Mines* (1950), a dashing, child-friendly smuggler in **Fritz Lang's** *Moonfleet* (1955), and a sensitive British officer very understandably in love with the sublime **Ava Gardner** in **George Cukor's** *Bhowani Junction* (1956). After all this, one ends up being rather grateful for the Grangers of this world, who never took either themselves or their art too seriously, but were, nonetheless, consummate professionals. Granger really showed what he could do when given the chance in **Richard Brooks's** little known and elegiac **Western**, *The Last Hunt* (1956).

Other Key Films: *The Man In Grey* (1943); *Fanny By Gaslight* (1944); *Love Story* (1944); *Madonna Of The Seven Moons* (1944); *Waterloo Road* (1945); *Saraband For Dead Lovers* (1948); *Scaramouche* (1952); *The Prisoner Of Zenda* (1952); *Young Bess* (1953); *Green Fire* (1954); *North To Alaska* (1960); *The Wild Geese* (1978)

Key Line: 'Weren't we both beautiful?' [In a touching late-night phone call to his friend, Ava Gardner, just before her death in 1990, after having seen a rerun of *Bhowani Junction* on television]

Grant, Cary

Let's clear up any misunderstandings here and now – Cary Grant was the best light comedian who ever lived, and probably the best all-round screen actor to boot. His timing was perfect, he was a master of nuance, he aged better than any other actor ever, and to blazes with his private life and his five marriages and all the other irrelevant details biographers sniff out in an effort to dilute his indissoluble star. Stick a Grant film in the DVD machine, and you just know that you're going to be entertained and taken out of yourself for the next ninety minutes. Even better, watch him on the big screen and see how a master makes the most of every precious moment of screen time without taking anything away from his fellow actors – more than that, he gives them face, even when they don't deserve it, by playing *off* them, as well as *to* them. He was never given an Oscar, but he deserved at least ten, and it is to Hollywood's eternal shame that they could only come up with a belated award that read, in pitiful fashion: 'with the respect and affection of his colleagues'. Humbug! Catch his Janus-like abilities in **Josef von Sternberg's** *Blonde Venus* (1932), or in **Leo McCarey's** *The Awful Truth* (1937), or maybe in **Howard Hawks's** *Only Angels Have Wings* (1939) or in **Alfred Hitchcock's** *Suspicion* (1941), or **Joseph L Mankiewicz's** *People Will Talk* (1951). Better still, see just about anything in the list below, and marvel.

Other Key Films

She Done Him Wrong (1933); *I'm No Angel* (1933); *The Last Outpost* (1935); *Topper* (1937); *Bringing Up Baby* (1938); *Holiday* (1938); *Gunga Din* (1939); *In Name Only* (1939); *His Girl Friday* (1940); *My Favourite Wife* (1940); *The Philadelphia Story* (1941); *The Talk Of The Town* (1942); *Mr Lucky* (1943); *Arsenic And Old Lace* (1944); *Notorious* (1946); *The Bachelor And The Bobby-Soxer* (1947); *The Bishop's Wife* (1947); *Mr Blandings Builds His Dream House* (1948); *I Was A Male War Bride* (1949); *Monkey Business* (1952); *To Catch A Thief* (1955); *An Affair To Remember* (1958); *Indiscreet* (1958); *Houseboat* (1958); *North By Northwest* (1959); *Charade* (1963); *Father Goose* (1954)

1. 'I intended to be with you on our honeymoon, Hildy, honest I did.' [Howard Hawks's *His Girl Friday*]
2. 'See, when a girl's under twenty-one, she's protected by law. When she's over sixty-five, she's protected by nature. Anywhere in between, she's fair game.' [**Blake Edwards**'s *Operation Petticoat* (1959)]

Grant, Hugh

It's a tricky thing to have to follow the alphabetical likes of **Cary Grant** in a book like this, especially if one happens to be a light comedian too, but it says much for Hugh Grant that he needn't blush and retire modestly, for he's an extremely talented and professional actor in his own right, and such comparisons are always monstrous anyway. Putting aside his excellent performances in Mike Newell's *Four Weddings And A Funeral* (1994), Roger Michell's *Notting Hill* (1999), and Sharon Maguire's *Bridget Jones's Diary* (2001) in which he turned his usual good guy persona on its head, Grant was very good indeed as Frederic Chopin in James Lapine's *Impromptu* (1990), and outstanding in **Ang Lee's** *Sense And Sensibility* (1995) and **Michael Apted's** much underrated thriller, *Extreme Measures* (1996). Grant's modest and rather shy outer skin disguises a true professional flair, and one anticipates with interest the eventual outcome of his rather classically old-fashioned (in the best sense of the word) career.

Other Key Films: *Maurice* (1987); *White Mischief* (1988); *Bitter Moon* (1994); *Sirens* (1994); *Nine Months* (1995); *Restoration* (1995); *Mickey Blue Eyes* (2000); *Small Time Crooks* (2000); *About A Boy* (2002); *Two Weeks Notice* (2002); *Love Actually* (2003); *Bridget Jones: The Edge Of Reason* (2004); *American Dreamz* (2006); *Music And Lyrics By* (2006)

Grant, Richard E

The third light comedian by the name of Grant in a row, and another real talent, blissfully shown to its full extent in **Bruce Robinson's** cult masterpiece *Withnail & I* (1987). Why is the film so good? And why is Grant so good in it? Talent. And a rigorous understanding of the camera and of what it shows and (sometimes) conceals. Grant's neologism-filled autobiography, *With Nails* (1996), is very entertaining indeed on the pretty much random way Hollywood garners its leading players from the howling pack of wannabe stars, and it is no surprise at all that Grant has floated to somewhere near the top of the character actor pond (and one confidently anticipates him remaining there). People (the present author included) will probably be collaring Grant in the street, right up until his dotage, and spluttering in his face about how much his *Withnail* reminds us of our misspent youth. But what Grant and his director/screenwriter Bruce Robinson identified so effectively and so elusively in the character of *Withnail* was not, of course, ourselves, but rather someone we had known and admired, sported with, despaired of, and eventually lost.

Other Key Films: *How To Get Ahead In Advertising* (1989); *Mountains Of The Moon* (1990); *Henry And June* (1990); *L.A. Story* (1991); *The Player* (1992); *Jack And Sarah* (1995); *Portrait Of A Lady* (1996); *Twelfth Night* (1996); *Spice World* (1997); *Food Of Love* (1997); *The Match* (1999); *The Little Vampire* (2000); *Gosford Park* (2001); *Bright Young Things* (2003); *Wah-Wah* [dir.] (2005)

Greenaway, Peter

Greenaway appeals to the French (his greatest fans) because he encapsulates and seems to give credence to the 1954 concept of the **auteur theory** promulgated for so long by its Cahiers du Cinéma originator, **François Truffaut**. Greenaway claims not to give a damn about his audience, but simply to make films to suit himself, and one can believe him insofar as his films abound in intellectuality (the bane of that institutional and insecure British philistine, the television film critic) but sometimes lack heart, in the grand old *nouveau roman* style. Any commercial success Greenaway enjoys comes almost by default, and we are apparently to applaud this, while brushing aside the fact that his very seriousness is his worst characteristic, and one that can occasionally verge on the pretentious. All that aside, one would rather know that Greenaway is out there beavering away at his conceits, fay as some of them are, than not have Greenaway at all. For all his showiness and the high-minded jargon with which his auxiliaries surround him, he does in fact boil down to a rigorous and professional filmmaker who resolutely refuses to be bound by either the creative ether of money, or the necessity of making it.

Key Films: *The Falls* (1980); *The Draughtsman's Contract* (1983); *A Zed And Two Noughts* (1985); *The Belly Of An Architect* (1987); *Drowning By Numbers* (1988); *The Cook, The Thief, His Wife, & Her Lover* (1989); *Prospero's Books* (1991); *The Baby Of Macon* (1993); *Darwin* (1993); *Pillow Book* (1997); *Death Of A Composer* (1999); *8 _ Women* (1999); *A Life In Suitcase* (2005)

Greenstreet, Sidney

Greenstreet only started acting when he was sixty-one years old, and although his career spanned a brief nine years, he instantly became one of the most recognisable of all 'faces' following his performance as the 'Fat Man', Kaspar Gutman, alongside **Humphrey Bogart** and **Peter Lorre** in **John Huston's** *The Maltese Falcon* (1941). Greenstreet supported the pair once again in **Michael Curtiz's** *Casablanca* (1942) and *Passage To Marseille* (1944), though his best film is probably **Jean Negulesco's** classic *film noir* *The Mask Of Dimitrios* (1944). Come to think of it, he was pretty good in **Michael Curtiz's** *Flamingo Road* (1949), playing Sheriff Titus Semple, the very incarnation of evil intent to **Joan Crawford's** not-so-innocent social climber, Lane Bellamy.

Other Key Films: *They Died With Their Boots On* (1941); *Across The Pacific* (1942); *Conflict* (1945); *Three Strangers* (1946); *The Verdict* (1946); *The Hucksters* (1947); *Ruthless* (1948); *The Woman In White* (1948)

Key Line:
1. 'As the leader of all illegal activities in Casablanca, I am an influential and respected man.' [*Casablanca*]
2. 'I tell you right out, I'm a man who likes talking to a man who likes to talk.' [*The Maltese Falcon*]

Greer, Jane

One of the few really good female baddies (if that's not a contradiction in terms), Greer kept **Robert Mitchum** reeling in **Jacques Tourneur's** *film noir* masterpiece *Out Of The Past* [a.k.a. *Build My Gallows High*] (1947) because she always behaved worse than even he expected. She played a similar trick on **Dick Powell** in Sidney Lanfield's *Station West* (1948) – of course she had to die in both movies, unlike **Kathleen Turner** in **Lawrence Kasdan's** *Body Heat* (1981), who, with Linda Fiorentino in John Dahl's **The Last Seduction** (1994), has come closest in recent years to inheriting the Greer mantle. Greer's greatest strength in these, her two best movies, and also in one or two of the others listed below, was that she didn't mind alienating her audience, and for the exceptionally pretty woman that she was, her lack of obvious vanity in this regard was exemplary at a time when Hollywood was busy churning out sycophantic little starlets by the bus load.

Other Key Films: *Dick Tracy* (1945); *The Big Steal* (1949); *The Company She Keeps* (1950); *The Prisoner Of Zenda* (1952); *Desperate Search* (1952); *The Clown* (1953); *Down Among The Sheltering Palms* (1953); *Man Of A Thousand Faces* (1958); *The Outfit* (1973); *Against All Odds* (1984)

Key Line: Dick Powell: 'Are you always this sweet to the men who fight over you?' Greer: 'Only the winners.' [*Station West*]

Griffith, D W

An old-fashioned Southerner, and the son of a Civil War veteran who finally succumbed to his war wounds in 1885, Griffith allowed his gentlemanliness to leach into his films, particularly in his depictions of women, and it is this sentimentality, together with his intuitive racism, that may prevent some modern audiences from realising what an extraordinarily innovative man Griffith really was in his tally of more than 500 shorts and feature films. *Birth Of A Nation* (1915) and *Intolerance* (1916) were unique in their scope, accurately reflecting an American nation intent on temporarily damping down creativity in favour of productivity, in the aftermath of the US entry into the First World War. Griffith's way of alternating close-ups and long-shots, his fastidious editing and his enlightened use of ace cinematographer, **Billy Bitzer**, led directly to the widespread exploitation of such techniques as the flashback, the matte shot, the use of a split screen to show different actions happening simultaneously, and soft focus photography. Following the financial failure of *Intolerance*, into which Griffith had poured the major part of his personal fortune, he was forced to narrow the focus of his storytelling, and this led to the magnificent quartet of *Hearts Of The World* (1918), *Broken Blossoms* (1919), *True Heart Susie* (1919) and *Orphans Of The Storm* (1922). Despite being co-founder of United Artists with **Mary Pickford**, **Charles Chaplin** and **Douglas Fairbanks Sr**, the studios sidelined Griffith at the coming of sound, despite such incontrovertible proof as the **Walter Huston**-dominated *Abraham Lincoln* (1930), that Griffith was perfectly capable of mastering that technique too. Griffith died in 1948, in the latest of a succession of apartment hotels that he called home, just four years after his equally neglected colleague, the by then alcoholic Bitzer.

Other Key Films: *The Violin Maker Of Cremona* (1909); *The Unseen Enemy* (1912); *Judith Of Bethulia* (1913); *The Mother And The Law* (1914); *The Great Love* (1918); *A Romance Of Happy Valley* (1919); *The Fall Of Babylon* (1919); *The Idol Dancer* (1920); *Way Down East* (1920); *Dream Street* (1921); *The White Rose* (1923); *Sally Of The Sawdust* (1925); *The Sorrows Of Satan* (1926); *The Battle Of The Sexes* (1928); *The Struggle* (1931)

Key Line: 'It is like writing history with lightning. And my only regret is that it is all so terribly true.' [President Woodrow Wilson on seeing *The Birth Of A Nation* (1915)]

Guinness, Alec

Guinness died, aged eighty-seven, on the seventh August 2000 – his death was a huge loss as it was he almost alone among the actor/knights of his generation who embraced the 'new' with pleasure, and it was he, of them all (**John Gielgud**, **Ralph Richardson**, **Laurence Olivier** and **Michael Redgrave** included) who recognized cinema early on for the great art form that it undoubtedly was. His Herbert Pocket, in **David Lean's** *Great Expectations* (1946), and his Fagin, in the same director's *Oliver Twist* (1948), exuded an energy that only Olivier could match, although Olivier persisted in thinking, right to the end, that cinema was a second-rate art compared to the theatre. Guinness had no such qualms, and his portrayals of Sidney Stratton in **Alexander Mackendrick's** *The Man In The White Suit* (1951), and Lt. Col. Jock Sinclair in Ronald Neame's *Tunes Of Glory* (1960), were masterpieces of rigorously controlled emotional acting. Most think his greatest performance came as Col. Nicholson in Lean's *The Bridge On The River Kwai* (1958), but, paradoxically, his greatest moment may well have been on television, as the downbeat George Smiley in the magnificent 1979-1982 BBC series based on the John le Carré spy novels.

Other Key Films: *Kind Hearts And Coronets* (1949); *The Mudlark* (1950); *The Lavender Hill Mob* (1951); *The Captain's Paradise* (1953); *Father Brown* (1954); *The Ladykillers* (1955); *The Horse's Mouth* (1958); *The Scapegoat* (1959); *Our Man In Havana* (1959); *Lawrence Of Arabia* (1962); *The Fall Of The Roman Empire* (1964); *Doctor Zhivago* (1965); *The Quiller Memorandum* (1966); *The Comedians* (1967); *Cromwell* (1968); *A Passage To India* (1984); *Little Dorrit* (1987); *A Handful Of Dust* (1988); *Kafka* (1992); *A Foreign Field* (1993); *Mute Witness* (1994)

Hackman, Gene

A subtle, controlled screen actor, who can fairly claim to be one of the most successful living masters of his profession given his extensive, and often surprising, filmography, Hackman played mavericks during the 1970s and early 1980s, then graduated through heavies to warped establishment figures by way of the occasional iconoclast. His best films capture his capacity for single-minded intensity, and include **William Friedkin's** *French Connection* (1971), **Francis Ford Coppola's** *The Conversation* (1974) and **Clint Eastwood's** *Unforgiven* (1992), in which his performance as Sheriff 'Little Bill' Daggett spans the otherwise heady gulf between the violent and the homespun. Hackman's greatest strength lies in his ability to suggest the values the common man holds dear, together with his occasional ability to transcend them.

Other Key Films: *Bonnie And Clyde* (1967); *Prime Cut* (1972); *Scarecrow* (1973); *French Connection II* (1975); *Superman* (1978); *Reds* (1981); *Eureka* (1983); *No Way Out* (1987); *Mississippi Burning* (1988); *Narrow Margin* (1990); *Get Shorty* (1995); *Extreme Measures* (1996); *Twilight* (1998); *Enemy Of The State* (1998); *Under Suspicion* (2000); *The Replacements* (2000); *The Mexican* (2000); *Heartbreakers* (2001); *Heist* (2001); *The Royal Tenenbaums* (2001); *Runaway Jury* (2003); *Welcome To Mooseport* (2004)

Haller, Ernest

Haller shared an Oscar with Ray Rennahan and **Lee Garmes** for his Technicolor cinematography on **Victor Fleming's** *Gone With The Wind* (1939), but his real forte lay in black-and-white, and he was the man behind the lighting behind **Bette Davis** in **William Wyler's** *Jezebel* (1938) and **Edmund Goulding's** *Dark Victory* (1939). **Joan Crawford** must have been impressed with the results because she insisted on Haller filming her as **Michael Curtiz's** *Mildred Pierce* (1945) when she had reached the tricky age of forty-one – needless to say Haller contrived to make her look as unblemished and as beautiful as her hard and somewhat unforgiving features would allow.

Other Key Films: **Raoul Walsh's** *The Roaring Twenties* (1939); Anatole Litvak's *All This And Heaven Too* (1940); **Nicholas Ray's** *Rebel Without A Cause* (1955); **Robert Aldrich's** *Whatever Happened To Baby Jane?* (1962)

Hamer, Robert

One of the lost souls of the British film industry, Hamer died at the early age of fifty-two after a long fight with alcoholism. He was, however, responsible for four remarkable films that ensure him a place in the pantheon. *It Always Rains On Sunday* (1947) was the first of a long and influential line of British underworld thrillers that include Mike Hodges's *Get Carter* (1971), John Mackenzie's recently re-released *The Long Good Friday* (1980), and Guy Ritchie's *Lock, Stock And Two Smoking Barrels* (1999), while Hamer's *Kind Hearts And Coronets* (1949) took dry humour to its zenith. *The Long Memory* (1952) featured a brilliantly intense **John Mills**, fine location work and a magnificently extended revenge motif, and the icing on this extraordinary director's cake comes with his early 'Haunted Mirror' sequence in the genuinely creepy *Dead Of Night* (1945), which knocks such modern variants as Eduardo Sanchez and Daniel Myrick's *The Blair Witch Project* (1999) into the proverbial cocked hat.

Other Key Films: *Pink String And Sealing Wax* (1947); *The Spider And The Fly* (1949); *The School For Scoundrels* (1960)

Hammerstein, Oscar II

A lawyer turned lyricist (the man must have had a way with words) Hammerstein's most fruitful partnership was with composer Richard Rodgers, and between them they produced such perennial favourites as Walter Lang's *State Fair* (1945) and *The King And I* (1956), **Fred Zinnemann's** *Oklahoma!* (1955), Joshua Logan's *South Pacific* (1958) and **Robert Wise's** *The Sound Of Music* (1965). It was also Hammerstein who penned the words to the immortal 'Ol' Man River' during an earlier pairing with **George Gershwin**.

Other Key Films: James Whale's *Showboat* (1936); Julien Duvivier's *The Great Waltz* (1938); Norman Z McLeod's *Lady Be Good* (1941)

Hammett, Dashiell: Ex-Pinkerton operative Hammett all but invented **pulp fiction**, and while he wrote relatively few original screenplays, the style of his greatest books leached through Hollywood like sulphuric acid through the face of a rogue gunsel. His pared-down and sometimes brutal prose was categorically different to that of **Raymond Chandler**, to whom many wrongly compare him; and **Humphrey Bogart** was the perfect personification of his Sam Spade in **John Huston's** *The Maltese Falcon* (1941), in a way that he never managed as Chandler's **Philip Marlowe** – that distinction would go to **Robert Mitchum**, in **Dick Richards's** sublime *Farewell My Lovely* (1975). Excoriated by the House Un-American Activities Committee for his alleged communist sympathies, the awesomely well-read Hammett gave up writing novels in favour of drink – a decision that finally killed him in 1961.

Hanks, Tom

Now a very big name indeed thanks largely to Robert Zemeckis's *Forrest Gump* (1994), Hanks, to look at, seems hardly cut out for stardom. Beginning his career as a comedian, most notably in **Ron Howard's** *Splash* (1984), he has steadily moved towards more serious roles, such as Aids-victim Andrew Beckett in **Jonathan Demme's** *Philadelphia* (1993), and as the embattled Captain Miller in **Steven Spielberg's** *Saving Private Ryan* (1998), for which he netted a paltry $40 million gross. The voice of Sheriff Woody in Disney's *Toy Story* (1995) and *Toy Story 2* (1999), Hanks has recently tried to consolidate his 'serious' acting credentials, by doing a **Robert De Niro** in reverse – this time slimming down 25lbs to play the (reasonably) emaciated Chuck Noland in Robert Zemeckis's *Cast Away* (2000).

Comparable as a light dramatic actor to, say, **James Stewart**, Hanks made a surprisingly good stab at directing, acting and scripting, in *That Thing You Do!* (1996), and has recently turned to producing, once again alongside Steven Spielberg, with the $100 million TV wartime drama *Band Of Soldiers* (2001). Turn to **Worst Films** for a review of Hanks's recent turn in **Ron Howard's** *The Da Vinci Code* (2006).

Other Key Films: *Bachelor Party* (1984); *The Money Pit* (1986); *Dragnet* (1987); *Big* (1988); *Turner And Hooch* (1989); *Sleepless In Seattle* (1993); *Apollo 13* (1995); *The Celluloid Closet* (1995); *You've Got Mail* (1998); *The Green Mile* (1999); *Road To Perdition* (2002); *The Ladykillers* (2004); *The Terminal* (2004)

Key Line: 'My momma always said life was like a box of chocolates…you never know what you're going to get.' [*Forrest Gump*]

Harlow, Jean

Killed by kidney failure at the age of twenty-six due to her Christian Scientist mother's refusal to allow the appropriate treatment when her daughter lapsed into a coma, Harlow was a true one-off, and her nickname 'The Blonde Bombshell' doesn't come remotely near to doing her justice. A wonderful comedienne, Harlean Carpenter, or 'Babe' as she was known to her friends, lit up any film in which she appeared. Notorious for seldom wearing underwear – something that can be deduced only too easily from a close perusal of George Cukor's *Dinner At Eight* (1933) – she excelled as the sassy platinum blonde adept at keeping virile men's men like Clark Gable in their place – at her feet, of course – in movies like **Victor Fleming's** *Red Dust* (1932), and Tay Garnett's *China Seas* (1935). Catch her in **Frank Capra's** underrated *Platinum Blonde* (1931), with the great Robert Williams, which also happens to contain, in the butler's 'puttering' scene, the best shaggy-dog dialogue in movie history.

Other Key Films: *The Public Enemy* (1931); *Bombshell* (1933); *Hold Your Man* (1933); *Libeled Lady* (1936); *Wife vs. Secretary* (1936); *Personal Property* (1937)

Key Lines: Harlow: 'I was reading a book the other day.' Marie Dressler (starting back): 'Reading a book?' Harlow: 'Yes. It's all about civilization or something – a nutty kind of a book. Do you know that the guy said that machinery is going to take the place of every profession?' Marie Dressler: 'Oh, my dear, that's something you need never worry about.' [*Dinner At Eight*]

Harris, Ed

One of the best-kept secrets of mainstream and independent Hollywood, Harris has an impressive body of work behind him for a man who didn't get his first big break until thirty-three, and then only as astronaut John Glen in Philip Kaufman's *The Right Stuff* (1983). An unassuming man who disguises his total commitment to every part he plays behind the skilful wall of his acting, Harris, with **Robert Duvall** and **John Malkovich**, is one of that great trio of talented baldies who have had to make their way in the cutthroat world of movies through talent rather than surface comeliness. Even in an otherwise flawed but interesting film such as Victor Nuñez's *Flash Of Green* (1985) Harris's trademark of quiet and focused concentration shines through, and he was, quite definitely the very best thing in **Jean-Jacques Annaud's** *Enemy At The Gates* (2001) [see **Worst Films**], as icy master sniper, Major Erwin König.

Other Key Films: *Under Fire* (1983); *Places In The Heart* (1984); *Walker* (1987); *To Kill A Priest* (1988); *Glengarry Glen Ross* (1992); *The Firm* (1993); *China Moon* (1994); *Nixon* (1995); *The Rock* (1996); *Absolute Power* (1997); *The Truman Show* (1998); *Walking The Dead* (1999); *The Prime Gig* (2000); *Pollock* [also director] (2000); *Buffalo*

Soldiers (2001); *A Beautiful Mind* (2001); *The Hours* (2002); *The Human Stain* (2003); *A History Of Violence* (2005); *Copying Beethoven* (2006)

Harris, Richard

Following **Oliver Reed's** unexpected death on the set of **Ridley Scott's** *Gladiator* (2000) [in which Harris played Marcus Aurelius], Harris duly proclaimed himself the last great survivor. An all-round hell-raiser, womaniser, and self-declared 'holy terror', Harris eventually outlived his friend Ollie by a mere three years. With nearly seventy films, two wives, and a couple of hundred sexual conquests behind him, Harris felt that he had some right to crow. **Lindsay Anderson's** *This Sporting Life* (1963) made him, Joshua Logan's *Camelot* (1967) gave him an international following, and both Jim Sheridan's *The Field* (1990) and Randa Haines's *Wrestling Ernest Hemingway* (1993) secured him a critically acclaimed dotage. What more could a man want?

Other Key Films: *The Long And The Short And The Tall* (1961); *Mutiny On The Bounty* (1962); *The Red Desert* (1964); *The Heroes Of Telemark* (1965); *A Man Called Horse* (1970); *The Molly Maguires* (1970); *The Wild Geese* (1978); *Cry The Beloved Country* (1995); *Smilla's Sense Of Snow* (1997); *To Walk With Lions* (1999); *The Barber Of Siberia* (2000); *The Count of Monte Cristo* (2001); *My Kingdom* (2001); *Harry Potter and the Sorcerer's Stone* (2001); *The Count Of Monte Cristo* (2002); *Harry Potter And The Chamber Of Secrets* (2002)

Key Line: 'The role of husband was never one of my strongest.' [Harris on marriage]

Harrison, Rex

Known as 'Sexy Rexy' to his friends – and to his six ex-wives? – most people remember Harrison as Professor Higgins in **George Cukor's** *My Fair Lady* (1964), but in actual fact, he only got the part by default after **Cary Grant** refused it and insisted that Harrison be allowed to repeat his Broadway success on the big screen. His early work was actually far better, and one remembers with affection his spoiled would-be novelist, Charles Condomine, in **David Lean's** *Blithe Spirit* (1945). He was perfect casting, also, for Sidney Gilliat's *The Rake's Progress* [a.k.a. *Notorious Gentleman*] (1945), and he injected real pathos into his role as defunct sea captain Daniel Gregg, in **Joseph L Mankiewicz's** magisterial *The Ghost And Mrs Muir* (1947).

Other Key Films: *Night Train To Munich* (1940); *Major Barbara* (1941); *Unfaithfully Yours* (1948); *The Reluctant Debutante* (1958); *Midnight Lace* (1960); *Staircase* (1969)

Harryhausen, Ray

Harryhausen is renowned to this day for the magical fighting skeletons that appeared in both Nathan Juran's inspired fantasy *The Seventh Voyage Of Sinbad* (1958) and in Don Chaffey's *Jason And The Argonauts* (1963). Harryhausen animated the skeletons through his own variation on the stop motion technique, Superdynamation, with which he recreated scenes that a 1950s child might well have been able to imagine, thanks to comics, but would never have dreamed of actually seeing re-enacted on the screen. Despite all the encroachments made by modern computer and digital technology, Harryhausen's effects still impress because they were based on a resolutely human scale, and were, as such, always believable.

Other Key Films: Eugene Lourie's *The Beast From 20,000 Fathoms* (1953); Jack Sher's *The Three Worlds Of Gulliver* (1960); Don Chaffey's *One Million Years B.C.* (1967); Desmond Davis's *Clash Of The Titans* (1981)

Hartley, Hal

Hartley is the director of such medium budget and quirkily independent movies as *Trust* (1991), and also the whimsically perverse *Amateur* (1994), which starred Hartley's alter ego, Martin Donovan, and the luminous **Isabelle Huppert** as an ex-nun who decides to branch out into writing pornography. Both these two small films are far more satisfying in their scope than the blockbusters turned out by some of Hartley's more lucratively employed contemporaries. Hartley's is the cinema of intelligence, in which preconceptions are challenged, assumptions suborned, and expectations over-turned – this alone is enough to ensure, thank God, that the doors to the major Hollywood studios are probably now forever closed to him. Hartley's most approachable film, *Simple Men* (1992), was a touching and genuinely eccentric insight into the convolutions that families can put themselves through in their search for identity.

Other Key Films: *The Unbelievable Truth* (1990); *Ambition* (1991); *Flirt* (1995); *Henry Fool* (1997); *The Book Of Life* (1998); *No Such Thing* (2001); *The Girl From Monday* (2005); *Fay Grim* (2006)

Hathaway, Henry

They don't make them like Hathaway anymore, especially in the lengths of their careers – his amounted to an impressive forty-two years, all spent directing, with variable, if always entertaining results. Perhaps it was because he was so resolutely anti-intellectual that he lasted so long, for he was certainly not unintelligent, as he showed with the very strange, heady, and really rather fantastical *Peter Ibbetson* (1935). In that same year he had the dubious distinction of directing Adolf Hitler's favourite film, *The Lives Of A Bengal Lancer* (1935), although one can hardly blame Hathaway for whatever message Hitler may have derived from it. Later successes include *Kiss Of Death* (1947) – a first-class *film noir* with the serially underrated **Victor Mature** – *The Desert Fox* (1951), with the ever-excellent **James Mason** as Erwin Rommel, and *True Grit* (1969), for which **John Wayne** finally won the Oscar that had been his due for over thirty years.

Other Key Films: *The Trail Of The Lonesome Pine* (1936); *Johnny Apollo* (1940); *The Shepherd Of The Hills* (1941); *13 Rue Madeleine* (1947); *Call Northside 777* (1948); *Niagara* (1953); *The Sons Of Katie Elder* (1965); *Nevada Smith* (1966)

Key Line: 'Henry Hathaway is very easy for a writer to work with. He's absolutely dreadful for actors to work with: he's probably the toughest son of a bitch in Hollywood…he's doing it deliberately, because this is the way he's discovered he can work.' [Wendell Mayes, who co-scripted Hathaway's *From Hell To Texas* (1958)]

Hawkins, Jack

Hawkins ended his film career miming his words and being dubbed by other actors, due to an operation for throat cancer that permanently damaged his vocal chords. This was a double tragedy for him, for Hawkins *was* his voice – a stiff upper-lip British one, to be sure, but with the capacity for sudden, surprising bursts of raw emotion. His best-known role was as General Allenby, in **David Lean's** *Lawrence Of Arabia* (1962), although he was perhaps most memorable as the Pharaoh in **Howard Hawks's** wonderfully kitsch *Land Of The Pharaohs* (1955), in which Hawkins was for once allowed to show the inherent vulnerability that lay behind his otherwise ultra-dominant characters.

Other Key Films: *The Fallen Idol* (1948); *The Small Back Room* (1948); *Mandy* (1952); *The Cruel Sea* (1953); *The Bridge On The River Kwai* (1958); *Zulu* (1964); *Lord Jim* (1965); *Waterloo* (1970); *Young Winston* (1972)

Hawks, Howard

Hawks is one of the all-time greats, and proof that the Hollywood studio system of the 1930s and 1940s was every so often capable of throwing up a talent of genuine and sometimes brilliant originality. Hawks acknowledged early on that men and women are fundamentally incompatible, and then took it as his life's challenge to engender situations in which that very incompatibly would provide the fundamental attraction. It is almost impossible to sift out just a few films from Hawks's litany of 24-carat gems and near masterpieces, but most enlightened beings would probably agree that his best comedies were the sublime *Twentieth Century* (1934), twinned with *Bringing Up Baby* (1938), *His Girl Friday* (1940), *Ball Of Fire* (1942), *I Was A Male War Bride* (1949), *Monkey Business* (1952), *Gentleman Prefer Blondes* (1953) and *Rio Bravo* (1959). But *Rio Bravo*, I hear you cry, is a **Western**. Not so. All Hawks's films sneered at genres, and therein lay his greatest talent – he simply didn't care what people expected of him. He was always going to make his own choice of films (which the studios would graciously fund) and follow his own star, and if this involved joking with his friends, throwing in a song or two, or having his characters debate seriously on trivial subjects, then so be it. The General Sternwood orchid-house episode in *The Big Sleep* (1946) lasts a good ten minutes, and really has nothing to do with the film at all beyond providing **Humphrey Bogart** with a good excuse to begin investigating and to fall in love with **Lauren Bacall**. But it was a great scene, and continues to give pleasure however many times one sees it. Similarly, the 'was you ever stung by a dead bee' running gag, with the inimitable **Walter Brennan** in *To Have And Have Not* (1944) – on paper, it shouldn't even be funny, but it is as often as not triumphantly remembered after the rest of the movie has retreated back into the darkness from when it came. And what the blazes was Hoagy Carmichael doing in the same movie beyond providing a few brilliant musical interludes and a lot of innocent pleasure? Yes, it may be easy to pick at Hawks, but it has proved impossible to recreate him, and on the fifteenth watching of *El Dorado* (1967) – which itself only came about because Hawks had had so much fun making *Rio Bravo* that he thought, well why not do it again? – it becomes obvious that Hawks is Hawks because his movies find time to be human. His heroes, in spite of their own better judgement, are forever dragging along unwanted sidekicks, wastrels, rummies and wild animals, so that when we emerge from the shadowy enchantment of one of Hawks's pictures, our world seems bathed in that same illogical but infinitely precious glow of optimism. See **Heartstopping Moments**

Other Key Films: *Trent's Last Case* (1929); *The Dawn Patrol* (1930); *Scarface: The Shame Of A Nation* (1932); *Barbary Coast* (1935); *Only Angels Have Wings* (1940); *Sergeant York* (1941); *The Outlaw* [uncredited] (1943); *Red River* (1948); *The Big Sky* (1952); *Land Of The Pharaohs* (1955); *Hatari!* (1962); *Man's Favourite Sport?* (1964); *Rio Lobo* (1970)

Key Line: **Robert Mitchum's** drunken sheriff, J. P. Hannah: 'What are you doing here?' **John Wayne's** Cole Thornton: 'I'm looking at a tin star with a drunk pinned on it.' [Howard Hawks's *El Dorado* (1967)]

Hayden, Sterling

Always something of an octagonal peg in a round hole, Hayden captained one of the last of the square-rigged schooners as a young man and never lost his passion for sailing – a passion which he would fund from his erratic acting career – occasionally disappearing for lengthy periods to complete yet another leg of his ongoing round-the-world journey. A novelist as well as an actor, Hayden's good looks weathered over the years into something far more interesting, and he was well used by **John Huston** in *The Asphalt Jungle* (1950), by **Nicholas Ray** in *Johnny Guitar* (1953), and by **Stanley Kubrick** in *The Killing* (1956) and *Dr Strangelove* (1964). In 1951 he named names before the House Committee On Un-American Activities (HUAC) in order to save his career, an act he deeply regretted and later publicly apologized for, and he subsequently made a number of short-lived comebacks in later life, most notably as Roger Wade, the irascible, hell-raising writer in **Robert Altman's** *The Long Goodbye* (1973). An interesting curiosity.

Other Key Films: *Arrow In The Dust* (1954); *Suddenly* (1954); *Terror In A Texas Town* (1958); *Hard Contract* (1969); *1900* (1977); *King Of The Gypsies* (1978)

Hayworth, Rita

Although gorgeous to look at and a very fine dancer and singer (as well as an often underrated actress – one of the inevitable perils, one supposes, of too much beauty), there was something fatally vulnerable about Hayworth, and the fates really did seem to conspire against her during her terrible downhill battle, towards the end of her life, with both alcohol and Alzheimer's Disease. Her second husband, **Orson Welles**, captured the essence of her charms, together with the often contradictory nature of her screen image, in the form of the perverse and manipulative Elsa Bannister in his *The Lady From Shanghai* (1948), but Hayworth was also superb in **Charles Vidor's** stupendous *film noir*, *Gilda* (1946). At her best she lit up the screen, and for some reason it is only *on* the big screen, in a darkened cinema, that she really comes to life.

Other Key Films: *Only Angels Have Wings* (1939); *You'll Never Get Rich* (1941); *You Were Never Lovelier* (1942); *Cover Girl* (1944); *Miss Sadie Thompson* (1954)

Key Line: 'I can never get a zipper to close. Maybe that stands for something? What do you think?' [*Gilda*]

Head, Edith

Head's name appeared on more movie credit rolls than did the copyright symbol during the 1930s, 1940s and 1950s, as she designed clothes for every great star of Hollywood's golden era. Even her mistakes, as in **Bette Davis's** scene-stealing off-the-shoulder number in **Joseph L Mankiewicz's** *All About Eve* (1950), were serendipitously perfect. Head was the mistress of the human form, and she had collected so many academy awards as a costumier by the end of her fifty-year career, that it's a wonder she didn't set herself to designing outfits for them too.

Other Key Films: Howard Hawks's *Ball Of Fire* (1941); **Preston Sturges's** *Sullivan's Travels* (1941); **Billy Wilder's** *Five Graves To Cairo* (1943), *Double Indemnity* (1944) and *Sunset Boulevard* (1950); **George Stevens's** *Shane* (1953); **Alfred Hitchcock's** *Rear Window* (1953) (notably **Grace Kelly's** sublime frock in the dinner from Ciro's scene), *To Catch A Thief* (1955), *The Birds* (1963) and *Marnie* (1964)

Heart-stopping Moments:

1. **Jean Renoir's** *La Grande Illusion* (1937). When the soundtrack goes silent and the men in the prisoner-of-war camp suddenly become aware of a British soldier in the process of dressing up as a woman for a theatrical pageant. The muted camera tracks all the way along their faces, and in each face we are privileged to see the beyond-sexual yearning every man has for home, for female companionship, and for softness, after the

vindictive harshness of their collective experience of war.

2. **John Huston's** *Night Of The Iguana* (1964). When **Richard Burton** returns to **Ava Gardner** at the end of the film (following his polite, prescient rebuff by **Deborah Kerr**) to tell her that he will be staying after all, and the hard-nosed Gardner turns quickly away from him in an effort to hide her emotions (although not, of course, from the camera). This scene unfailingly procures sobs from all sensitive members of any audience who are viewing this magnificent film as it should be viewed, on a full-sized screen, in a proper cinema, and preferably in Paris.

3. **Howard Hawks's** *To Have And Have Not* (1945). That little wiggle of a dance that **Lauren Bacall** does at the end of the film, to Hoagy Carmichael's music, as she walks towards **Humphrey Bogart**, and which is far more redolent of her happiness that he has accepted her than if she were to express those emotions in words. Like the *Night Of The Iguana* moment, it is pure, unadulterated, cinema.

4. George Marshall's *The Blue Dahlia* (1946). Although not a good film in the strictest sense, there is a magic moment when **Alan Ladd** is brought up short by the luminous **Veronica Lake** when she asks him, 'Have you seen me before?' and he utters the following words (penned by **Raymond Chandler**) in a flat, resigned tone, as if he has lived with them all his life – 'Every guy's seen you before. Somewhere. The trick is to find you.'

5. **Joseph L Mankiewicz's** *The Ghost And Mrs Muir* (1947). When the shadow of **Rex Harrison's** ghostly sea captain falls across **Gene Tierney's** now aged features at the exact moment of her death – superbly accompanied, of course, by **Bernard Hermann's** swooping music. The scene appeals to the visceral instinct we all have towards the possibilities of reincarnation, and to any eventual prospect we might still entertain of finding a more than fleeting happiness.

6. **John Ford's** *My Darling Clementine* (1946). When **Henry Fonda** first sees Clementine alighting from the stagecoach, and stands up, from his habitual prone position, almost in exaltation.

7. **Alexander Korda's** *Rembrandt* (1936). When **Charles Laughton** silences a roomful of cynical and worldly men and their mistresses by admitting his love for his wife, Saskia, and describing her as all women to him. A moment later we realise that, during those few brief moments in which he has been extolling her virtues, she has died. Magic.

8. **Federico Fellini's** *La Strada* (1954). The scene after a wedding, in which **Giulietta Masina** follows the children of a large, strange house, up to the first floor and into the isolated bedroom of a boy with an enlarged head, and we realise, in the magical transition from adult to child's view (and without the need for any words) that this is where she really belongs, in the children's world, the place from which she was taken at the beginning of the film.

9. **Akira Kurosawa's** *The Seven Samurai* (1954). The scene in which the young Samurai is told that he cannot go to fight with the older men, in the peasant village. What follows is a series of close-ups, during which Kombei tells of the years he has followed the code of Bushido, and which culminates in the grim, noble face of Kyuzo, the greatest of all the Samurai, arriving at the door.

10. **Billy Wilder's** *Sunset Boulevard* (1950). The moment when one of the technicians, who would conceivably have been only an apprentice in the 1920s, recognizes Norma Desmond/**Gloria Swanson** on **Cecil B DeMille's** set, where she is sitting, alone and unnoticed, in the Director's chair. Slowly he spotlights her. She raises her face to the light. Gradually and magically all the extras come flocking around her, like moths to the light of a lamp. This particular scene is one of the greatest of all mute illustrations of the fundamental magic of the movies.

11. **Jean Renoir's** *Les Bas-Fonds* (1936). The moment when **Louis Jouvet** and **Jean Gabin** lie on the grass reminiscing, and an unscripted snail walks up Jouvet's arm which he incorporates, with a great actor's instincts, into the scene.

12. **John Ford's** *The Grapes Of Wrath* (1940). The moment when Ma Joad (played by Jane Darwell), about to leave her condemned farm for the last time, silently tries on an old pair of earrings that she has found in a box. Ford shows us her broken, and briefly young, reflection in an old mirror. The scene is silent. Words aren't necessary.

13. **Robert Bresson's** *Mouchette* (1967). When a fourteen-year-old schoolgirl, clad only in a simple shift and a pair of wooden clogs, allows herself to roll slowly down the bank of a river towards her certain death. She fails the first time, gets up, and in one of the greatest and most heart-rending moments in all cinema, makes her way slowly up the bank, in a despair so deep that nothing can break through it, before rolling down once again, this time to her death.

14. Jacques Feyder's *Knight Without Armour* (1937). When Russian aristocrat, **Marlene Dietrich**, in an all-but-diaphanous white nightgown, races across the empty lawns of her father's stately home, fearful that she has been abandoned to the mob by her servants and entourage. She comes to a stop by the lake, upon which a thousand angry peasants approach her from over the lee of the hill, their pitchforks and sickles held high. Hesitant at first, Dietrich slowly draws herself up and proudly faces them.

15. **Josef von Sternberg's** *Dishonoured* (1931). Another Dietrich moment, this time she is about to be shot as a spy. No mercy is possible. She asks for decent clothes, a lipstick, the chance to wash, and a piano. A young officer brings her these things, then breaks down at the thought of a woman suffering such a death. Dietrich comforts him before striding out to the firing squad, looking immaculate, with a cigarette dangling nonchalantly from her lips.

16. **Ernst Lubitsch's** *The Shop Around The Corner* (1940). When Margaret Sullavan's Clare Novak, in love with a man (**James Stewart**) she thinks she knows only by correspondence (but who is also, unbeknown to both of them, her co-worker), searches with her gloved hand inside her post-box, only to discover that there is no letter there. The shot of her bereft face as she realises her loss is one of the most poignant moments in all cinema, and a worthy tribute to the lessons all sound directors might profitably learn, if only they had the inclination, from the art of silent filmmaking.

17. The moment in **David Lean's** *Brief Encounter* (1945) when **Trevor Howard's** Dr Alec Harvey finally declares his love for Celia Johnson's Laura Jesson in the boat shed.

Hecht, Ben

Hecht is the screenwriter most people think of when they think of the wisecracking Hollywood movies of the 1930s, in which the girls are just as sassy as the boys (without feeling the need to emasculate them) and in which the screenwriter, for perhaps the very last time, occasionally succeeds in stealing the show. Hecht worked on an extraordinary succession of hit movies, often collaborating with I A L Diamond or Charles Macarthur, and as often as not received little or no billing for his pains, as in his work for **John Ford's** *The Hurricane* (1937) and **Victor Fleming's** *Gone With The Wind* (1939). His masterpieces are **William Wellman's** *Nothing Sacred* (1937) and **Alfred Hitchcock's** *Notorious* (1946), in both of which Hecht's obsession with hypocrisy, and of what constituted truth, were most apparent. He is best remembered for his play, *The Front Page*, co-written with Macarthur, that spawned two outstanding movies, Lewis Milestone's *The Front Page* (1931) and **Howard Hawks's** *His Girl Friday* (1940), and one pretty good one, **Billy Wilder's** *The Front Page* (1974).
Other Key Films: Howard Hawks's *Twentieth Century* (1934) and *Monkey Business* (1952); **George Stevens's** *Gunga Din* (1939); Alfred Hitchcock's *Spellbound* (1945); **Otto Preminger's** *Where The Sidewalk Ends* (1950);
Key Line: 'The sonofabitch stole my watch!' [*The Front Page*]

Heflin, Van:

Heflin never really made it as a big star despite a number of leading-man roles, but he was more than good in the series of varied films he did get to make. Belying his all-American boy-next-door looks, he brought a considerable emotional range to Lewis Milestone's *The Strange Love Of Martha Ivers* (1946), to Curtis Bernhardt's *Possessed* (1947), and, in particular, to his obsessed, dissatisfied policeman, Garwood, in **Joseph Losey's** first class *film noir*, *The Prowler* (1951). His most famous role was as the homesteader, Joe Starrett, in **George Stevens's** *Shane* (1953).
Other Key Films: *The Outcasts Of Poker Flat* (1937); *Santa Fe Trail* (1940); *Madame Bovary* (1949); *Battle Cry* (1955); *3:10 To Yuma* (1958); *They Came To Cordura* (1959)

Heist Movies

Heist movies are films in which the central action revolves around a robbery, and whose plots generally follow, in consecutive order, conception, perpetration, and implication. Notable examples include **John Huston's** *The Asphalt Jungle* (1950), **Jules Dassin's** *Rififi* (1954), **Stanley Kubrick's** *The Killing* (1956), and Peter Collinson's *The Italian Job* (1969). Literary-minded fans of the caper, or heist movie, might like to try the Parker books of Richard Stark, the acknowledged master of caper fiction and the originator of some of the best Hollywood heist movie clones.

Hepburn, Audrey

Hepburn may be dearly loved and esteemed by her long-standing fans, but even they cannot dispute the fact that she was never much of an actress, and that her fame lies more in her persona, her gamine charm, and the glamour she so exceptionally personified, than in any thespian talent. The only notable exception to this is

Audrey Hepburn in Breakfast at Tiffany's, directed by Blake Edwards (1961).

Paramount/The Kobal Collection

her role of Sister Luke/GabrielleVan Der Mal in **Fred Zinnemann's** *The Nun's Story* (1959). Her skills were tailor-made for the sophisticated and still elitist 1950s, when the post-war boom had yet to impact on the ability of the under-classes to derive any benefit from it – instead, as a temporary placebo, they watched Hepburn, in films like **Stanley Donen's** *Funny Face* (1958) and *Charade* (1963), or **Blake Edwards's** *Breakfast At Tiffany's* (1961), and dreamed.

Other Key Films: *Roman Holiday* (1953); *Sabrina* (1954); *Love In The Afternoon* (1958); *The Nun's Story* (1959); *My Fair Lady* (1964); *Two For The Road* (1967); *Robin And Marian* (1976); *Always* (1989)

Hepburn, Katherine

Hepburn was the most stylised actress of her generation, and it is to her credit that she managed to ensure that the public mood accorded with her stylisations, rather than the other way around. No one ever talked or acted like Hepburn *except* Hepburn, and it was this very eccentricity and self-absorption that allowed her to extend her career beyond all reasonable limits and to virtually monopolize that singular and rarefied niche of 'Oscars for the elderly', that so warms the cockles of the Academy's ageing hearts. She acted in surprisingly few films for someone whose career spanned close to sixty-five years, and she made a conspicuous number of duds – even stranger than that was her reputation, during the 1940s, of being box-office poison, the feeling being that her upper-class accent grated on the newly democratic aspirations of the returning soldiers and their girls. Hepburn swept these minor problems aside, of course, becoming democracy personified in such films as **George Cukor's** *Adam's Rib* (1949) and *Pat And Mike* (1952), just as she'd been elitism personified in **Howard Hawks's** *Bringing Up Baby* (1938) and Cukor's earlier, and arguably best comedy of the sexes, *The Philadelphia Story* (1940). Later in life, following long-term lover **Spencer Tracy's** death, she became wise and somewhat distant, reminding us, in such films as Mark Rydell's *On Golden Pond* (1981) and Glenn Gordon Caron's *Love Affair* (1994), what a peculiarly *American* phenomenon we had for so long been attracted to.

Other Key Films: *A Bill Of Divorcement* (1932); *Little Women* (1933); *Stage Door* (1937); *Holiday* (1938); *Woman Of The Year* (1942); *State Of The Union* (1948); *The African Queen* (1951); *Summertime* (1955); *Suddenly Last Summer* (1959); *The Lion In Winter* (1968); *Rooster Cogburn* (1976)

Key Lines:

1. 'Nature, Mr Allnutt, is what we are put into this world to rise above.' [*The African Queen*]

2. 'I never dreamed that any mere physical experience could be so s timulating.' [*The African Queen*]

3. 'She, Kate Hepburn, is a very bossy, humourless lady. She has a sense of wit, but no sense of humour whatsoever…and nobody is going to tell Kate Hepburn anything!' [Screenwriter Arthur Laurents on Hepburn, who starred in **David Lean's** film of Laurents's play, *Summertime* (1955)]

Herrmann, Bernard

Herrmann composed the music for **Alfred Hitchcock's** *Psycho* (1960) – the famous bit when **Janet Leigh** is driving alone in her car with the rain pounding onto the windscreen so hard that she can scarcely see, and she's just peering through the struggling wipers trying to get her bearings when…bang!…up looms the Bates Motel and perdition. And how about the shrieking *Tsi… Tsi… Tsi…* of the violins when Leigh is being slaughtered in the shower? A certain sort of genius, allied with a supreme confidence in one's animal abilities, is needed to achieve such an effect. It is inconceivable that it could be bettered, just as it is inconceivable to imagine **Orson Welles's** horse rearing up over the terrified **Joan Fontaine** in Robert Stevenson's *Jane Eyre* (1944) without the awesome background music, or **Robert De Niro's** Travis Bickle cruising like a shark through the mean streets of New York in **Martin Scorsese's** *Taxi Driver* (1976), without Hermann to lead us inside the tortured recesses of Bickle's mind. Hermann's music acts as a metaphorical voice-over to the narrative, and he is the greatest master of all at framing alienation in sound, as he did so sublimely and so categorically in the case of **Robert Ryan's** disenchanted cop in **Nicholas Ray's** magnificent *On Dangerous Ground* (1951).

Other Key Films: Orson Welles's *Citizen Kane* (1941) and *The Magnificent Ambersons* (1942); **Joseph L Mankiewicz's** *The Ghost And Mrs. Muir* (1947) and *Five Fingers* (1952); Alfred Hitchcock's *The Man Who Knew Too Much* (1956), *North By Northwest* (1959) and *Marnie* (1964); J Lee Thompson's *Cape Fear* (1962); **François Truffaut's** *Fahrenheit 451* (1966)

Herzog, Werner

The **auteur theory** of directorial supremacy promulgated by the Cahiers du Cinéma boys seems tailor-made for the philosophically inclined Herzog. Indeed his single-mindedness in getting his visions onto celluloid has sometimes more resembled the compulsive tic of an incipient madman, particularly when twinned with the complementary mania of actor **Klaus Kinski**, whom Herzog, despite his better judgement, and at some considerable risk to what remained of his own sanity, persisted in using as his alter ego on screen. But *Aguirre, Wrath Of God* (1972) is a unique experience, and it is hard to imagine a better or more understandable vampire than Kinski's *Nosferatu* (1979), a more complex *Woyzeck* (1979), or a more incomplete *Fitzcarraldo* (1982). Herzog's best film, however, was as far removed from Kinski's creative histrionics as it is possible to be – *The Enigma Of Kaspar Hauser* (1975) was a gentle, rigorously controlled and almost documentary insight into a truly simple man, who appeared as if from nowhere, lingered briefly to remind us that we do not possess all the answers, and then was roughly torn from the world by a man (his father perhaps) whom we neither know nor, to all intents and purposes, see. Herzog is obsessed with God, with fate and with the meaning of creation, and at the end of *Kaspar Hauser* we are left with the uncomfortable feeling that Adam and Eve's loss of the Garden of Eden may well have been occasioned by nothing more profound than a temporary fit of pique on the part of its erstwhile creator.

Other Key Films: *Signs Of Life* (1968); *Even Dwarfs Started Small* (1970); *Fata Morgana Frustrated Future* [doc.] (1971); *Land Of Silence And Darkness* [doc.] (1972); *Heart Of Glass* (1976); *Stroszek* (1977); *The Ballad Of The Little Soldier* (1984); *Where The Little Ants Dream* (1984); *Cobra Verde* (1988); *It Isn't Easy Being God* (1989); *Scream Of Stone* (1991); *Lessons In Darkness* (1992); *Mein Liebster Feind – Klaus Kinski* [doc.] (1999); *Invincible* (2001); *Grizzly Man* (2005); *Rescue Dawn* (2006)

Heston, Charlton

Heston is a king-actor (using **Orson Welles's** definition of a man with such innate presence that his incarnation as a mere common man would appear absurd). The two king-actors met and matched each other in Welles's magisterially expressionistic *Touch Of Evil* (1958), in which the real-life Heston, through his character of Mike Vargas, possibly began to infer, in the downfall of Welles's monstrous Hank Quinlan, the fate that was to befall his own screen persona many years later. Heston bravely championed the unchampionable Welles ever after, and this courtesy – call it niceness if you will – was always a part of his charm, and was evident even when he was at his most martial, as in **William Wyler's** *Ben-Hur* (1959) or **Anthony Mann's** *El Cid* (1961). Heston allowed one to believe, even if ever so briefly, that history might be influenced by individuals, and the gradual tendency of his later career towards fantasy, as in Franklin J Schaffner's *Planet Of The Apes* (1968) and Richard Fleischer's *Soylent Green* (1973), revealed an awkward but undoubtedly conscious acknowledgment, that time and tide (and the coming of the common man) were beginning to pass him by.

Other Key Films: *Dark City* (1950); *The Naked Jungle* (1954); *Secret Of The Incas* (1954); *The Ten Commandments* (1956); *The Big Country* (1958); *The Wreck Of The Mary Deare* (1959); *55 Days At Peking* (1963); *Major Dundee* (1965); *The Agony And The Ecstasy* (1965); *The War Lord* (1965); *Khartoum* (1966); *Will Penny* (1968); *Call Of The Wild* (1972); *Gray Lady Down* (1978); *Tombstone* (1993); *Hamlet* (1996); *Illusion Infinity* (1998); *Toscano* (1999); *Any Given Sunday* (1999); *Town And Country* (2001); *Planet of the Apes* [Remake] (2001); *The Order* (2003); *My Father, Rua Alguem 5555* (2003); *Genghis Khan* (2005)

Hitchcock, Alfred

It is impossible for anyone who has seen even one of his films to deny Hitchcock his place inside the cinema's pantheon of greats, for his was the most 'cinematic' mind of all, and at the same time the most isolated from 'real life' of all the great directors. Cinema made Hitchcock just as surely as the stage made **Laurence Olivier**, and he was equally in thrall to it, subsuming his unconscious mind, and ours, to its magic. He worked in England until 1939, turning out a series of bravura films including *The 39 Steps* (1935), *Young And Innocent* (1937) and *The Lady Vanishes* (1938) and then, as if he

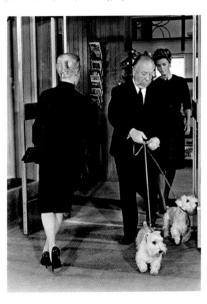

Tippi Hedren and Alfred Hitchcock making his cameo appearance in his film The Birds (1963).

Universal/The Kobal Collection

instinctively understood how the Second World War would swing the fulcrum of power ever further westwards, he moved to America, where he began work on a new series of films. These proved unique in the annals of commercial cinema in that they successfully spanned the two worlds of the critically acclaimed and the financially viable over the immense period of thirty-six years. *Rebecca* (1940), *Suspicion* (1941) and *Saboteur* (1942) initially harked back to his English years, but with *Spellbound* (1945) he discovered his lodestone, namely the American film with an English sensibility, and this was to become his stock-in-trade during the remainder of his career. *Notorious* (1946), *Strangers On A Train* (1951), *Rear Window* (1954), *Vertigo* (1958) and *North By Northwest* (1959) showed the Americans themselves as they wished to be, all the while craftily mining the very Cold War insecurities such films were ostensibly designed to obviate. *Psycho* (1960), *The Birds* (1963) and *Marnie* (1964) were the late *chef d'oeuvres* of a master never content to rest upon his laurels, and the relative weakness of his last films can hardly, in the circumstances, afford us much cause to grumble.

Other Key Films: *The Lodger* (1926); *Blackmail* (1929); *The Man Who Knew Too Much* (1934); *The Secret Agent* (1936); *Sabotage* (1937); *Jamaica Inn* (1939); *Foreign Correspondent* (1940); *Shadow Of A Doubt* (1943); *Lifeboat* (1944); *The Paradine Case* (1948); *Rope* (1948); *Under Capricorn* (1949); *I Confess* (1953); *Dial M For Murder* (1954); *To Catch A Thief* (1955); *The Wrong Man* (1958); *Torn Curtain* (1966); *Topaz* (1969); *Frenzy* (1972); *Family Plot* (1976)

Key Lines:

1. 'Actors should be treated like cattle.' [Hitchcock on the acting profession]
2. 'Television has brought back murder into the home – where it belongs.' [Hitchcock on murder]
3. 'There is no terror in a bang, only in the anticipation of it.' [Hitchcock on suspense]
4. 'His whole life was motion pictures; there didn't seem to be much else in it. He just loved what he was doing, and he transmitted that feeling to you, rather than hovering over you like a giant genius.' [Screenwriter John Michael Hayes after his four-time collaboration with Hitchcock, on *Rear Window* (1954), *The Trouble With Harry* (1955), *To Catch A Thief* (1955) and *The Man Who Knew Too Much* [co-script] (1956)]
5. 'The thing that amuses me about Hitchcock is the way he directs a film in his head before he knows what the story is.' [**Raymond Chandler**, during the co-writing of *Strangers On A Train* (1951)]

Hoffman, Dustin

Hoffman, like his co-star **Tom Cruise** in Barry Levinson's *Rain Man* (1988), makes a virtue of his diminutive size, using it to gather in parts that larger, more obvious men, would never find it in themselves to attempt. He was an overnight sensation in **Mike Nichols's** *The Graduate* (1967), and his Ratso in **John Schlesinger's** *Midnight Cowboy* (1969) was an utterly cinematic creation; the character's link with everyday reality was tenuous, in other words, while its link with cinematic reality was absolute. And that is Hoffman's strength – he never forgets that he's in a movie, and his Michael Dorsey/Dorothy Michaels in **Sydney Pollack's** *Tootsie* (1982) succeeds for that very reason. Hoffman can play a loser better than anyone, and even when his loser occasionally wins through, as in **Arthur Penn's** magisterial *Little Big Man* (1970), or **Sam Peckinpah's** ultra-violent *Straw Dogs* (1971), we are left, not with the taste of champagne, but with the taste of bitter aloes. In recent years Hoffman seems to have lost his way a little, and has fallen back on his reputation to the extent that he has chosen to appear in one or two no-doubt lucrative pot-boilers, for example **Stephen Frears's** *Hero* (1992) and **Wolfgang Petersen's** *Outbreak* (1995). However he did partially redeem himself in Michael Corrente's *American Buffalo* (1996), and his seriousness in the face of Hollywood madness should carry him triumphantly through to a critically acclaimed dotage.

Other Key Films: *Papillon* (1973); *Lenny* (1974); *All The President's Men* (1976); *Marathon Man* (1976); *Agatha* (1979); *Kramer Vs. Kramer* (1979); *Death Of A Salesman* [TVM] (1985); *Family Business* (1989); *Billy Bathgate* (1991); *Hook* (1991); *Sleepers* (1996); *Mad City* (1997); *Sphere* (1998); *Messenger: The Story Of Joan Of Arc* (1999); *Runaway Jury* (2003); *Finding Neverland* (2004); *Meet The Fockers* (2004); *Stranger Than Fiction* (2006)

Key Line: 'Mrs Robinson, you're trying to seduce me, aren't you?' [*The Graduate*]

Holden, William

After changing his name from William Beedle Jr. (for obvious reasons), Holden first made his mark in Rouben Mamoulian's *Golden Boy* (1939). Always destined for virile parts due to his peculiarly American brand of masculine good looks, Holden gradually drank himself to death – killing, in the process, the innocent bystander at one of his numerous car accidents. Holden seemed to coast along for much of the time in his movies, but when good directors did get hold of him, and when they succeeded in galvanizing him out of his lethargy, he could prove excellent, as with his Joe Gillis in **Billy Wilder's** *Sunset Boulevard* (1950), his Sefton in *Stalag 17* (1953), and his Pike Bishop in **Sam Peckinpah's** *The Wild Bunch* (1969). It was in this role that for the first and only time, Holden allowed his personal despair to show through.

Other Key Films: *Born Yesterday* (1950); *Union Station* (1950); *Escape From Fort Bravo* (1953); *The Country Girl* (1954); *Sabrina* (1954); *Picnic* (1955); *Love Is A Many Splendored Thing* (1955); *The Bridge On The River Kwai* (1958); *The Horse Soldiers* (1959); *Network* (1976); *Fedora* (1978)

Hope, Bob

Is Hope really funny? Or do we simply laugh at him because we are expected to do so? There is an element of the after-dinner speaker in all his performances, testing out that last tentative joke for the possibility that it might elicit one final chortle. Hope, among all screen comedians, is the most obvious product of the 'one by the many' – he is the gagman of the nineteenth tee, a placator of the middle-classes and the comforting presence that persuades us that niceness comes rewarded with riches, and that studied modesty (disguised by braggadocio) will bring with it the laurels and the reassurances of a ripe old age. That said, his is an essentially innocent and pain-free talent, best summed up in his most successful screen performance as Wallie Campbell in Elliott Nugent's *The Cat And The Canary* (1939).

Other Key Films: *Road To Singapore* (1940); *Road To Zanzibar* (1941); *Caught In The Draft* (1941); *Road To Morocco* (1942); *Road To Utopia* (1946); *Road To Rio* (1947); *The Paleface* (1948); *Fancy Pants* (1950); *Road To Bali* (1952); *The Iron Petticoat* (1956); *The Facts Of Life* (1960); *Critic's Choice* (1963)

Hopkins, Anthony

It is hard to see the later, confident Hopkins, in the early, ersatz *James Bond* clone he played in Etienne Perier's *When Eight Bells Toll* (1971), but the nervous intensity of his acting showed through even then, as if this elusive man always had something better to do, some other place to go, and that he was aching to get on with it despite the expectations of his foolish audience. We now know that his impatience was for the stardom he knew he merited (an instinctive rather than a studied haste, perhaps), and that what we had allowed ourselves to miss in his youth, we would belatedly have to make up for in his prime. For Hopkins *is* the finest British screen actor of his generation, and his subtlety and dedication to his craft should serve as lessons to the short-shrifters and the ease-merchants who make up such a large proportion of the present-day generation of wannabes. Hopkins's Captain Bligh in Roger Donaldson's *The Bounty* (1984) is the genuine article – a vulnerable, self-made man with homoerotic tendencies who is entirely of his time, not ours, and who is only understandable in that context. In **James Ivory's** *Howard's End* (1992), Hopkins was a high Victorian monolith washed up in Edwardian England, and in the same director's *Remains Of The Day* (1993) he played a man so straightened by his sense of duty that love, even the very possibility of it, remains utterly and disastrously marginalized. **Richard Attenborough's** *Shadowlands* (1993) leavened the post-Edwardian despair that Hopkins controls so well, and allowed a fleeting and shocking happiness to a man nominally incapable of even comprehending it. Now that he is in such demand in Hollywood, following his bravura performances as Hannibal Lecter in **Jonathan Demme's** *Silence Of The Lambs* (1991) and Ridley Scott's *Hannibal* (2001), it is comforting to know that habit, together with an ingrained artistic integrity, will simply not allow him to give anything but his best. Note for Film Buffs: Hopkins is actually a few months younger than **Dustin Hoffman**.

Other Key Films: *The Lion In Winter* (1968); *The Looking Glass War* (1970); *A Doll's House* (1973); *Magic* (1978); *The Elephant Man* (1980); *The Good Father* (1986); *Blunt* (1986); *84 Charing Cross Road* (1987); *Desperate Hours* (1990); *Legends Of The Fall* (1994); *Nixon* (1995); *Surviving Picasso* (1996); *Amistad* (1997); *The Edge* (1997); *The Mask Of Zorro* (1998); *Instinct* (1999); *Titus* (1999); *Mission: Impossible 2* (2000); *Hearts in Atlantis* (2001); *The Devil and Daniel Webster* (2001); *Red Dragon* (2002); *The Human Stain* (2003); *Alexander* (2004); *Proof* (2005); *The World's Fastest Indian* (2005); *Fracture* (2006); *Bobby* (2006)

Key Line: 'A census taker once tried to test me. I ate his liver with some fava beans and a nice Chianti.' [*The Silence Of The Lambs*]

Hopper, Dennis

Hardly the great figure he has sometimes been portrayed as, though certainly an interesting one – if only because he has survived a level of substance and alcohol abuse that has already dispatched those of his generation with somewhat lesser constitutions – Hopper's main claim to fame lies in his early link with **James Dean** in **Nicholas Ray's** *Rebel Without A Cause* (1955) and **George Stevens's** *Giant* (1956), and for his direction of the **cult**, though ultimately disappointing, *Easy Rider* (1969). When not too vociferously method acting, he has turned in some fine performances, particularly in **David Lynch's** *Blue Velvet* (1986) and Tony Scott's *True Romance* (1993). He has also directed a *film noir* thriller, *The Hot Spot* (1990), which proved very good indeed.

Other Key Films: *True Grit* (1969); *The American Friend* (1977); *Apocalypse Now* (1979); *Out Of The Blue* (1980); *Rumble Fish* (1983); *Paris Trout* (1991); *Red Rock West* (1993); *Waterworld* (1995); *The Source* [doc.] (1999); *Bad City Blues* (1999); *The Spreading Ground* (2000); *Luck Of The Draw* (2000); *Knockaround Guys* (2001); *The Piano Player* (2002); *The Night We Called It A Day* (2003); *The Keeper* (2004); *House Of 9* (2005); *Land Of The Dead* (2005); *10ᵗʰ & Wolf* (2006)

Best **Horror Films**

Roy Ward Black's *Asylum* (1972); **Roger Corman's** *The Mask Of The Red Death* (1964); **Wes Craven's** *A Nightmare On Elm Street* (1984); **Jonathan Demme's** *Silence Of The Lambs* (1991); Ruggiero Deodato's *Cannibal Holocaust* (1980); **Samuel Fuller's** *Shock Corridor* (1963); Robin Hardy's *The Wicker Man* (1973); **Werner Herzog's** *Nosferatu The Vampyre* (1979); **Alfred Hitchcock's** *Psycho* (1960) and *The Birds* (1963); **Stanley Kubrick's** *The Shining* (1980); **F W Murnau's** *Nosferatu* (1922); **Roman Polanski's** *Repulsion* (1965) and *Rosemary's Baby* (1968); **Sam Raimi's** *Evil Dead* (1982); George A Romero's *The Night Of The Living Dead* (1968); Kaneto Shindo's *Onibaba* (1964); **Jacques Tourneur's** *Cat People* (1942) and *Curse Of The Demon* [a.k.a. *Night of the Demon*] (1958); Robert Wiene's *The Cabinet Of Dr Caligari* (1919)

Hoskins, Bob

A former Covent Garden Porter, Hoskins is at his best playing raw, emotional men thrown into situations where they find themselves suddenly out of their depth, as in his breakthrough TV performance as Arthur Parker, in Dennis Potter's magisterial *Pennies From Heaven* (1978), directed by Piers Haggard. His gang boss, Harold, in John Mackenzie's recently re-released *The Long Good Friday* (1980) is a case in point, as is his towering performance as the lovesick petty crook in **Neil Jordan's** *Mona Lisa* (1986). Hoskins had a surprise success in Robert Zemeckis's *Who Framed Roger Rabbit* (1988), which had the virtue of making him a rich man overnight, as he received a percentage cut. Since then his roles have varied alarmingly in quality, but it is unlikely that we have heard the last of his talent.

Other Key Films: *The Cotton Club* (1984); *Brazil* (1985); *The Lonely Passion Of Judith Hearne* (1988); *Shattered* (1991); *Nixon* (1995); *Cousin Bette* (1998); *Felicia's Journey* (1999); *Enemy At The Gates* (2001); *The Sleeping Dictionary* (2001); *Last Orders* (2001); *Maid In Manhattan* (2002); *Den Of Lions* (2003); *Vanity Fair* (2004); *Beyond The Sea* (2004); *Mrs Henderson Presents* (2005); *Hollywoodland* (2006)

Howard, Leslie

Howard was the man who gave **Humphrey Bogart** his first big screen break by insisting that he play the part of Duke Mantee in Archie Mayo's *Petrified Forest* (1936). It is perhaps hard for present-day audiences to appreciate that an actor as elusive as Howard ever had that sort of influence in Hollywood, but his was an indefinable talent, perfect for the asexual and somewhat fatalistic version of romantic idealism that flourished, very briefly, in the inter-war years. This was encapsulated best by his Holger Brandt in Gregory Ratoff's *Intermezzo: A Love Story* (1939), and by his brief appearance as Philip Armstrong Scott (shades of the even more fatalistic Robert Falcon Scott?) in **Michael Powell's** *The 49th Parallel* (1941). Howard played passive, end-of-empire men, and he would have made a marvellous Sir Edward Leithen if John Buchan's Leithen books had ever come to be filmed. His Ashley Wilkes in **Victor Fleming's *Gone With The Wind*** (1939), so often criticized in favour of **Clark Gable's** more virile, thrusting Rhett Butler, is a pretty much perfect rendition of the lost, probably apocryphal spirit of the American South, and it is entirely fitting that Scarlett O'Hara should be idealistically attached to him, while being not so much wooed as ravished by the newly anti-heroic future incarnated by Gable. Howard died in 1943, shot down by the Nazis while travelling by air from Lisbon to London – while hesitating to call this a fitting end for such an elusive man, one is nonetheless forced to accord a measure of appropriateness to the manner of his leaving.

Other Key Films: *Berkeley Square* (1933); *The Lady Is Willing* (1934); *Of Human Bondage* (1934); *The Scarlet Pimpernel* (1935); *Pygmalion* (1938); *Pimpernel Smith* (1941); *The First Of The Few* (1942)

Howard, Ron

A former child star and veteran of such TV classics as *Happy Days* and *The Andy Griffith Show*, Howard found his epiphany in **George Lucas's** *American Graffiti* (1973) as Steve, but he has since given up acting in favour of becoming a highly bankable director with a penchant for one-word movie titles. *Splash* (1984), which was an adult breakthrough for both Disney and Howard himself, was followed by the slightly sickly *Cocoon* (1985). Howard redeemed himself, however, with *Willow* (1988), followed by the very exciting *Backdraft* (1991). His best film to date has been

Apollo 13 (1995), and if there were still a studio system, it would be just to say that Howard is the perfect encapsulation of it. But there isn't. So he isn't. See **Worst Films** for a review of Howard's *The Da Vinci Code* (2006).

Other Key Films: *Parenthood* (1989); *Far And Away* (1992); *The Paper* (1994); *EdTV* (1999); *How The Grinch Stole Christmas* (2000); *A Beautiful Mind* (2001); *The Missing* (2003); *Cinderella Man* (2005)

Howard, Trevor

Howard came from another generation entirely to his partial namesake, **Leslie Howard**, a generation that grew up in more or less total ignorance of the utter emasculation of England during the First World War. And it showed. Howard was a tougher customer altogether, a man whom one imagined *doing* things, rather than passively contemplating the past. After being wounded in action in 1943, he was taken up by director **Carol Reed** for a small part in *The Way Ahead* (1944), and it is somewhat miraculous to see him so quickly transformed into the confident Alec Harvey, in **David Lean's** *Brief Encounter* (1945). He was barely thirty at the time (though he looked much older) but he had already formed the exact persona he was to inhabit in the ensuing forty-two years. Reed understood Howard better than any other director he worked with, and it is for his role as Major Calloway in Reed's *The Third Man* (1949) that Howard will probably be best remembered, although his most complex and satisfying performance for Reed came later, as Peter Willems in *Outcast Of The Islands* (1951). Howard's later films, excellent though they are, cannot stand comparison with those of his prime.

Other Key Films: *Passionate Friends* (1948); *The Golden Salamander* (1949); *Odette* (1950); *The Gift Horse* (1952); *The Heart Of The Matter* (1953); *The Roots Of Heaven* (1958); *Sons And Lovers* (1960); *Mutiny On The Bounty* (1962); *Von Ryan's Express* (1965); *The Charge Of The Light Brigade* (1968); *Ryan's Daughter* (1970); *Kidnapped* (1971) *The Offence* (1973); *Conduct Unbecoming* (1975); *Sir Henry At Rawlinson End* (1980); *White Mischief* (1987)

Key Line: 'Death is at the bottom of everything, Martins. Leave death to the professionals.' [*The Third Man*]

Howe, James Wong

One of Hollywood's greatest cinematographers (he first started work in **Cecil B DeMille's** cutting room in 1917), Howe undoubtedly influenced the look of Orson Welles's ***Citizen Kane*** (1941) with his extraordinarily expressive camerawork on William K Howard's similarly themed *The Power And The Glory*. Howe's mastery of contrast and movement was also wonderfully evident in Jack Conway's *Viva Villa!* (1934), but it was only later, with Robert Rossen's *Body And Soul* (1947), **Alexander Mackendrick's** *The Sweet Smell Of Success* (1958) and **Martin Ritt's** *Hud* (1963), that his total mastery of the black-and-white medium became apparent.

Other Key Films: W S Van Dyke's *The Thin Man* (1934); John Cromwell's *The Prisoner Of Zenda* (1937) and *Algiers* (1938); **William Dieterle's** *Dr. Ehrlich's Magic Bullet* (1940); **Sam Wood's** *Kings Row* (1942); Daniel Mann's *The Rose Tattoo* (1955); Joshua Logan's *Picnic* (1956); Martin Ritt's *Hombre* (1967)

Hudson, Rock

Hudson gave every appearance of being heterosexual beefcake personified, a fact made all the more poignant by his forcibly unacknowledged homosexuality (except within the closed Hollywood film community) and by his death in 1985, bravely if belatedly acknowledged, from the AIDS virus. Given his physical qualifications as a heartthrob, Hudson developed into a better actor than he had any right to be given Hollywood's inevitable pigeon-holing of his talents. He predated **Randolph Scott** as a sensitive **Budd Boetticher** hero in *Seminole* (1953); and **Douglas Sirk**, who had directed him in a bit part in *Has Anybody Seen My Gal?* (1952), decided that there was something more than pure beefcake in this 6ft 4in hunk, and went on to prove so in the quartet of high-quality melodramas that were to make Hudson's name – *Magnificent Obsession* (1954), *All That Heaven Allows* (1955), *Written On The Wind* (1956) and *The Tarnished Angels* (1958). Other excellent Hudson roles came as Bick Benedict in **George Stevens's** *Giant* (1956), and later as Antiochus 'Tony' Wilson in **John Frankenheimer's** underrated *Seconds* (1966).

Other Key Films: *Winchester '73* (1950); *Bend Of The River* (1952); *A Farewell To Arms* (1958); *Pillow Talk* (1959); *Blindfold* (1966); *Tobruk* (1967); *Ice Station Zebra* (1968); *The Undefeated* (1969)

Hughes, Howard

A true eccentric in later life, Hughes exhibited, from his very first venture into film production with Lewis Milestone's *Two Arabian Knights* (1927), a compulsive need for control. The older he got, the more inspired by his actresses and his toys and his dreams did he become, culminating in the heady and Machiavellian saga of *The Outlaw* (1940-1946) in which his obsession for both the physical and the metaphysical dimensions of **Jane Russell's** cleavage took on something of an endearingly epic quality. Hughes was the reluctant hedonist personified, and he came to represent the quintessence of a mainland America largely unscathed by two world wars and which had come to believe that money and the convulsive spending of it were sufficient and valid compensations for vacuity. Almost despite himself, Hughes encouraged the talents of others, and it is for this, as well as for his extraordinary life, that he should be remembered.

Other Key Films: *Hell's Angels* (1930); Lewis Milestone's *The Front Page* (1931); **Howard Hawks's** *Scarface* (1932); **Victor Fleming's** *Bombshell* (1933); **Don Siegel's** *The Big Steal* (1949); John Cromwell's *The Racket* (1951); **Josef Von Sternberg's** *Jet Pilot* (1951) and *Macao* (1952); **Nicholas Ray's** *Flying Leathernecks* (1951); **John Farrow's** *His Kind Of Woman* (1951); **Otto Preminger's** *Angel Face* (1952)

Huppert, Isabelle

An actress like Huppert would be impossible in the US, for she comfortably spans both extremes of the commercial and the outré in films as disparate as **Claude Chabrol's** *Violette Nozière* (1978) and **Jean-Luc Godard's** *Sauve Qui Peut* (1980). She first made her mark in **Bertrand Blier's** *Les Valseuses* (1971), and it is arguable that her films as a teenager and as a young woman, up to and including Claude Goretta's *The Lacemaker* (1976), were her best, in that she was so astonishingly confident and evocative an actress so early in her career. Of her later films, Maurice Pialat's *Loulou* (1980), in which she played the bourgeoise to **Gérard Depardieu's** *rustre*, is perhaps the highlight, but she was characteristically excellent in **Bertrand Tavernier's** *Coup De Torchon* (1981), **Paul Cox's** *Cactus* (1986), **Hal Hartley's** *Amateur* (1994) and Claude Chabrol's *L'Ivresse Du Pouvoir* (2006).

Other Key Films: *César Et Rosalie* (1972); *Glissements Progressifs Du Plaisir* (1974); *Le Juge Et L'Assassin* (1976); *Heaven's Gate* (1980); *La Truite* (1982); *La Femme De Mon Pote* (1983); *Madame Bovary* (1991); *Elective Affinities* (1996); *La Vie Moderne* (1999); *Clara* (2000); *La Pianiste* (2001); *8 Femmes* (2002); *Deux* (2002); *La Vie Promise* (2002);

Le Temps Du Loup (2003); *Ma Mère* (2004); *I Heart Huckabees* (2004); *Les Soeurs Fâchées* (2004); *Gabrielle* (2005)

Hurt, John

John Hurt is an actor whose face has corrugated and whose voice has coarsened in recent years, taking on something of the quality of a British version of France's Philippe Léotard (whom in many ways he resembles). Hurt, at his best, suggests a mixture of enlightened irony and knowing perverseness, aspects which were best used by **Stephen Frears** in *The Hit* (1984) and by Michael Caton-Jones's inspired casting of him as Stephen Ward in *Scandal* (1989). Richard Kwietniowski's *Love And Death On Long Island* (1997) has revived what had begun to seem (outside television, at least) a somewhat moribund career, and his recent outing as Dr Iannis in John Madden's *Captain Corelli's Mandolin* (2001) [while drawing a veil over the rest of the movie] has brought him rightfully back to the forefront of character acting (which he still persists in doing, as in Jon Jones's *The Alan Clark Diaries* (2004), a good deal better on television).

Other Key Films: *A Man for All Seasons* (1966); *10 Rillington Place* (1971); *The Disappearance* (1977); *Midnight Express* (1978); *Alien* (1979); *The Elephant Man* (1980); *Heaven's Gate* (1980); *The Osterman Weekend* (1983); *Champions* (1984); *1984* (1984); *White Mischief* (1987); *The Field* (1990); *Contact* (1997); *The Commissioner* (1998); *New Blood* (1999); *Lost Souls* (2000); *Tabloid* (2001); *Harry Potter And The Sorcerer's Stone* (2001); *Crime And Punishment* (2002); *Owning Mahowny* (2003); *Hellboy* (2004); *The Proposition* (2005); *Shooting Dogs* (2005); *V For Vendetta* (2005)

Hurt, William

Hurt has never fulfilled the potential so many were so keen to see in him during the 1980s, and this is because his strangely passive persona is such a dominant one – it is almost as though he believes that things should happen to him rather than that he must engender them himself. The majority of his best parts came early on in his career, with **Ken Russell's** oddly compulsive *Altered States* (1980) and **Lawrence Kasdan's** immaculate *Body Heat* (1981) (which still thrills with its bravura confidence), and in which Hurt reached the apogee of his rather masochistic self-regard. He was good, certainly, as Luis Molina in **Hector Babenco's** *Kiss Of The Spider Woman* (1985), and fully deserved his Oscar, but he was already on his way to

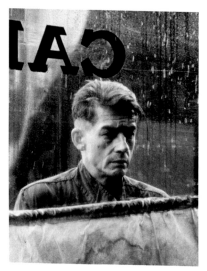

John Hurt in the film 1984, directed by Michael Radford (1984).

Umbrella/Rosenblum/ Virgin Films/The Kobal Collection

becoming too pernickety an actor, prey to odd tics and compulsive habits, and Kasdan's *Accidental Tourist* (1988) seems perilously close to self-caricature. It would be nice to be proved wrong, for Hurt is an attractive, subtle actor, but one suspects he was unsuited or in some way unprepared for stardom when it came, and that celebrity eased him, very slightly, off track.

Other Key Films: *Eyewitness* (1981); *The Big Chill* (1983) *Gorky Park* (1983); *Children Of A Lesser God* (1986); *Broadcast News* (1987); *Alice* (1990); *The Doctor*

(1991); *Until The End Of The World* (1992); *Smoke* (1995); *Jane Eyre* (1996); *Lost In Space* (1998); *Do Not Disturb* (1999); *The Contaminated Man* (2000); *Artificial Intelligence: A.I.* (2001); *The Blue Butterfly* (2004); *The Village* (2004); *The King* (2005); *A History Of Violence* (2005); *Syriana* (2005); *Beautiful Ohio* (2006)

Huston, Anjelica

Huston has grown with the years, her face maturing, her presence strengthening, and in this respect she resembles her father, **John Huston**, and her grandfather, **Walter Huston**, who both produced their best work in mid to later life. As Lilly Dillon, in **Stephen Frears's** *The Grifters* (1990), Huston with her frantic rejection of any signs of self-weakness, beautifully complemented her earlier performance in John Huston's *The Dead* (1987), in which she was all vulnerability, but distant, as if her husband, Donal McCann, had been worshipping a statue for all the years he had so misjudged her. Huston is an actress writers should be writing fresh material for; not wasting their time trying to lever her into existing vehicles that may not suit her abilities.

Other Key Films: *A Walk With Love And Death* (1969); *The Postman Always Rings Twice* (1981); *Prizzi's Honour* (1985); *Gardens Of Stone* (1987); *A Handful Of Dust* (1988); *Mr North* (1988); *Crimes And Misdemeanors* (1989); *Enemies, A Love Story* (1989); *The Witches* (1990); *Manhattan Murder Mystery* (1993); *The Crossing Guard* (1995); *Phoenix* (1998); *The Golden Bowl* (2000); *The Royal Tenenbaums* (2001); *The Life Aquatic With Steve Zissou* (2004); *These Foolish Things* (2006); *Seraphim Falls* (2006); *Material Girls* (2006)

Huston, John

Huston engenders mixed emotions in just about anyone brave enough to take a view on him – he has been venerated, bitched about, envied by those of lesser talent, and stabbed in the back by the very people who should have been most supportive of him. Yet even though the work, the intelligence, and the paradoxical manifestations of vainglory remain, it is still hard to decide if he is a major artist or merely a talented dilettante who found that cinema was a convenient outlet for a creative energy that could just as well have chosen any one of a dozen other paths for its fulfilment. And yet there are so many wonderful films – *The Maltese Falcon* (41), in which **Bogart** is recognisably Bogart for the first time – the war documentaries, a serious project to which he devoted three of the most creative years of his life – *The Treasure Of The Sierra Madre* (47) and *Key Largo* (48), both films dealing with men forced out of their normal rut and faced with the nightmare of moral choice – and *The Asphalt Jungle* (50), which bursts the glamorous balloon of the major crime **heist** to show the vulnerability beneath the tough outer sleeve of its protagonists. His late masterpieces, *The Misfits* (1961), *Night Of The Iguana* (1964) and *Fat City* (1971), downgrade plot in favour of characterisation, and his people, even if they don't suffer fundamental change by the end of the film, are at least conscious of their humanity, and of the fact that, unlike Bogart's Fred C Dobbs in *The Treasure Of The Sierra Madre*, they can no longer make it on their own. Huston was a fine filmmaker, literate, adventurous and moral, who sometimes achieved, and this is no mean feat, the semblance of an enlightened understanding. See **Heartstopping Moments**

Other Key Films: *We Were Strangers* (1949); *The Red Badge Of Courage* (1951); *The African Queen* (1951); *Moulin Rouge* (1952); *Beat The Devil* (1954); *Moby Dick* (1956); *Heaven Knows, Mr. Allison* (1958); *Reflections In A Golden Eye* (1967); *The Man Who Would Be King* (1975); *Wise Blood* (1979); *Under The Volcano* (1984); *Prizzi's Honour* (1985); *The Dead* (1987)

Key Line: 'John Huston was a very interesting man. He could recite Shakespeare, the whole of Shakespeare, when he had a few drinks. I knew all of his wives. If I could live it all over again, I would like to live his life.' [Screenwriter Curt Siodmak, brother of director **Robert Siodmak**, on his friendship with Huston.]

Huston, Walter

Walter Huston was one of the finest screen actors of his or any other generation, and it is astonishing to realise that he only starred in his first feature film at the age of forty-six, after spending the previous twenty-five years on the stage and in vaudeville. To watch him enter into a part and then allow it to take him over, as with the elusively simple Sam Dodsworth in **William Wyler's** *Dodsworth* (1936), or the wise escaped convict in **Jean Renoir's** *Swamp Water* (1941), or as the compulsive but generous Howard in his son, **John Huston's**, *The Treasure Of The Sierra Madre* (1948), is to see a master of instinctive, intelligent acting working at the peak of his craft. Even in such heady oddities as **Josef Von Sternberg's** *The Shanghai Gesture* (1941) and **Howard Hughes's** *The Outlaw* (1947), Huston towers sanely over his often hysterically overacting counterparts.

Other Key Films: *The Virginian* (1929); *Abraham Lincoln* (1930); *Rain* (1932); *Gabriel Over The White House* (1933); *Rhodes* (1936); *The Light That Failed* (1940); *Edge Of Darkness* (1943); *Dragonwyck* (1946); *Duel In The Sun* (1947); *Summer Holiday* (1948); *The Furies* (1950)

Ingram, Rex

The famous, visually innovative silent filmmaker who gave both **Rudolf Valentino** and **Ramon Navarro** their first big breaks, Ingram was the massively influential director of *The Four Horsemen Of The Apocalypse* (1921), *The Prisoner Of Zenda* (1922) and *Scaramouche* (1923), as well as being the founder of the famous Victorine Studios in Nice. His later films came out under his own aegis, following a dispute with MGM's **Louis B Mayer,** who had refused to put Ingram in charge of *Ben-Hur* (1926) – a row which eventually led to the movie being directed, very effectively, by Fred Niblo. Ingram gave up making films just after the coming of the sound era, citing, in explanation, his disgust at the venality and artistic philistinism of the Hollywood Mafiosi.

Other Key Films: *Trifling Women* (1922); *Where The Pavement Ends* (1923); *Mare Nostrum* (1926); *The Magician* (1926); *The Garden Of Allah* (1927); *Baroud* (1932)

Irons, Jeremy

Irons is a master of inhibition, bringing to it all the subtlety and despair that the British class system can provide. However, this very talent seems to have limited the scope of his work, and one cannot fail to make the comparison with **Dirk Bogarde**, whom Irons somewhat arcanely resembles, but whose later range he has yet to emulate. Irons was excellent in **David Cronenberg's** *Dead Ringers* (1988), although he failed to show us the full possibilities of conventional bourgeois passion in **Louis Malle's** sadly underrated *Damage* (1992), leading one to question whether he isn't best suited to playing the warped outcasts of an established order, rather than the denizens of the established order itself – for Irons achieved exactly this trick in Adrian Lyne's outstanding version of *Lolita* (1997), making of Humbert Humbert a truly tragic figure, driven not only by lust but also by the exigencies of a seemingly inexorable fate.

Other Key Films: *The French Lieutenant's Woman* (1981); *Moonlighting* (1982); *The*

Mission (1986); *Reversal Of Fortune* (1990); *Kafka* (1991); *Waterland* (1992); *Stealing Beauty* (1996); *The Man In The Iron Mask* (1998); *Dungeons & Dragons* (2000); *The Fourth Angel* (2001); *Callas Forever* (2001); *Being Julia* (2004); *The Merchant Of Venice* (2004); *Casanova* (2005); *Inland Empire* (2006)

Ivory, James

For some reason the critics have always enjoyed slamming the Ivory/Ismail Merchant/Ruth Prawer Jhabvala triumvirate, but even a quick glance at Ivory's filmography will show that he is an unselfconscious director (along the lines of a **Henry King**) who, had he lived in the days of the great studios, would surely have turned out first-rate and highly literate commercial entertainment decade after decade. The fact that Merchant/Ivory have managed to finance and bring to fruition so many good films in the present anti-independent climate is something of a small miracle. Ivory's best films came early, with *Shakespeare Wallah* (1965), *Bombay Talkie* (1970) and *Heat And Dust* (1983), but of his later films, pick of the bunch is undoubtedly the masterly *Howards End* (1992), closely followed by the equally well-made and impeccably acted *Remains Of The Day* (1993). Ivory is that rarity among modern-day filmmakers – a man who plays to his strengths.

Other Key Films: *The Wild Party* (1975); *The Europeans* (1979); *Quartet* (1981); *The Bostonians* (1984); *A Room With A View* (1986); *Maurice* (1987); *Jefferson In Paris* (1995); *Surviving Picasso* (1996); *A Soldier's Daughter Never Cries* (1998); *The Golden Bowl* (2000); *Le Divorce* (2003); *The White Countess* (2005)

Jackson, Glenda

Now a sober and responsible UK Labour Party member of parliament, it is hard to believe that Jackson was once feted as a sex symbol. However she certainly did exude a somewhat earthy sensuality in her first films, often quite literally, as, for example, when **Oliver Reed's** Gerald Crich ravished her Gudrun Brangwen in **Ken Russell's** *Women In Love* (1969), with the mud from his father's grave still fresh on his hands. She went on to do further excellent work for Russell in *The Music Lovers* (1971), but her finest and most sensitive performance came as Alex Greville in **John Schlesinger's** *Sunday Bloody Sunday* (1971), one of the most literate and elegant films British cinema has ever produced. Jackson was a household name during the 1970s, taking parts, and a second Oscar, in Melvin Frank's *A Touch Of Class* (1972) and **Michael Apted's** underrated *Triple Echo* (1972), but she appeared to lose interest in acting during the 1980s, ending with a token appearance as Gudrun Brangwen's mother in Russell's *The Rainbow* (1989) – D H Lawrence's precursor to *Women In Love* – and a lesser film in every way than its excellent, ground-breaking progenitor.

Other Key Films: *The Marat-Sade* (1967); *The Boy Friend* (1971); *Mary Queen Of Scots* (1971); *The Maids* (1974); *Hedda* (1975); *Stevie* (1978); *The Return Of The Soldier* (1981); *Turtle Diary* (1985); *Doombeach* (1990)

Jackson, Peter

Obsessed by movies since the age of eight, the swarthy, furry, and undeniably diminutive Jackson somewhat resembles the hobbits that he has since made so famous. The film that launched him at Cannes was the four-years-in-the-making *Bad Taste* (1987), which led directly to his first professional film, the hilariously gore bespattered *Braindead* (1992). *Heavenly Creatures* (1994) confirmed his talent, and his extended homage to the effect ***King Kong*** had on him as a child, exemplified in his masterpiece *The Lord Of The Rings Trilogy* (2001-2003) and in his own *King Kong*

(2005), has raised him to the very forefront of the commercial movie world in terms of both quality and heart.

Other Key Films: *The Lord Of The Rings: The Fellowship Of The Ring* (2001); *The Lord Of The Rings: The Two Towers* (2002); *The Lord Of The Rings: The Return Of The King* (2003)

Key Line: 'I doubt I could ever control myself sufficiently to make a serious horror film.' [Jackson on self-knowledge]

Jackson, Samuel L

Jackson had been in the business a long time before **Quentin Tarantino's** *Pulp Fiction* (1994) shot the then forty-five-year-old former theatre star into the stratosphere – and to give Jackson credit, celebrity doesn't seem to have gone to his head. He was excellent in **Spike Lee's** *Jungle Fever* (1991), and he can call upon a fine talent for offbeat comedy, as displayed in **Steve Buscemi's** *Trees Lounge* (1996), to counteract his otherwise outstanding capacity for invoking menace. A stayer.

Other Key Films: *Ragtime* (1981); *Sea Of Love* (1989); *Betsy's Wedding* (1990); *Mo' Better Blues* (1990); *GoodFellas* (1990); *White Sands* (1992); *True Romance* (1993); *Losing Isaiah* (1995); *Deep Blue Sea* (1999); *Shaft* (2000); *The Caveman's Valentine* (2001); *The 51st State* (2001); *Changing Lanes* (2002); *Star Wars: Episode II – Attack Of The Clones* (2002); *Country Of My Skull* (2004); *Kill Bill: Vol. 2* (2004); *Star Wars: Episode III – Revenge Of The Sith* (2005); *Freedomland* (2006); *Black Snake Moan* (2006)

Key Line: 'Oh I'm sorry. Did I break your concentration?' [Jackson to one of his many victims in *Pulp Fiction*]

Jarman, Derek

A cheerfully iconoclastic product of the 1960s art scene, Jarman began his professional career set designing for **Ken Russell** on *The Devils* (1971). His first feature, *Sebastiane* (1975), was made on a shoestring budget and bears absolutely no resemblance whatsoever to the 1968 **Dirk Bogarde** vehicle of (roughly) the same name, apart, perhaps, from the sexual orientation of its leading men: the one proudly acknowledged; the other resolutely unacknowledged, it must be said. A gay-rights activist who died from the AIDS virus in 1994, Jarman was a brave and intelligent maverick who had very little time for those who did not at least partially share the tenor of his personal and professional predilections. His last full-length feature, *Blue* (1993), was a meditation on AIDS, the colour blue, and on the dreadful paradox of an extraordinarily gifted visual artist gradually losing his sight.

Other Key Films: *Jubilee* (1978); *The Tempest* (1979); *Caravaggio* (1986); *The Last Of England* (1987); *Aria* ['Louise' segment only] (1988); *War Requiem* (1989) *The Garden* (1990); *Edward II* (1991) *Wittgenstein* (1993); *Glitterbug* [compilation of fragments from home movies] (1994)

Jarmusch, Jim

Jarmusch looks a little like his films – individual, curious, otherworldly – and classes himself as a comedy writer rather than as the avant-garde director he is so often taken for. Rigorously independent, he retains total control over his negatives, which include his breakthrough movie, *Stranger Than Paradise* (1984), and the sublimely comic *Down By Law* (1986), which introduced Italian humorist Roberto Benigni to American audiences. Something of a loner himself, Jarmusch revels in the idiosyncrasies of alienation, and enjoys dropping visual and verbal quotes from his favourite directors inside the fabric of his films.

Other Key Films: *Mystery Train* (1989); *Night On Earth* (1991); *Dead Man* (1995); *Ghost Dog: The Way Of The Samurai* (1999); *Coffee And Cigarettes* (2003); *Broken Flowers* (2005)

Key Line: 'I wanted to have always known him.' [Actor Stephen Saban, about Jarmusch]

Jarre, Maurice

Jarre has to be considered one of the most successful of all screen composers, if only for his contribution to the films of **David Lean.** *Lawrence Of Arabia* (1962), *Doctor Zhivago* (1965), *Ryan's Daughter* (1970) and *A Passage To India* (1984) can all boast immaculate and often unnervingly intrusive Jarre scores. Noted for his inventive use of instrumentation and his subtly textured orchestrations, Jarre is equally at home composing for such cold-blooded commercial ventures as **Roger Vadim's** *Barbarella* (1968) and **Clint Eastwood's** *Firefox* (1982), as he is for more esoteric fare, such as Volker Schlöndorff's *The Tin Drum* (1979) and **Peter Weir's** *The Year Of Living Dangerously* (1983). He is the father of Jean-Michel Jarre, himself the ex-husband of **Charlotte Rampling** and master of city-centre laser lighting spectaculars – a true chip off the old block.

Other Key Films: Serge Bourguignon's *Sundays And Cybele* (1962); **Georges Franju's** *Judex* (1964); **John Frankenheimer's** *The Fixer* (1968); **John Huston's** *The Man Who Would Be King* (1975); **Peter Weir's** *Witness* (1985) and *Dead Poets Society* (1989); **Adrian Lyne's** *Jacob's Ladder* (1990); **Mike Figgis's** *Mr. Jones* (1993); **Michael Cimino's** *Sunchaser* (1996); Hugh Hudson's *I Dreamed Of Africa* (2000)

Jeanson, Henri

Jeanson, together with poet **Jacques Prévert**, was the power behind the words that gave the films in the French **poetic realism** tradition their peculiarly seductive style. Jeanson's greatest screenplays were for Julien Duvivier's *Pépé Le Moko* (1937), *Un Carnet De Bal* (1937), and **Marcel Carné's** outstanding *Hôtel Du Nord* (1938). Jeanson later went on to write a series of comedies and swashbucklers during the 1950s and 1960s, the best of which was Christian-Jaque's *Fanfan La Tulipe* (1951), in which an athletic **Gérard Philipe** leaps gamely from pillar to post just nine years before his untimely death of a heart attack, aged thirty-seven.

Other Key Films: Christian-Jaque's *Boule De Suif* (1945); **René Clément's** *The Damned* (1947)

Johansson, Scarlett

It is hard to believe that Johansson (born in 1984) has already acted in upwards of thirty-two films. She played Grace MacLean in **Robert Redford's** *The Horse Whisperer* (1998) when she was only fourteen, and it was a mere five years later, in 2003, that she had her annus mirabilis, in which she incarnated the neglected Charlotte, in **Sofia Coppola's** *Lost In Translation* (2003), and the bewildered Griet, in Peter Webber's *Girl With A Pearl Earring* (2003). Since then she's more than held her own against the **Kate Winslets** and the **Gwyneth Paltrows** of this world, in terms of both the quality of her playing and her star charisma, with notable parts in Mike Barker's *A Good Woman* (2004) and **Woody Allen's** *Match Point* (2005).

Other Key Films: *North* (1994); *The Man Who Wasn't There* (2001); *Eight Legged Freaks* (2002); *A Love Song For Bobby Long* (2004); *The Island* (2005); *Scoop* (2006); *The Black Dahlia* (2006)

Key Line: 'I was driving through Los Angeles and I look up and see the biggest photo of me I have ever seen in my life on a massive ad space. I screamed and slammed on the brakes. I couldn't believe it. It's very strange to see my cleavage the size of a brontosaurus.' [Johansson on biological diversity]

Johnson, Ben

An excellent character actor who left his lazy Oklahoman mark on virtually every film in which he ever acted (usually taking the nominal part of a Texan, for to this day few people in the US, let alone abroad, can readily find Oklahoma on the map), Johnson was a **John Ford** protégé and one of the best natural horsemen the screen has ever seen. As a man, he was possessed of a quiet, countryman's integrity that Ford used to best advantage in the last two films of his cavalry trilogy, *She Wore A Yellow Ribbon* (1949) and *Rio Grande* (1951). However Johnson really came into his own when he was given the co-lead role, alongside Harry Carey Jr, in Ford's outstanding *Wagonmaster* (1950). This was a film which benefited immeasurably from having no real stars among its cast list, and which is now rightly considered to be one of the finest of all the great director's **Westerns** (as well as being one of the closest to his heart). In later life Johnson became something of an iconic figure to directors such as **Sam Peckinpah** and **Peter Bogdanovich** who, along with **Lindsay Anderson**, did the most to protect Ford's posthumous reputation. Bogdanovich used Johnson to Oscar-winning effect as Sam The Lion, in *The Last Picture Show* (1971), playing brilliantly on the instinctive sense of loss that Johnson brought to all his later roles.
Other Key Films: *Three Godfathers* (1949); *Shane* (1953); *One-Eyed Jacks* (1961); *Major Dundee* (1965); *Will Penny* (1968); *The Wild Bunch* (1969); *The Undefeated* (1969); *Chisum* (1970); *The Getaway* (1972); *Junior Bonner* (1972); *The Sugarland Express* (1974); *The Hunter* (1980)
Key Line: 'Being crazy about a woman like her is always the right thing to do.' [Johnson to Timothy Bottoms in *The Last Picture Show*, about Ellen Burstyn's Lois Farrow]

Jolson, Al

Star of Alan Crosland's *The Jazz Singer* (1927) – the first ever part-talkie feature – Jolson was a master of music hall and revue, where he was renowned for his trademark 'black-face' routine. With his moribund career resuscitated due to *The Jazz Singer's* extraordinary success, he went on to star in a number of other musical films built around his powerful, cantor's voice, culminating in his very own biopic, Alfred E Green's *The Jolson Story* (1946), for which he provided the songs and Larry Park the histrionics. If Jolson had nothing else, he certainly had energy.
Other Key Films: *The Singing Fool* (1928); *Hallelujah, I'm A Bum* (1933); *Rose Of Washington Square* (1939); *Swanee River* (1940)
Key Line: 'Wait a minute! Wait a minute! You ain't heard nothin' yet!' [Jolson's catchphrase, or shtick, which he used in *The Jazz Singer*]

Jones, Jennifer

Jones was a true oddity. Her career was the product, not of any particular talent (although she had that too) but of a passion – the passion of *Gone With The Wind* producer **David O. Selznick**. The passion, in its way, was fine, (**Howard Hughes** entertained a similar one for **Jane Russell**), but in Selznick's case the passion gradually became an obsession that threatened to destroy them both, to the extent that Jones attempted suicide on a number of occasions and Selznick's career limped into a neglected decline. And what came of it all? Perhaps the most notorious film of the Selznick/Jones cycle is **King Vidor's** *Duel In The Sun* (1946), in which Jones was inspirationally miscast as half-breed Pearl Chavez alongside Gregory Peck's sensationally demonic 'Lewt' McCanles – but then the film, too, was misguided, and became a success almost despite itself. One watches it today with a sort of awe that so much money and effort could have been spent on a project that so accurately mirrored, in psychological terms at least, the story-to-be of its star and of its producer. Jones's best role, in what was an exceedingly mixed career, came in **Michael Powell's** *Gone To Earth* (1950), in which she played Hazel Woodus, a hunter's quarry (in this case **David Farrar's** Squire Reddin), as if she were born for the part – which, in a way, of course, she was.

Other Key Films: *The Song Of Bernadette* (1944); *Love Letters* (1945); *Cluny Brown* (1946); *Portrait Of Jenny* (1949); *Madame Bovary* (1949); *Carrie* (1952); *Ruby Gentry* (1953); *Beat The Devil* (1954); *The Man In The Gray Flannel Suit* (1956); *The Barretts Of Wimpole Street* (1958); *A Farewell To Arms* (1958)

Jones, Tommy Lee

An odd choice for stardom, Jones seems far too intelligent to have reached the heady Hollywood heights – he's quite simply a first-rate screen actor with an eye-catching (although hardly drop-dead gorgeous) face, who ploughed a lonely groove for upwards of twenty years in a succession of often very good TV movies. He appeared to have achieved a career breakthrough in **Michael Apted's** *Coal Miner's Daughter* (1980), but it was only eleven years later, with his sizzling performance as Clay Shaw in **Oliver Stone's** *JFK* (1991), that the Academy sat up and took notice of him. The part of Deputy US Marshal Samuel Gerard, in Andrew Davis's *The Fugitive* (1993) won him his best supporting actor Oscar, and levered him up (or down, depending on one's viewpoint) to such big-budget films as Joel Schumacher's *The Client* (1994) and Barry Sonnenfeld's *Men In Black* (1997). Catch him in **Tony Richardson's** *Blue Sky* (1991) for a reminder of what we've lost.

Other Key Films: *Rolling Thunder* (1977); *Eyes Of Laura Mars* (1978); *The River Rat* (1984); *Stormy Monday* (1988); *Natural Born Killers* (1994); *Volcano* (1997); *U. S. Marshals* (1998); *Space Cowboys* (2000); *Rules Of Engagement* (2000); *The Hunted* (2003); *The Missing* (2003); *Man Of The House* (2005); *The Three Burials Of Melquiades Estrada* [also dir.] (2005); *A Prairie Home Companion* (2006)

Jordan, Neil

One of the most interesting directors to work largely outside the Hollywood system, Jordan began strongly with *Angel* (1982), in which he first used actor Stephen Rae, now one of his regulars, and followed up with the challenging *The Company Of Wolves* (1984), which divided the critics but worked wonderfully well on the screen. *Mona Lisa* (1986) cemented his reputation, and *The Crying Game* (1992) finally seduced Hollywood into making overtures, which Jordan responded to with *Interview With The Vampire* (1994). Far more interesting was his 1991 film, *The Miracle*, in which his obsession with identity, friendship and the intemperate morality of trust received full measure. His recent, underrated, *The End Of The Affair* (1999), continues his preoccupation with the melancholy paradoxes inherent in moral choice.

Other Key Films: *High Spirits* (1988); *We're No Angels* (1989); *Michael Collins* (1996); *The Butcher Boy* (1997); *In Dreams* (1998); *The Good Thief* (2002); *Breakfast On Pluto* (2005)

Jouvet, Louis

Jouvet is one of the top ten screen actors who have ever lived, but his name is hardly known outside France except to the occasional wild-eyed film buff emerging from the depths of a Parisian flea-pit. Jouvet never rated film as he did theatre, but despite his devil-take-it attitude, he turned in four or five performances during the 1930s that are so majestic, so true, that any potential film actor or actress should be forced to watch them as part of their essential training. His greatest performance came as the Baron, in **Jean Renoir's** *Les Bas-Fonds* (1936), a noble work, based on the writings of Maxim Gorky, but it remains a hard film to find, and potential aficionados will probably come across **Marcel Carné's** *Hotel Du Nord* (1938), Julien Duvivier's *La Fin Du Jour* (1939) or **Henri-Georges Clouzot's** *Quai Des Orfèvres* (1947) with greater ease. Either way, they should endeavour to see the films in a cinema, as part of a director's season perhaps, rather than on the television.

Other Key Films: *Topaze* (1933); *La Kermesse Héroïque* (1935); *Mister Flow* (1935); *Mademoiselle Docteur* (1936); *Un Carnet De Bal* (1937); *Drôle De Drame* (1937); *L'Alibi* (1937); *La Marseillaise* (1938); *Entrée Des Artistes* (1938); *Le Drame De Shanghai* (1938); *Volpone* (1940); *Sérénade* (1940); *Untel Père Et Fils* (1940); *Un Revenant* (1946); *Les Chouans* (1946); *Entre Onze Heures Et Minuit* (1948); *Retour À La Vie* (1949); *Lady Paname* (1949); *Miquette Et Sa Mère* (1950); *Une Histoire D'Amour* (1951)

Jean Gabin (left) and Louis Jouvet in Jean Renoir's 1936 film, Les Bas-Fonds (The Lower Depths/Underground/ Underworld)

Junge, Alfred

A great art designer, and the man who injected his trademark look of heightened romanticism into many of the best pre- and post- Second World War British films, most notably Robert Stevenson's *King Solomon's Mines* (1937) and Sam Wood's *Goodbye Mr Chips* (1939), Junge succeeded best of all in the extraordinary series of masterpieces he made with **Michael Powell** and Emeric Pressburger. These included *The Life And Death Of Colonel Blimp* (1943), *A Canterbury Tale* (1944), *I Know Where I'm Going* (1945), *A Matter Of Life And Death* (1946) and also the magnificent *Black Narcissus* (1947), which was entirely shot at Pinewood and Denham studios, and in the gardens of Leonard's Lee in Sussex but which gave the impression of having been at least partly shot on location in Nepal. Junge is one of the hidden, faceless men of the cinema, without whose contribution, the filmic world would be a very second-rate place indeed.

Other Key Films: **King Vidor's** *The Citadel* (1938); Richard Thorpe's *Ivanhoe* (1952); **John Ford's** *Mogambo* (1953)

Jürgens, Curt

Jürgens epitomized a desperate perversity on the screen, as if there were something not quite savoury beneath his smooth and handsome exterior. As a result of this he was at his best in tense dramas, playing men who have in some way been tricked out of what they feel to be their just deserts. He was, as such, perfectly cast in **Roger Vadim's** *And God Created Woman* (1956) as **Brigitte Bardot's** frustrated older swain, Eric, and in **Nicholas Ray's** *Bitter Victory* (1958) as Major Brand. a basically decent man warped by jealousy (shades of Macbeth), who conspires, in his madness, to bring down a better one.

Other Key Films: *The Last Waltz* (1953); *The Devil's General* (1955); *The Enemy Below* (1958); *The Inn Of The Sixth Happiness* (1958); *Ferry To Hong Kong* (1959); *Miracle Of The White Stallions* (1963); *Lord Jim* (1965); *Nicholas And Alexandra* (1971); *The Spy Who Loved Me* (1977)

Karloff, Boris

Karloff was always the most human of monsters, a cricket-loving gentleman of the Raj who, by some extraordinary mixture of talent and serendipity, ended up in Hollywood playing ghouls, which, though terrifying, were at the same time perversely understandable. His monster, in **James Whale's** *Frankenstein* (1931), was more victim than perpetrator, and the dignity inherent in Karloff's personality was beautifully brought out by **Peter Bogdanovich** in his debut film, *Targets* (1968), in which the elderly horror actor offers himself in sacrifice to save the innocent victims of a demented sniper.

Other Key Films: *The Prisoner* (1923); *Man In The Saddle* (1926); *The Criminal Code* (1931); *The Man Who Dared* (1932); *Scarface* (1932); *The Mummy* (1932); *The Old Dark House* (1932); *The Ghoul* (1933); *The Lost Patrol* (1934); *The Raven* (1935); *The Bride Of Frankenstein* (1935); *Tower Of London* (1939); *Devil's Island* (1940); *The Body Snatcher* (1945); *Bedlam* (1946); *Corridors Of Blood* (1962)

Kasdan, Lawrence

With a partial writing credit on **George Lucas's** *The Empire Strikes Back* (1980) and *Return Of The Jedi* (1983), and a full credit on **Steven Spielberg's** *Raiders Of The Lost Ark* (1981), Kasdan could have happily sat back and watched the dollars roll in for any number of Hollywood script doctoring and screenwriting jobs. Following the success of his first feature, *Body Heat* (1981), however, he chose the infinitely more frustrating director's path, successfully, in *The Big Chill* (1983), worthily, in *Wyatt Earp* (1994), and nobly, in *Grand Canyon* (1991). His most enjoyable film is *Accidental Tourist* (1988), in which he brings to life the characters of best-selling novelist, Ann Tyler. The film was a success, despite the mannered, but for once forgivable, presence of Geena Davis.

Boris Karloff in
Frankenstein, directed
by James Whale (1931).

*Universal/The Kobal
Collection*

Other Key Films: *Silverado* (1985); *I Love You To
Death* (1990); *French Kiss* (1995); *Mumford* (1999);
Dreamcatcher (2003)

Kaurismäki, Aki & Mika

An odd-ball pair of brothers who have (double-
handedly?) placed Finland back on the
cinematic map, Aki and Mika began as
iconoclasts and have since become cosy
members of the insider's club they started out
satirising in such films as Mika's *The Clan* (1984)
and Aki's *Crime And Punishment* (1983), *Ariel*
(1989), *Match Factory Girl* (1990), *I Hired A
Contract Killer* (1990) and *Leningrad Cowboys Go
America* (1990). By turns brutal, miraculous, offbeat and tender, most of their best films deal with
losers who somehow contrive to pull back just a
little dignity from the dud cards their characters
are invariably dealt. Film buffs extraordinaire, the
brothers run their own Midnight Sun film
festival, and are doyens of a chain of art-house movie theatres in Helsinki.
Other Key Films: Aki's *Calamari Union* (1985); *Hamlet Goes Business* (1987);
Bohemian Life (1992); *Tatjana* (1994); *The Man Without A Past* (2002); *Laitakaupungin
Valot* (2006); and Mika's *Zombie And The Ghost Train* (1991); *Drifting Clouds* (1996);
L.A. Without A Map (1998); *Julia* (1999); *Highway Society* (2001); *Honey Baby* (2003)

Kaye, Danny

It is hard to like Kaye's screen persona, even in retrospect, because it likes itself so
much. As a talented ex-Vaudevillian, he chose his moment well and made the most
of it. Norman McLeod's *The Secret Life Of Walter Mitty* (1947) undoubtedly struck a
chord with a public fed up with the mock reality of years of war newsreels and now
wanting a real bite of ersatz Never Never land, but Thurber it certainly wasn't. Charles
Vidor's *Hans Christian Andersen* (1952), in which Kaye played the title role, is one of
the worst examples ever of Hollywood's repellent desire to foment entertainment
even to the brain-dead, and is the direct precursor to dreck such as **Carol Reed's**
mind-numbingly trivial *Oliver!* (1968). Enough said.
Other Key Films: *Up In Arms* (1944); *Wonder Man* (1945); *A Song Is Born* (1948);
The Inspector General (1949); *Knock On Wood* (1954); *White Christmas* (1954); *The
Court Jester* (1956); *Merry Andrew* (1958)
Key Line: 'The pellet with the poison's in the vessel with the pestle. The chalice from
the palace has the brew that's true.' [*The Court Jester*]

Kazan, Elia

With numerous Academy Awards under his belt, Kazan should have been the toast of
Hollywood; instead, he became increasingly marginalised following his agreement to
name names before Senator Macarthy's House of Un-American Activities
Committee (HUAC). Co-founder of the New York Actor's Studio, Kazan directed a
series of critically acclaimed and commercially successful movies in the early 1950s,
amongst which *Panic in the Streets* (1950), *A Streetcar Named Desire* (1951), *Viva
Zapata!* (1952) and *On the Waterfront* (1954) stand out. He helped launch many

careers, most notably that of **Marlon Brando** in *Streetcar*, **James Dean** in *East of Eden* (1955) and **Warren Beatty** in *Splendor in the Grass* (1961). His forte was always in social realism, allied with a poetic nostalgia for a simpler time, and his later films suffer from the lapse into sentimentality that such a preoccupation can engender.

Other Key Films: *Pinky* (1949); *Man on a Tightrope* (1953); *Baby Doll* (1956); *A Face in the Crowd* (1958); *America, America* (1963); *The Arrangement* (1969); *The Visitors* (1972); *The Last Tycoon* (1976)

Keaton, Buster

Joseph Francis Keaton vies with **Charlie Chaplin** and **W C Fields** as the greatest of all screen comedians, and one has only to look at a still of his face to be convinced that he held within himself the secret of disguising tragedy with farce. Only really recognised as a genius toward the end of his life, in the self-directed *The Playhouse* (1921), *The Navigator* (1924), *Sherlock Jr.* and *The General* (1927), Keaton lifted comedy to sublime levels of creativity. His mistake in abandoning his own production company, and the artistic freedom it guaranteed, for a contract with MGM, may now be seen as a tragedy as acute, in its way, as the massacre of **Orson Welles's** *The Magnificent Ambersons* (1942) or the critical disregard which attended the first screening of **Charles Laughton's** masterpiece, *The Night Of The Hunter* (1955). <u>Note for Film Buffs:</u> Watch out for a brief appearance by Keaton sitting around a table playing bridge at Norma Desmond's house in **Billy Wilder's** *Sunset Boulevard* (1950).

Buster Keaton in *The Cameraman*, directed by Edward Sedgwick (1928).

MGM/The Kobal Collection

Other Key Films: *The Scarecrow* (1920); *The Haunted House* (1921); *The Boat* (1921); *The Paleface* (1921); *The Frozen North* (1922); *Our Hospitality* (1923); *Seven Chances* (1925); *Go West* (1925); *Battling Butler* (1926); *The Cameraman* (1928); *Spite Marriage* (1929)

Keaton, Diane

Keaton's fashion statement (or rather lack of it) in **Woody Allen's** *Annie Hall* (1977) started something of a trend, and for a brief moment during the late 1970s, she seemed to encapsulate everything that the modern woman thought and represented. She still retains her mannerisms, but as with all fashions, Keaton has been left to tidy up the bricks of a career founded, not so much upon talent (although she has that), as upon a fundamental misunderstanding. The difficulty was that Keaton's persona in the Allen films was simply a female extension of the director's own, and it is only when she occasionally shook off the Allen mantle, as in **Francis Ford Coppola's** *The Godfather* trilogy (1972-

90), in Richard Brooks's grotesquely disturbing *Looking For Mr. Goodbar* (1977), and **Warren Beatty's** *Reds* (1981), that she began to reveal something of herself. In recent years she has joined the middle-aged 'Hollywood worthies' charivari – something of a tragedy when weighed against the bitter-edged performances she gave at her best.
Other Key Films: *Play It Again Sam* (1972); *Interiors* (1978); *Manhattan* (1979); *Shoot The Moon* (1982); *The Little Drummer Girl* (1983); *Mrs. Soffel* (1984); *Radio Days* (1987); *Manhattan Murder Mystery* (1993); *The First Wives Club* (1996); *The Other Sister* (1999); *Town And Country* (2001); *Plan B* (2001); *Something's Gotta Give* (2003); *The Family Stone* (2005)

Keitel, Harvey

Yet another ex-marine actor [see **Steve McQueen** and **Lee Marvin**], live-wire Keitel worked for **Martin Scorsese** in *Mean Streets* (1973) and *Taxi Driver* (1976), before making his European mark (in more ways than one) in **Ridley Scott's** *The Duellists* (1977). A subtle, sympathetic actor, even when playing borderline psychotics such as in **Abel Ferrara's** *Bad Lieutenant* (1992), Keitel was one of the main reasons for the success of **Quentin Tarantino's** debut movie *Reservoir Dogs* (1992), which he both backed and acted in. At his strongest, as in the small but crucial role of Hal in Ridley Scott's *Thelma And Louise* (1991), Keitel can underplay with the best of them, manifesting a quality of restraint that make his sudden, frenetic outbursts all the more effective.
Other Key Films: *Alice Doesn't Live Here Anymore* (1975); *Bad Timing* (1980); *The Last Temptation Of Christ* (1988); *The Two Jakes* (1990); *The Piano* (1993); *Pulp Fiction* (1994); *Smoke* (1995); *From Dusk Till Dawn* (1996); *Cop Land* (1997); *Holy Smoke* (1999); *U-571* (2000); *Little Nicky* (2000); *Nailed* (2001); *Red Dragon* (2002); *Crime Spree* (2003); *Dreaming Of Julia* (2003); *The Gypsy's Curse* (2005); *The Shadow Dancer* (2005); *A Crime* (2006)

Kelly, Gene

Kelly was destined, from the very beginning, to be compared to **Fred Astaire**, for no other reason than that they inhabited (for want of a better word) the same profession. Kelly, however, was muscular where Astaire was elegant, and he was modern, too, (in cinematic terms at least), where Astaire was comfortably old-fashioned. Astaire comparisons aside, one is left with Kelly as a dancer and singer of great talent, who genuinely stimulated a revival in the musical and in modern ballet at a time when both were in danger of conking out for lack of fuel. **Vincente Minnelli's** *An American In Paris* (1951) may have fomented the vomit-inducingly romanticized view of the French that held sway until only relatively recently, but it also incorporated a ballet sequence, inspired by the canvases of Raoul Dufy, of astonishing ingenuity. Similarly, **Stanley Donen's** *Singin' In The Rain* [Kelly co-directed] (1952) is genuinely uplifting, and is the musical of all musicals as far as the non-musical loving public is concerned. It's a pretty good record, and Kelly was a pretty nice guy.
Other Key Films: *Cover Girl* (1944); *Anchors Aweigh* (1945); *The Pirate* (1948); *On The Town* (1949); *It's Always Fair Weather* (1955); *Invitation To The Dance* (1956); *Inherit The Wind* (1960); *Les Demoiselles De Rochefort* (1967); *That's Entertainment Trilogy* [compilation] (1974-1994)

Kelly, Grace

Kelly was sex personified (or sex sanctified, depending on your point of view), and it was patently obvious to every man watching her on the screen that, ice-cold and frozen as she seemed, there were as yet unseen fires simmering within. Corny? Perhaps. Yet it sold films, and allowed Kelly to appeal as strongly to men as to the women she awed with her Dior, Chanel and Balenciaga frocks, and with her more than other-worldly elegance – if a woman such as she couldn't end up marrying a prince in real life, then who could? She did find her prince, of course, and lost her career in the process, and there was something acutely touching about her later appearances, now slightly bloated, as Prince Rainier of Monaco's consort – the victim, as we belatedly found out, of strange, if rather innocent, cultish compulsions. At her best, in **Alfred Hitchcock's** *Rear Window* (1954) and *To Catch A Thief* (1955), and as the spoilt heiress every woman secretly yearns to be in Charles Walters's *High Society* (1956), Kelly epitomized a quasi-insane standard of everyday glamour and made it seem something to be desired – to that extent she is one of the great daughters of the cinema, where the dream is always more important than its interpretation.

Other Key Films: *Fourteen Hours* (1951); *High Noon* (1952); *Mogambo* (1953); *Dial M For Murder* (1954); *The Country Girl* (1954); *Green Fire* (1954); *The Bridges At Toko-Ri* (1955); *The Swan* (1956)

Key Lines:

1. 'Well, if there's one thing I know, it's how to wear the proper clothes.' [*Rear Window*]
2. 'You want a leg, or a breast?' [Kelly to **Cary Grant** in *To Catch A Thief*]

Kerr, Deborah

There was something magnificent about Deborah Kerr, as though her steel had been tempered at a familiar forge but was somehow stronger, more durable, than that of her contemporaries. She was un-neurotic and everyday, but with a luminous beauty that sometimes shone, sometimes took a back seat. Her glamour was innate, and she appeared to scorn artifice and the sins of over-emoting, and to that extent her admissions of weakness, as Sister Clodagh in **Michael Powell** and Emeric Pressburger's *Black Narcissus* (1946), and as Hannah Jelkes in **John Huston's** *The Night Of The Iguana* (1964), were all the more touching. Strangely, it is in the smaller films that one often appreciates her the most – as Catherine Parr in George Sidney's *Young Bess* (1953), for example, or as Laura Reynolds in **Vincente Minnelli's** *Tea And Sympathy* (1956) – where her innate good nature and gentleness stand out like beacons in the otherwise sargassic sea of Hollywood sharkdom.

Other Key Films: *Major Barbara* (1941); *The Life And Death Of Colonel Blimp* (1943); *Perfect Strangers* (1945); *I See A Dark Stranger* (1946); *King Solomon's Mines* (1950); *The Prisoner Of Zenda* (1952); *Julius Caesar* (1953); *From Here To Eternity* (1953); *The End Of The Affair* (1954); *The King And I* (1956); *Heaven Knows Mr. Allison* (1958); *An Affair To Remember* (1958); *Separate Tables* (1958); *The Sundowners* (1960); *The Innocents* (1961); *The Chalk Garden* (1963); *The Assam Garden* (1985)

Key Line: 'Years from now, when you talk about this – and you will – be kind.' [*Tea And Sympathy*, on letting the marginally effeminate John Kerr (no relation) make love to her]

Kidman, Nicole

Kidman is famous as much for her marriage to **Tom Cruise,** and its much publicised break-up in 2001, as for her own star power, which probably galls her, but which may yet shed light on her innate talent. She impressed in the choice part of Rae Ingram in Phillip Noyce's *Dead Calm* (1989), but Charles Williams's book is so strong that any one of a dozen actresses could have played the part as successfully. She was effective again in **Jane Campion's** otherwise disappointing (because loaded) *The Portrait Of A Lady* (1996), but what, one asks, would **Emma Thompson** have made of the part? Such comparisons are odious, it is true, but there is something about Kidman that engenders them, as if she were to some extent a cipher, and her position as yet unresolved. Perhaps we came closest in **Stanley Kubrick's** *Eyes Wide Shut* (1999), where Kidman's Alice Harford watches herself in the mirror, just as Kidman seems to in so many of her movies. One wishes she would release herself.

Other Key Films: *Days Of Thunder* (1990); *Billy Bathgate* (1991); *Emerald City* (1991); *Far And Away* (1992); *To Die For* (1995); *The Peacemaker* (1997); *Eyes Wide Shut* (1999); *Birthday Girl* (2000); *Moulin Rouge* (2001); *The Hours* (2002); *Dogville* (2003); *The Human Stain* (2003); *Cold Mountain* (2003); *The Stepford Wives* (2004); *Birth* (2004); *The Interpreter* (2005); *Bewitched* (2005), *Fur* (2006)

Kieslowski, Krzysztof

It still seems something of a miracle that we had Kieslowski with us for so long – he was a director torn from the bowels of film, who crept up on those of us who were despairing, in the depths of the 1980s, of ever feeling enthusiasm for a modern film-maker again. But then came *The Double Life Of Veronique* (1991). Initially repelled (for at first glance the film can seem over-contrived) one returns to it despite one's initial reservations, only to be won over, and then again, by the acute sensibility to nuance and to visual design exhibited by its maker. *Blue* (1993), *White* (1994) and *Red* (1994) followed, and it became apparent that Kieslowski was almost alone among modern filmmakers in thinking along metaphysical, rather than along political or sociological lines. His death, aged fifty-four, was a dreadful blow to what used, with reason, to be called Art-House film; in other words, films where the intellect is first brought into play and then subsumed by the instinctive answers to the questions that have been asked under its aegis.

Other Key Films: *Camera Buff* (1979); *Talking Heads* (1980); *No End* (1984); *The Dekalog [The Ten Commandments]* (1988)

King, Henry

An extraordinarily versatile studio director of the old school, King spent forty-six years in the business, starting with *Who Pays* (1916) and ending with *Tender Is The Night* (1962). In between, he entertained untold millions with such high-quality and intelligently thought-out star vehicles as *Tol'able David* (1921), *State Fair* (1933), the exquisitely photographed *Jesse James* (1939), and the excellent, and still underrated *The Sun Also Rises* (1958). King loved America, and his best films are imbued with a sense of its possibilities, thus making him a rare optimist in a film world populated largely by would-be cynics.

Other Key Films: *Lloyds Of London* (1936); *Old Chicago* (1938); *Alexander's Ragtime Band* (1938); *The Black Swan* (1943); *Captain From Castile* (1948); *Twelve o' Clock High* (1949); *The Gunfighter* (1950); *The Snows Of Kilimanjaro* (1952); *Carousel* (1956); *The Bravados* (1958)

King Kong

Merian C Cooper and Ernest B Schoedsack's *King Kong* (1933) is important in the history of film because, for once, Hollywood (in the person of **David O. Selznick**) allowed itself to be carried along in an experiment that, on paper, had little or no chance of succeeding. The film cost close to $700,000 to make and grossed an incredible $1,761,000 on its initial release – incredible, seeing as how the stop-motion special effects could just as easily have engendered humour, rather than awe. But the story was so strong and so resonant, above all in archetypal terms, that audiences seldom even knew why they were finding the film so satisfying. The Kong we see in the jungle and on top of the Empire State Building (an inspired touch) was in reality an eighteen-inch model designed by special-effects guru Willis O'Brien – RKO's initial plan had called for a man in a monkey suit. The film was re-released five years later, but this time with the sex removed, the gore mopped up and the monster emasculated. Modern filmmakers and scriptwriters might profitably learn from the fact that in the case of *King Kong*, the script came first and the means afterwards. Oh yes, and a mention ought to be made here of **Peter Jackson's** *King Kong* (2005), which emerged, against all the odds, as a successful and enlightened tribute to a masterpiece that the movie-obsessed Jackson must have known and loved since childhood.

Key Line: 'Oh no, it wasn't the aeroplanes. It was Beauty killed the Beast.' [*King Kong*]

Kingsley, Ben

An elusive screen presence, who almost disappears behind the parts he plays, Kingsley first reached a large international audience with his portrayal of the title role in **Richard Attenborough's** *Ghandi* (1982). More than good, as well, in John Irvin's *The Turtle Diary* (1986) and **Steven Spielberg's** *Schindler's List* (1993), Kingsley seems set – and is probably content – to remain on the periphery of stardom, just so long as he receives parts as challenging as his Roberto Miranda in **Roman Polanski's** *Death And The Maiden* (1995), in which he was so convincing that one almost ends up rooting for him over his erstwhile victim, **Sigourney Weaver,** and also in Jonathan Glazer's outstanding *Sexy Beast* (2000), in which Kingsley's Don Logan took borderline psychosis across the frontier and well into nomansland.

Other Key Films: *Fear Is The Key* (1972); *Betrayal* (1983); *Maurice* (1987); *Bugsy* (1991); *Sneakers* (1992); *Species* (1995); *Parting Shots* (1998); *Rules Of Engagement* (2000); *The Triumph of Love* (2001); *House Of Sand And Fog* (2003); *Oliver Twist* (2005); *Mrs Harris* (2005); *Lucky Number Slevin* (2006)

Kinski, Klaus

Demented German actor who spent the better part of a decade believing he was the Second Coming, Kinski was actually (when he was able to control his temper) a consummate screen actor with an extraordinary instinct for visual and emotional subtleties. Forever associated with his counterpart and sometime nemesis **Werner Herzog**, Kinski starred in four of the director's most outstanding films: *Aguirre, Wrath Of God* (1972), *Nosferatu* (1978), *Woyzeck* (1979) and *Fitzcarraldo* (1982). These two highly disparate characters alternately brought out the best and the worst in each other, and Herzog's recent TV documentary tribute to Kinski, *Mein Liebster Feind – Klaus Kinski* (1999), shows how close each came to (quite literally) driving the other mad.

Other Key Films: *Ludwig II* (1954); *For A Few Dollars More* (1965); *Dr Zhivago* (1965); *Circus Of Fear* (1967); *Venus In Furs* (1970); *Burden Of Dreams* (1982); *The Little Drummer Girl* (1984)

Kline, Kevin

Kline should really have been born around 1910, so that he could have given **Errol Flynn** a run for his money during the Golden Era of the 1930s, for he was made for swashbuckling – he even looks better in a moustache. Given that he was actually born in 1947, he still hasn't done too badly for himself, revealing a wondrous comic touch in Charles Crichton's *A Fish Called Wanda* (1988) – a gift which was already apparent in his high-octane performance as **Meryl Streep's** schizophrenic lover, Nathan Landau, in **Alan J Pakula's** *Sophie's Choice* (1982). His best work to date has been as adulterer Ben Hood in **Ang Lee's** *The Ice Storm* (1997).

Other Key Films: *The Big Chill* (1983); *Silverado* (1985); *Cry Freedom* (1987); *The January Man* (1989); *Grand Canyon* (1991); *Dave* (1993); *French Kiss* (1995); *Fierce Creatures* (1997); *The Ice Storm* (1997); *In & Out* (1997); *Wild Wild West* (1999); *The Anniversary Party* (2000); *The Emperor's Club* (2002); *De-Lovely* (2004); *The Pink Panther* (2006); *A Prairie Home Companion* (2006); *As You Like It* (2006)

Korda Family, The

The three Korda brothers: Alexander, a director and producer; Vincent, an art director; and Zoltán, an editor and director, were God's greatest gift to the crisis-stricken British film industry of the 1930s. Between them they made a series of what are unquestionably the most prestigious films ever produced in Great Britain. This includes Alexander Korda's own *The Private Life Of Henry VIII* (1933), *The Private Life Of Don Juan* (1934), *Rembrandt* (1936) and *That Hamilton Woman* (1941), together with an extraordinary list of productions by other directors, all notable for their outstanding quality and scrupulous design, including **René Clair's** *The Ghost Goes West* (1935), Jacques Feyder's *Knight Without Armour* (1936), Zoltan Korda's *The Four Feathers* (1939), the multi-directed *The Thief Of Bagdad* (1940) and **Carol Reed's** *The Fallen Idol* (1948). Alexander also happened to be one of the nicest men in movies. See **Heartstopping Moments**

Other Key Films: **Anthony Asquith's** *The Winslow Boy* (1948); **Michael Powell's** *The Small Back Room* (1949); Carol Reed's *The Third Man* (1949) and *Outcast Of The Islands* (1951)

Korngold, Erich Wolfgang

A classic product of the late nineteenth-century Viennese style of music (despite his 1897 'beginning of modernism' birth date), Korngold was proclaimed a child genius by Mahler, but finally settled for a high-profile career in Hollywood and the composition of such lushly romantic repertoire works as his Violin Concerto. His ecstatic scores for **Michael Curtiz's** magnificent quartet of *Captain Blood* (1935), *The Adventures Of Robin Hood* (1938), *The Private Lives Of Elizabeth And Essex* (1939) and *The Sea Hawk* (1940), contributed enormously to the atmosphere and longevity of what would otherwise have been a series of only vaguely memorable swashbucklers.

Other Key Films: **William Dieterle's** *A Midsummer Night's Dream* (1935); **Mervyn LeRoy's** *Anthony Adverse* (1936); William Keighley's *The Prince And The Pauper* (1937); Michael Curtiz's *The Sea Wolf* (1941); **Sam Wood's** *King's Row* (1942); **Edmund Goulding's** *The Constant Nymph* (1943)

Kovacs, Laszlo

An ex-lighting cameraman, Kovac made his real debut as a cinematographer with **Peter Bogdanovich's** *Targets* (1968) and **Dennis Hopper's** *Easy Rider* (1969), but his true mastery of lighting and the camera only became apparent with **Bob Rafelson's** *Five Easy Pieces* (1970). Since then Kovacs has worked with the smart pack, the art pack and the brat pack, and has been responsible for the look of some of the most inventive and influential movies of the era, including stints as a co-photographer, for example on **Steven Spielberg's** *Close Encounters Of The Third Kind* (1977) and **Martin Scorsese's** entertaining documentary about The Band, *The Last Waltz* (1978).

Other Key Films: Bob Rafelson's *The King Of Marvin Gardens* (1972); Hal Ashby's *Shampoo* (1975); Graeme Clifford's *Frances* (1982); Ivan Reitman's *Ghostbusters* (1984); P J Hogan's *My Best Friend's Wedding* (1997); Troy Miller's *Jack Frost* (1998); Bunny Hunt's *Return To Me* (2000); Donal Petrie's *Miss Congeniality* (2000); Marc Lawrence's *Two Weeks Notice* (2002);

Krasna, Norman

One of the most independent-minded of all the mainstream studio era screenwriters, Krasna liked to adapt his own storylines for the screen, and constructed a remarkable rags-to-riches career for himself in the process. His solo credits include **Fritz Lang's** *Fury* (1936) [for the screen story], **Alfred Hitchcock's** *Mr And Mrs Smith* (1941), and **Stanley Donen's** *Indiscreet* (1958). Krasna emigrated to Europe at the height of his success, an act that, quite literally, stopped his career dead in its tracks.

Other Key Films: Mitchell Leisen's *Hands Across The Table* (1935); **Clarence Brown's** *Wife Versus Secretary* (1936); Fritz Lang's *You And Me* (1938); **Sam Wood's** *The Devil And Miss Jones* (1941); **George Cukor's** *Let's Make Love* (1960)

Kristofferson, Kris

Sexy (or so my wife tells me) and multi-talented (he also has a successful career as a singer songwriter), the Kristofferson persona shouldn't really work on the screen, but it does. He was good in B Norton's *Cisco Pike* (1972) and better in **Sam Peckinpah's** *Pat Garrett And Bill The Kid* (1973), but the undoubted highpoint of his film career has come recently, in **John Sayles's** utterly magnificent *Lone Star* (1996), the best film about America by an American for easily a generation. Kristofferson's performance as corrupt sheriff Charlie Wade explores every false American myth going, and strikes notes that many actors spend their lifetimes trying to achieve.

Other Key Films: *Alice Doesn't Live Here Anymore* (1974); *Songwriter* (1984); *Trouble In Mind* (1985); *Pharaoh's Army* (1995); *Lone Star* (1996); *Blade* (1998); *Payback* (1999); *Planet Of The Apes* (2001); *D-Tox* (2002); *Silver City* (2004); *The Jacket* (2005); *Disappearances* (2006)

Kubrick, Stanley

Kubrick's recent death has robbed cinema of a true iconoclast, able to woo actors of the box-office calibre of **Tom Cruise** to take time off from other, more lucrative work, to appear in what has unfortunately turned out to be the director's last film, *Eyes Wide Shut* (1999). Kubrick's greatest days came earlier, however, with such classics as *The Killing* (1956), *Paths Of Glory* (1958) and the one and only *Dr Strangelove; Or How I Learned To Stop Worrying And Love The Bomb* (1963), a film so undeniably perfect of its type that it still improves after repeated watching. Many consider *2001: A Space Odyssey* (1968) to be Kubrick's masterpiece, but his most controversial film, which has recently been re-released following the director's death, must be *A Clockwork Orange* (1971), which set out to challenge existing preconceptions concerning violence and sexuality, and succeeded all too well. With an astonishing knowledge of cinema history, and a fastidious nature that involved him in frenzied and lengthy preparations for all his films, it is something of a miracle that he left us a filmography quite so rich and varied in its content.

Other Key Films: *Fear And Desire* (1953); *Killer's Kiss* (1955); *Spartacus* (1960); *Lolita* (1962); *Barry Lyndon* (1975); *The Shining* (1980); *Full Metal Jacket* (1987)

Key Line: 'What are you? Some kind of a pre-vert?' [Keenan Wynn to **Peter Sellers** in *Dr. Strangelove*]

Kurosawa, Akira

The extraordinary thing about *The Seven Samurai* (1954) – the film for which Kurosawa is most famous in the West – is that even an eight-year-old child [in this case, my son] can watch all three hours twenty minutes of it without twitching and without showing signs of boredom. It can't simply be the story, for at the age of eight many of the nuances will inevitably pass a child by. So it must be the visual quality – the editing, the composition, the whole look of the film. In just the same way a child can look at the paintings of Paul Gauguin, Vincent Van Gogh, or Paul Cézanne, and be seduced by their design, without understanding the theory behind it. Kurosawa is a naturalistic director, in direct line to the poets, the philosophers and the painters that Japan has produced so fruitfully over a period of more than 3,000 years. His greatest films have a visual and literary universality, which explains why he was so attracted to that other master of the universal, William Shakespeare, whose *Macbeth* Kurosawa turned into *Throne Of Blood* (1958), and whose *King Lear* he turned into *Ran* (1985). Following a failed suicide attempt in 1970 after the failure of the studio-bound *Dodeska-den* (1970), Kurosawa was invited to the Soviet Union to film *Dersu Uzala* (1975), a film about the friendship, based on absolute trust, between a fur trapper and the Russian leader of a topographical expedition in nineteenth-century Siberia. The result is a masterpiece, and its success with audiences ushered in the last great creative period of this noble director – an era which encompassed not only *Ran* but also its predecessor, the visually awe-inspiring and sublimely literate *Kagemusha* (1980). See **Heartstopping Moments**

Other Key Films: *Judo Saga* (1943); *Drunken Angel* (1948); *Stray Dog* (1949); *Rashomon* (1950); *The Idiot* (1951); *The Lower Depths* (1958); *The Hidden Fortress* (1958); *Yojimbo* (1961); *Sanjuro* (1962); *Dreams* (1990); *Rhapsody In August* (1991)

Kusturica, Emir

Kusturica astonished everyone with his *Time Of The Gypsies* (1989) – the film was at once so real and so magical, as if an entirely new voice and eye were making itself felt in the cinema. Awards poured down on Kusturica's head and he received the usual dread summons from Hollywood. It is to his great credit, therefore, that *Arizona Dream* (1993), the film that emerged from the summons, is no worse. The film is part indisputably brilliant, part turgid, and it is only with his return to Yugoslavia and to his roots, that Kusturica re-emerged, not unscathed exactly, but at the very least chastened, to direct the picaresque, Palme D'Or winning *Underground* (1995). Kusturica ploughed a new and very different furrow with *Black Cat, White Cat* (1998), a slapstick gypsy comedy with some of the best music and some of the funniest set pieces put on film since **Mel Brooks's** *The Producers* (1968), thirty years before.

Other Key Films: *Do You Remember Dolly Bell?* (1981); *When Father Was Away On Business* (1985); *Life Is A Miracle* (2004)

Ladd, Alan

Shy and retiring in everyday life, Ladd was a boy's-own hero in his films, appealing to a younger audience than almost any of his contemporaries. A natural athlete, his deep voice belied his five-foot six-inch frame, and when paired with the equally diminutive **Veronica Lake**, he gave an impression of stature twinned with serenity. At his best when playing loners bruised by, and wary of, women, his finest performance was undoubtedly in **George Stevens's** *Shane* (1953), where, in some strange way, he managed to transcend himself and become the sort of actor he always, by implication at least, could have been.

Other Key Films: *The Glass Key* (1942); *This Gun For Hire* (1942); *The Blue Dahlia* (1946); *Calcutta* (1947); *The Great Gatsby* (1949); *Appointment With Danger* (1951); *The Badlanders* (1958); *The Carpetbaggers* (1964)

Key Lines:
1. 'Call me Shane.' [*Shane*]
2. 'I never saw another actor who moved as gracefully as Alan, who had that kind of coordination. A beautiful, deep voice. Everybody said he was a non-actor, but they were wrong. He knew what he was doing.' [Richard Maibaum, who scripted Irving Pichel's *O.S.S.* (1946) and co-scripted Elliott Nugent's *The Great Gatsby* (1949), on working with Ladd]

Lake, Veronica
Often twinned with **Alan Ladd** in hard-boiled thrillers (although they reputedly couldn't stand each other), the peek-a-boo-coiffed Lake was actually an extremely talented comedienne, as she proved in **Preston Sturges's** comic masterpiece *Sullivan's Travels* (1941) and **René Clair's** delightfully idiosyncratic *I Married A Witch* (1942). Her career as a top-rank star really only spanned five years, however, from 1941-1946, and ended with a final outing in **George Marshall's Raymond Chandler-**scripted *The Blue Dahlia* (1946). All her later attempts at a comeback, even with Ladd at her side once again, fizzled out. Note for film buffs: Eighteen years after her last Hollywood film, Lake co-produced and starred in one of the worst and most surreally dotty horror films in movie history, B F Grinter's *Flesh Feast* (1970), in which she tortures Hitler to death and ends up by shrieking anti-Nazi inanities at the audience.

Other Key Films: *The Glass Key* (1942); *This Gun For Hire* (1942)

Lancaster, Burt
Endowed by nature with a fine physique and an even finer toothy smile that, out of the blue, could light up and transform his face, Lancaster began his acting career in **Robert Siodmak's** *film noir* masterpiece *The Killers* (1946), in which his brooding, panther-like presence (the result of his former career as a circus acrobat) immediately gave him entrée to the select club of Hollywood leading men. By 1948 he had formed his own production company, and he spent the rest of his life alternating (rather in the manner of **Clint Eastwood**) between art and commerce. Two great performances stand out – as J J Hunsecker, the amoral gossip columnist in **Alexander Mackendrick's** *Sweet Smell Of Success* (1958), and as Lou Pasco, the self-deluding minor hood in **Louis Malle's** *Atlantic City* (1980).

Other Key Films: *Brute Force* (1947); *I Walk Alone* (1947); *Criss Cross* (1949); *Come Back Little Sheba* (1952); *From Here To Eternity* (1953); *Apache* (1954); *Separate Tables* (1958); *Elmer Gantry* (1960); *Birdman Of Alcatraz* (1962); *The Leopard* (1963); *The Train* (1965); *The Swimmer* (1968); *1900* (1977); *Local Hero* (1983); *Tough Guys* (1986); *The Jeweller's Shop* (1988); *Rocket Gibraltar* (1988); *Field Of Dreams* (1989)

Key Line: **Tony Curtis**: 'Can I come in, J J?' Lancaster: 'No. You're dead, son. Get yourself buried.' [*The Sweet Smell Of Success*]

Lang, Charles B
Even a cursory glance at Lang's filmography will explain why he was nominated on eighteen separate occasions for academy awards for his cinematography. Ever the total professional, Lang was director of photography on such films as **Frank Borzage's** *A*

Farewell To Arms (1933), **Henry Hathaway's** *The Lives Of A Bengal Lancer* (1935), **Joseph L Mankiewicz's** *The Ghost And Mrs. Muir* (1947), **Fritz Lang's** *The Big Heat* (1953) and **Anthony Mann's** *The Man From Laramie* (1955). A consummate lighting technician and one of the most respected men in the Hollywood artistic hierarchy, **Billy Wilder** chose the, by then, freelancing Lang for *Sabrina* (1954) and *Some Like It Hot* (1959), while **Marlon Brando**, fastidious as ever and anxious about the look of his debut film, soon found that Lang's touch had not deserted him. The film which emerged from their collaboration *One-Eyed Jacks* (1961) with its surging, romantic shots of the coast of California, is surely one of the most beautifully photographed of all late period black-and-white films.

Other Key Films: John Cromwell's *Tom Sawyer* (1930); Elliott Nugent's *The Cat And The Canary* (1939); Lewis Allen's *The Uninvited* (1944); **Billy Wilder's** *Ace In The Hole* (1951); Delbert Mann's *Separate Tables* (1958); **Stanley Donen's** *Charade* (1963)

Lang, Fritz

Lang cut his teeth in the German **Expressionist** Movement of the 1920s with *Die Nibelungen* (1924), the ground-breaking *Metropolis* (1926), and *M* (1931), in which **Peter Lorre** played a tormented child-murderer. A convinced Nazi hater, Lang fled Germany for Hollywood (after an uncomfortable interview with Joseph Goebbels), where he directed **Spencer Tracy** in *Fury* (1936), an anti-mob indictment that MGM, to Lang's unutterable horror, massacred on the cutting-room floor. Lang's continuing obsession with the psychology of human weakness made him the ideal thriller and *film noir* director, with masterpieces such as *The Big Heat* (1953), *Clash By Night* (1955), and *While The City Sleeps* (1956) to his credit. But Lang didn't have an easy time of it in Hollywood (he was used to total control, something which the studios felt was their prerogative) and he reluctantly returned to Germany in 1956, where his last film, *The 1000 Eyes Of Dr Mabuse* (1960) was made under trying circumstances. Lang was an iconoclast in a world of clones, and his fascination with the underside of life and with the pathological and morphological motivations of evil was always going to set him at odds with a studio system with a vested interest in the preservation of the status quo.

Other Key Films: *Dr Mabuse* (1921); *Western Union* (1941); *Man Hunt* (1941); *Hangmen Also Die* (1943); *The Woman in the Window* (1945); *Scarlet Street* (1945); *House By The River* (1950); *Rancho Notorious* (1952); *The Blue Gardenia* (1953); *Human Desire* (1954); as actor, in **Jean-Luc Godard's** *Contempt* [*Le Mépris*] (1963)

Key Line: 'I liked Fritz. He was a hell of a good talker. He said funny things, mostly of a dry wit and mostly detrimental about other people.' [Ring Lardner Jr, who co-scripted *Cloak And Dagger* (1946), on its director, Lang]

Lange, Jessica

A complex and sadly underused actress, Lange's *annus mirabilis* came in 1982, when she should have won a Best Actress Oscar for her performance in Graeme Clifford's *Frances* (1982), but had to content herself with Best Supporting Actress in **Sydney Pollack's** *Tootsie* (1982) instead. Other fine performances followed, notably as doomed country singer Patsy Cline in **Bruce Beresford's** *Crimes Of The Heart* (1986), and in **Tony Richardson's** marvellous last film *Blue Sky* (1991), for which Lange won the Best Actress Oscar that had eluded her nine years before. Even in supporting roles, such as that of the bandit's wife in Michael Caton-Jones's *Rob Roy* (1995), she always retains her integrity and refuses to take the easier path of browbeating her audience into submission.

Other Key Films: *King Kong* (1976); *The Postman Always Rings Twice* (1981); *Country* (1984); *Far North* (1988); *Cape Fear* (1991); *Night And The City* (1992); *A Thousand Acres* (1997); *Cousin Bette* (1998); *Titus* (1999); *Prozac Nation* (2000); *Big Fish* (2003); *Don't Come Knocking* (2005)

Lanza, Mario

They tried to turn cheerful, promiscuous, golden-throated Lanza into a film star, but his eating (in the light of which his second movie, Norman Taurog's *The Toast Of New Orleans* (1950), takes on an entirely new connotation), his temper and his unfortunate propensity for drink and drugs (quite a list, if you think about it) led to a fatal heart attack, aged thirty-eight. His voice was brilliant but untrained ('canned belto' some wit called it), and Lanza was never able to see live performances right through thanks to shortcomings in his breathing technique. But on film, when he stopped acting and began to sing, he was magic, and Richard Thorpe's *The Great Caruso* (1951) will have to stand as his epitaph – although Lanza was never really great, and he certainly wasn't Caruso. Even so, and bearing in mind the Technicolor commerciality of his career, there are odd times, usually in the shower, when it is hard to get 'Call Me Fool' out of one's head and down the plughole, where it probably belongs.

Other Key Films: *That Midnight Kiss* (1949); *Because You're Mine* (1952); *Serenade* (1956) [forget the film – go read the James M Cain novel instead]; *The Seven Hills Of Rome* (1958); *For The First Time* (1959)

Laszlo, Ernest

Laszlo received a total of eight Oscar nominations for cinematography throughout his career, and deserved at least eight more, with films such as **Billy Wilder's** *Stalag 17* (1953), **Robert Aldrich's** *Kiss Me Deadly* (1955) and **Fritz Lang's** *While The City Sleeps* (1956) under his belt. He went commercial during the 1960s and 70s and the quality of his work suffered as a result, but his photography on Stanley Kramer's *Ship Of Fools* (1965) won him a well-deserved Academy Award, and everyone is allowed a few duds like George Seaton's *Airport* (1970) when they have such exquisite-looking black and whiters as Rudolph Maté's *D.O.A.* (1950) to their credit.

Other Key Films: **John Farrow's** *Two Years Before The Mast* (1946); **Joseph Losey's** *M* (1951); Richard Fleischer's *Bandido* (1956); Stanley Kramer's *Inherit The Wind* (1960)

Lathrop, Philip H

Lathrop is another underrated cinematographer whose name is hardly known outside film-buff circles. Well he certainly deserves to be more highly regarded, for it is with some astonishment that one realises the consistent, frequently ground-breaking quality of his work. Look at this list: David Miller's *Lonely Are The Brave* (1962), Norman Jewison's *The Cincinnati Kid* (1965), **John Boorman's** *Point Blank* (1967), **Sam Peckinpah's** *The Killer Elite* (1975), Walter Hill's *The Driver* (1978), and **Wim Wenders's** *Hammett* (1982). Elegant stuff.

Other Key Films: Blake Edwards's *Days Of Wine And Roses* (1963); **Sydney Pollack's** *They Shoot Horses Don't They?* (1969); Jean-Claude Tramont's *All Night Long* (1981); **Wes Craven's** *Deadly Friend* (1986)

Laughton, Charles

Indisputably rotund, and with his vocal cords damaged by a First World War gassing, Laughton was, on the surface, a curious candidate for international stardom.

Mercurial and insecure by nature, and deeply uneasy about his homosexuality, Laughton delighted the film world with his astonishing portrait of the king in **Alexander Korda's** *The Private Life Of Henry VIII* (1933). He went on to one of the finest of all screen careers, incarnating Captain Bligh in Frank Lloyd's *Mutiny On the Bounty* (1935), and Quasimodo in **William Dieterle's** *The Hunchback Of Notre Dame* (1939). In 1955, he directed possibly the finest debut film ever achieved within the Hollywood system, the **James Agee-**scripted *Night Of The Hunter*. Alas, although critically well-received and widely, if belatedly, viewed as the masterpiece it is, it was commercially unsuccessful and proved to be Laughton's only film as a director.

Other Key Films: *If I Had A Million* (1932); *Les Misérables* (1935); *Rembrandt* (1936); *The Beachcomber* (1938); *Jamaica Inn* (1939); *The Tuttles Of Tahiti* (1942); *The Canterville Ghost* (1944); *The Paradine Case* (1948); *The Big Clock* (1948); *The Bribe* (1949); *Hobson's Choice* (1954); *Witness For The Prosecution* (1958); *Advise And Consent* (1962)

Key Line: 'I no got wife no make happy, and I no got kids to make rich and big and strong, like me. Someday Tony die, sure. Who'll cry for Tony?' [Charles Laughton as Tony Patucci, in Garson Kanin's *They Knew What They Wanted* (1940)]

Laurel and Hardy

When they were great they were very, very great, and when they were bad they were still pretty good. Paradoxically, skinny Stan Laurel was the driving force behind this sublime comic pairing, but Oliver Hardy more than held his own (on-screen as well as off) even though he received only half Laurel's salary. Leo McCarey directed many of their early shorts, but with the coming of sound they moved on to full-length features, such as **Hal Roach** and Charles Rogers's *Fra Diavolo* (1933) – the mere thought of which, more than thirty years later, could still cause the author's father to giggle uncontrollably. Their relationship started to disintegrate after James W Horne's *Way Out West* (1937), but they made films for a further twelve years, and together, as is only right, they still added up to considerably more than the sum of their parts.

Other Key Films: *The Battle Of The Century* (1927); *Two Tars* (1928); *Night Owls* (1930); *Another Fine Mess* (1930); *The Music Box* (1932); *Sons Of The Desert* (1933); *Blockheads* (1938); *A Chump At Oxford* (1940)

Key Line: 'Another fine mess you've gotten me into.' (Hardy)

Law, Jude

Law's early theatre career was a spectacular one, with an Olivier award for Outstanding Newcomer and a Tony nomination for Outstanding Supporting Actor – his film career has taken off, too (aside from the occasional blip, usually occasioned by an all too conventional love life lived within the unconventional glare of an ever-burning, ever-churning publicity machine). Law found himself unexpectedly launched into the stratosphere following his brilliant performance as Dickie Greenleaf, in **Anthony Minghella's** *The Talented Mr. Ripley* (1999). Quite apart from his perfect mastery (as an Englishman) of a particularly difficult American idiom, he managed to submerge himself inside the part to such an extent that one was left at the end of the film with the impression that one had been privileged to see a major new talent in the making. Has he been able to take advantage of his running start? Well, apart from a few turgidly commercial roles, such as his Russian sniper, Vasilli Zaitsev, in **Jean-Jacques Annaud's** overblown *Enemy At the Gates* (2001), and his misjudged *Alfie* (2004), for Charles Shyer, one would have to say yes. Law's finest role (and his most catastrophically underappreciated) came as Inman, in Anthony Minghella's masterful *Cold Mountain* (2003), and on the strength of that alone one can

only look forward with a sharpened interest to his artistic (and emotional) maturity.
Other Key Films: *Gattaca* (1997); *Bent* (1997); *Midnight In The Garden Of Good And Evil* (1997); *Final Cut* (1998); *eXistenZ* (1999); *Love, Honour And Obey* (2000); *Artificial Intelligence: A.I.* (2001); *Road To Perdition* (2002); *I Heart Huckabees* (2004); *Closer* (2004); *The Aviator* (2004); *All The King's Men* (2006)

Lawton, Charles, Jr

Lawton is the man responsible for the camerawork on two of **Budd Boetticher's** outstanding Ranown cycle of **Westerns** featuring the great **Randolph Scott**, *Ride Lonesome* (1959) and *Comanche Station* (1960). These late films in the cycle have a particular look, an elegiac touch that seeks to remind us of what was lost when civilization and its minions took over the great plains from the men and women whose spiritual home they were. It is arguable that on the basis of his work on those two films, and also on Phil Karlson's *They Rode West* (1954), Delmer Daves's *Jubal* (1956), *3:10 To Yuma* (1958) and *Cowboy* (1958) along with **John Ford's** *Two Rode Together* (1961), that Lawton is one of the greatest and most unsung of all cinematographers, Western-oriented or otherwise. And as if that wasn't enough, Lawton also photographed **Orson Welles's** *The Lady From Shanghai* (1948), which has to be one of the most gorgeously perverse-looking films ever made, with its deep contrasts, surprising angles, and massive, almost ugly close-ups.

Other Key Films: Charles Riesner's *The Big Store* (1941); **Allan Dwan's** *Brewster's Millions* (1945); Curtis Bernhardt's *Miss Sadie Thompson* (1953)

Charles Laughton in The Hunchback of Notre Dame, directed by William Dieterle (1939).

RKO/The Kobal Collection/Alex Kahle

Lean, David

Renowned (and sometimes criticized) for his later epics such as *The Bridge On The River Kwai* (1958), *Doctor Zhivago* (1965), *Ryan's Daughter* (1970) and *A Passage To India* (1984), Lean was actually a far better film-maker before he discovered wide-screen CinemaScope. Early classics such as *Brief Encounter* (1945), *Great Expectations* (1946), *Oliver Twist* (1948) and *The Passionate Friends* (1949), although smaller in scale, were larger in heart, and benefited from Lean's own concise editing, a talent that seemed to become looser with each successive larger-than-life blockbuster. There is no doubt that *Lawrence Of Arabia* (1962) is wonderfully professional and gives much pleasure visually, but it has always seemed (dare one say it?) just a little cold at the centre.

Other Key Films: *Blithe Spirit* (1945); *Madeleine* (1949); *The Sound Barrier* (1952); *Hobson's Choice* (1954); *Summer Madness* (1955)

Léaud, Jean-Pierre

Léaud was destined for stardom the moment director **François Truffaut** chose him as his alter ego in the Antoine Doinel cycle of films, consisting of *The 400 Blows* (1959), *Love At Twenty* (1962), *Stolen Kisses* (1968), *Bed And Board* (1970) and *Love On The Run* (1979). Léaud represented the quintessential French young man – with his chiselled looks and floppy hair, he could never be anything else – at the same time existentialist and conservative, hedonistic and ascetic, aesthete, philosopher and *érotomane*. **Jean-Luc Godard** saw the visual manifestations of such paradoxes in Léaud too, using him in *Masculine-Feminine* (1966), *Made In USA* (1966), *La Chinoise*

(1967) and *Weekend* (1968). Léaud truly reached the heights in one great film by one great director, **Jean Eustache's** *La Maman Et La Putain* (1973), which more than rustles the laurels of even **Bernardo Bertolucci's** magnificent *Last Tango In Paris* (1972) in which Léaud had featured the year before. Since then, as if exhausted by his heady early fame, Léaud has fallen a little by the wayside, even though directors such as Agnes Varda, **André Téchiné** and **Aki Kaurismäki** doggedly continue to use him.
Other Key Films: *Le Testament D'Orphée* (1960); *Pierrot Le Fou* (1965); *Pigsty* (1969); *Les Deux Anglaises Et Le Continent* (1971); *Day For Night* (1973); *Détective* (1985); *I Hired A Contract Killer* (1990); *J'Embrasse Pas* (1991); *Personne Ne M'Aime* (1994); *Irma Vep* (1996); *Innocent* (1999); *L'Affaire Marcorelle* (2000); *Dark Circles* (2001); *Le Pornographe* (2001); *Folle Embellie* (2004)

Leconte, Patrice
A 1969 graduate of the prestigious Institut Des Hautes Etudes Cinématographiques, Leconte began his professional career as a cartoonist on *Pilote* magazine, before returning to film six years later to make his directorial debut with *Les Vécés Étaient Fermés De L'Intérieur* (1975) – the film flopped, but his next film, *Les Bronzés* (1978), a spoof on Club Mediteranée-style holidays, was a tremendous success. Concentrating on the three themes of male bonding, deviant sexuality and incipient madness, Leconte made the tragicomic *Tandem* (1987), followed by the even darker *Monsieur Hire* (1989). *Le Mari De La Coiffeuse* (1990) was as light as a soufflé in comparison, and gave Leconte his greatest international success, and his best films since have spanned both sides of his personality – the deviant and the comedic – and include the black humour of *Tango* (1993), and the brilliantly realised *Ridicule* (1996), whose melding of wit, costume and politics affords a marvellously sophisticated entertainment in the grand French rococo style.
Other Key Films: *Les Spécialistes* (1984); *Contre L'Oubli* (1991); *Le Batteur Du Boléro* (1992); *Le Parfum D'Yvonne* (1994); *Lumière Et Compagnie* (1995); *Les Grands Ducs* (1996); *Une Chance Sur Deux* (1998); *La Fille Sur Le Pont* (1999); *La Veuve De Saint-Pierre* (2000); *Felix Et Lola* (2000); *Rue Des Plaisirs* (2001); *L'Homme Du Train* (2002); *Confidences Trop Intimes* (2004); *Mon Meilleur Ami* (2006)

Lee, Ang
Lee had already established himself as a major director with *The Wedding Banquet* (1993) and *Eat Drink Man Woman* (1994) before the lure of Europe, and of **Emma Thompson's** immaculate screenplay, persuaded him to try his hand at an English period drama. The result was *Sense And Sensibility* (1995), an unlikely subject at first glance, but one that Lee triumphantly made his own. *The Ice Storm* (1997) followed, a subtle and very dark investigation into the moral fall-out from the upheavals of the 1960s in American suburbia, proving, beyond a doubt, that Lee's forte was character, atmosphere and emotional truth. Lee respects the conventions of whatever period he is filming, and it is notable that, unlike many of his New York University Institute of Film and Television counterparts, he has not, as yet, been swayed by the unholy burden of contemporary rectitude. Lee's recent *Crouching Tiger, Hidden Dragon* (2000) has proved itself a most improbable triumph with the chattering classes, selling itself as a message movie to people who wouldn't be seen dead attending a swashbuckler – which is what it really is, of course – whilst *Brokeback Mountain* (2005) has managed the almost impossible task of making latent homosexuality sexy.
Other Key Films: *Ride With The Devil* (1999); *Chosen* [short] (2001); *Hulk* (2003)

Lee, Bruce

Less a film star than a phenomenon, Bruce Lee was the first great martial-arts entertainer to successfully make the crossover from China to the US. Lee's early death at the age of thirty-three from a brain oedema guaranteed his already burgeoning cult status, but it is only in three films, the best of which was Robert Clouse's *Enter The Dragon* (1973), together with an entertaining bit part in Paul Bogart's *Marlowe* (1969), that his grace and talent really showed to the full.

Other Key Films: *Fist Of Fury* (1972)

Key Line: 'I owe my spirituality to Bruce Lee. In my lifetime I never met another man who was even remotely at his level of consciousness.' [Sterling Silliphant, who scripted *Marlowe* (1969), in which Lee famously destroyed private eye James Garner's office with his bare hands and feet]

Lee, Christopher

Born Christopher Frank Cardini, beanpole Lee is renowned for his horror roles, in particular for his incarnation of *Dracula* in the Hammer Horror series. A better actor than his career might at first glance indicate, he has recently done some fine television work, notably in the BBC television adaptation of *Gormenghast* (2000), but film buffs (a law unto themselves) will always cherish his eccentric performance as the dancing, daemonic Lord Summerisle in Robin Hardy's curious *The Wicker Man* (1973). In a remarkable career comeback, Lee was offered the part of Saruman the White in Peter Jackson's *Lord Of The Rings* trilogy (2001-2003), a move which virtually coincided with a series of *Star Wars* appearances for George Lucas (2002 & 2005). 'May the ring force be with you, oh precious master…' Harry Potter next?

Key Films: *The Curse of Frankenstein* (1958); *Dracula* (1959); *Dr. Terror's House Of Horrors* (1965); *The Man with the Golden Gun* (1974); *Circle Of Iron* (1979); *The Salamander* (1981); *Howling II* (1985); *Funny Man* (1994); *Sleepy Hollow* (1999); *Greyfriars Bobby* (2005); *Charlie And The Chocolate Factory* (2005)

Lee, Spike

In many ways an unprepossessing and rather vainglorious figure, Lee has real talent hidden beneath his agitprop façade. *Malcolm X* (1992) is a superb meditation on commitment, but its very success shows the rest of Lee's films up in a poorer light. *She's Got To Have It* (1986) and *Do The Right Thing* (1989), though streetwise on the surface, seem somewhat shallow and one-track minded by comparison, but his recent outing into thriller territory, *Inside Man* (2006), garnered some useful reviews – it would be best to draw a veil, perhaps, over *She Hate Me* (2004), however.

Other Key Films: *School Daze* (1987); *Mo' Better Blues* (1990); *Jungle Fever* (1991); *Crooklyn* (1994); *Clockers* (1995); *He Got Game* (1998); *Summer Of Sam* (1999); *Bamboozled* (2000); *25th Hour* (2002)

Lehman, Ernest

One of the most versatile and successful of all Hollywood screenwriters, Lehman's masterpiece was the adaptation of his own novella for **Alexander Mackendrick's** *Sweet Smell Of Success* (1958). His own personal favourite remains his version of Rocky Graziano's autobiography in **Robert Wise's** *Somebody Up There Likes Me* (1956), but many movie fans consider Lehman's script for **Alfred Hitchcock's** *North By Northwest* (1959) as coming perilously close to Hollywood perfection. His final list of credits reads like a who's who of the Hollywood mainstream.

Other Key Films: **Billy Wilder's** *Sabrina* (1954); Walter Lang's *The King And I*

(1956); Robert Wise and Jerome Robbins's *West Side Story* (1961); Robert Wise's *The Sound Of Music* (1965); **Mike Nichols's** *Who's Afraid Of Virginia Woolf?* (1966); **William Wyler's** *Funny Girl* (1968); **John Frankenheimer's** *Black Sunday* (1977)

Leigh, Janet

Leigh had a lot of bad years when she was forced into trivial fare by her contract with MGM, but suddenly, around 1958, she found herself – or rather **Orson Welles** found her, in *Touch Of Evil* (1958) – identifying a strange, almost innate masochism that the camera brought out, and which audiences, sadists all, lapped up. **Alfred Hitchcock**, the cinema audience's favourite ersatz sadist, sniffed fresh blood, and pounced on Leigh for the role of Marion Crane in *Psycho* (1960), after which Leigh's masochism reigned supreme with put-upon roles in **John Frankenheimer's** *The Manchurian Candidate* (1962) and Jack Smight's *Harper* (1966), culminating in her being attacked by monster rabbits in William F Claxton's *Night Of The Lepus* (1972) and menaced by a billow of angry miasma in **John Carpenter's** *The Fog* (1980). And who said careers don't run in cycles?

Other Key Films: *That Forsyte Woman* (1949); *Scaramouche* (1952); *The Naked Spur* (1953); *The Black Shield Of Falworth* (1954); *Pete Kelly's Blues* (1955); *The Vikings* (1958); *Wives And Lovers* (1963); *Halloween H 20: Twenty Years Later* (1998); *A Fate Totally Worse Than Death* (2005)

Leigh, Jennifer Jason

Leigh is a true oddity in Hollywood terms – an attractive actress who decided, early on in her career, that character parts and not glamour were to be her forte. One can only utter an awestruck 'bravo!'. Fine but curious in **Paul Verhoeven's** *Flesh And Blood* (1985), she was even better in Robert Harmon's *The Hitcher* (1986), and really found her stride in **Barbet Schroeder's** otherwise pretty much over-the-top *Single White Female* (1992), and in **Robert Altman's** *Short Cuts* (1993) – her incarnation of Dorothy Parker in **Alan Rudolph's** *Mrs. Parker And The Vicious Circle* (1994) was as eccentric as it was masterly, and remains in the memory long after the film itself has been forgotten. **Taylor Hackford's** excellent *Dolores Claiborne* (1995) followed, as well as the role of **Jean Harlow**-loving Blondie O'Hara in Robert Altman's *Kansas City* (1996). If Leigh can keep her nerve, and if she can avoid lesser, misdirected films such as Jocelyn Moorhouse's *A Thousand Acres* (1997) and Agnieszka Holland's *Washington Square* (1997), her career must surely go from strength to strength.

Other Key Films: *The Big Picture* (1989); *Miami Blues* (1990); *Crooked Hearts* (1991); *Rush* (1992); *The Hudsucker Proxy* (1994); *Georgia* (1995); *eXistenZ* (1999); *Skipped Parts* (2000); *The King Is Alive* (2000); *The Anniversary Party* (2001); *Road To Perdition* (2002); *In The Cut* (2003); *El Maquinista* (2004); *Rag Tale* (2005)

Leigh, Mike

Along with fellow-iconoclast **Ken Loach**, Leigh has resolutely ignored mainstream British cinema to concentrate on such improvisational set-pieces as *Life Is Sweet* (1991), *Naked* (1993) and *Secrets And Lies* (1996), which was the first of his films to benefit from anything like a universal release. He followed this up with the remarkable *Career Girls* (1997), and his standing in France (and indeed anywhere where integrity is valued over bankability) is very high. *Secrets And Lies* won the Palme D'Or at the 1995 Cannes Film Festival, and is notable for the fact that, due to Leigh's insistence that his actors improvise towards a plot rather than having a plot foisted upon them, no one knew what the upshot of the film would be until it happened.

Leigh, Vivien

Justly famous for landing the part of Scarlett O'Hara in **David O Selznick's** production of *Gone With The Wind* (1939) and for what she subsequently made of it, Leigh's later career was blighted by tuberculosis, and, to an increasing extent, by manic depression. Superb alongside husband **Laurence Olivier** in *That Hamilton Woman* (1941), she also registered strongly in **Mervyn LeRoy's** *Waterloo Bridge* (1940) and opposite **Marlon Brando** as Blanche DuBois in **Elia Kazan's** *A Streetcar Named Desire* (1951). A tragic figure, she died at the age of fifty-four in 1967, leaving us with only the memory of her fragile beauty in the relatively small number of films she managed to make while in her prime.

Other Key Films: *Fire Over England* (1937); *Caesar And Cleopatra* (1945); *Anna Karenina* (1948); *The Roman Spring Of Mrs Stone* (1961)

Key Line: 'After all, tomorrow is another day.' [*Gone With The Wind*]

Lemmon, Jack

Lemmon became something of an institution in the US, alongside the recently deceased **Walter Matthau**, for his ability to instil hysteria with humour (and drama with hysteria). Some of his early film performances were exceptional, most notably in **John Ford** and **Mervyn LeRoy's** *Mister Roberts* (1955), **Billy Wilder's** *Some Like It Hot* (1959) and *The Apartment* (1960), **Blake Edwards's** *Days Of Wine And Roses* (1962) and Gene Saks's *The Odd Couple* (1968), but a glance through Lemmon's filmography suggests that he was far more of a one-track player than is currently acknowledged. Even in such nominally dramatic roles as his Jack Godell in James Bridges's *The China Syndrome* (1979) and his excellent Shelley 'the Machine' Levine in James Foley's *Glengarry Glen Ross* (1992), it is the same Lemmon that tried to *Save The Tiger* in John G Avildsen's 1973 movie, or find his son in **Constantin Costa-Gavras's** *Missing* (1982), who consistently reappears. It eventually comes down to a question of believability rather than talent (for Lemmon had oodles of that) – his anti-heroic characters, in the final analysis, seem contrived, as though the process from conception to finalization were merely an intellectual equation, with no place left for instinct.

Other Key Films: *It Should Happen To You* (1954); *The Cowboy* (1958); *Bell Book And Candle* (1959); *Irma La Douce* (1963); *How To Murder Your Wife* (1965); *The Fortune Cookie* (1966); *The Out-Of-Towners* (1970); *The Front Page* (1974); *The Prisoner Of Second Avenue* (1975); *Macaroni* (1985); *JFK* (1991); *Short Cuts* (1993); *The Legend Of Bagger Vance* (2000)

Leonard, Robert Z

Leonard (the Z stands for Ziegler) directed one of the most underrated **Greta Garbo** vehicles, *Susan Lenox: Her Fall and Rise* (1931), one of the best-ever Jane Austen adaptations, *Pride And Prejudice* (1941), and one of the fruitiest quasi-*film noirs* ever conceived of in a Hollywood story department, *The Bribe* (1949), and yet his name is little known outside the demented cognoscenti (this author included) who derive a vicarious pleasure from the endless perusal of screen credits. His career (he started out as an actor before turning to directing) lasted fifty years, and more than half his films are silents, now rarely seen outside the archives, but this cheerful Chicagoan whose name will be forever linked to the heyday of MGM was a brilliant craftsman and a thoroughgoing professional, and even the froth on the froth of his froth has a distinctive and decidedly pleasant taste.

Other Key Films: *The Master Key* (1914); *Modern Love* (1918); *Fashion Row* (1923); *Bright Lights* (1925); *Adam And Evil* (1927); *Let Us Be Gay* (1930); *Strange Interlude* (1932); *The Great Ziegfeld* (1936); *Maytime* (1937); *When Ladies Meet* (1941); *The Secret Heart* (1946); *In The Good Old Summertime* (1949); *The King's Thief* (1955)

Leone, Sergio

One of the screen's most instinctive visual masters, Leone used the full spectrum of CinemaScope with controlled abandon, and will forever be remembered for the awe-inspiring crane-tracking shot in his masterpiece *Once Upon A Time In The West* (1968). To the swelling lyricism of **Ennio Morricone's** music, he follows **Claudia Cardinale** as she alights from a train, then swoops over the station-house as she enters, only to pick her up again on the far side as she stares down the main street of one of the mythical West's most consummately convincing border towns. It is one of the greatest moments in all cinema – and Leone, when he was on his best form, as in *The Good, The Bad, And The Ugly* (1968) and *Once Upon A Time In America* (1983), *was* cinema.

Other Key Films: *A Fistful Of Dollars* (1964); *For a Few Dollars More* (1966); *Fistful Of Dynamite* [a.k.a. *Duck, You Sucker*] (1972)

LeRoy, Mervyn

The diminutive LeRoy, or Le Roy, as he was sometimes known, had tried just about every job going in films (including wardrobe, acting, lab work, assistant cameraman, gag writing and comedy construction) before Warners tried him out as a director on *No Place To Go* (1927). Just three years later he was directing **Edward G Robinson** in *Little Caesar* (1931) and **Gloria Swanson** in her last major role – if one excepts **Billy Wilder's** *Sunset Boulevard* (1950) – in *Tonight Or Never* (1931). It wasn't long before LeRoy began fronting Warners' social dramas with the powerful and still affecting *I Am A Fugitive From A Chain Gang* (1932). This success led to a sequence of high-profile films including *Gold Diggers Of 1933* (1933) and *Anthony Adverse* (1936), followed by a lucrative, but ultimately deadening move to MGM, where he worked as a producer as well as a director on a series of increasingly bland commercial vehicles, including *Waterloo Bridge* (1940), *Random Harvest* (1942) and *Little Women* (1949). He had a minor return to form (and to Warners) in the mid-1950s, most notably with *The FBI Story* (1959), which harked back to his *Little Caesar* heyday, but the spark was gone and LeRoy retired, still only in his mid sixties, to rest on his laurels and to contemplate the Irving Thalberg Memorial Award that, in 1975, the Academy chose to award him for his lifetime's achievement.

Other Key Films: *The Heart Of New York* (1932); *Tugboat Annie* (1933); *Elmer The Great* (1933); *I Found Stella Parish* (1935); *Blossoms In The Dust* (1941); *Madame Curie* (1943); *Thirty Seconds Over Tokyo* (1944); *Quo Vadis* (1951); *Home Before Dark* (1958); *Gypsy* (1962)

Lewin, Albert

Lewin was a genuine oddity in a Hollywood devoted to conformity. An intellectual in a world of boastful philistines, he worked as **Irving Thalberg's** assistant at MGM before moving to Paramount, again as a producer, in 1937. In 1942 he was finally given the chance to direct, and during the next fifteen years he produced, wrote and directed six films, all of which were quirky, and one or two downright perverse.

Lewin's headiest concoction was the desperately romantic *Pandora And The Flying Dutchman* (1951), which featured a brilliantly on-form **James Mason** as the Dutchman, and an **Ava Gardner** at the peak of her beauty (and immaculately photographed by **Jack Cardiff**) as the spoilt Pandora, who eventually finds an enduring love (to say the very least) with her sea-borne cavalier. Lewin's first three films had been quirky literary tales, all with a sadomasochistic bent, and all featuring the laconic talents of the doomed **George Sanders**, but his follow-up *Saadia* (1954), was unfortunately a failure, marginally redeemed by his final film, *The Living Idol* (1956), which returned to the strange world which Lewin had inhabited so well in *Pandora*. For a long time it was fashionable to pan Lewin for his intellectual and literary aspirations, but the Sanders films are fascinating, every one, and *Pandora* is one of those odd little miracles that occasionally thrust themselves to the surface of even the most pacific of seas.

Other Key Films: *The Moon And Sixpence* (1942); *The Picture Of Dorian Gray* (1945); *The Private Affairs Of Bel Ami* (1947)

Lewis, Jerry

Lewis is the Prince of hysteria, the man who could cause even a convention of Buddhist monks to tear out their non-existent hair. It is irritating even to have to talk about him, let alone think about him, but his position in the contemporary US unconscious is secure, not so much on account of his movies (which few young people have probably seen) but more on account of his demented charitable activities, which satisfy an apparently profound Western need to be seen to be doing something, rather than just to do it. Following his seven-year stint as **Dean Martin's** stooge (or was it the other way around?) from 1949 to 1956, Lewis directed himself in a series of increasingly demented, increasingly bathetic films, which include *The Bellboy* (1960), *The Nutty Professor* (1963) and *The Patsy* (1964). Something of an institution in France, where for a long time he was preferred to the home-grown talent of **Jacques Tati**, Lewis made an unlikely sort of comeback with his appearance, as Jerry Langford, in **Martin Scorsese's** *The King Of Comedy* (1983).

Other Key Films: *The Ladies' Man* (1961); *The Errand Boy* (1961); *The Family Jewels* (1965); *Three On A Couch* (1966); *The Big Mouth* (1967); *One More Time* (1969); *Which Way To The Front?* (1970); *Arizona Dream* (1993); *The Nutty Professor* (1996)

Lewis, Joseph H

Lewis was that rare thing – a B-Movie director who transcended his calling. His best films, like the sublime *Gun Crazy* (1950), work on a deep psychological level. Because he wasn't a slave to highly-paid, and very often vain, stars, Lewis was able to take more risks than many of his better-known contemporaries. Catch **Cornell Wilde** in *The Big Combo* (1955), or **Sterling Hayden** in *Terror In A Texas Town* (1958), to see both men give the sort of edgy, committed performances that simply weren't required of them in the bigger-budget movies they sometimes made.

Other Key Films: *My Name Is Julia Ross* (1946); *So Dark The Night* (1947); *Undercover Man* (1949); *A Lady Without Passport* (1952); *Desperate Search* (1953); *Cry Of The Hunted* (1954); *Lawless Street* (1956)

Lewton, Val

Lewton was the expressionist maestro of the B-Movie genre, and he was largely responsible for returning horror to the mind, from where, after all, it had sprung, claws unsheathed, in the first place. His dark reign began when he joined RKO as a producer in 1942, and the next four years saw him responsible for **Jacques Tourneur's** *Cat People* (1942), *I Walked With A Zombie* (1943) and *The Leopard Man* (1943), Mark Robson's *The Seventh Victim* (1943), *The Ghost Ship* (1943), *Youth Runs Wild* (1944), *Isle Of The Dead* (1945) and *Bedlam* (1946), and **Robert Wise's** *The Curse Of The Cat People* (1944) [co-directed by Gunther von Fritsch], *Mademoiselle Fifi* (1944) and *The Body Snatcher* (1945). Not all these were the successes that Lewton devotees would have them be, but they were all inspired as much by intelligence and visual daring (often in the interests of economy), as they were by the desire to rake in the dollars and cents. *I Walked With A Zombie*, for instance, is genuinely eerie, and *The Curse Of The Cat People* is an odd little tale, more psychological fairytale than horror flick, and impossible to contemplate outside the freedom afforded by the B-Movie genre. Lewton died of a heart attack, aged just forty-six, having produced only three mediocre films in his last five years of life, although it must be said that Hugo Fregonese's curious little **Western** *Apache Drums* (1951) has its moments.

Livesey, Roger

Seductively gravel-voiced star of British film throughout the 1940s and 50s, Livesey will be forever remembered for his role in **Michael Powell's** cult love story *I Know Where I'm Going* (1945), in which he starred opposite **Wendy Hiller**, and whose burgeoning number of fans will secure his otherwise almost certainly fragmented posthumous reputation. Memorable as a tramp forced to sit, against his better judgment, for **Charles Laughton's** momentarily inspired *Rembrandt* in **Alexander Korda's** magnificent 1936 biopic, Livesey customarily played sensitive, old-school Englishmen, who yet had a glitter in their rheumy, pipe-smoke-laden eyes. His finest performance came in Powell's *A Matter Of Life And Death* (1946) in which he diagnosed a cerebrally-stricken **David Niven** while at the same time charming (quite innocently, of course) the gorgeous Kim Hunter. He and his gentlemanly like, though bitterly missed in this most ungentlemanly of ages, at least remain captured for posterity on celluloid.

Other Key Films: *The Life And Death Of Colonel Blimp* (1943); *Vice Versa* (1947); *That Dangerous Age* (1949); *The Master Of Ballantrae* (1953); *The Intimate Stranger* (1956) *The League Of Gentlemen* (1960); *The Entertainer* (1960); *Of Human Bondage* (1964); *Hamlet* (1969)

Lloyd, Harold

Lloyd was the great survivor. Of all the silent stars of comedy, it was he who glided athletically through to a comfortable and secure old age, free from obvious vices and other self-destructive inroads. His two stock characters, 'Willie Work' and 'Lonesome Luke', both reflect this serene confidence in ordinariness, and even in Sam Taylor and Fred Newmeyer's *The Freshman* (1925), Lloyd's eager college boy is notable for his pathetic desire to belong, at any cost, even if it means becoming a laughing stock. Lloyd's most celebrated scene, the clock-dangling trick in Taylor and Newmeyer's *Safety Last* (1923), came about in an ordinary way too – his stuntman had inadvertently broken his leg and the star thought, oh well, he may as well do it himself.

Other Key Films: *Algy On The Force* (1913); *Lonesome Luke* (1915); *The Big Idea* (1918); *Bumping Into Broadway* (1919); *His Royal Slyness* (1919); *Haunted Spooks* (1920); *A Sailor-Made Man* (1921); *Grandma's Boy* (1922); *Girl Shy* (1924); *Hot Water* (1924); *The Kid Brother* (1927); *Speedy* (1928); *Welcome Stranger* (1929); *The Cat's Paw* (1934); *The Milky Way* (1936)

Loach, Ken

Loach is a committed socialist whose films reflect that commitment, concentrating on the marginal and the dispossessed, and endeavouring to throw a little light on their otherwise forgotten lives. His first feature, *Poor Cow* (1969), remains in the memory more than thirty years after its first showing thanks to its scathing depiction of the commonplace brutality of an allegedly caring State apparatus – in a Loach film, it is people who care and who can make a brief difference to lives, never institutions. *Raining Stones* (1993) was a magnificently human film, finding comedy in horror and yet never losing sight of the deadening, brutalising effect poverty can have on even decent people, and *Ladybird, Ladybird* (1994) deserved every critical accolade it received. Loach is that rare thing – a political filmmaker who never preaches, but simply shows.

Other Key Films: *Kes* (1969); *Wednesday's Child* (1971); *The Gamekeeper* (1978); *Black Jack* (1979); *Looks And Smiles* (1982); *Singing The Blues In Red* (1986); *Hidden Agenda* (1990); *Riff Raff* (1991); *Land And Freedom* (1995); *Carla's Song* (1996); *The Flickering Flame* (1997); *My Name Is Joe* (1998); *Bread And Roses* (2000); *The Navigators* (2001); *Sweet Sixteen* (2002); *Fond Kiss…, Ae* (2004); *The Wind That Shakes The Barley* (2006)

Lombard, Carole

Lombard was **Clark Gable's** great love, and one of the funniest women in movies (try Gregory La Cava's *My Man Godfrey* (1936) or **William Wellman's** *Nothing Sacred* (1937) for an exquisite taste). She was beautiful, too, in a radiant, laconic way, as if she couldn't quite understand what all the fuss was about but, well, if men were made that way, who was she to cavil? Her life and career are made all the more poignant by the manner of her death – happily married to Gable, she briefly left his side to go on tour selling US war bonds, and her returning aircraft crashed. Gable was distraught for years, and Lombard's fans, which included President Roosevelt, bereft. Her swansong was Ernst Lubitsch's magnificent *To Be Or Not To Be* (1942), a comedy beyond time itself, just as she is.

Other Key Films: *The Arizona Kid* (1930); *Ladies' Man* (1931); *No Man Of Her Own* (1932); *Twentieth Century* (1934); *Hands Across The Table* (1935); *Love Before Breakfast* (1936); *Made For Each Other* (1939); *In Name Only* (1939); *Mr. And Mrs. Smith* (1941)

Key Line:
'How would you like this spaghetti applied to your person?' [Carole Lombard as Amy Peters, in Garson Kanin's *They Knew What They Wanted* (1940)]

Lord Of The Rings, The

The first live action film adaptation of John Ronald Reuel Tolkien's perennially bestselling *The Lord Of The Rings* (1954-1955) must surely rank as one of the most audacious endeavours in movie-making history. Shot simultaneously, but released in three instalments as *The Lord of the Rings: The Fellowship of the Ring* (2001), *The Lord of the Rings: The Two Towers* (2002), and *The Lord of the Rings: The Return of the King* (2003), it drew to a close director **Peter Jackson's** lifelong cinematic ambition of adapting the book for the screen. Making excellent use of Jackson's native New Zealand scenery, the three films not only put New Zealand onto the map as a major movie-making destination, but reinvigorated the NZ tourist industry to boot. The trilogy did sensationally well at successive Academy Awards ceremonies, winning seventeen Oscars in total – *The Return Of The King* was notable for winning all of the eleven awards for which it was nominated, matching the total garnered by **James Cameron's** *Titanic* (1997) and **William Wyler's** *Ben-Hur* (1959), and surpassing the previous 'clean sweep' record of nine Oscars out of nine nominations for **Vincente Minnelli's** *Gigi* (1958) and **Bernardo Bertolucci's** *The Last Emperor* (1987).

Loren, Sophia

When the German army withdrew from Naples in 1944, Loren was barely ten-years old, and the experiences she had then, of fear, hunger and uncertainty (readers of Norman Lewis's brilliant *Naples '44* will have some idea of the hell on earth the place then was) must have gone a long way towards forming the joyful, yet intrinsically serious woman we see on the screen in such films as **Vittorio De Sica's** *Two Women* (1960), **Anthony Mann's** *El Cid* (1961) and **Stanley Donen's** *Arabesque* (1966). Always a luminous beauty, Loren has aged wonderfully well, and though she rarely appears in films now, she carries her deserved celebrity lightly and with panache.

Other Key Films: *Quo Vadis* (1951); *The Anatomy Of Love* (1953); *The Miller's Beautiful Wife* (1955); *Boy On A Dolphin* (1958); *Houseboat* (1958); *That Kind Of Woman* (1959); *The Millionairess* (1960); *The Condemned Of Altona* (1962); *The Fall Of The Roman Empire* (1964); *Lady L* (1965); *The Voyage* (1974); *A Special Day* (1977); *Sun* (1997); *Destinazione Verna* (2000); *Between Strangers* (2002); *Too Much Romance* (2004)

Lorre, Peter

One of the funniest of all Spike Jones's song spoofs is his band's version of 'My Old Flame', sung in a Peter Lorre voice. For Lorre *was* his voice, and it's uncanny just how many people can actually imitate it very well indeed. His nervous tics, his arching eyebrows and his smarmy, too-smooth-by-half mannerisms all went to making him, along with **Walter Brennan, Thelma Ritter**, and **Sidney Greenstreet**, one of the most instantly recognisable character actors of them all. Think of his Joel Cairo in **John Huston's** *The Maltese Falcon* (1941), or his Señor Ugarte in **Michael Curtiz's** *Casablanca* (1942) – just what nationality was Ugarte meant to be? Or didn't it matter? Earlier, before his passage to Hollywood (not to Marseille), he was the cringing, murderous, doomed Franz Becker in **Fritz Lang's** *M* (1931), and a superbly chilling assassin, known only as The General, for **Alfred Hitchcock** in *Secret Agent* (1936) – a man so single-minded in his hatred of the enemy that even otherwise placid allies like **John Gielgud's** Edgar Brody feared him.

Other Key Films: *Pionier In Ingolstadt* (1928); *The Man Who Knew Too Much* (1934); *Crime And Punishment* (1935); *Think Fast Mr. Moto* (1937); *Strange Cargo* (1940); *All Through The Night* (1942); *The Constant Nymph* (1943); *Background To Danger* (1943); *Passage To Marseille* (1944); *The Mask Of Dimitrios* (1944); *Arsenic And Old Lace* (1944);

Confidential Agent (1945); *The Beast With Five Fingers* (1946); *Black Angel* (1946); *Beat The Devil* (1954); *Tales Of Terror* (1962); *The Raven* (1963)

Losey, Joseph

An American director, working in England, and venerated by the French – a contradiction in those terms and many others – Losey made films that are often perverse, sometimes hysterical, but consistently interesting. Driven out of the US by Senator Macarthy's House Un-American Activities Committee (HUAC), Losey, who had shown himself capable, with *The Prowler* (1951) and *The Concrete Jungle* (1960), of making commercially successful mainstream scorchers, now found himself, a bare three years later, making convoluted and pretentious trash like *Eve* (1963). That, fortunately, was the low point, although the sheer unlikeability of many of his characters militated against the undoubted success of such otherwise astute social satires as *The Servant* (1964) and *Accident* (1968). The *Go-Between*, in 1971, was a second marvellous return to form, but still, damn it, there was no one the viewer could actually empathise with, thanks to Losey's humans-as-ants obsession.

Other Key Films: *The Boy With The Green Hair* (1949); *The Lawless* (1951); *The Big Night* (1952); *The Sleeping Tiger* (1955); *Finger Of Guilt* [a.k.a. *The Intimate Stranger*] (1958); *Chance Meeting* [a.k.a. *Blind Date*] (1960); *King And Country* (1966); *Mr Klein* (1978)

Best Love Films

Frank Borzage's *A Farewell To Arms* (1932) and *Strange Cargo* (1940); **Frank Capra's** *The Bitter Tea Of General Yen* (1932); **Marcel Carné's** *Quai Des Brumes* (1938) and *Les Visiteurs Du Soir* (1942); **Henry Hathaway's** *Peter Ibbetson* (1935); **Alfred Hitchcock's** *Rebecca* (1940); **Krzysztof Kieslowski's** *The Double Life Of Véronique* (1991); **David Lean's** *Brief Encounter* (1945); **Albert Lewin's** *Pandora And The Flying Dutchman* (1951); **Ernst Lubitsch's** *The Shop Around The Corner* (1940); Rouben Mamoulian's *Queen Christina* (1933); **Joseph L Mankiewicz's** *The Ghost And Mrs Muir* (1947); **Anthony Minghella's** *The English Patient* (1996) and *Cold Mountain* (2003); **Max Ophüls's** *Liebelei* (1932); Nagisa Oshima's *Ai No Corrida* (1976); **Michael Powell** and Emeric Pressburger's *I Know Where I'm Going* (1945) and *A Matter Of Life And Death* (1946); **Nicholas Ray's** *They Live By Night* (1949); **Douglas Sirk's** *A Time To Love And A Time To Die* (1958); **Josef von Sternberg's** *The Blue Angel* (1929-1930), *Morocco* (1930) and *Shanghai Express* (1932); **François Truffaut's** *Jules Et Jim* (1962); **William Wyler's** *Roman Holiday* (1953)

Lubitsch, Ernst

A former actor himself, Lubitsch just occasionally took his direction of other actors to exaggerated, not to say fetishistic lengths, while still leaving one to emerge from any cinema showing his films with a gleeful grin on one's face. His best films are a delight to the eye and the ear, and are possibly the most good-natured and innocently decadent ever to have come out of Hollywood. Frequently working with screenwriter Samson Raphaelson, Lubitsch treated sex as a pleasure (something a little strange to Puritan and Prohibition-minded America) whether it was in such frothy operettas as *The Merry Widow* (1934), featuring **Maurice Chevalier** and Jeannette Macdonald; or such sophisticated sex comedies as *Trouble In Paradise* (1932), *Angel* (1937) and *Ninotchka* (1939); or in romance, with the delightful *The Shop Around The Corner* (1940); satire (with a little sex thrown in, of course) in the sublime *To Be Or Not To Be* (1942); or whimsy, with *Heaven Can Wait* (1943). The 'Lubitsch touch' was a light one – Teutonic in concept and production values, maybe, but never so in the resolution. See **Heartstopping Moments**

Other Key Films: *The Eyes Of The Mummy* (1918); *The Oyster Princess* (1919); *Madame Du Barry* (1919); *Anna Boleyn* (1920); *The Marriage Circle* (1924); *The Patriot* (1928); *The Love Parade* (1929); *Design For Living* (1933); *Bluebeard's Eight Wife* (1938); *That Uncertain Feeling* (1941); *Cluny Brown* (1946); *That Lady In Ermine* [completed by **Otto Preminger**] (1948)

Lucas, George

Lucas began his career making promotional shorts for the films of his friend and erstwhile mentor **Francis Ford Coppola**. His first feature was an expanded version of his University of Southern California short, *THX 1138* (1971), which already pointed the way to his trademark of astonishing visuals and underwritten scripts. *American Graffiti* followed in 1973, coincidentally launching the careers of a number of now veteran stars, including **Richard Dreyfuss** and **Harrison Ford**. Having earned only $20,000 from *American Graffiti* (the film, made on a tight budget of $70,000, went on to gross $55 million), Lucas was forced to forgo the opportunity to collaborate with Coppola on *Apocalypse Now* (1979), in order to work on his brainchild, *Star Wars*. Launched in 1977 but three years in the making, this proved to be a science-fiction fairy tale which borrowed freely from just about every lucrative genre in the book, from war movies and screwball comedies, to **Westerns** and edge-of-the-seat, 'Perils Of Pauline'-type cliff-hangers. Equally influential off-screen as a first-rate cutter and editor, Lucas was also the producer (through Lucasfilm) of **Akira Kurosawa's** *Kagemusha* (1980), **Steven Spielberg's** *Indiana Jones* tetralogy (1981 onwards), Jim Henson's *Labyrinth* (1986) and **Ron Howard's** *Willow* (1988), and the driving force behind such technical innovations as THX sound and the Industrial Light & Magic special-effects company.

Other Key Films: *Star Wars Episode 1 – The Phantom Menace* (1999); *Star Wars Episode 2 – Attack Of The Clones* (2002); *Star Wars Episode 3 – Revenge Of The Sith* (2005)

Lumet, Sidney

He started strongly, with *12 Angry Men* (1958), peaked with *A Long Day's Journey Into Night* (1962), *The Pawnbroker* (1965) and *The Hill* (1965), fought bravely on the way down with *The Anderson Tapes* (1972), *The Offence* (1973) and *Serpico* (1973), and finally hit rock bottom with *A Stranger Among Us* (1992). It's an odd career, almost as if two men were taking it in turns to direct Lumet's films. Recently, with *Guilty As Sin* (1992) and *Night Falls In Manhattan* (1997), he has shown a welcome, if hesitant, return to form. Lumet had been both overrated and underrated in his time, and it is probably a tribute to his intelligence that, despite a career which has lasted for upwards of fifty years, he is still impossible to pigeon-hole.

Other Key Films: *The Fugitive Kind* (1959); *A View From The Bridge* (1962); *The Appointment* (1969); *Dog Day Afternoon* (1975); *Network* (1976); *The Verdict* (1982); *The Morning After* (1986); *Gloria* (1999); *Find Me Guilty* (2006);

Lumière, The Brothers

Louis and Auguste Lumière were the first people to envisage the motion picture as something that might appeal to a mass, rather to an individual audience, as was the case with **Thomas Edison's** peep-show *Kinetoscope*, the machine upon which their subsequent invention was based. They built and patented the Cinématographe in

1895, a dual-purpose camera/projector capable of foxing the eye into believing that what it was seeing on the screen was actually moving. Following their successful showing of *Workers Leaving The Lumière Factory* [*La Sortie Des Usines Lumière*], on 22 March 1895, they went on to present twelve short films in the cellar of the Grand Café, Boulevard des Capucines, Paris, on 28 December of the same year, which included what was probably the first-ever piece of filmed slapstick comedy, the brilliantly self-explanatory (Hollywood pitch artists please note) *Watering The Gardener* [*L'Arroseur Arrosé*]. It was at that exact moment that the cinema, as we know it, was born.

Lupino, Ida

Descended from a long line of English stage entertainers, Lupino became one of the only women directors to work successfully within the 1950s Hollywood system. Her best film as director was *The Hitch-Hiker* (1953), a convincing portrait of criminal schizophrenia, but Lupino was better known for her acting, and her waif-like, girl-of-the-people looks allowed her to shine in a variety of roles, most notably opposite **John Garfield** in **Michael Curtiz's** *The Sea Wolf* (1941), in **Jean Negulesco's** intriguingly offbeat *film noir* *Road House* (1948), and best of all in **Nicholas Ray's** *On Dangerous Ground* (1951), where her utterly convincing blind woman (watch how she uses the hanging plants as an orientating device) finally contrives to soften the embittered heart of **Robert Ryan's** self-hating cop.
Other Key Films: *Her First Affaire* (1933); *Peter Ibbetson* (1935); *Sea Devils* (1937); *The Adventures Of Sherlock Holmes* (1939); *They Drive By Night* (1940); *High Sierra* (1941); *Devotion* (1946); *Escape Me Never* (1947); *Beware, My Lovely* (1952); *The Big Knife* (1955); *While The City Sleeps* (1956); *Junior Bonner* (1972)

Lynch, David

After debuting with the extraordinary, low-budget, *Eraserhead* (1977), Lynch joined the mainstream with *The Elephant Man* (1980), a high-quality but rather empty piece of work, and *Dune* (1985), which lost a fortune, and which some die-hard fans still persist in viewing as a flawed masterpiece. His next film, *Blue Velvet* (1986), *was* an undisputed masterpiece, and would, in itself, be enough to secure him a niche in the ultimate movie pantheon in the sky (if there is such a place). *Wild At Heart* (1990), another fervid, surreally perverse mini-masterpiece followed, upon which Lynch branched out into television with the cult *Twin Peaks* series – the disastrous *Fire Walk With Me* (1992) [See **Worst Films**], was a *Twin Peaks* spin-off. Well, *plus ça change…* Fans living on in the hope of a renaissance have recently derived fresh optimism from the outstanding *Mulholland Drive* (2001).
Other Key Films: *Weeds* (1987); *The Cabinet Of Dr Ramirez* (1991); *Lumière Et Compagnie* [one section] (1995); *Lost Highway* (1997); *The Straight Story* (1999); *Inland Empire* (2006)

McCrea, Joel

An understated and modest actor who shone in both comedic and dramatic roles, McCrea graced two of the funniest films ever to come out of the Hollywood studio system – **Preston Sturges's** *Sullivan's Travels* (1941) and *The Palm Beach Story* (1942). Both films relied on him as the earnest straight man, baffled by the chaos surrounding his every move. Later he moved back into **Westerns**, making a fine career for himself in a series of **Jacques Tourneur** films, which included *Stars In My Crown* (1950) and *Wichita* (1955). His career ended on a high, with the superb **Sam**

Peckinpah Western, *Ride The High Country* (1962).
Other Key Films: *The Silver Cord* (1933); *Barbary Coast* (1935); *These Three* (1936); *Wells Fargo* (1937); *Union Pacific* (1939); *Foreign Correspondent* (1940); *The More The Merrier* (1943); *The Great Moment* (1944); *Fort Massacre* (1958)
Key Line: 'Everybody's a flop until he's a success.' [McCrea to **Claudette Colbert** in *The Palm Beach Story*]

McDormand, Frances

A favourite with independent filmmakers on account of her offbeat good looks and inspired capacity for eccentricity, McDormand has been a **Coen Brothers** regular [she is married to Joel] since her first appearance in *Blood Simple* (1984), and made a strong impression as pregnant police officer Marge Gunderson in *Fargo* (1996), for which she received a best-actress Oscar. That same year she gave another knockout performance as the Daddy-dominated Bunny in **John Sayles's** magnificent *Lone Star* (1996), and she bids fair to continue her run as one of the finest character actresses working in American cinema.

Other Key Films: *Raising Arizona* (1987); *Mississippi Burning* (1988); *Chattahoochee* (1989); *Hidden Agenda* (1990); *The Butcher's Wife* (1991); *Crazy In Love* (1992); *Passed Away* (1992); *Short Cuts* (1993); *Primal Fear* (1996); *Paradise Road* (1997); *Talk Of Angels* (1998); *Wonder Boys* (2000); *Almost Famous* (2000); *The Man Who Wasn't There* (2001); *Laurel Canyon* (2002); *City By The Sea* (2002); *North Country* (2005); *Friends With Money* (2006)

Key Line: 'There's more to life than a little money, you know. Don't you know that? And here you are. And it's a beautiful day. I just don't understand it.' [McDormand's Marge Gunderson to captured killer Gaear Grimsrud (Peter Stormare) on his way to jail]

McDowell, Malcolm

McDowell had a remarkable beginning to his career, acting in a trio of arguably the most important British films to emerge from the dying fall of the 1960s – **Lindsay Anderson's** *If…* (1968) and *O Lucky Man!* (1973), and **Stanley Kubrick's** *A Clockwork Orange* (1971). McDowell's rather repellent screen persona did not wear well, however, and he began to appear in a series of increasingly turgid commercial vehicles during the late 1970s and early 1980s, **Paul Schrader's** *Cat People* (1982) notwithstanding. His recent demented lead performance in Paul McGuigan's ultra violent thriller *Gangster No 1* (2000) may go some way towards resuscitating an, of late, rather moribund (but nevertheless dementedly busy) screen career.

Other Key Films: *Figures In A Landscape* (1970); *Aces High* (1976); *Caligula* (1979); *Britannia Hospital* (1982); *Gulag* (1985); *Bopha!* (1993); *Star Trek: Generations* (1994); *The Gardener* (1998); *Just Visiting* (2001); *The Company* (2003); *Rag Tale* (2005); *Exitz* (2006); *Cut Off* (2006)

Mackendrick, Alexander

One of Britain's greatest directors, Sandy Mackendrick proved himself that rare thing – a man who could successfully direct comedy, with *Whisky Galore!* (1949) and *The Ladykillers* (1955), satire, with *The Man In The White Suit* (1951), romance, with *Saraband For Dead Lovers* (1948), tragedy, with his American masterpiece, *The Sweet Smell Of Success* (1958), and even children's films, with *Sammy Going South* (1963). It's as if he had to test himself, at least once, in every possible category – and it worked. What more need be said?

McLaglen, Victor

McLaglen was a genuine tough, with his barrel chest and cocky, big-man's walk. An ex-boxer and inveterate fighter, he was a strange choice as **Marlene Dietrich's** romantic leading man in **Josef von Sternberg's** *Dishonored* (1931), but he made a more than adequate stab at the part. **John Ford** used him in a number of films, most notably as Gypo, in *The Informer* (1935), for which McLaglen won a well-deserved Oscar. Hardly a great actor, he was rather wonderful, in a comic buffoon sort of a way, in Ford's great trilogy of **Westerns**, *Fort Apache* (1948), *She Wore A Yellow Ribbon* (1949), and *Rio Grande* (1950), as Sgt. Festus Mulcahy, Sgt. Quincannon, and Sgt. Major Quincannon, respectively. The sly, drunken characterization, of course, was always delightfully the same.

Other Key Films: *The Call Of The Road* (1920); *Winds Of Chance* (1925); *Beau Geste* (1926); *Mother Machree* (1928); *A Devil With Women* (1930); *The Lost Patrol* (1934); *Wee Willie Winkie* (1937); *The Quiet Man* (1952)

MacMurray, Fred

MacMurray played charming and faintly stressed pipe-smoking family men and he played *film noir* crooks. The *film noir* crooks were better. The best of all was his Walter Neff in **Billy Wilder's** *Double Indemnity* (1944), entangled in **Barbara Stanwyck's** platinum blonde coils; but he reprised the idea, if not the role, of the honest man drawn into deceit, in **Richard Quine's** *Pushover* (1954), this time with a deceptively innocent-looking **Kim Novak** to tempt him. When you've seen those two, go back to Chester Erskine's *The Egg And I* (1947) and weep.

Other Key Films: *The Texas Rangers* (1936); *Remember The Night* (1940); *Virginia* (1941); *The Lady Is Willing* (1942); *Above Suspicion* (1943); *Murder He Says* (1945); *Singapore* (1947); *An Innocent Affair* (1948); *Never A Dull Moment* (1950); *Fair Wind To Java* (1953); *The Caine Mutiny* (1954); *Woman's World* (1954); *Day Of The Badmen* (1958); *Face Of A Fugitive* (1959)

McQueen, Steve

Always a man's man, McQueen's weather-beaten face perfectly echoed the deprived, institutional background that made him that way. Catapulted to stardom (although not over the border into Switzerland) in **John Sturges's** *The Great Escape* (1963), he was a massively successful actor despite, in many ways, running against the grain of his own times. Often playing detached, sporadically charming loners, he excelled as a high-stakes poker player in **Norman Jewison's** *The Cincinnati Kid* (1965), and also as the hard-boiled cop in Peter Yates's *Bullitt* (1968). His best performance came as *Junior Bonner* (1972) for director **Sam Peckinpah**, in which McQueen looked wryly back at the traditions and culture that had formed him, while they disappeared, literally in a cloud of dust, beneath his eyes. He died, tragically, of an asbestos-related cancer at the age of only fifty.

Other Key Films: *The Magnificent Seven* (1960); *Love With The Proper Stranger* (1963); *Soldier In The Rain* (1963); *Nevada Smith* (1966); *The Sand Pebbles* (1966); *The Thomas Crown Affair* (1968); *The Reivers* (1969); *The Getaway* (1972); *Junior Bonner* (1972); *Papillon* (1973); *The Towering Inferno* (1974); *An Enemy Of The People* (1977); *Tom Horn* (1980); *The Hunter* (1980)

Key Line: '…McQueen was an impossible bastard. A third of the way through the picture, McQueen took charge. I had to rewrite his scenes and rearrange them…oh, he drove you crazy.' [Scriptwriter **W R Burnett** on the making of **John Sturges's** *The Great Escape* (1963), which he co-scripted with novelist James Clavell]

Mahin, John Lee

Mahin was that strange example of Hollywood citizenry, the highly paid and committed studio-system screenwriter. His output was astonishing and his professionalism was complete – even Scott Fitzgerald acknowledged him as, 'among the half dozen best picture writers in the business.' Mahin virtually created **Clark Gable's** royal persona, and even his lesser films, of which there were few, were interesting as much for the particular quality of their flaws as for their virtues. He had a hand (sometimes uncredited) in practically all **Victor Fleming's** greatest movies including *Red Dust* (1932), *Treasure Island* (1934), *Captains Courageous* (1937), *Test Pilot* (1938), ***Gone With The Wind*** (1939), *The Wizard Of Oz* (1939), *Dr Jekyll And Mr Hyde* (1941) and *Tortilla Flat* (1942), as well as scripting Jack Conway's *Boom Town* (1940), **John Ford's** *Mogambo* (1953) and **John Huston's** *Heaven Knows Mr Allyson* (1958). And that's just a fraction of his output.

Other Key Films: **Howard Hawks's** *Scarface* (1932); W S Van Dyke's *Naughty Marietta* (1935); **Mervyn LeRoy's** *Quo Vadis* (1951); John Ford's *The Horse Soldiers* (1959)

Maibaum, Richard

Another great pro, but well below **John Lee Mahin** on the studio scale of greatness, Maibaum has impressive screen credits that conjure up a mixture of the commercial and the literate, with the commercial predominating. With co-script credits on a total of eleven (yes, eleven) ***James Bond*** films, it would be easy to forget Maibaum's earlier scripts of the quality of Elliott Nugent's *The Great Gatsby* (1949) – which was far better than the **Robert Redford** version – Terence Young's *Paratrooper* (1954), Jose Ferrer's *Cockleshell Heroes* (1956) and **Nicholas Ray's** *Bigger Than Life* (1956).

Other Key Films: Terence Young's *Dr No* (1963), *From Russia With Love* (1964) and *Thunderball* (1965); Guy Hamilton's *Goldfinger* (1964), *Diamonds Are Forever* (1971) and *The Man With The Golden Gun* (1974); John Glen's *For Your Eyes Only* (1981), *Octopussy* (1983) and *A View To A Kill* (1985)

Malick, Terrence

Malick represents the obverse of the usual Hollywood coin – an erudite, literate man who chose not to make any movies for twenty years because he wasn't prepared to settle for second best. *Badlands* (1973) was his first feature as producer/director/screenwriter, a canny film that took some of the elements from **Nicholas Ray's** *They Live By Night* (1949) and some of the elements from **Joseph H Lewis's** *Gun Crazy* (1949), and combined them into a modern parable. *Days Of Heaven* (1978) was more original if marginally less satisfying, and it wasn't until the release of *The Thin Red Line* (1998) that it became clear that Malick's somewhat elusive reputation was justified – it was as if (were one to believe the news reports) J D Salinger had at last brought out his long-awaited masterpiece. *The Thin Red Line* wasn't as good as all that, but it wasn't bad either. If Malick keeps up his production ratio, he'll have three more films in him before he hits eighty.

Other Key Films: *The New World* (2005)

Malkovich, John

A stage actor and director who just happens to make films, Malkovich made his first mark in the movies playing a blind man, in Robert Benton's *Places In The Heart* (1984). In that same year he began to construct his international reputation with Roland Joffé's *The Killing Fields* (1984), but he had a setback the following year when he botched the lead role in Peter Yates's *Eleni* (1985). He was far better as Tom in **Paul Newman's** *The Glass Menagerie* (1987), but he really found his feet as the lubricious Vicomte de Valmont in **Stephen Frears's** *Dangerous Liaisons* (1988), which may still be his best film performance. Now something of a self-referential icon following the surprise success of Spike Jonze's *Being John Malkovich* (1999), he is counted among those rare actors who are equally at home on stage or on celluloid.

Other Key Films: *Empire Of The Sun* (1987); *The Sheltering Sky* (1990); *Of Mice And Men* (1992); *Shadows And Fog* (1992); *In The Line Of Fire* (1993); *Beyond The Clouds* (1995); *Mulholland Falls* (1996); *The Portrait Of A Lady* (1996); *Con Air* (1997); *The Man In The Iron Mask* (1998); *Shadow Of The Vampire* (2000); *Les Âmes Fortes* (2001); *Knockaround Guys* (2001); *The Dancer Upstairs* [dir.] (2002); *Ripley's Game* (2002); *The Libertine* (2004); *Colour Me Kubrick* (2005); *Klimt* (2006)

Malle, Louis

Malle began his directing career by making one of the best thrillers ever to come out of France, *Ascenseur Pour L'Échafaud* (1958) – which also benefited from a terrific Miles Davis score – which he followed up with *Les Amants* (1958). With a beginning like that, it was odds on that he would fall flat on his face, and it redounds to his eternal credit that after such a garishly commercial film as *Viva Maria* (1965) he was able to come back as subtly as he did in *Le Voleur* (1967), *Le Souffle Au Coeur* (1971) and the magnificent *Lacombe Lucien* (1973). But it is his later films, beginning with *Atlantic City* (1981), and moving through *My Dinner With André* (1981) and *Au Revoir Les Enfants* (1987) to the delightful *Milou En Mai* (1989), that have permanently secured the reputation of this elusive, deeply committed, and much lamented filmmaker.

Other Key Films: *Le Monde Du Silence* (1956); *Zazie Dans Le Métro* (1960); *Pretty Baby* (1978); *Damage* (1992); *Vanya On 42nd Street* (1994)

Mankiewicz, Joseph L

One of the most erudite of all Hollywood writer/directors, this former producer and screenwriter became an actor's dream when he finally took up directing (after nearly twenty years in the movie business) with such masterpieces of commercial cinema as *A Letter To Three Wives* (1949), the nail-bitingly good *Five Fingers* (1952) and the **Humphrey Bogart/Ava Gardner** vehicle *The Barefoot Contessa* (1954). Even when he stuck his neck out with more controversial material, as in Tennessee William's *Suddenly Last Summer* (1959), he was always interesting and sometimes, as in his earlier *All About Eve* (1950) and *People Will Talk* (1951), sublime. See **Heartstopping Moments**

Other Key Films: *Dragonwyck* (1946); *The Ghost And Mrs Muir* (1947); *No Way Out* (1950); *Julius Caesar* (1953); *Guys And Dolls* (1955); *The Quiet American* (1958); *Cleopatra* (1963); *Sleuth* (1972)

Mann, Anthony

Anthony Mann made **Westerns**, thrillers and sword-fight movies, and he was, quite simply, one of the best directors ever to come out of the Hollywood system. He understood early on that making a genre or a commercially viable film did not mean that you couldn't also probe the human condition, just as more pretentious directors might claim and signally fail to do. From his early **film noir**, *Raw Deal* (1948), through his magnificent series of psychological Westerns with **James Stewart,** which included *Winchester 73* (1950) and *The Naked Spur* (1953), right down to the outstanding and critically underrated *El Cid* (1961), Mann made magic out of material that, in other hands, might have remained simply mundane.

Other Key Films: *T-Men* (1948); *Border Incident* (1949); *Side Street* (1949); *The Tall Target* (1951); *Bend Of The River* (1952); *Thunder Bay* (1953); *The Man From Laramie* (1955); *The Tin Star* (1958); *Man Of The West* (1958); *The Fall Of The Roman Empire* (1964); *The Heroes Of Telemark* (1965)

Key Line: 'I avoided him because I figured, Jeez, this is a no-talent guy. You couldn't even have a conversation with him, he was so ignorant. And it turns out we made ten, eleven pictures together...he understood the camera...understood concept.' [Screenwriter **Philip Yordan** on Mann, with whom he collaborated on, among other movies, *The Man From Laramie* [co-script] (1955), *El Cid* [co-script] (1961) and *The Fall Of The Roman Empire* [co-script] (1964)]

March, Frederic

March had what **Thelma Ritter** would have called 'class', meaning that whatever he touched was never less than impressive, and often far more. He was a character actor at a time when character actors were usually quirky, eccentric individuals with one or two standard strings to their bows and little else – but March was considerably better than that. There are moments in Rouben Mamoulian's *Dr Jekyll And Mr Hyde* (1932), **William Wellman's** *A Star Is Born* (1937) and John Cromwell's *Victory* (1940), when we feel we are in the presence of screen greatness, and looking back to those films, one realises that March's innate modesty of performance was the only thing that stood between him and the superstar celebrity of, say, a **Spencer Tracy**.

Other Key Films: *My Sin* (1931); *Design For Living* (1933); *The Barretts Of Wimpole Street* (1934); *Anna Karenina* (1935); *Anthony Adverse* (1936); *Nothing Sacred* (1937); *I Married A Witch* (1942); *The Best Years Of Our Lives* (1946); *Christopher Columbus* (1949); *Man On A Tightrope* (1953); *Executive Suite* (1954); *The Desperate Hours* (1955); *Inherit The Wind* (1960); *Seven Days In May* (1964); *Hombre* (1967); *The Iceman Cometh* (1973)

Marlowe, Philip

Fictional character created by **Raymond Chandler** and the main protagonist in all his novels, Marlowe was a Los Angeles private eye of a rather unique ilk – he had to be 'the best man in his world and a good enough man for any world'. Such a moral dimension was virtually unique in the **pulp fiction** realm of *Black Mask* and the many other magazines that catered to this most hard-boiled of genres. **Dick Powell, Robert Montgomery, Humphrey Bogart, Robert Mitchum, Elliot Gould** and James Garner all made a stab at the part, but Mitchum, for whom Marlowe could have been written, won hands down in Dick Richards's late but masterful *Farewell My Lovely* (1975). Bogart certainly made a brave shot at him in *The Big Sleep* (1946), but he wasn't Marlowe, he was Bogart.

Martin, Dean

Martin seemed as easy-going in private life as he was on the screen, and with his good looks, fine voice and apparently innate capacity to suggest that he was drunk even when perfectly sober, he was able to make a natural transition from the stage to the movies. He was **Jerry Lewis's** straight man for nearly eleven years and sixteen movies, providing the music, the romance and the shrugs, but when he branched out on his own he made an equal success of it, much to everyone's surprise. His best dramatic screen performance came in **Edward Dmytryk's** *The Young Lions* (1958) – in which he got to kill reformed-Nazi **Marlon Brando** in one of the most unnecessary murders in screen history – but his highpoint came as Dude, in **Howard Hawks's** *Rio Bravo* (1959). The film is so absurdly enjoyable, and Martin so utterly perfect as **John Wayne's** wreck of a friend, that even when he picks up his guitar and duets with Ricky Nelson, we smile in happy satisfaction, knowing that in the fantasy world we are inhabiting, all is indisputably well. It was all the sadder, then, when **Frank Sinatra's** Rat Pack finally got him, ensuring that the promise he had shown at the beginning of his solo career should turn to spoof.

Other Key Films: *The Stooge* (1953); *Artists And Models* (1955); *Hollywood Or Bust* (1956); *Some Came Running* (1959); *Ocean's Eleven* (1960); *The Sons Of Katie Elder* (1965); *The Silencers* (1966); *Bandolero!* (1968); *Five Card Stud* (1968)

Key Line: 'He liked to swing his golf clubs, and I had heard about his drinking; but when he had something to do on the set, he was very professional.' [Screenwriter Walter Bernstein, who was working on **Marilyn Monroe's** final, unfinished project, *Something's Got To Give*, on co-star, Martin]

Martin, Steve

A former stand-up gagman (and warm-up act for The Carpenters), Martin has carved a strange niche for himself in Hollywood as the thinking man's comedian. From his first manic performance in Carl Reiner's *The Jerk* (1979), through his underrated and wrongfully panned turn as the disillusioned music salesman in Herbert Ross's *Pennies From Heaven* (1981), up to and beyond his quasi straight-man role in John Hughes's *Planes, Trains And Automobiles* (1987), Martin has both written and acted with a full understanding of the long tradition of which he forms a part. Something of an acquired taste, when he really hits the spot, as in **Fred Schepisi's** *Roxanne* (1987) [which he scripted], Martin is probably the finest screen comedian of his generation.

Other Key Films: *Dead Men Don't Wear Plaid* (1982); *All Of Me* (1984); *Little Shop Of Horrors* (1986); *Dirty Rotten Scoundrels* (1988); *Parenthood* (1989); *LA Story* (1991); *HouseSitter* (1992); *A Simple Twist Of Fate* (1992); *Sgt. Bilko* (1996); *Bowfinger* (1999); *Novocaine* (2001); *Bringing Down The House* (2003); *Cheaper By The Dozen* (2003); *Shopgirl* (2005); *The Pink Panther* (2006)

Key Line: 'I punched a totally innocent Hungarian.' [*HouseSitter*]

Marvin, Lee

Marvin had seen darkness during his war service with the Marines, and the look and very often even the scent of death seemed to follow him throughout his career. He was a hard man in a pretty soft racket, and when he found a film to suit that hardness, as he did in **John Boorman's** *Point Blank* (1967), the audience were brought just a little closer to their primitive selves, all the time wary and a little anxious that such a man may one day come their way. Marvin, of course, could ham it with the best of them, and it was only rarely that a director could lever below the surface to the heart of darkness within. His most authentic films, for just that reason, were **Fritz Lang's** *The Big Heat* (1953), in which he threw boiling hot coffee in **Gloria Grahame's** face, **Michael Curtiz's** *The Comancheros* (1961), **John Ford's** *The Man Who Shot Liberty Valance* (1962), **Don Siegel's** *The Killers* (1964) and John Boorman's elliptical *Hell In The Pacific* (1968), in which Marvin was persuaded to go back over the spirit of his own war and turn it into parable.

Other Key Films: *Eight Iron Men* (1952); *Gun Fury* (1953); *The Wild One* (1954);

The Caine Mutiny (1954); *Bad Day At Black Rock* (1955); *Violent Saturday* (1955);
Attack! (1956); *Donovan's Reef* (1963); *Cat Ballou* (1965); *The Professionals* (1966); *The
Dirty Dozen* (1967); *Prime Cut* (1972); *The Iceman Cometh* (1973); *Shout At The Devil*
(1976); *The Big Red One* (1980); *Gorky Park* (1983)

Marx Brothers, The

Chico was the eldest, followed by Harpo, Groucho, Gummo and Zeppo (something
of an afterthought ten years later), but the Marx Brothers as we know them
consisted of Chico, with the hat and piano, Harpo, with the hair and harp, and
Groucho, with just about everything else, but mostly the moustache and the cheap
cigar. Schooled by their vaudeville-performing mother, the boys finally hit Broadway
in 1924, where they were snapped up by the movies. Their anarchic humour (and it
was anarchy – no normal life could continue in their nihilistic presence) spawned a
series of demented works in which they played havoc with bourgeois values and
restored to childhood what the adult world had stolen from it. Their greatest film
together is **Leo McCarey's** *Duck Soup* (1933), and though the humour palls
occasionally, and their self-obsession has a tendency to turn the audience into tourists
ogling through the bars at a cage full of chimpanzees, at his best, Groucho's insane
flights of fancy incorporate all the frustrations, longings and absurdities inherent in
the American male, and leave us with the ghostly impression of a vulnerable person
hidden behind the carapace of levity.

Other Key Films: *Animal Crackers* (1930); *Monkey Business* (1931); *Horse Feathers*
(1932); *A Night At The Opera* (1935); *A Day At The Races* (1937); *At The Circus* (1939);
The Big Store (1941); *A Night In Casablanca* (1946)

Key Lines:

    1.   Groucho: 'That's in every contract. That's what they call a sanity clause.'

Chico: 'You can't fool me. There ain't no Sanity Clause.' [*Night At The Opera*]

2. 'I wasn't kissing her. I was just whispering in her mouth.' [Chico to his wife, on being discovered *in flagrante delicto*]

3. 'Either he's dead, or my watch has stopped!' [Groucho: *A Day At The Races*]

4. 'If you can't leave in a taxi you can leave in a huff. If that's too soon, you can leave in a minute and a huff.' [Groucho: *Duck Soup*]

5. 'Remember, you're fighting for this woman's honour…which is probably more than she ever did.' [Groucho: *Duck Soup*]

6. 'Why, a four-year-old child could understand this report. Run out and find me a four-year-old child. I can't make head or tail of it.' [Groucho: *Duck Soup*]

7. Telegram – PLEASE ACCEPT MY RESIGNATION. I DON'T WANT TO BELONG TO ANY CLUB THAT WILL ACCEPT ME AS A MEMBER. [*Groucho And Me*]

8. 'I never forget a face, but in your case I'll be glad to make an exception.' [Groucho on relationships]

Mason, James

Silky-toned and suave charmer whose performances varied widely in quality, Mason was at his best in such films as **Carol Reed's** *Odd Man Out* (1947), **Albert Lewin's** *Pandora And The Flying Dutchman* (1951) and **Joseph L Mankiewicz's** *Five Fingers* (1952), where he matched, and indeed surpassed, nearly all his contemporaries. What Mason had was mystery, and virtually no other male actor of his time could equal him for haunted charm – his Rommel, in **Henry Hathaway's** *The Desert Fox* (1951), was definitive, and he impressed, too, as Humbert Humbert in **Stanley Kubrick's** *Lolita* (1962). In both the morning and the late afternoon of his career he played attractive villains best, but there was a time, somewhere in the late 1940s and early 1950s, where he incarnated doomed lovers in such a fated yet detached way that he managed to carve out a romantic niche for himself that has never quite been refilled. **Other Key Films**: *Thunder Rock* (1943); *The Man In Grey* (1943); *The Wicked Lady* (1946); *The Prisoner Of Zenda* (1952); *Face To Face* (1952); *Julius Caesar* (1953); *Charade* (1953); *A Star Is Born* (1954); *Bigger Than Life* (1956); *North By Northwest* (1959); *Lord Jim* (1965); *Georgy Girl* (1966); *The Mackintosh Man* (1973); *Cross Of Iron* (1977); *The Shooting Party* (1984)

Mastroianni, Marcello

Renowned both for his charm and for his unabashed philandering, Mastroianni was Italy's most famous actor, and retained this status until his death in 1996. **Federico Fellini's** screen alter ego, and a favourite of such directors as **Luchino Visconti** and **Michelangelo Antonioni**, he first made his international mark standing in the Trevi fountain alongside the voluptuous Anita Ekberg's breasts in Fellini's *La Dolce Vita* (1960). A subtle actor, and not afraid of showing his insecurities on screen, Mastroianni could often miss the mark, and he (correctly) ascribed such occasional lows in his career to a consummate, though always charming, idleness. **Other Key Films**: *White Nights* (1958); *La Notte* (1961); *Vie Privée* (1962); *Marriage, Italian Style* (1963); *The Tenth Victim* (1965); *Leo The Last* (1970); *Blow-Out* (1973); *La Nuit De Varennes* (1981); *Ginger And Fred* (1985); *Dark Eyes* (1987); *Stanno Tutti Bene* (1990)

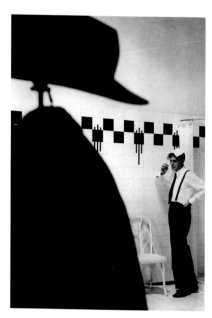

Marcello Mastroianni in Otto e Mezzo (8½), directed by Federico Fellini (1963).

Cineriz/The Kobal Collection

Matthau, Walter

With his craggy features and loping, uncoordinated walk, Matthau was instantly recognisable in whatever role he played. Often teamed with **Jack Lemmon** in such comedic hits as Gene Saks's *The Odd Couple* (1968), and **Billy Wilder's** *The Fortune Cookie* (1966) and *The Front Page* (1975), Matthau was also capable of effectively playing straight roles, such as the reluctant district Marshall in David Miller's *Lonely Are The Brave* (1962), and as the eponymous hero in the smooth **Don Siegel** thriller *Charley Varrick* (1973), which has since become something of a **cult**, thanks to Matthau getting away with the heist, the dosh, *and* the acting honours.

Other Key Films: *Charade* (1963); *A Guide For The Married Man* (1967); *Hello Dolly!* (1969); *A New Leaf* (1970); *Plaza Suite* (1971); *The Taking Of Pelham One Two Three* (1974); *The Sunshine Boys* (1975); *Buddy Buddy* (1981); *I.Q.* (1994); *Grumpier Old Men* (1995); *Out To Sea* (1997); *Hanging Up* (2000)

Mature, Victor

Often relegated as an also-ran in the acting stakes on account of his muscles and his glamorous good looks, Mature was actually a professional and versatile leading man who could often carry a film on his star allure alone. Excellent in *film noirs* such as Bruce Humberstone's *I Wake Up Screaming* (1941) and **Henry Hathaway's** *Kiss Of Death* (1947), he was the best-ever screen Doc Holliday in **John Ford's** superb *My Darling Clementine* (1946), knocking later aspirants such as **Kirk Douglas** and Val Kilmer into a cocked hat. <u>Thought For The Day</u>: Never judge an actor or actress by their looks alone.

Other Key Films: *The Shanghai Gesture* (1941); *Cry Of The City* (1948); *Easy Living* (1949); *Samson And Delilah* (1949); *Violent Saturday* (1955); *The Last Frontier* (1956); *After The Fox* (1966); *Head* (1968)

Mayer, Louis B

Marcus Loew merged his controlling interest in Metro and the Goldwyn Company with Louis B Mayer Pictures in 1924 to create MGM. He then instantly appointed Mayer vice president and general manager of the new conglomerate. Always power hungry, Mayer, the quintessential Hollywood mogul, soon bent MGM to his will, creating a dictatorship where his every whim was instantly gratified, and from which he could foment wholesome family values and the conservative, not to say reactionary, patriotic principles he held so dear. This said, he was a hard worker, and an even harder, some-times whimsical taskmaster, and his enlightened choice of **Irving G Thalberg** to head MGM operations from 1924-33 did somewhat lessen his otherwise deadening effect. Mayer left MGM in 1951, after having created the longest string of feel-good pap in the history of movies – material like the *Andy Hardy* series, interspersed with such occasional gems as Robert Z Leonard's *Pride And Prejudice* (1940).

Méliès, Georges

Méliès was the magician of early cinema, and it was through the aegis of his magic show that he first conceived of a camera to suit his fantastical requirements. By 1896 he had already made nearly eighty short films, and had fully understood the lucrative possibilities of transposing magic to the movies, dropping his live act, and simply showing film scenes to the ever-eager punters queuing at the doors of his theatre. In 1897 he built Europe's first film studio outside Paris, at Montreuil, and it was there that he made *Cinderella* (1899), *Jeanne D'Arc* (1900) and his most famous film, *Le Voyage Dans La Lune* (1902). The public, however, soon tired of Méliès's tricks, and by the 1915 showing of his masterpiece, *À La Conquête Du Pole*, he was a virtual bankrupt. In desperation he sold most of his assets and reverted to the magic tricks that had pointed the way to his interim career – but by 1927 he was a totally forgotten man. Four years later, in one of the *volte-faces* that only the French contrive so well, he was abruptly recognised for his contribution to film history by the Government, awarded the *Légion D'Honneur*, and settled in a rent-free apartment for the remaining seven years of his life.

Other Key Films: *Après Le Bal* (1897); *Le Magicien* (1898); *Les Miracles Du Brahmine* (1899); *L'Homme-Orchestre* (1900); *Le Temple De La Magie* (1901); *Eruption Volcanique À La Martinique* (1902); *Damnation Du Docteur Faust* (1904); *Voyage À Travers L'Impossible* (1904); *Le Palais Du Mille Et Une Nuits* (1905); *Le Tunnel Sous La Manche* (1907) [somewhat prescient, that one]; *Le Raid Paris-New York En Automobile* (1909)

Melville, Jean-Pierre

Melville's first film was *Le Silence De La Mer* (1949), in which he used his experience in the French Resistance to explore the paradox of warfare between neighbouring countries. This was quickly followed by the intriguing *Les Enfants Terribles* (1950), which heralded a welcome new talent in the now rather moribund French film industry. Melville really hit his stride with the then underrated *Bob Le Flambeur* (1955), presaging the superb series of gangster films which was to follow and which reached its apotheosis with *Le Samourai* (1967), a masterpiece of late-period *film noir* which has influenced just about anybody who has attempted the genre ever since.

Other Key Films: *Léon Morin – Priest* (1961); *Le Doulos* (1963); *L'Armée Des Ombres* (1969); *Le Cercle Rouge* (1970); *Un Flic* (1972)

Mifune, Toshiro

The most internationally renowned of all Japanese film actors, Mifune collaborated for many years with the great **Akira Kurosawa**, most notably in *Rashomon* (1950), *The Seven Samurai* (1954), *I Live In Fear* (1955) and *Yojimbo* (1961). As comfortable in broad comedy and domestic drama as he is wielding a samurai sword, Mifune was superb as the marooned Japanese soldier opposite **Lee Marvin's** equally marooned marine in **John Boorman's** offbeat masterpiece *Hell In The Pacific* (1969), and deserves to be counted, on the strength of his Kurosawa films alone, as one of the greatest screen actors of all time. A director and producer in his own right, Mifune made a strong impression as Lord Toranaga in the 1980 television miniseries based on James Clavell's best-selling *Shogun*, in which he once again demonstrated his power for stillness and facial control.

Other Key Films: *The Idiot* (1951); *The Life Of Oharu* (1952); *The Lower Depths* (1958); *Throne Of Blood* (1958); *The Hidden Fortress* (1958); *The Bad Sleep Well* (1960); *Sanjuro* (1962); *Red Beard* (1965); *Red Sun* (1971); *Midway* (1976); *Winter Kills* (1979); *Inchon* (1982); *Jinsei Gekijo* (1983); *Taketori Monogatari* (1987); *The Death Of A Tea Master* (1989); *Picture Bride* (1995)

Milland, Ray

In many ways a run-of-the-mill leading man, the former Reginald Truscott-Jones surpassed himself in one or two quite remarkable films, before descending into a late-career burst as an effective lead in a series of outstanding horror movies. The high point of his career came in **Billy Wilder's** *The Lost Weekend* (1945), where he played a desperate alcoholic, Don Birnam, who was incapable of staying on the wagon, and for which he won a well-deserved Best Actor Oscar. Another highlight came with his performance as **Grace Kelly's** murderous husband in **Alfred Hitchcock's** *Dial M For Murder* (1954). Even in the B-features of which he was a staple during the late 1950s and early 1960s, Milland always gave of his best, and his capacity for playing subtly eccentric characters inside an environment of Eisenhower-era conformity marks him out as one of the more interesting and idiosyncratic of second rankers.

Other Key Films: *The Glass Key* (1935); *French Without Tears* (1939); *Beau Geste* (1939); *The Major And The Minor* (1942); *The Big Clock* (1948); *Alias Nick Beal* (1950); *Bugles In The Afternoon* (1952); *A Man Alone* [also dir.] (1955); *The Girl In The Red Velvet Swing* (1955); *The Premature Burial* (1962); *X – The Man With X-Ray Eyes* (1963); *Love Story* (1970); *The Thing With Two Heads* (1972); *Gold* (1974)

Miller, George

Action aficionados will be forever indebted to Miller for his magnificent Mad Max duet starring **Mel Gibson** – *Mad Max* (1979) and *Mad Max 2: The Road Warrior* (1981). (The third film in the series, *Mad Max Beyond Thunderdome* (1985), simply doesn't have what it takes.) Miller took action sequences that had been done a thousand times before – the car chase, the helicopter after the runaway truck, the escape by night, the idyllic lull before the storm – and transformed them into something utterly different and surprisingly original. From the very first moment of the *Mad Max 2* 'war-of-the-nations' montage, we know we are in for a treat, and by the end of the film (big-screen of course), we emerge, sweating and bleary-eyed into the street, half expecting to see Humungus howling towards us on his mighty roadster, his duelling pistol primed with the last of his precious stock of gold-tipped bullets.

Other Key Films: *The Witches Of Eastwick* (1987); *Lorenzo's Oil* (1992); *Over The Hill* (1992); *Babe: Pig In The City* (1998)

Mills, John

Mills acted in a series of fascinating and very English films during the late 1940s and early 1950s, some of which deserve reassessment, if only for the low-key, curiously hard-boiled energy that Mills brought to his roles. Roy Ward Baker's *The October Man* (1947), Anthony Kimmins's *Mr. Denning Drives North* (1951), and **Robert Hamer's** *The Long Memory* (1952) are all fascinating for their use of location, their tiny eccentricities, tight observations of character and occasional black humour. They are the British equivalent of 1930s French **Poetic Realism** and 1940s American *film noir*, and it is very possibly because they did such a brilliant job in reflecting a psychologically ravaged, war-sick and unglamorous England (in all its curious drabness and downbeat reality) that they are so little known and appreciated now.

There was something about Mills, some indefinable Everyman aspect, that was curiously impressive. Forget the war films and the stiff-upper-lip baloney, and go check out Mills in Anthony Pelissier's *The Rocking Horse Winner* (1949), or in J Lee Thompson's *Ice Cold In Alex* (1958) or Ronald Neame's *Tunes Of Glory* (1960) – not many screen actors have such range and quality, and few, if any, have been so persistently undervalued.

Other Key Films: *The Midshipmaid* (1932); *Goodbye Mr. Chips* (1939); *Cottage To Let* (1941); *In Which We Serve* (1942); *We Dive At Dawn* (1943); *This Happy Breed* (1944); *The Way To The Stars* (1945); *Great Expectations* (1946); *Scott Of The Antarctic* (1948); *The History Of Mr. Polly* (1949); *Hobson's Choice* (1954); *The Colditz Story* (1955); *Town On Trial* (1956); *The Chalk Garden* (1963); *Oh! What A Lovely War* (1969); *Ryan's Daughter* (1970); *Gandhi* (1982); *Hamlet* (1996); *Bean* (1997); *Bright Young Things* (2003)

Minghella, Anthony

Minghella is a consummate professional, both as screenwriter and director, and his films hark back, in their quality and the care with which they are constructed, to the great melodramas of 1940s Hollywood. *Truly, Madly, Deeply* (1991) worked on a number of levels, as comedy, drama and romance, and *The English Patient* (1996) continued this eclectic trail, once again satisfying both the intellectual and the romantic in a way that has hardly been bettered in recent years. *The Talented Mr. Ripley* (1999) was a deserved success, but one still finds it astonishing that Minghella's magisterial *Cold Mountain* (2003) did not garner every award in the book and cement his reputation as one of the finest mainstream filmmakers living, for it is brilliant, sophisticated cinema-making at its best, and Minghella's is a rare talent.

Other Key Films: *Mr. Wonderful* (1993); *Play* [short] (2000)

Minnelli, Vincente

Minnelli made smooth, dark chocolaty entertainment (a bit like **Douglas Sirk**, but with music), which was always satisfying, always immaculately produced, and which occasionally, just occasionally, touched real heights of intensity. *The Clock* (1945) was his first near-masterpiece, starring a still unspoiled **Judy Garland** (whom he was to marry in 1945) and the brilliant, doomed **Robert Walker**. *The Bad And The Beautiful* (1952) featured a sneering **Kirk Douglas**, a sublimely winsome **Gloria Grahame**, and a pipe-chewing, typewriter-tapping **Dick Powell**, and *The Band Wagon* (1953) gave much-needed late-career kudos to the inimitable Jack Buchanan, more than ably and equally elegantly abetted by the one and only **Fred Astaire**. On top of all this, Minnelli managed a really brilliant Vincent Van Gogh biopic in *Lust For Life* (1956), and possibly the most outrageously charming Maurice Chevalier vehicle ever, with *Gigi* (1958). Whoever said that the Hollywood studio system couldn't produce the goods when it tried?

Other Key Films: *Cabin In The Sky* (1943); *Meet Me In St. Louis* (1944); *Ziegfeld Follies* (1946); *The Pirate* (1948); *Madame Bovary* (1949); *Father Of The Bride* (1950); *An American In Paris* (1951); *Brigadoon* (1954); *Tea And Sympathy* (1956); *Designing Woman* (1958); *The Reluctant Debutante* (1958); *Some Came Running* (1959); *Two Weeks In Another Town* (1962); *The Sandpiper* (1965)

Mitchum, Robert

Consummate screen presence and iconoclast (he was sentenced to sixty days on a work farm for possession of marijuana in 1948) Mitchum paved the way for many of today's quasi-tough leading men – the only difference being that Mitchum really *was* tough, yet somehow managed to retain his appeal to women as well as to men, despite that apparent handicap. The perfect **Philip Marlowe**, he encapsulated **Raymond Chandler's** dictum that 'down these mean streets a man must go who is not himself mean, who is neither tarnished nor afraid…' Unfortunately Mitchum only got to play Marlowe when he was rising fifty-eight – his was the definitive version, however, ably abetted by Dick Richards's sublime reworking of *Farewell My Lovely* (1975). Another career high was his performance as the preacher in **Charles Laughton's** unjustly neglected (until recently) *Night of the Hunter* (1955).

Other Key Films: *The Locket* (1946); *Pursued* (1947); *Crossfire* (1947); *Out Of The Past [a.k.a. Build My Gallows High]* (1947); *Blood On The Moon* (1948); *Where Danger Lives* (1950); *Macao* (1952); *The Lusty Men* (1952); *Angel Face* (1953); *Bandido* (1956); *Heaven Knows Mr Allison* (1958); *The Enemy Below* (1958); *Thunder Road* (1958); *The Sundowners* (1960); *Cape Fear* (1962); *El Dorado* (1967); *Villa Rides* (1968); *Ryan's Daughter* (1970); *The Friends Of Eddie Coyle* (1973); *The Yakuza* (1975); *Maria's Lovers* (1985); *Mr. North* (1988); *Cape Fear* [remake] (1991); *Tombstone* (1993); *Dead Man* (1996)

Key Lines:

1. 'One of the biggest stars in the world was Rin Tin Tin. And that was a dog. So there can't be too much of a trick to it.' [Mitchum on stardom]
2. 'Whatever he does he always comes back to the family.' [Dorothy Mitchum on fidelity – she was married to Mitchum for fifty-six years, until his death in 1997, aged seventy-nine]

Mizoguchi, Kenji

Mizoguchi is one of the great masters of world cinema, an assertion borne out by even the few of his films that are currently available to Western audiences. The two masterpieces we know best are *The Life Of Oharu* (1952) and *Ugetsu Monogatari* (1953), an exquisitely photographed tale of ambition, betrayal and partial redemption, in which each movement of the camera, each fastidious set-up adds to the story, so that we find ourselves locked inside Mizoguchi's world, where character, moral force and psychological constraint vie with each other, highlighted by his elucidatory camera, until we are entirely subsumed by the drama unfolding in front of us. Mizoguchi died, after a lengthy battle against ill-health, at the age of only fifty-eight, leaving a legacy of more than eighty films of which only a fraction have ever been seen outside his native Japan.

Other Key Films: *Blood And Soul* (1923); *A Man's Life* (1928); *The Dawn Of Manchuria And Mongolia* (1932); *Osen Of The Paper Cranes* (1934); *The Story Of the Late Chrysanthemums* (1939); *The Woman Of Osaka* (1940); *The Loyal 47 Ronin* (41-2); *The Love Of Sumako The Actress* (1947); *Women Of The Night* (1948); *Miss Oyu* (1951); *A Geisha* (1953); *Chikamatsu Monogatari* (1954); *Street Of Shame* (1956)

Monroe, Marilyn

Born Norma Jean Mortenson, Monroe became, during her brief thirty-six-year life, the ultimate Hollywood sex symbol. Following a deeply troubled childhood and a failed marriage (entered into when she was just fourteen), she first came to the public's notice as a bit player in two excellent films – **John Huston's** *The Asphalt Jungle* (1950) and **Joseph L Mankiewicz's** *All About Eve* (1950). Just two years and eleven movies later she was the most famous film star in the world. In 1954 she got married again, this time to baseball star Joe DiMaggio, then, a year after that, to playwright **Arthur Miller**, who wrote her final, elegiac film, Huston's *The Misfits*

(1961), in which she played the fragile, otherworldly Roslyn Taber opposite **Clark Gable's** unregenerate Gay Langland. Following her apparent and much-debated suicide in 1962, rumour had it that Monroe had conducted unhappy affairs with two of the Kennedy brothers, Robert and Jack. True or not, her image is synonymous with sex, and, for many, she remains the ultimate screen goddess.

Other Key Films: *Clash By Night* (1952); *Gentlemen Prefer Blondes* (1953); *Niagara* (1953); *How To Marry A Millionaire* (1953); *River Of No Return* (1954); *The Seven Year Itch* (1955); *Bus Stop* (1956); *Some Like It Hot* (1959); *Let's Make Love* (1960)

Key Lines:

1. 'All they have to do is play eight bars of 'Come To Me, My Melancholy Baby', and my spine turns to custard, I get goose pimply all over, and I come to them.' [*Some Like It Hot*]

2. 'What was interesting is that nobody really liked Monroe... Monroe was totally unreliable. Nobody knew what she was going to do.' [Screenwriter Walter Bernstein, co-writer on Monroe's final, unfinished project, *Something's Got To Give*, from which she was fired two months before her death, in August 1962]

3. 'She was a sad, sad, sad creature. She was sick. In a rightly ordered world, she would have been in a nuthouse. She was psychotic. Once you got to know her, one couldn't feel sexy about her.' [George Axelrod, who wrote the original play and co-scripted **Billy Wilder's** *The Seven Year Itch* (1955), and scripted Joshua Logan's *Bus Stop* (1956), on the Monroe myth]

Marilyn Monroe in How to Marry a Millionaire, directed by Jean Negulesco (1953).

20th Century Fox/The Kobal Collection

***Best* Monster Films**: Jack Arnold's *Creature From The Black Lagoon* (1954) and *Tarantula* (1955); Larry Cohen's *It's Alive!* (1973); **Merian C Cooper** and Ernest Schoedsack's *King Kong* (1933); Inoshiro Honda's *Godzilla* (1955); George McCowan's *Frogs* (1972); John McTiernan's *Predator* (1987); Kurt Neumann's *The Fly* (1958); Christian Nyby's *The Thing* [a.k.a. *The Thing From Another World*]; **Peter**

Julie Adams and Ben Chapman who played the part of the Gill-Man out of the water (though he was uncredited) in Creature from the Black Lagoon, directed by Jack Arnold (1954).

Universal/The Kobal Collection

Jackson's *King Kong* (2005); **Ridley Scott's** *Alien* (1979); **James Whale's** *Frankenstein* (1931) and *The Bride Of Frankenstein* (1935); Irvin S Yeaworth Jr's *The Blob* (1958) [all right, the film isn't any good, but think of the **cult**]

Montand, Yves

A fine cabaret singer, an elegant dancer and a more than competent actor, Montand seemed to have it all – but his background was actually one of grinding poverty and uprootal. Born Ivo Levi, in Italy's Monsummano Alto, Montand's family fled to Marseilles when Mussolini's fascist party came to power, and he never forgot the sense of political injustice he derived from his truncated youth. The often penniless Montand became a protégé of Edith Piaf, and later conducted a curious on/off marriage with **Simone Signoret** interspersed with numerous affairs, one of which involved the still-married **Marilyn Monroe**. Montand electrified the screen as Mario in **Henri-Georges Clouzot's** *The Wages Of Fear* (1952), and later collaborated on a series of first-rate political thrillers with director **Constantin Costa-Gavras**, which included his propaganda masterpiece *Z* (1969). At the end of his life he was something approaching a French national institution.

Other Key Films: *Les Portes De La Nuit* (1946); *The Wolves* (1956); *Aimez-Vous Brahms?* (1961); *Goodbye Again* (1962); *Vivre Pour Vivre* (1967); *The Confession* (1970); *State Of Siege* (1973); *Jean De Florette* (1986); *Manon Des Sources* (1986)

Moore, Roger

Suave leading man of the ironical 'I may be English but I'm certainly no gentleman' school of acting, Moore found his feet playing Maverick, Ivanhoe and the Saint for television, then landed the plum role of *James Bond*, which he incarnated, more than adequately, in seven films. Often criticized for being rather wooden, Moore is one of those rare actors who are happy sending up their own image, and his charm and unfailing modesty when teased about his apparent shortcomings have endeared him to generations of fans. Just occasionally, as in **Basil Dearden's** *The Man Who Haunted Himself* (1970), Moore has proved that he is more than just a pretty face.

Other Key Films: *Crossplot* (1969); *Live And Let Die* (1971); *Gold* (1974); *The Man With The Golden Gun* (1974); *Shout At The Devil* (1976); *The Spy Who Loved Me* (1977); *The Wild Geese* (1978); *Moonraker* (1979); *The Sea Wolves* (1980); *For Your Eyes Only* (1981); *Octopussy* (1983); *A View To A Kill* (1985); *Bed & Breakfast* (1992); *The Quest* (1996); *Spice World* (1997); *The Enemy* (2001)

Moreau, Jeanne

Moreau was the art-house director's darling during the 1960s, and rightly so, for she brought an earthy and utterly European sensuousness to all her roles, in direct opposition to the **Doris Day** and **Julie Andrews** caricatures of the US mainstream. Working for such directors as **Louis Malle** in *L'Ascenseur Pour L'Echafaud* (1958), and **Michelangelo Antonioni** in *La Notte* (1961), Moreau reminded audiences of what sex was really about – the overwhelming desire of one human being for another. Her Catherine in **François Truffaut's** *Jules Et Jim* (1961) became the personification of female sexuality for countless young Frenchwomen of her time, who were themselves to prove influential in the heady Paris riots of May 1968. Addressed simply as Mademoiselle Jeanne Moreau, she received a well-deserved homage at the Berlin Film Festival 2000, and remains, to this day, very much the grande dame of European cinema.

Other Key Films: *Touchez Pas Au Grisbi* (1953); *Les Liaisons Dangereuses* (1959); *Eva* (1962); *Diary Of A Chambermaid* (1963); *Chimes At Midnight* (1966); *The Sailor From Gibraltar* (1967); *The Immortal Story* (1968); *Les Valseuses* (1974); *Mr Klein* (1977); *Plein Sud* (1980); *Querelle* (1982); *La Femme Nikita* (1990); *Until The End Of The World* (1992); *Map Of The Human Heart* (1992); *Beyond The Clouds* (1996); *The Prince's Manuscript* (2000); *Lisa* (2001); *Cet Amour Là* (2001); *Les Parents Terribles* (2003); *Le Temps Qui Reste* (2005); *Go West* (2005)

Key Line: 'Age doesn't protect you from love, but love, to some extent, protects you from age.' [Moreau on enlightened pragmatism]

Monica Vitti and Jeanne Moreau in La Notte (The Night), directed by Michelangelo Antonioni (1960).

NEPI/SOTILEDIP/ Silver Films/The Kobal Collection

Morricone, Ennio

Best known as composer-in-residence to **Sergio Leone** on his **Spaghetti Westerns** series, Morricone is a master musician who has worked with directors of the stature of **Federico Fellini**, **Pier Paolo Pasolini**, **Bernardo Bertolucci**, **Gillo Pontecorvo** and **Brian De Palma**. Composer of more than 570 film scores, Morricone uses anything and everything to create his effects, most notably the human whistling in Leone's *The Good The Bad and The Ugly* (1966), and the swooping harmonica in the same director's *Once Upon A Time In The West* (1968). He was also responsible for the much borrowed and infinitely haunting xylophone music in **Terrence Malick's** *Days Of Heaven* (1978).

Other Key Films: Henri Verneuil's *The Sicilian Clan* (1969); Elio Petri's *Investigation Of A Citizen Above Suspicion* (1970); Edouard Molinaro's *La Cage Aux Folles* (1979); Roland Joffé's *The Mission* (1986); **Mike Nichols's** *Wolf* (1994); **Oliver Stone's** *U Turn* (1997); Adrian Lyne's *Lolita* (1997); **Warren Beatty's** *Bulworth* (1998); Roland Joffé's *Vatel* (2000); Guiseppe Tornatore's *Malèna* (2000); Liliana Cavani's *Ripley's Game* (2002); **Quentin Tarantino's** *Kill Bill Vol. 1* and *Vol. 2* (2003 & 2004); Guiseppe Tornatore's *La Sconosciuta* (2006)

Murnau, F W

Virtually nothing survives of Murnau's early work (pre-1921), but his *Nosferatu – Eine*

Symphonie Des Grauens [*Nosferatu The Vampire*] (1922) is a round peg in the rhomboid hole of German **expressionism**, and has been massively influential, to this day, with its use of real locations, grotesque design and atmospheric lighting. It caused filmmakers to start to think laterally, and to use the whole of their available space rather than merely to view on-camera space as an extension of the theatre. Murnau completed two other masterpieces, *The Last Laugh* (1924) and the exquisite, heart-breaking *Sunrise* (1927) [his first Hollywood film], before his death in a car accident, aged just forty-two, on a location scouting trip from Los Angeles to Monterey.
Other Key Films: *Schloss Vögelöd* (1921); *Der Brennende Acke* (1922); *Faust* (1926); *Four Devils* (1928); *City Girl* (1930); *Tabu* [co-dir. **Robert Flaherty**] (1931)

Murphy, Eddie
Brooklyn-born Murphy, who was a successful stand-up comedian before he ever dreamed of a screen career, appeared to have the golden touch following his first star-making screen appearance in Walter Hill's *48 Hrs* (1982). He came out with a string of scrupulously fabricated comedy hits including Martin Brest's *Beverly Hills Cop* (1984) and John Landis's *Coming To America* (1988). Then his luck, and a goodly part of his audience, suddenly left him, and he found himself forced back into such increasingly moderate rehashes as Landis's *Beverly Hills Cop III* (1994) and **Wes Craven's** *Vampire In Brooklyn* (1995), before Tom Shadyac's *The Nutty Professor* (1996) lifted him back out of the soup. Murphy's films are notable for their cheek, their energy and their visual inventiveness, but also for their uncomfortably partial plots and often dubious moral imperatives.
Other Key Films: *Trading Places* (1983); *Beverly Hills Cop II* (1987); *Coming To America* (1988); *Another 48 Hrs.* (1990); *Boomerang* (1992); *The Distinguished Gentleman* (1992); *Metro* (1997); *Dr Dolittle* (1998); *Bowfinger* (1999); *Nutty Professor II:The Klumps* (2000); *Shrek* (2001) [he voiced the donkey]; *Dr Dolittle 2* (2001); *I Spy* (2002); *Dreamgirls* (2006)

Best Musical Films
Lloyd Bacon's *42nd Street* (1933); Alain Corneau's *Tous Les Matins Du Monde* (1991); **Clint Eastwood's** *Honkytonk Man* (1982); **Milos Forman's** *Amadeus* (1984); Bob Fosse's *Cabaret* (1972); François Girard's *Thirty-Two Short Films About Glenn Gould* (1994); Taylor Hackford's *Hail! Hail! Rock n' Roll* (1987); **Howard Hawks's** *Gentlemen Prefer Blondes* (1953); **Gene Kelly** and **Stanley Donen's** *On The Town* (1949) and *Singin' In The Rain* (1952); **Mervyn LeRoy's** *Gold Diggers Of 1933* (1933); **Vincente Minnelli's** *The Bandwagon* (1953); **G W Pabst's** *Die Dreigroschenoper* [*The Threepenny Opera*] (1930); **Alan Parker's** *The Commitments* (1991); **Michael Powell** and Emeric Pressburger's *The Red Shoes* (1947); Herbert Ross's *Pennies From Heaven* (1981); Mark Sandrich's *Top Hat* (1935); Bert Stern's *Jazz On A Summer's Day* (1959); **George Stevens's** *Swing Time* (1936); **Bertrand Tavernier's** *Autour Du Minuit* [*Around Midnight*] (1986); **John Waters's** *Cry-Baby* (1990); **Robert Wise's** *West Side Story* (1961) and *The Sound Of Music* (1965)

Neeson, Liam
Neeson can be a rather intense actor, but his mercurial tendencies are more than matched by his striking talent in such challenging parts as that of Oskar Schindler, in **Steven Spielberg's** outstanding *Schindler's List* (1993), and his brilliant turn in John Madden's *Ethan Frome* (1993). One of the masochistic school of screen actors (whose other adepts include **Marlon Brando** and **Ralph Fiennes**) Neeson was as good in

Michael Caton-Jones's *Rob Roy* (1995) as **Mel Gibson** was conventional in that same year's self-directed *Braveheart* (1995).

Other Key Films: *Excalibur* (1981); *The Bounty* (1984); *The Mission* (1986); *Darkman* (1990); *Under Suspicion* (1991); *Nell* (1994); *Before And After* (1996); *Michael Collins* (1996); *Les Misérables* (1998); *The Hunting* (1999) *Gun Shy* (2000); *Gangs Of New York* (2002); *Love Actually* (20030; *Kinsey* (2004); *Kingdom Of Heaven* (2005); *Batman Begins* (2005); *Seraphim Falls* (2006)

Negulesco, Jean

There is no real comparison between the early Negulesco, before *How To Marry A Millionaire* (1953), say, and the later, post-Cinemascope Negulesco of *Three Coins In The Fountain* (1954) and *Woman's World* (1954) fame. In fact it is hard to believe that the director of such tight little ***film noir*** thrillers as *The Mask Of Dimitrios* (1944) and *Road House* (1948) is the very same man who subsequently made *Boy On A Dolphin* (1958), which is notable for nothing more than its wet-blouse publicity shot of Sophia Loren. Hmm. Perhaps his self-acknowledged, impenetrable Hungarian accent was to blame? Or could it have been Hollywood's fault?

Other Key Films: *The Conspirators* (1944); *Three Strangers* (1946); *Nobody Lives Forever* (1946); *Humoresque* (1946); *Deep Valley* (1947); *Johnny Belinda* (1948); *The Mudlark* (1950); *The Rains Of Ranchipur* (1955); *A Certain Smile* (1958); *Jessica* (1962)

Neo-realism

The style which transfigured Italian cinema during the 1940s and early 1950s, Neo-realism came about partially as the result of the incredibly harsh conditions suffered by virtually all Italians in the aftermath of the Nazi pull-out of 1944. Dependent on a non-intrusive camera and on storylines that highlighted the lives of ordinary people, the cycle is often considered to have begun with **Luchino Visconti's** *Ossessione* (1942), but the genuine first film of the movement was **Roberto Rossellini's** *Rome: Open City* (1945), a heady mélange of documentary, sensodrama, and direct filming on the streets, and a precursor to the Italian preference for overdubbing as later epitomised by the films of **Federico Fellini**. Prominent neo-realist films include Aldo Vergano's *Outcry* (1947), **Vittorio De Sica's** *Bicycle Thieves* (1948) and Guiseppe De Santis's *Bitter Rice* (1949). The movement petered out in the mid-1950s when the horrors of the war had been partially forgotten, and young Italians, in thrall to an economic revival and a hero-worshipping of America, began looking to glamour, and Vespas, and girls in fluffy skirts, rather than to the lessons of the past, for inspiration.

Other Key Films: Vittorio De Sica's *The Children Are Watching Us* (1943) and *Shoeshine* (1946); Roberto Rossellini's *Paisan* (1946), *Germany Year Zero* (1947) and *Stromboli* (1949); Alberto Lattuada's *Without Pity* (1948); Pietro Germi's *Mafia* (1949) and *The Path Of Hope* (1950)

Newman, Paul

Newman's reputation is healthier than it ought to be, notwithstanding the undoubted talent he showed in such excellent movies as **Arthur Penn's** *Left-Handed Gun* (1958) and **Martin Ritt's** *Hud* (1963), which, as the amoral Hud Bannon, contained his best-ever performance. In his many subsequent films he has often allowed his undoubted charm to get the better of him, losing the hard edge he showed in Stuart Rosenberg's *Cool Hand Luke* (1967), or, even worse, endeavouring to recreate it artificially, as in George Roy Hill's utterly contrived *Slap Shot* (1977).

The film that most successfully combined both key elements of Newman's appeal – his coldness and his charm – was Robert Rossen's *The Hustler* (1961), but in the forty years since then the star (and star he certainly is) may have offered much immediate gratification, but rather less long-lasting pleasure.

Other Key Films: *Somebody Up There Likes Me* (1956); *The Long Hot Summer* (1958); *Cat On A Hot Tin Roof* (1958); *Sweet Bird Of Youth* (1962); *Harper* (1966); *Hombre* (1967); *Butch Cassidy And The Sundance Kid* (1969); *Sometimes A Great Notion* (1971); *The Mackintosh Man* (1973); *The Sting* (1973); *The Verdict* (1982); *Mr. And Mrs. Bridge* (1990); *The Hudsucker Proxy* (1994); *Nobody's Fool* (1994); *Twilight* (1998); *Where The Money Is* (2000); *Road To Perdition* (2002)

Key Line: 'The only question I ever ask any woman is what time is her husband coming home?' [*Hud*]

New Wave

The French New Wave was a reaction against what its adherents, **Claude Chabrol**, Jacques Demy, **Jean-Luc Godard**, **Louis Malle**, **Alain Resnais**, Jacques Rivette, **Eric Rohmer** and **François Truffaut**, felt was the post- Second-World-War 'embourgeoisification' of French film. Using theories formulated through articles in the influential *Cahiers du Cinéma* magazine, the group suggested a new order in which film would be given back to the young, with directors signing their work rather as painters like Paul Cézanne and Paul Gauguin would have done seventy years earlier. During the brief five-year life of the movement, which spanned 1958-62, there really did seem to be a new feeling afoot, of cupboards dusted out and skeletons shaken. But the iconoclasts soon found themselves 'embourgeoisified' in their turn, and the movement, as do all movements, eventually petered out, having afforded much pleasure and not a little lucrative employment to the usual phalanx of film theorists and vainglorious critics bringing up the rear.

Key Films: Claude Chabrol's *Le Beau Serge* (1958) and *Les Cousins* (1959); François Truffaut's *Les Quatre Cents Coups* [*The 400 Blows*] (1959) and *Jules Et Jim* (1961); Jean-Luc Godard's *À Bout De Souffle* [*Breathless*] (1960) and *Une Femme Est Une Femme* [*A Woman Is A Woman*] (1961); Jacques Rivette's *Paris Nous Appartient* (1960)

Nichols, Mike

A strangely inconsistent filmmaker, Nichols was an Actor's Studio protégé, and proved his theatrical worth with his effective handling of Edward Albee's *Who's Afraid Of Virginia Woolf* (1966). It is hard, in retrospect, to remember how influential his next film, *The Graduate* (1967), really was, but he certainly succeeded in capturing the Zeitgeist once again with *Carnal Knowledge* (1971), in which he dissected the sexual illusions of an entire generation of American men. *Wolf* (1994), once again with **Jack Nicholson**, and the more recent *Primary Colors* (1998) showed a welcome return to form after a string of rather moderate precursors, which included the seriously overrated *Postcards From The Edge* (1990). His recent *Closer* (2004), however, was a magnificent return to form, and played up to just those strengths of character, human motivation, and the workings of random fate, that have imbued all Nichols's best work. **Other Key Films:** *Catch-22* (1970); *Silkwood* (1983); *Working Girl* (1988); *Regarding Henry* (1991); *The Bird Cage* (1996); *What Planet Are You From?* (2000)

Nicholson, Jack: A perennially popular and notably promiscuous hell-raiser and rabble-rouser, Nicholson also has one of the finest bodies of work of any actor of his generation streaming along behind him. First spotted at the somewhat advanced age of thirty-two (after more than a decade in pot-boilers) in **Dennis Hopper's *Easy Rider*** (1969), Nicholson surprised everybody with the depth and commitment of his performances in such outstanding films of the 1970s as **Bob Rafelson's** *Five Easy Pieces* (1970), **Mike Nichols's** *Carnal Knowledge* (1971), Hal Ashby's *The Last Detail* (1973), **Roman Polanski's** *Chinatown* (1974), **Michelangelo Antonioni's** *The Passenger* (1975), and **Milos Forman's** *One Flew Over The Cuckoo's Nest* (1975). Few actors, if any, can have achieved so much, and turned public perceptions so unequivocally around, in so short a time. His later work has varied between magnificence – his Eugene O'Neill in **Warren Beatty's** *Reds* (1981) – and commercial expediency, with his Joker in **Tim Burton's** *Batman* (1989). He has however had a most welcome recent return to form as Alex in Bob Rafelson's *Blood and Wine* (1996), and as irascible novelist, Melvin Udall, in James L Brooks's *As Good As It Gets* (1997) (at least in the first half, until the film became mawkish).

Art Garfunkel and Jack Nicholson in Carnal Knowledge, directed by Mike Nichols (1971).

Avco Embassy/The Kobal Collection

Other Key Films: *The King Of Marvin Gardens* (1972); *Goin' South* (1978); *The Shining* (1980); *The Postman Always Rings Twice* (1981); *The Border* (1983); *Terms Of Endearment* (1983); *Prizzi's Honour* (1985); *The Witches Of Eastwick* (1987); *The Two Jakes* (1990); *A Few Good Men* (1992); *The Crossing Guard* (1995); *Mars Attacks!* (1996); *The Pledge* (2001); *About Schmidt* (2002); *Anger Management* (2003); *Something's Gotta Give* (2003); *The Departed* (2006)

Key Lines:

1. 'Women today are better hung than men.' [*Carnal Knowledge*]
2. Secretary/Breathless Fan: 'How do you write women so well?' Irascible author Melvin Udall (Jack Nicholson): 'I think of a man, and take away reason and accountability.' [*As Good As It Gets* (1997)]

Niven, David

Suave leading man and notorious roisterer (with his chum and housemate, **Errol Flynn**) Niven turned in some fine performances during his more than forty-year career, notably in **Michael Powell** and Emeric Pressburger's *A Matter of Life and Death* (1946) and in Delbert Mann's *Separate Tables* (1958). As effective in light comedy as he was in romantic derring-do, Niven was a renowned raconteur and practical joker, and wrote two best-selling autobiographical books in later life. He died in 1983 after a long, un-winnable battle against motor neurone disease.

Other Key Films: *The Charge of the Light Brigade* (1936); *The Prisoner Of Zenda* (1937); *Bluebeard's Eighth Wife* (1938); *Dawn Patrol* (1938); *Wuthering Heights* (1939); *The Real Glory* (1939); *Raffles* (1940); *The Bishop's Wife* (1947); *The Elusive Pimpernel* (1950); *Carrington V.C.* (1955); *Around The World In 80 Days* (1956); *Bonjour Tristesse* (1958); *The Guns Of Navarone* (1961); *55 Days At Peking* (1963); *The Pink Panther* (1964); *The Sea Wolves* (1980)

Noiret, Philippe

One of France's greatest and most prolific actors, Noiret has the sort of acting range that most movie stars can only dream of. He first won international plaudits for his performance in **Louis Malle's** *Zazie Dans Le Métro* (1961), and again for his role as the boring husband in **George Franju's** *Thérèse Desqueyroux* (1962). His career now belatedly in gear, the sombre-faced Noiret began his slow rise to stardom with movies such as Marco Ferreri's *La Grande Bouffe* (1973) and **Bertrand Tavernier's** *The Clockmaker* (1973), which marked the start of a fruitful collaboration between the two men. Since then he has been directed by virtually every first-class French director in the business – and a good few Italian ones as well – but paradoxically, as these things so often happen, his greatest international success came with one of his lesser films, Giuseppe Tornatore's *Cinema Paradiso* (1989), which, while still immensely enjoyable, can hardly bear comparison with a performance of the calibre he gave for Tavernier that same year as Commandant Dellaplane in *La Vie Et Rien D'Autre* (1989).

Other Key Films: *Alexandre Le Bienheureux* [a.k.a. *Happy Alexander*] (1969); *Le Vieux Fusil* (1975); *Le Juge Et L'Assassin* (1975); *Coup De Foudre* (1978); *La Mort En Direct* (1979); *Three Brothers* (1981); *Coup De Torchon* (1981); *L'Étoile Du Nord* (1982); *Le Cop* (1984); *Round Midnight* (1986); *Tango* (1993); *Il Postino* (1994); *Les Grands Ducs* (1996); *Soleil* (1997); *Le Bossu* (1997); *Le Pique-Nique De Lulu Kreutz* (2000); *Un Honnête Commerçant* (2002); *Père Et Fils* (2003); *Les Côtelettes* (2003); *Ripoux 3* (2003); *Edy* (2005)

Nolte, Nick

Following what studio pundits usually call an 'interesting youth', Nolte got his big break in 1976, at the ripe old age of thirty-five, in the television saga *Rich Man, Poor Man*. A year later he was still playing beefcake opposite Jacqueline Bisset in Peter Yates's *The Deep* (1977), but that all changed with **Karel Reisz's** *Dog Soldiers* [a.k.a. *Who'll Stop The Rain*] (1978), in which Nolte first suggested the true depth of his talent. He then began the roller-coaster ride he's been on ever since, both film-wise and weight-wise, and whose highlights include Paul Mazursky's *Down And Out In Beverly Hills* (1986), **Martin Scorsese's** *New York Stories* (1989), and **Sidney Lumet's** *Q & A* (1990). Even his failures, such as **James Ivory's** *Jefferson In Paris* (1995) are interesting, if only because of the intensity with which he approaches every part, however unworthy some of them are of his talents.

Other Key Films: *Cannery Row* (1982); *48 Hrs* (1982); *Under Fire* (1983); *Farewell*

To The King (1989); Cape Fear (1991); The Prince Of Tides (1991); Mulholland Falls (1996); U-Turn (1997); The Thin Red Line (1998); The Best Of Enemies (1999); The Golden Bowl (2000); Investigating Sex (2001); Hulk (2003); Hotel Rwanda (2004); Peaceful Warrior (2006); Quelques Jours En Septembre (2006)

Novak, Kim

Novak grows on you. At first you say to yourself, oh, another big, blowzy be-sweatered blonde, where's the point? Then you may be fortunate enough to see her in a Richard Quine movie – *Pushover* (1954) perhaps, or *Bell Book And Candle* (1958), or *Strangers When We Meet* (1960), or maybe even in Joshua Logan's *Picnic* (1955), or in that breathtaking study of incipient paranoia, **Alfred Hitchcock's** *Vertigo* (1958) – and everything suddenly falls into place. Novak shouldn't work on screen but she does. There is a mystery about her, an allure, that a thousand other actresses can try for and fail to get, but with Novak it comes naturally, as if she is ever so slightly lost, but determines to make the best of it until someone should happen along and show her the way to the exit. This is devastatingly attractive to men, and unthreatening to women, and therein lies Novak's power and the reason why she was the US's biggest female draw in 1957.

Other Key Films: The Man With The Golden Arm (1955); Jeanne Eagels (1958); Pal Joey (1958); Of Human Bondage (1964); Kiss Me Stupid (1964); Liebestraum (1991)

Novarro, Ramon

The Durango-born Novarro was the third of the great trio of Latin lover-type silent stars, along with **John Gilbert** and **Rudolf Valentino**, and now he is forgotten by all but the cognoscenti, apart from the occasional rerun of Fred Niblo's *Ben-Hur* (1925) (usually consisting of just the chariot race), or George Fitzmaurice's *Mata Hari* (1931), in which he co-starred with **Greta Garbo**. He made one or two lacklustre Mexican films before his final fall from grace – his last Hollywood film was **George Cukor's** aptly named *Heller In Pink Tights* (1960) – when he was found battered to death on the floor of his Hollywood Hills mansion, in 1968, the victim of some venal young hustlers he had unwisely picked up earlier that day.

Other Key Films: The Prisoner Of Zenda (1922); Scaramouche (1923); The Arab (1924); The Student Prince (1927); The Pagan (1929); In Gay Madrid (1930); Laughing Boy (1934); The Sheik Steps Out (1937); The Big Steal (1949)

Nykvist, Sven

Ingmar Bergman's preferred cinematographer, and the quietly presiding genius behind the look of more than a hundred films, Nykvist is a master of natural light and heightened chiaroscuro. A fine director in his own right, as with his unrelentingly downbeat *The Ox* (1991), Nykvist was responsible for the gorgeous look of Charles Jarrott's underrated *The Dove* (1974), as well as for the recreation of the *feel* of old New Orleans in **Louis Malle's** *Pretty Baby* (1978). Although **Bob Rafelson's** *The Postman Always Rings Twice* (1981) failed to match up to its 1946 Tay Garnett predecessor, no one in their right mind could deny that Nykvist conjured up depression-era America with awesome skill.

Other Key Films: Ingmar Bergman's The Virgin Spring (1960); Caspar Wrede's One Day In The Life Of Ivan Denisovich (1971); **Woody Allen's** Crimes And Misdemeanors (1989) and Celebrity (1998); **Lasse Halstrom's** What's Eating Gilbert Grape (1993); Norman Jewison's Only You (1994); Peter Yates's Curtain Call (1999)

Oates, Warren

Oates was suitably named, for his forte was in oaters, and in fact he looked as if he were bean-scrunching in just about every film in which he featured, his eyes permanently crinkled against the sun, his teeth, conceivably rotten, picked with whatever came closest to hand (in one movie, even a knife). Dead from a heart attack at fifty-three, Oates really made his mark as Lyle Gorch in **Sam Peckinpah's** *The Wild Bunch* (1969), and followed this up as the aptly named GTO in his friend Monte Hellman's excellent *Two-Lane Blacktop* (1971). Another great Hellman movie starring Oates was the underrated *Cockfighter* (1974), which came as good as dammit to recreating the magnificent Charles Willeford novel it sprang from – something of a miracle given that the main protagonist spends virtually the whole book refusing to talk.
Other Key Films: *Ride The High Country* (1962); *Major Dundee* (1965); *In The Heat Of The Night* (1967); *Barquero* (1970); *The Hired Hand* (1971); *Badlands* (1974); *Bring Me The Head Of Alfredo Garcia* (1974); *Race With The Devil* (1975); *92 In The Shade* (1975); *The Border* (1982); *Blue Thunder* (1983)

Oberon, Merle

Alexander Korda, whom Oberon later married in 1939, first became obsessed by her curious, almost Asiatic beauty in 1933, when he cast her as Anne Boleyn in his *The Private Life Of Henry VIII*. Although she was a passably good actress, Oberon hardly deserved her ensuing roles in Korda's *The Private Life Of Don Juan* (1934) and Harold Young's *The Scarlet Pimpernel* (1935). She was much better in **William Wyler's** *Wuthering Heights* (1939), but, despite her fervid private life, she never became the stuff of screen legend, as the infatuated Korda had so obviously hoped.
Other Key Films: *I Claudius* [unfinished] (1937); *Lydia* (1941); *The Lodger* (1944); *Berlin Express* (1948); *Hotel* (1967)
Key Line: 'I'd masturbate about her all night – with the lights off, so God couldn't see me.' [Richard Harris, on his juvenile fascination with Oberon, whom he claims he finally did get to bed]

O'Hara, Maureen

O'Hara was the perfect foil for the men's men of 1940s and 1950s Hollywood, and was used to good effect by **John Ford** opposite **John Wayne** in *Rio Grande* (1950) and *The Quiet Man* (1952). Never a great actress, O'Hara was nonetheless an extremely professional one, and many of her roles tapped into the vein of acceptable sentimentality that audiences, deadened by the horrors of the Second World War, seemed to find necessary at the time.
Other Key Films: *Jamaica Inn* (1939); *The Hunchback Of Notre Dame* (1939); *A Bill Of Divorcement* (1940); *How Green Was My Valley* (1941); *The Foxes Of Harrow* (1947); *Our Man In Havana* (1960); *McLintock!* (1963)
Key Line: 'She looked as though butter wouldn't melt in her mouth – or anywhere else.' [Elsa Lanchester on O'Hara]

Oldman, Gary

A fine theatrical actor, Oldman uses stage technique to good effect in the handful of first-class films he has made since bursting into public awareness with Alex Cox's *Sid And Nancy* (1985), in which he played the part of doomed punk-rocker, Sid Vicious. This was closely followed by his brilliant portrayal of Joe Orton in **Stephen Frears's** *Prick Up Your Ears* (1987), which finally tipped off the US market to his precocious talent. He was astonishing as a crazed drug-dealer in Tony Scott's *True Romance* (1993), and equally good in the role of a crooked policeman in Peter Medak's *Romeo Is Bleeding* (1994) and **Luc Besson's** *Léon* (1994). His best performance to date has been as Beethoven, in Bernard Rose's much-underrated *Immortal Beloved* (1994), but he was also a wonderfully overblown Count Dracula in **Francis Ford Coppola's** *Bram Stoker's Dracula* (1992).

Other Key Films: *Remembrance* (1982); *Rosencrantz And Guildenstern Are Dead* (1990); *JFK* (1991); *The Scarlet Letter* (1995); *Basquiat* (1996); *The Fifth Element* (1997); *Lost In Space* (1998); *The Contender* (2000); *Hannibal* (2001); *Nobody's Baby* (2001); *Interstate 60* (2002); *Dead Fish* (2004); *Harry Potter And The Prisoner Of Azkaban* (2004) *Harry Potter And The Goblet Of Fire* (2005); *Bosque De Sombras* (2006)

Olivier, Laurence: Considered by many to be the greatest screen actor of them all (and by others a boring old ham), Olivier burst onto the screen (quite literally) in **William Wyler's** *Wuthering Heights* (1939), followed, in the same year, by **Alfred Hitchcock's** awesomely romantic *Rebecca* – then, to complete the hat-trick, he was the definitive Darcy in **Robert Z Leonard's** *Pride and Prejudice* (1940). He starred as Horatio Nelson, alongside his then wife **Vivien Leigh**, in **Alexander Korda's** *That Hamilton Woman* (1941), and, to cap what was already a fine career, he went on to act in and direct a ground-breaking *Henry V* (1944) and a *Hamlet* (1948). His final screen triumph came playing Archie Rice in **Tony Richardson's** *The Entertainer* (1960), from which moment, due to increasing ill-health, he only took occasional, largely character, roles to provide for the future of his family.

Other Key Films: *As You Like It* (1936); *Fire Over England* (1937); *49th Parallel* (1941); *Carrie* (1952); *The Beggar's Opera* (1953); *The Prince and the Showgirl* (1958); *The Devil's Disciple* (1959); *Spartacus* (1960); *Othello* (1965); *Khartoum* (1966); *Oh! What A Lovely War* (1969); *Sleuth* (1972); *Marathon Man* (1976); *The Boys From Brazil* (1978); **Dracula** (1979); *The Bounty* (1984)

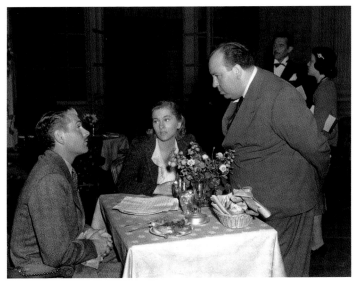

Laurence Olivier, Joan Fontaine and Alfred Hitchcock in 1940.

Selznick/United Artists/The Kobal Collection

Ophüls, Max: A cult director obsessed by the cyclical nature of human emotions and, as such, comparable in essence to the great **Jean Renoir**, Ophüls was falsely accused of sentimentality by some, but in fact he had recognized the fragile nature of human sexuality far better than many of the so-called 'realistically-inclined' directors who surrounded him. A true poet of the cinema, his bittersweet *Letter From An Unknown Woman* (1948) predated the full flowering of his talent in such films as *La Ronde* (1950), *Le Plaisir* (1952), *Madame de...* (1953), and his masterpiece, *Lola Montés* (1955).

Other Key Films: *Die Verkaufte Braut* (1932); *La Signora Di Tutti* (1934); *La Tendre Ennemie* (1936); *Caught* (1949); *The Reckless Moment* (1949)

Orry-Kelly, John

Along with his contemporary, **Edith Head**, Orry-Kelly was one of the greatest-ever costume designers for the cinema, being responsible for much of the Warners look during the 1930s and early 1940s. A master of period detail, Orry-Kelly was at home in both black and white and colour, and was most often associated with **Bette Davis**, although he designed costumes, at one time or another, for virtually every great star of Hollywood's Golden Era.

Other Key Films: Mervyn LeRoy's *I Am A Fugitive From A Chain Gang* (1932) and *Gold Diggers Of 1933* (1933); **William Wyler's** *Jezebel* (1938); **John Huston's** *The Maltese Falcon* (1941); **Michael Curtiz's** *Casablanca* (1942); Irving Rapper's *Now Voyager* (1942); **Frank Capra's** *Arsenic And Old Lace* (1944); Curtis Bernhardt's *A Stolen Life* (1946); **Vincente Minnelli's** *An American In Paris* (1951); **Billy Wilder's** *Some Like It Hot* (1959)

O'Sullivan, Maureen

O'Sullivan is now primarily remembered for being **John Farrow's** wife, Mia Farrow's mother and for wearing the miraculous side-split loincloth in **Jack Conway's** *Tarzan And His Mate* (1934) that has fed the fantasies of millions of young cinephilic schoolboys ever since. Following her marriage in 1936 she produced seven children, giving her, one would suppose, very little time for the pursuit of her acting career. She was excellent, however, as **Greer Garson's** nicest sister, Jane, in **Robert Z Leonard's** *Pride And Prejudice* (1940), a part typical of the role of sidekick, favourite sister and best friend that she honed throughout her early career.

Other Key Films: *Strange Interlude* (1932); *The Barretts Of Wimpole Street* (1934); *David Copperfield* (1935); *Anna Karenina* (1935); *A Day At The Races* (1936); *Tarzan Escapes* (1936); *Tarzan Finds A Son* (1939); *Tarzan's New York Adventure* (1942); *The Big Clock* (1948); *Where Danger Lives* (1950); *The Tall T* (1958)

Key Line: 'You Tarzan, me Jane.' [*Tarzan The Ape-Man*]

O'Toole, Peter

A good-looking hell-raiser and a passable, if wildly over-stylised actor, O'Toole carved a career of sorts during the 1960s on the back of his glamorous appearance and on his capacity for shouting his dialogue, somewhat along the lines of **Laurence Olivier's** rather more controlled shouting in *Henry V* (1945). O'Toole shouted his way through the part of T E Lawrence in **David Lean's** *Lawrence Of Arabia* (1962) and then continued shouting as Michael James in Clive Donner's *What's New Pussycat?* (1965), as King Henry II in Anthony Harvey's *The Lion In Winter* (1968), and as Jack, 14th Earl of Gurney, in Peter Medak's *The Ruling Class* (1972). Later, when he took to parodying himself in such films as Richard Rush's *The Stunt Man*

Johnny Weismuller
and Maureen
O'Sullivan in Tarzan
and His Mate,
directed by Cedric
Gibbons (1934).

*MGM/The Kobal
Collection*

(1980), one became almost nostalgic for the time when the shouting was real, and not put on, and by the time of Richard Benjamin's delightfully silly *My Favourite Year* (1982), one had begun to miss the devil-may-care O'Toole of the early days, and to regret the dilution of his often-inspired vamping. Is it a case of 'they don't make them like that anymore?' What does it matter? One turns to O'Toole's films with a sentimental if bemused attachment, just as one turns on the critics of certain of his stage performances with the words, 'a gentleman never shoots at a sitting target'.

Other Key Films: *Becket* (1962); *Lord Jim* (1965); *The Night Of The Generals* (1967); *Murphy's War* (1971); *Under Milk Wood* (1971); *Caligula* (1979); *The Last Emperor* (1987); *High Spirits* (1988); *King Ralph* (1991); *Fairytale: A True Story* (1997); *Phantoms* (1998); *The Manor* (1999); *The Final Curtain* (2001); *Bright Young Things* (2003); *Troy* (2004)

Key Line: 'I'm not an actor. I'm a movie star!' [*My Favourite Year*]

Outlaw, The: Howard Hughes's

The Outlaw (1943), beautifully shot by **Greg Toland**, was originally intended as a backdrop to **Jane Russell** and her extraordinary cleavage, but she hardly appears in it except to pout at the way Billy The Kid treats her. **Walter Huston** plays it brilliantly straight, as an icy and unpredictable Doc Holliday, while Thomas Mitchell, of all people, plays Pat Garrett, with more than a dash of his Gerald O'Hara in **Victor Fleming's** *Gone With The Wind* (1939). Jack Beutel, who is prettier even than Russell, despite lacking her womanly advantages, plays Billy The Kid as a bona fide New Mexican (which he wasn't), and with such a heady variation of mannerisms that some scenes, especially when taken with Huston's slow, steady, delivery, become so curiously fascinating that one is forced to keep on watching despite the utter absurdity of what is actually going on. Top marks must go to Hughes for daring to use a stock-in-trade porn shot in a major Hollywood vehicle – a close-up of Russell's face turns into a close-up of her mouth quite literally going down on the recumbent Beutel, although we are deprived of the actual detail, except in fade-to-black. The shot was so outré that filmmakers such as **Henri-Georges Clouzot** in *Quai Des Orfèvres* (1947) [see **Erotic Moments**] have been copying it ever since, showing that high-quality dementia can sometimes excel even itself in its unplanned and unintentional originality.

Ozu, Yasujiro

Ozu represented the heart of Japanese cinema – he watched the world and its people with unalloyed tenderness, recording their fears, their mistakes, the complications they as often as not foisted on themselves, with a rare and paradoxically objective sensitivity. There is no escape in Ozu-land, only acceptance of one's lot, coupled with a generous, if sometimes tentative, encouragement by one generation of another. His films were little known in the West until *Tokyo Story* (1953), but each is a miniature masterpiece, slow moving, sometimes discursive, always heartfelt. His usually static camera watches, records, but never judges – that is left to the viewer – and we find ourselves learning tolerance, during an Ozu film, just as we learn it from a film by **Robert Bresson**, or **Jean Renoir**. In his world, if there is to be no escape, then there must be reconciliation, accommodation, peace. It is a simple message, but can take a lifetime to understand. Ozu helps.

Other Key Films: *The Life Of An Office Worker* (1929); *I Was Born, But...* (1932); *A Tokyo Woman* (1933); *A Story Of Floating Weeds* (1934); *The Record Of A Tenement Gentleman* (1947); *A Hen In The Wind* (1948); *Late Spring* (1949); *Early Summer* (1951); *The Flavour Of Green Tea Over Rice* (1952); *Early Spring* (1956); *Twilight In Tokyo* (1958); *Equinox Flower* (1958); *Late Autumn* (1960); *The End Of Summer* (1961); *An Autumn Afternoon* (1962)

Pabst, G W

Outside film-buff circles Pabst is largely renowned for his extraordinary and wildly stylised *Pandora's Box* (1929), which introduced the ill-fated but infinitely fascinating **Louise Brooks** to international audiences. The film is still powerful, with its expressionistic sets, flowing camerawork and extremities of decadent passion, but Pabst's *Die Dreigroschenoper* [*The Threepenny Opera*] (1931) is the greater film, with its bizarre, nineteenth-century central character, played by the great Rudolf Forster, who gets closer to the heart of a Victorian pimp, both visually and through characterization, than any number of present-day actors, tied, as they so often are, by the bonds of social and political expedience.

Other Key Films: *Die Freudlose Gasse* (1925); *Geheimnisse Einer Seele* (1926); *Westfront 1918* (1930); *A Modern Hero* (1934); *Le Drame De Shanghai* (1938); *Das Bekenntnis Der Ina Kahr* (1954)

Pacino, Al

At his best he is one of the finest screen actors working in America today, using his face, eyes and body with a confidence born, one suspects, of despair, and his best parts, as Michael Corleone in **Francis Ford Coppola's** *The Godfather* (1972) and as vulnerable cop Frank Keller in Harold Becker's *Sea Of Love* (1989), reflect this. His recent form has been less impressive, and Martin Brest's *Scent Of A Woman* (1992) gave the impression that a lot of effort had been expended for little in the way of insight. His performance as Ricky Roma in James Foley's *Glengarry Glen Ross* (1992), on the other hand, was superb, and it was wonderful to see Pacino so confident and so enthusiastic in the self-directed *Looking For Richard* (1996), in which he indulges in a fascinating thespian trawl through the making of Shakespeare's *Richard III*. He is an actor who plays to his strengths, and most of his best film roles hover within scenting distance of the US Eastern Seaboard.

Other Key Films: *The Panic In Needle Park* (1971); *Scarecrow* (1973); *Serpico* (1973); *Dog Day Afternoon* (1975); *Bobby Deerfield* (1977); *Scarface* (1983); *Dick Tracy* (1990); *Carlito's Way* (1993); *Heat* (1995); *Donnie Brasco* (1997); *Any Given Sunday* (1999); *Chinese Coffee* (2000) [also dir.]; *Insomnia* (2002); *The Recruit* (2003); *The Merchant Of Venice* (2004); *88 Minutes* (2006)

Pakula, Alan J

A curious hybrid in Hollywood terms, Pakula started out as a producer then turned to directing when he was more than forty. Occasionally misled by his own intelligence, Pakula directed two of the best thrillers of the 1970s – *The Parallax View* (1974) and *All The President's Men* (1976) – both of which were marred by an overly self-conscious use of film trickery to obtain their effects (form over substance, if you like). That said, his 1982 film of William Styron's *Sophie's Choice* worked on a number of interesting levels, and *Presumed Innocent* (1990) was a more than professional stab at that most elusive of rogue elephants, an international best-seller. Pakula was killed, on 19 November 1998, when a metal pipe thrown up by another vehicle smashed through the windscreen of his car. He left a sadly curtailed legacy, always fascinating, but at the same time curiously unengaging, as if its perpetrator had been conducting, not a film career, exactly, but more a lengthy experiment into the parameters of credulity.

Other Key Films: *Klute* (1971); *Comes A Horseman* (1978); *Rollover* (1981); *Orphans* (1987); *The Pelican Brief* (1993); *The Devil's Own* (1997)

Palance, Jack

Palance was destined never to be offered anything but tough guy roles after his face was severely burned during the Second World War, but he successfully negotiated his way through this unwelcome rite of passage (and that of being a professional heavyweight boxer – he fought under the name Jack Brazzo) to prove himself worthy of stronger parts, thanks to the anguished depth he managed to give to roles that other, lesser actors, would simply have coasted through. Following his sinister but profound villain, Wilson, in **George Stevens's** *Shane* (1953), Palance surprised every-one with his tormented performance as neurotic actor, Charles Castle, in **Robert Aldrich's** *The Big Knife* (1955), and his excellent turn as Jeremiah 'Jerry' Prokosch, in **Jean-Luc Godard's** *Le Mépris* [*Contempt*] (1963). He made a particularly welcome comeback as amorous painter Rudi Cox in Percy Adlon's *Bagdad Café* (1988).

Other Key Films: *Panic In The Streets* (1950); *Sudden Fear* (1952); *I Died A Thousand Times* (1955); *Torture Garden* (1967); *The Professionals* (1966); *The Horsemen* (1971);

City Slickers (1991); *Salmonberries* (1992); *Tombstone* (1993); *Cops & Robbersons* (1994); *Treasure Island* (1999)

Paltrow, Gwyneth

A skilful and attractive actress and something of a mistress of accent and vocal nuance, Paltrow has constructed her early career with care, and is now justifiably enjoying its fruits. Douglas McGrath's *Emma* (1996) ensured international interest in her, and her recent performances in John Madden's *Shakespeare In Love* (1998), **Anthony Minghella's** *The Talented Mr. Ripley* (1999), and Christine Jeffs's *Sylvia* (2003), have cemented her reputation as a dependable and talented leading lady. Whether she has the long-term staying power of a **Jessica Lange**, a **Michelle Pfeiffer** or a **Meryl Streep** remains to be seen.

Other Key Films: *Hook* (1991); *Flesh And Bone* (1993); *Malice* (1993); *Mrs Parker And The Vicious Circle* (1994); *Jefferson In Paris* (1995); *Seven* (1995); *Great Expectations* (1998); *Sliding Doors* (1998); *Duets* (2000); *Bounce* (2000); *Possession* (2002); *Sky Captain And The World Of Tomorrow* (2004); *Proof* (2005); *Infamous* (2006)

Gwyneth Paltrow and Jude Law in The Talented Mr Ripley, directed by Anthony Minghella (1999).

Paramount/Miramax/The Kobal Collection/Phil Bray

Parker, Alan

Something of a self-proclaimed iconoclast of British cinema, Parker has actually made a sequence of very conventional films very well, beginning with his debut success,

Bugsy Malone (1976), a film which still has the capacity to please and to entertain. His best film is *Mississippi Burning* (1988), in which he investigated the roots of racism, although a cult has formed around *Midnight Express* (1978), which provided Parker with that initial, precious key to the Hollywood studio restrooms. *The Commitments* (1991), about a talented Irish band doing uncannily good cover versions of Otis Redding songs, gave his career a much needed and well-deserved mid-flow boost – it's just a bit of shame he chose *The Road To Wellville* (1994) to follow it up with. His *Life Of David Gale* (2003), however, was a serially underrated and most pleasant surprise.

Other Key Films: *Fame* (1980); *Shoot The Moon* (1981); *Pink Floyd – The Wall* (1982); *Birdy* (1985); *Angel Heart* (1987); *The Road To Wellville* (1994); *Evita* (1996); *Angela's Ashes* (1999)

Pasolini, Pier Paolo

A multi-talented iconoclast, Pasolini delighted in shocking the Italian bourgeois church and laity from its customary inertia. A master of both the beautiful and the grotesque, Pasolini lived as he died, violently and without remorse, and in *Accatone!* (1961), *Theorem* (1968) and *Pigsty* (1969) he genuinely took the tradition of Italian neo-realist cinema a step further than it had ever intended to go. An extreme Marxist in his political views, Pasolini was, paradoxically perhaps, deeply religious, although his personal dogma was definitely not that of his baptismal Catholic Church. The victim of many censorship attempts while he was alive, Pasolini met his death at the hands of a seventeen-year-old youth who claimed that the maestro had importuned him, an act that only added to the mystique that still surrounds this bizarre and talented man.

Other Key Films: *Mama Roma* (1962); *The Gospel According To St Matthew* (1964); *Oedipus Rex* (1967); *The Decameron* (1970); *Medea* (1970); *The Canterbury Tales* (1971); *The Arabian Nights* (1974); *Salo – The 120 Days Of Sodom* (1975); *La Ricotta* (1976)

Passer, Ivan

Yet another talented European director and screenwriter who, despite one or two successes, has seemingly been humbled by the Hollywood machine. Passer had it within him to be a top-rank director, given the promise that he showed with his two early Czechoslovakian films, *A Boring Afternoon* (1965) and *Intimate Lightning* (1965), and with his scripts for **Milos Forman**. His talent seemed born out by his best US film to date, the outstanding *Cutter's Way* [original title *Cutter And Bone*] (1981), which used **Jeff Bridges**, John Heard and Lisa Eichhorn in ways that they must only dream of now, lost as they are in the commercial mainstream or on its peripheries. What happened? Who knows? Hollywood (whatever that may be) is not renowned for either its sensitivity or its subtlety when dealing with artists who concentrate on character and atmosphere over plot. God knows what they would have made of a genius such as **Jean Renoir** today – he, like Passer, would probably have sunk without critical trace, hoist by his inability to perfect the elusive, nay ineffable, art of the two-minute pitch.

Other Key Films: *Law And Disorder* (1974); *Crime And Passion* (1976); *Silver Bears* (1978); *Creator* (1985); *Haunted Summer* (1988); *The Wishing Tree* (1999); *Nomad* (2004)

Peck, Gregory

Peck often gave the impression of being something of a goody-goody, a mix between a school headmaster and a lay preacher, and even when he went counter to that image, there was still always something cosy in the evil he portrayed, as with Lewt, his lusty cowboy, in **King Vidor's** wildly over-the-top *Duel In The Sun* (1946). Even when he kissed a girl, one half expected Peck to step back and mildly berate her for her forwardness, but this is not to say that he was in any way a bad actor, for Peck occasionally transcended even his own saintly image and turned in excellent performances, particularly as Atticus Finch, the liberal hayseed lawyer in Robert Mulligan's *To Kill A Mockingbird* (1963), and as the embattled husband and father, Sam Bowden, in J Lee Thompson's *Cape Fear* (1961). Having outlasted virtually all his contemporaries, Peck's films remain as testimony to the cautiously burgeoning liberal conscience of 1940s and 1950s Hollywood.

Other Key Films: *Days Of Glory* (1944); *Spellbound* (1945); *The Yearling* (1946); *The Paradine Case* (1947); *Twelve O'Clock High* (1949); *Captain Horatio Hornblower* (1951); *The Snows Of Kilimanjaro* (1952); *Roman Holiday* (1953); *The Purple Plain* (1955); *Moby Dick* (1956); *On The Beach* (1959); *Mirage* (1965); *Arabesque* (1966); *I Walk The Line* (1970); *Billy Two Hats* (1973); *The Omen* (1976); *MacArthur* (1977); *Boys From Brazil* (1978); *Old Gringo* (1989); *Cape Fear* (1991)

Key Line: 'If you have to tell them who you are, you aren't anybody.' [Peck on celebrity]

Peckinpah, Sam

Always larger than life, Peckinpah was a man's man in what was rapidly becoming (to his eyes at least) a feminised world. His heroes reflect himself – in other words they are men who have outstayed the welcome of their own times, and indulge in 'beserker' fits of suicidal bravura in a (usually) vain effort to reverse the tide. *Ride The High Country* (1962), in which he paired ageing **Western** star **Randolph Scott** with **Joel McCrea**, and *The Wild Bunch* (1969), in which modern life saw off **William Holden** and tamed **Robert Ryan**, are cases in point, but his most complex work (in its complete form) was *Pat Garrett And Billy The Kid* (1973), in which Peckinpah appeared to suggest that nothing, despite his earlier protestations, was forever. Some of his later films slipped into self-parody, but *Junior Bonner* (1972), in which Peckinpah transferred some of his real fear of change onto **Steve McQueen's** stonily bewildered face, was very fine indeed.

Other Key Films: *Major Dundee* (1965); *The Ballad Of Cable Hogue* (1970); *Straw Dogs* (1971); *The Getaway* (1972); *Bring Me The Head Of Alfredo Garcia* (1974); *The Killer Elite* (1975); *Cross Of Iron* (1977); *The Osterman Weekend* (1983)

Key Line: 'I liked what I heard he was about – a guy who gave everybody a lot of shit and stood his ground...frankly, I never saw him behave badly.' [Screenwriter Waylon Green, who co-scripted *The Wild Bunch* (1969), on the allegedly 'mercurial' Peckinpah]

Penn, Arthur

Penn is the classic example of a fine director touching his peak, wobbling a little, re-finding himself, and then going completely off the boil. He touched commercial heaven with *Bonnie And Clyde* (1967), surpassed it with *Little Big Man* (1970), which was a justifiable critical and commercial success and which remains in the memory long after the hype has been forgotten, and then, apart from two or three well-crafted thrillers, including the underrated *Night Moves* (1975), made nothing of any real consequence ever again. There are too few directors of Penn's particular talent around today and it is something of a tragedy that either Hollywood, or the sum of his own particular idiosyncrasies, has let him down.

Other Key Films: *The Left-Handed Gun* (1958); *The Miracle Worker* (1962); *Mickey One* (1965); *The Chase* (1966); *Alice's Restaurant* (1969); *The Missouri Breaks* (1976); *Target* (1985); *Penn & Teller Get Killed* (1988)

Penn, Sean

Only three years older than **Brad Pitt** and four years older than **Johnny Depp**, Penn seems somehow of a different generation; more of a flashback to the late 1940s **John Garfield** and the early 1950s **Marlon Brando** than the modern **Tom Cruise**-like hominid. A fervid, highly-strung brawler, Penn is also a remarkably talented actor and director whose own *The Indian Runner* (1991) was disastrously underrated on its release. Penn roused himself from a premature retirement to script and direct his friend **Jack Nicholson** in *The Crossing Guard* (1995), only to find this interesting movie meeting the same fate as its predecessor. Penn is a talented and conscientious actor, and he was as outstanding as death-row victim, Matthew Poncelet, in **Tim Robbins's** unsentimental *Dead Man Walking* (1995), as he was in **Oliver Stone's** unjustly maligned *U-Turn* (1997). His recent performances as vainglorious jazz guitarist, Emmet Ray, in **Woody Allen's** *Sweet And Lowdown* (1999) and as tormented bereaved father Jimmy Markum in **Clint Eastwood's** *Mystic River* (2003), can only add to his reputation as Hollywood's most magnetically problematic son.

Other Key Films: *Taps* (1981); *The Falcon And The Snowman* (1985); *At Close Range* (1986); *Colors* (1988); *Casualties Of War* (1989); *State Of Grace* (1990); *Carlito's Way* (1993); *The Thin Red Line* (1998); *Up At The Villa* (2000); *Before Night Falls* (2000); *The Weight Of Water* (2000); *The Pledge* [dir.] (2001); *I Am Sam* (2001); *21 Grams* (2003); *The Assassination Of Richard Nixon* (2004); *The Interpreter* (2005); *All The King's Men* (2006)

Key Line: 'Acting is the girl who's unattractive to me. I don't enjoy it. Ever.' [Penn on acting]

Périnal, Georges

Périnal was poached from his native France by Britain's **Alexander Korda** on the strength of his extraordinary body of work for **René Clair**, and for his one-off triumph with **Jean Cocteau** on *Le Sang D'Un Poète* (1931). Périnal went on to photograph Korda's *The Private Life Of Henry VIII* (1933), Paul Czinner's *Catherine The Great* (1934), Korda's exquisite *Rembrandt* (1936), the utterly sublime multi-directed *The Thief Of Bagdad* (1940), and **Michael Powell** and Emeric Pressburger's *The Life And Death Of Colonel Blimp* (1943). A magnificent career, particularly when seen in conjunction with his early sequence of films for Clair, which included *Under The Roofs Of Paris* (1930) and *Le Million* (1931), after which Clair, too, was poached by Korda, for *The Ghost Goes West* (1936), a film coincidentally photographed by the excellent Harold Rossen, and not Périnal, for a change.

Other Key Films: Zoltan Korda's *The Four Feathers* (1939); **Carol Reed's** *The Fallen Idol* (1948); **Otto Preminger's** *Bonjour Tristesse* (1958)

Perkins, Anthony

An intense, nervous and rather mannered actor, Perkins had his most famous incarnation as Norman Bates, in **Alfred Hitchcock's** *Psycho* (1960), which both made his reputation and at the same time destroyed him for the more conventional roles to which his talents might better have suited him. Perkins never wholly shook off the gawky, hesitant adolescent that he played in so many of his earlier films, and his best performance came, surprisingly, not in the cinema, but on television, as a superb Javert in Victor Hugo's *Les Misérables* (1978).

Other Key Films: *Friendly Persuasion* (1956); *Fear Strikes Out* (1958); *The Matchmaker* (1958); *Tall Story* (1960); *The Trial* (1963); *The Champagne Murders* (1966); *Ten Days' Wonder* (1971); *Pretty Poison* (1968); *Crimes Of Passion* (1984)

Key Line: 'A boy's best friend is his mother.' [*Psycho*]

Petersen, Wolfgang

A German art-film director who has gradually moved across to the US mainstream while nevertheless managing to keep certain key elements of his early sensitivity intact, Petersen wowed international audiences with *Das Boot* (1981), his claustrophobic tale of life aboard a German submarine during the Second World War, and followed up with the effective and pleasantly offbeat thriller *Shattered* (1991). His **Clint Eastwood** movie, *In The Line Of Fire* (1993), further confirmed his capacity for reinvention, but *Air Force One* (1997), with **Harrison Ford**, was as grotesque as it was conventional, and one fancies that Petersen, while cheerfully pocketing the loot, must secretly have hated kowtowing to the twin exigencies of both star and blockbusting potential. He looked much more comfortable directing **George Clooney** in *The Perfect Storm* (2000), where his sea skills honed on (or in) *Das Boot* were once more called into play, and he made a surprising and probably rather gratifying success of *Troy* (2004).

Other Key Films: *Einer Von Uns Beiden* (1973); *Die Konsequenz* (1977); *Schwarz Und Weiss Wie Tage Und Nächte* (1978); *The Neverending Story* (1984); *Enemy Mine* (1985); *Outbreak* (1995); *Poseidon* (2006)

Pfeiffer, Michelle

Despite her beauty (welcome distraction though it is) and despite a recent spate of rather worthy roles, Pfeiffer remains a serious contender for best mainstream actress of the 1980s and early 1990s, with her string of first-rate performances in such films as John Landis's *Into The Night* (1985), **George Miller's** *The Witches Of Eastwick* (1987), **Jonathan Demme's** *Married To The Mob* (1988), **Stephen Frears's** *Dangerous Liaisons* (1988) and Steve Kloves's *The Fabulous Baker Boys* (1989). This magical run continued with **Fred Schepisi's** *The Russia House* (1990), Jonathan Kaplan's *Love Field* (1992), **Martin Scorsese's** *The Age Of Innocence* (1993) and **Mike Nichols's** *Wolf* (1994) – few actresses in recent years, without the safe studio structure of the 1930s and 1940s behind them, can have managed their careers and chosen their vehicles so well.

Other Key Films: *Scarface* (1983); *Ladyhawke* (1985); *Tequila Sunrise* (1988); *Frankie And Johnny* (1991); *Batman Returns* (1992); *Up Close And Personal* (1996); *A Thousand Acres* (1997); *The Deep End Of The Ocean* (1999); *What Lies Beneath* (2000); *I Am Sam* (2001)

Key Line: 'You can have it all, but you can't do it all.' [Pfeiffer on life]

Philipe, Gérard

Dead from heart failure at the age of thirty-six, Philipe crammed a great deal of life into his fifteen-year screen career, becoming, in that short time, France's most popular romantic lead and one of the most successful stage actors of his generation. He managed that peculiarly French trick of mixing commercial nous with critical acuity and making a success of them both, and his capacity for plain-speaking leavened with tenderness and a melancholia that seemed in some way to foreshadow his early death, ensures him perpetual cult status with enlightened audiences. As happy in swashbuckling roles [Christian-Jaque's *Fanfan La Tulipe* (1952)] as he was in romantic comedy [**René Clair's** *Les Belles De Nuit* (1952)], Philipe's death in 1959 spans the exact crossover point between the old guard and the French **New Wave**.

Key Films: *L'Idiot* (1946); *Le Diable Au Corps* (1946); *La Chartreuse De Parme* (1947); *Une Si Jolie Petite Plage* (1948); *Souvenirs Perdus* (1949); *La Ronde* (1950); *La Beauté Du Diable* (1950); *Juliette Ou La Clé Des Songes* (1951); *Knave Of Hearts* (1954); *Le Rouge Et Le Noir* (1954); *Le Joueur* (1958); *Les Liaisons Dangereuses* (1959)

Gerard Philipe and Jeanne Valerie in Les Liaisons Dangereuses (Dangerous Liaisons), directed by Roger Vadim (1959).

Films Marceau/The Kobal Collection

Pialat, Maurice

One of the foremost French directors of his generation, Pialat brings a naturalistic painter's eye to his film work, most notably in *Loulou* (1980), in which yuppie **Isabelle Huppert** and butch **Gérard Depardieu** ignite chemically and sexually (if not intellectually), and *A Nos Amours* (1983), a paean to adult/teenage misunderstandings. He won the Cannes Palme D'Or for *Sous Le Soleil De Satan* (1987), a brooding, almost **Bressonian** exercise in misplaced spirituality, and racked up a further success with *Van Gogh* (1991), in which he endeavoured to come to terms with the final few months of Vincent Van Gogh's extraordinary life, daringly using Jacques Dutronc, a French pop star, in the title role – a risk, incidentally, that paid off handsomely.

Other Key Films: *L'Enfance Nue* (1968); *La Gueule Ouverte* (1974); *Passe Ton Bac D'Abord* (1979); *Police* (1985); *Le Garçu* (1996)

Piccoli, Michel

Piccoli is French cinema's sophisticated Mr Sardonicus, forever taken aback by the callowness and idiocy of his fellow man, then shrugging his shoulders at his inability to do anything about it. He spans, at his best, both the avant-garde and the commercial mainstream in a way that few American actors can ever aspire to, and one relishes his powerful and often anarchical screen presence in such films as **Jean-Luc Godard's** *Le Mépris* [*Contempt*] (1963), **Luis Buñuel's** *Belle De Jour* (1967), Marco Ferreri's *La Grande Bouffe* (1973), and, more recently, as the simple, almost saintly Milou, in **Louis Malle's** *Milou En Mai* (1989).

Other Key Films: *Le Doulos* (1963); *Diary Of A Chambermaid* (1964); *Les Demoiselles De Rochefort* (1967); *The Discreet Charm Of The Bourgeoisie* (1972); *Atlantic City* (1980); *La Nuit De Varennes* (1982); *Viva La Vie* (1985); *Death In A French Garden* (1985); *La Belle Noiseuse* (1991); *Bête De Scène* (1994); *Tykho Moon* (1997); *Rien Sur Robert* (1999); *Tout Va Bien, On S'En Va* (2000); *Je Rentre À La Maison* (2001); *Espelo Mágico* (2005); *Belle Toujours* (2006)

Brigitte Bardot and Michel Piccoli in Le Mepris (Contempt), directed by Jean-Luc Godard (1963).

Rome Paris Films/The Kobal Collection

Pickford, Mary

Known as 'America's Sweetheart', Pickford was, in reality, a tough cookie who knew how to cut a good deal with the studio bosses. She was still playing little girls with ringlets in her late twenties, in Marshall Neilan's *Daddy Long Legs* (1919) and Paul Powell's *Pollyanna* (1920), because that's what the public wanted. Together with **D W Griffith**, **Charlie Chaplin** and **Douglas Fairbanks Sr.** she formed United Artists in 1919. Already hugely wealthy, she married Fairbanks in 1920 and built Pickfair, their exotic mansion in Beverly Hills, in which they reigned together in state as king and queen of silent Hollywood. The coming of sound, twinned with the shearing of her golden locks, finally put paid to Pickford's screen career, but she lived on, occasionally appearing on radio, occasionally bringing out a book of memoirs, something of a belated grand dame of cinema, until her death in 1979.

Other Key Films: *In Old Kentucky* (1909); *The Little Teacher* (1910); *Tess of the Storm Country* (1913); *Rebecca of Sunnybrook Farm* (1917); *A Romance Of The Redwoods* (1917); *Stella Maris* (1918); *Little Lord Fauntleroy* (1921); *Rosita* (1923); *The Gaucho* (1927); *The Taming Of The Shrew* (1929); *Kiki* (1931)

228

Pitt, Brad

Along with **Johnny Depp**, Pitt has risen steadily to the top of his generation of actors, proving that he is as discriminating in his choice of parts as he is ambitious in his eventual intentions. He made his first international mark at the age of twenty-eight, in **Ridley Scott's** *Thelma And Louise* (1991), in which he played J D (**James Dean**?), a capricious and venal drifter who nevertheless gives Geena Davis's Thelma the best sex of her life. He followed this breakthrough, however, with a rather moribund turn as Paul MacClean in **Robert Redford's** *A River Runs Through It* (1992). He then resurrected himself with Edward Zwick's *Legends Of The Fall* (1994) [based on a brilliant Jim Harrison novella] in which he gave an almost Dean-like cast to his performance as Tristan Ludlow. David Fincher's recent *Fight Club* (1999), together with Guy Ritchie's *Snatch* (2000), Gore Verbinski's *The Mexican* (2001), and **Wolfgang Petersen's** *Troy* (2004) have certainly done no harm to his bankability after the box-office fiasco of Martin Brest's *Meet Joe Black* (1998).

Other Key Films: *Across The Tracks* (1991); *Johnny Suede* (1991); *Kalifornia* (1993); *True Romance* (1993); *Seven* (1995); *Twelve Monkeys* (1995); *Sleepers* (1996); *The Devil's Own* (1997); *The Spy Game* (2001); *Ocean's Eleven* (2001); *Ocean's Twelve* (2004); *Mr & Mrs Smith* (2005); *Babel* (2006)

Pleasence, Donald

Pleasence could play sinister and he could play kind, but sinister brought in the money, and Pleasence made a virtue of his myopic gaze and his faculty for turning the guilty sweats on or off at will in a long sequence of films from the late 1950s to his death in 1995, amongst which Clive Donner's *The Caretaker* (1964), **Roman Polanski's** *Cul-De-Sac* (1966) and Delbert Mann's *Kidnapped* (1971) (Pleasence's performance, and not the film) stand out. Latterly, Pleasence became something of a *rentier* in a succession of movies based on the characters from **John Carpenter's** massively successful *Halloween* (1978-1995), but at his best, he was one of the most subtle screen actors of his generation, whose greatest skill lay in his capacity to play common men made briefly uncommon by the events surrounding them. The best example of this came in the BBC TV series based on Anthony Trollope's *Barchester Chronicles* (1982), in which Pleasence brilliantly incarnated the near-saintly Septimus Harding.

Other Key Films: *The Beachcomber* (1954); *1984* (1956); *Sons And Lovers* (1960); *The Hands Of Orlac* (1961); *Dr. Crippen* (1963); *Maniac* (1964); *Eye Of The Devil* (1967); *The Eagle Has Landed* (1976); *Dracula* (1979); *Escape From New York* (1981); *Shadows And Fog* (1992)

Plummer, Christopher

Plummer is the **Peter Finch** of his generation, a fine screen actor who has never quite enjoyed the superstar success that his skills and his talents should have warranted. Was it because of his looks, which were pleasant, though unconventional? Or was it because, like **Orson Welles** and **Charlton Heston**, he was a King-actor, unable to play common men with any real degree of verisimilitude? Whatever the case, in his best performances he shows a rare integrity and a total commitment to the cinema, and one remembers him fondly as the young schoolteacher in **Nicholas Ray's** *Wind Across The Everglades* (1958), as the squeaky-voiced Emperor Atahualpa in Irving Lerner's *The Royal Hunt Of The Sun* (1969), and as the aristocratic, worldly-wise, indeed rather gentle Duke of Wellington, in Sergei Bondarchuk's *Waterloo* (1970).

Other Key Films: *The Sound Of Music* (1965); *The Night Of The Generals* (1967); *The Man Who Would Be King* (1975); *The Disappearance* (1977); *Murder By Decree* (1978); *The Silent Partner* (1978); *Somewhere In Time* (1980); *Eyewitness* (1981); *Wolf* (1994); *12 Monkeys* (1995); *Dolores Claiborne* (1995); *Black Heart* (1998); *The Dinosaur Hunter* (2000); *A Beautiful Mind* (2001); *Alexander* (2004); *Must Love Dogs* (2005); *Syriana* (2005); *The New World* (2005); *Inside Man* (2006)

Poetic Realism

Originally a uniquely French genre, but later taken up and transmogrified into a particularly American form of heightened realism by directors such as **Nicholas Ray** in *They Live By Night* (1949) and **Charles Laughton** in *Night Of The Hunter* (1955), poetic realism combined a consuming interest in everyday life and ordinary people with an intensified, often poeticised dialogue that could, on occasion, seem deliriously opposed to the dramatic events unfolding on the screen. Notable films in the genre include **Jean Renoir's** *Le Crime De M. Lange* (1935), *Les Bas-Fonds* (1936), *La Grande Illusion* (1937) and *La Règle Du Jeu* (1939), **Julien Duvivier's** *Pépé Le Moko* (1937), and **Marcel Carné's** *Quai Des Brumes* (1938), the last two of which benefited from scripts by **Henri Jeanson** and **Jacques Prévert** respectively (Prévert also wrote *Le Crime De M. Lange*) – who between them constituted the two greatest literary exponents of the poetic realism style. There was always a strong element of despair in the original stories (an aspect later taken up by a succession of *film noir* directors in the United States), but this despair was mitigated by an existential desire to live for the moment, to take happiness, however brief it might be, and wring as much juice from it as possible before fate, or the machinations of an antagonistic state machine, could snatch it away.

Other Key Films: Pierre Chenal's *La Rue Sans Nom* (1933) and *Le Dernier Tournant* (1939); Julien Duvivier's *La Bandera* (1935) and *Un Carnet De Bal* (1937); Jean Grémillon's *Gueule D'Amour* (1937) and *Remorques* (1939); Marcel Carné's *Jenny* (1936), *Hôtel Du Nord* (1938), *Le Jour Se Lève* (1939) and *Les Visiteurs Du Soir* (1945); Albert Valentin's *L'Entraîneuse* (1938); Christian-Jaque's *Boule De Suif* (1945)

Poitier, Sidney

Poitier was the first mainstream actor to appeal, on equal terms, to both black and white audiences. This remarkable crossover, which first manifested itself in **Joseph L Mankiewicz's** *No Way Out* (1950) and culminated in Stanley Kramer's *The Defiant Ones* (1958), paved the way for the gradual liberalisation of a screen that has, to this day, still not reached the stage of being totally colour-blind. Such a thing *is* possible, however, despite the carping of cynics, for it already exists in Cuba and Brazil, and should it ever be achieved in the United States and Western Europe, Poitier's name deserves to go high on the roll of honour, for he afforded the beginnings of public dignity to an enforced underclass, at a time when the night seemed at its longest.

Other Key Films: *Cry The Beloved Country* (1952); *Red Ball Express* (1952); *The Blackboard Jungle* (1955); *Edge Of The City* (1958); *Porgy And Bess* (1960); *A Raisin In The Sun* (1961); *Paris Blues* (1961); *In The Heat Of The Night* (1967); *Sneakers* (1992); *The Jackal* (1997)

Polanski, Roman

Polanski steadfastly maintains that his childhood in the Cracow ghetto, the gassing of his mother at Auschwitz, the murder of his pregnant wife by drug-crazed drop-outs, and his belated flight from America to avoid a further prison term for his alleged rape of a thirteen-year-old girl at **Jack Nicholson's** house, have nothing whatsoever to do with the underlying feeling of alienation and hostility that permeates most of his films. And he may be right. He is an intelligent, self-possessed man, who has survived, apparently intact, horrors that would have crippled lesser men, and it seems patronising in the extreme not to listen to him (as Mark Cousins refused to do in an interview Polanski granted to the BBC in 2001). A graduate of the Lodz Film School, Polanski has always been a master of many genres, and he proved this by following the cult success of the art-house *Repulsion* (1965) with *Rosemary's Baby* (1968), one of the most genuinely frightening of all horror films, and *Chinatown* (1974), a masterpiece of enlightened filmmaking and the greatest of all latter-day *film noirs*. *Death And The Maiden* (1994) marked a fine return to his old form, and this was followed by critical plaudits for *The Pianist* (2002), proving that, despite his amused variability, Polanski still remains a master of the medium he respects and loves so much.

Other Key Films: *Knife In The Water* (1962); *Cul-De-Sac* (1966); *Dance Of The Vampires* (1967); *Macbeth* (1971); *The Tenant* (1976); *Tess* (1979); *Frantic* (1988); *Bitter Moon* (1992); *The Ninth Gate* (1999); *Oliver Twist* (2005)

Polglase, Van Nest

Polglase's name is so achingly familiar from its appearance on so many Golden Age Of Hollywood credit and title rolls, that it comes as something of a surprise to discover that most people have no clear idea what he did. Well, Polglase was the foremost art director and production designer of his generation, and was responsible for the overall look of the sets on such ground-breaking movies as **Merian C Cooper** and Ernest Schoedsack's *King Kong* (1933), **John Ford's** *The Lost Patrol* (1934) and *The Informer* (1935), **William Dieterle's** *The Hunchback Of Notre Dame* (1939), **Orson Welles's** *Citizen Kane* (1941), and **Charles Vidor's** *Gilda* (1946). Quite a record and, despite the drinking problems which caused his untimely dismissal from RKO, quite a man.

Other Key Films: George Cukor's *Little Women* (1933); Thornton Freeland's *Flying Down To Rio* (1933); **George Stevens's** *Gunga Din* (1939); **Alfred Hitchcock's** *Suspicion* (1942)

Best **Political/Satirical Films**

Lindsay Anderson's *If...* (1969); Clarence Brown's *Intruder In The Dust* (1949); **Frank Capra's** *Mr Smith Goes To Washington* (1939); **Constantin Costa-Gavras's** *Z* (1969); **Sergei Eisenstein's** *Ivan The Terrible Parts 1 & 2* (1943-1945); **Federico Fellini's** *La Dolce Vita* (1960); **John Ford's** *The Grapes Of Wrath* (1940) and *Sergeant Rutledge* (1960); **Jean-Luc Godard's** *Pierrot Le Fou* (1965); **Stanley Kubrick's** *A Clockwork Orange* (1971); Gregory La Cava's *Gabriel Over The White House* (1933); **Fritz Lang's** *While The City Sleeps* (1955); **Mike Leigh's** *Secrets And Lies* (1996); **Ken Loach's** *Raining Stones* (1993); **Sydney Pollack's** *They Shoot Horses, Don't They?* (1969); **Gillo Pontecorvo's** *The Battle Of Algiers* (1966); **Leni Riefenstahl's** *Triumph Of The Will* (1936); **Tony Richardson's** *The Loneliness Of The Long-Distance Runner* (1962); **Volker Schlöndorff's** *The Tin Drum* (1979); Lee Tamahori's *Once Were Warriors* (1994); **Jean Vigo's** *Zéro De Conduite* (1933); **Luchino Visconti's** *The Leopard* (1963); **Peter Weir's** *The Year Of Living Dangerously* (1982); **William Wellman's** *Nothing Sacred* (1937)

Pollack, Sidney

Pollack likes to work regularly with his actors, initially with **Burt Lancaster** (who acted as something of a mentor before his death in 1994), and later with **Robert Redford**, whom he directed in, amongst others, *This Property Is Condemned* (1966), *Jeremiah Johnson* (1973), *The Way We Were* (1975) and *Out Of Africa* (1985). An ambitious director who can nevertheless miss the mark badly, as in *Havana* (1990), Pollack may have resuscitated **Dustin Hoffman's** career with *Tootsie* (1982), but his best film is still *The Yakuza* (1975), in which a suitably embittered **Robert Mitchum** literally lights up the screen as private eye Harry Kilmer. A rather good occasional actor, Pollack appeared (very effectively) in **Stanley Kubrick's** final film, *Eyes Wide Shut* (1999).

Other Key Films: *The Scalphunters* (1968); *They Shoot Horses, Don't They?* (1968); *Three Days Of The Condor* (1973); *Bobby Deerfield* (1977); *The Electric Horseman* (1979); *Absence Of Malice* (1981); *The Firm* (1993); *Sabrina* (1995); *Random Hearts* (1999); *The Interpreter* (2005)

Pontecorvo, Gillo

Pontecorvo, a leading anti-Fascist partisan in Italy during the Second World War, deserves to be remembered for more than merely his extraordinary *The Battle Of Algiers* (1966), a film which still retains its capacity to shock with the audacity of its criticism of the monolithic French state. Pontecorvo was always something more than a left-wing propagandist, and his understanding of the humanity and vulnerability of even his enemies, as shown in the much underrated *Quemada!* (1969), gave added power to his attacks on Imperialism and on the men and women in whose vested interest many of its horrors were undertaken.

Other Key Films: *The Long Blue Road* (1958); *Kapò* (1960); *The Tunnel* (1979); *Ogro* (1979); *I Corti Italiani* [segment only] (1997)

Powell, Dick

Powell started his career in the early 1930s as a light tenor crooner in **Busby Berkeley's** sexy series of Gold Diggers musicals, and continued it into the 1940s and 50s as the often beaten-up protagonist of a convincing sequence of *film noir* thrillers. He played **Philip Marlowe** in *Murder My Sweet* (1944) [a.k.a. *Farewell My Lovely*], and convincingly took on the roles of driven men in **Edward Dmytryk's** *Cornered* (1945) and André de Toth's *The Pitfall* (1948). In 1953 he directed his own tough little 'nuclear threat' B-movie thriller, *Split Second*.

Other Key Films: *42nd Street* (1933); *Gold Diggers Of 33* (1933); *Dames* (1934); *A Midsummer Night's Dream* (1935); *Johnny O'Clock* (1947); *Station West* (1948); *The Bad And The Beautiful* (1952); [and as director] *The Enemy Below* (1958) and *The Hunters* (1958)

Key Line: 'I'm flattered you want me and bitter you got me.' [**Vincente Minnelli's** *The Bad And The Beautiful*]

Powell, Michael

The Michael Powell and Emeric Pressburger directing/writing team, under their trade name of The Archers, can now be seen, with the convenient hindsight of time, to have been almost single-handedly responsible for the post-war revival of quality British Cinema. Cult icons to a younger generation of filmmakers in America (including **Steven Spielberg** and **Martin Scorsese**) this strange and talented duo were responsible for *The Life And Death Of Colonel Blimp* (1943), the exquisitely quirky *I Know Where I'm Going* (1945), and the brilliantly designed *Black Narcissus* (1947). Their masterpiece was *A Matter Of Life And Death* (1946), in which heaven, and the endless staircase leading to it, was paradoxically filmed in black and white, while the earth, with all its emotional frailty, appeared in colour. Following the dissolution of their partnership in 1956, Powell went on to direct the remarkable *Peeping Tom* (1960), a film which so outraged the censors with its graphic yet sympathetic portrayal of a voyeuristically obsessed serial killer, that it effectively ended this extraordinary man's career.

Other Key Films: *49th Parallel* (1941); *A Canterbury Tale* (1944); *The Red Shoes* (1948); *The Small Back Room* (1949); *Gone To Earth* (1950); *Tales Of Hoffman* (1952); *The Battle Of The River Plate* (1956); *Ill Met By Moonlight* (1958); *Age Of Consent* (1969)

Powell, William

Powell was **Dashiell Hammett's** suave Nick Charles (wrongly known as the Thin Man – that was someone else in the movie), with sexy **Myrna Loy** as his Nora, in the long-running series of comedy thrillers which began with W S Van Dyke II's *The Thin Man* (1934), and ended, twelve pairings later (not all of them in the Thin Man series) with Edward Buzzell's *Song Of The Thin Man* (1947). In-between times, Powell played in some excellent comedies, including Gregory La Cava's delightful *My Man Godfrey* (1936) and Jack Conway's equally splendid *Libeled Lady* (1936), plus some first-rate little thrillers, too, including Conway's remake of Kurt Bernhardt's 1938 pre-war French thriller *Carrefour* [renamed *Crossroads*] (1942), and Chester Erskine's *Take One False Step* (1949). Powell lived to the ripe old age of ninety-two despite (or perhaps because of) his famous dallyings (and occasional marriages) with such luminous ladies as **Carole Lombard** and **Jean Harlow**.

Other Key Films: *Outcast* (1922); *Romola* (1924); *Beau Geste* (1926); *The Great Gatsby* (1926); *The Canary Murder Case* (1929); *The Key* (1934); *Double Wedding* (1937); *I Love You Again* (1940); *Love Crazy* (1941); *Ziegfeld Follies* (1946); *The Senator Was Indiscreet* (1948); *How To Marry A Millionaire* (1953); *Mr. Roberts* (1955)

Power, Tyrone

One of the pretty boys of the Hollywood star factory, Power showed in later, riskier films, that he really could act. He played wildly against type in **Edmund Goulding's** *Nightmare Alley* (1947), as the vainglorious Stanton Carlisle, who ends his career as a carnival 'geek' biting the heads off chickens, and also in **Henry King's** *The Sun Also Rises* (1958), in which he took the part of Ernest Hemingway's impotent alter ego, Jake Barnes, in love with **Ava Gardner** but utterly incapable of consummating his passion (how one feels for him). He was more than good, too, in **Rouben Mamoulian's** superb *The Mark Of Zorro* (1940), and also as the protagonist in King's gorgeously coloured *Jesse James* (1939). Power, scion of an Irish acting dynasty of eighteenth century origin, died of a heart attack, whilst filming, at the tragically early age of forty-five, just as his father had done before him.

Other Key Films: *Lloyd's Of London* (1936); *In Old Chicago* (1938); *The Black Swan* (1942); *Captain From Castile* (1947); *King Of The Khyber Rifles* (1953); *Witness For The Prosecution* (1958)

Preminger, Otto

Preminger fell between two stools – the intellectual and the expedient. The expedient finally won out, but the intellectual had quite a good run of it, with movies as idiosyncratic as his two brilliant *film noirs*, *Laura* (1944) and *Where The Sidewalk*

Ends (1950). Also included in this list would be the seriously melodramatic *Angel Face* (1953), a restrained **Marilyn Monroe** performance in *River Of No Return* (1954), and the outstanding did-he-do-it-or-didn't-he *Anatomy Of A Murder* (1959), which predated the permissive 60s in its candid discussion of sex. The film for which he is best known is *Exodus* (1966), which, although excellent of its kind, pales into worthy insignificance when compared to his stylish earlier films.

Other Key Films: *Forever Amber* (1947); *Daisy Kenyon* (1947); *Whirlpool* (1949); *The Court-Martial Of Billy Mitchell* (1955); *Bonjour Tristesse* (1958); *Advise And Consent* (1962); *The Human Factor* (1980)

Presley, Elvis

One hardly thinks of Presley first and foremost as a film star, but he made a number of movies before his death at the age of forty-two, and one or two were actually quite good, notably **Don Siegel's** *Flaming Star* (1960) and Phil Karlson's *Kid Galahad* (1962). Die-hard fans will, of course, watch anything at all with Presley in it, and good luck to them. He is, after all, one of the greats.

Other Key Films: *Love Me Tender* (1956); *King Creole* (1958); *Fun In Acapulco* (1963); *Roustabout* (1964); *Frankie And Johnny* (1965)

Prévert, Jacques

Prévert was a poet who just happened to write for films. He mixed street intellectualism, popular ballad making and a high-minded intensity of emotion in a way that it would be almost impossible to replicate today. His moment, curiously enough, came during the 1950s (and not during the 1930s, when he was writing most frequently), when his brand of elegant, existential despair struck a retrospective chord with a youth culture still overwhelmed by the war memories of its parents, and still struggling to find a philosophy that encompassed both fatalism and hope. The team of Prévert and **Marcel Carné** had already turned out such films during the 1930s, in the form of *Quai Des Brumes* (1938) and *Le Jour Se Lève* (1939), and when the young painter in *Quai Des Brumes* tells **Jean Gabin** that he can no longer paint because when he looks at a tree he sees not only the tree, but a man hanging from it, and when he looks at the sea it is not the wind or the surf that he hears, but the cry of drowning men, young 1950s France responded to his nihilism, dressing themselves in black, reading Jean-Paul Sartre and Albert Camus, and turning to literature and music, rather than to the cult of consumerism, for their sustenance. One wishes that the same could be said of today's youth.

Other Key Films: **Jean Renoir's** *Le Crime De M. Lange* (1936); Marcel Carné's *Jenny* (1936), *Drôle De Drame* (1937), *Les Visiteurs Du Soir* (1942), *Les Enfants Du Paradis* (1945) and *Les Portes De La Nuit* (1946)

Price, Vincent

Price was the horror supremo *par excellence* (though he began life as a straight actor), and he was possessed of a wry and endearing capacity to take himself off. With his laconic voice and indissoluble confidence, Price carried literally dozens of low-budget horror movies in the 1960s and 1970s, and one or two real stinkers as well. Something of an epicure in real life, Price gave some notable, not over-the-top performances in films such as **Otto Preminger's** *Laura* (1944) and **Fritz Lang's** *While The City Sleeps* (1956) before he succumbed, with an elegant disdain, no doubt, to the horror industry. His personal favourite of all his films was **Samuel Fuller's** *The Baron Of Arizona* (1950) – an odd choice at first glance, but typical of Price's delight-

fully idiosyncratic nature. To see Price in full ham thespian swing, you could do worse than tune into **John Farrow's** *His Kind Of Woman* (1951), in which his jaded swashbuckler, Mark Cardigan, belatedly discovers that he really is a brave man after all.
Other Key Films: *The Private Lives Of Elizabeth And Essex* (1939); *The Bribe* (1949); *House Of Wax* (1953); *The Fly* (1958); *Fall Of The House Of Usher* (1960); *The Pit And The Pendulum* (1961); *The Raven* (1963); *Masque Of The Red Death* (1964); *Edward Scissorhands* (1990)

Best **Psychological Dramas**: **Bernardo Bertolucci's** *Last Tango In Paris* (1972); **Peter Bogdanovich's** *The Last Picture Show* (1971); Youssef Chahine's *Central Station* [*Bab El-Hadid*] (1958); **Milos Forman's** *One Flew Over The Cuckoo's Nest* (1975); **Alfred Hitchcock's** *Spellbound* (1945) and *Vertigo* (1958); **John Huston's** *The Treasure Of The Sierra Madre* (1947) and *Fat City* (1972); **Neil Jordan's** *The Crying Game* (1992); **Emir Kusturica's** *Time Of The Gypsies* (1989); **Fritz Lang's** *The Woman In The Window* (1944); Rouben Mamoulian's *Dr Jekyll And Mr Hyde* (1931); **Joseph L Mankiewicz's** *Suddenly Last Summer* (1959); **Alexander Mackendrick's** *Sweet Smell Of Success* (1957); **Bob Rafelson's** *Five Easy Pieces* (1970); **Roberto Rossellini's** *Voyage To Italy* (1953); Charles Vidor's *Gilda* (1946); **Raoul Walsh's** *Pursued* (1946); **Billy Wilder's** *Sunset Boulevard* (1950) and *Ace In The Hole* [a.k.a. *The Big Carnival*] (1951)

Pulp Fiction

Hard-boiled pulp fiction (the pulp referred to what happened to the paper after the disposable piece was read) first appeared in the United States during the 1920s, in such magazines as *Black Mask*, *Spicy Stories*, *Ace-High*, *Amazing*, *Astounding*, *Detective Magazine*, etc., and directly fomented the 1930s genre of Warner gangster movies, which began with **Mervyn LeRoy's** *Little Caesar* (1931) and **William Wellman's** *Public Enemy* (1931), and which culminated in the doom-laden and visually poetic 1940s and 1950s *film noir* cycle. Its principal literary progenitors and adherents were **Dashiell Hammett**, **Raymond Chandler**, John D MacDonald, Paul Cain, Howard Browne, Jim Thompson, Donald E Westlake, Dorothy B Hughes, Mickey Spillane, Henry Kane, William S Prather, Stephen Marlowe, Charles Williams, Ross MacDonald and **James M Cain**, and their tight, no-nonsense style of writing, which concentrated on the ordinary man and woman caught up in the toils of fate, proved enormously influential in both verbal and visual terms to the history of American cinema, and, through that medium, to the history of European cinema as well.

Vincent Price in Return of the Fly, directed by Edward Bernds (1959).
20th Century Fox/The Kobal Collection

Key Line: 'When I went to college and took writing courses, they would always talk about the distinctions between the pulp writer and the slick writer and the art writer. I came to realize that was ridiculous. There are only interesting stories and dull stories, no matter where they're printed.' [Richard Matheson, prolific cult author of novels such as *I Am Legend* (1956), and scripts the quality of Jack Arnold's *The Incredible Shrinking Man* (1957) [from his own novel] and Jeannot Szwarc's *Somewhere In Time* (1980), based on his novel *Bid Time Return*]

Quaid, Dennis

Quaid always seems to have been born just a little out of his own time, as if he should have been an actor during the 1940s or 1950s rather than now. He has chosen his parts well, by and large, and has shone rather than gleamed in them, possibly on account of his marginally offbeat looks, which give him an edge over some of the purely pretty-boy actors of his generation. He was excellent in his first film, Peter Yates's *Breaking Away* (1979), and followed that up with a brilliant performance as Gordon Cooper in Philip Kaufman's *The Right Stuff* (1983). His best part to date, though, has been that of Remy McSwain, in Jim McBride's *The Big Easy* (1986), where he suggested what a versatile actor he could be if someone only knew how to use him. Steve Kloves's *Flesh And Bone* (1993) has come nearest to fulfilling that potential, but to date Quaid must be counted as one that got away.

Other Key Films: *The Long Riders* (1980); *All Night Long* (1981); *Suspect* (1987); *DOA* (1988); *Come See The Paradise* (1990); *Postcards From The Edge* (1990); *Wyatt Earp* (1994); *Dragonheart* (1996); *SwitchBack* (1997); *The Parent Trap* (1998); *Any Given Sunday* (1999); *Frequency* (2000); *Traffic* (2000); *Far From Heaven* (2002); *The Alamo* (2004); *In Good Company* (2004); *Flight Of The Phoenix* (2004); *American Dreamz* (2006)

Quayle, Anthony

Quayle played decent, modest men, and embodied a particular sort of Old Rugbeian Englishness which is now majestically out of fashion. Even when he played a baddie, as with his Captain Van Der Poel in J Lee Thompson's *Ice Cold In Alex* (1958), he was a decent baddie (apart from those awful shorts, that is), and he seemed content to reserve his real talents for the stage, where he excelled. He was admirable, however, as Frank O'Connor in **Alfred Hitchcock's** *The Wrong Man* (1958), and his Colonel Brighton in **David Lean's** *Lawrence Of Arabia* showed his screen persona at its humane, sensitive, but nevertheless rather ineffectual best.

Other Key Films: *Hamlet* (1948); *Battle Of The River Plate* (1956); *The Guns Of Navarone* (1961); *Operation Crossbow* (1965); *Anne Of The Thousand Days* (1969); *The Tamarind Seed* (1974); *The Eagle Has Landed* (1976); *Murder By Decree* (1979)

Quinn, Anthony

Quinn had a long wait for stardom, being called upon to play a bewildering variety of parts in his sixteen years as a character actor in the Sargasso sea of Hollywood minor stardom. Then came an Oscar as **Marlon Brando's** brother in **Elia Kazan's** *Viva Zapata* (1952). More disasters followed, however, among them Pietro Francisci's *Attila The Hun* (1955), a strong each way bet in the Turkey-of-all-time Olympics. Meanwhile **Federico Fellini** had directed Quinn in *La Strada* (1954), and his luck began to change again. A second Oscar for his role as Gauguin, in **Vincente Minnelli's** excellent *Lust For Life* (1956), and parts in **David Lean's** *Lawrence Of Arabia* (1962) and Michael Cacoyannis's *Zorba The Greek* (1964) followed, and he soon became the mighty, macho Quinn we all came to know and love, still showering the world with his progeny at an advanced age, until his death, of respiratory failure, in June 2001.

Other Key Films: *Against All Flags* (1952); *The Hunchback Of Notre Dame* (1958); *The Guns Of Navarone* (1961); *Barabbas* (1962); *A High Wind In Jamaica* (1965); *Marseilles Contract* (1974); *Lion Of The Desert* (1981); *Last Action Hero* (1993); *A Walk In The Clouds* (1995); *Oriundi* (1999)

Rafelson, Bob

One of the miracles of 1970s post-*Easy Rider* US cinema, Rafelson seemed to have the future in his hands for a brief moment, but in fact it turned out to be the past – a knowledge of it and of its effects and importance on the present. *Five Easy Pieces* (1970) and *The King Of Marvin Gardens* (1972) can now be seen, with the vast privilege of hindsight, to be key films in the melding of two eras – the pre-1960s and the post-1960s – for they tell of the marginal people who stumbled between the slats, not really of one era or another, but out of time, just as their music, and their dreams are out of time. Rafelson has never surpassed those two movies, not even with his recent *Blood And Wine* (1997), which showed a marked return to form after nearly twenty-five years in the wilderness of commercial vacuity. Just briefly, in *Blood And Wine*, in the character played by **Judy Davis**,

Rafelson achieves again that otherness which had marked him out, so early in his film career, as a potentially great auteur/filmmaker.

Other Key Films: *Head* (1968); *Stay Hungry* (1976); *The Postman Always Rings Twice* (1981); *Black Widow* (1987); *Mountains Of The Moon* (1990); *Man Trouble* (1992); *The House On Turk Street* (2002)

Raft, George

One of the great bad guys of the cinema, Raft was a actually a pretty terrible actor who managed, through a process of luck, good publicity and a dead-pan face, to carve himself a particular niche (that of a gangster) and stick to it. No gangster, though, ever remotely looked or acted like Raft, and his alleged Mafia connections remain strictly that – alleged. He was OK, in a Raftian way, in **Howard Hawks's** *Scarface* (1932), but when he was paired with a not-yet-iconic **Humphrey Bogart** in **Raoul Walsh's** *They Drive By Night* (1940), it rapidly became apparent that Raft did not have the capacity to cast off his former mantle and don a new one. He is the sort of actor who is better in the memory than in the flesh.

Other Key Films: *Night Court* (1932); *Night After Night* (1932); *Every Night At Eight* (1935); *The Glass Key* (1935); *You And Me* (1938); *Background To Danger* (1943); *Cairo* (1953); *Black Widow* (1954); *Some Like It Hot* (1959)

Raimi, Sam

Cult horror director best known for his *The Evil Dead* series (1983-2006 and counting) and the rather more sophisticated *Darkman* (1990), which starred an unlikely **Liam Neeson**, Raimi is a film buff with a finger in a lot of pies as occasional actor, screenwriter, producer and director. The original *The Evil Dead*, made on a spectacularly low budget, and spawner of an awful lot of junky imitations, was a witty, literate slant on the usual Hammer-horror clichés, and still manages to entertain, amuse and scare through its imaginative use of film trickery and the exuberance and ironical humour with which its excesses are perpetrated.

Other Key Films: *Crimewave* (1985); *Evil Dead 2* (1987); *Army Of Darkness* (1993); *The Quick And The Dead* (1995); *A Simple Plan* (1998); *For Love Of The Game* (1999); *The Gift* (2000); *Spider-Man* (2002); *Spider-Man 2* (2004)

Raimu

A great French actor who will be forever linked with, and loved for, his role as César in **Marcel Pagnol's** sublime film trilogy comprising **Alexander Korda's** *Marius* (1931), **Marc Allégret's** *Fanny* (1932) and Pagnol's own *César* (1936), Raimu went on to delight his legion of fans in Pagnol's self-directed follow-up to the trilogy, *The Baker's Wife* (1938), as Aimable, the melancholic baker who loses the will to make bread when his wife, Aurelie, leaves him for the local shepherd. In perfect Gallic fashion the deprived villagers rally together to restore both the status quo and their access to Aimable's wonderful bread. These four films between them are the best example of what French cinema can bring us that American cinema never can, namely a profoundly sophisticated insight into simplicity.

Other Key Films: *Le Blanc Et Le Noir* (1931); *Tartarin De Tarascon* (1934); *Gribouille* (1937); *Un Carnet De Bal* (1937); *Noix De Coco* (1939); *La Fille Du Puisatier* (1940); *L'Arlésienne* (1942); *Le Colonel Chabert* (1943)

Rains, Claude

A wonderful character actor and leading man whose smooth bedside manner belied the steel that he could, on occasion, summon from his heart, most notably in **Alfred Hitchcock's** *Notorious* (1946), in which his Nazi sympathiser, Alexander Sebastian, married, bedded, and then tried to kill **Ingrid Bergman**, despite **Cary Grant's** rather belated objections. Rains left poor Ingrid more or less alone in **Casablanca** (1942), although not for want of carnal intent, for he concentrated his attentions in a heady – but unacknowledged, one must assume – homoerotic manner, on **Humphrey Bogart's** Rick instead. Rains carried irony and sardonic levity to extremes that only **George Sanders**, another expatriate Brit in the Hollywood maelstrom, could equal, and remained happily and fruitfully in work almost to his death, in 1967. *Pace* Paul Bettany (who was excellent in the part), Rains, in his prime, would have made a perfect Stephen Maturin, in **Peter Weir's** *Master And Commander: The Far Side Of The World* (2003).

Other Key Films: *The Invisible Man* (1933); *Anthony Adverse* (1936); *The Prince And The Pauper* (1937); *The Adventures Of Robin Hood* (1938); *Four Daughters* (1938); *The Sea Hawk* (1940); *Now Voyager* (1942); *Mr Skeffington* (1944); *Caesar And Cleopatra* (1945); *Deception* (1946); *The Unsuspected* (1947); *The Passionate Friends* (1949); *Where*

Rank, J Arthur

The devoutly Methodist J Arthur Rank became one of the biggest names in the British Film Industry during the 1940s and 1950s, expanding into most of the post-colonial markets and owning more than a thousand cinemas in the UK mainland alone, including the Gaumont and the Odeon chains. In his heyday, Joseph Arthur had control of both **Denham** and **Pinewood** studios, together with a considerable number of peripheral interests such as hotels, amusement arcades and Xerox copying facilities. His trademark was, and still is, known throughout the world, and consists of a bare-chested 'Bombardier' Billy Wells striking an enormous papier-mâché gong – James Blades, the much-loved percussionist who actually made the sound of the gong, delighted a generation of young children by carting around the ersatz gong and its smaller progenitor and giving lively school demonstrations during the 1950s and 1960s.

Rathbone, Basil

Rathbone was one of the screen's most effective villains – one has only to think of his appallingly cold Mr Murdstone in **George Cukor's** *David Copperfield* (1935) or his heartless Sir Guy Of Gisbourne in **Michael Curtiz's** *The Adventures Of Robin Hood* (1938) – while at the very same time playing, in a lengthy series of films (1939-1946), the screen's most enduring hero, **Sherlock Holmes**. Rathbone brought two very different aspects of his personality to bear on both archetypes, focusing on acute intelligence in the case of Holmes, most notably in Sidney Lanfield's *The Hound Of The Baskervilles* (1939), and sophisticated ambition in the case of such supreme villains as his Richard III in Rowland Lee's *Tower Of London* (1939). With his mellifluous voice, elegant figure and fencer's way with the sword, Rathbone was one of the great stalwarts of the Golden Age of Hollywood.

Other Key Films: *The Great Deception* (1926); *The Last Days Of Pompeii* (1935); *A Tale Of Two Cities* (1935); *Captain Blood* (1935); *The Adventures Of Marco Polo* (1938); *Dawn Patrol* (1938); *The Mark Of Zorro* (1940); *The Black Cat* (1941); *Frenchman's Creek* (1944); *The Last Hurrah* (1958)

Ray, Nicholas

It was the French who first called Ray one of the greatest of all Hollywood directors, and his debut film, *They Live By Night* (1948), must vie with **Charles Laughton's** *Night Of The Hunter* (1955) as one of the best-ever first features by a debut director. It was the French, too, with their long visual tradition, who best understood the concept of Ray's 'poetry of the screen', which used lighting, sound and close-ups to heighten the dramatic effect of dialogue. In *On Dangerous Ground* (1951), a 'cop and blind girl' story that might have seemed simply mawkish in any other hands is turned into a profound character study of an alienated man, with Ray using the exterior landscapes of town and country to mirror his character's mental state – it is Ray's genius that in a number of brilliantly constructed extended scenes **Robert Ryan's** disenchanted cop always seems to be on the verge of some fundamental revelation about the intricacies of his own heart. Ray's *In a Lonely Place* (1950) is arguably **Humphrey Bogart's** best and most complex film, while his *Johnny Guitar* (1954) raised **Joan Crawford** from the mundane to the peculiar. Other notable films include the teen classic *Rebel Without a Cause* (1955), and the underrated **Robert Mitchum** vehicle *The Lusty Men* (1952). Even Ray's sublimely dotty gypsy musical,

Hot Blood (1954), somehow contrives to work when seen on the big screen. **Wim Wenders** recorded Ray's final illness in his documentary *Lightning Over Water* (1980).
Other Key Films: *Born To Be Bad* (1950); *On Dangerous Ground* (1951); *Run For Cover* (1955); *Bitter Victory* (1958); *Party Girl* (1958); *Wind Across The Everglades* (1958); Wim Wenders's *The American Friend* [as actor] (1977)
Key Lines:

1.   'Oh, Nick could give you cancer. Actually, I think he died of cancer. He had the most miserable life of anybody I have ever known. Nobody liked him. Nobody was close to him… It was very difficult to get anything out of him, except when he recognised it was right.' [Screenwriter **Philip Yordan**, who may or may not have scripted *Johnny Guitar* (1954), on director Ray]

2.   'I don't think he was either a compulsive liar or a Hollywood rat. I think he was a man who was *hungry* for recognition, who really didn't trust that his talent was authentic.' [Screenwriter Stewart Stern, who scripted *Rebel Without A Cause* (1955), on director Ray]

Ray, Satyajit

Considered the doyen of all Indian filmmakers, Ray was instrumental in alerting notoriously xenophobic western audiences to the fact that there was a film industry in India, and that it was of an extremely high quality. Ray virtually beggared himself in order to complete his first film, *Pather Panchali* (1955), but the film was such a success at the Cannes Film Festival that both Ray's future as a director, and, just as importantly, the financial backing necessary to construct further films, was assured. He completed what is now called the Apu trilogy, with *Aparajito* (1956) and *The World Of Apu* (1959), before embarking on a series of films that not only changed the view the West had of India, but also the view India, or at the very least educated India, had of itself. Perhaps Ray's most exquisite film, and the one which best highlights the extraordinary paradoxes inherent in Indian society, is *The Music Room* (1963), for which Ray also wrote the score. The image of the final, glorious concert held in the crumbling palace (so earnestly resented by the up-and-coming yet deeply philistine middle classes) is an enduring image of the capacity of the noumenal to transcend the present and take on the mantle of myth.
Other Key Films: *The Goddess* (1960); *Two Daughters* (1961); *The Lonely Wife* (1964); *The Coward And The Holy Man* (1965); *Days And Nights In The Forest* (1970); *Distant Thunder* (1973); *The Golden Fortress* (1974); *The Chess Players* (1977); *The Visitor* (1992)

Redford, Robert

The big screen's original golden boy, Robert Redford has made the most of his career, acting, producing, directing, and founding the world-famous Sundance Institute for independent films and filmmakers. Despite all this, his screen persona remains more or less static, just as his looks do – one emerges from his movies impressed by their professionalism but just a little dissatisfied, as if one has been momentarily tempted by a luxurious lifestyle and then thought better of it. This is not to say that Redford is a bad actor, merely a mannered one. His directing, on the other hand, starting with *Ordinary People* (1980), through *The Milagro Beanfield War* (1987) and *The River Runs Through It* (1993), and in particular *Quiz Show* (1995), has improved with each film, and there is no earthly use denying his charm, and his obvious intelligence, and the diligence with which he has tried to follow the tenets of his own conscience.

Other Key Films: *The Chase* (1966); *Barefoot In The Park* (1967); *Butch Cassidy And The Sundance Kid* (1969); *Tell Them Willie Boy Is Here* (1969); *Jeremiah Johnson* (1972); *Three Days Of The Condor* (1975); *All The President's Men* (1976); *Out Of Africa* (1985); *Havana* (1990); *Indecent Proposal* (1993); *The Horse Whisperer* [also dir.] (1998); *The Legend Of Bagger Vance* [dir.] (2000); *Spy Game* (2001); *The Clearing* (2004); *An Unfinished Life* (2005)

Redgrave, Michael

A fine screen actor and the father of an acting dynasty in **Vanessa**, Lynn and Corin, Redgrave was a Janus-like figure, uncomfortable with both his sexuality and his obvious, though frequently underused talent. His best performances came early, in **Alfred Hitchcock's** *The Lady Vanishes* (1938), the multi-directed *Dead Of Night* (1945) and **Anthony Asquith's** *The Browning Version* (1951), but he also brought his trademark nervous worthiness to **Tony Richardson's** *The Loneliness Of The Long Distance Runner* (1962) and to Stuart Burge's film of the National Theatre's *Uncle Vanya* (1963).

Other Key Films: *Thunder Rock* (1942); *The Way To The Stars* (1945); *The Captive Heart* (1946); *Mourning Becomes Electra* (1947); *The Importance Of Being Earnest* (1952); *Mr Arkadin* (1955); *1984* (1956); *The Quiet American* (1958); *The Hill* (1965); *The Go-Between* (1971)

Key Line: 'Ah, Sir Michael Redgrave, I'll be bound!' [Sir John Gielgud, reportedly alluding to Redgrave's purported liking for homosexual bondage during their meeting in the street after hearing of Redgrave's 1959 knighthood]

Redgrave, Vanessa: On top of her form, Redgrave is one of the greatest of all screen actresses, remarkable both for her involvement with and utter commitment to any part she agrees to play. **Karel Reisz's** *Morgan!* (1966) first gave an inkling of her possible range, and **Fred Zinnemann's** *A Man For All Seasons* (1966) confirmed it – whether on screen or on stage she is luminous, exuding a transcendental calm that other actresses can only marvel at. She thoroughly deserved her Oscar for Zinnemann's *Julia* (1977), but in recent years there has been a deepening, a greater force to her now fully mature presence, that was absent before. Her small part in **James Ivory's** *Howard's End* (1992) was utterly sublime, and she literally carried Marleen Gorris's otherwise variable *Mrs. Dalloway* (1998) with the integrity and grace of her performance.

Other Key Films: *Blowup* (1966); *Camelot* (1967) *The Sailor From Gibraltar* (1967); *The Charge Of The Light Brigade* (1968); *The Sea Gull* (1968); *The Devils* (1971); *Mary Queen Of Scots* (1971); *The Seven Percent Solution* (1976); *Agatha* (1979); *The Bostonians* (1984); *Wetherby* (1985); *Prick Up Your Ears* (1987); *Little Odessa* (1995); *Wilde* (1997); *An Interesting State* (1999); *A Rumor of Angels* (2000); *The Pledge* (2001); *The Fever* (2004); *The White Countess* (2005)

Reed, Carol

Reed thought and lived in terms of cinema and of visual images, and it is curious, but somehow uplifting, to think of this illegitimate child of the great Edwardian actor, Herbert Beerbohm Tree, sloughing off the traditional English obsession with words and the workings of the intellect, to direct intuitively, in the French style, using words to fuel images, rather than vice versa. After the somewhat conventional, but still entertaining *Night Train To Munich* (1940) and *The Way Ahead* (1944), Reed stunned those who thought of him as unadventurous with his **expressionist** depiction of treachery, betrayal and remorse in *Odd Man Out* (1947), in which **James Mason's** wounded Johnny McQueen flails through an increasingly fantastic Dublin. *Fallen Idol* (1948) followed, and was an exquisite character study into the relationship between a child and **Ralph Richardson's** Baines the butler, the only person ever to show him any kindness, and who may, or may not be a killer – rarely has the dark side of a child's natural ignorance of the workings of adult hearts been more sensitively shown. Reed's masterpiece is *The Third Man* (1949), in which, from the very first, we are aware of Reed's total creative control over his material – from Robert Krasker's extraordinary shots of post-war Vienna to **Orson Welles's** inspired scene-stealing, to Anton Karas's haunting zither-music accompaniment, the film is an almost perfect example of cinema's capacity for intelligent, enlightened entertainment. Many critics believe that Reed faltered after *The Third Man*, but this is not strictly correct. *Outcast Of The Islands* (1951) is an extraordinary film, and can bear repeated viewings, and **Trevor Howard** gives the performance of his life as Peter Willems, a man whom evil creeps up on, despite the almost saintly protection of Ralph Richardson's Captain Lingard, and in the face of Robert Morley's brilliantly hypocritical Almayer. For those four sublime films one can even forgive Reed for having agreed to direct *Oliver!* (1968), which is really saying something.

Other Key Films: *Midshipman Easy* (1935); *Bank Holiday* (1938); *Kipps* (1941); *The Young Mr. Pitt* (1942); *The Man Between* (1953); *A Kid For Two Farthings* (1955); *Trapeze* (1956); *The Key* (1958); *Our Man In Havana* (1959); *The Running Man* (1963); *Follow Me* (1972)

Reed, Oliver

A renowned piss artist and sometime heroic drunk, Reed began his screen career as a nervous, vibrant actor in a series of barely remembered B-movies. His uncle, **Carol Reed**, used him as Bill Sykes in the movie version of the hit musical *Oliver!* (1968), where he was spotted by **Ken Russell** who, in turn, cast him as Gerald in *Women In Love* (1969), which proved to be possibly Reed's most subtle screen performance. Parts in Russell's *The Devils* (1971) and Richard Lester's *The Three Musketeers* (1973) followed, but Reed's decline was long. He died while co-starring in what might well have been his comeback film, **Ridley Scott's** *Gladiator* (2000), and he would have been amused had he known that his final scenes would have to be computer aided with the help of Soft Image.

Other Key Films: *Hannibal Brooks* (1969); *The Hunting Party* (1971); *Tommy* (1975); *The Prince And The Pauper* (1977); *Lion Of The Desert* (1979); *Castaway* (1986); *Prisoner Of Honour* (1991); *Funny Bones* (1995)

Reeves, Keanu

Reeves is a high-profile actor of no outstanding talent who yet possesses that rare thing – screen charisma. This is despite the po-faced look he has worn for virtually every role since *Bill & Ted's Excellent Adventure* (1989). His female following is immense (and notably eclectic) and his recent role of Neo (yes, Neo) in Larry and Andy Wachowski's *The Matrix* trilogy (1999-2003) has done nothing to dent Reeves's otherworldly reputation with a set of fans who will hear no ill of their hero whatsoever.

Other Key Films: *The Prodigal* (1984); *River's Edge* (1987); *Dangerous Liaisons* (1988); *Parenthood* (1989); *Point Break* (1991); *My Own Private Idaho* (1991); *Much Ado About Nothing* (1993); *Speed* (1994); *A Walk In The Clouds* (1995); *Feeling Minnesota* (1996);

Devil's Advocate (1997); *The Replacements* (2000); *The Gift* (2000); *Sweet November* (2001); *Hard Ball* (2001); *Something's Gotta Give* (2003); *Constantine* (2005); *The Lake House* (2006)

Reisz, Karel

Possibly the most influential of the 'kitchen-sink drama' school of British directors, Reisz was actually Czechoslovakian, and served in the wartime RAF following the death of both his parents in a Nazi concentration camp. His first feature was *Saturday Night And Sunday Morning* (1960), which launched **Albert Finney's** screen career and which was the precursor to a seemingly endless stream of less well-made clones. *Morgan: A Suitable Case For Treatment* (1966) cleverly isolated the half-manic, half-intellectual background to swinging London, and *The Gambler* (1974) showed Reisz's keen eye for American nuances. *The French Lieutenant's Woman* (1981) is still his most successful film to date, but *Dog Soldiers* (1978) [a.k.a. *Who'll Stop The Rain*], with Reisz's perennial leading man, **Nick Nolte**, is oddly memorable, if only for its extraordinary atmosphere.

Other Key Films: *Night Must Fall* (1964); *Isadora* (1968); *Sweet Dreams* (1985); *Everybody Wins* (1990)

Renoir, Jean

Arguably the greatest of all film directors, Renoir belonged to a long line of creative individuals which included his artist father, Auguste, his actor brother, Pierre, and his nephew, Claude Renoir, a fine cinematographer who photographed many of his uncle's films. A visual philosopher of the highest sensibility, Renoir was a down-to-earth man, obsessed by the individual and by the crucial relationship such an individual must forge between society and the natural environment. A master of extempore, Renoir extended the bounds of the cinema with such masterpieces of **poetic realism** as *Toni* (1935), *La Grande Illusion* (1937) and *La Règle Du Jeu* (1939), exploring not only the social strati of his times, but also defining them by reference to the past and to the lessons of the importance of dignity, respect, duty and consistency already learned under its aegis. Like **John Ford**, with whom, in many ways, he can be compared, Renoir made films that exude humanity and an understanding of the disparate characteristics that differentiate people, as well as of what brings them together. His artistry, magnificent though it was, was always transcended by his search for understanding. See **Heartstopping Moments**

Other Key Films: *La Chienne* (1931); *Boudu Sauvé Des Eaux* (1932); *Madame Bovary* (1934); *Une Partie De Campagne* (1946); *Les Bas-Fonds* (1936); *Le Crime de Monsieur Lange* (1936); *Une Partie de Campagne* (1936); *La Marseillaise* (1938); *La Bête Humaine* (1938); *Swamp Water* (1941); *The Southerner* (1945); *The Diary Of A Chambermaid* (1946); *The Woman On The Beach* (1947); *The River* (1951); *La Carosse d'Or* (1952); *Eléna Et Les Hommes* (1956)

Key Line: 'Is it possible to succeed without any act of betrayal?' [Renoir on life]

Resnais, Alain

Resnais came closer than any other film director to bringing the subtleties of the novelistic form to the screen. What he attempted in *Hiroshima Mon Amour* (1959) was so original in terms of film, and yet so commonplace in terms of literature, that it deserves mention. In short, he endeavoured to remake time. By using narration, story fragmentation, and by juxtaposing documentary images with filmed narrative, Resnais used the audience's existing knowledge of literary forms to widen the scope of the purely filmic dialogue he was conducting with them. *Last Year In Marienbad* (1961) was his second essay into such inherently ambiguous territory, but it is with *Muriel* (1963) that he succeeded best in terms of his own cinematic ambitions. The film remains a curious and rather moving hybrid, less successful than *Hiroshima* in subverting the audience's expectations and in reaching a satisfying resolution, perhaps, but rich and dense of image, leaving the strange impression that one has inhabited, rather than merely voyeuristically viewed, the lives of its protagonists.

Other Key Films: *Nuit Et Brouillard* [docu] (1956); *The War Is Over* (1966); *Je T'Aime Je T'Aime* (1968); *Stavisky* (1974); *Providence* (1977); *Mon Oncle D'Amérique* (1980); *Life Is A Bed Of Roses* (1983); *Love Unto Death* (1984); *Mélo* (1986); *I Want To Go Home* (1989); *Smoking/No Smoking* (1993); *On Connaît La Chanson* (1997)

Reynolds, Burt

It may be hard to believe now, but Reynolds was hot commercial property during the late 1970s to early 1980s, topping the Quigley Publications Poll from 1978-1982, thanks to such movies as Hal Needham's *Smokey And The Bandit* (1977) and *The Cannonball Run* (1981), films which appealed to an all-teenage, all-redneck audience. Despite the usual run of duds and box-office fodder, Reynolds aspired to greater things, and he made one or two excellent films to offset the inevitable commercial dross. Such highlights included **John Boorman's** *Deliverance* (1972), and the underrated *Sharkey's Machine* (1981), which he also directed. He has recently made something of a comeback in Paul Thomas Anderson's excellent *Boogie Nights* (1997), as, of all paradoxical things, an artistically pretentious pornographer.

Other Key Films: *Sam Whiskey* (1969); *Shamus* (1973); *The Man Who Loved Cat Dancing* (1973); *White Lightning* (1973); *Hooper* (1978); *The Man Who Loved Women* (1983); *Mad Dog Time* (1996); *Bean* (1997); *Pups* (1999); *The Crew* (2000); *The Last Producer* [also dir.] (2000); *The Librarians* (2000); *Driven* (2001); *Hotel* (2001); *Time Of The Wolf* (2002); *The Longest Yard* (2005); *Forget About It* (2006)

Reynolds, Debbie

Comparable, in effect if perhaps not in intent, to actresses such as **Julie Andrews** and **Doris Day**, Reynolds was a very talented singer and dancer with a titillating, because repressed, 1950s style sexuality. Her best part was undoubtedly in **Stanley Donen** and **Gene Kelly's** *Singin' In The Rain* (1952), in which her ebulliently virginal, yet somehow still inflammatory attractions were used to good effect. <u>Note For Film Buffs</u>: Reynolds must be the only female dancer in the history of the movies to be seen smoothing down her skirt so as *not* to show off her panties in an energetic dance routine during *Singin' In The Rain*.

Other Key Films: *The Daughter Of Rosie O'Grady* (1950); *Hit The Deck* (1955); *The Tender Trap* (1955); *The Catered Affair* (1956); *This Happy Feeling* (1958); *The Rat Race* (1960); *Goodbye Charlie* (1964)

Richardson, Ralph

A profoundly eccentric and lovable man, Richardson was one of the foremost Shakespearian stage actors of his age, and, rather like his contemporary, **John Gielgud**, he slipped into acting for motion pictures almost by default. However, his majestic performances in **Carol Reed's** *The Fallen Idol* (1948), **Julien Duvivier's** *Anna Karenina* (1948), **William Wyler's** *The Heiress* (1949), and **Sidney Lumet's** *Long Day's Journey Into Night* (1962) proclaim him as one of the greatest – albeit one of the most arbitrary in his choice of parts – of all screen actors. His farewell performance as the 6th Lord Greystoke in Hugh Hudson's *Greystoke* (1984), in which he recreates, in full mess kit, a famed tray slide down a set of marble steps, fatally injuring himself in the process, succeeds in bringing tears to the eyes each time one sees it, not so much on account of his performance, good as it is, but more on account of what Richardson represented as a man.

Other Key Films: *Things To Come* (1936); *The Citadel* (1938); *The Four Feathers* (1939); *Outcast Of The Islands* (1951); *The Sound Barrier* (1952); *Richard III* (1955); *The Passionate Stranger* [a.k.a. *A Novel Affair*] (1954); *Our Man In Havana* (1960); *Woman Of Straw* (1964); *The Looking-Glass War* (1969); *O Lucky Man!* (1973)

Key Line: 'The art of acting consists in keeping people from coughing.' [Richardson on acting]

Richardson, Tony

Richardson came to maturity in the rapidly changing social and industrial milieu of post-Second-World-War England, and he wisely made it his principal subject. With films such as *A Taste Of Honey* (1961) and *The Loneliness Of The Long Distance Runner* (1962), he challenged the formal authority of the unthinking middle classes, and his film version of John Osborne's seminal *Look Back In Anger* (1959) was very nearly as influential as the original play. *Tom Jones* (1963) was a rip-roaring and anarchically picaresque tilt at class windmills, as was his excellent *The Charge Of The Light Brigade* (1968). A former husband of the actress **Vanessa Redgrave**, Richardson's work fell off in later years, but he had a marvellous and well-earned return to form with the posthumously released *Blue Sky* (1994).

Other Key Films: *The Entertainer* (1960); *Saturday Night And Sunday Morning* (1960); *The Loved One* (1965); *The Border* (1981)

Rickman, Alan

Neither exceptionally handsome nor exceptionally well endowed with athletic grace, what Rickman has going for him is that he can act – his most oleaginous of Mr Slopes in BBC TV's masterly *Barchester Chronicles* (1982), suggested it, his Jamie in **Anthony Minghella's** *Truly Madly Deeply* (1991) proved it, and his Colonel Brandon in **Ang Lee's** *Sense And Sensibility* (1995) compounded that proof, for Rickman turned the nominally unglamorous, unthankful part of a retired, middle-aged army officer into a tour-de-force of virile acting, totally in keeping with the period in which the story was set. And that is another of Rickman's strengths – he is sufficiently confident of his skills to allow the audience time to appreciate them, rather than ramming them, in the fashion of certain celebrity actors, down people's throats.

Other Key Films: *Die Hard* (1988); *The January Man* (1989); *Close My Eyes* (1991); *Closet Land* (1991); *Robin Hood: Prince Of Thieves* (1991) *Bob Roberts* (1992); *An Awfully Big Adventure* (1995); *Michael Collins*

A still from Leni Riefenstahl's 1938 documentary Olympia which covered the eleventh Olympic Games held in Berlin in 1936.

Olympia-Film/The Kobal Collection

(1996); *The Winter Guest* [dir.] (1997); *Judas Kiss* (1998); *Galaxy Quest* (1999); *Dark Harbor* (1999); *Blow Dry* (2001); *Harry Potter And The Sorcerer's Stone* (2001); *Love Actually* (2003); *Harry Potter And The Prisoner Of Azkaban* (2004); *Snowcake* (2005); *Harry Potter And The Goblet Of Fire* (2005); *Nobel Son* (2006)

Key Line: 'Cancel the kitchen scraps for lepers and orphans. No more merciful beheadings. And call off Christmas!' [Rickman as the Sheriff of Nottingham in Kevin Reynolds's *Robin Hood: Prince Of Thieves*]

Riefenstahl, Leni

Excoriated and imprisoned for her adherence to and friendship with Adolf Hitler, no one can deny that Riefenstahl has been one of the most influential filmmakers of the past century, even if that influence can now be perceived, with the benefit of hindsight, to have been largely malevolent. Professing her innocence right to the end, Riefenstahl nonetheless encapsulated the horrible and empty beauty of fascism in two masterpieces of heroic contrivance: *Triumph Of The Will* (1936), which purported to be a documentary about the Nüremberg rallies but was, in fact, a Goebbels-inspired hymn to Nazi hysteria, and the two-part *Olympia* [*Fest Der Schönheit* and *Fest Der Völker*] (1938) which again purported to be a documentary, this time about the 1936 Berlin Olympics but was, in fact, a Goebbels-motivated paean to Arian supremacy. The answer to the enigma of Riefenstahl may lie in such earlier pantheistic 'mountain' films as *The Blue Light* (1932), which she both directed and acted in, and in which Germanic neo-poetic idealism finds itself allied to a curious sort of romantic folly.

Other Key Films: *Victory Of The Faith* [*Der Sieg Des Glaubens*] (1933); *Day Of Freedom* (1935); *Berchtesgarten Uber Salzburg* (1935); *Tiefland* (1954); *Impressionen Unter Wasser* [Docu.] (2002)

Riskin, Robert

New Yorker Riskin wrote the screenplays or assisted with the dialogue on a number of **Frank Capra** comedies, including *Platinum Blonde* (1931), *It Happened One Night* (1934) [for which he won an Oscar], *Mr. Deeds Goes To Town* (1935) and *Meet John Doe* (1941). An absolute ace with the one and two liners, Riskin was also used on the *Thin Man* series, most notably as the scriptwriter on Richard Thorpe's *The Thin Man Goes Home* (1944), which, not surprisingly, proved to be one of the funniest of the whole sequence. Another significant achievement was his script, based on James Hilton's best-selling novel, for Capra's resolutely non-comedic *Lost Horizon* (1937).

Other Key Films: **John Ford's** *The Whole Town's Talking* (1935); **Henry Hathaway's** *The Real Glory* (1939); **William Wellman's** *Magic Town* (1947)

Ritt, Martin

A politically conscientious director whose work could, on occasion, slip into a somewhat bathetic earnestness, Ritt was at his best coaxing anti-heroic performances out of otherwise heroically inclined actors. *Hud* (1963), with an electric **Paul Newman** and an unsentimentally realist Patricia Neal, was his finest film, while *The Spy Who Came In From The Cold* (1966) saw **Richard Burton** plumb the depths of existential despair. Later films, such as *The Front* (1976) and *Norma Rae* (1979) were thoroughly professional, but just a little worthy.

Other Key Films: *Edge Of The City* (1958); *The Long Hot Summer* (1958); *The Sound And The Fury* (1959); *Hombre* (1967); *The Molly Maguires* (1970); *Conrack* (1974); *Cross Creek* (1983); *Murphy's Romance* (1985); *Stanley & Iris* (1990)

Key Line: 'The immediate recognition that we were dealing with a man of principle, a man with a wonderful mind, a man who was absolutely honest and direct… He fought a lot of battles for us. We were a gang of three.' [Irving Ravetch and Harriet Frank Jr on Ritt, for whom they scripted *The Long Hot Summer*, *The Sound And The Fury*, *Hud*, *Hombre*, *Conrack*, *Norma Rae*, *Murphy's Romance* and *Stanley & Iris*]

Ritter, Thelma

One of the best-loved and most instantly recognizable of all character actresses, Ritter specialized in playing weary, caustic, blue-collar working women in what now seems a plethora of the best 1940s and 1950s films. Although Ritter was inevitably typecast in this way, she never cheated her audience, and there are a few real gems among her performances, particularly as **Bette Davis's** conscience in **Joseph L Mankiewicz's** *All About Eve* (1950), as the murdered saleswoman in **Samuel Fuller's** *Pickup On South Street* (1953), and as **Marilyn Monroe's** cynical friend in **John Huston's** *The Misfits* (1960).

Other Key Films: *A Letter To Three Wives* (1949); *Perfect Strangers* (1950); *Titanic* (1953); *Rear Window* (1954); *Pillow Talk* (1959); *A Hole In The Head* (1959); *Birdman Of Alcatraz* (1962)

Key Line: 'Listen mister. When I come in here tonight you seen an old clock running down. I'm tired. I'm through. Happens to everybody sometime. It'll happen to you too someday.' [*Pickup On South Street*]

Roach, Hal

Roach lived to be a hundred, and was finally honoured with a special Oscar, at the age of ninety-one, for his extraordinary contribution to film comedy. As producer to the Greats, he discovered and cosseted the likes of **Laurel and Hardy**, **Harold Lloyd** and the Our Gang team, while at the same time aiding and abetting the early careers of directors such as **Leo McCarey**, **George Marshall** and **George Stevens**, and, hardly coincidentally, generating some of the best and most enduring of all film comedies.

Other Key Films: Edgar Kennedy's *From Soup To Nuts* (1928); Roach's own *Men Of The North* (1930); Roach and Charles Rogers's *Fra Diavolo* (1933); Norman McLeod's *Topper* (1937); James W Horne's *Way Out West* (1937); Lewis Milestone's *Of Mice And Men* (1939); Gordon Douglas's *Saps At Sea* (1940)

Road Movies

The United States is a country of travellers, of people who come from somewhere, stay a little, and then move on; it is natural, therefore, that a genre of film should spring up to reflect this. Road movies take place during the course of journeys, journeys that can function either as an escape from discovery or as a means of discovery. Like the best short stories, such films are about change; about the effects a stranger's passing can have on an otherwise closed community. Many of the greatest **Westerns** are road movies, as are some of the finest *film noirs*. Each generation of filmmakers rediscovers the archetype and makes it their own.

Key Films: **Frank Capra's** *It Happened One Night* (1934); **John Ford's** *The Grapes Of Wrath* (1940); **Preston Sturges's** *Sullivan's Travels* (1941); Tay Garnett's *The Postman Always Rings Twice* (1946); **Jacques Tourneur's** *Out Of The Past* (1947); **Nicholas Ray's** *They Live By Night* (1949); **Joseph H Lewis's** *Gun Crazy* (1949); **Anthony Mann's** *Winchester '73* (1950); John Ford's *The Searchers* (1956); **Dennis Hopper's** *Easy Rider* (1969); **Bob Rafelson's** *Five Easy Pieces* (1970); **Terrence**

Malick's *Badlands* (1973); **Stephen Frears's** *The Hit* (1985); **David Lynch's** *Wild At Heart* (1990); **Ridley Scott's** *Thelma And Louise* (1991); **Hal Hartley's** *Simple Men* (1992); **Patrice Leconte's** *Tango* (1993)

Robbins, Tim

Robbins began at the very bottom – which doesn't mean auditioning and giving away his tapes to every producer going; it means all that and then finding that four consecutive big movies you have a major part in are flops. Yes, Robbins featured in Willard Huyck's *Howard The Duck* (1986), Bill Fishman's *Tapeheads* (1988), Terry Jones's *Eric The Viking* (1989) and Roger Donaldson's *Cadillac Man* (1990) in the space of just five years. It is to his eternal credit (and a tribute to his talent) that he survived the sort of career vicissitudes that would have floored more fragile actors. Between 1992 and 1994 Robbins played the title role of Griffin Mill in **Robert Altman's** *The Player* (1992), directed and took the lead in *Bob Roberts* (1992), shone as randy cop Gene Shepard in Altman's *Short Cuts* (1993), redeemed *The Shawshank Redemption* from worthiness, won over waverers to **Fred Schepisi's** marginally cute *I.Q.* (1994), and made sense of the **Coen Brothers'** Pythonesque *The Hudsucker Proxy* (1994). All something of a miracle when one looks at his inauspicious beginnings. Other Key Films: *Toy Soldiers* (1984); *The Sure Thing* (1985); *Top Gun* (1986); *Bull Durham* (1988); *Dead Man Walking* [dir. only] (1995); *Nothing To Lose* (1997); *Arlington Road* (1999); *Cradle Will Rock* [dir.] (1999); *High Fidelity* (2000); *AntiTrust* (2001); *Human Nature* (2001); *Mystic River* (2003); *War Of The Worlds* (2005); *La Vida Secreta De Las Palabras* (2005); *Catch A Fire* (2006)

Roberts, Julia

The girl with the biggest grin in the world, Roberts has every reason to be happy, for she had a string of five consecutive hits between 1997 and 2001: P J Hogan's *My Best Friend's Wedding* (1997), Roger Michell's *Notting Hill* (1999), Gary Marshall's *Runaway Bride* (1999), **Steven Soderbergh's** *Erin Brockovich* (2000) and Gore Verbinski's *The Mexican* (2001). Now on $20 million a picture, with fifteen per cent of the gross thrown in for good measure, Roberts is the eternally thirty-something woman *par excellence* (she was actually born in 1967), representing female middle America's most fervid aspirational dreams. Hardly great shakes as an actress, her stage presence, however, is electrifying, and she has that rare charisma that all major stars need if they are going to make the most of their all-too-brief time at the very top. Other Key Films: *Mystic Pizza* (1988); *Steel Magnolias* (1989); *Pretty Woman* (1990); *Flatliners* (1990); *Sleeping With The Enemy* (1991); *Dying Young* (1991); *The Pelican Brief* (1993); *Mary Reilly* (1996); *Michael Collins* (1996); *Conspiracy Theory* (1997); *Stepmom* (1998); *America's Sweethearts* (2001); *Ocean's Eleven* (2001); *Mona Lisa Smile* (2003); *Closer* (2004); *Ocean's Twelve* (2004)

Robinson, Bruce

Robinson is a fine screenwriter, an occasional actor and a subtle, sensitive director, but any notionally constructive critique of his work fetches up against the phenomenon of *Withnail & I* (1986), which, to its many adherents [and this author is one], is quite simply the best British film (dare one say English?) of the past twenty years. Forget Robinson's screenplay for Roland Joffé's *The Killing Fields* (1984), magnificent though it is. Forget his scripts for Joffé's *Fat Man And Little Boy* (1989), and for his own *How To Get Ahead In Advertising* (1989) and *Jennifer 8* (1992), excellent though they are. A *Withnail & I* only comes along once in a lifetime, and that should be enough for any man. Without wishing to blow an already battered trumpet, the film is virtually faultless as both a comedy and as a record of the social mores of a recent but already bygone era, and can bear any number of repeated viewings. It thoroughly deserves its **cult**, and Robinson thoroughly deserves the credit for forcing through an idea that must have sounded terminally dire on paper. If there is any justice in the world, battered geriatrics will still be watching *Withnail* in thirty years time and muttering, 'Yes, that was how it was…' through their nicotine and vomit-stained beards, '… or, just maybe, how it should have been.'

Other Key Films: **Sidney Poitier's** *Ghost Dad* [co-sc] (1990); **Neil Jordan's** *In Dreams* [script] (1998);

Key Lines:

1. 'Getinthebackofthevan!!' [A sublimely irritated police constable in *Withnail & I*]

2. 'Baaaastards!!!' [Withnail's worldview from *Withnail & I*]

Robinson, Casey

Robinson was one of the Hollywood studio system's best literary adaptors, and his scope was quite extraordinarily wide, spanning such masterpieces of commercial cinema as **Michael Curtiz's** *Captain Blood* (1935), **Edmund Goulding's** *Dark Victory* (1939) and *The Old Maid* (1939), **Anatole Litvak's** *All This And Heaven Too* (1940) and **Irving Rapper's** *Now, Voyager* (1942), in which Robinson penned a number of the most familiar lines in Hollywood movie history. His extraordinary capacity for empathy and for delving deep down to the essence of a novel without losing sight of the author's intentions, mark him out as one of the unsung greats of the screenwriting profession.

Other Key Films: **Sam Wood's** *Kings Row* (1941) and *Saratoga Trunk* (1946); **Henry King's** *The Snows Of Kilimanjaro* (1953); **Fritz Lang's** *While The City Sleeps* (1956)

Key Line: 'Oh Jerry. Don't let's ask for the moon. We have the stars.' (*Now, Voyager*)

Robinson, Edward G

At first glance a most unlikely candidate for major stardom, the Romanian-born Emmanuel Goldenberg constructed his career very well. He cemented his initial reputation with mean gangster roles such as that of Little Rico in **Mervyn LeRoy's** *Little Caesar* (1930) and only latterly, once his reputation and name (changed to Edward G Robinson) were firmly established, moved to more challenging roles, including that of the man who invented the cure for syphilis in **William Dieterle's** *The Story Of Dr Ehrlich's Magic Bullet* (1940), which, despite its subject matter, remains one of the best-ever Hollywood biopics. A renowned collector of Impressionist paintings, Robinson made a fine series of *film noirs* during the 1940s, which included **Billy Wilder's** *Double Indemnity* (1944), and two **Fritz Lang** sizzlers, *The Woman In The Window* (1944) and *Scarlet Street* (1945). Possibly his finest performance, however, involved a sinister reprise of Little Rico (Johnny Rocco, this time) in **John Huston's** *Key Largo*, in which Robinson's face takes on an almost reptilian malevolence.

Other Key Films: *The Man With Two Faces* (1934); *Barbary Coast* (1936); *Kid Galahad* (1937); *Brother Orchid* (1940); *The Sea Wolf* (1941); *The Stranger* (1946); *The Night Has A Thousand Eyes* (1948); *House Of Strangers* (1949); *Nightmare* (1956); *Sammy Going South* (1963); *Cheyenne Autumn* (1964); *The Cincinnati Kid* (1965); *Soylent Green* (1973)

Key Line: 'Is this the end of Johnny Rocco?' [*Key Largo*]

Rodgers, Richard

First with lyricist Lorenz Hart, and then with **Oscar Hammerstein II**, Rodgers created a bevy of the most brilliant musical shows in cinema history, filmed versions of which include **Busby Berkeley's** *Babes In Arms* (1939), A Edward Sutherland's *The Boys From Syracuse* (1940), **Fred Zinnemann's** *Oklahoma!* (1955), Walter Lang's *The King And I* (1956), George Sidney's *Pal Joey* (1958), Joshua Logan's *South Pacific* (1958) and **Robert Wise's** *The Sound Of Music* (1965). A filmed biopic, Norman Taurog's *Words And Music* (1948), featuring Tom Drake as Rodgers and **Mickey Rooney** as Lorenz Hart [which included a smash Vera-Ellen and **Gene Kelly** dance version of 'Slaughter On Tenth Avenue'] was made about Rodgers's and Hart's early lives – early, for Rodgers was only forty-six and in mid-career when the film came out.

Other Key Films: A. Edward Sutherland's *Mississippi* (1935); **Mervyn LeRoy's** *Fools For Scandal* (1938); Tim Whelan's *Higher And Higher* (1944)

Roeg, Nicholas

A former clapper boy, lighting cameraman and cinematographer who belatedly moved into directing, Roeg never seemed totally at ease in front of the camera (or, perhaps more accurately, beside it). His visuals are often wonderful, but his later scripts can be woeful, particularly in the case of *Eureka* (1983). *Don't Look Now* (1973), however, in which a Venetian serial killer becomes the final, deadly catalyst in the story of two people torn apart by the loss of their child, is a first-rate and disciplined thriller, and *Bad Timing* (1980), though intellectually rather perverse, still holds together visually. Roeg's first film, *Performance* (1970), which he co-directed with Donald Cammell, is now something of a **cult** favourite, more due to Cammell's wayward genius and Mick Jagger's iconic presence (and swoopingly variable accent), than to Roeg's own input. *The Man Who Fell To Earth* (1976) was a genuine oddity – a brilliant idea, with striking visuals, and a magnetic star presence in David Bowie, but which nevertheless contrived to verge on the incoherent. If this all sounds unduly critical, it shouldn't be taken as such, for Roeg's standards and his expectations of himself are high, and his is a genuinely eclectic talent which can provoke, puzzle and satisfy in roughly equal measures.

Other Key Films: *Walkabout* (1971); *Insignificance* (1985); *Castaway* (1986); *Aria* (1987); *The Witches* (1990); *Cold Heaven* (1992); *Heart Of Darkness* (1994); *Two Deaths* (1995); *Puffball* (2006)

Rogers, Ginger

A scintillating dancer, notably alongside **Fred Astaire** in Mark Sandrich's *The Gay Divorcée* (1934) and *Top Hat* (1935), not to mention **George Stevens's** *Swing Time* (1936), Rogers (whose career was almost entirely run by her mother) was also a more than passable, sometimes even raunchy, comedienne, as witnessed by her earlier work in Lloyd Bacon's *42nd Street* (1933) and **Mervyn LeRoy's** *Gold Diggers Of 1933* (1933). Rogers had more serious aspirations, however, than hoofing and comedy, and she single-mindedly pursued them (and an Oscar) in **Sam Wood's** *Kitty Foyle* (1940). She never really reclaimed the ground she lost when her partnership with Fred Astaire broke up in 1939 (to be briefly revived in 1949 with **Charles Waters's** The Barkleys Of Broadway), but her talent for mimicry was shown to good effect in **Billy Wilder's** entertaining oddity *The Major And The Minor* (1942), while her capacity for melodrama took pride of place in Alex Segal's *Harlow* (1965).

Other Key Films: *Flying Down To Rio* (1933); *Rafter Romance* (1934); *Roberta* (1935);

Vivacious Lady (1938); *The Primrose Path* (1940); *Tom, Dick And Harry* (1941); *Roxie Hart* (1942); *Forever Female* (1953)

Rogers, Roy

Rogers asked to be skinned and stuffed and placed on his beloved horse, Trigger, when he died, and one suspects that if this had been legally possible, it would have been done, and the defunct cowboy and his erstwhile steed would now be waiting to greet their guests at the entrance to the Roy Rogers Museum in Victorville, California, with 'Happy Trails' gently playing in the background. Rogers made people feel good in his movies, and advocated the sort of clean-living, clean-thinking life that now seems so resolutely out of fashion (except with the silent majority, of course). In movies such as Joseph Kane's *King Of The Cowboys* (1943) and William Witney's *Roll On Texas Moon* (1947) and *Heart Of The Rockies* (1951), Rogers, with his wife, Dale Evans, and his chum, Gabby Hayes, by his side, suggested security to a whole generation of children who grew up in the aftermath of the Second World War only to find themselves trapped afresh within the toils of the lengthy and paranoid Cold War which followed it. And that's quite some achievement.

Other Key Films: *Under Western Stars* (1939); *Dark Command* (1940); *Sons Of The Pioneers* (1942); *The Cowboy And The Señorita* (1944); *My Pal Trigger* (1946); *Springtime In The Sierras* (1947); *North Of The Great Divide* (1950)

Rogers, Will

Will Rogers was the master of the sort of ersatz homespun philosophy that had Americans queuing to see his talking pictures – he was a bit of a flop in silent movies, for obvious reasons – exactly when they were at their most vulnerable, i.e. during the Great Depression. His great art lay in reminding people that the common man has something to say too, if he can only spit out of his chaw, clear his throat and get a word in edgewise. By the time of his death, in a plane crash in 1935, the fifty-five-year-old Rogers was reportedly the most famous man in America after the President. In movies such as **John Ford's** *Doctor Bull* (1933), *Judge Priest* (1934) and *Steamboat Round The Bend* (1935), Rogers charmed his way into American folklore, and his polo ranch above Malibu is now something of a national shrine.

Other Key Films: *Happy Days* (1929); *A Connecticut Yankee* (1931); *State Fair* (1933); *Mr. Skitch* (1933); *Doubting Thomas* (1935); *In Old Kentucky* (1935)

Key Line: 'There is only one thing that can kill the movies, and that is education.' [Rogers on film]

Rohmer, Eric

An early editor of *Cahiers du Cinéma*, Rohmer turned to directing in the 1960s with his series of moral tales (*Les Contes Moreaux*), which featured the celebrated *Claire's Knee* (1971), in which a lust-tormented Jean-Claude Brialy spends most of the film debating whether or not to touch his friend's daughter's patella. Rohmer's genius, of course, lies in his concentration on the mundane to highlight the larger emotional issues that face adolescents and adults. He continued this delicate process both with his comedies and proverbs (*Comédies et Proverbes*) of the 1980s, and with his more recent seasonal tales, building an impressive body of work notable for its delicate subtleties and complete lack of ostentation.

Other Key Films: *La Collectioneuse* (1967); *Pauline À La Plage* (1983); *L'Ami De Mon Ami* (1987); *Conte De Printemps* (1990); *Conte D'Hiver* (1992); *Conte D'Été* (1996); *Conte D'Automne* (1998); *L'Anglaise Et Le Duc* (2000); *Triple Agent* (2004)

Rooney, Mickey

Rooney epitomized what young America thought it might like to be during late 1930s and early 1940s. A wisecracking, anti-intellectual ball of fire, he would probably have been sat upon at the earliest opportunity in real life, and he actually *was* sat upon after his return from an unlikely war service. To foreign audiences, there was always something sensationally curious about Rooney, but then there seems something sensationally curious about the America he represents, an America which still mystifies onlookers with its self-defeating charivaris, and in the light of which Rooney's nine marriages, and assorted bankruptcies, comebacks, sentimental outings and tough-minded statements of intent seem perfectly normal, everyday matters. That said, Rooney managed to transcend his image on one or two occasions, proving that there was indeed chicken-wire behind the papier-mâché. He was genuinely good as Puck in Max Reinhardt and **William Dieterle's** *A Midsummer Night's Dream* (1935), and genuinely tough in **Don Siegel's** *Baby Face Nelson* (1958). In the interim he gave America what it seemed to want, and then reminded them of the cost involved in getting it.

Other Key Films: *A Family Affair* (1937); *Boys Town* (1938); *The Adventures Of Huckleberry Finn* (1939); *Strike Up The Band* (1940); *Babes On Broadway* (1942); *National Velvet* (1944); *Words And Music* (1948); *The Bridges At Toko-Ri* (1955); *Breakfast At Tiffany's* (1961); *It's A Mad Mad Mad Mad World* (1963); *The Black Stallion* (1979); *Maximum Force* (1992); *Lightning, The White Stallion* (1996); *The First Of May* (1999); *Paradise* (2003); *Strike The Tent* (2005); *Bamboo Shark* (2006)

Rossellini, Roberto

Rossellini is the man who snatched **Ingrid Bergman** from her adoring fans (and her adoring husband) in the United States, impregnated her (twice), then sent her packing following his affair and subsequent (one presumes) impregnation of the Indian screenwriter, Somali Das Gupta. That's how the newspapers had it, anyway. All that aside, Rossellini just happens to be one of the main progenitors of the **neo-realist** movement in Italy, and a filmmaker, perhaps more influential than tender, more intellectual than wry, whose obsession with the necessity of 'seeing' everything, whether from the point of view of the actor or of the audience, could serve, and sometimes did, to alienate both. His greatest films were his war trilogy, *Roma Città Aperta* [*Open City*] (1945), *Paisà* [*Paisan*] (1946) and *Germania Anno Zero* [*Germany Year Zero*] (1947), followed by *L'Amore* (1948), in which his then lover Anna Magnani portrayed two enduring Italian archetypes, the scorned lover and the saintly peasant, and finally the extraordinary *Viaggio In Italia* (1958), which succeeds despite (or perhaps because of) the fact that its two stars, Bergman and **George Sanders**, didn't have the faintest idea what the film they were in the process of making was about.

Other Key Films: *Stromboli* (1949); *The Seven Deadly Sins* (1952); *Europa '51* (1952); *Joan Of Arc At The Stake* (1954); *General Della Rovere* (1959); *Agostino Di Ippona* (1972)

Roth, Tim

Roth is one of only a handful of British actors to have made a successful long-term crossover to American cinema. Following his extraordinary performance as Mr. Orange/Freddy in **Quentin Tarantino's** *Reservoir Dogs* (1992) (one assumes that Tarantino had seen Roth's performance in **Stephen Frears's** *The Hit* (1984), and cast him on the strength of it), he went on to feature as Pumpkin, in the same director's *Pulp Fiction* (1994), and as Joshua, a hit man with family problems, in James Gray's

Little Odessa (1994). He played bravely against type as an English aristocrat in Michael Caton-Jones's *Rob Roy* (1995), before reverting once again to lucrative gangster-hood in Bill Duke's *Hoodlum* (1997). All humour aside, Roth is an excellent actor who deserves to be challenged by rather more than a gun, a sword or a hypodermic syringe. Other Key Films: *The Cook The Thief His Wife And Her Lover* (1989); *Vincent And Theo* (1990); *Rosencrantz And Guildenstern Are Dead* (1990); *Bodies, Rest & Motion* (1993); *Captives* (1995); *Everyone Says I Love You* (1996); *Gridlock'd* (1997); *Vatel* (2000); *Lucky Numbers* (2000); *Planet Of The Apes* (2001); *Invincible* (2001); *To Kill A King* (2003); *Silver City* (2004); *Don't Come Knocking* (2005); *Dark Water* (2005)

Rourke, Mickey

Rourke had a good run during the 1980s, trading on the success of his curiously memorable cameo as Teddy Lewis, an ex-con arsonist, in **Lawrence Kasdan's** *Body Heat* (1981), to garner parts in **Michael Cimino's** *Year Of The Dragon* (1985), Adrian Lyne's curious psycho-sexual hodgepodge, *9 1/2 Weeks* (1986), and **Alan Parker's** underrated *Angel Heart* (1987) – and yes, Rourke doesn't dress in period, but in the context of a fantasy film like *Angel Heart*, what does it matter? His best part to date has come as Henry Chinaski (alter ego of cult author, Charles Bukowski) in **Barbet Schroeder's** *Barfly* (1987), and even though his recent star has set a little despite a number of perfectly respectable performances, there is still something about his mannered style and his existentialist, bloody-minded off-screen troublemaking that appeals. With everyone against him but the French, the guy must be doing something right.

Other Key Films: *Heaven's Gate* (1980); *Diner* (1982) *Eureka* (1983); *Rumble Fish* (1983); *A Prayer For The Dying* (1987); *White Sands* (1992); *The Rain Maker* (1997); *Point Blank* (1997); *Shergar* (1999); *Get Carter* (2000); *The Pledge* (2001); *Claire's Hat* (2001); *Spun* (2002); *Once Upon A Time In Mexico* (2003); *Sin City* (2005); *Domino* (2005); *Stormbreaker* (2006); *Killshot* (2006)

Rozsa, Miklós

Rozsa wrote fulsome music that didn't cloy, something of a cute trick in a Hollywood whose view of old Vienna involved *Sachertorte*, Sigmund Romberg (who was actually born in Hungary, just as Rozsa was) and Lily Pons trilling 'Tales Of The Vienna Woods' (or something remarkably like it) to a somewhat bemused **Henry Fonda**, in John Cromwell's *I Dream Too Much* (1935). Hearing a Rozsa score winding itself up as a prelude to **Billy Wilder's** *Five Graves To Cairo* (1943) or *Double Indemnity* (1944), for instance, or maybe in **Alfred Hitchcock's** *Spellbound* (1945), **Robert Siodmak's** *The Killers* (1946), **John Huston's** *The Asphalt Jungle* (1950) or George Sidney's *Young Bess* (1953), has been know to cause grown men and women to rub their hands together in lurid anticipation of a *real* Hollywood movie, something with love and passion, drama and guts in it. Rozsa and other composers of his ilk, including **Bernard Hermann**, **Max Steiner**, **Frederick Hollander** and **Erich Wolfgang Korngold**, are more than a little responsible for the *feeling* that remains of a movie after the plot and the characters and even the context in which one saw it have long been forgotten.

Other Key Films: Jacques Feyder's *Knight Without Armour* (1937); **Alexander Korda's** multi-directed *The Thief Of Bagdad* (1940); Billy Wilder's *The Lost Weekend* (1945); **Jules Dassin's** *Brute Force* (1947); **George Cukor's** *Bhowani Junction* (1956); **William Wyler's** *Ben-Hur* (1959)

Rudolph, Alan

Rudolph is the quirky, quasi-independent director of such fascinating after-dinner movies as *Choose Me* (1984), *Trouble In Mind* (1985) and the curious *Mortal Thoughts* (1991), which featured the realistically slumming team of Demi Moore and **Bruce Willis**, in their one and only non-mainstream movie. *The Moderns* (1988) and *Mrs. Parker And The Vicious Circle* (1994) represent Rudolph in full period fig, and they are both remarkably successful at conjuring up a jaded epoch in which style was seen to equate to talent – something which is unfortunately all too true of our own generation, and so gives the films an added resonance. His recent *Afterglow* (1997) continues the vein of character over story which Rudolph has mined so well, and it is extremely heartening to know that Rudolph is out there, like his near contemporary, **John Sayles**, quietly notching up an impressive list of recognisably consistent films.

Other Key Films: *Buffalo Bill And The Indians, Or Sitting Bull's History Lesson* (1976); *Welcome To LA*(1977); *Remember My Name* (1979); *Roadie* (1980); *Endangered Species* (1982); *Songwriter* (1985); *Equinox* (1993); *Breakfast Of Champions* (1999); *Trixie* (2000); *Investigating Sex* (2001); *The Secret Lives Of Dentists* (2002)

Russell, Gail

The only girl whose limpid eyes could look blue in black and white, Russell never made it to the big time, and died tragically, aged thirty-six, after a long fight against alcoholism. A shy, unarguably beautiful woman, Russell was at her best in roles that brought out her innate masochism, and one feels almost guilty about calling her the most alluring victim in cinema history. **John Wayne**, who was rumoured to be in love with her, partnered her to good effect in two of his lesser but still underrated films, James Edward Grant's *The Angel And The Badman* (1947) and Edward Ludwig's *Wake Of The Red Witch* (1948), and she was also very good in **John Farrow's** *Calcutta* (1947). **Joseph Losey**, too, recognised the power of those extraordinary, fated eyes, in his otherwise unremarkable *The Lawless* (1950).

Other Key Films: *The Uninvited* (1944); *The Unseen* (1945); *The Night Has A Thousand Eyes* (1948); *Captain China* (1949); *Seven Men From Now* (1956); *The Tattered Dress* (1958)

Russell, Jane

Russell is fun, and her movies, while never taking themselves too seriously, always reflect her buoyant nature and are consequently redeemed from the mediocrity that might otherwise have been their lot. Despite the mixed blessing(s) of a world-famous bust, Russell proved she could sass with the best of them, standing up to **Robert Mitchum** in **Josef von Sternberg's** *Macao* (1952), to just about everybody in **Howard Hawks's** *Gentlemen Prefer Blondes* (1953), and to the King himself, **Clark Gable**, in **Raoul Walsh's** *The Tall Men* (1955). Mention, too, has to be made of **Howard Hughes's** *The Outlaw* (1943), the film in which Russell was first exposed to an eagerly waiting world.

Other Key Films: *The Paleface* (1948); *His Kind Of Woman* (1951); *Double Dynamite* [one hell of a title, in the circumstances] (1951); *The Las Vegas Story* (1952); *Underwater!* (1955); *Hot Blood* (1956); *The Revolt Of Mamie Stover* (1956); *Darker Than Amber* (1970)

Key Line: 'I like a man who can run faster than I can.' [*Gentlemen Prefer Blondes*]

Russell, Ken

The iconoclastic director of some of the best television documentaries ever made (for the BBC *Monitor* programme), Russell had considerable success with his biographies of composers Frederick Delius, Edward Elgar and Claude Debussy and this paved the way for his extraordinary debut in feature films, *Women In Love* (1969), which remains one of the best-ever big-screen adaptations of D H Lawrence. Always a little prone to creative hysteria, Russell allowed his fervid love of music and his inordinate pleasure in shocking his audience to coalesce in *The Music Lovers* (1971), which took viewers on a heady ride to an inspired, rather than a base, camp. *The Devils* (1971), though much reviled at the time, was brilliantly designed and as feverishly true to its origins as its author was anarchic – British cinema had never known his mainstream equal. Russell's first US film, *Altered States* (1980), was a great success (despite author Paddy Chayefsky's appalled disclaimers), and Russell continues to this day, alternately missing and hitting the mark, his cherubic smile and radical intelligence intact. There is no one else quite like him.

Other Key Films: *The Boy Friend* (1971); *Savage Messiah* (1972); *Mahler* (1974); *Tommy* (1975); *Lisztomania* (1975); *Valentino* (1977); *Crimes Of Passion* (1984); *Gothic* (1987); *The Rainbow* (1989); *Whore* (1991); *MindBender* (1996); *The Fall Of The Louse Of Usher* (2002)

Ryan, Meg

Ryan is an intelligent actress, somewhat along the lines of a Lee Remick, whose success seems, in some strange way, rather out of proportion to her talent. Looking through her filmography one is hard put to select an especially memorable film, and the inevitable conclusion to be drawn (and this is not meant pejoratively) is that Ryan is an actress of the moment, a condition that incorporates both her strength and her weakness. Strength, because her enjoyment of her stardom is, after all, now; weakness, in that her films, even such period dramas as Michael Hoffman's *Restoration* (1995), resolutely fail to transcend the era in which they happen to be filmed. Ryan is a 1980s woman, and she carries this unfortunate condition through to any part she plays. The upside is that in the films where she plays to type, as in Rob Reiner's *When Harry Met Sally...* (1989) and Nora Ephron's *Sleepless In Seattle* (1993), she is magnificently successful, and in thirty years time, people will look back at the results with fascinated horror, rather as today they look back at bell-bottomed trousers, the zoot suit, and the beehive hairdo.

Other Key Films: *D.O.A.* (1988); *Flesh And Bone* (1993); *I.Q.* (1994); *When A Man Loves A Woman* (1994); *French Kiss* (1995); *Addicted To Love* (1997); *You've Got Mail* (1998); *Hanging Up* (2000); *Proof Of Love* (2000); *In The Cut* (2003); *Against The Ropes* (2004)

Ryan, Robert

Ryan is a movie connoisseur's actor – an adept at darker roles, he was the protagonist of choice for a number of the great **film noir** directors, who understood that Ryan had that rare thing, the ability to live a role, even if that role happened to be unsympathetic. A pronounced liberal by conviction, Ryan portrayed an anti-semite in **Edward Dmytryk's** *Crossfire* (1947), a has-been boxer in **Robert Wise's** superb *The Set-Up* (1949), and a disenchanted cop on the verge of a nervous breakdown in **Nicholas Ray's** sensational *On Dangerous Ground* (1951). Head and shoulders above many of the more mundane leading men of his day, Ryan improved even bad movies by his presence, and some aspects of his performances remain deep in the mind long after the movies themselves have been forgotten.

Other Key Films: *The Woman On The Beach* (1947); *Berlin Express* (1948); *The Secret*

Fury (1950); *The Racket* (1951); *Beware, My Lovely* (1952); *Clash by Night* (1952); *The Naked Spur* (1953); *Bad Day At Black Rock* (1955), *Day Of The Outlaw* (1959); *Odds Against Tomorrow* (1959) *Billy Budd* (1962); *The Wild Bunch* (1969); *The Outfit* (1973)

Ryder, Winona

With her unconventional childhood (she is the god-daughter of LSD-exponent Timothy Leary) and her delicate good looks, Ryder might easily have drifted into feisty victim movies, along the lines of Wes Craven's *Scream* (1996), but her winsomeness is cut with intelligence, and her art with cunning, as she showed from very early on, as **Dennis Quaid**/Jerry Lee Lewis's cousin Myra in Jim McBride's *Great Balls Of Fire* (1989). She has chosen well since then, alternating canny commercial fare like Gillian Armstrong's *Little Women* (1994), Ben Stiller's *Reality Bites* (1994) and Jocelyn Moorhouse's *How To Make An American Quilt* (1995), with more esoteric material, such as **Tim Burton's** *Edward Scissorhands* (1990), Richard Benjamin's *Mermaids* (1990) and **Jim Jarmusch's** *Night On Earth* (1991). If she ignores her agent's advice and remembers to leaven her moneymaking with riskier projects, such as her Abigail Williams in Nicholas Hytner's *The Crucible* (1996), she will have a career to be proud of.

Other Key Films: *Beetlejuice* (1988); *The Age Of Innocence* (1993); *The House Of The Spirits* (1994); *Celebrity* (1998); *Autumn In New York* (2000); *Lost Souls* (2000); *S1m0ne* (2001); *Mr Deeds* (2002); *The Darwin Awards* (2006); *A Scanner Darkly* (2006)

Sanda, Dominique

Sanda was the intellectual film buff's pin-up during the 1970s, and something of a hit with art-house directors too, who saw in her glacial beauty a metaphorical canvas on which their visual and verbal conceits could be played out. She was the last major actress to have an air of mystery about her (excepting, perhaps, Irene Jacob and **Juliette Binoche**), and following her debut in **Robert Bresson's** *Une Femme Douce* (1969), in which Bresson perfectly captured the elusive, instinctual intelligence which was her stock-in-trade, Sanda found herself cast as **Bernardo Bertolucci's** Anna Quadri in *The Conformist* (1970), a woman destroyed by the very object of the fascination she so knowingly exerted. The third film in that great early trilogy of hers (she was aged between twenty-one and twenty-three at the time) was **Vittorio De Sica's** *The Garden Of The Finzi-Continis* (1971), which proved to be a metaphor as much for the loss of Eden as it was for the lurid attractions of the snake that precipitated its fall.

Other Key Films: *Without Apparent Motive* (1971); *L'Impossible Objet* (1973); *Steppenwolf* (1974); *1900* (1976); *Eredità Ferramonti* (1976); *Caboblanco* (1980); *Les Mendiants* (1988); *Nobody's Children* [TVM] (1994); *Garage Olimpo* (1999); *Les Rivieres Pourpres* (2000); *The Island Of The Mapmaker's Wife* (2000)

Sanders, George

Sanders carried the world-weary, more-than-marginally cynical sophisticate that he played, often indifferently, in a host of sometimes indifferent films, through into his real life, when he picked up a bottle of pills, downed them, and proceeded to shuffle off his mortal coil in as elegant and flippant a manner as possible, aged sixty-five, thus fulfilling a promise he had made to himself in a typical fit of prescience nearly thirty years earlier. At his best, in **Albert Lewin's** cad-trilogy comprising *The Moon And Sixpence* (1942), *The Picture Of Dorian Gray* (1945) and *The Private Affairs Of Bel Ami* (1947), and also in **Joseph L Mankiewicz's** *All About Eve* (1950), Sanders played the quintessential, albeit occasionally tender-minded bounder, whose concept the eighteenth century had inadvertently bequeathed to the twentieth. Just once, however, in **Roberto Rossellini's** magnificent *Viaggio In Italia* (1953), did he stumble upon a director and a film that managed to cut beneath the glitteringly, sneeringly barbed carapace that he wore as armour, and down to the livid, inhibited flesh underneath. Sanders never repeated the exercise, and he went on to die, nineteen years later, just as he had chosen to live – by a process of enlightened default.

Other Key Films: *Confessions Of A Nazi Spy* (1939); *Rebecca* (1940); *Foreign Correspondent* (1940); *The Lodger* (1944); *Hangover Square* (1945); *The Ghost And Mrs Muir* (1947); *Ivanhoe* (1952); *While The City Sleeps* (1956); *Village Of The Damned* (1960)

Key Line: 'Dear World, I am leaving because I am bored. I feel I have lived long enough. I am leaving you with your worries in this sweet cesspool. Good luck.' [Sanders's suicide note]

Sarandon, Susan

Sarandon briefly flirted with the big time following her success in **Ridley Scott's** *Thelma And Louise* (1991), but it hardly suited her, as she is a movie connoisseur's actress, renowned more for subtlety than glitz, and more for insight than excitement (despite those famous breasts). Her best roles, but not necessarily her best performances, came early, as Sally Matthews in **Louis Malle's** *Atlantic City* (1980) and as Aretha Tomalin in **Paul Mazursky's** *Tempest* (1982). Her best recent performances have come in two somewhat flawed films, **Tim Robbins's** *Dead Man Walking* (1995), and John Turturro's *Romance & Cigarettes* (2005). Now something of a feminist icon (her roles have suffered and become a little cloying as a result), she seems a strangely European actress in an American skin.

Other Key Films: *The Rocky Horror Picture Show* (1975); *The Great Waldo Pepper* (1975); *Pretty Baby* (1978); *King Of The Gypsies* (1979); *The Witches Of Eastwick* (1987); *Bull Durham* (1988); *The January Man* (1989); *Light Sleeper* (1992); *Lorenzo's Oil* (1992); *Little Women* (1994); *The Client* (1994); *Dead Man Walking* (1995); *Twilight* (1998); *Cradle Will Rock* (1999); *Time Of Our Lives* (2000); *Igby Goes Down* (2001); *Noel* (2004); *Irresistible* (2006); *Bernard And Doris* (2006)

Saura, Carlos

Saura reflects the paradox of Spain as no one else does, for he understands the dual nature of a Spanish people whose temperament requires the presence of both a bullfighter and a bull, as opposed to, say, the English temperament, which of recent years seems to feel that it can get away with just the bull (and a castrated one, at that). Following a series of necessarily elliptical films produced under the totalitarian regime of Francisco Franco and which include the internationally successful *La Caza* (1966) and *Peppermint Frappé* (1967), Saura made a trio of films soon after Franco's death in 1975 – *Cria Cuervos* (1976), *Elisa, Vida Mia* (1977) and *Los Ojos Vendados* (1978), all attempted to come to terms with the personal and familial sense of guilt left by even an unconscious participation in Franco's tyranny. Saura is now best known for his flamenco trilogy, incorporating the superb *Blood Wedding* (1981), *Carmen* (1983), and *El Amor Brujo* (1986).

Other Key Films: *Los Golfos* (1960); *La Madriguera* (1969); *El Jardin De Las Delicias* (1970); *Ana Y Los Lobos* (1973); *El Dorado* (1988); *La Noche Oscura* (1989); *Ay Carmela!* (1990); *Flamenco* (1997); *Tango* (1998); *Goya En Burdeos* (1999); *Buñuel Y La Mesa Del Rey Salomón* (2001); *Salomé* (2002); *The Seventh Day* (2004); *Iberia* (2005)

Sayles, John

One of the best and most literate of director/screenwriters working anywhere today (a modern **Joseph L Mankiewicz**?), Sayles surpassed even himself with his recent *Lone Star* (1996), the finest and most perspicacious film about the American experience to have hit the screens since **Bob Rafelson's** *Five Easy Pieces* (1970). A novelist, hack-for-hire, teacher and occasional actor, Sayles funds his films through these peripheral activities, creating, as a result, miracles of integrity in the sea of incipient mire that is Hollywood. *The Return Of The Secaucus Seven* (1981) alerted the alertable to Sayles's talent, while *Lianna* (1983) and *Matewan* (1987) triumphantly confirmed the sighting. His strange and delightful children's film, *The Secret Of Roan Inish* (1994), simply added yet another string to this extraordinarily talented man's bow, proving that if sensibility is sufficiently refined, it will become apparent in whatever it touches.

Other Key Films: *The Brother From Another Planet* (1984); *Eight Men Out* (1988); *City Of Hope* (1991); *Men With Guns* (1997); *Limbo* (1999); *Sunshine State* (2002); *Casa De Los Babys* (2003); *Silver City* (2004)

Schepisi, Fred

Schepisi is a very successful and commercially literate director who achieved the crossover to the US with his *The Chant Of Jimmy Blacksmith* (1978), a harrowing account of tacit racism against both Aboriginals and those of mixed blood in his home country of Australia. On his arrival in North America, Schepisi made one of the most delightful and unexpected of recent **Westerns** with *Barbarosa* (1982), in which Willie Nelson and Gary Busey literally eat up the screen as two of the most unlikely but touching heroes in horse-opera history. His follow-up features, including the entertaining *Six Degrees Of Separation* (1993), have, without exception, been intelligently made and stimulating to watch, marking Schepisi out as one of the more interesting mainstream directors working today.

Other Key Films: *Iceman* (1984); *Plenty* (1985); *Roxanne* (1987); *A Cry In The Dark* (1988); *The Russia House* (1990); *Mr. Baseball* (1993); *I.Q.* (1994); *Fierce Creatures* (1997); *Last Orders* (2001); *It Runs In The Family* (2003)

Schlesinger, John

Schlesinger directed one of the finest and most adult of all British films, *Sunday Bloody Sunday* (1971), and arguably one of the best American films, too, in *Midnight Cowboy* (1969). With such a reputation behind him, one may be forgiven for feeling a little disappointed at much of his subsequent, large-scale US work, especially when one remembers the delightful *Billy Liar* (1963), and his fine evocation of Thomas Hardy's tragic world in *Far From The Madding Crowd* (1967). However he made a steady and remarkable comeback, especially after the horror of *Honky Tonk Freeway* (1981), on the smaller scale that suits his fastidious and rarefied talents, with *An Englishman Abroad* (1983), *A Question Of Attribution* (1991) and *Cold Comfort Farm* (1996), all initially made for television but proving so popular that they were given limited cinematic releases in the United States. If he had stuck to what he was good at, rather than being drawn into the commercial and moral morass, Schlesinger's reputation would not have suffered the ups and downs it has, and he would now be regarded, not merely by the few, but by the many, as one of the finest directors of the past half century.

Other Key Films: *A Kind Of Loving* (1962); *Darling* (1965); *The Day Of The Locust* (1975); *Marathon Man* (1976); *Yanks* (1979); *The Falcon And The Snowman* (1985);

Madame Sousatzka (1988); *Pacific Heights* (1990); *The Innocent* (1993); *Eye For An Eye* (1996); *The Next Best Thing* (2000)

Schoonmaker, Thelma

One of the acknowledged greats of the editing world (and the wife, from 1984 until his death in 1990, of **Michael Powell**), Schoonmaker has worked almost exclusively with **Martin Scorsese**, whom she got to know when they were both freshmen at NYU. Her brilliant work on Michael Wadleigh's famous documentary about the 1969 Woodstock Festival (which she co-edited with Scorsese), followed hard on the heels of her collaboration on Scorsese's first feature, *Who's That Knocking At My Door?* (1968), a film which predated her Oscar-winning work on *Raging Bull* (1980) by a surprising twelve years. Since then she's worked on virtually all the director's films, and her editing is notable both for its fluency and for its technical brilliance.

Other Key Films: *The King Of Comedy* (1983); *After Hours* (1985); *The Color Of Money* (1986); *The Last Temptation Of Christ* (1988); *Goodfellas* (1990); *Cape Fear* (1991); *Age Of Innocence* (1993); *Casino* (1995); Alison Anders's *Cradle Of My Heart* (1996); *Kundun* (1997); *Bringing Out The Dead* (1999); *Gangs Of New York* (2002); *The Aviator* (2004); *The Departed* (2006) [all directed by Martin Scorsese unless otherwise indicated]

Schrader, Paul

Schrader began his film career as a screenwriter, working with **Robert Towne** on **Sidney Pollack's** *The Yakuza* (1975). He followed this with a solo credit for **Martin Scorsese's** *Taxi Driver* (1976), a film which, not unsurprisingly, afforded him a relatively easy entrée into Hollywood's exclusive writer/director's list. His directional debut, *Blue Collar* (1978), was an underrated little film and may just have influenced **Quentin Tarantino's** sassy dialogue for *Reservoir Dogs* (1992) and *Pulp Fiction* (1994). Since then he has proved himself an edgy, intellectual director, who has always stood on the periphery of the mainstream, choosing subjects that mark him out as a marginal independent. Following his commercial success with *American Gigolo* (1980), and his critical success with *Cat People* (1982), Schrader has alternated between scriptwriting jobs for other directors, and the making of his own tormented films, which include the excellent *Mishima: A Life In Four Chapters* (1985), and the extremely overwrought *The Comfort Of Strangers* (1990). A philosophy major and film theoretician, Schrader has the courage to take risks, but his self-awareness can sometime backfire on him, as he showed in *Light Sleeper* (1992), a film supposedly based (let's hope only in part) on one of Schrader's own 'lost weekends'.

Other Key Films: *Hardcore* (1979); Martin Scorsese's *Raging Bull* [script] (1980) and *The Last Temptation Of Christ* [script] (1988); **Peter Weir's** *Mosquito Coast* [script] (1986); *Light Of Day* (1987); *Patty Hearst* (1988); *Touch* (1996); *Forever Mine* (1999); *Auto Focus* (2002); *Dominion: Prequel To The Exorcist* (2005)

Schroeder, Barbet

Schroeder started off by producing a number of **Eric Rohmer's** early films, including *La Collectioneuse* (1966) and *Ma Nuit Chez Maud* (1969), before branching out into directing with the curious *More* (1969), a film which has aged better than many of its psychedelic contemporaries, and can now be seen as remarkably true to the particular period of the mid-1960s it is depicting. A number of documentaries followed, before Schroeder, inflamed perhaps by **Bernardo Bertolucci's** *Last Tango In Paris* (1973), attempted his own investigation into the subtleties of sexual role-play and power games with *Maîtresse* (1976), in which **Gérard Depardieu** gets in over his head following an affair he instigates with professional dominatrix, Bulle Ogier. During the 1980s Schroeder showed his versatility by directing four very different films in succession: *Tricheurs* (1984) about gambling; the Charles Bukowski/Henry Chinaski/**Mickey Rourke** curiosity *Barfly* (1987); *Reversal Of Fortune* (1990), which told of the Claus and Sunny von Bulow case; and *Single White Female* (1992), a horror film masquerading as a psychological study. Schroeder's films entertain, stimulate and tease in roughly equal proportions, and unlike those of many of his brasher contemporaries, they grow better with time.

Other Key Films: *Kiss Of Death* (1995); *Before And After* (1996); *Desperate Measures* (1998); *Our Lady Of The Assassins* (2000); *Murder By Numbers* (2002)

Schwarzenegger, Arnold

Big Arnie is not everyone's cup of goulash soup, but what he does, he does very well, and with an entirely commendable lack of restraint. He first showed us how prepossessing he could be on screen in **Bob Rafelson's** excellent *Stay Hungry* (1976), and went on to incarnate (as no one else could possibly have done in quite the same way) **John Milius's** *Conan The Barbarian* (1982), which is a far better film, along the lines of the **Alexander Korda**-produced *The Thief Of Bagdad* (1940), than many otherwise enlightened critics gave it credit for being. With his moulded grin, twinkling eyes and stupendous physique, and despite his recent brush with heart disease, Arnie remains obstinately larger-than-life, and his performances in **James Cameron's** *The Terminator* (1984), **Paul Verhoeven's** *Total Recall* (1990) and, in particular, Cameron's follow-up in the Terminator series, *Terminator 2: Judgment Day* (1991), are very nearly perfect examples of their kind – heroic, self-conscious, eager, and at the same time wryly amused both at the vagaries of the world and at a determined person's ability to manipulate them.

Other Key Films: *Pumping Iron* (1977); *Commando* (1985); *Predator* (1987); *Red Heat* (1988); *Last Action Hero* (1993); *True Lies* (1994); *Eraser* (1996); *Batman & Robin* (1997); *End Of Days* (1999); *The 6th Day* (2000); *Collateral Damage* (2001)

Key Line: John Connor: 'Jesus! You were going to kill that guy.' Big Arnie: 'Of course. I'm a Terminator.' [*Terminator 2: Judgment Day*]

Science Fiction

One of the oldest of all cinema genres (**Georges Méliès** dazzled audiences in 1898 with his *L'Homme Dans La Lune*, again in 1900 with his *Mésaventures D'Un Aéronaute*, and then in 1902 with his version of Jules Verne's *Le Voyage Dans La Lune*) in almost all cases science-fiction film is simply a transposition of other ideas and genres into space, the future, or both. Science-fiction movies have included horror films [**Ridley Scott's** *Alien* (1979)], **Westerns** [Peter Hyams's *Outland* (1981) was a virtual remake of **Fred Zinnemann's** *High Noon* (1952)], fairytales [**George Lucas's** *Star Wars* series, from 1977-2005] and even Shakespeare [Fred McLeod Wilcox's *Forbidden Planet* (1956) was a reworking of *The Tempest*]. Sci-fi movies tend to come in waves, usually allied to some major technical innovation in special effects, one prime mover being **Stanley Kubrick's** *2001: A Space Odyssey* (1968), which preceded the moon landing by one year. However it was undoubtedly the prodigious success of *Star Wars* that really brought science fiction to a wider audience and made it acceptable.

Best Science-fiction Films

Jack Arnold's *The Incredible Shrinking Man* (1958); **Luc Besson's** *The Fifth Element*

(1997); Gordon Douglas's *Them!* (1954); Richard Fleischer's *Soylent Green* (1973); **Jean-Luc Godard's** *Alphaville* (1965); Val Guest's *The Quatermass Experiment* (1955); Peter Hyams's *Outland* (1981); L Q Jones's *A Boy And His Dog* (1974); Philip Kaufman's *Invasion Of The Body Snatchers* (1978); **Stanley Kubrick's** *2001: A Space Odyssey* (1968); **Fritz Lang's** *Metropolis (1927)* and *The Girl In The Moon (1929)*; Wolf Rilla's *Village Of The Damned* (1960); **George Lucas's** *Star Wars* (1977); Christian Nyby's *The Thing* (1951); **Ken Russell's** *Altered States* (1981); **Ridley Scott's** *Blade Runner* (1982); **Don Siegel's** *Invasion Of The Body Snatchers* (1956); **Steven Spielberg's** *Close Encounters Of The Third Kind* (1977); **Paul Verhoeven's** *Robocop* (1987) and *Total Recall* (1990); **Robert Wise's** *The Day The Earth Stood Still* (1951)

Grant Williams and Randy Stuart in The Incredible Shrinking Man, directed by Jack Arnold (1956).

Universal/The Kobal Collection

Scorsese, Martin

Scorsese is an enthusiast. It comes through in the way he talks (hardly stopping to draw breath) and in the way he makes his movies – passionately, with one wary eye on the past, measuring himself – a little like Ernest Hemingway in his famous letter to Maxwell Perkins – prior to trading punches with the greats. Scorsese, to give him credit, is a more humble man than Hemingway, but he is possibly less talented too, and one can sometimes become aware, in his most prestigious films, of a process of stretching, as though he knows that he is busy composing his own epitaph and wants it to be a good one. Perhaps Scorsese's greatest gift to cinema is not so much his work as his generosity – he is a man who values others, and goes out of his way to encourage them, and he has rescued one or two reputations, **Michael Powell's** amongst them, which might otherwise have languished in the anteroom of fame. In purely filmic terms, Scorsese's real talent lies in his capacity to mould dialogue, movement and sound into one fluid, cinematic whole, and he achieves this effect most consistently with *GoodFellas* (1990), which, despite its unpleasant subject matter, still succeeds in rising above its bitter roots in a marvellous series of inspired set pieces. See **Thelma Schoonmaker**

Other Key Films: *Mean Streets* (1973); *Alice Doesn't Live Here Anymore* (1975); *Taxi Driver* (1976); *New York New York* (1978); *Raging Bull* (1980); *The King Of Comedy* (1983); *After Hours* (1985); *The Last Temptation Of Christ* (1988); *Cape Fear* (1991); *The Age Of Innocence* (1993); *Casino* (1995); *Kundun* (1997); *Bringing Out The Dead* (1999); *Gangs Of New York* (2002); *The Aviator* (2004); *The Departed* (2006)

Scott, Randolph

Scott was the tall-riding, slow-drawling star of the magnificent Ranown cycle of **Budd Boetticher** horse operas (the name was an elision of Scott's Christian name and producer Harry Joe Brown's surname) but Scott, who was born in 1898 and lived to be ninety years old, was a very different **Western** hero from the younger, brasher **John Wayne**, who was born nine years later. One always believed that Scott had *come* from somewhere, and that he would eventually move on once the action was over. His wonderful, deeply human films were always in passing; transitional movies, so to speak. Scott never explained himself, but let people think what they wanted, and if they came to the right decision, that was OK by him, and if they came to the wrong one – well, they took their own chances. His philosophy was that a man could make up his own mind – ride his own road – and any time he wanted he could change it. It's hard to believe that Scott was already sixty-two when he and Boetticher made their final film together, *Comanche Station* (1960), and that it was to be another two years before **Sam Peckinpah** asked him to buckle on his spurs one final time, together with co-star **Joel McCrea**, for the elegiac *Ride The High Country* (1962). A great man, and a great legacy – in many ways Scott *was* the myth of the West. Or how it should have been.

Other Key Films: *Roberta* (1935); *Last Of The Mohicans* (1936); *Frontier Marshall* (1939); *Jesse James* (1939); *Western Union* (1941); *Captain Kidd* (1945); *Albuquerque* (1947); *Santa Fe* (1951); *Carson City* (1952); *The Bounty Hunter* (1954); *Lawless Street* (1955); *Ten Wanted Men* (1955); *Seven Men From Now* (1956); *The Tall T* (1958); *Decision At Sundown* (1958); *Buchanan Rides Alone* (1958); *Ride Lonesome* (1959); *Westbound* (1959)

Scott, Ridley

From his starting point in British television commercials, Scott has risen to become one of the most trusted names on the Hollywood director's circuit. Since his wonderfully assured debut in *The Duellists* (1977), through *Alien* (1979), *Blade Runner* (1982) and *Thelma And Louise* (1991), most of his films have hit the mark both visually and verbally. When they do miss – apart from the excruciatingly embarrassing *GI Jane* (1997) – they always miss worthily, and never for want of trying. His recent $100,000,000 blockbuster *Gladiator* (2000), has revived yet another neglected Hollywood genre – the 'sword, vandals and sandals' epic. Even if *Gladiator* is historically inaccurate – Scott has Caesar signing letters with a wooden pen and passing them across to his secretary, whereas paper only came to Europe from China in around the year 600 – it is always, at the very least, entertaining.

Other Key Films: *Legend* (1985); *Someone To Watch Over Me* (1987); *Black Rain* (1989); *1492: Conquest Of Paradise* (1992); *White Squall* (1996); *Hannibal* (2001); *Black Hawk Down* (2001); *Matchstick Men* (2003); *Kingdom Of Heaven* (2005); *A Good Year* (2006)

Scott-Thomas, Kristin

She's a curiously passive actress, but her very passivity contains the emotional core that is her forte, for Scott-Thomas has a rare capacity for drama, a talent which harks back to such great screen performers as **Bette Davis** and **Barbara Stanwyck**. She can play tough, as in her magnificently horrid Brenda Last in Charles Sturridge's *A Handful Of Dust* (1988), a performance so accurate that it raised hisses in certain French cinemas, and she can play tender, as in her Katherine Clifton in **Anthony Minghella's** *The English Patient* (1996). Hers is a face and a technique which will age well, and one would like to see her really stretched now that she is in her prime – as Emma Bovary perhaps, or, better still, as Lawrence Durrell's Constance, a book and a character that cry out to be filmed.

Other Key Films: *The Tenth Man* (1988); *Bitter Moon* (1992); *Four Weddings And A Funeral* (94); *An Unforgettable Summer* (1994); *Angels & Insects* (1995); *Richard III* (1995); *Le Confessionale* (1997); *The Horse Whisperer* (1998); *Souvenir* (1998); *Random Hearts* (1999); *Up At The Villa* (2000); *Gosford Park* (2001); *Petites Coupures* (2003); *Arsène Lupin* (2004); *Man To Man* (2005); *Keeping Mum* (2005); *La Doublure* (2006)

Screwball Comedies

The Golden Age of depression-busting and war-fatigue-alleviating screwball comedies came during the 1930s and 1940s, incorporating fast-talking, fast-gagging, often ludicrous plots, in which eccentric characters, notably out of synch with the status quo, get themselves into ever increasing spirals of inspired mayhem. Screwball stars included **Cary Grant**, **Jean Harlow**, **Katherine Hepburn**, **William Powell**, **Carole Lombard**, **Frederic March**, **Myrna Loy** and **Claudette Colbert**, and they were directed, as often as not, by **Ernst Lubitsch**, **Preston Sturges**, **Frank Capra** or **Howard Hawks**.

Key Films: Ernst Lubitsch's *Trouble In Paradise* (1932), *Ninotchka* (1939), and *To Be Or Not To Be* (1942); Preston Sturges's *The Lady Eve* (1941), *Sullivan's Travels* (1941), *The Palm Beach Story* (4) and *The Miracle Of Morgan's Creek* (1944); Frank Capra's *It Happened One Night* (1934), *You Can't Take It With You* (1938), and *Arsenic And Old Lace* (1944); Howard Hawks's *Twentieth Century* (1934), *Bringing Up Baby* (1938), *His Girl Friday* (1940), *I Was A Male War Bride* (1949) and *Monkey Business* (1952); Gregory La Cava's *My Man Godfrey* (1936); Leo McCarey's *The Awful Truth* (1937); **William Wellman's** *Nothing Sacred* (1937); **George Cukor's** *Holiday* (1938); **René Clair's** *The Ghost Goes West* (1936) and *I Married A Witch* (1942)

Sellers, Peter

An inspired comic actor with a notably difficult and complex personality, Sellers learnt his trade the hard way, firstly as part of his parents' music-hall comedy act, and then as the immortal Bluebottle in the long-running 1950s BBC radio show, *The Goons*. Sellers began his assault on the big screen as supporting actor in a number of Ealing Comedies, most notably **Alexander Mackendrick's** *The Ladykillers* (1955), and these were followed by lead roles in the **Boulting Brother's** *I'm All Right Jack* (1959) and Sidney Gilliat's *Only Two Can Play* (1962). His big break came with **Stanley Kubrick's** *Dr. Strangelove Or: How I Learned To Stop Worrying And Love The Bomb* (1963), in which he played not only Group Capt. Lionel Mandrake (to whom **Sterling Hayden's** Gen. Jack D. Ripper confides his 'precious bodily fluids' theory), but also long-suffering President Merkin Muffley and the insane, wheelchair-ridden, false-hand-possessing Doctor Strangelove, whose ill-concealed devotion to the Führer is only eclipsed by his glee at the thought of proactively repopulating a world devastated by a nuclear holocaust he himself has largely been instrumental in fomenting. Sellers's most lucrative creation was the bumbling Inspector Clouseau, protagonist of five and a half feature films – five and a half, because one of them, **Blake Edwards's** *The Trail Of The Pink Panther* (1982), which was released three years after Sellers's death from a heart attack, consisted only of out-takes. Sellers's finest performance, and the one which brought him his only Oscar, came late, as Chauncey (Chance), the simple gardener turned Presidential advisor and celebrity in Hal Ashby's *Being There* (1979).

Other Key Films: *The Smallest Show On Earth* (1958); *The Mouse That Roared* (1959); *Waltz Of The Toreadors* (1962); *Lolita* (1962); *The Wrong Arm Of The Law* (1963); *The Pink Panther* (1964); *A Shot In The Dark* (1964); *What's New Pussycat?* (1965); *After The Fox* (1966); *The Party* (1968); *Hoffman* (1970); *There's A Girl In My Soup* (1970); *The Return Of The Pink Panther* (1975); *The Pink Panther Strikes Again* (1976); *Revenge Of The Pink Panther* (1978)

Peter Sellers in the Pink Panther film A Shot in the Dark, directed by Blake Edwards (1964).

United Artists/The Kobal Collection

Selznick, David O.

One of the greatest of all Hollywood producers, Selznick is renowned both for his demented single-mindedness in bringing Margaret Mitchell's best-selling novel *Gone With The Wind* to the screen in 1939, and for inveigling England's **Alfred Hitchcock** over to Hollywood to direct *Rebecca* (1940). **George Cukor's** magnificent *David Copperfield* (1935) was another of his babies, as was **King Vidor's** wildly over-the-top but astonishingly successful *Duel In The Sun* (1947). A renowned workaholic and worrier, Selznick's final production was Charles Vidor's remake of Ernest Hemingway's seminal novel *A Farewell To Arms* (1958).

Other Key Films: **George Cukor's** *A Bill Of Divorcement* (1932); **Merian C. Cooper** and Ernest B. Schoedsack's *King Kong* (1933); **Clarence Brown's** *Anna Karenina* (1935); **Jack Conway's** *A Tale Of Two Cities* (1935); **William Wellman's** *Nothing Sacred* (1937); John Cromwell's *The Prisoner Of Zenda* (1937); **Alfred Hitchcock's** *Spellbound* (1945); **Carol Reed's** *The Third Man* (1949); **Michael Powell** and Emeric Pressburger's *Gone To Earth* (1950)

Sennett, Mack

Sennett, together with his producer/director rival **Hal Roach**, were the two silent era kings of slapstick comedy. Sennett's contribution included the Keystone Cops, the Sennett Bathing Beauties, and an astonishing series of comedies starring the likes of **Charlie Chaplin**, Harry Langdon, Mabel Normand, and the ill-fated '**Fatty' Arbuckle**. Sennett's intense sense of fun did not outlast the silent era in terms of film productions, but his greatest comedies continue to give immense pleasure to those still fortunate enough to possess a simple heart.

Key Films: *Mabel At The Wheel* (1914); *The Little Teacher* (1915); *Home Talent* (1921); *The Lion's Roar* (1928); *The Chumps* (1930)

Best Sentimental Films

Gabriel Axel's *Babette's Feast* (1987); Jean Becker's *Les Enfants Du Marais* (1999); **Frank Capra's** *It's A Wonderful Life* (1946); John Cromwell's *The Enchanted Cottage* (1945); Julien Duvivier's *Poil De Carotte* (1932) and *Sous Le Ciel De Paris* (1950); **John Ford's** *Three Godfathers* (1948); **Akira Kurosawa's** *Dersu Uzala* (1974); **Ernst Lubitsch's** *Heaven Can Wait* (1943); Robert Mulligan's *Summer of 42* (1970); **Jean Renoir's** *The River* (1950); **Bertrand Tavernier's** *Un Dimanche A La Campagne* (1984) and *Daddy Nostalgie [These Foolish Things]* (1990); Giuseppe Tornatore's *Cinema Paradiso* (1989)

Serrault, Michel

An outstanding screen actor and one of France's most successful exports if one takes into account his role of Albin/Zaza in Edouard Molinaro's *La Cage Aux Folles* trilogy (1978, 1980, 1985), Serrault has an enormous range which spans his Raymond in **Henri-Georges Clouzot's** sensational *Les Diaboliques* (1955), to the title role in Christian De Chalonge's grotesque *Dr. Petiot* (1990). Serrault's greatest performance came as the lawyer, Jérome Martinaud, in Claude Miller's *Garde À Vue* (1981), accused of the rape and murder of two schoolgirls by police inspectors Guy Marchand and **Lino Ventura**, and for which he won a formidably well-deserved César.

Other Key Films: *Candide* (1960); *King Of Hearts* (1966); *Le Viager* (1972); *Buffet Froid* (1979); *Mortelle Randonée* (1983); *Le Miraculé* (1987); *Ennemis Intimes* (1987); *Haute Époque* (1994); *Nelly And Monsieur Arnaud* (1995); *Rien Ne Va Plus* (1997); *Le Libertin* (2000); *Une Hirondelle A Fait Le Printemps* (2000); *Belphégor – Le Fantôme Du Louvre* (2001); *Vajont* (2001); *24 Heures De La Vie D'Une Femme* (2002); *Le Furet* (2003); *Grabuge!* (2005); *Les Enfants Du Pays* (2006); *Le Bénévole* (2006)

Sharif, Omar

One would imagine that Sharif thoroughly enjoyed his time as a romantic lead in such European films as **David Lean's** *Doctor Zhivago* (1965) and Terence Young's *Mayerling* (1969), following his stunning first introduction to non-Arab audiences in Lean's *Lawrence Of Arabia* (1962) – but one suspects that his subsequent bridge-playing and horse-racing career have given him far more satisfaction. A former Copt who converted to Islam, Sharif would possibly concur with the view that his strengths lie in his celebrity status rather than in his acting abilities, but, that said, he was considerably more than merely adequate in **James Clavell's** *The Last Valley* (1970) and **John Frankenheimer's** *The Horseman* (1971).

Other Key Films: *The Night Of The Generals* (1967); *Funny Girl* (1968); *Mackenna's Gold* (1969); *The Tamarind Seed* (1974); *Funny Lady* (1975); *Bloodline* (1979); *Green Ice* (1981); *Top Secret!* (1984); *The Rainbow Thief* (1990); *Heaven Before I Die* (1997); *The 13th Warrior* (1999); *The Parole Officer* (2001); *Monsieur Ibrahim Et Les Fleurs Du Coran* (2003); *Hidalgo* (2004)

Sherlock Holmes

Holmes was the creation of novelist/physician Arthur Conan Doyle (1859-1930), and most of the sixty-eight novels and stories he wrote about his hero were intended for a weekly magazine audience, forcing Doyle to keep the thrills and surprises coming, rather than to save them for the very end of the piece. Of course, this accords perfectly with the needs of the cinema and of the film screenplay, which is normally written in a three-act sequence, and the stories have proved immensely popular with movie audiences since the very inception of the medium. Holmes's first cinematic outing came only thirteen years after the famous detective's first appearance in print, in the movie short, *Sherlock Holmes Baffled* (1900). Holmes has been played by upwards of eighty actors since then, in something approaching 250 films, but his most convincing incarnation (even though Holmes found himself unwillingly modernized for wartime audiences) was by **Basil Rathbone**, with Nigel Bruce as his endearingly bumbling Dr Watson. The most successful and intelligent long-term pairing came on television, however, with Jeremy Brett's definitive Holmes beautifully complemented by David Burke's intelligent (for once) Watson.

Other Key Films: Buster Keaton's *Sherlock Jr.* (1924); Sidney Lanfield's *The Hound Of The Baskervilles* (1939); **Billy Wilder's** *The Private Life Of Sherlock Holmes* (1970); Herbert Ross's *The Seven Percent Solution* (1976); **Disney's** *Basil, The Great Mouse Detective* (1986); Barry Levinson's *Young Sherlock Holmes* (1986); Fraser C. Heston's *The Crucifer Of Blood* (1991)

Siegel, Don

Siegel is a frequently underrated director whose rite of passage came as a lowly member of the Warner Brothers' insert department, where he even got to do a little work on **Casablanca** (1942). His first feature, *The Verdict* (1946), starring **Sidney Greenstreet**, was a first-class *film noir*, and Siegel went on to direct the critically acclaimed semi-documentary *Riot In Cell Block 11* (1954), and the seminal *Invasion Of The Body Snatchers* (1956), one of the best of all **science fiction** films. He teased out **Elvis Presley's** finest screen performance in *Flaming Star* (1960), and later directed his friend, **Clint Eastwood**, in the curious but effective *The Beguiled* (1971). His best late-career thriller is *Charley Varrick* (1973), with **Walter Matthau**, and he also excelled directing **John Wayne's** subtle and moving swansong movie, *The Shootist* (1976).

Other Key Films: *The Big Steal* (1949); *Hell Is For Heroes* (1962); *The Killers* (1964); *Madigan* (1968); *Dirty Harry* (1971); *Telefon* (1977); *Escape From Alcatraz* (1979)

Key Line: 'If you had fought in a platoon in Vietnam, Don would have been the kind of lieutenant you'd have hoped you were lucky enough to have leading your scared ass.' [Sterling Silliphant, who scripted *The Lineup* (1958) and *Telefon* (1977) for Siegel]

Signoret, Simone

Similar to Shelley Winters in build (both began as slender blondes, then somewhat ballooned) Signoret tempered her innate masochism with intelligence, particularly in such early films as Jacques Becker's *Casque D'Or* (1952), and **Henri-Georges**

Clouzot's *Les Diaboliques* (1954), in which she played Nicole Horner, the murderous mistress of Paul Meurisse's cold-blooded schoolteacher, Michel Delasalle. Following her Oscar success as Alice Aisgill in *Room At The Top* (1958), Signoret moved on to character roles in her later films, most notably as Auschwitz-survivor Rosa in Moshe Mizrahi's *Madame Rosa* (1977), for which she won a César. She enjoyed (endured?) a tempestuous thirty-four-year marriage to honorary Frenchman **Yves Montand**, with whom she co-starred in a number of films, and whose serial infidelity with the likes of **Marilyn Monroe** she seemed to take, if not in her stride, then at the very least philosophically.

Other Key Films: *La Ronde* (1950); *Thérèse Raquin* (1953); *Naked Autumn* (1961); *L'Armée Des Ombres* (1969); *L'Aveu* (1970); *Chère Inconnue* (1980); *L'Étoile Du Nord* (1982)

Best Silent Films

Luis Buñuel and Salvador Dali's *Un Chien Andalou* (1929); **Charles Chaplin's** *The Gold Rush* (1925) and *City Lights* (1930); Benjamin Christensen's *Haxan* (1921); **Carl Dreyer's** *The Passion Of Joan Of Arc* (1928); **Sergei Eisenstein's** *Battleship Potemkin* (1925); **Abel Gance's** *Napoléon* (1925); **D W Griffith's** *The Birth Of A Nation* (1915) and *Intolerance* (1916); **Buster Keaton's** *The General* (1926); **Fritz Lang's** *Metropolis* (1927); **F W Murnau's** *Faust* (1926) and *Sunrise* (1927); **G W Pabst's** *Pandora's Box* (1929); Curt Siodmak, **Robert Siodmak**, **Edgar G Ulmer** & Fred Zinnemann's *Menschen Am Sonntag* [**Billy Wilder** has a writing credit] (1930); **Erich von Stroheim's** *Foolish Wives* (1921) and *Greed* (1923)

Simmons, Jean

Simmons was a big star during the 1950s, and one of the select few British actresses (**Elizabeth Taylor** and **Deborah Kerr** notwithstanding) to manage the tricky crossover to Hollywood, which she did accompanied by her then husband, **Stewart Granger**. She was arguably one of the most beautiful women ever to grace the big screen, and her career was a distinguished one, with notable parts, during her *annus mirabilis* of 1953, in George Sidney's *Young Bess* (1953), **Otto Preminger's** *Angel Face* (1953) and Henry Koster's *The Robe* (1953) – she later followed up with **William Wyler's** *The Big Country* (1958), **Stanley Kubrick's** *Spartacus* (1960), and husband-to-be **Richard Brooks's** *Elmer Gantry* (1960). She continued her career during the 1960s and 1970s, but at a less frenetic pace, delivering a series of typically committed performances, and she made a small but telling comeback in Jocelyn Moorhouse's *How To Make An American Quilt* (1995).

Other Key Films: *Great Expectations* (1946); *Black Narcissus* (1947); *Hamlet* (1948); *Desiree* (1954); *Guys And Dolls* (1955); *Life At The Top* (1965); *The Happy Ending* (1969)

Simon, Michel

One look at Simon, with his weather-beaten features, his misdirected teeth, his stand-up hair and his multitudinous chins, would be enough to persuade most sane people that the man would never stand a chance of becoming a screen actor, let alone a star. But his face and his voice were Simon's stock-in-trade, and in a career spanning fifty years, he proved to be one of the greatest actors of this or any other era. He had a natural integrity on the screen, even in the most obnoxious of parts, such as his lascivious tramp, Boudu, in **Jean Renoir's** *Boudu Sauvé Des Eaux* (1932), or his Zabel in **Marcel Carné's** *Quai Des Brumes* (1938). Simon contrived to inject a grotesque, heightened reality into even such nominally sympathetic roles as his Père Jules in **Jean Vigo's** L'Atalante (1934), and it was this consistent refusal to mar greatness with sentiment that raises him so high, and which was shown, in its ultimate perfection, in **Julien Duvivier's** La Fin Du Jour (1939).

Other Key Films: La Passion De Jeanne D'Arc (1928); La Chienne (1931); Drôle De Drame (1937); Vautrin (1944); Panique (1946); Le Poison (1951); Le Vieil Homme Et L'Enfant (1967); L'Ibis Rouge (1975)

Sinatra, Frank

Sinatra took the cult of celebrity to places it had never been, loafing, in purposeful cognito, with his minders massed around him like frigates to a destroyer, through bars, hotel lobbies, casinos, airports, always the centre of attention, and always oh-so conscious of it. His career came in three stages: the bobby-soxer years (1939-1945), in which his voice and his willowy form set the hearts of countless teenage girls pounding; his film-and-swing years (1953-1970), from his breakthrough Maggio in **Fred Zinnemann's** From Here To Eternity (1953) to his eponymous anti-hero in Burt Kennedy's Dirty Dingus Magee (1970); and his comeback years (1975-1993), in which he always seemed on the point of leaving us, only to hove back into view again, his flotilla and status miraculously intact, for just one final concert. He was one of the greatest popular singers of all time, a more than passable actor, and an occasionally philanthropic man.

Other Key Films: Anchors Aweigh (1945); On The Town (1949); Suddenly (1954); Young At Heart (1955); Guys And Dolls (1955); The Tender Trap (1955); The Man With The Golden Arm (1955); High Society (1956); Pal Joey (1958); The Manchurian Candidate (1962); Von Ryan's Express (1965); The Naked Runner (1967); Tony Rome (1967); The Detective (1968); Lady In Cement (1968); The First Deadly Sin (1980)

Key Line: 'Everyone in the whole world who hates me is now here.' [Guys And Dolls]

Siodmak, Robert

Siodmak (yet another German/US transplant) may be one of the greatest of all **film noir** directors, but his best films, Phantom Lady (1944), The Killers (1946), Cry Of The City (1948), Criss Cross (1949) and The File On Thelma Jordon (1950), transcend the genre to become a series of awesome character studies of losers, marginals and the hope-stricken, each one battling to retain a little dignity in an inimical world. He returned to Germany in 1953, and continued making films such as Die Ratten (1955) and L'Affaire Nina B (1962). However, once in Germany, he was no longer the outsider he had been in the United States, and this loss of role seemed to result in the demise of the edgy, chippie part of his morbid, doom-laden talent. See **Best Silent Films**

Other Key Films: Son Of **Dracula** (1943); The Spiral Staircase (1945); The Dark Mirror (1946); The Great Sinner (1949); Deported (1950); The Whistle At Eaton Falls (1951); The Crimson Pirate (1952)

Sirk, Douglas

If it hadn't been for the **auteur theory**, promulgated so serendipitously by the Cahiers du Cinéma, Sirk would be remembered now as merely a melodramatic precursor of the soap-opera movement, hardly worthy of more than an enlightened footnote in cinema textbooks. An expatriate Dane born in Germany, Sirk had a very real sense of not belonging to the American culture which eventually employed him and this imbues all his finest films. Sirk's movies are often about people, nominally belonging, but yet pushed to the margins of their natural milieus through selfishness, in *Magnificent Obsession* (1954), ill-advised love affairs, in *All That Heaven Allows* (1956) and *Written On The Wind* (1958), and unacknowledged longings and thwarted ambitions, in *The Tarnished Angels* (1958) and *Imitation Of Life* (1959). All Sirk's Hollywood films combine a comforting, almost fetishistic love of detail and texture, with story-lines that continually undermine the assumptions of a society apparently so firmly and permanently anchored in the material – to that extent he may be seen as one of the most visionary of all mainstream Hollywood directors of his era. **Other Key Films**: *La Habañera* (1937); *Zu Neuen Ufern* (1937); *Die Heimat Ruft* (1937); *Hitler's Madman* (1943); *Shockproof* (1949); *Thunder On The Hill* (1951); *Meet Me At The Fair* (1952); *All I Desire* (1953); *Sign Of The Pagan* (1954); *Captain Lightfoot* (1955); *There's Always Tomorrow* (1956); *Interlude* (1958); *A Time To Love And A Time To Die* (1958)

Slasher Movies

Films in which the principal interest lies in when and whom the cleaver/pickaxe/chainsaw/meat-hook-wielding protagonist will target next. Pointed examples might include Tobe Hooper's *The Texas Chainsaw Massacre* (1974), Wes Craven's *The Hills Have Eyes* (1977), **John Carpenter's** *Halloween* (1978) and **Abel Ferrara's** *Driller Killer* (1979). Classic devices include blades (of varying sorts) descending through walls, up bath plugs and out of graves. The title 'King Of The Slashers' must go to **Jack Nicholson's** Jack Torrance, in **Stanley Kubrick's** *The Shining* (1980), which, while hardly constituting a slasher movie *per se*, brilliantly invoked slasherdom in the infamous bathroom scene in which Torrance tries to claw his way through Shelley Duvall's bathroom door with an axe.

Slocombe, Douglas

An eminent British cinematographer, Slocombe began his career photographing seventeen-years-worth of Ealing Studios productions including the multi-directed *Dead Of Night* (1945), **Robert Hamer's** *It Always Rains On Sundays* (1947) and *Kind Hearts And Coronets* (1949), Charles Crichton's *The Lavender Hill Mob* (1951) and **Alexander Mackendrick's** *The Man In The White Suit* (1951). He then turned freelance, where the quality of his work has sustained him through **Joseph Losey's** *The Servant* (1963), **Roman Polanski's** *Dance Of The Vampires* (1967) and **Steven Spielberg's** *Indiana Jones* trilogy (1981-1989), garnering, in the process, a heady succession of Academy Award nominations. As a former journalist and Second-World-War newsreel cameraman, Slocombe created one of his most beautifully shot films with Alexander Mackendrick's CinemaScope-friendly *A High Wind In Jamaica* (1965). **Other Key Films**: **John Huston's** *Freud* (1962); Anthony Harvey's *The Lion In Winter* (1968); **Ken Russell's** *The Music Lovers* (1971); **Fred Zinnemann's** *Julia* (1977); Irvin Kershner's *Never Say Never Again* (1983)

Smith, Maggie

Although essentially a stage actress and comedienne, Maggie Smith customarily acts everyone else off the screen when she does deign to trip the light fantastic and appear in a film. Her landmark performance came in Ronald Neame's *The Prime Of Miss Jean Brodie* (1969), but she was even better in Herbert Ross's *California Suite* (1978) and Jack Clayton's *The Lonely Passion Of Judith Hearne* (1988). Catch her on the stage, if you can, before she retires – a rare spirit, she has remarkable sympathy for the people she plays.

Other Key Films: *The VIP's* (1963); *The Pumpkin Eater* (1964); *Oh! What A Lovely War* (1965); *Quartet* (1981); *The Missionary* (1982); *A Private Function* (1985); *A Room With A View* (1985); *Hook* (1991); *Sister Act* (1992); *Secret Garden* (1993); *Richard III* (1995); *The First Wives Club* (1996); *Washington Square* (1997); *Tea With Mussolini* (1999); *The Last September* (1999); *Curtain Call* (1999); *Gosford Park* (2001); *Harry Potter Series* (2001-2007); *Ladies In Lavender* (2004); *Keeping Mum* (2005)

Key Line: 'Give me a girl at an impressionable age, and she is mine for life.' [*The Prime Of Miss Jean Brodie*]

Smith, Will

The popular star of television's *The Fresh Prince Of Bel-Air*, and an esteemed rap singer – if that's not a contradiction in terms – and light comedian, Smith starred in **Fred Schepisi's** *Six Degrees Of Separation* (1993), a pointed satire on the hypocrisy inherent in much New York upper class liberalism. He then went on to achieve star status in Michael Bay's *Bad Boys* (1995), Roland Emmerich's *Independence Day* (1997) and Barry Sonnenfeld's *Men In Black* (1997). His recent *Wild Wild West* (1999) took implausibility to new heights, but provided Smith with a nice little earner and a hit record to boot, while his excellent performance as Muhammad Ali in Michael Mann's *Ali* (2001), marked the highpoint of his career to date. With his films grossing $1400 million dollars up to 2003, Willard will doubtless go far.

Other Key Films: *Where The Day Takes You* (1992); *Enemy Of The State* (1998); *The Legend Of Bagger Vance* (2000); *I, Robot* (2004); *Hitch* (2005); *The Pursuit Of Happyness* (2006)

Soderbergh, Steven

Soderbergh started at the top, with *sex, lies and videotape* (1989), which won him the Palme D'Or at the Cannes Film Festival, and then horrified his fans with *Kafka* (1991), which was actually very good indeed, followed by *King Of The Hill* (1993) and *Schizopolis* (1996), which were even better. Somewhat bewildered, no doubt, by his unjustified blackballing, Soderbergh fought back with the excellent *Out Of Sight* (1998), starring **George Clooney** and Jennifer Lopez, a film which must have brought him to the attention of **Julia Roberts**, whom he then directed in the commercially lucrative though intellectually vapid *Erin Brockovich* (2000). Now on something of a streak, thanks to the runaway success of *Traffic* (2000) and *Ocean's Eleven* (2001), Soderbergh is happy proof that, even in Hollywood, talent will eventually out.

Other Key Films: *The Underneath* (1994); *Gray's Anatomy* (1996); *Out Of Sight* (1998); *The Limey* (1999); *Solaris* (2002); *Bubble* (2005); *The Good German* (2006)

Spacek, Sissy

Definitely one of the most interesting of the 1970s vintage of actresses, Spacek is an Actor's Studio disciple who always wore her Strasbergian credentials lightly, and with grace, from the moment of her very first appearance (naked) on screen in Michael Ritchie's pulpish *Prime Cut* (1972). She made her name as Holly in **Terrence Malick's** *Badlands* (1973), and confirmed her initial promise with a sensational performance in **Brian De Palma's** *Carrie* (1976), returning from beyond the grave in one of the snazziest schlock finales in movie history. A very impressive sequence of films followed, including Jack Fisk's curious little love story, *Raggedy Man* (1981), and **Constantin Costa-Gavras's** *Missing* (1982). In recent years, however, she seems to have gone a little out of fashion as a leading lady, and this is sad, for Spacek at her best, was always the thinking person's alternative to the Hollywood heavy brigade.

Other Key Films: *Welcome To LA*(1976); *Three Women* (1976); *Heartbeat* (1980); *Coal Miner's Daughter* (1980); *The River* (1984); *Crimes Of the Heart* (1986); *The Long Walk Home* (1990); *JFK* (1991); *The Grass Harp* (1996); *Blast From The Past* (1999); *The Straight Story* (1999); *In The Bedroom* (2001); *Tuck Everlasting* (2002); *North Country* (2005); *An American Haunting* (2005)

Spacey, Kevin

It suddenly occurred to Hollywood that Spacey was more than just a simple character actor when his Roger 'Verbal' ('So who is Keyser Soze?') Kint stole Bryan Singer's *The Usual Suspects* (1995) from under the noses of a stellar array of the usual oddball leading men, including **Gabriel Byrne**, Stephen Baldwin and Chazz Palminteri. A veteran stand-up comedian and Tony award-winner, Spacey already knew how to milk his audience, and the best-supporting Oscar he took for Kint paved the way for the roles in Curtis Hanson's *L.A. Confidential* (1997) and Sam Mendes's *American Beauty* (1999) which have since made his name.

Other Key Films: *Heartburn* (1986); *Working Girl* (1988); *Henry & June* (1990); *Glengarry Glen Ross* (1992); *Seven* (1995); *A Time To Kill* (1996); *The Negotiator* (1998); *Hurlyburly* (1998); *Ordinary Decent Criminal* (2000); *Pay It Forward* (2000); *The Shipping News* (2001); *The Life Of David Gale* (2003); *Beyond The Sea* (2004); *Edison* (2005); *Superman Returns* (2006)

Spaghetti Westerns

Spaghetti **Westerns** are cowboy movies made during the 1960s and 1970s by Italian directors, usually in Spain, and normally with over-the-hill or still nascent US actors in the lead roles. **Sergio Leone** is the acknowledged master of the genre, which took the gentle loner that **Randolph Scott** played in the Ranown series of **Budd Boetticher** Westerns during the 1950s, and gave him a Japanese Samurai attitude. Prominent Leone films such as *A Fistful Of Dollars* (1964) and *For A Few Dollars More* (1965) began the series, with **Clint Eastwood** starring, and these were followed by a whole series of spaghettis starring Terence Hill (born Mario Girotti) and Bud Spencer (born Carlo Pedersoli), which mixed broad comedy with almost continuous gunplay. The genre began (somewhat inevitably) satirising itself with Tonino Valerii's *My Name Is Nobody* (1973), and petered out soon afterwards, but not before making its influential mark on such worthy American heirs as Clint Eastwood's *High Plains Drifter* (1973) and **Fred Schepisi's** *Barbarosa* (1982). See *Best* **Western Films**

Spielberg, Steven

Director, producer, and sometime writer, Spielberg had made a number of successful shorts and television features before his TV movie, *Duel* (1971/1983) – the one in which a gigantic, driverless truck threatens home-bound salesman Dennis Weaver – cemented his reputation as a budding director, and gave him the opportunity to direct the well-received *Sugarland Express* (1974). Universal then offered him *Jaws* (1975), and so began the Spielberg legend; a legend based on the three all-American virtues of mechanical talent, energy and the capacity to make enormous quantities of money. It is to Spielberg's credit that he has rarely allowed his power or influence to cloud his judgement, and despite one or two fiascos (no doubt necessary, in psychological terms, to prevent vainglory), he has weaved his way skilfully between the twin pillars of popular culture and genuinely heartfelt projects with commendable restraint. *Close Encounters Of The Third Kind* (1977), *Raiders Of The Lost Ark* (1981), *E.T. The Extra-Terrestrial* (1982) and *Jurassic Park* (1993) were all brilliant forays into populist myth-making, but he has leavened these with more adult material, such as *The Color Purple* (1985), *Empire Of The Sun* (1987), *Amistad* (1997), and *Saving Private Ryan* (1998). The brightest star in Spielberg's firmament, however, is still *Schindler's List* (1993), a brilliantly successful and emotionally nourishing account of the effect one person can have on a culture designed to deaden morality and replace it with a form of expedient insanity. There is hardly a false note in *Schindler*, and when Spielberg mounted the rostrum to collect his first Academy Award for Best Director, he could do so in the certain knowledge that he had justified his place in a world more notable for its moral deficiencies than for its eagerness to stand up and be counted.

Susan Backlinie and director Steven Spielberg on the set of Jaws (1975).

Universal/The Kobal Collection

Other Key Films: *1941* (1979); *Indiana Jones And The Temple Of Doom* (1984); *Indiana Jones And The Last Crusade* (1989); *Always* (1989); *Hook* (1991); *The Lost World: Jurassic Park* (1997); *Artificial Intelligence: A.I.* (2001); *Minority Report* (2002); *Catch Me If You Can* (2002); *The Terminal* (2004); *War Of The Worlds* (2005); *Munich* (2005)

Spy Films

The film world has been obsessed with spies ever since the dancer and courtesan, Mata Hari, was shot dead by a French firing squad in the forests of Vincennes, on 5 October 1917, for what may (or may not) have been her spying activities on behalf of the Germans. **Greta Garbo** played her in George Fitzmaurice's *Mata Hari* (1931), **Marlene Dietrich** played a variation on her (agent X27) in **Josef von Sternberg's** *Dishonored* (1931), **Jeanne Moreau** played her in Jean-Louis Richard's *Mata Hari, Agent H21* (1964) [co-scripted by **François Truffaut**, no less] and even Sylvia Kristel (of Emmanuelle fame) took a stab at her in Curtis Harrington's absurd *Mata Hari* (1985). But spies and secret agents really came into their own after the Second World War, when a plethora of films purporting to tell the true story of this or that hero or heroine (or villain) appeared. Two of the best biopics, largely because the stories they told were so fascinating in themselves, were Lewis Gilbert's *Carve Her Name With Pride* (1958), in which Virginia McKenna played Violette Szabo, and Herbert Wilcox's *Odette* (1950), in which Anna Neagle played Odette Churchill. With the publication of best-selling author, John Le Carré's 1963 novel, *The Spy Who Came In From The Cold*, the spy film took on a different, more self-consciously literary emphasis, as manifested by **Martin Ritt's** 1965 film of the book, starring an on-form **Richard Burton** as tormented master spy, Alec Leamas. The flip side of the coin came with the gadget-driven *James Bond* franchise, although some of Ian Fleming's original books were actually plot-driven and quite dark – read his 1953 *Casino Royale*, for instance. Recently, the spy film has taken on something of a comic, post-Graham Greene twist, with **John Boorman's** excellent *The Tailor From Panama* (2001) [based on another Le Carré novel], and the spoof Mike Myers hits, Jay Roach's *Austin Powers: International Man Of Mystery* (1997) and *Austin Powers: The Spy Who Shagged Me* (1999).

Key Lines:

1: 'I am married to an American agent.' [**Claude Rains's** astonished Nazi agent, Alexander Sebastian, to his dominating mother, eerily played by Leopoldine Konstantine, in **Alfred Hitchcock's** *Notorious* (1946)]

2: 'A beautiful, mysterious woman pursued by gunmen. Sounds like a spy story.' [**Robert Donat** as John Buchan's Richard Hannay, in Alfred Hitchcock's *The Thirty-Nine Steps* (1935)]

Best Spy Films: Michael Anderson's *The Quiller Memorandum* (1966); **John Frankenheimer's** *The Manchurian Candidate* (1962); Guy Hamilton's *Goldfinger* (1964); **Alfred Hitchcock's** *Foreign Correspondent* (1940) and *Notorious* (1946); **Joseph L Mankiewicz's** *Five Fingers* (1952); Ronald Neame's *The Odessa File* (1974); **Martin Ritt's** *The Spy Who Came In From The Cold* (1966); **Josef von Sternberg's** *Dishonored* (1931); **Billy Wilder's** *Five Graves To Cairo* (1943); Terence Young's *From Russia With Love* (1963)

Stallone, Sylvester

Stallone has always been an edgier actor than his great competitor in the action-movie stakes, Big **Arnie Schwarzenegger**. When this aspect of the man is allowed to come to the fore, as in Ted Kotcheff's excellent first contender in the Rambo series, *First Blood* (1982), we are at once aware why Stallone managed to keep his place in the blockbuster stakes throughout the 1980s and most of the 1990s. The ensuing Rambo films, however, were turgidly run-of-the-mill, in the same way that, as the Rocky films played on, they signally failed to improve on their progenitor, John G Avildsen's *Rocky* (1976). Stallone has occasionally tried to break out from the big-action straightjacket, most notably in Roger Spottiswoode's *Stop! Or My Mom Will Shoot* (1992) and James Mangold's *Cop Land* (1997), but sadly it seems that his cupidity has forever consigned him to a pumped-up, hyper-muscled, but increasingly toothless version of the Sartrean Huis Clos scenario.

Other Key Films: *Farewell My Lovely* (1975); *Paradise Alley* (1978); *Tango & Cash* (1989); *Cliffhanger* (1993); *Demolition Man* (1993); *Daylight* (1996); *Cop Land* (1997); *Get Carter* (2000); *Driven* (2001); *D-Tox* (2002); *Avenging Angelo* (2002); *Rocky Balboa* (2006)

Key Line: 'Stallone has one talent – that is to have soaked up all the bullshit which has accumulated in La La Land over the years, coated it with an ersatz patina of culture and love of fine art, and created from his bootstraps a genuine, authentic

Monster.' [Sterling Silliphant, who co-scripted Menahem Golan's *Over The Top* (1986), which starred Stallone as a tender-hearted arm-wrestler]

Stanwyck, Barbara

Feisty leading lady who had the courage to play a number of unsympathetic characters, the former Ruby Stevens was orphaned at the age of thirteen and literally *did* start her fifty-year career in the chorus line. With a degree of maturity well beyond her twenty-five years, she shone as the missionary's wife who falls under the spell of **Nils Asther's** decadent Chinese warlord in **Frank Capra's** *The Bitter Tea Of General Yen* (1932). The moment when, returning downriver to Shanghai after Yen's suicide, she turns her face up to the clouds to recall the memory of her strange lover, is undoubtedly one of cinema's greatest **Heartstopping Moments**. The perfect *film-noir* scheming Vamp in **Billy Wilder's** *Double Indemnity* (1944), Stanwyck also excelled at playing fallen women, as Mae Doyle, for instance, in **Fritz Lang's** underrated *Clash By Night* (1952), or as Thelma Jordon, in **Robert Siodmak's** *The File On Thelma Jordon* (1949), which also featured a brilliant performance by the eccentric Wendell Corey.

Other Key Films: *Ten Cents A Dance* (1931); *Baby Face* (1932); *Gambling Lady* (1934); *The Woman In Red* (1935); *Stella Dallas* (1937); *Union Pacific* (1939); *The Lady Eve* (1941); *Meet John Doe* (1941); *Ball Of Fire* (1942); *Lady Of Burlesque* (1943); *The Strange Love Of Martha Ivers* (1946); *The Two Mrs Carrolls* (1947); *Sorry Wrong Number* (1948); *No Man Of Her Own* (1950); *Titanic* (1953); *Executive Suite* (1954); *The Night Walker* (1965)

Key Lines:

1. 'If I ever loved a man again, I'd bear anything – he could have my teeth for watch fobs.' [*Clash by Night*]

2. 'If you waited for a man to propose to you from natural causes, you'd die of old maid-hood.' [*The Lady Eve*]

Star Trek

Cult US television series (1966-1968), *Star Trek*, with its seventy-nine episodes, spawned four further spin-offs, ten movies (and counting) and a dedicated following of Trekkies. For them, *Star Trek* is a passion, a way of life, and sometimes even a religion; for non-Trekkies, *Star Trek* is a cause for derision and linguistic misgivings due to the most famous split infinitive in entertainment history ('to boldly go…'). *Star Trek* lore – based on the current sample of ten films – has it that only the even-numbered movies pass muster.

Key Line: 'Live long and prosper!'

Stars Wars

Star Wars is without doubt the most valuable movie franchise of all time. It is the brainchild of Californian-born **George Lucas**, who obstinately persisted with his 1977 project despite the scepticism of backers, 20th Century-Fox. The film eventually grossed $194,000,000, a sum that has since been dwarfed by the film's re-release in 1997, together with its two sequels, *The Empire Strikes Back* (1980) and *The Return Of The Jedi* (1983). Lucas has now completed a trilogy of prequels, *Star Wars: Episode 1 - The Phantom Menace* (1999), *Star Wars: Episode II - Attack of the Clones* (2002) and *Star Wars: Episode III - Revenge of the Sith* (2005), all three box-office, if not critical, successes.

Key Line: 'A long time ago, in a galaxy far, far away…' [*Star Wars* (1977)]

Steiger, Rod

Steiger was method acting personified, for its influence seems to leach off the screen and into real life with him, until it was sometimes hard to tell the characters from the man who played them. His first conspicuous success was as **Marlon Brando's** crooked brother, Charley Malloy, in **Elia Kazan's** *On The Waterfront* (1954), and this began the period when Steiger played heavies, deviants, venal producers and sweaty crooks, in such movies as **Robert Aldrich's** *The Big Knife* (1955), Mark Robson's *The Harder They Fall* (1956), **Samuel Fuller's** *Run Of The Arrow* (1958) and Richard Wilson's *Al Capone* (1958). Steiger always took himself very seriously indeed as an actor, and there were times when one felt that he tried on his parts much as a young girl will try on a new dress, twirling for all to see and praise her. Steiger's most memorable performance came as Bill Gillespie in Norman Jewison's *In The Heat Of The Night* (1967), but he was most convincing in a now little-seen Peter Hall film, *Three Into Two Won't Go* (1969), as the unfaithful husband of (his then real-life wife) Claire Bloom – and also, of course, as the haunted Sol Nazerman in **Sidney Lumet's** devastating *The Pawnbroker* (1965).

Other Key Films: *Oklahoma!* (1955); *Jubal* (1956); *The Court Martial Of Billy Mitchell* (1955); *The Mark* (1961); *Dr. Zhivago* (1965); *No Way To Treat A Lady* (1968); *Waterloo* (1960); *A Fistful Of Dynamite* (1971); *The Amityville Horror* (1979); *Lion Of The Desert* (1981); *Der Zauberberg* (1982); *The Ballad Of The Sad Café* (1991); *Mars Attacks!* (1996); *Crazy In Alabama* (1999); *End Of Days* (1999); *Cypress Edge* (1999); *The Flying Dutchman* (2000); *Lightmaker* (2001); *A Month Of Sundays* (2001); *Poochall Junkies* (2001)

Steiner, Max

Steiner was one of the great composers of Hollywood's Golden Age of the 1930s and 1940s, scoring such films (among 200-odd others) as **John Ford's** *The Informer* (1935), **Victor Fleming's** *Gone With The Wind* (1939), **Michael Curtiz's** *Casablanca* (1942), Irving Rapper's *Now, Voyager* (1942) and **John Huston's** *The Treasure Of The Sierra Madre* (1948) and *Key Largo* (1948). Yet another expatriate Austrian (what would Hollywood have done without them?), Steiner had actually studied under Gustav Mahler at Vienna's Imperial Academy Of Music, and was so precocious a talent that he was already conducting professionally at the age of sixteen. His scores have a *fin-de-siècle* lushness and heady romanticism that ensured him a total of three Oscars and twenty-three further nominations.

Other Key Films: **George Cukor's** *A Bill Of Divorcement* (1932) and *Little Women* (1933); **William Wellman's** *A Star Is Born* (1937); John Cromwell's *Since You Went Away* (1944); **Howard Hawks's** *The Big Sleep* (1946); John Ford's *The Searchers* (1956)

Sternberg, Josef von

There is no other director remotely like von Sternberg, and it is sometimes hard to conceive how he managed to get away with his delirious visual fantasies for quite so long in a Hollywood devoted to mammon and to mammaries. An expatriate Austrian, brought to the US when he was not yet ten, the adult von Sternberg drifted to Hollywood and found himself work as an assistant director. Following the release of his first film, *The Salvation Hunters* (1925), **Charlie Chaplin** declared him a genius, and the epithet stuck. Silent success followed, leading to a series of sound films starring his discovery and fetish object, **Marlene Dietrich**, notable for their dense, heady atmosphere, exotic lighting and mannered, almost other-worldly dialogue. The first was *The Blue Angel* (1930), filmed bilingually in Germany, which introduced von Sternberg's trademark masochistic male and the song 'Falling In Love Again', that was to follow Dietrich like a lucky charm throughout her career. Von Sternberg could undoubtedly be a tyrant on set, and his artistic credo, which valued atmosphere above story, poetry above logic, allowed his actors, who were often chosen more for their looks than their acting ability, little leeway. However, his magnificent sequence of films for Paramount, all starring Dietrich, and which include *Morocco* (1930), *Dishonored* (1931), *Blonde Venus* (1932), *Shanghai Express* (1932), *The Scarlet Empress* (1934) and *The Devil Is A Woman* (1935), took cinema to realms it had never before inhabited, via visual imagery that has rarely been bettered, using sound and movement, light and darkness, in a way that no other director, before or since, has ever used them. See **Heartstopping Moments**

Other Key Films: *Underworld* (1927); *The Last Command* (1928); *An American Tragedy* (1931); *Crime And Punishment* (1935); *The King Steps Out* (1936); *I Claudius* [unfinished] (1937); *The Shanghai Gesture* (1941); *Jet Pilot* (1950) [released 1957]; *Macao* (1952); *The Saga Of Anatahan* (1953)

Stevens, George

Stevens took his personal cine camera with him during his time as a Major with the Army Signals Corps Unit during the Second World War, and used it to take some extraordinary colour footage, most notably of the relief of Dachau concentration camp. The experience obviously changed him, for the films he made after the war are notable for their gentle humanity and attempt to understand human motivation. *A Place In The Sun* (1951) sets the audience a moral conundrum that only *Shane* (1953), arguably one of the best **Westerns** ever, succeeds in answering – namely that love alone is not a sufficient foundation for happiness. When **Alan Ladd's** Shane rides off into the sunset, he is not simply abrogating responsibility, but also taking it – for were he to stay, he might destroy the very thing that he had belatedly begun to cherish. People always count in a George Stevens film, and it is notable that even in his early comedies (and very good they are too), and in his later melodramas, he never quite allows sentiment to take over from sense, and so retains his capacity to move, rather than merely tug at, the heartstrings.

Other Key Films: *Alice Adams* (1935); *Swing Time* (1936); *Quality Street* (1937); *A Damsel In Distress* (1937); *Gunga Din* (1939); *Penny Serenade* (1941); *Woman Of The Year* (1942); *The Talk Of The Town* (1942); *The More The Merrier* (1943); *I Remember Mama* (1948); *Giant* (1956); *The Diary Of Anne Frank* (1959); *The Only Game In Town* (1970)

Key Line: 'A great man and a marvellous drinking companion, but sometimes you never knew what the hell he was shooting. Still, it all added up.' [Screenwriter Allan Scott, who co-scripted *Swing Time* (1936) and *Quality Street* (1937), on director Stevens]

Stewart, James

Popular with both the public and the studios, Stewart's Princetonian drawl masked an acute intelligence and a forceful integrity. These served him well in both his film and his wartime career, where, after flying numerous bombing missions over Germany, he rose to the heady rank of Air Force brigadier general. **Frank Capra** first recognized Stewart's 'Everyman' nature in *You Can't Take It With You* (1938) and *Destry Rides Again* (1940), but it was only after the war that Stewart really came into his genuine, rather darker self, in a wonderful run of **Anthony Mann** Westerns – which includes that picaresque oddity *Winchester 73* (1950) – and in the series of films he did for **Alfred Hitchcock**, most notably as driven ex-police officer, John 'Scottie' Ferguson, in the sublimely perverse *Vertigo* (1958).

Other Key Films: *The Shopworn Angel* (1938); *Mr Smith Goes To Washington* (1939); *The Philadelphia Story* (1940); *It's A Wonderful Life* (1946); *Call Northside 777* (1948); *Broken Arrow* (1950); *Harvey* (1950); *The Naked Spur* (1953); *Rear Window* (1954); *The Man From Laramie* (1955); *Anatomy Of A Murder* (1959); *Flight Of The Phoenix* (1966)

Key Lines:
1. 'Well I... I always feel I belong where I am.' [*The Man From Laramie*]
2. 'I wouldn't give you two cents for all your fancy rules if behind them they didn't have a little bit of plain, ordinary kindness and a little looking out for the other feller.' [*Mr Smith Goes To Washington*]

Stone, Oliver

Stone dropped out of Yale and into Hollywood with a similar alacrity, directing the minor cult movie *Seizure* (1974), and penning the script for **Alan Parker's** *Midnight Express* (1978), before taking joint writing credit on John Milius's *Conan The Barbarian* (1981) and finally graduating into the super-writing league via **Brian De Palma's** *Scarface* (1983). His first directing success came with *Salvador* (1986), closely followed by *Platoon* (1986), which was the film that finally projected him into the big-time. With his emphasis on power, greed and the destructive capacity of the male when society's harness is temporarily lifted by war, great wealth or political power, Stone fits neatly into the Ernest Hemingway, Norman Mailer, Charles Bukowski line of self-abusing iconoclasts. *Wall Street* (1987), *Born On The Fourth Of July* (1989) and *JFK* (1991) were all good in their way, but Stone excels at more out-of-the-way material, such as his underrated *U-Turn* (1997), in which an increasingly disorientated **Sean Penn** backs through the door marked *film noir* and emerges somewhere close to hell.

Other Key Films: *The Hand* (1981); *Talk Radio* (1988); *The Doors* (1991); *Heaven & Earth* (1993); *Nixon* (1995); *Any Given Sunday* (1999); *Alexander* (2004); *World Trade Center* (2006)

Storaro, Vittorio

One of the all-time Greats of cinematography, Storaro adapts himself to each director, fleshing out their visions with the brilliance of his lighting and camerawork. Working regularly with **Bernardo Bertolucci**, for whom he created the dazzling visual tapestry of *The Conformist* (1970), and the darkened, often candle-lit entrances to the soul in *Last Tango In Paris* (1973), he was also responsible for the look of **Francis Ford Coppola's** masterpiece *Apocalypse Now* (1979), and the strange, comic-book intensity of **Warren Beatty's** *Dick Tracy* (1990), which consisted, astonishingly, of only a six-colour sequence.

Other Key Films: **Michael Apted's** *Agatha* (1979); Warren Beatty's *Reds* (1981) and *Bulworth* (1998); Francis Ford Coppola's *One From The Heart* (1982) and *Tucker: The Man And His Dream* (1988); Bernardo Bertolucci's *The Last Emperor* (1987) and *The Sheltering Sky* (1990); **Carlos Saura's** *Tango* (1997) and *Goya En Burdeos* (1999); **Alfonso Arau's** *Picking Up The Pieces* (2000)

Streep, Meryl

Adored by some, excoriated by others, Streep has often been compared, unfavourably, to her perceived 1980s archrival, **Jessica Lange**. Bitterness peaked in 1982 with Streep's Oscar success in **Alan J Pakula's** *Sophie's Choice*, when the critics were all for Lange's performance in Graeme Clifford's *Frances*. Streep may be a detached actress, seeming to approach a part from the outside in, but this should not detract from her often remarkable interpretations. She's a **Bette Davis**, not a **Barbara Stanwyck**, and one still remembers that first haunted look she gave **Jeremy Irons** in **Karel Reisz's** marvellously flawed *The French Lieutenant's Woman* (1981). In her recent films she seems to have been searching for some role that would carry her through middle-age towards a comfortable and garlanded semi-retirement, but having tried action, pseudo-feminism, worthiness and romance, she still appears to be flailing a little in her choices. This is a shame, for her serious approach to screen acting should rightly be serving as an example to younger actors still uncertain of the parameters of their profession.

Other Key Films: *Julia* (1977); *The Deer Hunter* (1978); *Kramer vs. Kramer* (1979); *Silkwood* (1983); *She-Devil* (1989); *Death Becomes Her* (1992); *The Bridges Of Madison County* (1995); *Marvin's Room* (1996); *Dancing At Lughnasa* (1998); *Music Of The Heart* (1999); *Adaptation* (2002); The Hours (2002); *The Manchurian Candidate* (2004); *Prime* (2005); *A Prairie Home Companion* (2006); *The Devil Wears Prada* (2006)

Streisand, Barbra

In the same league as **Judy Garland** and **Al Jolson** when it comes to belting out a melody, it could perhaps be said that Streisand has been over-praised, over-humoured and over-the-top in just about equal measures during her overlong screen career. Her début movie, **William Wyler's** *Funny Girl* (1968), could surely only appeal to the sort of people who hang flying ducks in their living rooms and shuffle around the parquet floor on cloth pantoufles [see **Philippe Noiret** in **Patrice Leconte's** *Tango* (1993) for a polished example] and its follow-up, **Gene Kelly's** *Hello Dolly!* (1969), did for matchmaking and **Louis Armstrong** what Elaine May's *Ishtar* (1987) did for the art of comedy. Her directorial debut, *Yentl* (1983) was so sublimely unconvincing that it arguably set back the cause of cross-dressing by ten years, and *The Mirror Has Two Faces* (1996) took a first-class little French thriller, André Cayette's *Le Miroir A Deux Faces* (1958), and turned it into a dirge. Opinion is, of course, divided and Barbrolaters will no doubt disagree vociferously with such a summary of their heroine's career.

Other Key Films: *On A Clear Day you Can See Forever* (1970); *What's Up Doc?* (1972); *The Way We Were* (1973); *A Star Is Born* (1976); *The Prince Of Tides* [also dir.] (1991); *Meet The Fockers* (2004)

Stroheim, Erich von

His real name was Erich Oswald Stroheim, and he was the son of a maker of straw hats, and his Hollywood incarnation, in all its demented and sometimes ill-judged glory, was largely the creation of his own fervid and obsessive imaginings. The assumed name of von Nordenwall part of his double act was, however, the genuine product of the young Erich Stroheim's observation of the decadent Viennese *fin de siècle* that gave us Freud, Mahler and Schoenberg. In his greatest films as director and star, *Foolish Wives* (1921), *Greed* (1925), *The Wedding March* (1928) and the unfinished *Queen Kelly* (1928), von Stroheim perfectly inhabited that very same sensuous, disordered and fallible Hapsburg Empire of the senses while remaining only too well aware of the reasons for its demise. **Jean Renoir** and **Billy Wilder** were the two great directors who understood and valued him as an actor, and in his extraordinary performances in Renoir's *La Grand Illusion* (1937), and in Wilder's *Five Graves To Cairo* (1943) and *Sunset Boulevard* (1950), von Stroheim occasionally came close to

being the man whose Golem-like image he had so fastidiously created.
Other Key Films: as director, *Blind Husbands* (1918); *The Devil's Passkey* (1919); *The Merry Widow* (1928); as an actor in *The Lost Squadron* (1932); *As You Desire Me* (1932); *So Ends Our Night* (1941); *The Great Flamarion* (1945); *La Danse De Mort* (1947)

Key Lines:

1: 'The Man You Love To Hate.' [Erich von Stroheim's publicity billing for *The Heart Of Humanity* (1918)]

2: 'I don't like women in the morning. Go away!' [Von Stroheim's Erwin Rommel in *Five Graves To Cairo* (1943)]

Sturges, John

A top-rank action director who specialized in **Westerns** and adventure films, Sturges made his mark directing **Spencer Tracy** as one-armed war veteran John J MacReedy in *Bad Day at Black Rock* (1955), before hitting the big time with *The Magnificent Seven* (1960), in which he cast virtually every key male actor of the next ten years. *The Great Escape* (1963) consolidated his position in the Hollywood hierarchy, and he became the director of choice of the tough-guy acting school, and, as such, he directed **Clint Eastwood** in *Joe Kidd* (1972) and **John Wayne** in *McQ* (1974). Sturges's final film, *The Eagle Has Landed* (1976), with **Michael Caine**, is a superb example of the successful adaptation of a best-selling novel.
Other Key Films: *The Capture* (1950); *Escape From Fort Bravo* (1953); *Gunfight At The OK Corral* (1958); *Last Train From Gun Hill* (1959); *Hour Of The Gun* (1967); *Ice Station Zebra* (1968)

Sturges, Preston

Scion of a rich and artistically rarefied world, and, incidentally, inventor of the kiss-proof lipstick, Sturges also made a sequence of the funniest and most inventive films ever to come out of Hollywood. He began his career as a screenwriter on such movies as A Edward Sutherland's *Diamond Jim* (1935) and Mitchell Leisen's *Easy Living* (1937), and this discipline stood him in good stead when he was given the opportunity to direct his own script of *The Great McGinty* (1940). Already Hollywood's highest-paid writer, the floodgates then opened and in the next four years he wrote and directed *Christmas In July* (1941), *The Lady Eve* (1941), *Sullivan's Travels* (1941), *The Palm Beach Story* (1942), *The Miracle Of Morgan's Creek* (1944) and *Hail The Conquering Hero* (1944). These films are miracles of demented, satirical humour, and it is something of a tragedy that Sturges, exhausted perhaps by such a burst of immaculately sustained creativity, should have produced only five more films (three of which were happily up to his old standards) before his untimely death in 1959 at the predictably eccentric venue of the Algonquin Hotel in New York. It is impossible ever to forget such magnificent creations as the shotgun toting, hound-like baying Ale and Quail Club, the Weenie King, or Rudy Vallee's J. D. Hackensacker III, and it is for the consistent gentleness and humanity of his humour, and his acceptance of oddity as simply a minor variation on the normal, that Sturges deserves to be honoured.
Other Key Films: *The Great Moment* (1944); *The Sin Of Harold Diddlebock* [a.k.a. *Mad Wednesday*] (1947); *Unfaithfully Yours* (1948); *The Beautiful Blonde From Bashful Bend* (1949); *Les Carnets Du Major Thompson* (1955)

Sutherland, Donald

Sutherland had been languishing in the doldrums for seven years before **Robert**

Altman's *M★A★S★H* (1970), in which he played the lazily anarchic Hawkeye Pearce, and Brian G Hutton's *Kelly's Heroes* (1970), made him famous. He has since steered a clever course between commercial expedience and artistic integrity, and he is one of the few actors still in work to have retained, and even improved, his reputation over a forty-five year career. He was impressive as John Klute, in **Alan J Pakula's** *Klute* (1971), and even more so as John Baxter in **Nicholas Roeg's** *Don't Look Now* (1973), and he has used his engaging quirkiness and his versatile Canadian accent to promote a steady following both in the US and in Europe, in a sequence of roles as disparate as his Calvin in **Robert Redford's** *Ordinary People* (1980) (possibly the best role of his career), and Ivan in **Werner Herzog's** *Scream Of Stone* (1991).

Other Key Films: *Steelyard Blues* (1972); *The Day Of The Locust* (1975); *1900* (1975); *The Eagle Has Landed* (1976); *Casanova* (1976); *Blood Relatives* (1978); *The Disappearance* (1978); *Invasion Of The Body Snatchers* (1978); *Bear Island* (1979); *Eye Of The Needle* (1981); *The Winter Of Our Discontent* (1983); *Crackers* (1984); *The Wolf At The Door* (1987); *Lock Up* (1989); *A Dry White Season* (1989); *Backdraft* (1991); *JFK* (1991); *Six Degrees Of Separation* (1993); *Fallen* (1998); *Instinct* (1999); *Space Cowboys* (2000); *The Art Of War* (2000); *The Italian Job* (2003); *Cold Mountain* (2003); *Pride & Prejudice* (2005); *An American Haunting* (2005); *Land Of The Blind* (2006); *Ask The Dust* (2006)

Swank, Hilary
Hilary Swank earned $3000 for her part in Kimberley Peirce's *Boys Don't Cry* (1999), and it has proved to be the best investment of her life. She won a best actress Oscar for the part of cross-dressing Brandon Teena, and another for the role of boxing casualty Maggie Fitzgerald in **Clint Eastwood's** *Million Dollar Baby* (2004), putting her on par with **Vivien Leigh**, Helen Hunt, Luis Rainer and **Jodie Foster** as a two-out-of-two nominations winner. Swank, like **Debra Winger** (whom she somewhat resembles in terms of talent) was born to play redneck girls, and it will be interesting to see whether she can broaden her range beyond such parts

Other Key Films: *Quiet Days In Hollywood* (1997); *Heartwood* (1998); *Insomnia* (2002); *The Black Dahlia* (2006)

Swanson, Gloria
Swanson's rise to silent fame is inextricably linked to the star of her mentor, **Cecil B DeMille**, and to those of two other directors, **Sam Wood** and Allen Dwan. Thanks to such films as DeMille's *Male And Female* (1919) and *The Affairs Of Anatol* (1921), Wood's *My American Wife* (1922) and *Bluebeard's Eighth Wife* (1923), and Dwan's *A Society Scandal* (1924) and *Wages Of Virtue* (1924), Swanson was earning $17,500 a week by the time she decided to opt out of the studio system and form her own production company. Vainglory, of course, has been the bane of many lesser mortals, and it was to prove Swanson's downfall, for she arranged to star in and produce *Queen Kelly* (1928), with **Erich von Stroheim** directing. The film ruined her, to the extent that she was still paying off the debts she had incurred while making it in 1950, when **Billy Wilder** offered her the poisoned chalice of yet another comeback, this time as a grotesque parody of herself. To Swanson's credit she said yes to Norma Desmond and *Sunset Boulevard* (1950), and, ironically, it is for this film that she is now best remembered, and not for the often baroque flights of fancy that were the products of her heyday.

Other Key Films: *Don't Change Your Husband* (1919); *The Great Moment* (1921); *Under The Lash* (1921); *The Impossible Mrs. Bellew* (1922); *Prodigal Daughters* (1923);

Manhandled (1924); *The Coast Of Folly* (1925); *The Love Of Sunya* (1927); *Sadie Thompson* (1928); *Indiscreet* (1931); *Father Takes A Wife* (1941); *Airport 1975* (1974)

Best **Swashbucklers**

Philippe de Broca's *Cartouche* (1962); Christian-Jaque's *Fanfan La Tulipe* (1951); **John Cromwell's** *The Prisoner Of Zenda* (1937); **Michael Curtiz** and William Keighley's *The Adventures Of Robin Hood* (1938); Michael Curtiz's *Captain Blood* (1935) and *The Sea Hawk* (1940); William Keighley's *The Master Of Ballantrae* (1952); **Akira Kurosawa's** *Yojimbo* (1961); **Ang Lee's** *Crouching Tiger, Hidden Dragon* (2000); Rouben Mamoulian's *The Mark Of Zorro* (1940); Fred Niblo's *The Three Musketeers* (1921); Jean-Paul Rappeneau's *Cyrano De Bergerac* (1990); George Sidney's *Scaramouche* (1952); Vincent Sherman's *The Adventures Of Don Juan* (1949); **Robert Siodmak's** *The Crimson Pirate* (1952); **Jacques Tourneur's** *The Flame And The Arrow* (1950); **Raoul Walsh's** *The Thief Of Bagdad* (1924)

Talmadge, Norma

Sister of silent actress Constance, who was herself married to the great **Buster Keaton**, Talmadge was the biggest star in Hollywood for a short period during the 1920s, earning $250,000 a film. Not especially beautiful, and with a rather square, Victorian figure, Talmadge nevertheless struck a chord with audiences in films such as Albert Parker's *Branded Woman* (1920), Clarence Brown's *Kiki* (1926) and Fred Niblo's *Camille* (1927), in which she played tragic heroines. When her squeaky voice was finally exposed with the coming of sound, Talmadge gracefully retired from the screen to live off her extensive real estate holdings.

Other Key Films: *A Tale Of Two Cities* (1911); *Panthea* (1917); *Bluebeard's Eighth Wife* (1923); *Secrets* (1924); *The Dove* (1928); *DuBarry Woman Of Passion* (1930)

Tarantino, Quentin

It's hard to believe that Tarantino was only born in 1963, for he appears to have gone through enough career restarts to satisfy a man twice his age. A former video-store clerk with an encyclopaedic knowledge of film (in California, video stores stock *all* the great films) Tarantino wrote his breakthrough script, *True Romance* (1993), for director Tony Scott, and it was a humdinger. His own debut as a director, *Reservoir Dogs* (1993), quickly followed, and afforded him instant entry to that select club of brilliant first-timers which includes **Charles Laughton**, **Nicholas Ray** and **Orson Welles**. He followed up with the sensational *Pulp Fiction* (1994) and then, when critics were just beginning to write him off as burnt-out case, he completed his miraculous hat-trick with *Jackie Brown* (1997). Long may he prosper.

Other Key Films: Oliver Stone's *Natural Born Killers* (1994); Robert Rodriguez's *From Dusk Till Dawn* (1996); *Kill Bill: Vol. 1* (2003); *Kill Bill Vol. 2* (2004)

Tarkovsky, André

Considered by some to be the greatest Russian director since **Sergei Eisenstein**, Tarkovsky began his career working within the system, and ended it as a voluntary exile, dying of lung cancer, looking distractedly back at the culture which had made him and which he had belatedly come to feel had let him down. Tarkovsky's films are first and foremost philosophical treatises, and this is their weakness as well as – paradoxically – being the basis for their awe-inspiring visual and poetic harmony, for they are all films in which one is allowed sufficient space and time in which to think. *Andrei Rublev* (1966), Tarkovsky's masterpiece, consists of a majestic and extended exploration into the significance of art and religion, but his first feature, *Ivan's Childhood* (1962), which tells the story of a doomed boy working for the Russian partisans during the Second World War, is possibly the better picture. His final films, *Nostalgia* (1983) and *The Sacrifice* (1986), were directed abroad, and reflect Tarkovsky's long-standing and well-documented obsession with the gradual dumbing down of mass culture – but it is certain scenes from *Stalker* (1979), of all his films, which linger longest in this writer's memory.

Other Key Films: *Solaris* (1972); *The Mirror* (1974)

Tarzan

The burly Elmo Lincoln was, to all intents and purposes, the first screen Tarzan, in Scott Sidney's *Tarzan Of The Apes* (1918), but five-time Olympic gold medal winner **Johnny Weissmuller** is the man most viewers – even now, nearly seventy years after he first appeared in the role – will forever associate with Edgar Rice Burroughs's aristocratic simian. Even **Sean Connery** has appeared in a Tarzan film, John Guillermin's *Tarzan's Greatest Adventure* (1959), but only as a heavy, O'Bannion, to Gordon Scott's ape-man. There have been Tarzan spoofs, and porn Tarzans; there have been Indian Tarzans, with Chandrakant's *Tarzan 303*, and there have been Chinese Tarzans, with the aptly named *The Adventures Of Chinese Tarzan* (1940) [director unknown]. There have been cartoon Tarzans, with Chris Buck and Kevin Lima's *Tarzan* (1999), and even documentaries investigating the history and cultural impact of the ape-man, including Alain d'Aix's *Investigating Tarzan* (1997). **Jean-Luc Godard**, of all people, even named one of his most famous films *Tarzan Versus IBM*; all right, the film was actually *Alphaville (Une Étrange Aventure De Lemmy Caution)* (1965), and the Tarzan bit was one of six alternative titles, but the trend is clear. All in all there have been well over one hundred Tarzan films and television series, and every generation seems to require their very own version of the hero. Probably the best, by public acclamation, have been W S Van Dyke's original *Tarzan The Ape Man* (1932), and its follow-up, **Jack Conway** [uncredited] and Cedric Gibbons's *Tarzan And his Mate* (1934), closely followed by Hugh Hudson's *Greystoke:The Legend Of Tarzan, Lord Of The Apes* (1984).

Key Line: 'Me Tarzan. You Jane.' [from *Tarzan The Ape Man* (1932)]

Tati, Jacques

It is an object of faith that Tati's sense of humour was never appreciated in his native France – like most objects of faith, this is palpable nonsense. What is true is that Tati died bankrupt, unable to raise the money for his final M. Hulot film, ironically due to be called *Confusion*. Tati became increasingly self-conscious and, dare one say it, artistic, following the success of his first three features, *Jour De Fête* (1949), *Monsieur Hulot's Holiday* (1953) and *Mon Oncle* (1958), and the French public dislikes nothing more than a message. The British and the Americans, on the other hand, adore messages (as long as they are telescoped) and they opened their hearts to Tati and Hulot, if not their wallets. *Playtime* (1967) and *Traffic* (1972) duly delighted the critics with their satirical edge, but alienated the French public, who preferred the less intellectual antics of **Bourvil** and **Louis de Funés**. There is no doubt that Tati was a comic genius, and an under-appreciated one, but the fickle general public sees a fine line between populist comedy and enlightened social commentary, and to many, at least in his native France, Tati was perceived to have crossed it.

Other Key Films: *Sylvie Et Le Fantôme* (1946); *Le Diable Du Corps* (1947); *Parade* [also dir.] (1974)

Tavernier, Bertrand

A literate, deeply cultured Lyonnais – just like his father, around whom he based a sublime 1988 TV documentary, 'Lyons, Le Regard Intérieur' – Tavernier is both critic, cinéphile and director, and his best work, while remaining resolutely French in sensibility, is nonetheless imbued with his long-standing love of American cinema. His first feature, *The Watchmaker* (1973), was an immediate success, and starred **Philippe Noiret**, who ended up performing the same mimetic function for Tavernier that **Jean-Pierre Léaud** had earlier done for **François Truffaut**. *Sunday In The Country* (1984) effectively put Tavernier on a par with the greatest French directors, and both *These Foolish Things* (1991), in which he drew out an absolutely luminous performance from **Jane Birkin**, and *La Vie Et Rien D'Autre* [*Life And Nothing But*] (1992), in which Noiret verges on greatness, have only further confirmed Tavernier's extraordinary talent.

Other Key Films: *Le Juge Et L'Assassin* (1975); *La Mort En Direct* (1980); *Une Semaine De Vacances* (1980); *Coup De Torchon* (1981); *Mississippi Blues* (1983); *Round Midnight* (1986); *La Fille De D'Artagnan* (1994) *L'Appât* (1995); *Ça Commence Aujourd'hui* (1999); *Laissez-Passer* (2002); *Holy Lola* (2004)

Taviani, Paolo & Vittorio

This extraordinary, film-obsessed duo has kept the reputation of Italian cinema alive throughout its recent period of apparent decline, with their poetic meditations on myth, memory and the power of allegory. Following their Palme D'Or success at the Cannes Film Festival with *Padre Padrone* (1977), the brothers made the magical *The Night Of The Shooting Stars* (1982), which continued their fascination with the Second World War and its effects upon Italian society, a fascination that first became manifest in their debut film, *San Miniato, July 44* (1954). Their later films have been much bound up with the machinations of fate and the possibilities of redemption, and *Kaos* (1985) remains perhaps their greatest and most poetically accomplished work.

Other Key Films: *Un Uomo Da Bruciare* (1962); *Allonsanfan* (1974); *Il Prato* (1979); *Good Morning, Babylon* (1987); *Night Sun* (1990); *Fiorile* (1993); *The Elective Affinities* (1996); *Tu Ridi* (1998); *Un Altro Mondo é Possibile* (2001)

Taylor, Elizabeth

The last of the great studio-era screen goddesses, this 'Made In England' beauty – she was recently made a Dame of the British Empire – left for America at the outbreak of the Second World War, aged seven. She was signed up by MGM three years later for a mind-boggling eighteen-year contract, and the rest is, as they say, screen history. From her first appearance in Fred M Wilcox's *Lassie Comes Home* (1943) it was obvious that Taylor was born to be a star, and she moved, with no apparent difficulty (thanks to MGM's star minders), from Clarence Brown's *National Velvet* (1944), through **Vincente Minnelli's** *Father Of The Bride* (1950) into the tentative maturity and passion of **George Stevens's** *A Place In The Sun* (1951), where she realised for the first time, watching **Montgomery Clift** at work, that acting took effort. Eight marriages later, she remains an icon, an indefatigable fund-raiser for AIDS charities, and the recipient of two Oscars, one for Daniel Mann's *Butterfield 8* (1960), a film she described as a 'heap of shit', and the other for **Mike Nichols's** *Who's Afraid Of Virginia Woolf* (1966), in which she gave the performance of a lifetime as Martha opposite **Richard Burton's** George.

Other Key Films: *Little Women* (1949); *Ivanhoe* (1952); *Giant* (1956); *Raintree County*

(1958); *Cat On A Hot Tin Roof* (1958); *Suddenly Last Summer* (1959); *Cleopatra* (1963); *Reflections In A Golden Eye* (1967); *Secret Ceremony* (1968); *Under Milk Wood* (1971); *Winter Kills* (1979); *The Flintstones* (1994); *The Visit* (1999)
Key Line: 'Tell Mama. Tell Mama all.' [*A Place In The Sun*]

Taylor, Robert

Taylor (a.k.a. Spangler Arlington Brugh) was renowned for his fine profile, for his hard work, and for his wooden acting style, which relied overmuch on a serious frown and a set of flashing eyes. However he remained a top MGM star for nearly thirty years, so he must have had something else to offer, but it is a little hard to decide what. He was inoffensive, like Robert Young, and handsome, like **Tyrone Power**, and he made an excellent corrupt lawyer in **Nicholas Ray's** *Party Girl* (1958), but the magic certainly came as much from Ray as it did from Taylor (although one hesitates to begrudge him one of the few meaty parts he was ever given). Kids always loved him though, when he buckled his swash in films like Richard Thorpe's *Ivanhoe* (1952), *Knights Of The Round Table* (1954) and *The Adventures Of Quentin Durward* (1956), and that's no small achievement.

Other Key Films: *Magnificent Obsession* (1935); *Camille* (1937); *Waterloo Bridge* (1940); *Billy The Kid* (1941); *Johnny Eager* (1942); *The Bribe* (1949); *Quo Vadis?* (1951); *All The Brothers Were Valiant* (1953); *The Law And Jake Wade* (1958); *Miracle Of The White Stallions* (1963); *The Night Walker* (1964)

Téchiné, André

The subtle and elegantly intimate French director of *Barocco* (1977), *Les Soeurs Brontë* (1979), *Rendez-Vous* (1985) and *Les Roseaux Sauvages* (1994), seemed to have achieved the crossover he deserved with the outstanding *Ma Saison Préferée* [*My Favourite Season*] (1993) and *Les Voleurs* (1996), both of which starred **Catherine Deneuve** and **Daniel Auteuil**. However, it was perhaps his concentration on character, maturity, and atmosphere at the expense of plot, that succeeded in alienating an English-speaking audience still made up of fifty per cent sentimentality and fifty per cent xenophobia. Apart from the handful of enlightened souls prepared to seek out Téchiné's films in the few remaining art theatres open to them, audiences are now forced to rely on rare television outings to keep up with his work. It's a sorry state of affairs when the latest **Tom Cruise** or **Julia Roberts** movie can monopolise every big screen in the country, whereas the wisdom and talent of a man like Téchiné is ghettoised. In an ideal world, shouldn't it be the other way around?

Other Key Films: *Paulina S'En Va* (1969); *Souvenirs D'En France* (1975); *Hôtel Des Amériques* (1981); *La Matiouette Ou L'Arrière-Pays* (1983); *Le Lieu Du Crime* (1986); *Les Innocents* (1987); *J'Embrasse Pas* (1991); *Alice Et Martin* (1998); *Loin* (2000); *Loin* (2001); *Les Égarés* (2003); *Les Temps Qui Changent* (2004); *Les Témoins* (2006)

Temple, Shirley

The most famous child star of them all, Temple, or 'little dimples' as some bright publicist called her, first worked when she was aged only three. A precocious dancer, and imbued with an apparent self-confidence verging on the criminal, Temple became the number-one box-office attraction in the US on her seventh birthday and remained so until beyond her tenth. If anyone imagines that merchandising only began with *Star Wars*, think again. There were Shirley Temple dolls, diapers, diaries and doilies – grown men like **Cary Grant**, **Gary Cooper** and **Victor McLaglen** were forced to kowtow and hootchy-kootchy with her on screen, knowing that if they clipped the little brat around the ear (as they doubtless wanted to) they would be excoriated by all America. She had talent, and a certain fey charm, and she cheered people up, in films like Irving Cummings's *Curly Top* (1935), William Seiter's *Dimples* (1936), **Allan Dwan's** *Heidi* (1937), and **John Ford's** *Wee Willie Winkie* (1937), during the appalling period of the Great Depression. Her career gave her up in the late 1940s, and she has spent the remainder of her life in public service, most notably as US Ambassador to Ghana and Czechoslovakia. Her autobiography was called *Child Star* (1988), but a better title might have been *From Dimples To Diplomat*.

Other Key Films: *Little Miss Marker* (1934); *Bright Eyes* (1934); *The Littlest Rebel* (1935); *Rebecca Of Sunnybrook Farm* (1938); *The Little Princess* (1939); *Susannah Of The Mounties* (1939)

Thalberg, Irving G

A sickly child, Thalberg grew into one of the best and most highly respected producers Hollywood has ever known, and the man who virtually ran MGM single-handed in the years from 1924 to 1933. It was during his tenure that MGM produced such commercial hits as Fred Niblo's *Ben-Hur* (1926), Clarence Brown's *Flesh And The Devil* (1927), **King Vidor's** *The Crowd* (1928) and Tay Garnett's *China Seas* (1935), alongside such long-term critical successes as **Tod Browning's** *Freaks* (1932), **Sam Wood's** *A Night At The Opera* (1935) and Sidney Franklin's *The Good Earth* (1937). Thalberg had been told by his doctors when he was only a teenager that he would never reach the age of thirty – in actual fact he reached thirty-seven, and left behind him a modestly won but mightily crafted legacy, and the reputation, rare in the cut-throat world of Hollywood film production, of being a decent man.

Other Key Films: Clarence Brown's *Anna Christie* (1930); **Ernst Lubitsch's** *The Merry Widow* (1934); Frank Lloyd's *Mutiny On The Bounty* (1935)

Thompson, Emma

Thompson had a magnificent run between 1992 and 1995, virtually unparalleled in terms of quality and achievement since the Golden Age of the 1930s and 1940s studio system. The run began with her luminous playing of Margaret Schlegel in **James Ivory's** *Howard's End* (1992), continued with her unrestrained performance as Beatrice in **Kenneth Branagh's** *Much Ado About Nothing* (1993), followed by her notably controlled Miss Kenton in Ivory's *Remains Of The Day* (1993). She then moved on to defending the Guilford Four as Gareth Peirce in Jim Sheridan's *In The Name Of The Father* (1993), transformed herself into a talented, touching Dora Carrington in Christopher Hampton's *Carrington* (1995), and then, *pièce de résistance*, both wrote the screenplay and acted as Elinor Dashwood in **Ang Lee's** *Sense And Sensibility* (1995). The other actresses of her generation must have heaved great sighs of relief when she took a break of a few years to start a family. As these things happen, of course, her post break career has not been as glittering as that which preceded it, but Thompson is far too talented an actress to write off quite yet.

Other Key Films: *The Tall Guy* (1989); *Henry V* (1989); *Impromptu* (1990); *Dead Again* (1991); *Peter's Friends* (1992); *Junior* (1994); *The Winter Guest* (1997); *Primary Colors* (1998); *Judas Kiss* (1998); *Maybe Baby* (2000); *Love Actually* (2003); *Imagining Argentina* (2003); *Nanny McPhee* (2005); *Stranger Than Fiction* (2006)

Thornton, Billy Bob

A character actor who found sudden fame (and an Oscar for the screenplay) as a result of his brilliant performance as the retarded murderer, Karl Childers, in the self-directed *Sling Blade* (1996), Thornton had paid his dues in a series of second-rate films which included Adrian Lyne's *Indecent Proposal* (1993) and Steven Seagal's *On Deadly Ground* (1994) before he managed to hit the big time. However for those

with the eyes to see, Thornton's talent was already on show in his magnificent script (co-written with Tom Epperson) and his excellent acting turn for Carl Franklin's still underrated edge-of-the-seat thriller, *One False Move* (1992), a movie that improves with each subsequent viewing.

Other Key Films: *For The Boys* (1991); *Tombstone* (1993); *The Stars Fell On Henrietta* (1994); *Dead Man* (1995); *Boogie Nights* (1997); *U-Turn* (1997); *Primary Colors* (1998); *A Gun, A Car, A Blonde* (1998); *Daddy And Them* [also dir.] (2000); *All The Pretty Horses* [dir.] (2000); *South Of Heaven, West Of Hell* (2000); *Daddy And Them* [also dir.] (2001); *The Man Who Wasn't There* (2001); *Wakin' Up in Reno* (2001); *Bandits* (2001)

Billy Bob Thornton in The Man Who Wasn't There, directed by Joel Coen (2001).

Working Title/The Kobal Collection

Thrillers

The normal definition of a thriller is a film that has you on the edge of your seat with psychological anxiety, without actually tipping you all the way over onto the floor in abject horror. The following *best* **Thrillers** selection fulfils that criterion admirably. All have some twist, some diabolical plot contrivance, that won't allow the audience a let-up before the director is good and ready. Will he or won't he kill her? Will she or won't she kill him? Will the assassin actually manage to kill De Gaulle even though we all know that that is impossible? Will the killer get away with it? And if so, how? Will the fact of being locked in a lift over a long weekend spoil the perfect crime? These are all staple thriller elements, fundamental to cinema and to the success of the mega-budget entertainment industry.

Key Lines:

1:    **Harrison Ford** as escaped murder suspect, Dr Richard Kimble: 'I didn't kill my wife.' **Tommy Lee Jones** as gun-threatened Deputy US Marshal Samuel Gerard: 'I don't care.' [*The Fugitive* (1993)]

2:    'Two fellows meet accidentally. Each one has someone that they'd like to get rid of, and they swap murders.' [The train scene between Farley Granger's Guy Haines and **Robert Walker's** Bruno Anthony, from **Alfred Hitchcock's** *Strangers On A Train* (1951)] Note For Film Buffs: Those immaculately written nineteen words, taken from the Patricia Highsmith novel and honed by one of the three script collaborators, **Raymond Chandler**, Czenzi Ormonde or Whitfield Cook, constitute an almost perfect movie pitch/concept. Chandler, given his form, must surely be the odds-on favourite to have penned them.

Best Thrillers

René Clément's *Plein Soleil* (1959); **Henri-Georges Clouzot's** *Le Corbeau* [*The Crow*] (1943) and *Les Diaboliques* (1954); Andrew Davis's *The Fugitive* (1993); Carl

Franklin's *One False Move* (1991); **Alfred Hitchcock's** *Strangers On A Train* (1951) and *North By Northwest* (1959); **Louis Malle's** *Ascenseur Pour L'Échafaud* (1957); Rob Reiner's *Misery* (1992); **Nicholas Ray's** *On Dangerous Ground* (1951); **Nicholas Roeg's** *Don't Look Now* (1973); **Martin Scorsese's** *Taxi Driver* (1976); **John Sturges's** *Bad Day At Black Rock* (1955); **Orson Welles's** *Confidential Report* (1954-1955); **Fred Zinnemann's** *The Day Of The Jackal* (1973)

Thurman, Uma

Another odd-ball looker, but seriously sexy with it, Uma Karuna Thurman has a strange, gawky grace on the screen, best seen in her early role of Cecile de Volanges, the young girl who is deflowered by **John Malkovich's** rapacious Vicomte de Valmont in **Stephen Frears's** *Dangerous Liaisons* (1988). More proof that Thurman has a very particular and natural screen presence came with the role of Glory in John McNaughton's excellent *Mad Dog And Glory* (1993), followed by her quirky turn as the overdosing Mia Wallace in **Quentin Tarantino's** brilliant *Pulp Fiction* (1994). Her recent work has been curiously chosen, and she remains a connoisseur's actress, who, like vintage wine, may well improve with age.

Other Key Films: *Adventures Of Baron Munchausen* (1989); *Henry & June* (1990); *Jennifer Eight* (1992); *Beautiful Girls* (1996); *The Truth About Cats And Dogs* (1996); *Batman And Robin* (1997); *Les Misérables* (1998); *The Avengers* (1998); *Sweet And Lowdown* (1999); *Vatel* (2000); *The Golden Bowl* (2000); *Tape* (2001); *Last Word on Paradise* (2001); *Kill Bill: Vol. 1* (2003); *Kill Bill: Vol. 2* (2004); *Be Cool* (2005); *Prime* (2005); *The Producers* (2005); *My Super-Ex Girlfriend* (2006)

Tierney, Gene

The upper-crust Tierney had an other-worldly and fragile beauty about her, which the studios, to their credit, recognised, using her as the physically elusive Laura, in **Otto Preminger's** *Laura* (1944), and as the ghost-driven Lucy, in **Joseph L Mankiewicz's** *The Ghost And Mrs. Muir* (1947). Tierney had a tragic life, giving birth to a mentally retarded child, and then succumbing to depression (following her break-up from **Rita Hayworth's** ex-husband, Aly Khan), a condition that necessitated a number of lengthy stays in sanatoria. At her best, as in John M. Stahl's *Leave Her To Heaven* (1945), or in the three first-rate *film noirs* she completed between 1949 and 1950 – Preminger's *Whirlpool* (1949) and *Where The Sidewalk Ends* (1950), together with **Jules Dassin's** fatalistic *Night And The City* (1950) – she transferred that other-worldliness to the screen in a way that few actresses, apart perhaps from **Kim Novak** in **Alfred Hitchcock's** *Vertigo* (1958), have ever achieved quite so well. At a 2006 showing of **Ernst Lubitsch's** *Heaven Can Wait* (1943) at the *Action Écoles* in Paris, the author witnessed a communal intake of breath from the entire cinema when Tierney first appeared on the screen, so radiantly beautiful did she seem to us all – and how often have you seen that happen?.

Other Key Films: *The Return Of Jesse James* (1940); *Tobacco Road* (1941); *The Shanghai Gesture* (1942); *Dragonwyck* (1946); *The Razor's Edge* (1946); *The Mating Season* (1951); *The Left Hand Of God* (1955); *Advise And Consent* (1962); *Toys In The Attic* (1963)

Best Titles

A particularly subjective one, this, but here are a few randomly chosen titles that might entertain, surprise and generally gladden the heart of film aficionados everywhere – they include the poetic, the inspired, and the downright schlocky, and

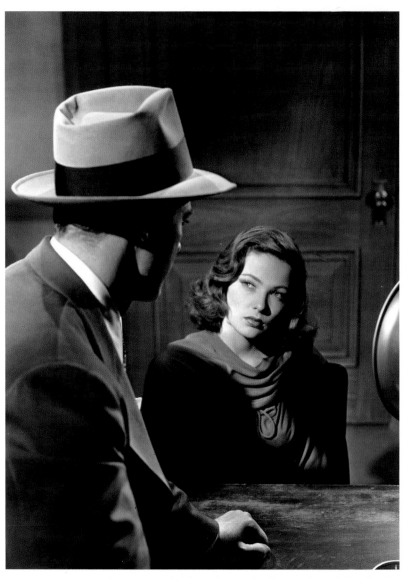

Dana Andrews and Gene Tierney in *Laura*, directed by Otto Preminger (1944).

20th Century Fox/The Kobal Collection

some are so descriptive one hardly needs to see the film in order to deduce the plot: **D W Griffith's** *The Musketeers Of Pig Alley* (1912); De Grasse's *Hell Morgan's Girl* (1917); Roy Del Ruth's *Love And Doughnuts* (1921); Muhsin Ertuğrul's *The Shirt Of Fire* (1923); Robert Z Leonard's *Adam And Evil* (1927) and *Let Us Be Gay* (1930); **Kenji Mizoguchi's** *Osen Of The Paper Cranes* (1934); **Edgar G Ulmer's** *Tomorrow*

We Live (1942); William A Seiter's *Four Jills In A Jeep* (1944); V Shantaram's *The Immortal Story Of Dr. Kotnis* (1946); Norman Foster's *Kiss The Blood Off My Hands* (1948); **Jean Negulesco's** *Johnny Belinda* (1948); Henry Levin's *The Mating Of Millie* (1948); **Preston Sturges's** *The Beautiful Blonde From Bashful Bend* (1949); **Howard Hawks's** *I Was A Male War Bride* (1949); **Vittorio De Sica's** *Indiscretion Of An American Wife* (1953); Ralph Thomas's *The Iron Petticoat* (1956); **Allan Dwan's** *Slightly Scarlet* (1956); Stan Brakhage's *Anticipation Of The Night* (1958), *Window Water Baby Moving* (1959) and *The Act Of Seeing With One's Own Eyes* (1971); **George Cukor's** *Heller In Pink Tights* (1960); Zhang Junli's *A Withered Tree Meets Spring* (1962); Dong Kena's *A Blade Of Glass On The Kunlun Mountains* (1962); Serge Bourguignon's *Sundays And Cybele* (1962); Don Owen's *Nobody Waved Goodbye* (1964); Aleksandar Petrovic's *I Even Met Some Happy Gipsies* (1967); Joyce Wieland's *Rat Life And Diet In North America* (1968); Alexander Kluge's *Artists At The Top Of The Big Top: Disorientated* (1968); Christopher Morahan's *All Neat In Black Stockings* (1969); Halit Refiğ's *I Lost My Heart To A Turk* (1969); Malcolm Le Grice's *Blackbird Descending* (1977); Tsui Hark's *All The Wrong Clues (For The Right Solution)* (1981); Katja von Garnier's *Abgeschminkt!* (1993); Zhang Yuan's *Beijing Bastards* (1993); Dwight Yoakam's *South Of Heaven, West Of Hell* (2000)

See also **Best Films**, **Erotic Moments**, **Heartstopping Moments**, **Worst Films**

Toland, Gregg

Orson Welles's cinematographer on *Citizen Kane* (1941), and the man who taught him the real potential of lighting and of deep focus photography, Toland was at the peak of his career when Welles was still panicking New York with his H G Wells radio spoof. Toland realised early on that great photography was all about catching emotion on the wing, and his camerawork in **William Wyler's** *Wuthering Heights* (1939), and **John Ford's** *The Grapes Of Wrath* (1940) and *The Long Voyage Home* (1940) testifies to his genius. His later work, however, is curiously unemotional, as if he had somehow burnt himself out during those fervid four years from 1939 to 1942 – a period which also included Wyler's *The Westerner* (1940) and **Howard Hawks's** comically sublime *Ball Of Fire* (1941). Toland died in 1948, aged only forty-four, and not a single star bothered to attend his funeral,

Other Key Films: Leo McCarey's *The Kid From Spain* (1932); **Rouben Mamoulian's** *We Live Again* (1934); Sidney Franklin's *The Dark Angel* (1935); William Wyler's *Dead End* (1937); Alfred Werker's *Kidnapped* (1938); Wyler's *The Best Years Of Our Lives* (1946); Henry Koster's *The Bishop's Wife* (1947)

Tourneur, Jacques

Tourneur is the thinking person's **cult** B-movie director, for his films grow on one over the years, showing up his A-feature commercial opposition as the also-rans they so often are. Tourneur had visual imagination, a rare attribute in the predominantly textually-orientated world of the Anglo-Saxon ascendancy. A Parisian by birth, and the inheritor of a Frenchman's eye for design, harmony and contrast, Tourneur first made his mark with a sensational trio of Val Lewton horror features: *Cat People* (1942), *I Walked With A Zombie* (1943) and *The Leopard Man* (1943). Just four years later he made one of the greatest and most perfect of all *film noir* thrillers, *Out Of The Past* [a.k.a. *Build My Gallows High*] (1947), which paired **Robert Mitchum's** Jeff Bailey as the fly to **Jane Greer's** Kathie Moffett's (Muffet?) spider, with rapacious **Kirk Douglas's** Whit Sterling circling, and gorgeous Virginia Huston's Ann waiting hopelessly in the wings. A series of fascinating **Westerns** followed, with *Great Day In*

The Morning (1956) notable amongst them, but the cherry on Tourneur's cake came, surprisingly, with a British horror movie, the one and only *Night Of The Demon* [a.k.a. *Curse Of The Demon*] (1958), in which an initially sceptical **Dana Andrews** combats the sinister and apparently all-powerful Niall MacGinnis. This is also the film in which we are privileged to be scared witless, first by a sensational magic-driven storm, and then by one of the most effective of all screen ghouls howling down at us from above the gushing boiler of the night express train.

Other Key Films: *Berlin Express* (1948); *The Flame And The Arrow* (1950); *Circle Of Danger* (1951); *Anne Of The Indies* (1951); *Way Of A Gaucho* (1952); *Appointment In Honduras* (1953); *Wichita* (1953); *Nightfall* (1958)

Towne, Robert
Towne wrote the script for **Roman Polanski's** sublime *Chinatown* (1974), and that has been enough, in Hollywood terms, to ensure his everlasting fame and the appearance of his work on any self-respecting screenwriting course – admittedly the script *is* just about perfect of its type, despite the fact that the ending was Polanski's, and not Towne's. If one is to believe the rumours, Towne has doctored just about every major and quite a few minor scripts that have appeared since then, but, joking aside, he has never produced anything else on the majestic scale of *Chinatown*, despite other notable successes such as Hal Ashby's *Shampoo* (1975) and *The Last Detail* (1983).

Other Key Films: Buzz Kulik's *Villa Rides* (1968); **Sydney Pollack's** *The Yakuza* (1975); *Greystoke: The Legend Of Tarzan* [using the alias of his dog, P. H. Vazak] (1984); *Tequila Sunrise* [also dir.] (1988); **Jack Nicholson's** *The Two Jakes* (1990); **Brian De Palma's** *Mission: Impossible* (1996); *Without Limits* [also dir.] (1998); **John Woo's** *Mission: Impossible II* (2000); *Ask The Dust* [wrote and dir.] (2006)

Tracy, Spencer
An actor's actor, Jesuit-educated Tracy won an unprecedented two consecutive Oscars for **Victor Fleming's** *Captains Courageous* (1937) and Norman Taurog's *Boy's Town* (1938). His multi-talented persona now established, he wowed audiences once again in Fleming's *Dr Jekyll And Mr Hyde* (1941), after which he began a fruitful nine movie screen partnership with **Katherine Hepburn**, beginning with **George Stevens's** *Woman Of The Year* (1942). The partnership between the two stars continued off-screen as well as on, until Tracy's death in 1967 – but the actor allegedly felt unable to divorce his wife and marry Hepburn because of his Catholic principles.

Other Key Films: *20,000 Years In Sing Sing* (1933); *Northwest Passage* (1940); *The Seventh Cross* (1944); *Adam's Rib* (1949); *Bad Day At Black Rock* (1955); *The Old Man And The Sea* (1958); *Inherit The Wind* (1960); *Judgement At Nuremberg* (1961)

Key Lines:

1. 'There were times my pants were so thin I could sit on a dime and tell if it was heads or tails.' [Tracy on poverty]

2. 'I like a he to be a he and a she to be a she.' [Tracy on sex, in **George Cukor's** *Pat And Mike* (1952)]

Travolta, John
Living proof that there can be life after career death (followed by death again), Travolta found himself top of the tree after appearing in John Badham's *Saturday Night Fever* (1977) and Randal Kleiser's *Grease* (1978), only to descend into the abyss (relatively speaking, for Travolta had invested his funds carefully) for nearly sixteen years, before triumphantly re-emerging as a sassy, wise-talking minor hood in

Quentin Tarantino's *Pulp Fiction* (1994). Since then, his now slightly fleshy face has shone out in video shops all over the world from action movies such as Barry Sonnenfeld's *Get Shorty* (1995), and **John Woo's** *Broken Arrow* (1996). A recent outing however, Roger Christian's *Battlefield Earth* (2000), based on Scientology founder L Ron Hubbard's erstwhile bestseller, has been welcomed by many as one of the single worst big-budget turkeys of the last hundred years of cinema. See **Worst Films**

Other Key Films: *Carrie* (1976); *Urban Cowboy* (1980); *Blow Out* (1981); *Face/Off* (1997); *Primary Colors* (1998); *The Thin Red Line* (1998); *The General's Daughter* (1999); *Lucky Numbers* (2000); *Swordfish* (2001); *Basic* (2003); *Be Cool* (2005); *Lonely Hearts* (2006)

Trintignant, Jean-Louis

Trintignant is a board on which directors can chalk whatever emotions, or lack of emotions they desire. He is such a consummate actor that even when he stands still, as in certain scenes during **Bernardo Bertolucci's** *The Conformist* (1970), the screen still seems nervously alive. The fifteen years before his breakthrough in *The Conformist*, however, were difficult ones for Trintignant, who was in danger of being typecast as a callow romantic lead in such mediocre fare as Claude Lelouch's *Un Homme Et Une Femme* [a.k.a. *A Man And A Woman*] (1966). Bertolucci's genius changed all that. It is arguable that Bertolucci must have seen Trintignant in **Eric Rohmer's** *My Night With Maud* (1969) and noticed his latent capacity for movement even in quietude. Whatever the case, Trintignant was suddenly in hot demand by non-commercial directors, and he made the most of his opportunities, starring in such films as Yves Boisset's *L'Attentat* (1972), Serge Leroy's *Les Passagers* (1976), Ettore Scola's *La Nuit De Varenne* (1983) and in **Krzysztof Kieslowski's** *Rouge* (1994), as the manipulative Judge Joseph Kern, faced with the innocence (or lack of it) of Irene Jacob's Valentine.

Other Key Films: *And God Created Woman* (1956); *Les Liaisons Dangereuses* (1959); *The Sleeping Car Murder* (1965); *Trans-Europ Express* (1967); *Les Biches* (1968); *Z* (1969); *Without Apparent Motive* (1971); *Flic Story* (1975); *Eaux Profondes* (1981); *Rendezvous* (1985); *Merci, La Vie* (1991); *Un Héros Très Discret* (1996); *Tykho Moon* (1997); *Ceux Qui M'Aiment Prendront Le Train* (1998); *Janis Et John* (2003)

Truffaut, François

Truffaut was a true enthusiast, a man for whom movies were life, and the filming of them the food that makes life liveable. He described much of his early childhood in his debut feature, *Les Quatre Cents Coups* [a.k.a. *The Four Hundred Blows*] (1959), in which his alter ego, **Jean-Pierre Léaud's** Antoine Doinel, compensates for an underprivileged childhood by escaping to the cinema – a habit which remained with Truffaut until his premature death of a brain tumour, aged fifty-two. André Bazin, the founder of the influential film magazine, *Cahiers du Cinéma*, first offered him a job as a film critic, and it was as such that he and his fellow cinéphiles devised what was later to become the **New Wave**. Following the success of *Les Quatre Cents Coups*, and its two brilliant follow-ups, *Tirez Sur Le Pianiste* (1960) and *Jules Et Jim* (1961), Truffaut became one of the most celebrated filmmakers in the world, but it is arguable that he had already given of his best. His ensuing films received mixed receptions, until he reached crisis point with the delightful *Day For Night* (1973), following which he took a much-needed sabbatical, emerging wiser perhaps, but with his creative energy impaired. *Le Dernier Métro* (1981) marked something of a final return to form, but Truffaut had scarcely two years left to live, and these were taken up with his new love, **Fanny Ardant**, and their infant daughter, Joséphine. Truffaut's success was, paradoxically, a triumph of the intellect over the heart, and it was this fundamentally rational approach to intuition that was to hamstring his later development as an artist.

Other Key Films: *La Peau Douce* (1964); *Fahrenheit 451* (1966); *The Bride Wore Black* (1968); *Stolen Kisses* (1968); *The Wild Child* (1970); *Les Deux Anglaises Et Le Continent* (1971); *The Story Of Adèle H.* (1975); *The Man Who Loved Women* (1977); *Vivement Dimanche* (1982)

Turner, Kathleen

Turner had one of the spunkiest starts of any actress, appearing opposite (and under, over and around) **William Hurt** in **Lawrence Kasdan's** *Body Heat* (1981), and reminding any who had been fortunate enough to see **Jacques Tourneur's** *Out Of The Past* [a.k.a. *Build My Gallows High*] (1947), of **Jane Greer's** wonderfully wicked Kathie Moffett. But then what? The talent was there, the beauty, the husky voice, the ne plus ultra *derrière*, but somehow everything was dissipated in roles that never really took her to the brink, in the way that she had been taken in *Body Heat*. Yes, she was entertaining and feisty in Robert Zemeckis's *Romancing The Stone* (1984) and Lewis Teague's *The Jewel Of The Nile* (1985), but it was a contrived feistiness, giving the impression that she was simply going through the motions in readiness for her large pay-check at the end. Her beauty solidified just a little in the early 1990s, opening up character roles to her which simply did not materialise, or which she refused. Looking through her filmography for another standout such as *Body Heat*, one comes across a plethora of adequate performances but absolutely nothing that has really challenged her. She would have been fine, for instance, in the **Annette Bening** part in **Sam Mendes's** *American Beauty* (1999), but Bening got that one and made it her own. Forget the fake Warshawskis, Kathleen, and convince some entrepreneurial producer to cast you in a remake of *Johnny Guitar*.

Other Key Films: *The Man With Two Brains* (1983); *Crimes Of Passion* (1984); *Prizzi's Honor* (1985); *Peggy Sue Got Married* (1986); *The Accidental Tourist* (1988); *The War Of The Roses* (1989); *House Of Cards* (1993); *A Simple Wish* (1997); *The Virgin Suicides* (1999); *Beautiful* (2000); *Prince Of Central Park* (2000); *Without Love* (2004)

Key Line: 'You're not too smart, are you? I like that in a man.' [*Body Heat*]

Turner, Lana

Turner was the epitome of the common girl plucked magically from the street (or, in her case, Schwab's drugstore) and turned into a star. The only snag was that she had little or no talent beyond a bright-eyed, artificial look of interest she could throw at any man, and a well-stacked bust which MGM showed off, as much as it dared, beneath a mind-boggling sequence of tightly fitting sweaters. Then Turner found her feet, and her milieu, in Tay Garnett's *The Postman Always Rings Twice* (1946), as the doomed Cora Smith, a small-town girl who marries up (to the sweating, amiable owner of a diner), and then tires of the deal, and the clammy, uxorial embraces that come with it. She was great in **Vincente Minnelli's** *The Bad And The Beautiful* (1952), and wonderfully schlocky in Mark Robson's *Peyton Place* (1958), then real life took over from screen drama when her daughter, Cheryl Crane, killed Turner's hoodlum lover, Johnny Stompanato, with a knife. Crane got off, and Turner wheeled out one final success, **Douglas Sirk's** *Imitation Of Life* (1959). But she had little but melodrama left in her, and her looks were beginning to blowse. What it all boils down to is that Turner was a natural B-movie actress thrown into the A-feature deep end, and it was only when her natural tackiness was coaxed into flame, as in **Mervyn LeRoy's** *Johnny Eager* (1942), or in Gottfried Reinhardt's *Betrayed* (1954), that she really shone.

Other Key Films: *Rich Man Poor Girl* (1938); *Ziegfeld Girl* (1941); *Dr. Jekyll And Mr. Hyde* (1941); *Honky Tonk* (1941); *Green Dolphin Street* (1947); *Cass Timberlane* (1947); *The Merry Widow* (1952); *Flame And The Flesh* (1954); *The Rains Of Ranchipur* (1955)

Ullmann, Liv

Lover and muse to director **Ingmar Bergman**, and a fine, intense actress in her own right, Ullmann starred in an extraordinary run of Bergman's films during the 1960s and 70s. As with her oft-times co-star **Bibi Andersson**, Bergman snatched Ullmann from the stage and cast her in a series of increasingly complex, emotionally searing parts in such films as *Persona* (1966), *Hour Of The Wolf* (1968), *Shame* (1968) and *Face To Face* (1976). Ullmann tried, in vain, to move across to the US mainstream, but soon realized that her forte was back in European art-house cinema, where she has more or less remained for the latter stages of her career.

Other Key Films: *The Passion Of Anna* (1969); *Cries And Whispers* (1972); *Scenes From A Marriage* (1973); *The Serpent's Egg* (1977); *Autumn Sonata* (1978); *Dangerous Moves* (1984); *The Ox* (1991); *The Long Shadow* (1992); *Zorn* (1994); *Faithless* [dir., with script by Ingmar Bergman] (2000)

Ulmer, Edgar G

Who knows how many films Ulmer actually made? What is indisputable is that he worked on smaller budgets, and turned out better films than many of his now forgotten, once more lauded, peers. His creative use of the camera, particularly in long takes (the main object of which was to save money) and in his enlightened composition and visual design, put to shame his more financially endowed colleagues.

Such films as *Isle Of Forgotten Sins* (1943), *Bluebeard* (1944), *Strange Illusion* (1945), *Ruthless* (1948) *The Naked Dawn* (1954), and Ulmer's masterpiece, *Detour* (1945), show a panache and a sense of style that have belatedly assured Ulmer of **auteur** status in the one country where such status still counts for something – France.

Other Key Films: *The Black Cat* (1934); *Tomorrow We Live* (1942); *Club Havana* (1945); *Her Sister's Secret* (1946); *The Strange Woman* (1947)

Unsworth, Geoffrey

Unsworth's rite of passage as a camera operator came with **Michael Powell** and Emeric Pressburger's superb duo, *The Life And Death Of Colonel Blimp* (1943) and *A Matter Of Life And Death* (1946). This then led to his promotion to officer class (*ergo* Director Of Photography status) on such alternately fervid and stiff-upper-lip classics as Marc Allégret's *Blanche Fury* (1948), Roy Ward Baker's Titanic movie, *A Night To Remember* (1958), **Stanley Kubrick's** *2001: A Space Odyssey* (1968), and Bob Fosse's *Cabaret* (1972). Unsworth's magnificent work on **Roman Polanski's** *Tess* (1979) was to prove an excellent, albeit posthumous, finale to an outstanding career.

Other Key Films: Charles Frend's *Scott Of The Antarctic* (1949); J Lee Thompson's *North West Frontier* (1959); Peter Glenville's *Becket* (1964); Richard Donner's *Superman* (1978); Michael Crichton's *The Great Train Robbery* (1979)

Vadim, Roger

French commercial filmmaker more notable for his marriages and liaisons with some of the most beautiful women in film history than for the quality of his work, Vadim launched first-wife **Brigitte Bardot's** 'sex-kitten' career (and completely sank St Tropez in the process, turning a pleasant fishing village into a poseur's paradise) with BB and her gingham bikini in *Et Dieu Créa La Femme [And God Created Woman]*

(1956). Following a well-publicised liaison in the early 60s with **Catherine Deneuve**, who bore him a child, he then launched third-wife **Jane Fonda's** brief career as a sex goddess with the titillating *Barbarella* (1967). Vadim must have had something, because a troop of his ex-wives, girlfriends and lovers reappeared on the occasion of his funeral in 1999, each manifesting signs of genuine regret.

Other Key Films: *Les Liaisons Dangereuses* (1958); *Les Parisiennes* (1962); *Ms Don Juan* (1973)

Lowell Sherman and Rudolph Valentino in Monsieur Beaucaire, directed by Sidney Olcott (1924).

Famous Players/ Paramount/The Kobal Collection

Valentino, Rudolf

The most perfect silent-age movie icon, Valentino died at the age of thirty-one just a few weeks before Warner Brothers inaugurated the sound era with its Vitaphone system. The émigré son of a down-at-heel family of Italian aristocrats, the di Valentina d'Antonguolas, Valentino first made his mark in **Rex Ingram's** *Four Horsemen Of The Apocalypse* (1921) – George Melford's *The Sheik* (1921) went on to cement his fervent female following, closely followed by Fred Niblo's *Blood and Sand* (1921). Two distraught women committed suicide on hearing of Valentino's death from peritonitis,

and more than a hundred were injured in the hysteria surrounding his funeral.
Other Key Films: *Monsieur Beaucaire* (1924); *The Eagle* (1925); *Son Of The Sheik* (1926)

Van Cleef, Lee

The 1960s **Spaghetti Western** explosion threw up a few strange characters who later made it to stardom (**Clint Eastwood** for one), but none stranger than Van Cleef, who was bald, almost indecently weird looking, and smoked a large corn-cob pipe for recreation. It was the eyes that did it, of course, and on such apparently insignificant features, movie fortunes have been made. Van Cleef could play mean, and he could play conservative/eccentric, and never more lucratively than in **Sergio Leone's** *For A Few Dollars More* (1966) and *The Good The Bad And The Ugly* (1966), which resuscitated the forty-one-year-old Van Cleef's flagging career (he always looked fifty whatever age he was) and ensured him hero status in France and Italy until his death in 1989. The one film he virtually carried on his own, Gordon Douglas's *Barquero* (1970), actually wasn't half bad of its type, proving that character actors can occasionally make good after all.
Other Key Films: *High Noon* (1952); *The Big Combo* (1955); *Tribute To A Bad Man* (1956); *The Young Lions* (1958); *Ride Lonesome* (1959); *Death Rides A Horse* (1967); *El Condor* (1970); *The Magnificent Seven Ride* (1972); *The Rip-Off* (1978); *Escape From New York* (1981); *Thieves Of Fortune* (1989)

Van Damme, Jean-Claude

Yes, he is the 'Muscles from Brussels' (or the 'Truffles from Brussels' as he prefers to call himself), and some of his movies may be a little over-sentimental and archetypal, but Van Damme brings a genuine and rather refreshing European sensibility to the best of his action films which give them an edge over their blustering and often inane US rivals. In Robert Harmon's *Nowhere To Run* (1993), his hero has a genuine love for children, and feet, if not of clay, at least of sand, and in Ringo Lam's *Maximum Risk* (1996), Van Damme reminds us not only that Europe and America are different continents containing different cultures, but also that heady, boy's-own action need not necessarily involve only the body, but can, on occasion, involve the head and the heart as well.
Other Key Films: *Double Impact* (1991); *Universal Soldier* (1992); *Hard Target* (1992); *Timecop* (1994); *Sudden Death* (1995); *Double Team* (1997); *Legionnaire* (1998); *Universal Soldier: The Return* (1999); *The Replicant* (2001); *The Order* (2001); *The Monk* (2001); *In Hell* (2003); *Wake Of Death* (2004); *Second In Command* (2006); *The Hard Corps* (2006)

Vanel, Charles

Vanel will be forever remembered by film buffs and edge-of-the-seat anxiety aficionados for his role as the tough/tender buddy of **Yves Montand** in **Henri-Georges Clouzot's** *The Wages Of Fear* (1952). Montand single-mindedly humiliates Vanel/Jo (who has set himself up as a man of means in the pestilential Central American oilfield community that none of them can afford to leave) before running over his legs with his truck in a mud-filled bog. The fact that Vanel can convince us of his utter change of heart and character is a testimony to his long and distinguished career in French cinema (let's face it, the best in the world), where he played parts ranging from the evil Javert in Raymond Bernard's *Les Misérables* (1934), to the tinder-dry Inspector Fichet in Clouzot's *Les Diaboliques* (1955). Extraordinarily,

Vanel made his first film, *Jim Crow*, in 1912, and his last, Francesco Rosi's *Three Brothers*, in 1980 – a magnificent career of sixty-eight years!

Other Key Films: *Waterloo* (1928); *L'Arlésienne* (1931); *Michel Strogoff* (1936); *Le Diable Souffle* (1947); *Si Versailles M'Était Conté* (1954); *To Catch A Thief* (1955); *Le Piège* (1958); *La Vérité* (1960); *Ballade Pour Un Chien* (1969); *Illustrious Corpses* (1976); *Ne Pleure Pas* (1978); *La Puce Et Le Privé* (1979)

Van Sant, Gus

An off-beat filmmaker whose best work, *Mala Noche* (1985), *Drugstore Cowboy* (1989) and *My Own Private Idaho* (1991) shows a particularly distinctive view of the United States underscored as much by drug abuse, bisexuality and incipient mania, as it is by friendship, the trust of strangers and the importance of country, and of the free passage within it to the heart. His people are searchers, movers and feelers, and Van Sant's films only fall down when they become static and overly intellectual.

Other Key Films: *Even Cowgirls Get The Blues* (1994); *To Die For* (1995); *Good Will Hunting* (1997); *Psycho* (1998); *Don't Worry, He Won't Get Far On Foot* (2000); *Finding Forrester* (2000); *Gerry* (2002); *Elephant* (2003); *Last Days* (2005)

Veidt, Conrad

Veidt became a British citizen in 1939 following Nazi threats against his Jewish wife, and he died three years later of a heart attack, aged just fifty. His German career had been a long and distinguished one, including the role of Cesare in Robert Wiene's *The Cabinet Of Dr. Caligari* (1919), and he and his extraordinary English accent were soon in great demand in France, Britain and the US. This led to parts in Walter Forde's *Rome Express* (1932), **Alexander Korda's** magical and multi-directed [by **Michael Powell** among others] *The Thief Of Bagdad* (1940), in which Veidt played the evil Jaffar, and **Michael Curtiz's** evergreen *Casablanca* (1942), as the sinister Major Heinrich Strasser. Veidt had a sudden posthumous burst of celebrity when his atrociously accented 1930s version of the song 'There's A Lighthouse Across The Bay' became a cult hit on disc jockey Terry Wogan's popular 1980s BBC radio programme.

Other Key Films: *Nocturno Der Liebe* (1918); *Around The World In 80 Days* (1919); *Lady Hamilton* (1921); *King Richard III* (1922); *Lord Byron* (1922); *William Tell* (1923); *The Hands Of Orlac* (1925); *Rasputin* (1932); *King Of The Damned* (1936); *The Spy In Black* (1939); *A Woman's Face* (1941); *All Through The Night* (1942); *Above Suspicion* (1943)

Ventura, Lino

Lino Ventura and pock-marked Eddie Constantine were France's tough men during the 1950s, 60s and early 70s – they played cops, thieves, crooks, thugs, hit men, bandits, private eyes, gunsels and murderers. Ex-boxer Ventura was the more talented actor of the two, and when he was paired with first-rate directors, as in **Louis Malle's** *Ascenseur Pour L'Echafaud* (1958) or Henri Verneuil's *The Sicilian Clan* (1969), he turned in performances of tremendous power. Francesco Rosi was also quick to recognize Ventura's star presence, using him to excellent effect in his *Illustrious Corpses* (1976) as the dogged police inspector uncovering a sinister and far-reaching right-wing conspiracy. The French counted on Ventura, for nearly thirty years, to turn out tough, unsentimental and utterly professional films, and he rarely, if ever, disappointed them.

Other Key Films: *Touchez Pas Au Grisbi* (1954); *Le Gorille Vous Salue Bien* (1958); *Taxi For Tobruk* (1961); *Les Barbouzes* (1964); *L'Armée Des Ombres* (1969); *The Valachi*

Verhoeven, Paul

Paul Verhoeven PhD (physics) has, it seems, always been fascinated by voyeuristic sex, even in his earlier Dutch films such as *Turkish Delight* (1973), *The Fourth Man* (1979) and *Spetters* (1980). However, after arriving in the US on a tide of dollars, either he or his producers had the bright idea of replacing the sex with violence (a taste much more to Hollywood's liking), leading to two mega hits, *Robocop* (1987) and *Total Recall* (1990). *Basic Instinct* (1992) marked a partial return to Verhoeven's original roots (if that is the right word) combining sex, violence *and* voyeurism to produce a third major commercial winner. No doubt inflamed by his success, Verhoeven tried to repeat the trick with *Showgirls* (1995), which proved so awful that it has now become a camp cult classic, somewhat along the lines of **Ed Wood's** *Glen Or Glenda* (1953). In an effort to redress the balance in his favour, Verhoeven made *Starship Troopers* (1997), which was seen by some as an attack on US militarism, and by others as a fundamental Nazi game plan. The talented Verhoeven, it seems, will always conjure up such paradoxes. It is, of course, possible that the man just may be the iconoclast he sells himself as, and he is certainly capable, when he wants to be, of almost visceral panache. Turn to *Basic Instinct* screenwriter Joe Esterhaz's astonishing *Hollywood Animal* (a book which, almost despite itself, throws open the lid to some awkward Hollywood truths) for more Verhoeven tales.

Other Key Films: *Business Is Business* (1971); *Flesh & Blood* (1985); *The Hollow Man* (2000); *Zwartboek* (2006)

Vidor, King

Vidor first made his mark with *The Big Parade* (1925), one of the greatest and most successful of all mainstream silent films, and which represented the peak of matinee-idol **John Gilbert** and silent-star Renee Adoree's screen careers. He followed this up with the considerably less lucrative, but equally penetrating *The Crowd* (1928), a film about the vicissitudes of poverty and the power of love to transcend it. Vidor cared about people, and his films, which include *Stella Dallas* (1937) (in which Barbara Stanwyck's Stella Dallas sacrifices her own happiness for that of her daughter), *The Citadel* (1938), *Duel In The Sun* (1947) and *Ruby Gentry* (1952) are noticeable, in particular, for their strong female roles.

Other Key Films: *Peg O' My Heart* (1922); *The Champ* (1931); *Cynara* (1932); *Northwest Passage* (1940); *Comrade X* (1940); *The Fountainhead* (1949); *Man Without A Star* (1955); *War And Peace* (1956); *Solomon And Sheba* (1959)

Key Line: 'Marriage isn't a word… it's a sentence!' [*The Crowd*]

Vigo, Jean

Vigo's is a tragic story. Stricken with tuberculosis following the mysterious death of his anarchist father in the infamous Fresnes prison in 1917 (when Vigo was just twelve-years old), Vigo produced only one forty-five-minute and one full-length feature, a documentary and a short, before succumbing to septicaemia at the age of twenty-nine. But his films have genius in them, and illustrate a sensibility so refined and so profoundly original in the context of the environment in which he was living (or in any context for that matter) that the French Government now belatedly awards an annual prize in Vigo's name for films that manifest a similar independence of spirit. Vigo's masterpiece is *L'Atalante* (1934), in which **Michel Simon** plays a free-thinking, foul-mouthed bargee, who at first challenges the swiftly consummated marriage of his beloved boss, and then becomes instrumental in its reinstatement. The film shows scenes as curious and as moving as they are universal, including the famous shot of Simon's tattooed belly button apparently smoking a cigarette. The earlier *Zéro De Conduite* (1933) was Vigo at his most anarchic and most influenced by his father, and the famous pillow fight (immaculately shot by Boris Kaufman) was later used as the basis for numerous theoretical arguments on existentiality and on the power of the young to challenge authority before their inevitable corruption by its influence. Regardless of fashion, mores, and the trivial vicissitudes of social expediency, Vigo's unique voice lives on.

Other Key Films: *Propos De Nice* (1930); *Taris, Champion De Natation* (1931)

Visconti, Luchino

Visconti was an aristocrat and a Marxist, two things that, in Milanese society during the time of Mussolini, were hardly as incompatible as they might seem elsewhere, and at other times. His first film was the magnificent *Ossessione* (1942), adapted, without permission, from **James M Cain's** novel *The Postman Always Rings Twice*, and by far the best film ever made on a subject that filmmakers as disparate as Tay Garnett (1946) and **Bob Rafelson** (1981) have since attempted. Visconti's most famous film is undoubtedly *Death In Venice* (1971), in which **Dirk Bogarde** gives a performance of such magnificent intensity that the entire film lurches headily around him like a frenzied, barely controllable merry-go-round. Visconti's most satisfying film, however, is his last, *L'Innocente* (1976), an extended paean to the concept of latifundium nestling in even the most aristocratic and enlightened of Sicilian souls.

Other Key Films: *La Terra Trema* (1948); *White Nights* (1958); *Rocco And His Brothers* (1960); *The Leopard* (1963); *The Damned* (1969); *Ludwig II* (1972); *Conversation Piece* (1975)

Voight, Jon

Voight had it all and then somehow lost it. He is a superb screen actor, as he proved beyond question in **John Schlesinger's** *Midnight Cowboy* (1969), **John Boorman's** *Deliverance* (1972) and Andrei Konchalovsky's *Runaway Train* (1985), but one now searches with increasing desperation for his appearance in parts that might afford him a filmography worthy of his talents. Instead he has appeared in such mundane films as **Brian De Palma's** *Mission: Impossible* (1996) and Luis Llosa's *Anaconda* (1997), although it remains patently obvious that Voight should be playing the sort of parts a great actor like **Robert Duvall** still contrives to find for himself.

Other Key Films: *Conrack* (1974); *Coming Home* (1978); *Heat* (1995); *Rosewood* (1997); *The General* (1998); *Enemy Of The State* (1998); *A Dog Of Flanders* (1999); *Pearl Harbor* (2001); *Lara Croft: Tomb Raider* (2001); *The Manchurian Candidate* (2004); *National Treasure* (2004)

Wajda, Andrzej

An eminent and brave filmmaker, Wadja became, during the 1950s, quite literally the voice of Poland. His masterwork is his trilogy – *A Generation* (1954), *Kanal* (1958) and *Ashes And Diamonds* (1958) – each of which starred the ill-fated Zbigniew Cybulski, who was known as the James Dean of Poland and who died in a railway accident in 1967 at the tragically early age of thirty-nine. Wajda later went on to map the original sources and progress of the solidarity movement in *Man Of Iron* (1981), but his main strength has always been in his instinctive understanding of how the past affects the present, a concept to which he has brought an often inspired visual slant, most notably in the scenes of the partisans' doomed escape through the claustrophobic Warsaw sewers in Kanal.

Other Key Films: *Lotna* (1959); *Ashes* (1965); *Everything For Sale* (1968); *Landscape After The Battle* (1970); *Man Of Marble* (1977); *Without Anaesthetic* (1979); *Danton* (1982); *The Possessed* (1987); *Nastazjai* (1994); *Pan Tadeusz* (1999); *Zemsta* (2002)

Walbrook, Anton

A marvellously romantic actor whose star shone briefly in a series of quality films during the 1940s and early 1950s, Walbrook had a marked advantage in his voice, an elegantly Austrian instrument that turned spoken English into something verging on the sublime. Scion of a family that had provided clowns for the Austro-Hungarian Empire's circuses for generations, Walbrook made his mature mark in Brian Hurst's *Dangerous Moonlight* (1941) and in **Michael Powell's** brilliant and perspicacious *The Life And Death Of Colonel Blimp* (1943), in which he played a sympathetic German, a rare role in wartime Britain. Walbrook's masterpiece, and the part for which he, above all men, was most perfectly suited, came as the master of ceremonies in **Max Ophüls's** *La Ronde* (1950). His career wound slowly down after that, and by the time of his death in 1967, he was something of a forgotten man.

Other Key Films: *Viktor Und Viktoria* (1933); *Maskerade* (1934); *Allotria* (1936); *Michael Strogoff* (1937); *Victoria The Great* (1937); *Gaslight* (1940); *49th Parallel* (1941); *The Red Shoes* (1948); *The Queen Of Spades* (1949); *Oh Rosalinda* (1955); *I Accuse!* (1958)

Walken, Christopher

An offbeat and intense character actor whose very frigidity on screen constitutes his main advantage over lesser performers, Walken first came to prominence in **Michael Cimino's** *The Deer Hunter* (1978), in which he played an action-addicted Vietnam veteran utterly unable to lay off the kick he got out of risking his life, again and again, at Russian roulette. He made a surprisingly effective all-singing, all-dancing pimp in Herbert Ross's sadly underrated *Pennies From Heaven* (1981), and his recent parts, though scarcer than one would wish, have all been effective, in particular Tony Scott's *True Romance* (1993) and John Badham's otherwise rather dotty *Nick Of Time* (1995). Walken is about the best baddie in the business, and his cold smile must be hell-on-earth if it's the final thing one sees before oblivion.

Other Key Films: *The Anderson Tapes* (1971); *Annie Hall* (1977); *Roseland* (1977); *The Dogs Of War* (1980); *Heaven's Gate* (1980); *Brainstorm* (1983); *The Dead Zone* (1983); *Biloxi Blues* (1988); *The Milagro Beanfield War* (1988); *King Of New York* (1990); *Things To Do In Denver When You're Dead* (1995); *Last Man Standing* (1996); *Sleepy Hollow* (1999); *The Opportunists* (2000); *Scotland, P.A.* (2001); *Joe Dirt* (2001); *America's Sweethearts* (2001); *Inside Job* (2001); *Man On Fire* (2004); *The Stepford Wives* (2004); *Romance & Cigarettes* (2005)

Walker, Robert

A sadly self-destructive actor, Walker had the chance to shine (which he did) in one utterly memorable performance, that of psychotic rich-boy Bruno Anthony in **Alfred Hitchcock's** *Strangers On A Train* (1951). Why is Walker so convincing in the part? It would be trite to ascribe his skill to his having lived on the psychological edge for most of his adult life – suffice it to say that in *Strangers*, and to a lesser extent in **Vincente Minnelli's** *The Clock* (1945), as the vulnerable young soldier who falls in love with, and marries, a non-singing **Judy Garland** during a forty-eight hour furlough, Walker hinted at a depth of characterization and a capacity for simplicity that must surely afford him a finer posthumous reputation than his tragically curtailed filmography would at first glance suggest.

Other Key Films: *Bataan* (1943); *Madame Curie* (1943); *Thirty Seconds Over Tokyo* (1944); *Since You Went Away* (1944); *The Sea Of Grass* (1946); *Till The Clouds Roll By* (1946); *One Touch Of Venus* (1948); *Vengeance Valley* (1951); *My Son John* (1952)

Key Line: 'Some people are better off dead. Like your wife and my father, for instance.' [Walker, making his proposition to Farley Granger, in *Strangers On A Train*]

Wallis, Hal B

The poor-boy-made-good producer of a quite extraordinary number of high-quality Hollywood mainstream films, ranging from **Mervyn LeRoy's** *Little Caesar* (1931) to **John Wayne's** *True Grit* follow-up, Stuart Miller's *Rooster Cogburn* (1975), Wallis could be said not only to have spanned, but to have more than partially created the great years of Hollywood cinema through which he lived. A modest man in comparison with some of his more bull-like contemporaries, Wallis had an astonishing filmography of more than 400 films, remarkably few of them clinkers, which attests both to his taste and to his fundamental humanity in a pit otherwise chock-full with ersatz vipers.

Other Key Films: Mervyn LeRoy's *I Am A Fugitive From A Chain Gang* (1932); **Michael Curtiz's** *Captain Blood* (1935); **William Wyler's** *Jezebel* (1938); Michael Curtiz's *The Adventures Of Robin Hood* (1938); **Raoul Walsh's** *High Sierra* (1941); Irving Rapper's *Now Voyager* (1942); Michael Curtiz's **Casablanca** (1943); **John Sturges's** *Last Train From Gun Hill* (1959); Peter Glenville's *Becket* (1964); **Henry Hathaway's** *True Grit* (1969)

Walsh, Raoul

Real-life cowboy and wearer of an eye-patch after an unfortunate collision with a flying rabbit, Walsh was one of the unsung paladins of Hollywood, producing splendid action films with often complex anti-heroes. After silent successes such as *What Price Glory?* (1926), he made **Humphrey Bogart's** name with *High Sierra* (1941), and provided **Errol Flynn** with one of his better roles, as Custer, in *They Died With Their Boots On* (1941). Director of more than a hundred films, Walsh was a true professional with a hint of genius, as was shown in *White Heat* (1949), in which **James Cagney** gets to immolate himself in a triumphant *Götterdämmerung* on top of a petrol refinery.

Other Key Films: *Sadie Thompson* (1928); *In Old Arizona* (1929); *The Big Trail* (1930); *The Roaring Twenties* (1939); *They Drive By Night* (1940); *Background To Danger* (1943); *Objective Burma!* (1944); *Pursued* (1947); *The Naked And The Dead* (1958)

War Films

When cinema started, circa 1895, war was one of the last things on people's minds. Twenty years later it was on everybody's mind, and cinema had found one of its great motifs. There have arguably been more great war films made than films in any other genre except the **Western**, and the list below represents some of the finest ones. War, by its very nature, can comprise horror, comedy, love, friendship, hate, and the solace of brief happiness – all the great themes, therefore. As with novels, so with movies: **Sergei Eisenstein's** *Alexander Nevsky* (1938) is cinema's *War And Peace*; **Jean Renoir's** *La Grande Illusion* (1937), is cinema's *Servitude Et Grandeur Militaires*; Lewis Milestone's *All Quiet On The Western Front* (1930) is at least comparable, in its cumulative effect, to the 1929 novel by Erich Maria Remarque that it was drawn from; **Francis Ford Coppola's** *Apocalypse Now* (1979) created a metaphor for the Vietnam conflict that is arguably stronger, and potentially more long-lasting, than true-life images from the war itself; and **Anthony Minghella's** *The English Patient* (1996) took war as the universal context for an exploration of love, friendship, and the mechanics of betrayal.

Key Lines:

1: 'You'll have to forgive me, comrade.' [**Lew Ayres** as Paul Baumer, in *All Quiet On The Western Front* (1930), asking the Frenchman he has just killed for understanding.

2: 'He wished that he, too, had a wound. A red badge of courage.' [From the narration accompanying **John Huston's** *The Red Badge Of Courage* (1951)]

Best War Films

Claude Autant-Lara's *La Traversée De Paris* (1956); **Bernardo Bertolucci's** *The Conformist* (1970); Sergei Bondarchuk's *Waterloo* (1970); **Robert Bresson's** *Un Condamné A Mort S'Est Échappé* (1956); Christian de Challonge's *Docteur Petiot* (1989); Grigori Chukrai's *Ballad Of A Soldier* (1959); **Michael Cimino's** *The Deer Hunter* (1979); James Clavell's *The Last Valley* (1970); **René Clément's** *Jeux Interdits* (1951); **Francis Ford Coppola's** *Apocalypse Now* (1979); **Sergei Eisenstein's** *Alexander Nevsky* (1938); **John Huston's** *The Red Badge Of Courage* (1951); **Stanley Kubrick's** *Paths Of Glory* (1958); **David Lean's** *The Bridge On The River Kwai* (1957); **Joseph Losey's** *Monsieur Klein* (1976); **Louis Malle's** *Lacombe Lucien* (1974); Jiri Menzel's *Closely Observed Trains* (1966); **Jean-Pierre Melville's** *L'Armée Des Ombres* (1969); **Lewis Milestone's** *All Quiet On The Western Front (1930)*; **Sam Peckinpah's** *Cross Of Iron* (1977); **Michael Powell** and **Emeric Pressburger's** *The Life And Death Of Colonel Blimp* (1943); **Nicholas Ray's** *Bitter Victory* (1957); **Jean Renoir's** *La Grande Illusion* (1937); **Roberto Rossellini's** *Paisà* (1946); **Steven Spielberg's** *Schindler's List* (1993); **Bertrand Tavernier's** *La Vie Et Rien D'Autre* (1989); **Billy Wilder's** *Five Graves To Cairo* (1943) and *Stalag 17* (1953)

Warhol, Andy

Warhol is seen by some as an avant-garde cultural icon and by others as a tiresome parvenu, and his film work falls somewhere in between the two camps but manages, nonetheless, to draw interminably pretentious twaddle from people one might otherwise assume should know better. Suffice it to say that Warhol took himself seriously, and that some of the work produced by his film 'factory' was highly prescient in its undermining of standard moral parameters (although it might conceivably be seen as splendidly irrelevant to those living outside such sophisticated cultural environments as New York). Paul Morrisey's *Flesh* (1968) and *Andy Warhol's Dracula* (1974) are the most celebrated of Warhol's post-gunshot creations, and will no doubt continue to delight and bore, for generations to come, the denizens of museum retrospective showings.

Other Key Films: *Sleep* (1963); *Harlot* (1964); *Bitch* (1965); *The Velvet Underground And Nico* (1967); *The Chelsea Girls* (1966); *L'Amour* (1973)

Washington, Denzel

Washington first attracted real notice as Pfc. Peterson in Norman Jewison's *A Soldier's Story* (1984), and the prestigious part of Steve Biko in **Richard Attenborough's** *Cry Freedom* (1987) soon followed. His best break, however, came in Edward Zwick's *Glory* (1989), and he has hardly looked back since. He was excellent as penniless private-investigator Easy Rawlins in Carl Franklin's *Devil In A Blue Dress* (1995), and looks set for a long, lucrative, if possibly somewhat over-earnest career.

Other Key Films: *For Queen And Country* (1988); *Ricochet* (1991); *Malcolm X* (1992); *Much Ado About Nothing* (1993); *The Pelican Brief* (1993); *Philadelphia* (1993); *Crimson Tide* (1995); *The Hurricane* (1999); *Remember The Titans* (2000); *Training Day* (2001); *John Q* (2001); *Out Of Time* (2003); *Man On Fire* (2004); *The Manchurian Candidate* (2004); *Inside Man* (2006)

Waters, John

Blissfully irreverent cult filmmaker who has flirted with the mainstream without ever actually choosing to go to bed with it, Waters first came to the attention of the moralists with his *Mondo Trasho* (1969), in which gargantuan transvestite Divine (an ex-school chum of Waters's) first erupted onto the big screen. History was made during Waters's follow-up, *Pink Flamingos* (1972), when Divine scoffed a dog turd. However, Waters's best film by far, *Cry-Baby* (1990), proved, paradoxically, to be a box-office failure, despite the presence of a tearfully tattooed **Johnny Depp** at the head of the cast list. The continentals loved it, though, and the film did much to bolster Depp's subsequent career as the thinking Frenchwoman's favourite American.

Other Key Films: *Female Trouble* (1972); *Desperate Living* (1977); *Polyester* (1981); *Hairspray* (1988); *Serial Mom* (1994); *Pecker* (1998); *Cecil B DeMented* (2000); *A Dirty Shame* (2004)

Key Line: 'Hysterectomy pants, I call them.' [*Cry-Baby*]

Waxman, Frank

One of the best of the romantic school of Hollywood film music composers, Waxman was responsible for a multitude of distinguished scores, including that for **Alfred Hitchcock's** *Rebecca* (1940), Peter Godfrey's *The Two Mrs Carrolls* (1947), Anatole Litvak's *Sorry Wrong Number* (1948), **Billy Wilder's** *Sunset Boulevard* (1950) and **George Stevens's** *A Place In The Sun* (1951). As with his distinguished colleagues, **Max Steiner**, Friedrich Hollander, **Bernard Hermann**, and **Erich Wolfgang Korngold**, Waxman was a classically trained musician who felt out of touch with modernism and preferred the well-staffed orchestras and well-stocked pocket books of Hollywood to the starvation on offer on the concert circuit.

Wayne, John

Arguably the best-loved and most enduring of all Hollywood stars, Marion Michael Morrison remains the focus of an ongoing cult that shows no sign of abating. Embodying the manly virtues of moral consistency and an invariable decency towards women, six-foot four-inch 'Duke' Wayne starred in more than 140 feature films during his fifty-year career. The chosen star for **John Ford** in his sublime cavalry trilogy, *Fort Apache* (1948), *She Wore a Yellow Ribbon* (1949) and *Rio Grande* (1950), Wayne was often reviled for his consistently held right-wing views, most notably by those who had failed either to see or to appreciate the profound humanism of his greatest films. Dignified to the last, he made his farewell to the screen in **Don Siegel's** *The Shootist* (1976), playing John Bernard Books, a gunfighter mortally ill with cancer (just as Wayne was at the time) and a man who was gently but resolutely concerned with the process of making his soul (and thus, coincidentally, cleansing the town of bad men) before dying.

Other Key Films: *The Oregon Trail* (1936); *Stagecoach* (1939); *The Long Voyage Home*

(1939); *They Were Expendable* (1945); *Red River* (1948); *Wake Of The Red Witch* (1948); *Three Godfathers* (1949); *The Quiet Man* (1952); *Hondo* (1953); *The Searchers* (1956); *Rio Bravo* (1959); *The Man Who Shot Liberty Valance* (1962); *El Dorado* (1967); *True Grit* (1969)

Key Line:

1. 'A long time ago I made me a rule – I let people do what they want to do.' [*Hondo*]
2. 'That'll be the day!' [*The Searchers*]
3. 'Don't apologize. It's a sign of weakness.' [*She Wore A Yellow Ribbon*]
4. 'I won't be wronged, and I won't be insulted, and I won't be laid a hand on. I don't do these things to other people, and I require the same from them.' [*The Shootist*]
5. 'John Wayne never blows a line. He'll come in letter perfect. The other actors will blow lines, but he will stand there patiently, wait for them to get their lines, then say his in his own way.' [Wendell Mayes, who scripted **Otto Preminger's** *In Harm's Way* (1965), which featured Wayne as Captain Rockwell Torrey]

Weaver, Sigourney

Refreshingly independent in a film world formed largely of wannabe clones, Weaver has constructed her career with care and has acted in remarkably few turkeys. She shot to fame, quite literally, as Ripley (shades of Patricia Highsmith?) in **Ridley Scott's** *Alien* (1979), and then consolidated her reputation for quality acting opposite **Mel Gibson** in **Peter Weir's** excellent *The Year Of Living Dangerously* (1982). She would have been sensational in **Lawrence Kasdan's** *Body Heat* (1981), which she turned down because of the sex scenes involved, while paradoxically agreeing to appear in Bob Swaim's much inferior *Half Moon Street* (1986), in which she cheerfully shed her clothes and cavorted in front of a mirror (and her audience) in stockings, suspender belt and precious little else. Since then she's been far more cautious (and just a little worthy).

Other Key Films: *Gorillas In The Mist* (1988); *Working Girl* (1988); *Dave* (1993) *Death And The Maiden* (1995); *Galaxy Quest* (1999); *Company Man* (2000); *Heartbreakers* (2001); The Guys (2002); Holes (2003); The Village (2004); Snowcake (2005); *The TV Set* (2006); *Infamous* (2006)

Webb, Clifton

A fondly remembered character actor who nevertheless had enough box-office clout to carry many films on his own, Webb Parmallee Hollenbeck specialised in over-bred, over-mannered know-it-alls with hearts of gold, as personified by his perennial Mr Belvedere in Walter Lang's *Sitting Pretty* (1948). Webb's best part, because it allowed full play to his innate waspishness, came as Waldo Lydecker in **Otto Preminger's** magnificent, ground-breaking *Laura* (1944).

Other Key Films: *The Dark Corner* (1946); *The Razor's Edge* (1946); *For Heaven's Sake* (1950); *Titanic* (1953); *Three Coins In A Fountain* (1954); *The Man Who Never Was* (1956)

Key Lines:

1. 'How I detest the dawn! The grass always looks like it's been left out all night.' [**Henry Hathaway's** *The Dark Corner*]
2. 'It's lavish, but I call it home.' [Waldo Lydecker, in *Laura*]

***Best* Weepies**
Marcel Carné's *Les Portes De La Nuit* (1946); **John Cromwell's** *The Enchanted Cottage* (1945); **Edmund Goulding's** *Dark Victory* (1939); Jean Grémillon's *Remorques* (1939-1940); **David Lean's** *Brief Encounter* (1945); **Ang Lee's** *Sense And Sensibility* (1995); **Mervyn LeRoy's** *Waterloo Bridge* (1940); **Joseph L Mankiewicz's** *A Letter To Three Wives* (1949); **Max Ophüls's** *Letter From An Unknown Woman* (1948); Irvin Rapper's *Now, Voyager* (1942); **Douglas Sirk's** *Magnificent Obsession* (1953) and *All That Heaven Allows* (1955); **Sam Wood's** *King's Row* (1942)

Weir, Peter
One of the best of Australia's 1970s 'New Wave' directors and something of a poet of emotional and physical claustrophobia, Weir is adept at maintaining the basic integrity of his films while still securing success at the box office. *Picnic At Hanging Rock* (1975) mystified an entire generation (and still persists in doing so – what really happened to those three girls, for God's sake?) whilst *Gallipoli* (1981), following the grand old filmic tradition of historical inaccuracy, was, emotionally-speaking at least, right on the nail, which can be the only conceivable justification, apart from propaganda, for tinkering with historical truth. Weir's best films to date are *The Year Of Living Dangerously* (1983) in which he successfully conjured up an entire lost decade that may be close to us in time but is far away in comprehension, and *Master And Commander: The Far Side Of The World* (2003), in which he so fastidiously recreated life aboard an early nineteenth century man-of-war that even die-hard Patrick O'Brian fans (like the author) were forced to acknowledge the brilliance of his adaptation. Fans of Weir's magnificent *Witness* (1985) and also of *Dead Poets Society* (1989), however, may wish to dispute these choices.
Other Key Films: *The Cars That Ate Paris* (1974); *The Last Wave* (1977); *The Plumber* (1980); *The Mosquito Coast* (1986); *Green Card* (1990); *Fearless* (1993); *The Truman Show* (1998);

Weissmuller, Johnny
Undeniably the greatest-ever screen *Tarzan*, Weissmuller was not in fact the first – that privilege fell to burly Elmo Lincoln, complete with impala loincloth and a shoulderful of coiled lianas, in Scott Sidney's *Tarzan Of The Apes* (1918). Weissmuller, however, brought an Olympic swimmer's physique to the part, and his initial success in W S Van Dyke's *Tarzan The Ape Man* (1932) led to a further eleven spin-offs, culminating in Robert Florey's *Tarzan And The Mermaids* (1948), in which good living and good loving had obviously taken their toll on our hero's once noble frame. During Weissmuller's brief but tempestuous marriage to Mexican firecracker Lupe Velez, the body make-up department were kept in a permanent state of mild hysteria by the marks Lupe's passionate temper and equally passionate carnality inflicted on the naked frame of their ape man. Fed up to the back teeth with Lupe's habit of flinging her skirt over her head in public places to reveal her invariable lack of underwear, Weissmuller divorced Velez in 1938 – sadly, she was to commit suicide six years and countless exhausted lovers later, by overdosing on Seconal tablets.
Other Key Films: *Tarzan And His Mate* (1934); *Tarzan Escapes* (1936); *Tarzan Finds A Son* (1939); *Tarzan's Secret Treasure* (1941); *Tarzan's New York Adventure* (1942); *Tarzan Triumphs* (1941); *Tarzan's Desert Mystery* (1943); *Tarzan And The Amazons* (1945); *Tarzan And The Leopard Woman* (1946); *Tarzan And The Huntress* (1947)

Welch, Raquel

Almost incapable of acting in the normal sense of the word, the half-Bolivian, half-English Welch founded and maintained her career on the triple assets of her face and figure, which, quite reasonably given the invariable laws of biology, have provided her with an extremely good living ever since. The famous image of her (in a leopard-skin loincloth and little else) which first skewered an entire generation of spotty adolescents by the groin, came in Don Chaffey's *One Million Years B.C.* (1966), a film which may well mark the high-water point of Welch's screen career. Welch has always been remarkably astute at marketing her sexuality and disguising her lack of real acting talent, and it would be absurd, in the context of her era, to have expected any more of her than that.

Other Key Films: *Fantastic Voyage* [in which she utters nary a word] (1966); *Fathom* (1967); *Bedazzled* (1967); *Bandolero!* (1968); *100 Rifles* (1969); *Myra Breckenridge* (1970); *The Magic Christian* (1970); *The Last Of Sheila* (1973); *The Three Musketeers* (1974); *Naked Gun 33_: The Final Insult* (1994); *Forget About It* (2006)

Key Line:

1. 'Being a sex symbol is rather like being a convict.' [Welch on the price of fame]
2. 'Tumak!' [*One Million Years B.C.*]

Welles, Orson

Welles was the closest Hollywood ever came to having a wayward genius in its commercially inhibited midst, and they made the worst of it. Whatever Pauline Kael or other carpers have to say about **Citizen Kane** (1941), the fact remains that Welles largely conceived and directed it, and absolutely certainly acted in it, and all this at the tender age of twenty-five, when most would-be geniuses are still busy chasing girls. Welles chased girls too, of course, and caught a good few of them, including **Rita Hayworth**, whom he married, then divorced, after showing her to the public in all her complexity in *The Lady From Shanghai* (1948). Six years before, his heart had been torn out, along with a good deal of his film, when RKO let editor **Robert Wise** loose on what might have proved to be Welles's greatest masterpiece, *The Magnificent Ambersons* (1942). His later films may have fallen off in budget terms as a result of the *Ambersons* failure, but they never fell off in imagination and creative design, and *Touch Of Evil* (1958) was masterly in all those departments, including Welles's acting. His Hank Quinlan, a grotesque yet strangely sympathetic human whale, out of place and out of mind in an imaginary borderland of the soul, lingers on in the memory as hardly any conventional film hero ever does. All through his life, Welles was obsessed with Shakespeare and with a merry, older England, where inhibitions do not stifle enterprise and where creativity isn't forced to feed off the fluff from its own navel, and his final mighty bow to that tradition came with *Chimes At Midnight* (1966), in which noble Falstaff is brought low by the iron hand of a soulless institution. Such was Welles's tragedy too, for he was *our* Falstaff figure, and his presence lingers in the ether, and will continue to linger, long after his tormentors, and their counterfeit memorials, have crumbled into dust.

Other Key Films: *Journey Into Fear* (1943) [co-dir]; *The Stranger* (1946); *Macbeth* (1948); *Othello* (1952); *Mr Arkadin/Confidential Report* (1955); *The Trial* (1962); *The Immortal Story* (1968); *F For Fake* (1975)

Key Lines:

1. 'In Italy for thirty years under the Borgias they had warfare, terror, murder, bloodshed – and they produced Michelangelo, Leonardo da Vinci

Although William Randolph Hearst successfully blocked the Radio City Music Hall première of Citizen Kane in 1941, it was successfully screened elsewhere.

RKO/The Kobal Collection

and the Renaissance. In Switzerland they had brotherly love, five hundred years of democracy and peace and what did they produce? The cuckoo clock.' [*The Third Man*]

2. 'I hate television. I hate it as much as peanuts. But I can't stop eating peanuts.' [Welles on nuts]

3. 'The biggest electric train set any boy ever had…' [Welles on the **RKO** studios]

4. 'He was some kind of a man. What does it matter what you say about people?' [**Marlene Dietrich** gives Hank Quinlan (and Welles?) his epitaph, in *Touch Of Evil*]

5. 'With Welles, everything began with the writing. And he was very good at it. He was a terrific guy…his wealth of information and background about story lines was inexhaustible. He was inventive. Fearless.' [Writer/Director **Richard Brooks** on Welles, with whom he worked on the Mercury Theatre radio series]

Wellman, William

One of the tough boys of the early US film industry, Wellman was a bona fide First World War aviation hero who simply could not shake off the habit of abrupt wartime command, even behind the camera. His tendency of treating his actors like recalcitrant fighter-bombers from the Lafayette Squadron got him into a fist-fight with **Spencer Tracy** and into a face-off with big **John Wayne**. Despite, or perhaps because of these eccentricities, he managed to make a number of very fine motion pictures, including *Wings* (1929), *The Public Enemy* (1931), *Call Of The Wild* (1935), *Nothing Sacred* (1937) and the magnificent *A Star Is Born* (1937), a film which showed a quite uncharacteristic understanding of women on Wellman's part.

Other Key Films: *Frisco Jenny* (1933); *Small Town Girl* (1936); *Beau Geste* (1939); *The Light That Failed* (1939); *Roxie Hart* (1942); *The Ox-Bow Incident* (1943); *Lady Of Burlesque* (1943); *Yellow Sky* (1948); *Battleground* (1949); *Across The Wide Missouri* (1951); *The High And The Mighty* (1954)

Wenders, Wim

Wenders is the classic example of a post-war German (he was born in 1945) who grew up in a country imbued, for the first time ever, with a totally alien yet heady sense of cultural freedom entirely emanating from the US. American films, books and music entered his native culture as if by osmosis, and his gentle and often sensitive films reflect this, in particular *The American Friend* (1977), *Hammett* (1982) and *Paris, Texas* (1984), for which he won the Palme D'Or at the Cannes Film Festival. His work turned increasingly fey during the late 1980s and early 90s, with *Wings Of Desire* (1987) and *Until The End Of The World* (1992), almost as if Wenders the filmmaker was seeing life from the very height of the angels he was depicting. But he came triumphantly down to earth again with his inspired documentary, *The Buena Vista Social Club* (1999), in which he resuscitated the careers of a group of sensational Cuban '*son*' musicians who had last enjoyed real success way back in the good old pre-Castro days.

Other Key Films: *The Goalkeeper's Fear Of The Penalty* (1971); *Alice In The Cities* (1974); *Wrong Move* (1975); *Kings Of The Road* (1976); *Lightning Over Water* (1980); *Tokyo-Ga* (1985); *Faraway, So Close* (1993); *Beyond The Clouds* [co-dir. with **Michelangelo Antonioni**]; *The End Of Violence* (1997); *The Million Dollar Hotel* (1999); *In America* (2001); *The Soul Of A Man* (2003); *Land Of Plenty* (2004); *Don't Come Knocking* (2005)

West, Mae

The mother of all vamps (with apologies to **Theda Bara**), West began by shocking Broadway with her play, *Sex*, then moved on to shock Hollywood in turn, almost single-handedly bringing down the wrath of the censorious Hays Office onto a mewling Tinseltown, on the strength of her fruity double entendres. Her screen career began at the age of forty, when her figure already resembled (even when corseted) the life-belt that the US Navy triumphantly named after it. But none of this mattered because West had that rare thing, innate sex-appeal, and she certainly knew how to use it, rattling the knees of screen swains such as **Cary Grant** with her straight from the shoulder invitations to 'come up sometime, and see me' in Lowell Sherman's *She Done Him Wrong* (1933). By 1935 she was the best-paid woman in Hollywood, but the high point of her camp, if not of her sex, appeal came five years later, when she starred opposite **W C Fields** in Edward Cline's *My Little Chickadee* (1940).

Other Key Films: *Night After Night* (1932); *I'm No Angel* (1933); *Belle Of The Nineties* (1934); *Goin' To Town* (1935); *Klondike Annie* (1936); *Go West Young Man* (1936); *Every Day's A Holiday* (1938); *The Heat's On* (1943); *Myra Breckenridge* (1970); *Sextette* (1978)

Key Lines:

1. 'I always say, keep a diary and some day it'll keep you.'
2. 'Beulah, peel me a grape.'
3. 'It's not the men in my life that counts, it's the life in my men.'
4. 'Is that a gun in your pocket, or are you just glad to see me?'
5. 'I used to be Snow White... but I drifted.'
6. 'You can say what you like about long dresses, but they cover a multitude of shins.'

Western, The

The Western is the song of the United States, a symbolic journey into just about every psychological and spiritual state imaginable, becoming, in the process, whatever the writer or the director chooses to make of it. It is for this reason that the Western will never die, despite numerous sombre warnings of its impending doom from the customary cluster of harbingers that hang around any genre open to disapproval. The Western can be about love, violence, brotherhood, sisterhood, poetry, or mental exploration, but it can just as easily be about heroes and heroines, bad guys and good guys, whores and goodtime girls, sanctity and perfidy. At its best, as in **John Ford's** *My Darling Clementine* (1946) or **Anthony Mann's** *Winchester '73* (1950), the Western takes on something of the characteristics of a country of the soul, where the landscape is of as much importance as the motives of the small, lonely characters within its often grotesque embrace. Sometimes, as in Ford's *The Searchers* (1956), the landscape *becomes* the soul, and a simple shot of a man riding away, framed through a doorway, with a woman standing to one side, back-on, watching, can transcend its own context, becoming a universal image of alienation and possible reconciliation in starkly silent, utterly visual terms – the essence, in other words, of the cinema. See **Spaghetti Westerns**

Key Lines:

1. 'Don't forget the Western is not only the history of this country, it is what the Saga of the Nibelungen is for the European.' [**Fritz Lang** on the Western]
2. Henry Fonda: 'Mac, you ever been in love?' Mac: 'No. I've been a bartender all my life.' [*My Darling Clementine*]
3. 'Badges? We ain't got no badges. We don't need no badges. I don't have to show you any stinking badges!' [Alfonso Bedoya to **Humphrey Bogart** in *The Treasure Of The Sierra Madre*]
4. 'Lady, the things I don't know you could herd like cows.' [Harry Carey, John Ford's 'bright star of the early Western sky', in Garson Kanin's *They Knew What They Wanted* (1940) – the film may not be a Western in the strictest sense, but Carey's sentiments exemplify the spirit of the Western, of which he was an icon]
5. 'I think all the stories about the West are probably full of shit. Cowboys were probably uneducated and very dull.' [Screenwriter **Julius J Epstein**, who co-scripted **Michael Curtiz's** *Casablanca* (1942) and **Frank Capra's** *Arsenic And Old Lace* (1944), on his detestation of Westerns – he didn't like **science fiction** either]
6. 'The Western hero is the last hero...he's a man who is accountable only to himself and God.' [Screenwriter **Philip Yordan**, who co-scripted **Nicholas Ray's** *Johnny Guitar* (1954) and **Anthony Mann's** *The Man From Laramie* (1955), on Westerns]

7. 'You name it. That's where I'm from. I'm the frommest man you ever did see.' Dale Robertson's John Banner, in Lewis R. Foster's *Dakota Incident* (1956)

Best Western Films

Budd Boetticher's *Seven Men From Now* (1956), *The Tall T* (1957), *Decision At Sundown* (1957), *Buchanan Rides Alone* (1958), *Comanche Station* (1960) and *Ride Lonesome* (1959); **Clint Eastwood's** *The Outlaw – Josey Wales* (1976) and *Unforgiven* (1992); **John Farrow's** *Hondo* (1953); **John Ford's** *Stagecoach* (1939), *My Darling Clementine* (1946); *Fort Apache* (1948), *She wore A Yellow Ribbon* (1949), *Rio Grande* (1950), *Wagon Master* (1950) and *The Man Who Shot Liberty Valance* (1963); **Henry Hathaway's** *True Grit* (1969); **Howard Hawks's** *Red River* (1948) and *Rio Bravo* (1959); **Fritz Lang's** *Rancho Notorious* (1952); **Sergio Leone's** *The Good, The Bad And The Ugly* (1966) and *Once Upon A Time In The West* (1969); **Anthony Mann's** *Winchester '73* (1950), *The Naked Spur* (1953), *The Man From Laramie* (1955) and *Man Of The West* (1958); George Marshall's *Destry Rides Again* (1939); David Miller's *Lonely Are The Brave* (1962); **Sam Peckinpah's** *Ride The High Country* (1961); **Arthur Penn's** *Little Big Man* (1969); **Nicholas Ray's** *Johnny Guitar* (1954) and *Run For Cover* (1955); **George Stevens's** *Shane* (1953); **John Sturges's** *The Magnificent Seven* (1960); **Raoul Walsh's** *Pursued* (1947); **Robert Wise's** *Blood On The Moon* (1948); **Fred Zinnemann's** *High Noon* (1952)

Whale, James

One of the great progenitors of the horror genre, Whale has recently been celebrated in a Hollywood biopic, Bill Condon's *Gods And Monsters* (1998), being played on screen by no less a figure than Ian McKellen. With *Frankenstein* (1931) [whose images would later run through and imbue **Victor Erice's** haunting *Spirit Of The Beehive* (1973)], *The Old Dark House* (1932), *The Invisible Man* (1933) and his camp masterpiece, *The Bride Of Frankenstein* (1935), Whale covered just about every conceivable variation, from outright comedy to naked fear, that later generations of **horror** filmmakers would so eagerly claim as their own. An ex-First World War prisoner-of-war, Whale knew both the darkness of the trenches, the humiliation of apparent defeat, and the joy of eventual victory, all of which are reflected in his films. This strange man eventually gave up films to paint full time, before dying, in rather odd circumstances, in his own swimming pool.

Other Key Films: *Journeys End* (1930); *By Candlelight* (1933); *Show Boat* (1936); *Sinners In Paradise* (1937); *The Man In The Iron Mask* (1939); *Green Hell* (1940); *They Dare Not Love* (1941)

Widmark, Richard

It's hard to pin Widmark down, because he was never really a leading man in the conventional sense of the term, although he was very certainly a star. Perhaps it was the mean streak that did it, constantly bubbling just below the surface and ready to erupt in grotesque violence at the slightest opportunity, as in **Henry Hathaway's** *Kiss Of Death* (1947), in which Widmark, shrieking with maniacal glee, sends a wheelchair-bound old lady to her death down a vertical flight of steps. But then the man could play gentle characters too, with that faraway look in his eyes and that sudden, boyish grin. Perhaps he was simply a one-off – a blond man in a predominantly dark world, who turned the tables on blondness, unlike his contemporary **Alan Ladd**, to become one of the very best screen villains going.

Whatever the case, it is impossible to forget his panting, petrified hood in **Jules Dassin's** *Night And The City* (1950), as he runs for his life, impervious even to the achingly beautiful, well-intentioned **Gene Tierney**, in his headlong descent into hell.

Other Key Films: *Road House* (1948); *Panic In The Streets* (1950); *No Way Out* (1950); *Pickup On South Street* (1953); *Broken Lance* (1954); *The Trap* (1958); *Warlock* (1959); *The Alamo* (1960); *Two Rode Together* (1961); *Cheyenne Autumn* (1964); *Madigan* (1968); *Death Of A Gunfighter* (1969); *To The Devil A Daughter* (1976); *Against All Odds* (1983)

Wilde, Cornel

Best seen as a top-of-the-tree B-movie actor, Wilde had a lot going for him in terms of looks and physique, and, remarkably for one of his beefcake calling, he also proved that he could, on occasion, act too. Similar in many ways to his near-contemporary **Dana Andrews**, his never-quite-conventional looks and obvious intelligence no doubt precluded him from rising any higher in the Hollywood firmament than he did. His best mainstream films were the tight little **Jean Negulesco** *film noir* *Road House* (1948), in which he was teamed with **Richard Widmark** and **Ida Lupino** in a scintillatingly murderous, hard-talking emotional triangle, and also **Joseph H Lewis's** sensational *The Big Combo* (1954) in which Wilde's eardrums were subjected to a particularly painful form of torture by a cold-blooded Richard Conte. Of the number of independent movies Wilde eventually directed under the aegis of his very own production company, it is *The Naked Prey* (1966), in which he finds himself stripped and allowed to run for his life from the bush tribe his clients have so unwisely and so lethally angered, that most stands out.

Other Key Films: *High Sierra* (1941); *A Song To Remember* (1946); *Leave Her To Heaven* (1946); *Forever Amber* (1947); *The Scarlet Coat* (1955); *Hot Blood* (1956); *Beach Red* [also dir.] (1968)

Richard Widmark in Night and the City, directed by Jules Dassin (1950).

20th Century Fox/The Kobal Collection

Wilder, Billy

If he's not the best comic director and scriptwriter the cinema ever produced, then Wilder comes pretty darned close. With his colleague, **Charles Brackett**, he co-wrote the words for **Ernst Lubitsch's** *Ninotchka* (1939) and for **Howard Hawks's** *Ball Of Fire* (1942), and his first directing success soon followed with the quirky and wonderful *Five Graves To Cairo* (1943). With *Double Indemnity* (1944), one of the greatest of all *film noirs*, under his belt, he then made the ultimate film about alcoholism, *The Lost Weekend* (1945), quickly followed by the best ever film about film, *Sunset Boulevard* (1950), and the best ever film about the newspaper business, *Ace In The Hole* (1951). And as if that wasn't enough, he then went on to make the best ever prisoner-of-war film, *Stalag 17* (1953), and the best ever 'itinerant musicians dressing up as women and being pursued by demented Mafiosi while taking time out to seduce Marilyn Monroe and Joe E Brown film'. Yes. You've guessed it. He made *Some Like It Hot* (1959) too. A master. No, *the* master. See **Heartstopping Moments**

Other Key Films: *The Major And The Minor* (1942); *The Emperor Waltz* (1948); *Sabrina* (1954); *The Seven Year Itch* (1955); *Love In The Afternoon* (1958); *Witness For The Prosecution* (1958); *The Apartment* (1960); *One Two Three* (1961); *The Fortune Cookie* (1966); *The Private Life Of Sherlock Holmes* [try and catch it — terminally underrated] (1970)

Key Lines:

1: Ninotchka: 'Why should you carry other people's bags?' Porter: 'Well, that's my business, Madame.' Ninotchka: 'That's no business. That's social injustice.' Porter: 'That depends on the tip.' [*Ninotchka*]

2: 'You have to be flexible. When CinemaScope came in, I thought about making the love story of two dachshunds.' [Wilder on enlightened pragmatism]

Wilder, Gene

A dotty and multi-talented comedian, Wilder will be forever cherished by film aficionados for his demented turn as Leo Bloom in **Mel Brooks's** *The Producers* (1968), which quite coincidentally happens to be one of the funniest films ever made. Wilder's 'Fat! Fat! Fat!' scene with Zero Mostel took neurosis to its illogical limits, and in doing so, became a classic, and nothing Wilder ever did later can really come close, although he was predictably splendid in Brooks's *Blazing Saddles* (1974) and in Arthur Hiller's immaculately timed *Silver Streak* (1976). Apropos of nothing whatsoever (and simply as a matter of passing interest) Wilder may be said to have the most unconventional hair (one assumes, still) of any major Hollywood star, always excepting that of Jack Nance in **David Lynch's** *Eraserhead* (1976).

Other Key Films: *Bonnie And Clyde* (1967); *Willy Wonka And The Chocolate Factory* (1971); *Young Frankenstein* (1974); *The Adventure Of Sherlock Holmes's Smarter Brother* (1975); *Stir Crazy* (1980); *The Woman In Red* (1984); *See No Evil, Hear No Evil* (1989); *Funny About Love* (1990); *Another You* (1991)

Williams, John

Composer of such majestic and stirring scores as **Steven Spielberg's** *Jaws* (1975), *Close Encounters Of The Third Kind* (1977), *Raiders Of The Lost Ark* (1981), *E. T. The Extra-Terrestrial* (1982), and *War Of The Worlds* (2005), not to mention **George Lucas's** entire *Star Wars* series (1977-2005), Williams seems to have been the composer of choice for just about any famous blockbuster one may care to mention during the 1970s and 1980s, and it is to his credit that his music does not seem to have turned either stale or predictable in the process. Some of his best work, however, has been on much smaller films, most notably for **Robert Altman's** *The Long Goodbye* (1973).

Other Key Films: Don Siegel's *The Killers* (1964); **Alfred Hitchcock's** *Family Plot* (1976); Richard Donner's *Superman* (1978); Mark Rydell's *The River* (1984); **George Miller's** *The Witches Of Eastwick* (1987); Steven Spielberg's *Jurassic Park* (1993); **Oliver Stone's** *Nixon* (1995); **Alan Parker's** *Angela's Ashes* (1999); Roland Emmerich's *The Patriot* (2000); Steven Spielberg's *Artificial Intelligence: A.I.* (2001); Rob Marshall's *Memoirs Of A Geisha* (2005); Steven Spielberg's *Munich* (2005); Bryan Singer's *Superman Returns* (2006)

Williams, Robin

Occasionally irritating but undoubtedly talented, Williams took a long time to get off the mark in movies, and he was all of thirty-five when Barry Levinson's *Good Morning Vietnam* (1988) notified the general public that he was here to stay. **Peter Weir's** *Dead Poets Society* (1989) made him something of a **cult** in continental Europe, and his recent form, both in a series of children's movies which includes Joe Johnston's *Jumanji* (1995), and also in more adult fare, such as **Gus Van Sant's** excellent *Good Will Hunting* (1997), indicates that the talent of this fine comedian should maintain him both in fine style and in close proximity to the top of the Hollywood heap.

Other Key Films: *Popeye* (1980); *The World According To Garp* (1982); *The Adventures Of Baron Munchausen* (1989); *The Fisher King* (1991); *Hook* (1991); *Mrs Doubtfire* (1993) *Father's Day* (1995); *Patch Adams* (1998); *Jakob The Liar* (1999); *Bicentennial Man* (1999); *One Hour Photo* (2001); *Insomnia* (2002); *The Final Cut* (2004); *The Big White* (2005); *The Night Listener* (2006)

Williams, Tennessee

A brilliant playwright, and the source for many a fervid, sometimes fetid, but always literate Hollywood film, Williams was the star of his own life, and virtually all the films made from his plays and scripts stem from this fact, as is shown in their treatment of adults as the unconscious progeny of their own sexual and emotional natures. For many viewers during the 1950s and 60s, Williams and his work represented the acme of what could or could not be acknowledged in terms of adult emotional truths – the highpoints of his career were consequently legion, and include **Elia Kazan's** *A Streetcar Named Desire* (1951), **Richard Brooks's** *Cat On A Hot Tin Roof* (1958), **Joseph L Mankiewicz's** *Suddenly Last Summer* (1959), and, best of all, **John Huston's** *The Night Of The Iguana* (1964).

Other Key Films: Irving Rapper's *The Glass Menagerie* (1950); Elia Kazan's *Baby Doll* (1956); José Quintero's *The Roman Spring Of Mrs Stone* (1961); Richard Brooks's *Sweet Bird Of Youth* (1962)

Willis, Bruce

One of the most intelligent and humorously self-deprecating of the latter-day big box-office macho men, Willis made his name in the television series *Moonlighting*, which gave him enough clout to land the star part in the *Die Hard* series of movie thrillers (1988-2007). Three successive turkeys, Norman Jewison's *In Country* (1989), **Brian De Palma's** *The Bonfire Of The Vanities* (1990) and Michael Lehmann's *Hudson Hawk* (1991), forced him to review his strategy, and he now seems to have plumped for the **Clint Eastwood** road of a big actioner, followed by a more thoughtful character performance, as in **Alan Rudolph's** *Mortal Thoughts* (1991), **Robert Altman's** *The Player* (1992) and **Quentin Tarantino's** *Pulp Fiction* (1994), to leaven the commercial sourdough. Willis has had a recent surprise hit with M Night Shyamalan's brilliant ghost story, *The Sixth Sense* (1999), and of all the blockbuster stars, he may still be the one to watch.

Other Key Films: *Blind Date* (1987); *Billy Bathgate* (1991); *The Last Boy Scout* (1991); *Death Becomes Her* (1992); *The Story Of Us* (2000); *The Kid* (2000); *Unbreakable* (2000); *The Whole Nine Yards* (2000); *Bandits* (2001); *Hart's War* (2002); *The Whole Ten Yards* (2004); *Hostage* (2005); *Sin City* (2005); *Lucky Number Slevin* (2006); *16 Blocks* (2006)
Key Line: 'I said to Bruce Willis, "Anyway, whoever you are, you're standing in my space – so f*** off!" ' [**Richard Harris**, on his first encounter with the star]

Willis, Gordon

Woody Allen's favourite cinematographer, Willis was the master behind the look of some of Allen's best loved films including *Annie Hall* (1977), *Manhattan* (1979), *Stardust Memories* (1980), *Zelig* (1983) and *The Purple Rose Of Cairo* (1985). He can also, when his director requires it, indulge in the sort of screen trickery seen in **Alan J Pakula's** *The Parallax View* (1974) and *All The President's Men* (1976), for which one easily forgives him, bearing in mind the conventional, yet magnificent work he did on **Francis Ford Coppola's** *The Godfather Parts I, II and III* (74–90).

Other Key Films: Alan J Pakula's *Klute* (1971) and ; **Herbert Ross's** *Pennies From Heaven* (1981); Alan J Pakula's *The Devil's Own* (1997)

Winger, Debra

A sadly underused actress who was, perhaps, simply not winsome enough for mass popular taste, Winger first made her mark in **Taylor Hackford's** *An Officer And A Gentleman* (1982) as the spunky (in more senses than one) working-class heroine whom **Richard Gere** gets to carry off in his willowy arms at the end of the movie (to well-earned cheers from the audience). Her best performance (*c'est la vie*) came in her biggest flop, **Bernardo Bertolucci's** disastrously underrated *The Sheltering Sky* (1990), although her understated playing of Joy Gresham in **Richard Attenborough's** *Shadowlands* (1993) was equally outstanding. She deserves better both from her public and the studios.

Other Key Films: *Urban Cowboy* (1980); *Terms Of Endearment* (1983); *Legal Eagles* (1986); *Black Widow* (1987); *Betrayed* (1988); *Forget Paris* (1995); *Big Bad Love* (2001); *Radio* (2003); *Eulogy* (2004)

Winslet, Kate

Flavour-of-the-year following her turn as Rose DeWitt Bukater in **James Cameron's** *Titanic* (1997), Winslet is a far better actress than her erstwhile co-star, **Leonardo DiCaprio**, is an actor, and her career, if she plays it right, should be considerably longer (if commensurately less lucrative). She was outstanding in her first big feature, **Peter Jackson's** *Heavenly Creatures* (1994), and she followed this up very effectively indeed, with a notable performance in **Ang Lee's** brilliant Jane Austen outing, *Sense And Sensibility* (1995), a film which almost single-handedly restored one's faith in the cinema's ability to produce emotionally satisfying, high-quality, mainstream entertainment. Michael Winterbottom's downbeat *Jude* (1996) was another career highlight, and one only hopes that this still maturing actress (she was born in 1975) can keep her nerve and talent intact over the long term.

Other Key Films: *Hamlet* (1996); *Hideous Kinky* (1998); *Holy Smoke* (1999); *Quills* (2000); *Thérèse Raquin* (2001); *Enigma* (2001); *Iris* (2001); *The Life Of David Gale* (2003); *Eternal Sunshine Of The Spotless Mind* (2004); *Finding Neverland* (2004); *Romance & Cigarettes* (2005); *All The King's Men* (2006)

Wise, Robert

Despite being the man whom RKO chose to massacre **Orson Welles's** *The Magnificent Ambersons* (1942) [he'd already been Welles's editor on **Citizen Kane** (1941)], Wise partially redeemed himself with a string of excellent *film noirs*, not to mention a further duet of screen musicals that included, yes, *The Sound Of Music* (1965) and *Star!* (1968). Wise's best movie is undoubtedly *The Set-Up* (1949), with **Robert Ryan** on top form as an ageing boxer playing out his final fight in tense real time, though Wise's earlier *Born To Kill* (1947) was another corker for the *film noir* connoisseur. The undervalued *Tribute To A Bad Man* (1956), a movie in which **James Cagney** managed the difficult task of moving from an unsympathetic to a sympathetic character without making the audience throw up in horror, fulfilled a similar function for **Western** aficionados. Come to think of it, *Blood On The Moon* (1948), with **Robert Mitchum** as its tormented post-Freudian protagonist, made a pretty good stab at being a double genre Western *film-noir*, and his two **science fiction** movies, *The Day The Earth Stood Still* (1951) and *The Andromeda Strain* (1971), were more than passable, stacking the odds even more in favour of Wise's post-Wellesian redemption.

Other Key Films: *The Body Snatcher* (1945); *Mystery In Mexico* (1948); *Executive Suite* (1954); *Run Silent Run Deep* (1958); *Odds Against Tomorrow* (1959); *West Side Story* (1961) [co-dir.]; *The Sand Pebbles* (1966); *Two People* (1973); *Audrey Rose* (1977); *Star Trek: The Motion Picture* (1974); *Rooftops* (1989)

Woo, John

Cantonese director of innovative, balletic action films, in which the editing, camera angles and cutting all play their part, Woo has continued his successful run with *Mission: Impossible 2* (2000), in which **Tom Cruise** reprised the same role of actor and producer that brought him a $75-million payout for *Mission: Impossible* (1995). Woo's cut of the *M:I2* take must have been pretty considerable too, based on his recent string of hits that includes *The Killer* (1989), *Hard Target* (1993), *Broken Arrow* (1996) and *Face/Off* (1997). An awesome technician, Woo woos his actors, allowing them to perform the sort of macho stunts that appeal to those who like their action both well done and bloody at the same time.

Other Key Films: *The Sunset Warrior* (1983); *Run Tiger Run* (1985); *A Better Tomorrow* (1986); *Bullet In The Head* (1990); *Once A Thief* (1991); *Hard-Boiled* (1992); *Wind Talkers* (2002); *Hostage* (2002); *Paycheck* (2003)

Key Line: 'Woo's action is like a dance, and he has that mythic quality in his pictures...' [Tom Cruise on Woo]

Wood, Ed

Considered by some to be the world's worst film director, Wood was the happy, albeit posthumous, beneficiary of a biopic to that effect in **Tim Burton's** *Ed Wood* (1994), which starred **Johnny Depp** as the eponymous hero. But Wood actually wasn't that bad if one takes into account his mania for cross-dressing (particularly in fluffy tops) and his rock-bottom budgets. Among his numerous masterpieces of retrospective camp, special acclaim must go to *Glen Or Glenda?* (1952) for its lessons in the use of voiceover, and to *Plan 9 From Outer Space* (1959) for just about everything, and particularly the ghoul.

Other Key Films: *Bride Of The Monster* (1953); *Jail Bait* (1954); *Night Of The Ghouls* (1960); *Necromancy* (1972)

Wood, Sam

Wood is the sort of director whose filmography looks considerably more impressive than the extent of his actual talent would suggest. He was put in charge of two of the greatest **Marx Brothers** films, *A Night At The Opera* (1935) and *A Day At The Races* (1937), but, according to Groucho, the films were successes despite, and not because of, Wood. He directed the sublime **Robert Donat** in *Goodbye Mr Chips* (1939), but the film was always Donat's, never Wood's, and the same can be said of *For Whom The Bell Tolls* (1943), which relies on the star chemistry of **Gary Cooper** and **Ingrid Bergman** to attract attention away from its stolid mechanics. All carping aside, Wood's best films came near the end of his career, with *The Devil And Miss Jones*

(1941) and *Ivy* (1947).

Other Key Films: *Madame X* (1937); *Raffles* (1939); *Kitty Foyle* (1940); *King's Row* (1942); *Guest Wife* (1945); *Command Decision* (1949); *Ambush* (1950)

Worst Films

There have been innumerable bad movies made over the past century of cinema and innumerable bad movie awards to celebrate them, and the subject must always, by its very nature, be an entirely subjective one. However some films are so bad that they simply transcend fashion, naturally falling into a category of their very own. Here are just a few from the past fifteen or so years, in date order, that were foisted upon us by directors who really should have known better:

1. **The Coen Brother's** *Barton Fink* (1991), in which a trio of otherwise excellent actors, John Turturro, John Goodman and **Judy Davis**, battle against the incoherence of a script which purports to examine the condition of writer's block and only succeeds in making one wish that it occurred more frequently. 'We all want it to have that Barton Fink feeling. I mean, I guess we all have that Barton Fink feeling, but since you're Barton Fink, I'm assuming you have it in spades.' [Studio boss Lipnick to Barton Fink – go to **Flynn**, **Errol** and check out the **key line** to find where this quote originated]

2. **David Lynch's** *Twin Peaks: Fire Walk With Me* (1992), in which pretension overcomes discretion and inanition replaces elucidation until…well, it just doesn't make any sense at all, even to those who consider the same director's *Blue Velvet* (1986) to be one of the very best and most original films of the past fifty years.

3. Manoel de Oliviera's appalling turkey *The Convent* (1995), in which **Catherine Deneuve** and **John Malkovich** walk from room to room looking uncomfortable. As well they might. Was Shakespeare really Spanish? And do we care? And is Luis Miguel Cintra really Mephistopheles? These abuses must be put an end to…

4. Claude Lelouch's *Les Misérables* (1995), in which an apparently disintegrating **Jean-Paul Belmondo** cavorts geriatrically around France, machine-gunning all and sundry in a demented attempt to mimic Victor Hugo's invariably unarmed Jean Valjean. And fails.

5. Michael Cacoyannis's *The Cherry Orchard* (1998), in which the acting is more wooden than the eponymous orchard, and the staccato, ill-edited direction obliterates all trace of Chekov's intended comic portrayal of the Russian ruling class in witless decline. The decelerating dénouement is relieved only by a convincingly purple-nosed Michael Gough as decaying butler Feers who, abandoned in the locked-up country house after its forced sale, is entrusted with the film's last line: 'My long life is coming to an end, and there has been no point to it.' A suitable valediction indeed.

6. Roger Christian's *Battlefield Earth* (2000), in which an ever-more porky **John Travolta** dresses up in dreadlocks and a metal tiara, with what appear to be two feeding tubes stuck up his nose, in a vain effort to frighten the rest of the world into embracing Scientology.

7. **Ron Howard's** *The Da Vinci Code* (2006), in which our intrepid director follows Dan Brown's book so slavishly that he succeeds in recreating all the book's vices without any of its virtues. Central to the disaster is a resolutely un-frightening performance by Paul Bettany as Silas, the

sadomasochistic albino monastic assassin (say that with your mouth full). Silas is meant to instil, quite literally, the fear of God in his victims, and he simply doesn't pull it off (and no, I don't mean the now near-ubiquitous cilice). So no baddy, no movie – Hollywood has always known that. And what about Audrey Tautou? Shouldn't she have been given just the faintest smattering of potential sanctity, being Jesus' g-g-g-g-g-g-g-g-g-g-g-granddaughter and all? Oh, what the hell...

See also **Best Titles, Erotic Moments, Heartstopping Moments**

Wyler, William

An obsessive perfectionist while on set, Wyler spanned the wholesome, culturally aspiring middle ground of the movie spectrum, and produced an extraordinary number of high-quality hits. His films were always literate if rarely deep, and *Dodsworth* (1936), which benefited from a superb **Walter Huston** performance in the title part, was his high-watermark artistically. The rest of his films, however, are both visually satisfying and downright enjoyable, and include *Dead End* (1937), *Jezebel* (1938), *Wuthering Heights* (1939), *Mrs Miniver* (1942) and *The Heiress* (1949). Highest profile of all was his 1959 epic version of *Ben-Hur*, though it is arguable that the lesser-known *Detective Story* (1951), which Wyler imbued with a semi-documentary feel, is the more challenging film. In later years Wyler began to take a few risks, most notably with *The Collector* (1965), a film based on the John Fowles novel of the same name, and which was considerably underrated at the time of its release.

Other Key Films: *These Three* (1936); *The Letter* (1940); *The Westerner* (1940); *The Little Foxes* (1941); *The Best Years Of Our Lives* (1946); *Carrie* (1952); *Roman Holiday* (1953); *The Desperate Hours* (1955); *The Children's Hour* (1962); *Funny Girl* (1968)

Yordan, Philip

Yordan is one of the near greats – a screenwriter who combines commercial nous with a critical and intellectual intensity that is only deepened by his uncanny way with vernacular and the red pencil – the so-called 'Yordan touch'. The 'near', however, came from his habit of hiring 'surrogates' (often consisting of blacklisted artists) to write some of his scripts, a practice which inevitably throws some doubt on one or two of his contributions to cinematic history, but none at all on his talent for incisive editing. Despite this proviso, Yordan's credits or co-credits read like a roll-call of intense and satisfying Hollywood movie-making, and include Max Nosseck's *Dillinger* (1945), **William Wyler's** *Detective Story* (1951), Byron Haskin's *Naked Jungle* (1954), **Nicholas Ray's** *Johnny Guitar* (1954), **Joseph H Lewis's** *The Big Combo* (1955) and Mark Robson's *The Harder They Fall* (1956). Whether Yordan wrote the finished scripts or not, his mark is all over these movies, and his uncanny way with dialogue puts him in the august company of such masters as **Ben Hecht** and Charles MacArthur.

Other Key Films: Frank Tuttle's *Suspense* (1946); **Anthony Mann's** *The Man From Laramie* (1955) & *El Cid* (1961); Nicholas Ray's *King Of Kings* (1961); Irving Lerner's *The Royal Hunt Of The Sun* (1969)

Young, Freddie

A doyen of British cinematography, Young photographed nearly all the large-scale **David Lean** movies, including *Lawrence Of Arabia* (1962), *Dr Zhivago* (1965) and *Ryan's Daughter* (1970). However, his best work (a contentious issue, this) came in black and white, and included **Sam Wood's** magnificent *Goodbye Mr Chips* (1939),

Michael Powell's *49th Parallel* (1941) and Young's masterpiece, **Richard Brooks's** *Lord Jim* (1965). The plot and treatment of *Lord Jim* may have been unfaithful to Joseph Conrad's original, but the film's lighting and photographic atmosphere, thanks to Young's brilliancy, were surely all that the creator of *Heart Of Darkness* could have desired.

Other Key Films: Carol Reed's *The Young Mr Pitt* (1942); **Anthony Asquith's** *The Winslow Boy* (1948); **John Ford's** *Mogambo* (1953); Franklin J Schaffner's *Nicholas And Alexandra* (1971)

Zaentz, Saul
Eminent producer who has almost single-handedly managed to corner the market in literary adaptations, Zaentz first made his mark co-producing **Milos Forman's** *One Flew Over The Cuckoo's Nest* (1975) alongside **Michael Douglas**. His follow-ups, apart from the occasional blip like **Peter Weir's** unjustly maligned *The Mosquito Coast* (1986), have been equally high-minded, whilst still retaining their capacity to pull in the dollars. In some ways, therefore, he's the model of the perfect producer, allowing directors like **Anthony Minghella** more or less free rein for their talents in movies such as *The English Patient* (1996).

Other Key Films: Ralph Bakshi's *The Lord Of The Rings* (1978); **Milos Forman's** *Amadeus* (1984); Philip Kaufman's *The Unbearable Lightness Of Being* (1988); Hector Babenco's *At Play In The Fields Of The Lord* (1991); Milos Forman's *Goya's Ghosts* (2006)

Zanuck, Darryl F
A tough-minded and old-fashioned movie mogul who fulfilled his lifelong ambition by taking over 20th Century-Fox in 1962, following the financial losses incurred by **Joseph L Mankiewicz's** mega-budget *Cleopatra* (1963) (it should be remembered that Zanuck had founded the original 20th Century Pictures in 1933, and been production manager at Fox itself until 1956, before turning independent) – all this accomplished, however, he then found that the movie industry had moved inexorably on while his back had been turned. Zanuck's greatest days were undoubtedly in the 1930s and early 1940s, when his word at Fox counted for everything, and during which he saw to fruition **Mervyn LeRoy's** *Little Caesar* (1931), John Ford's *The Grapes Of Wrath* (1940) and **Rouben Mamoulian's** *Blood And Sand* (1941). His later career encompassed a number of other classics, largely through his association with Mankiewicz and **Elia Kazan**, including Mankiewicz's *All About Eve* (1950) and *People Will Talk* (1951), and Kazan's *Pinky* (1949) and *Viva Zapata!* (1952). This aside, Zanuck is also remembered for smoking the largest cigars in the business.

Other Key Films: Henry King's *Jesse James* (1939); **John Ford's** *How Green Was My Valley* (1941); John Cromwell's *Anna And The King Of Siam* (1946); Robert Rossen's *Island In The Sun* (1958); the multi-directed *The Longest Day* (1962)

Key Lines:
1:   'For God's sake don't say yes until I finish talking!' [Zanuck on one-upmanship]
2:   'At MGM every picture was talked either to death or to life…whenever a picture got made, it was a miracle. At Fox there was only a script and Darryl Zanuck. He okayed it or he threw it out.' [Screenwriter Walter Reisch on the Zanuck touch]

Zavattini, Cesare

One of the greatest of all screenwriters and the founding father of Italian post-war **neo-realism**, Zavattini wrote the scripts for such disparate masterpieces as **Vittorio De Sica's** seminal *The Bicycle Thief* (1948) and the same director's hauntingly beautiful *The Garden Of The Finzi-Continis* (1971). A noted theoretician and an influential and iconic presence in Italian cinema, Zavattini never contemplated a formal move to the US, as so many of his contemporaries had done, but seemed content to work from his intellectually rewarding and esteemed European base.

Other Key Films: Vittorio De Sica's *Miracle In Milan* (1951); **René Clément's** *The Walls Of Malapaga* (1956); **Federico Fellini, Luchino Visconti** & Vittorio De Sica's *Boccaccio '70* (1962)

Zeffirelli, Franco

Zeffirelli's films are permeated with the happy fallout from their inceptor's early background as a set and costume designer for a number of Italian opera companies, and it is to this background as well that Zeffirelli owes his success at adapting Shakespeare to the cinematic medium. *The Taming Of The Shrew* (1967) marked his first tentative stab at the Bard, followed by the lush *Romeo And Juliet* (1968), which had the virtue of casting adolescents of a suitable age in the lead parts almost for the first time. A number of excellent opera adaptations followed before the inspired casting of **Mel Gibson** as *Hamlet* (1990) in a very effective if truncated version of the play.

Other Key Films: *Brother Sun, Sister Moon* (1973); *Endless Love* (1981); *La Traviata* (1982); *Otello* (1986); *Sparrow* (1993); *Jane Eyre* (1996); *Tea With Mussolini* (1999); *Callas Forever* (2001); *Tre Fratelli* (2005)

Zhang, Yimou

A fine director and cinematographer, Zhang has been consistently harassed by the Chinese authorities for his perceived criticism of the state apparatus. His first feature, *Red Sorghum* (1987), showed intense visual and intellectual promise, something borne out by his succeeding features, *Ju-Dou* (1990), the brilliant *Raise The Red Lantern* (1991), and *To Live* (1994). The latter includes one of the most magnificent crane shots in the history of cinema, in which two men, alone on a plain, are suddenly engulfed by an entire army of thunderously running soldiers.

Other Key Films: *The Story Of Qiu Ju* (1992); *Shanghai Triad* (1995); *Keep Cool* (1997); *The Road Home* (1999); *Not Less One* (1999); *Happy Times* (2000); *Hero* (2002); *House Of Flying Daggers* (2004); *Riding Alone For Thousands Of Miles* (2005); *Curse Of The Golden Flower* (2006)

Zinnemann, Fred

A thoroughly professional middlebrow director, Zinnemann was a technical perfectionist whose films always satisfied, although it is certain that he both hoped and believed they would do much more. Both *The Search* (1948) and *The Men* (1950) were worthy social and commercial vehicles, which, seen with hindsight and within the constraints of their time, now seem rather brave, while *High Noon* (1952) achieved a truly remarkable resonance, although to read the movie as a veiled comment on Cold-War America is palpably and retrospectively absurd. *From Here To Eternity* (1953) genuinely opened the can of worms that was America's prurient on-screen attitude to sex, whilst *The Sundowners* (1960) was simply first-rate family entertainment. Zinnemann's most accomplished and Oscar-garlanded film was *A*

Man For All Seasons (1966), although, paradoxically, it is in *The Day Of The Jackal* (1973), a film he made towards the end of his career, that his sheer technical ability reaches its apogee, for the film is a virtual blueprint of how to construct a taut, almost nihilistic thriller from a naturally extended bestseller source without losing any of the original fictional nuances.

Other Key Films: *Eyes In The Night* (1942); *Act Of Violence* (1949); *Oklahoma!* (1955); *The Nun's Story* (1959); *Behold A Pale Horse* (1964); *Julia* (1977); *Five Days One Summer* (1983)

Zsigmond, Vilmos

A hard-working and extremely professional mainstream cinematographer, Zsigmond is a master of light filters, and his name appears on some of the finest and most visually satisfying movies of the past thirty years. His masterpiece, purely in terms of cinematic atmosphere, is **Robert Altman's** *McCabe And Mrs Miller* (1971), but his sure touch with the camera and with lighting worked to equal effect in **Michael Cimino's** *The Deer Hunter* (1978) and in **George Miller's** *The Witches Of Eastwick* (1987).

Other Key Films: **John Boorman's** *Deliverance* (1972); Robert Altman's *The Long Goodbye* (1973); Michael Cimino's **Heaven's Gate** (1980); **Brian De Palma's** *Blow Out* (1981); **Sean Penn's** *The Crossing Guard* (1995); Stephen Hopkins's *The Ghost And The Darkness* (1996); Jonas McCord's *The Body* (2001); Kevin Smith's *Jersey Girl* (2004); **Woody Allen's** *Melinda And Melinda* (2004); Brian De Palma's *The Black Dahlia* (2006)

Zukor, Adolf

Founder of the star system and arguably the man who, with his Famous Players studio, put the very concept of the motion picture onto the map as a commercial reality, Zukor was renowned for his extraordinary tenaciousness in the face of adversity. It is to this that we owe the continued existence of Paramount studios, which was Zukor's baby ever since its takeover in 1917 and its first formal inception, in 1927, as the holding company for the Famous Players Lasky corporation. Zukor died in 1976 at the age of 103, still chairman emeritus of the company he had founded, fought for, and apparently lost. As such he spanned the entire history of the cinema, from its birth, through its adolescence, and into its full maturity.

Acknowledgements

Many people have supported me during the writing of this book, either through conversation, creative input, or inspired empathy. For instance I've enjoyed a number of extended debates with film buffs the calibre of Debbie Condon, daughter of Richard Condon of *The Manchurian Candidate* fame, playwright Kenneth Jupp, and Alastair, Lord Londonderry, a fellow *film noir* aficionado [who insists I give a special mention to Edgar G Ulmer's *Detour* (1945)]. Also with my nephew, Ole Rummel, and my son Lawrence, both of whose passion for film I somewhat deviously stoked at a criminally early age. I'd also like to thank Phill Walkley of Moviola, who kindly checked through the original manuscript for errors, and my editor (and Sophia Loren aficionado) Duncan Proudfoot, for his help with the pictures. Finally I'd like to thank my wife, Claudia, companion on a thousand heady days spent hurrying from one Paris art house cinema to another (with the occasional meal in between) in hot pursuit of Hawks, Lubitsch, Ray, Fellini, Carné, De Sica and all the many other ghosts of the silver screen who appear inside the pages of this book.

Dedication

For my wife, Claudia, and my son, Lawrence, boon companions in cinema's enchanted forests of the mind